Me & Lee

How I came to know, love and lose
Lee Harvey Oswald

By

JUDYTH VARY BAKER

Foreword by Edward T. Haslam

Afterword by Jim Marrs

ME & LEE: HOW I CAME TO KNOW, LOVE AND LOSE LEE HARVEY OSWALD

Published by:
Trine Day LLC
PO Box 577
Walterville, OR 97489
1-800-556-2012
www.TrineDay.com
publisher@TrineDay.net

Library of Congress Control Number: 2009943672

Baker, Judyth Vary,
Me & Lee: How I Came to Know, Love and Lose Lee Harvey Oswald—
1st ed.
p. cm.   (acid-free paper)
Includes references and index.
(ISBN-13) 978-0979988677 (ISBN-10) 0979988675
1. Oswald, Lee Harvey 2. Kennedy, John F. (John Fitzgerald), 1907-
1963—Assassination. 3. Baker, Judyth Vary 4. Cancer—United States—
Polio Vaccine (1954-1962) 4. United States—Politics and government—
History. I. Baker, Judyth Vary. II. Title

First Edition
10 9 8 7 6 5 4 3 2

Printed in the USA

Distribution to the Trade by:
Independent Publishers Group (IPG)
814 North Franklin Street
Chicago, Illinois 60610
312.337.0747
ipgbook.com

PUBLISHER'S FOREWORD

Tomorrow, and tomorrow, and tomorrow,
Creeps in this petty pace from day to day
~William Shakespeare, *Macbeth* – Act 5, Scene 5

Lee was a government agent.
~ Marguerite Oswald

What does it take to move people to take action? How can our republic be restored when many refuse to realize the sad state of our current affairs? Cloaked in America's Providence, our hijacked ship of state plunders the world for inbred criminal corporations leaving our collective fortunes tattered, tired and tied to exploitation, ignorance, greed, and gross injustice.

How did this happen? Did we just lose our way; get distracted; make some wrong decisions; morph into sleeping couch potatoes; or what?

My investigation of history tells me that something more than the simple foibles of man have led to today's dysfunctional corruption, something more than misguided misfits, malcontents and mavericks sullying our Pilgrims' Progress. Something more than "Lone Nuts."

Judyth Vary Baker's *Me & Lee – How I came to know, love and lose Lee Harvey Oswald* brings that point home in spades. Born out of a desire that children should know the truth about their father, Judyth's narrative of her meeting, and loving, Lee Oswald that humid summer of 1963 in New Orleans allows us all to know him, as we never have before.

Me & Lee gives us a deep glimpse of the man: his private and public world. A person we knew, and someone of whom we had no idea. Judyth's tale brings the light of understanding to bothersome breadcrumbs strewn about the dark forest of our national nightmare. Incongruent facts come out of the cold, forming a consistent detailed chronicle.

Contrary to published accounts, Lee Harvey Oswald was a patriot who loved his country. He submersed himself in an officially-sanctioned covert arena where one's inventive "legend" becomes entry into a netherworld of intrigue, compartmentalization, secret operations and contrived situations. Where one can be for or against something/someone, depending on whichever guise is called up by a taskmaster giving the high sign through the shadows of plausible deniability: a wilderness of chicanery, deceit and double/triple crosses.

According to all the major polls, no more than 36% of Americans have *ever* believed that Lee Oswald was the lone assassian, and the number has been generally around 15%, with a low of 10% in 1992 the year after Oliver Stone's epic *JFK*. The most recent polls show around 20% of the population believes Oswald "acted alone." This after nearly fifty years of an almost constant "Oswald=Lone Nut Assassin" media assault, including a 2003 fortieth anniversary special, where an august Peter Jennings informed the nation: Lee Harvey Oswald did the dirty deed all by his lonesome and ABC has the computer graphics to prove it!

Spin Control, Perception Management, Reality Engineering, Operation Mockingbird, the Great Wurlitzer, whatever you call it: the strategic psychological operations designed to manipulate our media and cover up the mega-misdeeds of flagrant corruption keep us all woefully unaware of the base reality engulfing our institutions, our history and ... our future. Ignorance is bliss?

Agnotology is the "scientific study of culturally induced ignorance": such as when intelligence agencies or other shadow players use their behind-the-scenes capabilities of media spin to conceal scurrilous activities and agendas. Gaming the system and us.

The cost of this mercenary connivance is our heritage, our liberty, our freedom, our country and ... *our future.* For without an honest dialogue, we become puppets of rhetoric: robotic serfs in a corporate-controlled world, mere pre-programmed economic units instead of vital sovereign human beings. As has been said, "Perfect slaves think they are free."

Me & Lee gives an opportunity for us to understand the depth of our "ignorance." We all owe Judyth Baker a huge debt and much thanks for her courage, forbearance, tenacity and grit in bringing to us all her very personal and revelatory story. A journey that has been beset with the trials and tribulations of exposing unwelcome truths.

Is America's destiny gone? Will it return? *Whither thou, O Columbia?*

I was in Mrs. Helser's eighth-grade Spanish class when the announcement of the assassination came over the room's loudspeaker. Soon there came a note: my work had called (I was a paperboy), and I was sent out on the streets to sell newspapers. I had never done that before and only did it one other time, two days later when Lee Harvey Oswald was murdered ... as the lies and legends arose.

Onwards to the Utmost of Futures
Peace,

Kris Millegan
Publisher
TrineDay
July 14, 2010

To Lee Harvey Oswald, my dearest friend, who gave his life for President John F. Kennedy, and to his family, who need to know that their husband and father was a brave, good man, a patriot, and a true American hero of whom they can be proud.

STATEMENT OF AUTHOR

This true story is presented in a very personal format. Records, chronology, details and evidence kept for over forty years have been thoroughly vetted and examined by the book's editors, as well as through a decade of investigation by seasoned researchers of good repute. The decision to add personal details was a difficult one, but the author believed it was important for the American people to understand the character and personality of the man falsely accused of killing President John F. Kennedy. I believe that any honest person reading this narrative, which offers a day-by-day account of Oswald's last months, will conclude that this government agent did not kill Kennedy, that he was framed, and that his actions were, in fact, courageous and heroic in his efforts to save Kennedy. But he knew too much, which was why he had to die. The author lives in exile due to death threats and is grateful to be alive.

With Gratitude To:

My beloved parents, my dear sister, my courageous oldest son, and my affectionate youngest daughter, who faithfully stood by my side. Also: to Sydney Wilkinson and Thom Whitehead, Edward T. Haslam, Jim Marrs, Edgar Tatro, Nigel Turner, Tom Rozoff, Kris Millegan, Dr. James Fetzer, Dr. John Williams and Kelly Thomas Cousins: my heartfelt thanks for caring about the truth without fear. Allan Mattsson and Kjell Berglund worked selflessly to keep me safe.

Special Acknowledgements:

John Allen Jr., Ed Bishop, Pamela McElwain-Brown, Martha Rose Crow, Wim Dankbaar, Peter deVries, Evelyn and Bill Hall, Joe and Martha Hall, Dean Hartwell, Don Hewitt and Phil Scheffler of *60 Minutes*, Jeffry King, Anna Lewis, William Livesay, Col. Dan Marvin, William "Mac" McCullough, Dr. Howard Platzman and family, Barbara and Jack Preston and family, K.J. Ray, Jamie Sawa, Martin Shackelford, Ed Sherry, and Jeff Worcester

Others Deserving Special Mention:

JoAnne Barbera, Gary Beebe, Gregory Burnham, Tony Carey, Jim Douglass, Chris and Steve Ege, Nora Fletcher, Lee Forman, Robert Groden , Gerry Hemming, Karyn Holt, Dr. John Hughes, Norman Kapoyos, Anita Langley, John Lebeau, Shawn Lessard, Howard Liebengood, Dr. J. W. Lindley, Harrison E. Livingstone, Martha Moyer, Lloyd Meijer, Al Maddox, Tricia and Steve Marcello, Dawn Meredith, Terry Mauro, Lea McGeHee, Linda Minor, Greg Parker, Jim Phelps, Joe and Barbara Preston, Pamela Ray, Debbee Reynolds, Tim Rian, Dr. Joseph Riehl, Robert Rozoff, Dick Russell , Dr. Kathy Santi, Anthony Summers, The Charles Thomas Family, Karl Vissers, Mary Jo Willis, John R. Woods, II.

Thanks to eBay seller *nicepictures* for many of the high-resolution photos of 1960s New Orleans used in this book.

TABLE OF CONTENTS

TABLE OF CONTENTS
(continued)

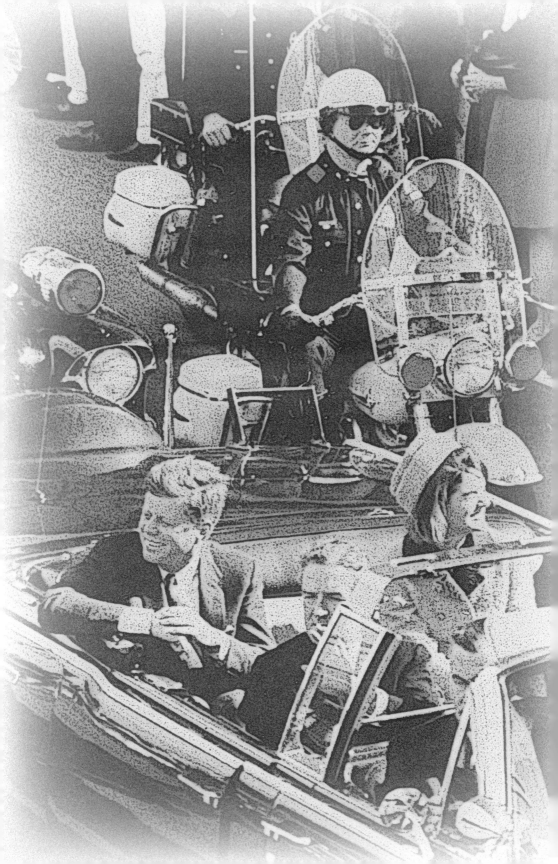

FOREWORD

A quick look at the cover of *Me & Lee* will tell you this is an auto-biographical book about a young woman named Judyth Vary Baker and her relationship with Lee Harvey Oswald in New Orleans in 1963. Lee was the 24-year-old man who burst upon the national stage faster than any person in American history. On November 22, 1963, his unknown name was transformed into a household phrase in a matter of hours, when he was publicly accused of murdering President John F. Kennedy.

President Kennedy had been gunned down by sniper fire in Dallas as his motorcade passed in front of the building where Lee worked. Denied his lawful right to an attorney, Lee Oswald vehemently denied committing the crime at every opportunity. In his words, "No, sir, I didn't shoot anybody." He then asked for legal representation.

Two days later, Lee was written into the history books himself for something he could not deny. He became the first person ever murdered on live television. The nation watched helplessly as Oswald was shot down before their eyes, while handcuffed and paraded through the basement of the Dallas police station. America heard the blast of Jack Ruby's .38 caliber pistol as he shot Lee Oswald at point-blank range, but we did not hear the screams of the 20 year-old girl watching from her television set in Gainesville, Florida – screams that echo throughout the pages of this book.

The narrative starts with that same young girl in Florida and drives patiently, but relentlessly, toward that infamous weekend in Dallas; a weekend that changed history. It would be reasonable to read such a story to gain new insights into what role Lee Harvey Oswald actually played in those events. This much you can expect. What is unexpected is the realization that you might have wound up reading a biography of Judyth Vary Baker even if she had never met Lee Oswald, but for a completely different set of reasons.

Here is an unusual tale about a remarkably talented young woman who used her unique combination of brains, beauty, personality, and determination to chase her dream of finding a cure for cancer. The astonishing thing is how successful she was in that effort, particularly at such a young age. Considered a scientific superstar by the press in her home town, and recognized for winning awards at prestigious science competitions, Judyth achieved prodigious feats while still in high school. These accomplishments attracted the attention of America's top scientists and some of the nation's most powerful political figures. Universities sent her offers. Scholarships were handed to her by prominent organizations. Newspaper articles enthusiastically praised her efforts to fight cancer and promoted her dream of finding a cure. All of this happened before she met Lee Oswald. In fact, the name Lee Harvey Oswald is not even mentioned in the first five absorbing chapters.

The fateful summer of 1963 in New Orleans derailed her life and cast her future into obscurity with the same vengeance that Oswald's name was cast into infamy. Fearing that she would be murdered, just as her friend Lee had been, she kept silent for decades. Warned that she would not be allowed to continue in the world of cancer research, she dropped out of science and abandoned her dream of finding a cure for cancer.

Instead she had five children and educated them to her own high standards. So, we are left to ponder the question: Would Judyth Vary Baker have found the cure for cancer if she had not been derailed? Or with her help, would we at least have a better weapon to fight the cancer epidemic that we face today? Is this omission part of the price we collectively pay for the subterfuge of the 1960s?

Like most biographies that are worth reading, this one presents a flawed hero who was exquisitely human. Judyth was an ambitious self-promoter who was both naïve and, at times, reckless. And she is full of contradictions: she loved animals, but killed hundreds of them by giving them cancer in her laboratory. Spoiled by her own success and cursed with questionable judgment, she zigged and zagged through life, running towards the things she loved and away from the things she loathed. She lunged from extreme to extreme with passion and conviction: From being an 18 year-old virgin who dreamed of becoming a nun, to committing adultery with a man who left a pregnant wife and baby alone at home in order to embrace her. What triggered her downfall, however, was not the fact that she strayed from her morality, but that she returned to it at an inconvenient moment. The problem was: She objected to intentionally killing a group of "human volunteers" in order to test the biological weapon which she and Lee had helped develop. In doing so, she endangered the reputation of a famous doctor - a sin that the doctor was not willing to forgive. Consequently, he banished her from medicine forever.

This is not a romance novel. It is a piece of history; a tile in our national mosaic that, once illuminated, changes the color of everything around it. It is the real-life story of a young girl trying to succeed in life. Trying to make her contribution. Trying to do something patriotic and important. Judyth Vary Baker is a witness, not a researcher.

Her tragic tale is an emotional odyssey told in the first person, but it is one with enormous political consequences. It shakes the very foundation of the explanations offered to the American people by their own government concerning the assassination of President Kennedy. Needless to say, getting her story out to the public has proven to be a long and difficult road. It presents new information which challenges the understanding of these important events. New information that is inconvenient for critics, historians and pundits, all of whom are vested in their own interpretations of these same events.

I was introduced to Judyth Vary Baker in 2000 by the staff of *60 Minutes*, the CBS News television program. I had written about the underground medical laboratory in New Orleans in which Judyth told them she had worked back in 1963. *60 Minutes* researched her story at their expense for 14 months, and their Executive Producer Don Hewitt called it "the biggest story of our times." So I was disappointed when *60 Minutes* decided not to air it. But I was interested in Judyth Vary Baker for my own reasons and subsequently arranged to meet with her in person. When we did, she allowed me to examine the volumes of evidence that she had organized into 3-ring binders. She was the witness that I had been missing in my investigation. She was "the technician" that I had predicted would have been necessary for the covert cancer laboratory that I had heard rumors of in the 1960s. A technician that had been trained to handle cancer-causing viruses.

I stayed in contact with Judyth over the years by phone and email. For the next nine years, I witnessed first-hand the difficulties and frustrations that she encountered as she tried to tell her story publicly. The reactions of both pro-conspiracy and anti-conspiracy JFK assassination groups on the internet was appalling. From either perspective, her story threatened their basic paradigms. They responded with insults, mockery and nit-picking. I begged her to stay off of the internet and to concentrate on writing a book that the public could read for themselves.

In 2003, I was encouraged when the History Channel aired "The Love Affair" as part of their popular series: *The Men Who Killed Kennedy*. This episode exposed for the first time that Judyth and Lee had been part of an effort to use cancer-causing viruses as a biological weapon. But it was withdrawn from circulation one week later, along with two other controversial episodes, for unexplained reasons.

In 2006, a long-awaited book was released, albeit in a print-on-demand format by a small publisher. It was withdrawn after only 85 copies had been printed. Its self-evident title was: *Lee Harvey Oswald: The True Story of the Accused Assassin of President John F. Kennedy by his Lover.* Fortunately, Judyth sent me one of the rare copies of that 700-page tome which, frankly, I struggled to read. But once I did, I found the basic evidence it contained so compelling, that I summarized the main points in two chapters of my 2007 book *Dr. Mary's Monkey.* Not only did the paper-trail support both her claims of knowing Lee Harvey Oswald and of being trained to handle cancer-causing viruses, but her narrative of the people and events in New Orleans in the summer of 1963 helped explain the maze of connections between the Mafia, the CIA, business leaders, politicians, and the medical community. It was a confederation of corruption which Jim Garrison's famous investigation had revealed.

The pursuit of power is a blood-thirsty game that knows few rules. It kills to silence. It punishes those who get in the way. It threatens those who might speak up. Lee was a casualty of this ugly game. His death preserved their secrets. He could not divulge his personal knowledge of the people and events leading up to Kennedy's assassination, and he could not disclose the details of the biological weapon intended to kill Fidel Castro. He could not say who he really worked for. Those who run this game deemed his death necessary for "the good of our country." Not only would it guarantee his silence, it would satisfy the public's lynch-mob anger over the death of their President. Such was their plan. And it worked. But they overlooked something: The girl in Gainesville.

This book is thick with political intrigue, but it is also a story about something else: something softer, but stronger. It is about that invisible force commonly called "love." A stubborn and enduring love, spiced with anger, frustration and yes, revenge. This is the story of the 20 year-old girl who screamed as she watched the man she loved murdered on national television, who saw him summarily convicted of the very crime that she knew he gave his life trying to stop. Judyth hid in silence for decades, afraid that she too would be murdered. But love eventually overcame fear. And love is ultimately the reason this woman decided to risk her life to tell the iconoclastic tale you are about to read.

You can listen to *Madame Butterfly*, or read *Romeo And Juliet*, but you are not likely to find a story about undying love in which a woman has "stood by her man" with more resolve. Despite their separation death, the horrible accusations made against him, or the crude insults she has endured publicly for pleading his case, the bottom line remains that Judyth Vary Baker loves Lee Harvey Oswald. And she wants you to know the man that she knew: the man who ultimately died because of his efforts to save John F. Kennedy. Here is her story at last.

Edward T. Haslam
November 2009

CHAPTER 1

TENDER YEARS

F ew people remember much of their lives before the age of five, but I certainly remember my fifth year clearly, since I nearly died. I got very sick: I had a fever and couldn't keep anything in my stomach. An intense pain developed in my abdomen, but my mother, the youngest in her own big family, had little experience with sick children. Busy hosting a family party that night at our home she simply had me curl up in bed, not realizing I had a ruptured appendix. There I was until about midnight when my grandfather decided to check in on me.

"My God!" he cried, "she's burning up!" My mother began to cry as she saw how sick I was. Grandpa scooped me up in his arms, hurried to his car and drove to us to the nearest hospital. It was cold outside, and he had my mother hold my head out the window to cool me down. The doctors later said that may have saved my life, but just barely. I was operated on immediately, but the situation was dire. My appendix had ruptured, and gangrene had spread everywhere. Massive amounts of penicillin and steroids were pumped into my body, along with blood transfusions. My family prayed. Father Rose, our family priest, came to administer Extreme Unction — the last rites.

They rolled me out of the operating room for the rites, then rolled me back in. Somehow, I made it through the night on the operating table, but there would be many more operations to come. Surgery after surgery, where they cut away infected tissues and even portions of my intestines. *Peritonitis, gangrene, abscesses, bowel obstruction ...* a hole developed in my stomach that allowed acids to leak into the upper portion of my torso. Unable to eat, I was fed by tubes snaked down my throat. Tubes were also in my arms, to add fluids, while tubes in my belly and abdomen drained fluids away. There is no describing the pain and helplessness I felt. I would gaze at a picture of the Virgin Mary hanging on the wall and try to deal with it. The nuns of Notre

Dame had brought the picture in, and learning that I begged for Holy Communion, though I was only five, priests came and celebrated Communion with me for months. It was there that I learned to pray.

Most of the time, I was totally dependent upon the care of the nursing staff for my daily needs. Catholic nuns sat at my bedside and prayed aloud. They called me their "Little Angel" and asked God to keep me alive. I needed so many transfusions that the hospital ran out of my blood type. My family was so desperate they recruited my Uncle Leo, who was considered the black sheep of the family because he had swindled half a million dollars from his own mother. But he had Type O blood in his veins, and I needed it in mine. My situation was so urgent that the transfusion was done directly, arm-to-arm. I guess one could say that Uncle Leo saved my life but, ironically, I never saw him again.

By the time the ordeal was over, I had spent a year and a half in the Pawating Hospital on St. Joseph's Avenue in Niles, Michigan. It was a dreadful experience for a young child. I remember thinking it would never end. But God delivered me from it, or so I was told.

I had missed nearly two years of school. My abdomen was scarred inside and out. I lived with abdominal pain so intense they finally operated on me again when I was ten to remove the adhesions caused by the earlier surgeries. Complications from the experience, such as extreme nearsightedness and a chronic problem with swallowing, have plagued me for the rest of my life. Eventually, I was told that due to all of the infections, abdominal surgeries and scarring, the doctors did not think I would ever be able to have children.

This was my introduction to the worlds of medicine and prayer. Needless to say, it was the major formative event of my early years, and it made me extremely close to my mother's large, affectionate Hungarian family, who visited me constantly during my long recovery, particularly my mother's older half-sister, Aunt Elsie. And the support of the nuns, who continued to educate me throughout my elementary school years, made me very religious. The long recovery also gave me lots of time to read and to draw.

I was born in Epworth Hospital in South Bend, Indiana on May 15, 1943, during the height of World War II. The hospital was so crowded with wounded soldiers that I was born in its corridor. My mother was very young — only 17 — but she'd already been married to my father for two years. My parents had eloped after my 15-year-old mother was forbidden to see 21-year-old Donald Vary anymore. But they were headstrong, and deeply in love.

My mother's big Hungarian family insisted that my father join the Catholic Church if he ever expected forgiveness. So he did, and a

Catholic wedding was held at a side altar. Only then did my grandparents recognize their daughter's marriage. My mother owned five acres of land in Bertrand, Michigan, where my father and his father George, who was a boatwright and carpenter, built her a lovely home. That house was beautiful, but it was wartime, and pipes for plumbing were impossible to find. Fifteen months after I was born, one more child joined the family: my sister, Lynda.

My father was a successful electrical engineer, and had invented some of the electronic parts used in the television sets of the day.[1]

Judyth's parents

He also owned stores that sold and repaired television sets and was part-owner of a local TV station where he worked as the managing engineer. We were not rich by any definition of the term, but my father had a good income and a bright future. We were "comfortable" economically.

When I was eleven, my father started doing engineering consulting at the Chrysler plant in Warren, Michigan, where Chrysler produced the Redstone missile.[2] As a result of this consulting work, he was offered a remarkable job at Sandia National Laboratory, a U.S. Government research facility in New Mexico. Sandia handled the engineering work for the better-known Los Alamos National Laboratory, home of the atomic bomb. The government planned to adapt the atomic bomb to use in rockets, and wanted to make sure no electrical problems would exist regarding the guidance system and its deadly payload.

It was a prestigious Cold War assignment, and my father eagerly accepted the offer. He had deep patriotic motives, as well. He'd injured his leg in a motorcycle accident and was classified 4-F (unsuitable for military service) — the only male in the whole family who hadn't served in any war — and my father felt it keenly. Having passed a lengthy security investigation, and with the imminent sales of his interest in the television station, our TV store and our home, in June 1955, my father drove us to the Sandia National Laboratories compound outside Albuquerque, New Mexico, two weeks before making the final leap. After all, we would be leaving our big extended family behind.

The Redstone Rocket Program

The Redstone rocket was the first U. S. ballistic missile to carry a nuclear warhead.

It had a range of 500 miles. Chrysler produced over 100 of these missiles, which were deployed in Germany between 1958 and 1964.

Problems with the guidance system led Chrysler to recruit new electrical engineers, like Judyth's father Donald Vary, from outside their organization. This highly classified work was to be done at the U.S. Government's Sandia National Laboratory on the grounds of Kirkland Air Force Base in Albuquerque, New Mexico.

This postcard, recently discovered by Donald Vary's granddaughter, establishes the date of his visit to New Mexico as June 29, 1955. Redstone's new guidance system was tested three months later, on September 22, 1955, at White Sands.

It missed its target by 74 miles, proving the guidance system still needed considerable improvement.

Donald Vary declined the assignment in New Mexico and moved to St. Petersburg, Florida in 1955.

There, my father encountered a problem he had not anticipated: barbed-wire fences. Scientists working on important national security projects, like missile guidance systems, were required to live on the grounds of the Air Force base which housed the laboratories. The base was surrounded by high chain-link fences topped with barbed-wire and protected by armed guards at the gates. My mother took one look at the fences and informed my father that she was not going to raise their children in a prison surrounded by barbed wire. It was an ultimatum made by a strong-willed woman who loved freedom. My father was forced to choose between his dream career and his family. He chose family. But it was a high price for him to pay, and the decision haunted him for the rest of his life.

Thanks to the sale of the TV station, the stores and the royalties he earned from his inventions, he had enough money to move us to St. Petersburg, near Tampa on the west coast of Florida. There we lived near other members of my mother's family, who followed us to the same area. It is in Florida that this story really begins.

"St. Pete", as it is commonly called, is on the north side of Tampa Bay. Its beaches are some of the most beautiful in America. The innocence of our life seems, in retrospect, like an idealized vision of suburban America in the 1950s. *Ozzie & Harriet, Leave it to Beaver,* and *Father Knows Best* played on the television sets my father had helped design. We were patriotic, middle-class and Catholic. America was at peace for the most part and the Cold War seemed far, far away.[3]

The fight against cancer, however, was much closer to home, at least for me. My beloved grandmother (my mother's mother, who lived near us) was dying from breast cancer. I visited her three times each week on my way home from school. I loved her dearly, and affectionately called her by her Hungarian nickname "Nanitsa." Watching her die was terribly painful, but not without purpose.

Judyth's maternal grandparents

It instilled within me a deep hatred of cancer. Being helpless to stop the insidious growth inside her was extremely frustrating to me. It was 1957.

Later that same year, our family moved once more, to nearby Bradenton, a smaller town on the south side of Tampa Bay. Bradenton is located on the banks of the Manatee River, a wide, peaceful waterway which flows into the Gulf of Mexico.

Once in Bradenton, I was enrolled in Walker Jr. High School, a public school whose campus adjoined Manatee High School.[4] Now in 8th grade, I had an art class, and my teacher gave us the assignment of painting a landscape. I set my easel up at the bridge that crossed the Manatee River near the hospital and began painting the river and the beautiful homes nestled along its banks.[5]

Before long, a woman came walking by and stopped to look at my painting. Slender, well-dressed, and older than my mother, she studied my work for a moment, then asked me politely where I had learned to paint. I told her I had been painting for many years and that my uncle, who was an artist, had bought me my first set of oil paints to get me started. When I told her that I was currently studying art at Walker Jr. High, she said she knew my art teacher, Mrs. DePew. As I would soon learn, this woman knew almost all of my teachers, and practically everyone else of significance in Bradenton. When she explained that she ran the local chapter of the American Cancer Society, I told her about my grandmother's cancer, and that I, too, wanted to help in the fight against cancer. She inquired as to my name and then introduced herself as Mrs. Georgianna Watkins. Then she politely excused herself and headed to a garden party at a nearby church.

Mrs. Watkins
by Judyth

Several days later, Mrs. Watkins contacted my art teacher at school and asked if I would be willing to paint posters for her American Cancer Society meetings. As it turned out, Mrs. Watkins lived in our neighborhood, just a few blocks away.[6] So, with my mother's permission, I began going to her house to help with her American Cancer Society work.

Mrs. Watkins was a widow who lived alone. Her home was basically devoted to her cancer society work. The front room was full of books and literature about cancer. Other rooms stored assorted medical supplies and various cancer society materials. At first, I simply helped her cut and fold bandages which she delivered to patients at the local hospital. Mrs. Watkins obviously had some kind of medical training (I think she had been a nurse), and I admired the way she spoke knowledgeably about medicine. She taught me my first medical lingo, and I spent my spare time at her house reading about cancer. Mrs. Watkins apparently enjoyed my company and became a mentor to me. She came to play an important role in my life for the next several years.

Back at home, my constant playmate was my sister Lynda. We did the things that teenage girls typically did back then. There was school, church, choir, Girl Scouts, sock hops, slumber parties, and, of course, we had boyfriends who took us roller-skating, to movies, horseback riding and water-skiing.

Both my parents were quite musical. Our father was a good pianist and entertained family and friends with his wide repertoire from jazz to Hungarian *czardas*. Our mother had a beautiful singing voice, and was well versed in the pop music of her day. They made sure we had piano lessons at an early age and later voice lessons.[7] We both sang in the glee club at school and in our church choir at St. Mary's.

At home, Lynda and I sang constantly, especially with our mother who was quite good at harmony. We practiced various duets and performed them on local television shows.[8] Our first such song was "The Cat Came Back." Later we sang "Tonight You Belong To Me" at a talent show in St. Petersburg and won a prize. I also sang solos in a number of programs.[9]

Judyth   *Mrs. Vary*   *Lynda*

Lynda winning 1st Prize at talent show

One year Lynda and I went to circus school. Bordering Bradenton to the south is Sarasota, the winter home of the Ringling Brothers Circus, and the location of the Ringling Museum. There is a school in Sarasota (today called the Sailor Circus) that trains school children in the performing arts, such as acrobatics, juggling, clowning, high-wire and trapeze, as well as backstage theatrical arts such as costume, lighting, make-up, and stage management. It started with a single gymnastics class in 1949, but today is a permanent 4-ring circus that bills itself as *The Greatest "Little" Show On Earth*.[10] Lynda and I enrolled in their summer program to study gymnastics and acrobatics, and we put together an act, which we performed around town at places like retirement homes.

Lynda and I studied hypnosis and hypnotized each other to improve our concentration and block out distractions. This, combined with my ability to block out pain acquired during my long hospital stay as a child, gave me an extraordinary ability to concentrate, which might help explain why I became such a fast reader. At one point my reading speed was reported to be 3,400 words-per-minute.

In high school, Lynda won baton trophies and became a majorette — a bubbly portrait of wholesome normalcy.[11] But I was being seduced by science, by great authors and poetry: I threw myself into books. Though Lynda and I continued our acrobatic act, a deep hunger to learn consumed me. I began reading the high school's Encyclopedia Britannica on a daily basis in the 9th grade. By the 10th grade I had completed all 24 volumes of the 1956 edition.

Bradenton looked like many other small Southern towns of that era, with a brick courthouse, a Rexall Drug Store, and a Woolworth's Department Store. I sometimes went shopping with my friends after school, and one day, after buying some Elvis records, we discovered that Woolworth's had some mollies (small black tropical fish) on sale. I noticed one molly had a rather large belly. The salesperson told us she was pregnant, and that this small fish was viviparous; she bore her young alive, instead of laying eggs. My parents had a big tank full of angelfish and other exotics, but none of them bore their young alive. Intrigued, I returned the Elvis records and purchased half a dozen mollies and a small tank.

Several days later, the pregnant molly (I named her "Miss Molly") gave birth. Her babies popped out one by one, but something was wrong. She still had a big lump, and I worried that she was retaining some unborn babies. But our veterinarian, who took care of my mother's poodles, was also an expert on fish and told me she probably had cancer. Nevertheless, Miss Molly was soon pregnant again, but as her time to deliver drew near, she struggled to swim, and gasped for breath. It was clear that she was dying.

As Miss Molly slowly sank to the bottom of the tank, all I could think of were the babies perishing inside her, so I took a razor blade, and with tears blurring my vision, cut off her head. Then I delivered her babies by C-section. It was my first "surgery." Each tiny molly was placed in a watch glass, and six of the eight babies survived.

My mother was proud of me for saving the lives of these little fish, but if I had not wept, she said, she would have been angry. That's how much she loved animals. Later, when I went off to college, she worried when I reported that my turtle, Fitzgerald (named after President Kennedy), had died. "I know you have to dissect mice all the time," she told me, "but promise me that you will never dissect a pet, that you will never have a heart that hard!"

But my parents were changing: without our big family nearby to steady their impetuous ways, they sometimes drank too much and treated us harshly, usually apologizing later. Earlier, they had often left us for months at a time in summer camps, or with grandparents, as they went traveling. Now, if they argued, they might roar off in their cars in different directions and leave us alone for days with our maid, or with our grandfather. This was stressful because Lynda and I worried they would split up for good.

Due to my interest in science, my parents had given me a good microscope for the small laboratory that I had set up in my bedroom. So when Molly died, I preserved her cancerous tissues in rubbing alcohol and examined them under my microscope. Next, I wanted to see the difference between cancerous tissue and normal tissue, so I took a healthy molly out of the tank, killed it, and cut off the corresponding portion of her tissue, to compare with the cancerous tissue under the microscope. It was my first "cancer experiment," and I hid it from my parents. They wouldn't have approved.

A few months later, I noticed that the female mollies I had rescued from the mother's second pregnancy began developing growths similar to their mother. When the next generation developed the same mysterious lumps, I suspected I was looking at the hereditary cancers I had read about. I felt this observation might be important, but I did not know what to do with my new discovery.

When I told Mrs. Watkins about my tumor-bearing fish, she encouraged me to continue studying them and to keep an accurate journal. She taught me how to enter times, dates, water temperature, diet... everything. She then suggested to my biology teacher that my fish project should be entered in the Walker Jr. High science fair. He agreed, and it won first prize — my first scientific success! I was on my way to becoming a cancer researcher. I knew my grandmother would have been proud, but had no idea how much I still had to learn. I'm grateful to Mrs. Watkins for not telling me how long and hard the road could be.

The following year I entered Manatee High School as a 9th grader and again entered my cancerous fish project in the Science Fair. I was disappointed to learn that I only placed third. Apparently, the judges felt that I had failed to prove that the fish actually had cancer, since I did not have a document from a qualified expert diagnosing the cancer. Certainly, I was not qualified to make such a determination myself. When I explained the problem to Mrs. Watkins, she decided it was time for me to meet some local doctors who might be willing to help.

"Have you been in a hospital before?" she inquired.

Yes, I said, for a year-and-a-half! Realizing that I had a first-hand view of life in hospitals, Mrs. Watkins started taking me with her to Manatee Memorial, where I met various cancer patients, doctors and staff. I observed that she never missed an opportunity to make the case for expanding cancer research in their hospital.

At the end of the school year, I turned fifteen. That summer, Mrs. Watkins received an invitation to the dedication ceremonies for a new critical care clinic in Lakeland, Florida. This was a large and impressive new facility financed with millions of dollars of taxpayer money. Mrs. Watkins invited me to accompany her to the opening of this new state-of-the-art clinic. She instructed me to bring along my cancerous fish so we could get an expert opinion. We transferred the fish to one of her Heinz pickle jars for the journey, a three-hour drive from Bradenton. There we stood in a crowd of well-dressed professionals inside this massive new hospital lobby that glistened with promise. Mrs. Watkins greeted local dignitaries who circulated through the crowd and introduced me to some of them, telling of my cancer-research project and my prizes at the science fairs. Yes, it was flattery, but she was making the point that bright young students should be recruited into cancer research.

The Guest of Honor at this event was Dr. Alton Ochsner, Sr., recently president of the American Cancer Society and founder of the Ochsner Clinic, a well-known medical center in New Orleans. As he worked his way through the crowd, Mrs. Watkins asked one of her local contacts to introduce us to Dr. Ochsner. When he did, she asked Dr. Ochsner if he thought my fish had cancer. Ochsner looked at my fish in the pickle jar and agreed that they appeared to have some kind of cancer. Learning that I had harvested the tumors and examined them under a microscope, he encouraged me to continue, adding that I might want to move up from fish to mammals for my next experiments. Then with the warmth and sparkle of a professional politician, he excused himself with a sunny smile and returned to meeting and greeting others at the reception, all of whom were anxious to hear him deliver the keynote address about lung cancer.

Dr. Ochsner's speech that day was impassioned, and it was easy to see why he had been president of the American Cancer Society. Before 1930 lung cancer was so rare, Ochsner explained, that it was not even listed on the International Classification of Disease system in the United States. Ochsner even recalled as a medical student that he was awakened in the middle of the night to witness an autopsy of a man who died of lung cancer, because his professors considered it to be a medical event so rare that he might not see another again in his lifetime.

A BOOK OF LIFE-AND-DEATH URGENCY FOR ALL SMOKERS, BY ONE OF THE WORLD'S LEADING CANCER SPECIALISTS.

SMOKING AND HEALTH

The past five years have brought to light startling new facts about smoking. Here is all the latest information, in a completely revised edition of Dr. Ochsner's earlier book, SMOKING AND CANCER.

ALTON OCHSNER, M.D.

But now, said Ochsner, there was an epidemic of lung cancer and the victims were overwhelmingly cigarette smokers. Lung cancer was a virtual death sentence for people at this time, but the link to cigarette smoking had not been proven to the satisfaction of the critics, the press or the government. There were no warnings on cigarette packages. Television and movie stars smoked freely on camera. Smoking was allowed in hospitals, offices, and restaurants. And people were getting lung cancer by the thousands.

Ochsner was the leader of a handful of determined doctors still trying to prove that smoking caused lung cancer, but their research was constantly attacked by the well-financed tobacco industry. Undeterred, Ochsner placed the blame for the huge increase squarely upon cigarette smoking, and urged us to join him in warning the public. If Ochsner's goal was to inspire, he succeeded. I, for one, was ready to join his cancer crusade. I resolved right there to graduate from fish to mice. I wanted to prove the connection between cigarettes and lung cancer through my own experiments. I told my dreams to Mrs. Watkins, and she said she would help me. It was August 3, 1958.

It was then that Mrs. Watkins really began to help me make my project a reality. We caught mice in traps, terminated them with ether and preserved them in pickle jars full of formaldehyde. Then she

THE DEATH OF A SMOKER
By Dr. Alton Ochsner

"When one puts a bullet in his head it is cheap, painless and quick. When one commits suicide by smoking it is prolonged, painful and expensive."

W-6145-LP

taught me how to dissect them. I learned mammalian anatomy in her living room, and she bought me my first set of medical instruments for dissecting these animals. As our friendship grew, Mrs. Watkins continued to bring me with her to the hospital whenever she could. I felt like I was now part of her cancer crusade. My enemy was cancer. It had killed my dear grandmother. With Mrs. Watkins and Dr. Ochsner on my side, I was ready to defeat it. Such is the stuff of dreams, and I had plenty of them.

---

1. My father's relatives were skilled craftsmen, such as boat-builders, wheelwrights and professional artists.
2. Chrysler Corporation began production of the Redstone missile in Warren, Michigan, on September 27, 1954 "Chrysler lifts NASA: the next step in the rocket story" http://www.allpar. com/history/military/chrysler-and-NASA.html.
3. Those who fought in the Korean War (1950-1953) may dispute whether we were at peace. But, officially, Korea was a "police action," and it was not treated as a real war in the mainstream media.
4. Walker Middle School (then called a Junior High School) was bulldozed to expand Manatee High School. So there is no longer a Walker Middle School in Manatee County Public Schools.
5. There were many artists in my family and I was well equipped with brushes, easels and paints. I had been drawing and painting for years by this time. I got my first set of oil paints and brushes at the age of five. My uncle Harold Vary was a professional artist and designed mobile home interiors. He also made illustrations for advertisers in South Bend. My grandmother Vary was also an artist. Her paintings paid for my grandparents' home and estate, as during the Depression my grandfather's boats, which were beautiful, just weren't selling. I designed the ads for my father's successful TV store business and even designed sets for his TV commercials, beginning when I was seven years old, and home from the hospital.

    My first portrait was of my aunt Elsie, when I was nine. I included all her wrinkles, which she didn't like, but she framed it anyway. It was done with charcoal I made myself.
6. At the time we rented an apartment in Le Chalet on Manatee Avenue called "The Le Chalet" by locals.
7. We took voice lessons from Sister Mary Cecilia, a missionary who had recently returned from China. She was yet another casualty of cancer in my early life. When Lynda and I knew her, she had already lost her right arm to cancer, and it eventually took her life.
8. There was much more live entertainment on television in the 1950s than there is today. It was common for television stations to present local acts to fill out their schedules.
9. I sang "The Lord Bless You and Keep You" in a program at Southside Jr. High School and later performed "Return to Sorrento" for a TV program shot at The Pier in St. Petersburg, FL
10. Visit SailorCircus.org to enjoy their videos. And be sure to visit their circus when you are in Sarasota.
11. Lynda was transferred to Palmetto High School in her junior year when my parents moved into a home they built nearby on Snead Island, while I continued to attend Manatee High School.

Raytheon Retailing

AD No. 2 ★ ★ ★   BELMONT RADIO CORP. 5011 W. Dickens Ave. Chicago 39, Illinois   AUG. 15, 1951

RETAILING DAILY, WEDNESDAY, AUGUST 15, 1951

The Raytheon Rambler . . .

THIS LITTLE PIG WENT AFTER A MARKET

TWO brothers in Savannah, Ga., today tie a successful merchandising story to the tale of a pig that went after a market. It was a plastic pig, of course, with a slot in the top to make it a bank.

LOOKING for a way to sell sewing machines, Leon and Bill Longwater, proprietors of the Longwater Appliance Co., bought plastic piggy banks to enable housewives to save the 25 cents daily claimed for the machine by the manufacturer's literature.

Salesmen passed out the piggy banks, radio commercials used the recorded squeal of a stockyard's pig, and sewing machine sales zoomed.

THAT'S turning a squeal into a profit. You can adapt this idea to the sale of Raytheon TV.

GOOD RAYTHEON TELEVISION merchandising by Exclusive Dealer Don Vary and his wife is described in another column on this page.

A "PLUS" value is added to his sales efforts, Don reports, every time his small daughters spend time in his showroom.

"When prospects see Judyth or Lynda operate our Raytheon receivers," Don said, "we frequently hear the remark, 'It must be easy if they can do it.'"

EVEN THE FARM MARKET

is special attention these days. FOR years farmers have been getting feed concentrates, and their bulk supplies in bags. First important change came when enterprising concerns started marketing supplies in attractively patterned cloth, suitable for dress-making after the feed had been dumped.

Now the women have to look elsewhere for dress material. A midwest manufacturer has come up with a truck designed to deliver feed direct to farm bins in bulk, with no bags in between.

ONE OF THESE DAYS a smart TV Dealer will suggest a new use of the cartons in which Raytheon TV sets are shipped . . . could be a doll house . . . or can you think of a better use?

Tips of Value
ON MERCHANDISING TV

Send your local promotion ideas, ones you've used for selling TV, to Raytheon Retailing, 5921 W. Dickens Ave., Chicago 39, Ill. The idea we select as "Merchandising Masterpiece" of the month we will reprint in this publication and pay twenty-five dollars for its use. Sorry—we cannot return or acknowledge your entries.

MERCHANDISING MASTERPIECE "A local promotion we have used with success for the past three years is the following: we give a 6 months subscription to the weekly TV guide with each TV sale. We also handle TV guide in our shop. Many customers come in for the weekly issues, giving us prospects for service, sale of antennas, etc., and we get a lot of competitors' customers.

"We have a list of almost all the TV owners in our area, and barrage them with Special Summer offers such as a complete antenna check-up for $9.95. This includes guy wires, if needed, tightening and a lot of miscellaneous for a reasonable price. We also rigged up a summer TV overhaul at a low price.

Walter J. Manola
Carlisle Radio and Television Company
Carlisle, Pa.

Exclusive Raytheon Dealer Sells TV 71 Miles From Transmitters

A likeable American of French descent and his wife have proved many times that they can successfully sell and service quality television 71 air miles away from networks' transmitters located above Chicago's Loop.

They are Don and Gloria Vary, owners and operators of State Line Television, situated 500 yards south of the state line on busy U. S. Highways 31 and 33, midway between Niles, Mich., and South Bend, Ind.

Don and Gloria are exclusive Raytheon dealers by choice. Don said:

"We have tried almost every kind of well-known television receiver, but none gets the result in this area that we obtain with Raytheon. One model of another manufacturer comes close, but it doesn't eliminate the automobile noises, and that is important to us in our location."

This visitor sat in State Line's showroom alongside the highway on a busy Friday afternoon when both pleasure cars and big transport trucks were rolling past in a steady stream. We watched the Cubs play ball via WGN-TV, Channel 9, whose transmitter is 71 air miles away. The picture was clear and the only noise that bothered us was that coming through the open door as the transport trucks roared past. Other channels did equally well.

"I love to sell Raytheon," Gloria said between innings. "It's the only television set I like, and it is bringing us repeat business."

"Repeat?" this visitor queried.

"What Gloria means," Don interjected, "is that most of our business this summer has come from the recommendations given Raytheon by people we previously sold."

In answer to questions, Don explained that their summer business "has not been bad."

"I don't see any reason to complain," he said. "We didn't expect to sell as fast as we will again in the Fall, but we have kept busy."

Don and Gloria provide proof of Raytheon quality to the thousands of motorists driving past State Line Television daily. They keep a Raytheon model with a 20-inch picture screen operating in the large display window, with the legend above it: "Look, no automobile interference!" The sign brings in plenty of prospects.

Inside the show room, the Varys prove their choice of Raytheon television to every prospect. Conspicuously posted is a statement of State Line policy that helps tell the truth about all television.

The Varys attribute their success in merchandising Raytheon television exclusively to a thorough knowledge of the electronics business, particularly its mechanics.

"We certainly can't sell any inside antennas," Don said. "In fact, our recommendations are for good outdoor installations. In addition, of course, we have studied many receivers and now recommend Raytheon exclusively as the set that delivers the best picture and sound in our territory.

"We have installed almost two hundred Raytheon sets in this area during the year since we opened our showroom near the state line. Those customers are sending in their friends, which adds up to about the best recommendation we can have."

Back at Engineering Specialty Company, Inc., Raytheon television distributor located in Gary, Ind., President E. M. Kirtland and his brother Dan spoke highly of the excellent job being done by Don and Gloria Vary.

"They not only sell television," Gene Kirtland said, "but they deliver on their promises that the Raytheon receivers installed by their men will bring in the Chicago stations people in their territory want to watch.

"Don goes even farther than Raytheon in claims for performance," Kirtland continued. "He ran a newspaper ad recently in which he said Raytheon would out-perform all other receivers. From the way he sells, I guess he must be proving it, at least to his customers' satisfaction."

Said Don Vary when asked about that statement:

"Nobody has proved me wrong yet. Raytheon does the best job in this area."

*Information supplied on written request.

LIFETIME GUARANTEE ON TUNER IS HOT SALES POINT
"Real Sales Clincher," Says Dealer

"There's one thing about people, their eyes . . . they can understand world and . . . that anything that has a guarantee Raytheon de . . . must be good. That's why lifetime . . . clincher. It's sort of famous "R . . . dependability of

The tu . . . outstanding Raytheon en . . . tuner . . . merely . . . radio; . . . parts . . . wrong . . . ance; accur . . .

Any . . . pend . . . it b . . . gua . . . tun . . . TV . . . on . . . ov . . . a . . . t . . .

sets on my floor . . . some of the background . . . its 25 years exclusively . . . its achievements in radio . . . and the like.

"Then, as a clincher, I bring . . . the fact that Raytheon's Raytheon Tuner is so good it carries a lifetime guarantee! That really . . .

GOOD FOR A LIFETIME

For the first time in the history of television, the heart of the TV set will carry a lifetime guarantee, according to W. L. Dunn, vice-president of Belmont Radio Corp. The lifetime warranty on the Raytheon tuner, displayed here, covers all parts except its two electronic tubes, which are covered in Raytheon's 1-year warranty. See story above for full information.

Sarasota Herald-Tribune   Sunday, Dec. 6, 1965

Manatee Hi Senior Hunts Cancer Cause

By JANE KOLB
Herald-Tribune Reporter

BRADENTON — A cure for the dreaded enemy—cancer—may yet be found in a high school laboratory.

If so, it certainly won't be by accident.

A blue-eyed senior at Manatee High School, Judy Vary, has developed a theory based on sound reasoning and spends every minute possible to the hope that the end result might "save just one human life."

"I believe wholeheartedly in the worth of my theory or else I wouldn't be working on it, but even if I do not find the answer I'm seeking, I will save another scientist from having to travel this same path," stated Judy.

Judy is a teenager with a vocabulary that is almost unbelievable, but even she admits frankly that she "can't communicate what this project means to me."

"The preservation of life is so very important that if just a single person can benefit from my experiments, then all the ..... duct experiments in a .....

SEEKING CANCER CURE—Judy Vary, a Manatee High School senior, is pictured above with one of the 90 white mice she is using to conduct experiments in a ...

Senior Attends National Meet With Scientists

With two Nobel Prize winners, and leaders in cancer research, Judy Vary, Manatee High School senior, recently attended the National American Cancer Society Seminar for 1961 in St. Petersburg.

Dr. Howard Moore, head of the Rosewell Park Memorial Institute for Cancer Research in Buffalo, New York, was so impressed by Judy and her cancer project that he offered her transportation to and from the Institute, room and board, plus $150 a month, to continue her research this summer in Buffalo.

She's Going

Judy is going; she's delighted! Of her work, she explains, "It's never been done before, and that's the reason these people are so interested." And "It's so encouraging," she adds, meaning the definite and positive results of her experiments.

DON'T WIGGLE — Judy Vary, top-notch MHS science student who has recently been honored in the Westinghouse Science Talent Search, administers cancer inducing materials into her white mouse — an important part of her cancer research project.

CHAPTER 2

WHIZ KID

In October 1957, an event occurred on the other side of the planet that was to impact lives all across America. The Soviets launched a 184-pound metal ball into orbit called Sputnik. The Space Race was suddenly on, and the Russians were in the lead!

Millions of Americans stood in their back-yards and watched the small shiny object cross the night sky like a moving star. On their radios and television sets, they could even hear it beep, like a time-bomb. The media brimmed with Cold War analysis. Space is the ultimate military high ground, and the Russians had gotten there before the Americans. Sputnik challenged the very idea of American military superiority. This was seen as having ominous implications for the future of democracy and the security of the world. U.S. Senator Lyndon Johnson summed up America's fear in one sentence: "The Communists could drop atom bombs on our heads from space if they wanted to."

Beyond the obvious military implications of the Russian launches, the Cold War commentators also saw broader political consequences of the Soviet success. To them, the race for scientific accomplishment was part of the struggle for global political leadership. If Democracy were to prevail, America would need to maintain a scientific lead over the Communists. May the best system win! And if America was going to win the Space Race, they needed to get their brightest students into the game early and give them the support they needed to succeed. Today's students would become tomorrow's scientists. Beating the Russians in the education game quickly became a patriotic cause, a new front in the Cold War. America's "Whiz Kids" suddenly became a strategic resource. Being young, smart and patriotic was "in." And I was all three.

In September 1958, I entered 10th grade. There I
met another person who came to have a profound
effect upon me: Lt. Col. Phillip V. Doyle, U.S. Army
retired, who taught physics and science at Manatee
High School.

Mr. Doyle

The combination of beautiful white sand beaches
and a low cost of living made Bradenton a popular
retirement spot for U.S. military personnel. Many of
them pursued second careers. Col. Doyle was one. He became a high
school teacher and guided not only my work at school, but facilitated
my ever-increasing network of contacts over the next three years. Beyond his understandable connections with local military retirees, he
also had links to scientists, doctors, and politicians around the country (and the world) which were harder to explain. It was my understanding Col. Doyle had worked with the OSS during WWII and possibly even with the CIA during its early years, though the details of his
service were never made clear to me. But he was certainly a patriotic
American military man who saw the world through Cold War glasses.

Col. Doyle took the Cold War challenge to heart and did his part
for this new crusade. He mobilized the resources and led the charge.
Doyle organized his brightest students into an elite team and arranged

Judyth with the Manatee High
Science Club

for them to meet important scientists
to advance their education and careers.
He also started a science club at our
school (I was voted the club's secretary). No ordinary science club sponsor, Doyle persuaded the local military
community to donate prize money and
equipment for science fairs, and asked
members of the local medical community to supply technical guidance for
students in the sciences.

Col. Doyle's contacts, however, extended well beyond the local community. This became clear to me in October 1958, when a scientist from Norway
named Dr. Canute Michaelson visited
our school. A specialist in genetics and
radiation, he was in the U.S. to attend
scientific conferences. Doyle hoped his
visit would inspire us to scientific careers.

Upon his arrival in Bradenton, Dr. Michaelson met with Col. Doyle
and Mrs. Grace McCarty, my biology teacher, who promised to intro-

duce him to their whiz kid. When Doyle introduced me to Dr. Michaelson, he surprised me by telling him that I had the highest IQ in the state of Florida. While I have no way of knowing the accuracy of Doyle's comment, it certainly makes the point that he held me in high esteem.

"Miss Vary," Dr. Michaelson said, "I hear you're breeding a line of fish that inherits cancer." I confirmed that, and explained my interest traced back to watching my beloved grandmother die from cancer. I was determined to learn all I could about the disease in hopes of conquering it. I showed him my cancerous fish and their breeding records. And I told him about my home-brewed efforts to induce cancer into mice. Liking what he heard, Dr. Michaelson openly insisted to Col. Doyle (and to our principal, Mr. Paul Davis) that the school provide me with a laboratory. He then gave Col. Doyle the names of scientists at Oak Ridge National Laboratory who could be helpful contacts for me, since they were on the cutting edge of medical uses of radiation.[1]

Col. Doyle told us that Dr. Michaelson had been a spy in the German underground that fought against Hitler, and that he considered Michaelson to be a hero. Scientist — Patriot — Spy — Hero! Oh, to be like Dr. Michaelson! I was so impressed that I started reading Ian Fleming's James Bond series to learn about the trade-craft used by spies.

Next, Col. Doyle organized a class known as the Science Research Seminar, for his top students. The idea of the seminar was actually the brain-child of two of his students (David Tracy and Dave Dietrich), and it included other talented students at Manatee High such as Bob Pope, Albert Freeman, Ray Nicoud and Helen Neel, all of whom I considered brilliant. Dave Dietrich became Valedictorian, and Helen Neel won all kinds of math scholarships and prizes. We all pursued special research projects over the next few years.

As a result of Dr. Michaelson's suggestion, in 1959 I was given the storage room in the new Science Building to use as a laboratory. I moved my brown mice to school so I could conduct my cancer experi-

---

Norwegian Scientist Visits MHS Classes

R 17, 1958   Page Th

Dr. Canute Michaelson, research scientist and professor of genetics (science of heredity) at Oslo University, Oslo, Norw visited various MHS classes last week. Dr. Michaelson is in No America for the annual Congress of Genetics and the Congress of Radiation. While in the U.S. he will visit several universities to study American methods of teaching and to collect material for a book.

Dr. Michaelson, who recently returned from a trip to Russia, was active in the underground during World War II, was captured by the Nazis and condemned to death, but managed to escape at the last possible moment. Among other things, he has taught the children of the King of Norway.

Speaking in Mrs. Dudley Key's college preparatory English class, he stressed Darwin's theory and the theory of mutation. In answering student questions, he stated that according to genetics and biology, there is a racial difference. He said, however, that there is no known intelligence differences in the races, but mainly a cultural difference. He explained briefly about the background of the races.

Western scientists, he said, believe that mutations are accidental, while Russian scientists say that they are not. In this way, he explained, the Russians have invented a biological excuse for Communism in that if all people lived in a Communistic environment, all would change or mutate to the Communist way of life.

While stating his theories on mutation caused by radiation, which is his special field, he said that ninety percent of the mutation caused by radiation is nonbeneficial to life. The lethal mutation causes death of the individual. That is the reason that geneticists are fighting for a ban on nuclear tests.

Educational T To Start Here On Channel 3

Educational television is sch uled to start October 27 at Ma tee High on channel 3.

Television sets will be availa to Mrs. Paul Parrish, Mrs. Le McLaughlin, and Miss Elizab Sloan's sixth period English cl es.

To Set Up Control Classes
Control classes will be set up test the effectiveness of this p gram. These classes will taught in much the same way without the use of television se Manatee County is one of se counties participating in this p gram. The other counties are H dy, Polk, Pinellas, Sarasota, Hi borough, and Pasco.

All programs telecast by station will fall into one of fe categories: pre-school progran in-school programs, adult edu tion, and civic and public serv programming.

Teacher Is Still Important
The teacher of the classro which is participating in any te vision lesson is the most import factor for success. Educational is not designed to replace t classroom teacher.

School superintendents, leade of business and civic affairs, a the heads of the colleges in o area, through their own tim founded the board of directors the Florida West Coast Educatic

ments under Col. Doyle's supervision. Being in such a group was an invigorating experience and made me feel like I was on the road to becoming the scientist I wanted to be.

My first major project for Doyle's seminar was inspired by my chemistry teacher Milton Scharer, a former industrial chemist. When he told me about the medicinal properties of magnesium, I became intrigued. "I want you to read *The Story of Magnesium,*" he said, handing me a small book he owned. I learned that 1,272 pounds of magnesium were hidden in each cubic mile of seawater. Seawater? One thing we had around Bradenton was plenty of seawater! "I want to get magnesium metal out of seawater," I told Scharer. "Do we have the equipment for a project like that?"

"I don't know if it's possible to get the pure metal itself," he replied. "This is just a high school. You'd need a refinery, if you got that far." Nevertheless, Scharer drove me to the beach, and we collected twenty gallons of seawater. Doyle quickly approved the proposal, excited by the project because he knew magnesium was an important lightweight metal that NASA was interested in for use in the Space Race. It fit perfectly into his "Cold War Whiz Kid Science Race" plan.

My experiment proposed a modest improvement to a process that had been invented in Germany. It took many hours to get the pure metal without access to a refinery. But I finally got the precise amount of metal available in one gallon of seawater, and using my art skills, created a display that helped the project stand out. "Magnesium from the Sea" won first prize in our school's science fair. Next came the Manatee County Science Fair. I won the Grand Prize there, qualifying me for the statewide competition in Melbourne, on the east coast of Florida, to be held April 8th and 9th, 1960.

Judyth's grandfather with her science project.

Col. Doyle drove Mrs. McCarty, Dave Dietrich, Bob Pope, Larry Jerome and me across the state to Melbourne for the competition. I'd spent summers at camps before, while my parents traveled, but this was the first time I had a generous personal allowance for food and souvenirs. I bought some chocolate-covered ants, and after everybody enjoyed a crunchy piece, I revealed the contents! The motel in Melbourne was up-scale, with a beautiful swimming pool, which made me realize how much money Doyle had raised for us to compete in these fairs.

In Melbourne, my "Magnesium from the Sea" project again won First Prize in the chemistry category and the Grand Prize in Physical Sciences. It was the "State Championship" in Science, catapulting me onto the radar screen of college recruiters and politicians anxious to share in my success. The American military was always present and supportive of these competitive events as a normal part of their recruiting and public relations activities. The Navy provided prizes, and 1st prize was traditionally a long cruise on one of their aircraft carriers. But my case presented a new problem: a girl had never won the Physical Science Grand Prize before, and females were not allowed on U.S. Navy warships, so they had to come up with another prize. They gave me a set of encyclopedias instead. I didn't know how to tell them that I already had a set of encyclopedias, so I graciously accepted their gift and gave the volumes to my parents, who happily added them to their library.

But the real prize for winning the Florida Science Fair was that it qualified me for the next rung of the competition, the National Science and Engineering Fair, to be held in Indianapolis, Indiana one month later, in May 1960. *My birth state!*

When I got home, the story of my winning the statewide science fair was hitting the local newspapers. Col. Doyle was pleased with the press coverage and took me with him to speak at civic groups. Meanwhile, I continued to work on my cancer projects in my own little laboratory at the new Science Building, though I fretted because I still needed pedigreed mice to do proper scientific experiments.

This was the research that Dr. Ochsner's speech had inspired me to do and which Mrs. Watkins had trained me for, all in the name of my dear grandmother. It was now the focal point of my life and I spent many hours in my lab between classes, in the evenings and on weekends.

The goal of my new experiment was to give mice lung cancer from extracts created from the tars in cigarette butts. Doyle soon secured 100 laboratory-grade mice for me, which I was busy breeding.[2] Friends helped me collect cigarette butts to supply my "gas chamber" where the mice would breathe carcinogen-laden smoke.

Doyle and Watkins arranged for me to work with two local radiologists who had recently trained at Oak Ridge (Drs. Shively and Roggenkamp) so that I could expose my mice to radiation, and pull down their immune systems in order to give them cancer faster.[3] This radiation work was always supervised. It began in the Professional Building, located near Manatee Memorial Hospital in downtown Bradenton. Later, I used other facilities.

One of the initial problems we encountered with radiation was figuring out what a lethal dose would be for a mouse. With the help of

The Bradenton Herald, Tuesday, April 12, 1960

City-County Ne

JUDY VARY

High School junior." It was like discovering a new world. I think Manatee High School is the most wonderful school, there are such great opportunities to express oneself."

'HARD WORK'

Milton W. Sharer, her chemistry teacher, who is accompanying Judy to Indianapolis, interrupted by saying that her praise for her school was quite typical of his modest pupil, but that it was her own hard work after school hours, even on Saturdays and holidays, that had been responsible for her prize winning project "Magnesium From The Sea."

Judy said she first got interested in her project after reading "The Story of Magnesium," especially one sentence which stated that 1272 pounds of magnesium may be found in one cubic mile of sea water. "I decided I'd try and find some of it."

The daughter of Mr. and Mrs.

the radiologists, I found information in the hospital's library which I used as a basis for our calculations. We then did an experiment intended to kill 25% of the mice in the group, but none died. My calculations were obviously wrong. I realized I needed to find someone who knew more about such things, and asked Dr. Shively if he knew anybody. Soon he came back with the name of a doctor in Tampa who was an expert in the experimental use of radiation on animals: Dr. James A. Reyniers, a bacteriologist.

During his 30 years at the University of Notre Dame, Dr. Reyniers pioneered the development of germ-free animals for use in laboratory research. Virtually all the germ-free mice colonies in a dozen medical centers on four continents stemmed from his research, and many were descendants of his original colonies. Recently, Dr. Reyniers had moved to Tampa where he started the Germ-Free Life Research Center in order to study the mysterious role of cancer-causing viruses. So I contacted Dr. Reyniers and asked for his help. He helped me figure out the correct amount of radiation to accomplish the task, and even donated some of his bacteria-free mice for my experiments.

The pace of my life was increasing dramatically, and I was busy all of the time. Meanwhile, the results of my award-winning project "Magnesium from the Sea" continued to generate interest.

U.S. Senator George Smathers heard of my winning the statewide competition in Chemistry and Physical Sciences and wrote me a standard letter of congratulation. It was nice, but was it special? Not really. It was the type of letter you keep for your portfolio knowing that it looks good, but means little. But several days later, I was called out of PE class and told to go to the school's office for a phone call. You can imagine the flood of possibilities that ran through my mind. Was there a problem? An accident? Was my grandfather sick?

When I got to the office, smiles were all around as the staff waited for me to pick up the phone. "Hello, this is Judy Vary," I said in earnest, not knowing what to expect. It was then I learned that it was Senator Smathers' office calling. In a minute, the Senator himself was on the phone, congratulating me for winning the Science Fair and inviting me to tour the campus of the University of Florida, his alma mater. He said he could arrange a scholarship for me there, and would set up a bank account for me in Bradenton where people could donate money for my educational expenses.

Senator Smathers

Smathers had a special interest in attracting Florida's top students in science and medicine to his alma mater, because he had funded dozens of research projects at UF and was the driving force behind the construction of their brand-new hospital. But then Smathers said something that really caught me by surprise. He said he would call the Governor and ask him to look into the commercial potential of my idea to extract magnesium from seawater. It was hard for a teenage girl in high school to know how to respond to such comments. Were these famous and powerful men really interested in my high school science project? Or was this just part of the public relations machinery that surrounds democratically elected politicians? While I welcomed the support and encouragement and knew that Col. Doyle and Mrs. Watkins would be pleased, I wondered if it was all for real, or just for show.

A week or two later, I was working with the mice in my lab when I got a second message summoning me to the school's office. This time I wasn't so afraid and when I arrived, the staff was smiling again, because Florida governor LeRoy Collins' office was on the phone. Yes, the governor had written too, saying he wanted to discuss the magnesium project with me. I had even called his office in response, but was told he was in a meeting. I assumed the governor was simply too busy to deal with a phone call from a high school student, and let it go. But I underestimated his interest.

Collins himself picked up the phone. He said he wanted me to tour a plant in Port St. Joe, Florida that was already pulling chemicals like magnesium out of the Gulf, but having problems with their process. We agreed I'd take the tour soon after school ended for the summer. I was keenly aware that I was only a high school student with a science project, but I realized I was being given access to very well connected people who were willing to help me. I was grateful for the support, and particularly for the offer of scholarships to finance my education.

Another month had passed since the Florida State Science Fair in Melbourne, and it was now time to go to the National Science Fair in Indianapolis for the national competition.

My chemistry instructor, Mr. Scharer, had plane tickets for us, but my mother was afraid of airplanes and insisted on driving me to Indianapolis herself. Oddly, once there, she dropped me off with Mr.

Scharer and continued on to see family members. I spent that night in a hotel, and didn't see her again until the event was over.

In Indianapolis I found my "Magnesium from the Sea" exhibit already set up for me right across from a computer science exhibit by an extraordinary (and cute) boy named Rob Strom. Rob had a fascinating exhibit that could be adapted to allow the computerized tracking of objects that swung around the moon and then orbited the earth. Already famous in some circles for having won the grand prize on the popular TV quiz show, *The Sixty-Four Thousand Dollar Question* some years before, Rob and his exhibit attracted a string of college recruiters, scientists, newspaper reporters and military officers. Frankly, his popularity helped the visibility of my exhibit as well.

Rob, by his own admission, was a liberal leftist and enjoyed the college recruiters and the scientists more than the military officers. I was far more conservative and patriotic. So when one these military officers asked me if I loved America, I boldly recited a poem I'd written about the American flag to make the point that, indeed, I did.

I spent the rest of the day with these scientists and military officers, who took a group of us kids to the headquarters of the Eli Lilly Company where we were introduced to other scientists and questioned about our science exhibits. I soon learned that Eli Lilly was a major pharmaceutical company with tens of thousand of employees marketing products in over 100 countries around the globe. Its 130-year history is studded with scientific breakthroughs and medical marketing success stories.[4] It was very "big league" business with billions of dollars of annual revenue and impressive marble office buildings with all the trimmings of corporate success. I was definitely impressed.

We were also taken to the University of Indiana School of Medicine. There, a reporter wanted to take some photographs, so our group of students was assembled in a hallway where a preserved human body was lying on a gurney. A doctor asked if one of us would make an incision into the cadaver for the photographer. Nobody said a word.

Finally, I took the scalpel and asked the doctor where he wanted the incision. I had to remind myself that you can't be squeamish if you want to be a scientist. "Can you find the trigeminal nerve?" the doctor asked. My grandmother, who died of breast and abdominal cancers, had suffered a metastasis to her trigeminal nerve, and by that mere accident of fate, I had studied its location. When I successfully located the nerve, the doctor was impressed.

The doctors, scientists and military officers accompanying us soon learned of my work with mice, hypothermia, and radiation to determine if low temperatures could reduce mouse metabolic rates, so irradiated cancerous tumors would spread more slowly. "Giving cancer to the mice has proven difficult," I told them, "but I can't do the hypo-thermia experiments without cancerous mice."

At this time, I was told that Russia's cancer research had sinister motives, and how we responded to this Soviet threat was just as important as the Space Race. I replied that I was determined to put forth my best efforts for America. If I was naïve, so were most Americans at that time. We still believed almost everything our government told us. At our interviews at Eli Lilly, some of us were asked to sign loyalty oaths, which were necessary to receive college scholarships from the State of Indiana.[5] I was happy to sign.

I apologized for not having finished my cancer research project in time for the 1960 science fairs. I explained that I was also trying to speed up the process of giving my mice cancer by exposing them to radiation. They had developed keratotic lesions, but were not getting cancer. How could I study cancer without a supply of cancerous mice?

I told them I intended to induce lung cancer in my new batches of mice using cigarettes, not realizing this was a task only sophisticated teams laboring in well-funded laboratories had ever accomplished. I had brought my lab records with me, and they were astonished by my claim that I had actually induced cancer in some mice by means of cigarette extracts, and that I had the evidence to support it. Now they were ready to help.

They gave me the name of the chief of radiobiology at the Walter Reed Army Institute of Research, and told me to write to him. They explained that he was the top expert in the field of radiation and hy-pothermia, and could supply me with specialized chemicals and information to support my work. Since I would be asking help from the U.S. Army, it was suggested that I also write to the President, offering my services to my country. I wrote the letter to Walter Reed promptly since I could see that it might produce tangible results. Less confident about writing a letter to President Eisenhower, a lame duck getting ready to retire, I put off the task for months. Eventually I wrote the letter to the newly elected President, John F. Kennedy.[6]

I was kept so long at Eli Lilly talking to the people that I missed the part of the event where the competitors explain their projects to the judges. Even without a presentation, my project finished fourth in my category. I was happy with that, and I knew that what I had accomplished at Eli Lilly would be far more important to my future than another prize. I felt that I had won in my own way.

When my mother returned, she apologized for not coming to the fair. When we got home, she then drove me to a large gathering of our relatives, all assembled to congratulate me. I had missed my Junior Prom to attend the fair, so I was asked to wear my prom gown, was photographed, and then asked to sing. I almost fainted with embarrassment! Then my mother took me horseback riding, one of my favorite activities. It was the perfect end to a wonderful week.

When I returned to Bradenton, there was press coverage in the local newspapers about my trip to Indianapolis, which dubbed me a "Science Whiz Kid". Doyle was happy about the newspaper coverage, as it helped his plan to get donations and support for his science crusade. And my "Magnesium from the Sea" exhibit was the featured project on the Science Club page of the school's yearbook.

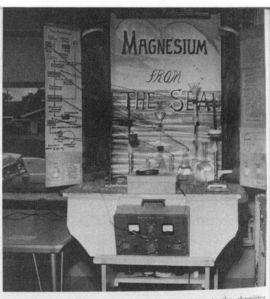

SCIENCE CLUB

Every study day the science club meets with Col. Philip Doyle, physics teacher, who assists the members as advisor and consultant.

Membership in the club is limited from necessity, and therefore the members are carefully selected on the basis of their academic ability, citizenship, and interest in science.

During the year the students work on a project. This year, projects included a Vandegraft generator, sound and optical experiments and the building of radio equipment.

"Magnesium from the Sea," is the prize winner in the chemistry division of Manatee's first Science Fair. This first place project was composed by Judy Vary.

The wave of attention created by "Magnesium from the Sea" continued to bear fruit. Colleges were contacting me and offering me admission to their schools. Here are the ones that I remember: MIT, UC-Berkeley, Purdue University, Indiana State University, Michigan State University, Rutgers, Duke, University of Florida and St. Francis College, a small Catholic school in Indiana. Many sent scholarship offers. I never actually applied in the traditional sense.[7] It was a nice way to pick a college! I had Col. Doyle to thank for that. As my junior year of high school ended, I turned seventeen.

During the summer, I took the bus to Florida's panhandle near Pensacola to tour the Port Saint Joe facility, as Governor Collins had arranged. It was a massive facility that looked like a giant chemistry set. When I arrived in Port Saint Joe, I was greeted by the plant manager. He then introduced me to U.S. Representative Robert L.F. Sikes.

Congressman Sikes, it was explained, was on the House Appropriations Committee. As Chairman of their Subcommittee for Military Construction, he presided over $3,500,000,000 of annual spending (1960 dollars) and had conveniently provided 14 military bases in his own Congressional District, in which we were standing. The Congressman eagerly expressed interest in an economical modification to the process, as presented in the "Magnesium from the Sea" project, as well as a second idea I offered for capturing the energy from lightning bolts by building strike towers in phosphate pits. (Florida has more lightning strikes than any other state in the nation — another untapped natural resource.) He said that he would be happy to discuss both ideas with Senator Smathers. I felt these important people were taking my ideas seriously.

That summer, I continued to care for my mice, conducting cancer experiments at school, at home and at the hospital. Col. Doyle scheduled me to speak to various civic organizations to help raise money for our science projects, and equipment for Manatee High's new science building. I made some impassioned speeches, and the response was generous. Even the local library donated an old display case to house my control mice. A group of doctors purchased steel mouse cages and other equipment for my research. Palmetto Savings & Loan paid for a genetically pure line of white mice. Bausch & Lomb, an optics company based in nearby Sarasota, donated a high quality oil-immersion microscope, and when they learned that I had lost my contact lenses in the swimming pool in Melbourne, they kindly gave me several sets of contacts lenses of different colors, and a special bifocal pair so I could use microscopes more effectively. Very scientific, and fun!

Tropicana Orange Juice began its operations in Bradenton, and their lab provided equipment for the local hospital's new oncology division, to which I was now permitted access for my cancer experiments.

Col. Doyle himself continued to donate his time and money, spending hours in medical libraries on my behalf (minors were not allowed). He would return with expensive copies of research reports paid for out of his own pocket. He even arranged for the school's shop class to save their sawdust as litter for my mice. And my friends continued to collect thousands of cigarette butts, which I needed to extract the tobacco carcinogens.

My experience in Indianapolis made me eager to study Russian. I wanted to decipher the Soviet scientific journals to figure out what they were working on. Doyle agreed that young American scientists should to be able to read Russian. Classes in Russian were being taught at Manatee Jr. College during the day, but I couldn't attend them, so Doyle and his military friends persuaded Dr. Theodore Concevitch to teach a night course. It was just an introduction to the language, but in my usual manner of plunging into things, I started reading English translations of Russian literature, listening to Russian music, and practicing simple Russian phrases on my family. In response, Mama nicknamed me "Juduffski."

As the summer ended, I anxiously awaited the start of my senior year. Football games! Homecoming! Parties! Boys!

In September of 1960, as school started, I received a package from Walter Reed Army Institute of Research. I admit that my expectations were low. I expected to find yet another polite letter saying "how nice" it was that I was interested in cancer research, with brochures about careers in the U.S. Army. But I was pleasantly surprised. The letter was from Dr. David Jacobus, the head of Walter Reed's Radiobiology Department. This was a group that worked with the lethal effects of radiation on human bodies. Dr. Jacobus had read my letter describing my research projects and responded with a two-page letter that carefully explained his thoughts about this field. He also sent some sophisticated chemicals to experiment with, which he thought might protect my mice from x-irradiation. Walter Reed, he said, was conducting research on hypothermia, just as I was. At the conclusion of his letter, he asked me to keep him posted on the results of my research.

Recently declassified documents show that Dr. Jacobus' research was so advanced that in 1964 he protected a group of monkeys from dying of lethal doses of radiation by giving them special chemicals — some of the same chemicals he sent me. Accompanying his letter, and these chemicals, were copies of scientific articles (some published, some unpublished), with the names of researchers interested in my area of inquiry, plus the dates and locations of scientific meetings and conferences.

As I eagerly searched the list, I noted that an important cancer research conference was coming to nearby St. Petersburg in the spring. Armed with exotic new chemicals, and inspired by Walter Reed's interest and support,

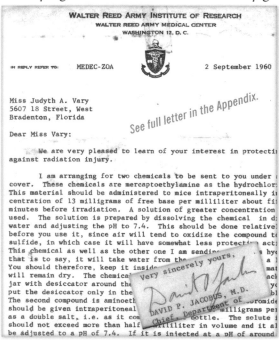

I plunged into months of work with a vengeance.

I had a laboratory full of Swiss-Webster mice, chemicals and equipment, the blessings of everybody, and supervised access to x-ray machines backed up by experts in radiation. By now, I also had unlimited access to medical libraries, including a pass to the library at the University of Florida. But my goal to attack cancer was hampered because it took so long to induce cancer in my mice. How could I speed up the process? How ironic that, in order to fight cancer, I had to find ways to make it flourish! It turned out to be expensive.

In December 1960, just when I needed more funds, a new round of publicity started that made my prior exposure pale in comparison. On Dec. 4th, the *Sarasota Herald-Tribune* ran a long article in the Sunday paper, saying that the cure for cancer might yet be found in a high school laboratory. I was the "young scientist" who was trying to do it. Dr. Jacobus, Walter Reed, my access to x-ray equipment, and other details filled half a page, along with a photo of me with the mice. Quoting the article: "Judy is a young woman very hard to explain with mere words. You must watch her and talk with her to understand the depth with which she experiences life." It concluded with a quote from me saying, "I do want to become

BRADENTON HERALD

The Bradenton Herald, Wednesday, Jan. 25, 1961   1-B

CITY-COUNTY NEWS

SCIENCE TALENT SEARCH

Manatee High Senior Joins Honors Group

By BOBBY BENNETT

Judy Vary, Manatee High School senior, has been named a member of the honors group from the Westinghouse Science Talent Search.

One of the five or six hundred honored, from a group of about 30 or 40 thousand who took the test, and one of 11 from Florida, Judy is now awaiting the February 1 announcement of the 40 top winners.

The 40 best students will be given all-expense paid trips to Washington, D. C., where for five days they will compete for scholarships ranging from three to seven thousand dollars.

Daughter of Mr. and Mrs. D. W. Vary, of Gulf and Bay Estates in Palmetto, Judy will probably be receiving scholarship bids from colleges around the country. Last year the dark-haired science student won first place in the State Science Fair with her project "Magnesium From The Sea." Going on to the National Science Fair, which was held in Indianapolis last year, she captured fourth place honors in nationa' competition.

Judy will now be invited to the Florida Talent Search in Lakeland in the near future. There, promising science students exhibit their projects before representatives of various colleges. Outstanding students are presented with scholarships to state schools.

PROJECT

Her senior project, which will be exhibited at the Florida Talent Search, is one of cancer research. Donated by Fred Langford, executive vice-president of the Palmetto Savings and Loan, Judy has 100 white mice which are the basis of her research.

The mice are being treated with substances from tobacco and cigarette filters which have been proven to cause cancer. After the cancer appears in the mice, Judy will use her new method of treatment to destroy it.

Although irradiation is often used to curb the spread of cancer, the radiation itself often has unpleasant effects on cells, sometimes causing them to be-

JUDY VARY
. . . In top group

come cancerous. Judy believes that anti-radioactive agents plus non-toxic stearates can be injected beneath the cancers to retard the movement of the cancer to other parts of the body.

Judy has received help on her project from many areas. Dr. David Jacobus, of the Walter Reed Army Medical Center in Washington, D. C., sent her $60 worth of chemicals, and each month Judy sends him a written report on the progress of her project.

Colonel Phillip Doyle and Milton Scharer, physics and chemistry instructors, respectively, at Manatee High, and Doctor John Shively, of Sarasota, have also contributed to Judy's success.

a scientist." The reporter concluded the article with a vote of confidence. "She'll make it, too."

The Associated Press ran a short version in newspapers across the country for the next six months. It is difficult to know how many papers actually ran it because there was no central archiving system, but the number appears to be over 100. After that, I had no more funding problems.[8]

In January 1961, another article ran in the *Bradenton Herald* reporting that I had been selected by the Westinghouse Talent Search as a state finalist for their grand prize, a paid trip to Washington, D.C. It also mentioned my cancer research project. While I did not win the trip to DC, I did get a $500 scholarship out of the deal.

A week later a similar story ran in my school newspaper with a photo of me with my mice, saying that I planned on making biochemical research my "life's work."

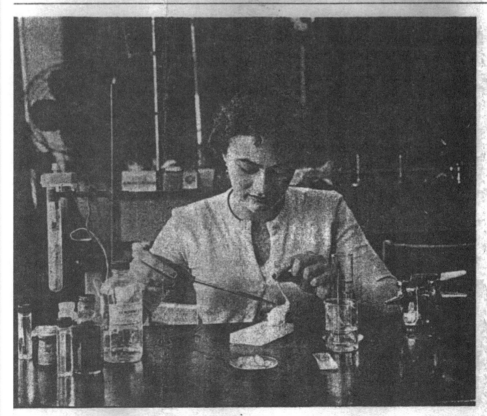

BRADENTON, FLORIDA, FRIDAY, FEBRUARY 3, 1961

DON'T WIGGLE — Judy Vary, top-notch MHS science student who has recently been honored in the Westinghouse Science Talent Search, administers cancer inducing materials into her white mouse — an important part of her cancer research project.

So, at the age of 17, I had my own cancer laboratory, supervised access to x-ray machines and un-supervised access to medical libraries, as well as the enthusiastic support of the local community, including Mrs. Watkins and the American Cancer Society. I had won statewide awards and national recognition for my "Magnesium from the Sea" science projects, money for college, scholarship offers from colleges I hadn't even applied to, promising political contacts with Florida's governor, a U.S. Senator and a U.S. Representative, plus an almost embarrassing amount of local press coverage.

Yes, it was an exciting time for me. Who wouldn't be pleased with all of that? I was grateful for what I had and thanked God for His bounty.

---

1. Two of the Bradenton radiologists, Dr. John Shively, and Dr. Milton Roggenkamp, who helped advise and guide me, received radiation and preclinical (tissue culture) training at Oak Ridge National Laboratories in 1959 and 1960 respectively. Harry S. Brown, CIA, was openly listed as a participant in 1960.

2. The Swiss-Webster mice were a gift from Palmetto Savings and Loan through Fred Langford, Pres.

3. The first radiation work was done at the Professional Building, with Dr. Shively, near Manatee Memorial Hospital. More radiation work followed at Sarasota Memorial Hospital's Tumor Clinic, thanks to a Century Club sponsor.

4. For a list of Eli Lilly's accomplishments see the http://www.lilly.com/about/history.

5. Such was the anti-Communist, "McCarthyite" atmosphere in Indiana: "In Indiana, a group of anti-Communists indicted *Robin Hood* (and its vaguely socialistic message that the book's hero had a right to rob from the rich and give to the poor), forcing librarians to pull the book from the shelves." (*The Coils of Cold War*, "Lecture 23," by S. K. Schultz)

6. My letter to the President is in the Appendix section in the back of the book. The reply I received from Ralph Dungan, a close advisor and friend of President Kennedy, is on page 28.

7. I thought any college, if they wanted me, would drop a scholarship in my lap. The fact that I didn't apply to the U of Chicago was due to my naïveté, as an MHS counselor said he'd informed them of my interests. Turned out he never wrote to anybody, and as many other offers just poured in that, when I found out, it was too late.

8. Here is a partial list from NewspaperArchive.com, which only reports a fraction of the newspapers nationally:[7]

1961 Jan. 24 — *Blytheville Courier News,* Blytheville, Arkansas

1961 Jan. 25 — *Greeley Daily Tribune,* Greeley, Colorado

1961 Jan. 27 — *Waterloo Daily Courier,* Waterloo, Iowa

1961 Jan. 30 — *Las Cruces Sun News,* Las Cruces, New Mexico

1961 Jan. 29 — *Corpus Christi Caller Times,* Corpus Christi, Texas

1961 Jan. 26 — *Stevens Point Daily Journal,* Stevens Point, Wisconsin

1961 Feb. 09 — *Pasadena Independent,* Pasadena, California

1961 Feb. 08 — *Star News,* Pasadena, California

1961 Feb. 26 — *News Tribune,* Fort Pierce, Florida

1961 Feb. 08 — *Mason City Globe Gazette,* Mason City, Iowa

1961 Feb. 01 — *Herald Press,* Saint Joseph, Michigan

1961 Feb. 02 — *Chillicothe Constitution Tribune,* Chillicothe, Missouri

1961 Feb. 18 — *Nashua Telegraph,* Nashua, New Hampshire

1961 Feb. 02 — *Times Record,* Troy, New York

1961 Feb. 28 — *Post Standard,* Syracuse, New York

1961 Feb. 27 — *Big Spring Daily Herald,* Big Spring, Texas

1961 Feb. 05 — *Paris News,* Paris, Texas

1961 Feb. 14 — *Bennington Evening Banner,* Bennington, Vermont

1961 Feb. 07 — *Manitowoc Herald Times,* Manitowoc, Wisconsin

1961 Mar. 16 — *Tucson Daily Citizen,* Tucson, Arizona

1961 Mar. 14 — *Fitchburg Sentinel,* Fitchburg, Massachusetts

1961 Mar. 29 — *Brainerd Daily Dispatch,* Brainerd, Minnesota

1961 Mar. 05 — *Ada Evening News,* Ada, Oklahoma

1961 Mar. 05 — *Progress Index,* Petersburg, Virginia

1961 Mar. 08 — *Sheboygan Journal,* Sheboygan, Wisconsin

1961 Apr. 12 — *Atchison Daily Globe,* Atchison, Kansas

1961 Apr. 03 — *Titusville Herald,* Titusville, Pennsylvania

1961 May 03 — *Daily Review,* Hayward, California

1961 May 17 — *Derrick,* Oil City, Pennsylvania

1961 Jul. 18 — *Evening Independent,* Massillon, Ohio

1961 Jul. 24 — *Daily Tribune,* Wisconsin Rapids, Wisconsin

1961 Sept. 15 — *Independent Record,* Helena, Montana

Newsaperachive.com, 2008.

9. The photo and article were published in MACOHI, the newspaper of Manatee County High School, on Feb. 3, 1961, p. 8. The article is entitled "Instructor Discusses High School Physics" and features my physics teacher Col. Phillip Doyle. The last three paragraphs are about me specifically and say, "Judy is hoping to attend either the University of Chicago, Duke University, or FSU. She will major in biochemistry and plans to make biochemical research her life's work."

BRADENTON, FLORIDA, FRIDAY, APRIL 14, 1961

'MEESES-MEESES-MEESES' — Admiring Judy Vary's science project, which centers around white mice, are Bob Pope, Charles Throckmorton, Frank Snydle, Judy, Jimmy Richards, Al Freeman; Larry Jerome and Colonel Philip Doyle. All of these students and Colonel Doyle, sponsor, attended the State Science Fair last week-end. (Photo by Curt Schulze).

Senior Attends National Meet With Scientists

With two Nobel Prize winners, and leaders in cancer research, Judy Vary, Manatee High School senior, recently attended the National American Cancer Society Seminar for 1961 in St. Petersburg.

Dr. Howard Moore, head of the Rosewell Park Memorial Institute for Cancer Research in Buffalo, New York, was so impressed by Judy and her cancer project that he offered her transportation to and from the institute, room and board, plus $150 a month, to continue her research this summer in Buffalo.

She's Going

Judy is going; she's delighted! Of her work, she explains, "It's never been done before, and that's the reason these people are so interested." And "It's so encouraging," she adds, meaning the definite and positive results of her experiments. What Judy is trying to do is to protect normal tissue from the adverse efefcts of irradia-

tion while this radioactive bombardment destroys cancerous tissue, and to retard the movement of the cancer to other parts of the body. She has tried her theories with white mice, keeping exact records and precise charts of all treatments and results.

1st High School Student

Judy was one of three Floridians at the Seminar, and the first high school student ever invited. Just 68 people were invited, Judy explained, and all except herself had doctor's degrees or better. During the five days, March 18-22, they discussed the most recent advances in cancer research, and released much information to the public.

Bring Home Awards

Arriving home from the State Science Fair last week-end, Judy brought with her six cash awards given to her for her outstanding research work. She was awarded a special scholar-

ship from the American Cancer Society . . . $250 to the college of her choice. The American Medical Association also presented her with a special $25 award.

In the Science Fair itself, Judy received a $15 prize in the Medical Arts division and was given a $25 Honorable Mention award by the Florida Medical Association. She is also the recipient of an Award of Excellence from the Science Talent Search.

Nine MHS Regional Fair winners traveled to the Fair, held in Lakeland. Senior Al Freeman was given a special $10 award for his project on astronomy. Sophomore Jimmy Richards also received a $25 award from the American Chemical Association.

Other travelers included Mike Harris, Bob Pope, Charles Throckmorton, Steve Bassett, Larry Jerome and Beth Holcombe.

John Alexander   William Kimber   Stanley Adamson
Helsa Servis   Moira Burke   Judith Vary

Dr. M. A. Bender

... Roswell scientist discusses radioactive isotopes with students

Students Start Roswell Park Work

By PAUL WIELAND

Scientific research with a high school beat began its eighth summer yesterday, brightening the ever-busy Roswell Park Memorial Institute with young people who want to be "in the know."

A group of 66 high school students and June graduates from five states and Canada started work at the cancer research institute under grants mainly supplied by the State of New York and the National Science Foundation.

But their work isn't on the high school level. Far from it.

Working closely with the institute's scientists, the students have plunged into the maze of highly - complicated research techniques being developed to fight cancer.

Officially titled the "Summer Research Participation Program," by its originator, Dr. Edwin A. Mirand, the summer study period provides outstanding science students with opportunities for original and sometimes rewarding research.

National Recognition

"Last summer we had a young lady studying here whose work in the sex determination of chickens was not only outstanding, but earned her national recognition," said Dr. Mirand, director of the program. "These young people are brilliant," he said, "and we try to give them the opportunity to display that brilliance usefully."

The teen-agers began their eight weeks yesterday with a battery of tests to determine their scientific "I-Q's," tests which will be repeated at the end of the program to ascertain the progress they have made.

Following tests, the youngsters were taken on a tour of the institute. The tour was punctuated by calculated once-overs of strange and complicated-looking pieces of scientific apparatus.

The conversation of the students was a strange mixture of the usual teen talk and an abundance of scientific words with little or no meaning to the layman.

Blond Helsa Servis, an 18-year-old June graduate from Silver City, N.M., said she would study neurosurgery techniques during her stay here. She'll attend San Jose State in San Jose, Calif., this fall.

To Study Radio Biology

Dark-haired Judith Vary, 18, from Palmetto, Fla., bubbled with the serious-sounding observation that the institute would "certainly be intellectually stimulating." She will study radio biology.

Dr. Mirand said "whatever they would study, they would study well," as he strode down the corridor to begin discussion of radioactive isotopes with a student.

— CHAPTER 3 —

CANCER GIRL

My father had turned down his opportunity to be part of the Cold War. He did not go to New Mexico to design guidance systems for ballistic missiles that could deliver nuclear warheads, incinerating millions of people in some distant land. Instead, we lived in a quiet little beach town in Florida. In the mid-fifties, we were here, and the Cold War was over there.

By 1960, however, all that was changing. The Cold War was getting closer by the day. Newspaper headlines screamed about "the Reds" at the breakfast table, and ominous voices from the television filled the air with threats of nuclear annihilation in our living rooms every night. The United States and the Soviet Union were locked in a high-stakes game of intimidation. Both sides were armed with diabolical weapons capable of carrying out their threats.

The arms race continued to escalate like an out-of-control poker game with both sides brandishing massive arsenals brimming with tanks, submarines, supersonic aircraft, nuclear bombs and missiles. And each side intimidated the other with a new generation of hydrogen bombs, which defied imagination. These radioactive super-weapons promised a blast equivalent to 100 million tons of dynamite, large enough to obliterate a huge city, while leaving a cloud of radioactive fall-out enshrouding the earth. A "Peace Summit" in Paris hoped to ease the tensions, but collapsed in bitter disarray a few days after the Russians shot down an American U-2 spy plane over Soviet air space.[1]

Raising the stakes further was the scheduled introduction of a new generation of missiles such as the Polaris and Minuteman that could be launched, as the name implied, at a moment's notice and strike deep inside Soviet territory. "Peace on Earth," was now based upon the official strategy cynically labeled MAD — Mutual Assured Destruction.

Polaris A1
1960

Minuteman I
1961

The American war-planners blamed the situation on Soviet aggression and their rhetoric about Soviet Communism could not have been sharper. It was a totalitarian dictatorship fixated on cradle-to-grave control internally, and global domination externally. The Soviet leadership saw the threat differently, and complained that America was  destabilizing the military balance between the two super-powers and fanning the arms race with a new generation of nuclear missiles. The American media portrayed Soviet leader Nikita Khrushchev as a crude and dangerous man who beat his fists and his shoe on his desk in the United Nations to disrupt disarmament meetings. *Time* magazine presented the Soviet leader to its audience standing in front of a mushroom cloud, to emphasize that the Soviets had resumed testing nuclear weapons, and announced their plans to develop a new 100-megaton bomb, a weapon twice as powerful as anything in the American arsenal.

In American culture, anti-Communism became a creed and spawned new organizations like the John Birch Society and the Minutemen, which were dedicated to fighting "the Red Menace." Fanatically patriotic expressions like "I'd rather be dead than Red" crept into the flag-wavers' phrase book and expressed the tone of the time. The nerve-wracking year ended with the election of a new president, John Fitzgerald Kennedy. The question loomed: Would this young untested man have the knowledge and experience to square off with the Soviets, without creating World War III?

On January 17, 1961, citizens across the country soberly watched their television sets as President Eisenhower made his farewell address to the American people. The venerable general, who had led America to victory over Hitler's Germany in World War II, and tried to maintain the peace in the tense years that followed, startled the country by warning about the danger to democracy from the unprecedented power being amassed by America's own "Military-Industrial Complex." He continued, "the potential for the disastrous rise of misplaced power exists, and will persist... we must never let the weight of this combination endanger our liberty or our democratic processes."

Three days later JFK was sworn in as the new president with these words: "Let the word go forth from this time and place, to friend and foe alike, that the torch has been passed to a new generation of Americans, born in this century, tempered by war, disciplined by a hard and bitter peace, proud of our ancient heritage; and unwilling to witness or permit the slow undoing of those human rights to which this nation has always been committed, and to which we are committed today at home and around the world." Then he reminded us, "Man holds in his mortal hands the power to abolish all forms of human poverty, and all forms of human life."

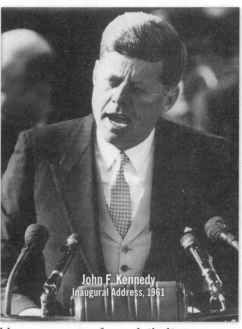

John F. Kennedy
Inaugural Address, 1961

Soon Kennedy announced the formation of the Peace Corps to bring much-needed technical assistance to alleviate poverty in the undeveloped Third World, and the Alliance for Progress, to bring economic development to Latin America in our own hemisphere. Somehow, under JFK's leadership, this new vision of hope surfaced to live side-by-side with the nightmare of global thermonuclear war, which had become part of our daily lives.

To those of us living in Florida, the Cold War and Communism seemed even closer than the abstract threats on the evening news. Less than 100 miles off Florida's coast, the revolution in Cuba had succeeded. Political refugees flocked to Florida as Cuban President Fidel Castro nationalized former American-controlled industries, and shut down the Mafia's beloved gambling and sex trade. The angry reaction of the U.S. government pushed Castro into the welcoming paws of the Russian Bear.

President Kennedy would soon be drawn into this conflict by a CIA-planned invasion of Cuba, a plot begun before he took office. The CIA had trained and armed angry Cuban exiles to overthrow Castro's new regime. The invaders landed on April 15, 1961 on a beach on the south side of Cuba known as the Bay of Pigs. But the Cuban military and their Russian advisers were prepared for the assault. Most of the 1,500 man invasion force was captured and imprisoned in Cuba under notorious conditions. The rest died on the beaches.

The Bay of Pigs failure embarrassed the U.S. in the eyes of the world, and strained already tense relations with the Soviet Union. While JFK publicly accepted the blame for the defeat, he privately felt that the CIA had manipulated him. He fired the CIA's top three officers.[2]

Inside Florida's Cuban exile community, however, the Bay of Pigs was seen differently. In their eyes, they had been betrayed. They already hated Castro with a passion. Now they distrusted Kennedy as well, particularly in Miami, where most of the exiled Cubans lived.

Back in Bradenton, I was still in high school. It was a warehouse of hormones, teeming with dreams, crowded with cliques, littered with romances, contaminated with rumors and decorated with the pageantry of sports teams, marching bands, cheerleaders and screaming crowds that made Friday night a spectacle to behold.

My father's new business was making money, and he built an impressive new house across the river with a dock and a pool, located on Snead Island on the outskirts of town. The move changed our school district, and my sister transferred to Palmetto High. Due to the work I was doing with Col. Doyle, I was allowed to continue at Manatee High School.

This was a busy time: though I was in no more class plays, as in my sophomore year, I stayed active in many clubs and committees — National Honor Society, Science Club, English Club, Art Club, Tri-High-Y, the Prom Committee, and *Societas Latina*. Manatee High held "Study Day" once a month, where students could attend club meetings all day if they didn't need tutoring. It was a wonderful incentive to keep good grades. My friends and I joined lots of clubs together. I got along well with most of my teachers, was on the newspaper staff, and had fun dating.

Of course, high school is still high school, and there were the petty jealousies that any form of success attracts, but I didn't let it get to me.[3] Those speeches to civic groups, meetings with reporters and doctors, work with handicapped kids in Sarasota at Happiness House, and the acrobatic acts my sister and I continued to perform for charities increased my self confidence. Nevertheless, I was on my knees every night. I believed God was guiding my research, and I prayed for breakthroughs. They came.

By now, I'd induced cancer in mice using tobacco tars. Now the focus was to give mice lung cancer with an aerosol form of the tars, for I needed lung cancers to test chemicals such as 2a-MDTP and MEA,[4] which I hoped would protect the normal tissues in these mice, if injected under their cancerous lungs before exposure to cancer-killing x-rays.

But my home life was starting to fracture. My father was no longer a promising scientist concerned about his reputation and the future of his career. He focused on making money and began drinking heavily. He frequently fought bitterly with my hot-blooded mother, who had her own set of problems and was excessively critical by nature. When they were not fighting, they escaped into a string of parties. My father's behavior, both at work and at home, became increasingly erratic.

His bad leg developed a painful bone infection. Desperate to avoid what would become a necessary amputation, my father drank even more to block out the pain. Bitter and angry, on some occasions he

actually hit my mother. That disgusted and frightened me. School became an attractive escape from home. All families have problems, and
we had ours.

My trip to the National Science Fair in Indianapolis the previous
spring had paid off. The batch of exotic chemicals that Dr. Jacobus had
sent me from the U.S. Army's Walter Reed Medical Research Institute
was successful in protecting my mice from the debilitating effects of
radiation long enough for their lung tissues to receive adequate doses
of cancer-killing x-rays.[5] The next step was to try the method on cancerous mouse lungs. Meanwhile, I eagerly bred my new mice so that I
would have enough for my experiments. Their population quickly grew
from 100 to 500. I had so many mice that I color-coded them with food
dye to keep the groups organized: white, purple, yellow and pink.

In the fall of 1960, perhaps an animal lover or maybe just a high
school prankster let all the mice in the biggest cage loose, and they ran
wildly throughout the science building. Imagine the chaos caused by
around one hundred multi-colored mice scampering around a high
school full of squealing teenage girls!

This memorable event was documented in Manatee High School's
1961 yearbook on the Science Club page "Hickory Dickory Dock."

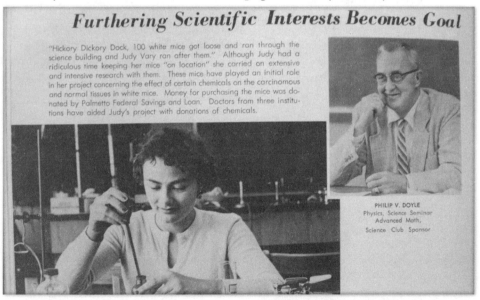

Furthering Scientific Interests Becomes Goal

"Hickory Dickory Dock, 100 white mice got loose and ran through the
science building and Judy Vary ran after them." Although Judy had a
ridiculous time keeping her mice "on location" she carried on extensive
and intensive research with them. These mice have played an initial role
in her project concerning the effect of certain chemicals on the carcinomous
and normal tissues in white mice. Money for purchasing the mice was donated by Palmetto Federal Savings and Loan. Doctors from three institutions have aided Judy's project with donations of chemicals.

PHILIP V. DOYLE
Physics, Science Seminar
Advanced Math,
Science Club Sponsor

In the lower right hand corner of that same page is a photograph of
my friend Tony López Fresquet, who was also a member of our Science Club. I had a huge crush on him, and we dated. He was charming, sophisticated, handsome and fun. Tony was Cuban, from a prominent and socially respected family that had lived there for generations.
His father, Rufo López Fresquet, was a banker and had been Trea-

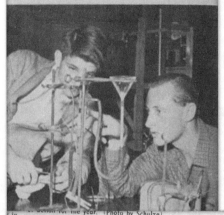

Larry Jerome points out to Tony Lopez-Fresquet the equipment he used for his project, experimenting with non-uniform electric fields. Larry is a member of the Seminor group.

Tony, Vince Lopez-Fresquet, Cuban Students, Attend MHS

By BETH CHAMPAGNE

Have you ever been shot at while driving home from the movies with your friends? Or attended a school where there are no electives (chemistry, physics, trigonometry, economics, and Spanish required in the junior year!) and had a holiday while Communists forced the school to be closed? Tony and Victor Lopez-Fresquet have had many experiences like these in Cuba during the past few years!

destitute but wishes an education, the public school is open to him until it is necessary that he work for a living. Victor and Tony were able to attend a private school.

Students Come To Learn

Since a formal education is not compulsory, most of the students at Tony and Victor's school came for one reason: They wanted to learn.

Tony and Victor's school began at 8:30 a.m. with an hour long study hall. Three classes, with 15 minute breaks between them, filled the remainedr of the morning. A recess of two hours was allowed for students to go home for lunch. At 2:00 p.m. the first of two afternoon classes began.

Teenagers Work

Cuban teenagers are working hard to improve their government, and have much hope for the future. Tony and Victor do not know when they will return to Cuba, but they will return, and do their best to make Cuba a strong and prosperous free nation.

Cuban boys, like Americans, enjoy cars, movies, baseball, basketball, and going steady. The only ones who have jobs are those who really need the

Tony   Vincent

Tony, a senior, and Victor, a junior, are native Cubans and have lived here for only a month. Their parents and young brother still reside in Havana, since their father's former government position prevents him from leaving the country. The boys' mother is an American.

Photo from news article about my Polar Bear Party, January 1961, in the chilly weather at my new house on Snead Island. I'm at far left. Tony López Fresquet is in the middle, massaging a girl's shoulders.

sury Minister in 1959 during the first 14 months of Fidel Castro's revolution, before falling out of favor for being too conservative.[6]

Fearing the turmoil and uncertainty of the political situation, Tony's father sent his two sons to live with their American grandmother in Bradenton. Tony was full of horror stories about Castro. Some of Tony's friends in Cuba had resisted Castro's takeover and been captured by soldiers. I felt his pain as I listened to his tales of resistance and torture.

Tony was the romantic flame of my high school years. But it was a flame that fizzled when he informed me that if he married me, he would require the right to have a mistress to entertain him outside of our marriage. Talk about a turn-off! This drastically violated my monogamist Catholic beliefs, and my vision of what a loving, faithful marriage would be like. I let Tony go from my heart and my life. But he taught me to see Fidel Castro through the eyes of someone who hated him with a personal passion.

As a result of the Great Mouse Stampede, a new laboratory was set up under the grandstands of our school's football stadium. The conditions were modest, if not primitive, but it was all I needed. There were two rooms. The first had a dirt floor covered in sawdust. This is where I kept the mice, and it was, of course, filled with cages. The second room became my workroom. It was more elaborate with a cement floor, fluorescent lights, a fan for ventilation and was equipped with a workbench, a stool, shelves for storing chemicals, and a propane tank. Running water came from a hose snaked over from one of the locker rooms.

By March of 1961, I could prove that cigarettes caused cancer. My 1961 science project was entitled *"Research on the Chemotherapeutic Action of AET, MEA and 2MDHTP on Irradiated Normal and Carcinomous Tissues in White Mice"* and it won 1st place in both the school's Science Fair and in the Regional Competition.[7]

But frankly, I was getting concerned that my experiments were beyond the skill sets of those selected to judge a high school science competition. In fact, I began to question whether they even understood my explanations, which had admittedly gotten quite technical and esoteric. Other than the scholarship money involved, the thrill of winning high school science competitions had started to fade. I wanted to show my results to professional cancer researchers, people with more knowledge and experience in cancer research than myself, who could help my career if they deemed my work important.

I mentioned earlier that Dr. Jacobus of Walter Reed had sent me a list of upcoming conferences. Now the long-awaited meeting of the American Cancer Society's Science Writers' Seminar in nearby St. Petersburg was imminent. The latest advances in cancer research would be revealed to the press. The country's most important cancer research scientists would be there, along with the media's most important health and science writers. All in the same room! So I asked Col. Doyle to arrange a way for me to attend.

Despite my eagerness and Col. Doyle's connections, he apologetically informed me that it would not be possible. The attendee list had been set for months, and only the most respected scientists and the top reporters from America's major media outlets were invited. This was a world-class professional event with no opportunity for a high school student, however curious or accomplished, to attend.

Col. Doyle was defeated, but I was not. Having more guts than good judgment, I thanked my mentor for his efforts, asked some friends to care for my mice for the next few days, and armed with my high school newspaper "Press Pass" and a stack of research records, I headed for the American Cancer Society's 4th Annual Science Writers' Seminar. It was March 20, 1961, the third day of their five-day conference. I soon confronted the obvious problem. St. Petersburg was 22 miles north, and I did not have a car. School was in session, and my friends who did have cars were in class. But I was young, healthy, and athletic. Marathon runners cover 26 miles in a few hours. Why couldn't a determined young person walk the same distance? So I set out on foot to walk from Bradenton to St. Petersburg. If my destiny was right, everything would work out. I walked for several hours, over the Manatee River Bridge and up the highway toward St. Pete.

I covered the first nine miles or so with little discomfort, but then I approached the formidable Skyway Bridge, which towered over the  entrance to Tampa Bay, and saw the miles of causeways which flanked it on either side. At first I was discouraged. Then it hit me. Why walk when I could ride? The highway was full of vehicles rushing by and headed in the right direction. I could hitchhike!

As I pondered the obvious dangers for a lone young female in a vehicle with a total stranger, I spotted a Trailways bus coming up the highway. I decided to try a trick that I had seen in a movie and raised the hem of my skirt enough to show a little thigh. It worked. The driver stopped, and let me on. I sat in the front and talked to him as we crossed the long Skyway causeway. I told him I was headed for the "The Doctors Motel" (its actual name). "Why, that's just a hop, skip and jump from the highway," he told me. "You can see the Skyway from there." What luck, as I could get lost just going around a corner. He dropped me off within sight of the big building.

I rushed over and entered the lobby. The Science Writers Seminar was about to start its next session. The last of the reporters were being hurried inside an already darkened meeting room, and they prepared to close the doors. I thrust myself between a pair of late-comers and flashed my high school "Press Pass" to the men at the door. They waved me inside with the others. I was in!

Inside the meeting room it was, however, hard to conceal the fact that I was a teenage girl in a room populated primarily by grown men in business suits. I was quickly noticed as I hunted for an empty seat. Surrounded by newsmen, scientists and doctors, I kept my head down and nervously took out my notebooks. I was crashing their meeting, and they knew it. The next presentation began with the air of routine. Slides began flashing on the screen at the front of the room. But people continued to whisper and peer at me. Maybe this wasn't such a good idea after all.

Suddenly the slide show came to a halt. Several men in suits approached me with a uniformed policeman. Busted! What could I do? Well, nothing. The policeman reached for my elbow and was helping me from my seat when a white-haired gentleman came over and interrupted them. He had no idea who I was, but he was intrigued that such a young person had dared to intrude on the meeting. He asked them to delay my eviction for a moment, while he conferred with a distinguished-looking couple sitting nearby. Then he returned and informed the security guards that everything was OK: I was now his guest, and I could stay. He walked me back to his table and invited me to sit beside him. Then he handed me a stack of papers to hold. When I quietly thanked him, he smiled at me and put a finger to his lips. The murmur in the room quickly faded, and the slide show resumed. I began taking notes.

During the break that followed the presentation, the white-haired gentleman finally introduced himself. He was Dr. Harold Diehl, the Senior Vice President of Research for the American Cancer Society. I thanked him for rescuing me. Then Dr. Diehl questioned me about my decision to crash his seminar. His attention increased when he heard that I had been conducting my own research on the connection between smoking and cancer, which he said he'd been keenly interested in since his days as Dean of the University of Minnesota Medical School.

Then he introduced me to the Robinsons, who had encouraged him to intervene on my behalf, and they asked me to lunch, along with Mrs. Diehl. At lunch, Dr. Diehl and his guests asked me many questions, such as how I found out about the conference and why I was so interested in attending a cancer seminar. I told them about watching my grandmother die, and about Mrs. Watkins and Col. Doyle, and finally about my own cancer research. I peppered my speech with as many scientific terms as I could think of, to make sure

HAROLD S. DIEHL, M.D. (1891-1973) was Dean of the University of Minnesota Medical School College of Medical Sciences (1935-1958) before becoming Senior Vice President for Research and Medical Affairs at the American Cancer Society (1957-1967). Diehl oversaw the ACS's scientific research programs and lead their crusade against lung cancer. This 1956 photograph highlights his early research linking lung cancer with smoking and shows a machine designed to chain smoke cigarettes in order to collect tar samples for research. In 1961 Diehl met Judyth Vary and inspected her cancer research laboratory at Manatee High School where she did similar research.

they knew I was serious. Finally, I told them I had induced cancer in mice in seven days.

My claim was met with a pregnant silence. Dr. Diehl gently informed me that only a select number of very sophisticated research laboratories in the country were actually able to give cancer to mice. Further, my claim of 'seven days' was faster than any of those laboratories had ever accomplished. If this was true, he said, he would like

Dr. Robert Robinson

to hear more. I offered to show him my records, which I had with me. He started looking through them right there at the lunch table. There I was, showing my research notes to the VP of Research of the American Cancer Society. But where would it lead?

Dr. Diehl then explained that he knew the world of tobacco, cigarette smoking, and lung cancer very well. He and a handful of like-minded doctors had organized an effort to convince the U.S. government to warn the American public about the dangers of tobacco. He, in fact, had recently testified before Congress on that subject. He asked me if I had heard of his friend Dr. Alton Ochsner who had been president of the American Cancer Society some years before. I confirmed that I did know of Dr. Ochsner and said that I had met him briefly at the opening of Dr. Watson's hospital in Lakeland. I said that I had shown Dr. Ochsner a pickle jar with my cancerous fish. I told Dr. Diehl that Dr. Ochsner had given an inspired speech about lung cancer, which had motivated me to do the research we were now discussing. He said that Dr. Ochsner had been Chief of Surgery at Tulane Medical School in New Orleans and that he enjoyed recommending promising students to this prestigious medical school. Dr. Diehl said he would try to contact Dr. Ochsner by phone on my behalf. Tulane? New Orleans? These were new ideas that I hadn't ever considered.

Ochsner with Dr. Matas, his predecessor at Tulane.

In the conversation that ensued, I could not help but notice that Dr. Diehl referred to Dr. Robinson as Sir Robert. This gracious and interesting man and his charming wife were both warm and personable to me, and he indulged me with talk about my research and about various approaches to designing experiments that I might consider. What I did not realize at the time was that Sir Robert Robinson was probably the most respected organic chemist in the world, with honorary degrees from no less than twenty universities, and had won the Nobel Prize for Chemistry. His title was not hereditary, but bestowed upon him by the British crown in appreciation for his contributions to science.

After lunch, Dr. Diehl stopped at a phone in the lobby and called Dr. Ochsner's office, as he had promised, and left a message.

I accompanied Mrs. Diehl back to their hotel room at her request. She was a charming elderly woman, and told me of her own battle with cancer. Her breasts had been surgically removed, as had the lymph glands, leaving her upper arms conspicuously swollen. I combed her hair as she sat before a mirror and removed her blouse to show me the scars from her surgery. It reminded me of the sufferings of my own grandmother. Mrs. Diehl talked at length of her long battle for life. This was the wife of one of the top cancer researchers in the world! Was this the best they had to offer, nothing but crude surgery and amputations?

When we returned to the seminar room, Mrs. Diehl introduced me to two doctors from the University of Chicago and explained that both had won the Nobel Prize. It would have been easy for a high school student to be intimidated by such credentials, but these men were relaxed and friendly to me. The room was full of scientific super-stars at the peak of their careers. But I was a teenager who was giving cancer to mice in her own laboratory. They were astonished at what I had done. They called me a medical Mozart. What a Cinderella experience!

After the seminar I again accompanied the Diehls back to their hotel suite. Dr. Ochsner rang up, returning Dr. Diehl's call. Dr. Diehl began in a friendly way and teased his old friend about what he had started, by inspiring a young girl to do her own cancer research. Then Diehl got down to business and started telling Ochsner about my research. He called it remarkable, and suggested to Ochsner that he come to the seminar to meet me. "Fat chance of that!" I thought quietly.

Then Diehl handed me the phone and said Dr. Ochsner wanted to speak to me. "So you have a project on smoking and cancer?" he inquired. "Good for you! What an excellent girl!" he said in his beautifully modulated voice. Somewhat embarrassed by his praise, but very aware that I was speaking with the former president of the American Cancer Society, I quickly told him as much as I could about my research project in the few minutes I had. When he had heard enough, he asked me to pass the phone back to Dr. Diehl.

When Diehl finished the phone call, he said that Ochsner would try to fly down to the seminar. Huh? It was hard to imagine that the famous Dr. Ochsner would actually fly to St. Petersburg just to meet me, but by this point everything already seemed like a dream. Why not?

Dr. Diehl then said that Dr. Ochsner had asked him to introduce me to the third player in their anti-smoking crusade, Dr. George Moore, who was already attending the conference. Dr. Diehl explained that Dr. Moore was the Director of Roswell Park Cancer Institute in Buffalo, New York, and he had known him since they both taught at the University of Minnesota Medical School. Each summer, Dr. Moore ran a program for promising students funded by the National Science Foundation. Ochsner thought I should attend Moore's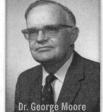

Dr. George Moore

training program and said he would talk to Moore about it. Moore and Ochsner were good friends with a history of professional cooperation in their war against cancer. Both were now involved in researching melanoma, an aggressive and deadly form of skin cancer.

Next, Dr. Diehl called Dr. George Moore's room and told him of his phone call with Alton Ochsner and said that Ochsner wanted him to meet me. Diehl invited Moore to join us and the Robinsons for dinner in the hotel's restaurant. When we arrived, Diehl introduced me to Dr. Moore, a genial man devoid of pretense. He praised Moore's cancer work and his role in their crusade against smoking, saying that Dr. Moore was the first hospital administrator in the country with the courage to ban cigarette vending machines from his hospital.

Then he told Moore about my claim of giving cancer to mice in seven days. Dr. Moore quickly became interested and began questioning me about my work. I did my best to respond, and unleashed my scientific vocabulary on him. Dr. Moore finally told me about his summer program for promising students and teachers, and said that he would like to find a way for me to attend, though all the slots had already been filled. "Oh!" I told him, "how I wish I could go! But I don't know how I'd be able to get there, even if you could slip me in." Then the Robinsons spoke up. They would pay for my transportation! Dr. Moore, impressed with their enthusiasm, came up with a solution: he would place me in his own personal lab, and arrange housing and a stipend for spending money. How could I say no?

When we were finished, Dr. Diehl invited me to attend the rest of the conference, and arranged for some of the writers to pick me up from my high school each morning and drive me home each evening.

The next day I heard a presentation that had a profound effect upon me. Dr. Ludwig Gross talked about his study of cancer, and of his conclusion that most cancers were, in fact, caused by viruses.[10] Cancer-causing viruses! Well, I had come to find out what was new, and I was getting it.

On the last day of the conference, Dr. Ochsner arrived. "So it's you again," he rumbled with his characteristic charm. "We want to take a look at your experiments."

When the seminar ended at noon that day, Dr. Ochsner, Dr. Diehl, a third gentleman and myself climbed in a car and drove back to Bradenton. All three were in their late-60s or 70s. The third man was Dr. Urey, whom I had not met previously. He was some type of chemist and had done something with radiation at the University of Chicago. I didn't ask to see his credentials.

The four of us arrived at Manatee High School, where Col. Doyle was summoned to join us. Doyle graciously greeted the group and offered to show them my laboratory. The three doctors inspected the lab (and the mice) under the stadium, and then followed Doyle back to his classroom, where they sat down and began going through my journals. While they were busy with the journals, Col. Doyle got out the hundreds of microscope slides and preserved lung cancer specimens that I had made. The trio agreed it was a well-designed research project that had produced lung cancer in mice faster than ever before. But there the praise suddenly ended. I had not anticipated what was about to happen next.

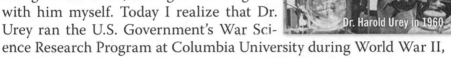

Dr. Urey expressed his concerns about the safety of using radiation and cancer in a high school laboratory with no security or safety equipment. Drs. Diehl and Ochsner concurred. Had I understood Dr. Urey's background better, I might have agreed with him myself. Today I realize that Dr. Urey ran the U.S. Government's War Science Research Program at Columbia University during World War II, which became known to history as the Manhattan Project.

Dr. Harold Urey in 1960

After some discussion of the dangers involved with my experiments, they concluded that no high school student should be allowed to do this kind of research, and that it should not happen again. In their words, I had been "playing with fire." Radiation, to be more precise. They saw the dangers clearly. But I had only learned about the possibility of triggering cancer-causing viruses the day before!

The doctors demanded that Col. Doyle shut down my lab immediately. Can you imagine how I felt? Poor Col. Doyle! I had knocked myself out to get these experts to come to our school and look at my research, which Doyle had supported so strongly. This was to be his moment of triumph. Instead, the most powerful and respected scientists in the country insisted that my laboratory be dismantled! Time to take a deep breath, and think.

A good chess player always thinks several moves ahead. While I was extremely unhappy about the recommendation to shut down my lab, I kept these thoughts to myself. I realized that their intent was not to punish me. These people were trying to help me. And high school was nearly over. I would be graduating in six weeks. What would happen to the lab, then? I couldn't show up at college dragging hundreds of mice in cages with me. I'd accomplished part of my dream, and some of the top cancer scientists in the country knew it. They would help the rest of it come true.

The three great men told Col. Doyle that I was invited to come to Roswell Park Memorial Institute in Buffalo, New York for a summer of fast-track training. The National Science Foundation would fund my work in Dr. Moore's own lab, where I would receive world class instruction on a project of my choice. I would also join the other students — already assigned to other labs — in scheduled seminars, and could choose an additional project, if I liked, which would be supervised by either Dr. Edwin Mirand or Dr. James T. Grace. These two scientists often worked together, and their cancer research was world-famous.

Dr. Urey

As his late-in-life title "Professor-at-Large" from the University of California indicates, Harold C. Urey was a huge intellect that was almost hard to categorize. He was best known for winning the Nobel Prize in Chemistry in 1934 and for being Director of War Research on the Atomic Bomb Project, Columbia University from 1940-1945. Born into a pioneer family in rural Indiana in 1893, he received his first college degree in Zoology. After working as a research chemist, he got his Ph.D. in Chemistry from the University of California and then studied at the prestigious Bohr's Institute for Theoretical Physics in Copenhagen before joining the faculty of Johns Hopkins University in 1929. His early research concerned the structure of atoms and molecules, and he co-authored a book on the subject called *Atoms, Molecules and Quanta*. Now a professor, Urey became editor of the Journal of Chemical Physics and soon joined the faculty of Columbia University where he won the Nobel Prize and where he became Director of War Research. He discovered heavy hydrogen, separated uranium-235 from uranium-238 and, after World War II, joined the Institute for Nuclear Studies, University of Chicago.

In the 1950s, his investigations into measurement of paleotemperatures led to his 1952 book *The Planets: Their Origin and Development*, which addressed the origin of the planets and the chemical problems of the origin of life on earth. Urey speculated that the early terrestrial atmosphere was probably composed of ammonia, methane and hydrogen, and it was one of his Chicago graduate students, Stanley L. Miller, who exposed these gases to simulated lightning and ultra-violet to produce amino acids, the building blocks of life. Later that decade he taught at the University of Oxford and was a member of both the Royal and American Astronomical Association. A crater on the moon is named in his honor. Professor Urey was awarded honorary Doctor of Science degrees from more than a dozen universities and received awards from organizations like the American Chemical Society, the Royal Society, and the National Academy of Sciences (1962). He was a member of many more important scientific societies around the world including the National Institute of Sciences of India and the Weizmann Institute of Science (Israel). He died in 1981.

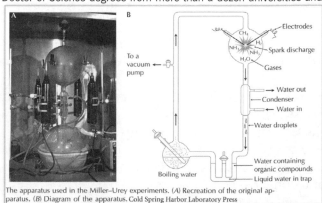

The apparatus used in the Miller–Urey experiments. (A) Recreation of the original apparatus. (B) Diagram of the apparatus. Cold Spring Harbor Laboratory Press

Adapted from http://nobelprize.org/nobel_prizes/chemistry/laureates/1934/urey-bio.html

The transportation funds were left with Col. Doyle, who understood the problems I was having with my father. After the good doctors left, seeing that I was scheduled to take a train from Tampa, I called Dr. Reyniers and left a message (he was out of town) with the good news. Then it was time to call Mrs. Watkins and rejoice with her!

On April 6, 1961, Col. Doyle and Mr. Scharer drove eight Science Seminar students (me included) to Lakeland, Florida, to compete in the State Science Fair. I won no grand prize this time: forbidden to bring my cancerous mice to the Fair, I didn't have the stars of the show with me. I could only display control animals, journals, stacks of x-rays and slides. The busy judges were overwhelmed, and moved on. I did receive a collection of small scholarships and minor awards from organizations like the American Cancer Society, the American Medical Association, and the Florida Medical Association. But I didn't want to let my school down, and there was one final event: the Science Talent Search finale, where hundreds gathered as I presented a paper and answered questions thrown at me by a panel of scientists truly qualified to judge my work. I received The Award of Excellence from the Westinghouse Science Talent Search, and was satisfied.

When we returned, my school newspaper ran an article about my adventures at the ACS Science Writer's Seminar: "Senior Attends National Meet with Sci-

Roswell Park Cancer Institute

Roswell Park Cancer Institute (RPCI) was the first facility in the world dedicated specifically to cancer research. Among its many historical achievements were the first observed immunological reactions to malignancy, the first cancer chemotherapy in the U.S., and the introduction of artificial respiration which revolutionized the field of anesthesiology. It was also the earliest example of government financing of cancer research.

Early Roswell Park X-ray room

In 1946, the RPCI became one of the first to study the effects of radiation on humans, under the direction of Dr. Joseph G. Hoffman, who had worked on the Manhattan Project. In the late 1950s and early 1960s, under the direction of Dr. George Moore, RPCI developed tissue culture media which had enormous impact on biological and pharmacological cell research. Today its Cancer Drug Center is capable of taking a drug from its conceptual stage in the chemistry laboratory through testing of the compound in clinical trials. The center is named after Dr. James T. Grace who co-authored "Human Susceptibility to Simian Tumor Virus." In 1971, RPCI hosted the U.S. House of Representatives hearings for the National Cancer Act which became known as President Nixon's "War on Cancer."

Today, it is one of only three facilities recognized as a National Cancer Institute and continues to receive millions of dollars of grants from the NCI each year. More history can be found at roswellpark.org/AboutUs/HistoricalHighlights

entists."[8] It featured a photo of Doyle with eight of his Science Club students gathered around one of my mice cages. The text mentioned my meeting two Nobel Prize winners and Dr. Moore, as well as my plans to attend the Roswell Park training program (see article opposite this chapter's title page).

Upon seeing this, my biology teacher, Mrs. McCarty suggested that I should write my own article about what I had learned at the conference. Perhaps Col. Doyle could help get it published in the local newspaper, and she would submit it to the trade magazine for the National Association of Biology Teachers.[9] I reviewed my notes from the conference and began working on an article about state-of-the-art cancer research.[10]

By the middle of April, the news about the Bay of Pigs invasion in Cuba broke. My friend Tony was devastated by its failure. One day in the chemistry lab, Tony suddenly grabbed a Bunsen burner and held it under his armpit! Horrified, I demanded that he explain his actions. He told me that was what Castro did to his prisoners. His hatred sharpened mine. Tony vowed to return to Cuba and assassinate Castro himself. Those brave words made me fear for him and his brother.

Then Senator Smathers contacted me again. He wanted me to commit to the University of Florida, and told me that he had arranged a scholarship and some jobs for me. I told him that I had not made up my mind yet, and wanted to think about it over the summer while I was working at Roswell Park Memorial Institute. With the news of the Bay of Pigs fresh on his mind, he inquired about the Lopez boys. I told him they were unhappy about the news from Cuba, but otherwise they were fine. (I omitted the Bunsen burner incident.) Smathers told me it would be better if I did not mention that he had inquired about them. Sorry, Senator. I told them anyway.

A few days later, on April 18th, another newspaper article appeared in the *Bradenton Herald* with a photo of me winning an art competition.[11] It was a welcome relief from the sour mood of my Cuban friends.

Now came the hard part: I had to terminate the remaining mice and clean out my lab. Many of the mice had already died from the cancer experiments, and I had euthanized others that had been contaminated with cancer or radiation. It was unpleasant, but necessary: part of a scientist's job. However, I had set aside about 50 uncontaminated mice as a control group. They presented no danger to anyone. I just couldn't kill them. I tried to find them homes, but nobody would take them. They were afraid of "catching" cancer. So I brought an empty aquarium with me to school and loaded them into it. I carried the aquarium on foot to a place by the river, near a wonderful banyan tree park where they could hide in the roots and build a new home for themselves. I set the aquarium down on the ground, tipped it over, and let them scamper.

On May 4, 1961, a 2,400-word article I had written about my experience at the Science Writers Seminar in St. Pete appeared in the *Bradenton Herald*, entitled: "Tremendous Efforts...".[12] But they didn't realize that I wrote it. My father called the *Herald* and the next day they printed a correction saying "Judy Vary wrote article."

On May 15, 1961, I turned eighteen. My world was full of birthday presents and invitations to graduation parties. I was busy obsessing over boys. But Dr. Ochsner was already responding to the disastrous Cuban situation in his own way. On that same day, he personally founded and financed an organization to fight Communism in Latin America called INCA — the Information Council for the Americas.[13] It would send anti-Communist tapes to radio stations all over Latin America. Then Dr. Ochsner invited his good friend Senator George Smathers to New Orleans to talk to business leaders about the Communist threat from Cuba.[14] Dr. Ochsner explained INCA's mission:

> *"As a surgeon, I know that in an emergency, sometimes you are forced to do things quickly or the patient will die ... We must spread the warning of the creeping sickness of Communism faster to Latin Americans, and to our own people, or Central and South America will be exposed to the same sickness as Cuba."*[15]

The end-of-year graduation parties continued. On June 2, 1961, the school newspaper ran a final article: "Talented Senior, Judy Vary, Takes Honors in Science, Art" and began with the words "Talent personified seems to be the best description of energetic, dark-haired senior Judy Vary." It was "Vary" embarrassing!

Just as classes were ending, I received a large envelope in the mail. It was from the White House. I had almost forgotten that I had written to the president, and hadn't really expected a response. I knew President Kennedy was busy playing nuclear chess with Khrushchev and trying to avert WW III, and didn't really think he had time to worry about Judy Vary. When I saw the envelope, I figured it would be a canned letter written by a secretary. But I was surprised to find a hand-signed letter from Ralph Dungan, President Kennedy's personal assistant, who enclosed a stack of materials about the Peace Corps.[16] I had asked how I could serve my country, and this thoughtful response on White House stationery thrilled me. What a great way to end high school! It was like the cherry on top of the sundae.

THE WHITE HOUSE
WASHINGTON

May 20, 1961

Dear Miss Vary:

The President has received your friendly letter, and he thanks you for the nice things you say about him. Your desire to be of service to your country has been noted and there are many ways you can help our country through responsible citizenship at the community, national, and international levels. I am enclosing several releases which include some of the things the President has mentioned in this respect.

With the President's best wishes,

Sincerely,

Ralph A. Dungan
Special Assistant
to the President

Miss Judyth Vary
4402 Pompano Lane
Palmetto, Florida

However, I still needed to pick a college, and I had a shoebox full of offers. My dream school was the University of Chicago, which sparkled with scientific super-stars and glistened with Nobel Prize winners. This school was founded and financed by the mega-wealthy Rockefeller Foundation and was the jewel in the crown of their medical interests. The school commanded respect from every corner of American science, and even from the lofty professors at the big name universities on the east and west coasts. They had not made me an offer, but I didn't let go of that dream, so I still wanted to be close to Chicago.

The fact that the universities in nearby Indiana were very strong in the sciences had been impressed upon me during the national science competition in Indianapolis in 1960. Purdue, Notre Dame, and Indiana University were all nationally recognized schools — and Indiana University was located in Indianapolis, where my cousins lived. Notre Dame needs little introduction, at least to football fans, but it was still male-only in 1961, so that question was moot. Purdue University was considered one of the great Midwestern universities and was famous for its engineering programs, especially in the highly competitive arenas of aviation and medicine. Even the ubiquitous MLA style sheet which rules "the formats and references of Academia" was developed there. Further, my paternal grandparents and most of my relatives still lived in Indiana.

Purdue's location in West Lafayette, Indiana, placed it about half-way between Indianapolis and Chicago, which made it only a few hours away by car from the University of Chicago itself. The history of Purdue University was closely tied to Indiana's pharmaceutical giants like Eli Lilly, where I knew I had supporters. It was also close to Notre Dame, which was packed with good Catholic boys. And Purdue's scholarship offer was more than adequate. It was also far away from Florida and the problems that had been growing at home with my father. This made Purdue more attractive to me than the University of Florida, only a few hours away from my parents. I decided in favor of Purdue, and wrote them a letter of acceptance.

Several days later, on June 6, 1961, I graduated from Manatee High School and was given the Art Award, but Colonel Doyle warned me that I would not be receiving the Science Award. It would be going to Larry Jerome, a good science student whose talents were obvious. "You have plenty of scholarships and awards already," he reminded me. I really didn't mind, but always felt there was a political element involved, because of the horror the great doctors had expressed about the dangers of my research. What is known for certain is that nobody at Manatee High School ever did research with white mice and cancer again.

A week later, I packed my bags for Buffalo, New York, where I would spend an exciting summer at Roswell Park. Had I known where the path I was entering would eventually take me, I might not have boarded that train.

---

1. Francis Gary Powers' U-2 spy plane was shot down on May 1, 1960.
2. After the Bay of Pigs fiasco, Kennedy fired Spymaster Allen Dulles, Deputy Director of the CIA, Richard Bissell, and Dulles' deputy, General Charles Cabell, who was the brother of Earle Cabell, the mayor of Dallas when Kennedy was shot.
3. To emphasize my point about petty jealousies, I will point to an unfortunate comment published in the press more than 45 years after it allegedly occurred. On 11/21/2008 the *Sarasota Herald-Tribune* (a newspaper owned by the *New York Times*) repeated a story by a classmate (Steve Bassett) that I became so nervous in an English class that I 'pee'd' in my pants. The reporter didn't ask me to confirm the story, which was published on the first page! It was raining hard that day, and I'd borrowed my English teacher's raincoat to cross over to the lab located under the stadium. While there, I turned and the raincoat's stiff sleeve accidentally knocked over a test-tube of mouse urine, which had been collected for chemical analysis. It splashed on me and on the raincoat, which I had to hose off.

    When I came to class, which was held in a cold, temporary building, the coat still smelled rank, and my skirt was wet on the left side all the way around to the back from the hosing. My English teacher was angry. I'd doused her raincoat with 'mouse pee'! She ordered me to stay in the coat, in my seat, until after class, at which time she told me to get the coat dry-cleaned with my own money. Needless to say, I did so. I was one of only four actors in our sophomore play, had won a Curtis Magazine Sales drive for my class selling magazines door to door, and had given speeches to civic groups, so Bassett's tale that I was so nervous about reciting in

English class that I wet myself would be funny if it weren't for its hint of malice. By 1961, Bassett was a Science Club rival whose science fair projects had been defeated by mine three years in a row. We called Steve a "jock" because of his dedication to sports and his fixation on his sports car. He wasn't part of our crowd. He considered himself superior to mere girls. He would end up with a West Point appointment, which is impressive, so he shouldn't have harbored such petty jealousy all those years — but it seems that he did..

4. MDTP (2MDHTP) is the anti-cancer androgen steroid 2 alpha-methyldihydrotestosterone propionate (example: http://cancerres.aacrjournals.org/cgi/reprint/26/11_Part_1/2329.pdf). Today, MEA is known as Cystagon (Cysteamine), used for treatment of radiation sickness (example: The protective effect of beta-mercaptoethylamine in acute radiation sickness.] ISAEV MS. *Azerbaidzhanskii Meditsinskii Zhurnal*. 1962 Oct;10:36-42. Russian.) PMID: 13956756 [PubMed - indexed for MEDLINE]

5. See Dr. Jacobus' letter in the Appendix.

6. *Time*, "The Triumvirate," Dec. 07, 1959. Tony' father, Rufo López Fresquet, was Castro's Treasury Minister in the first year of the Cuban Revolution. A moderate, he was loosely allied with Felipe Pazos, president of the powerful National Bank of Cuba who Castro fired. Tony's father requested permission to resign about one month later. Pazos was replaced by Ernesto ("Che")* Guevara, an Argentine-born physician who served as a Major in Castro's army and strongly supported the Socialistic reforms in Cuba. Che eventually headed to South America in hopes of spreading the Socialist Revolution there, and was captured and murdered in Bolivia. Tony's father wrote about his experiences in his book *My 14 Months with Castro*.

7. MaCoHi article, Mar. 16, 1961.

8. April 14, 1961 MaCoHi "Senior…" "Howard Moore" is a reporting error, apparently Col. Doyle's fault. Correct name was George Moore. It was Howard Diehl.

9. The National Association of Biology Teachers decided not to publish the paper.

10. *Bradenton Herald*, "Tremendous Efforts are being made in Fighting Cancer of All Kinds," by Judy Vary, May 4, 1961. A short article appeared on May 5 stating that the May 4 article had been written entirely by Judy Vary. See: http://www.judythvarybaker.com for full text

11. "Two share top honors in student show," Bradenton Herald, April 18, 1961.

12. The full text of "Tremendous Efforts" can be read at http://MeAndLee.com/TrEfforts. It displays an overview of the extent of my knowledge of cancer at that time.

13. May 15, 1961 — New Orleans. INCA was founded by public relations professional Edward Scannell Butler, under the direction of Alton J. Ochsner, who funded its creation. From the beginning its agenda was narrowly focused on Communism as an issue. INCA in fact sought support from liberal as well as conservative anti-Communists, asking liberal anti-Communist Smathers (U.S. Senator George Smathers, FL - Dem.) to speak at an organization function. http://cuban-exile.com/doc_076-100/doc0078.html

14. Source for Smathers speech at INCA, "A Short History of INCA," by Frank DeBenedictis, Cuban Information Archives, Document # 78, http://cuban-exile.com/doc_076-100/doc0078.html

15. "Dr. Ochsner Outlines anti-Red Tape Activity," New Orleans States Item, April 16, 1963, p. 33; clipping found in FBI file on Alton Ochsner.

16. Dungan had worked for JFK when Kennedy was a senator and advised him on matters related to the American Catholic community and Latin America, especially Cuba. Dungan summoned Paul C. Miller and R. Sargent Shriver to his office in the White House, to assist him in arranging President Kennedy's funeral ceremonies, as soon as Kennedy was declared dead. He worked with Lyndon Johnson for several months before being appointed U.S. Ambassador to Chile. He later became a member of the Council on Foreign Relations.

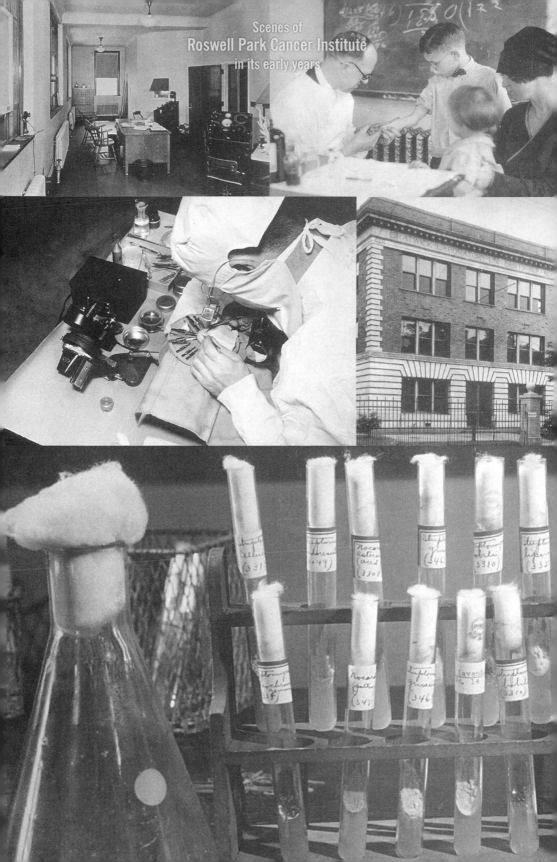

Scenes of
Roswell Park Cancer Institute
in its early years

Saint Francis of Assisi
patron saint of animals and the environment

Chapter 4

Higher Calling

Religion was a major part of my life from childhood. Catholic Sisters had prayed by my bedside for months at Pawating Hospital, and they had educated and guided me through years of elementary school. I was staunchly Catholic, faithfully attended Mass, sang sacred music in the church choir, loyally took Communion, went to Confession each week, prayed on both knees, did not eat meat on Fridays, and, like many Catholic girls, guarded my virginity like it was a national treasure. The catch was that I adored boys and, frankly, liked kissing them.

I have to laugh when I remember one night in high school when I was parked with a cute boy, and we began petting. As we came close to uncharted territory, and my heart started racing, I suddenly began to worry that my virginity might be lost that very night. How could I be a good girl, if I just let go with some guy that hadn't even married me? Thinking fast, I asked my heavy-breathing boyfriend to pray with me to seek God's guidance about whether I should remain a virgin until we got married. That put a quick end to our adventure into the unknown.

At age 18 I was a religious girl dedicated to finding a cure for cancer, who asked for God's guidance every day. The fact that I was now going to be trained by the nation's finest cancer research scientists was mind-boggling: God had answered my prayers! My gratitude was enormous.

Graduation was a time to think about those critical decisions that affect one's life forever. How could I serve God best? What would I do with this great gift of life? The best women I knew were Sisters — the outside world calls them "nuns." Serving God — and being a scientist or doctor at the same time — would be a great way to combine the pull of the world with the desire that burned in me to follow the example of the great female Catholic saints who were heroines in my eyes. Perhaps I could eventually serve as a medical missionary in Laos, as Tom Dooley did, or in Africa, as Dr. Schweitzer did! Such were my thoughts as I prepared for the big trip north, packing my bags to spend the summer at the Roswell Park Memorial Institute for Cancer Research in Buffalo, New York (today known as the Roswell Park Cancer Institute).[1]

I would be enrolled in an elite student program financed by the National Science Foundation. It was very competitive. 2,000 students from around the country applied for 70 positions, but my situation was somewhat different from the other students. I would also be working in Dr. Moore's personal laboratory on a melanoma project that Drs. Ochsner and Diehl were interested in. And Dr. Moore was the Director of the entire Roswell Park facility.

Mrs. Watkins was happy to hear that I'd be working in Dr. Moore's own laboratory.

"I have relatives in Philadelphia," she told me. "What if I ride the train with you as far as Penn Station? Then, later," she added, a bit sadly, "when I come up to Roswell Park to get evaluated, you can introduce me to Dr. Moore."

That's when I learned that my Mrs. Watkins had made an appointment to see if there was anything that could be done about her recently diagnosed advanced cancer of the stomach and pancreas. I was shocked. Stunned. Why would God let Georgia Watkins, who had helped so many people who suffered with cancer, get cancer herself? Unfair! Horrible! I went home and cried myself to sleep.

———

"I'll miss you so much, Juduffski," my mother said. "I don't want you to be lonely there," she went on, "so here..." I couldn't believe my eyes. My mother handed me a cage with two parakeets in it. I'd given them to her for Mother's Day, and now she was giving them back to me. Parakeets! It was the last thing I needed! Daddy hugged me, then put my suitcase in Col. Doyle's car, where Mrs. Watkins waited.

Col. Doyle drove us to the station in Tampa, and we boarded the train. I was happy to have her company on such a long trip, but inside I was gnawing on myself about her cancer. She had always been such an elegant lady — a pastor's wife and a prominent member of the community. Now, sick with cancer, she turned stoic and courageous. She tried to be discreet, but it was hard not to notice that she repeatedly coughed up blood into a neatly folded handkerchief.

At the Tampa train station, I stood in line to purchase two sandwiches. A poor elderly Negro woman stood in front of me, but was ignored until all "whites" were served. I couldn't believe it: they served a dozen people ahead of her. The old lady didn't have time to get the sandwich she paid for — the train came — so, on the train, I gave her my extra sandwich. I was just so angry about it. As for Mrs. Watkins, she ate almost nothing. She was quite weak and could hardly walk. It was a long train ride. When we finally arrived in New York City, I was so concerned about her that I got off the train to stay with her until her relatives arrived. Doing so meant that I missed my connection, but it gave us more time together. Through it all, Mrs. Watkins kept a cheery smile, and reminded me that her favorite "helper" was going to become a cancer researcher! When her relatives finally arrived, I offered them the parakeets, but they declined. When they left, I boarded the next train to Buffalo with my cage of parakeets. Once in Buffalo, I caught a taxi, and thankfully, the driver was glad to take the birds off my hands.

When I finally arrived at the cancer institute, I was four hours late and was welcomed by a critical voice that informed me that I was not only the last student to arrive, but that I had missed the IQ tests. This irritated Dr. Edwin A. Mirand, who ran the student program. He was a man with a very precise manner who liked things run his way and on time. To his credit, he took seriously the fact that he was responsible for the safety of the 67 students and teachers who would be working in a wide variety of cancer research projects, as

> **To Study Radio Biology**
>
> Dark-haired Judith Vary, 18, from Palmetto, Fla., bubbled with the serious-sounding observation that the institute would "certainly be intellectually stimulating." She will study radio biology.
>
> Dr. Mirand said "whatever they would study, they would study well," as he strode down the corridor to begin discussion of radioactive isotopes with a student.

well as around hospital patients who were mortally ill with cancer. But his admirable traits of discipline and responsibility did not mesh well with my growing independence, and both of us knew I would be working in the personal laboratory of his boss, Dr. Moore, which meant that some of my activities were out of Dr. Mirand's control. I probably should have shown Dr. Mirand more respect. He was, after all, one of the nation's leading experts on cancer-causing viruses. But to me, he was just the person running the student program.

It would be appropriate to mention here that Dr. Mirand co-authored an important medical article published in 1963, entitled "Human Susceptibility to a Simian Tumor Virus." "Simian" refers to apes and monkeys, and 'Tumor," of course, refers to a cancerous growth. So "simian tumor virus" really means "cancer-causing monkey virus." Why would the medical community want to know if humans could get cancer from a monkey virus? An important question! If you recall at the Science Writer's Seminar earlier that year, Dr.
Ludwig Gross discussed cancer-causing viruses, such as SV40 (Simian Virus #40).[2] SV40 had been traced to the Rhesus monkey. And the

kidneys of the Rhesus monkey had
been used to grow hundreds of millions of doses of the polio vaccines
distributed in the late-1950s.

After releasing tens of millions
of doses of the polio vaccine, the
scientific establishment found that
the cancerous SV40 had contaminated that same vaccine! The public
knew little about these matters at
the time, but the cancer researchers of the day were well-informed
about potential dangers... and consequences. They all knew there was
at least one cancer-causing monkey
virus in the polio vaccine, possibly
more. The critical question was:
Did SV40 cause cancer in humans?

The coauthor of the article was

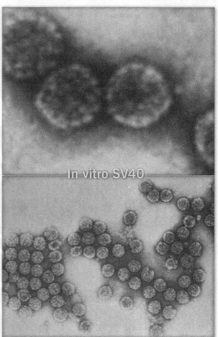

In vitro SV40

Dr. James T. Grace, also from the staff of the Roswell Park. Dr. Grace
had committed himself to cancer research after watching his two
year old son die of leukemia. Finally, I understood their interest in
me. Watching my grandmother die was "the price of admission" to
this strange and demanding world, populated by committed scientists
who had watched their loved-ones suffer from the common enemy
they fought daily.

Dr. Grace was a warm and personable man whose primary role in
the program was to teach the students to handle cancer-causing viruses safely. He taught me to propagate and handle the "Friend Virus"
(an unfriendly retrovirus that caused leukemia in mice)[3] and SV40 (the
DNA monkey virus that contaminated the polio vaccine and caused
cancer in a variety of mammals).

I was given a private room at the YWCA instead of a bed at the
university dorm where the majority of females in the program stayed.
The "Y" was a well-managed facility that was only ten minutes from
Roswell Park by bus. As such, it was a popular out-patient residence
for cancer patients being treated there. Being separated from most of
the other students had the effect of limiting my contact with them
after hours, and curtailing any gossip about the work being done in
Dr. Moore's lab.

In the room next to me, there was a beautiful young black woman
who was an opera singer. She had come to Roswell for treatment as a
patient. Ironically, she had throat cancer. She was educated, sophis-

ticated, and trained in classical opera. Plus she was always gracious and cordial to me. When I met her, she was still able to sing and spoke beautifully. I liked her and we became friends.

Our student program began the next day, and Dr. Mirand ran our seminars. I now saw why Dr. Mirand was selected to run the student program. His seminars were exciting and inspiring, precise and organized. He also had the "appointees," as they called us, attend the institute's staff sessions to learn how the day-to-day operations of a cancer research facility actually worked. After my classes, I reported to Dr. Moore's lab for the rest of the day. Dr. Moore was a genial and unpretentious man who kept himself in good shape by playing volleyball or basketball with the staff. But his work was his world. Once he got into his laboratory, he became uncommonly focused. Dr. Moore was also the director of the entire institute. So he came and went at will and left the day-to-day management of affairs in the lab to Dr. Haas and his wife, with whom I worked closely on a daily basis. Also part of this group was a brilliant college student named Art. This was his second summer working in Dr. Moore's lab, where he was wrapped up in the study of bacteriophages — viruses that destroy bacteria — which we believed could be adapted to selectively attack certain kinds of cancer cells in the body. This area of research continues to show promise today, which shows how far ahead of his time Art really was.

Medical articles by Drs. Grace and Mirand

These articles show the medical interests of Drs Grace and Mirand in the early 1960s:

"Roswell Park Research Participation Summer Program: Implications for professional education," J Med Educ. 1960 Jul; by E A MIRAND, G E MOORE, J T GRACE Jr

"Induction of leukemia in rats with Friend virus," Virology. 1962 Jun; by E A MIRAND, J T GRACE Jr

"Transmission of Friend virus disease from infected mothers to offspring," Virology. 1962 Mar; by E A MIRAND, J G HOFFMAN, J T GRACE Jr, P J TRUDEL

"Effect of chemotherapeutic agents on Friend virus induced leukemia in mice," Proc Soc Exp Biol Med. 1961 Nov; by E A MIRAND, J T GRACE Jr

"Morphology of viruses isolated from human leukemic tissue," Surg Forum. 1961; by J T GRACE Jr, S J MILLIAN, E A MIRAND, R S METZGAR

"Studies of leukemic cell antigens," Surgery. 1965 Jul; by E A MIRAND, G E MOORE, J T GRACE Jr

"Induction of tumors by a virus-like agent (s) released by tissue culture," Surg Forum. 1961; by E A MIRAND, D T MOUNT, G E MOORE, J T GRACE Jr, J E SOKAL

"Studies Of Leukemic Cell Antigens," Lab Animal Care. 1965 Feb ; by J T GRACE Jr, R F BUFFETT, E A MIRAND, V C DUNKEL

"Morphology of viruses isolated from human leukemic tissue," Proc Soc Exp Biol Med; by G OWENS, S J MILLIAN, E A MIRAND, J T GRACE Jr

"Relationship of viruses to malignant disease. Part I: Tumor induction by SE polyoma virus," Surgery. 1965 Jul; by E A MIRAND, J T GRACE, G E MOORE, D MOUNT

from the *BioInfoBank Library*

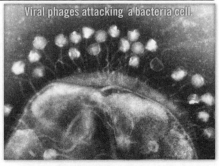
Viral phages attacking a bacteria cell.

Ongoing was a project to develop a liquid medium to keep cancer cells alive — a difficult task at the time. I worked with Dr. Moore and associates that summer in helping develop the basis of what is now the famed RPMI medium, still used worldwide to grow cancer cells in test tubes. By the end of that summer, I knew how to create these advanced mediums, which could keep cancer cells alive no matter where I ran a lab. That's important to remember in this story.

I had just begun my work when I received a phone call from Dr. Reyniers in Tampa. He had finally returned from his trip and had gotten my message about going to Roswell Park for the summer. He congratulated me and asked me to pass his regards on to Dr. Moore and his staff, many of whom he knew well. It was nice to be able to pass "regards" from someone so well-known to Dr. Moore, who said, "You do get around." Such social networking is as important in scientific careers as in any other. I promised myself that I would repay the favor to Dr. Reyniers one day if I could.

On many levels, this summer would be a rough emotional experience — a baptismal immersion into the tragedy of cancer. Day after day I saw people in the most advanced and dreadful stages of the disease, fighting for their lives. I saw patients exposed to radiation and injected with toxic chemicals in the attempt to poison their tumors. I saw their limbs amputated and their organs removed. I watched people die on the operating table. I saw patients so addicted to cigarettes that even when their cancerous tongues and jaws were removed, they still refused to quit, smoking their cigarettes through the red, wet hole that remained!

The laboratories at Roswell Park used animals for their experiments. I saw their suffering

James A. Reyniers

Bacteriologist James A. Reyniers pioneered the development of germfree animals for scientific research at the University of Notre Dame over a 30 year period. Virtually all the germfree colonies now multiplying in a dozen medical centers on four continents are either descended from Reyniers' stock or were developed using his methods.

Originally from Chicago, Reyniers was expert in the use of machine tools, a skill he learned in his family's business. He used these skills to develop laboratory equipment, such as isolation chambers for handling highly pathogenic organisms. He called himself a "bacteriological engineer," and it was said that his machine shop often dwarfed his laboratory.

Reyniers constructed a portable isolation system which integrated mechanical air filtration, steam sterilization, and specially constructed chambers. The military application of this technology was for biological weapons research in the 1940s. Records from the National Archives list him as participating in biowarfare research at that time. According to a 1961 article in TIME Magazine, Reyniers left Notre Dame in 1959 to set up the Germfree Life Research Center in Tampa, Florida, where he concentrated on the mysterious role of viruses as causes of cancer. He also co-authored an article on viruses in Japanese quail eggs in 1962 for the Laboratory of Viral Oncology, National Cancer Institute, U.S. Public Health Service, Bethesda, Maryland.

in a new light. I could see the sadness in their eyes as they looked upon a world composed of metal walls, monotony and pain. There was no hope for them. I saw their fear when their human keepers approached. One day my assignment was to watch five sedated dogs get 'de-barked' by having a hot cauterizing iron thrust down their throats to burn out their vocal cords. They could no longer bark, but they could still whine.

The animals were often shaved and wrapped in bloody bandages. One German shepherd mother had five puppies following a surgical procedure that removed her right lung. Nobody had guessed she was pregnant. She licked her newborn puppies clean, despite the agony imposed on her, only to watch them taken away. The sorrow in her eyes haunted me.

Marmoset

These experiences had a deep emotional impact on me. I felt guilty about the marmoset monkeys we were killing that summer in Dr. Moore's lab, and for the first time questioned the ethics of what I'd done to all those mice back in Bradenton.[4] A new part of my soul was beginning to open, and I became acutely aware of how much pain filled the world, like watching smoke slowly fill the hallway in a burning building.

About mid-summer, Mrs. Watkins arrived in Buffalo for her evaluation. It was good to see her, until she told me that the doctors had found that her cancer — already deadly — had now metastasized to both her kidneys. At her age, kidney transplants would not be a viable option. She knew her condition was terminal and understood, better than most people would, the sentence she had just received. She now faced the certainty of a slow, gruesome death.

There was nothing for her to do but go home. Needless to say, we had a long, sorrowful goodbye. Georgia Watkins had been the one who had started me on this path. She had been the one who helped me, encouraged me and trained me. Even in this dark hour, her confidence in my future remained unshaken: I would find a cure for cancer! Her life's work would not have been in vain!

I wept as she left, but I was now more determined than ever to fulfill Mrs. Watkins' prophesy and make her proud of me. Full of new resolve, I began staying later and longer than any of the other students at the labs, and took on extra projects. I gave myself little time for frills or fun.

I stopped attending the special weekend activities, such as canoe trips and visits to nearby Niagara Falls, which were intended to break the stress. Instead, I began reading cancer research journals, even tackling those written in foreign languages. Remembering how Dr. Reyniers had helped me, and hoping to donate to his cancer charity

("Research, Inc."), I purchased art supplies on my slim budget and began painting: I'd sell paintings to help his cause! Good luck was with
me: while jogging near the "Y" for exercise, I discovered D'Youville
College. I was allowed to set up a little studio after making friends with
some students there. The College soon agreed to put my paintings on
display to help raise funds for Dr. Reyniers' charity.[5] Particularly striking was the high quality of the medical technology program run by
this small Catholic college, which had been founded by Ursuline nuns.

"Small" did not mean "inadequate." I remembered that I'd
been offered a full scholarship
by St. Francis College — a small
Catholic college in Fort Wayne,
Indiana. I now learned that St.
Francis, too, had an excellent
medical technology program.
D'Youville was so friendly —
and so Catholic — that I began
to spend my Sundays there. I
was beginning to reconsider those plans to attend Purdue University.

As the days passed, the cancers that surrounded me seemed to be
closing in. My friend, the lovely opera singer who lived in the room
next to mine at the YWCA, was losing her battle. As the cancer —
and the debilitating radiation she was getting — pulled her down, she
became a ghost of her former self, not only losing her singing voice,
but even her ability to speak above a whisper. Yet she thanked God
for each day that she was able to utter a single word. It was unmistakable that she was dying. The dignity with which she faced her ordeal
humbled me.

Another woman living down the hall from me at the YWCA had
brain cancer, and they had surgically removed the cancerous part of
her brain. Now she suffered from sudden, dangerous seizures. In the
middle of the night I would hear her scream, and rush to her room.
By using a tongue depressor, I was able to keep her from seriously biting her tongue, but I didn't sleep well for fear she'd seize and I'd not
hear her. As we neared the end of the student program, I had a final
report to prepare for a seminar, which required long hours of work in
an alert state. I wasn't getting enough sleep. Then, on a D'Youville bulletin board, I noticed there was a room for rent in a nearby building
above the art gallery. After talking to the landlord, I went back to the
YWCA and got my things.

I had no idea that anyone would be upset, for the doctors never
came near the "Y." But they were. Somebody must have ratted on me,

because Dr. Mirand and a friend of his went looking for me immediately, frantic with worry. He thought he had *lost* a student! I probably should have told him what I was doing, but I didn't. Before long, they found me in the little garret room I'd rented, enjoying my spaghetti dinner straight from the can. Dr. Mirand, his face pale and his countenance furious, demanded my immediate return to the YWCA. "This place is a mile away from the Y!" he fumed. "We put you in the "Y" because it's only ten minutes away from the labs, so you can get more work done. That means, stay put! Those are the rules!" It was an order I had to obey.

I told Dr. Moore about the incident the next time I saw him, hoping I might position it in a better light than Dr. Mirand would. But Dr. Moore had far more serious things on his mind. He just chuckled at my story and said it was good that I gave "Edwin" something to fidget about.[6] The important thing was the work on melanoma that I was doing in his lab. He added that I did not need to continue in Dr. Mirand's program if I didn't want to.

The only place where I felt normal at this point was working in Dr. Moore's lab with Dr. Haas and his wife. It was where I belonged. One day we were discussing a young woman who had worked in their lab the year before: "What a waste!" they griped. "She became a nun!" I knew Dr. Haas and his wife were devout Catholics, so I was curious about their comment.

"Is she not going to become a scientist, or a doctor?" I asked.

"Yes, she still is," replied Dr. Haas, "but she'll never have children."

It was this comment that gave me the idea that I could be both a nun and a cancer researcher at the same time. Committed to finding a cure for cancer, and attracted to the idea of becoming a medical missionary for the Catholic Church, as had Dr. Tom Dooley, I'd not seriously considered becoming a "Sister" *and* a cancer research scientist. The idea was compelling. Peace and serenity! Life in a community that would always support my cancer research! I began to mull over what the doctors had told my mother when I was ten years old — that I'd never have children. Sadly, for the first time I realized that if I got married, the man I'd marry would be deprived of the massive joys of fatherhood. If I really loved that man, how could I let him marry somebody like me?

About this same time, Dr. Moore told me that Dr. Diehl was coming for a visit, and would be a guest at a dinner at Moore's home. Some students would be there, and he hoped I would come too, if I was free. *If I was free?* As if "No" was even an option. Yes, yes, yes, I would be there!

That evening Dr. Moore drove me from the lab to his beautiful home. The weather was perfect, so we ate outside on a patio in the back overlooking a lush wooded creek. Including myself, there were about fifteen students from the National Science Foundation program.

It was good to see Dr. Diehl again, and he was gracious and warm as usual. After dinner Dr. Moore took me aside to meet with Dr. Diehl in his study to discuss my future plans.

I was quite happy to have their interest and liked what I heard. They wanted me to continue my own research, instead of abandoning it and going to college as a normal freshman. Given that nothing was normal about my education at this point, the possibilities seemed limitless. I agreed with their suggestion, then told them about my desire to serve both God and humanity, perhaps as a combination doctor and nun in the Franciscan order. There I could devote 100% of my life to the fight against cancer. I told them about an offer sent to me by Saint Francis College (now the University of Saint Francis) in Fort Wayne, Indiana.[7] They understood that I was sincere, and took my proposal seriously, but they also exhibited a gentle fatherly concern that I might change my mind about "the nun thing" in time.

Dr. Moore and Dr. Diehl discussed my proposal and evaluated how it might impact the funding they had envisioned for my research. After some deliberation, they suggested that I could spend a year or two at St. Francis, before moving on to the University of Chicago. After all, St. Francis *did* have a fine medical technology department. They could arrange for grants, they said, to support a laboratory there for my use, so I could continue in my present course of research. I had just begun working with monkey viruses and radiation, under Dr. Grace, and was anxious to merge that new knowledge with my present work — facilitating the most rapid growth possible of human-based melanomas, in variants of our new, ground-breaking RPMI mediums. Dr. Diehl suggested that I could compare the growth rates of human melanomas infected with SV40 with that of uninfected human melanomas to determine what would make these fast-growing cancers even more deadly.

I was taken aback. Wasn't that just the opposite of what we were supposed to be doing?

"The key to defeating cancer is to understand it," Dr. Diehl reminded me. "If we learn what makes cancer more deadly, instead of what makes it weaker, we'll be forging ahead in brand new territory."

I understood. It was a "top-down" approach. What made cancer more deadly might just provide the key we needed to know how to defeat it.

None of this would interfere with any plans having to do with becoming a nun, they told me. And I'd be far away from my parents in Bradenton, and all their problems, which was what I wanted. That night, I wrote to Admissions at St. Francis College and accepted their offer. I would start in September, only weeks away. I also wrote to Purdue and formally declined their generous offer.

By the end of the summer training program, I had presented three papers to the program appointees and staff at Roswell Park.[8] Even Dr. Mirand begrudgingly complimented me on the quality of my final presentation at the last seminar session. "I don't know how you do it," he muttered.

As a result, I received several awards, including a grant from the National Science Foundation for my college tuition. Further, lab equipment and supplies would be sent to me, care of a lab in Fort Wayne, from the National Cancer Institute and the American Cancer Society. I would be getting a new strain of specially bred bacteria-free mice, tissue cultures with cancerous viruses like SV40, and cancerous tissues derived from human cells, like melanoma.[8] This is where Diehl and Ochsner wanted me to focus my research efforts. It would be quiet, low profile, with little red tape. Everything was set.

My parents called to tell me that Sister Mary Veronica had sent a letter. They were thrilled that I was going to attend a Catholic college. My time at Roswell now drew to a close, and yearning to see family and friends again before going to Fort Wayne, I took the train down to Tampa where I would then transfer to a bus for the final leg to Bradenton. But I had business in Tampa first. Dr. Moore had asked me to stop in and see Dr. Reyniers to arrange to get mice for my lab.

It was good to finally meet Dr. Reyniers in person, and I told him about donating the profits from my paintings to his research charity. In return Dr. Reyniers gave me a voucher I could use to get mice for the new laboratory I would be setting up at St. Francis.[9]

This stop in Tampa took longer than I expected. I had stopped in to see my grandfather who was in a hospital there. Grandpa had been exposed to mustard gas in World War I and had problems with his lungs. I missed the next several buses, and when I finally arrived back in Bradenton, my father picked me up at the bus station and brought me home... to a surprise party! My father had thrown a feast! Our house was jam-packed with friends. Two local beauties, Miss Manatee County and Miss Manatee County Fair, were there. My mother had bought a large cake topped with a white mouse sculpted out of frosting. Reporters and photographers from the local newspapers collected names

Mouse On The Cake

From Palmetto way comes news of **Judy Vary**, daughter of Mr. and Mrs. Donald W. Vary of Gulf to Bay estates. Judy was surprised recently at her home by 50 high school friends. She was home from Roswell Park Memorial Cancer Research Center in Buffalo, N.Y. Her time there was spent with white mice — every day, in fact. She did research work at the Center and worked under Dr. Howard Moore, the head of Roswell. They met last March when Judy was a guest writer at the National Science Writers Seminar in St. Petersburg.

and took photographs, and more articles appeared in the press about "Judy and her cancer research."

But my visit was brief. A few days later, in early September, 1961, I kissed my family goodbye and took a bus back to Tampa. There I boarded a train headed for Indiana, looking forward to setting up a lab as soon as possible that would be capable of handling the precious cancer cells that would soon arrive from Roswell Park.

Upon arrival at St. Francis College, I signed up for a full load of pre-med courses with organic chemistry, anatomy and physiology, math and a required English course taught by Dr. Fink! There's a name you don't forget. I quickly got into a religious routine by attending Mass every day.

By this time, I knew not to gossip about my work with other students. So I had the public face of a college freshman, and a secret life as a cancer researcher working on accelerated projects for the top scientists in that field in the country.

I settled into a room in the dormitory with two roommates. One of my roommates was a large girl with pendulous breasts and over-sized underwear. We were not close and I don't even recall her name. The other roommate, however, was quite memorable. This was Marilyn, an attractive girl armed with both a keen brain and a good sense of humor. Like me, she intended to combine medicine with a life of service to humanity, and was enrolled in premed classes, so we shared similar schedules, classes and interests. Every bit as religious as I, Marilyn told me how she had rejected her previous pursuit of earthly pleasures to pursue a higher purpose in life. She not only admitted she wasn't a virgin, but at night, after our third roommate fell asleep and began to snore, Marilyn would lie on her bed and recount her romantic adventures with various boyfriends, including intimate carnal details.

I was curious, as any girl would be. Marilyn was a gifted storyteller who laced her riveting tales with outrageous comments and delicious details. One comment stayed with me: as our roommate snored away, Marilyn said, in a stage whisper, "*Sex! Yes! I loved it!*" Then, with a deep sigh, she confessed, "The angels! They don't know what they've been missing!"

Marilyn became my closest friend at St. Francis. We both joined the choir and sang at Mass every morning. We both groaned over our comparative anatomy class, run by a tyrant nun. My small lab was now ready, but I still had no mice, so while waiting for their arrival, I had time to explore St. Francis' idyllic campus.

The architectural centerpiece of St. Francis is called "the castle." It was a lavish Victorian mansion built of sandstone in 1902 by industrialist John H. Bass, who became one of the wealthiest men in America by making wheels for railroad trains in the late 1800s.

The interior of the Bass Mansion was elaborately paneled with irreplaceable hardwood. In its center was an exquisite reading room with ornately carved cabinets holding treasured book collections. Carpeted stairs coiled down to a Gothic abyss of a basement where a huge collection of books, many very old, filled shelf after shelf in a labyrinthine maze. Hardly anyone was ever there, and the air was thick with silence. There was an occasional lamp, with an over-stuffed chair nearby to curl up in.

The library on the campus of St. Francis College on Spring Street, housed in the 33 room castle-like mansion called *Brookside,* named after the stream that crossed the 300 acre Bass estate.

Among this historic collection, I found treasures like a first edition of Milton's *Paradise Lost,* which I took from the shelf and started to read before I even reached the chair. At first, I eagerly inhaled it at my normal speed-reader pace, but soon I was reading slower and slower, as I was drawn into the depths of its beauty. I had finally found my sanctuary, and frequently returned to immerse myself in the mesmerizing solitude of those silent, subterranean rooms throughout the semester. Sometimes I would find myself reading alone into the night, feeling the great stone building shrouding the depth of human experience that lay between the dusty covers of the priceless collection. Here I read some of the great classics of Western literature: Blake, Dante, Hugo, as well as Russian authors like Pushkin and Dostoevsky. Some of the Russian works were published in dual language editions, so I got to practice reading in Russian to keep my meager skills alive.

It was great to be able to read literature instead of medical books, and to have a place where I could read in solitude. I relished my freedom from the daily control of my obsessive parents, and the meddlesome Dr. Mirand. Between the medical program, the religious atmosphere, and living in a tightly knit community of smart respectable young women, I felt I had really found my place in the world. I was on the road to having everything I had ever dreamed of.

But the American Cancer Society and the National Science Foundation were not paying my tuition and expenses so I could worship God, read Russian novels and listen to Marilyn's romantic adventures. I had work to do, involving cancer-causing monkey viruses like SV40 and human cells with melanoma. To this end, I had two laboratories. My main lab was not even on campus. It was housed at a nearby hospital, which was a convenient public front where things like radiation and handling viruses were not unusual. And it was just a brisk walk from St. Francis. The fact that the hospital had two new buildings under construction created an atmosphere of chaos that made it easy for me to slip in and out of my lab. I was hardly noticed, as the hospital was doubling in size with many new faces on the staff.

My concern about being noticed had to do with the fact that I was a minor who was officially not supposed to be working with viruses and radiation.

So not only did I try to keep a low profile around the hospital, but the paper trail for my project had to be protected. All items for my laboratory projects were shipped to me in care of a doctor in town. The doctor was Ray W. Fuller, a young biochemist who had just received his PhD from Purdue.[10] Fuller was the first director of the Biochemistry Research Laboratory at the Fort Wayne State Development Center

Dr. Ray W. Fuller

(a mental hospital), where he developed psychoactive drugs. Aware of the fragility of his new position, Fuller was anxious to please persons such as Dr. Diehl – the American Cancer Society's Vice President in charge of research, happily receiving shipments for me. In some cases, his lab actually did some of the initial processing of the cell cultures. After two years in Fort Wayne, Fuller officially joined the Eli Lilly company where he spent the next 33 years of his career. Today, Dr. Fuller is best known as coinventor of Prozac, the psychoactive drug that earns billions of dollars each year for Eli Lilly.[11]

I am not exactly sure how the chain of communication worked in Fort Wayne, but it appeared to involve Dr. Fuller, Eli Lilly, Roswell Park, and the American Cancer Society, all of whom were on our cancer team at the time. Bank-shooting deliveries through Dr. Fuller made it hard for anyone on the outside to trace the exact supply route to me. Since I was still a minor and was not supposed to be handling these types of materials without proper supervision, the paperwork said a qualified adult, Dr. Fuller, was my supervisor. The goal of my experiments was to see if the onset of melanoma was affected by the presence of SV40 (the monkey virus that had contaminated the polio vaccine). If I could learn under what circumstances the SV40 virus affected melanoma development – if indeed it did – perhaps I could then manipulate the virus to see what effect that had on melanoma development. At this time, I did not know that many thousands of people had actually been injected with the contaminated vaccine. The very thought of releasing that kind of loose cannon into masses of trusting people would have disgusted me. Aiming at the mechanics of the SV40 virus itself to make it fight cancer was a bold idea.[12] And if it worked, it would be what Dr. Ochsner called "Serendipity!" Cancer cells containing the SV40 virus arrived by early October 1961. They would be soon be followed by monkey kidney cells, through which the SV40 virus had spread like a fungus on old bread.

At the state hospital, Fuller's team processed my deliveries. They stabilized the tissue cell cultures in what today would be called a highly recommended precursor of RPMI 1640 (that's 1,640 variations of the medium that Dr. Moore and his assistants, such as myself, tested before the standard RPMI medium was perfected in 1967). When the cells were determined to be safely growing in the medium, it was sent to St. Joseph's Hospital — not far from St. Francis College — where I worked with the tissue cultures in their sparsely furnished oncology lab. I also brought cell cultures from that lab back to the St. Francis campus where my second lab was located. It was small and modest, but adequately equipped to nurture the cell cultures.

My initial task was to continue one of the three Roswell Park projects — growing hamster cell cultures in which a modified human melanoma had been established. I was testing a variety of RPMI mediums to determine which medium might speed up melanoma growth. Within two weeks, I revved the melanoma in those hamster cells into metabolic high gear. My reports were sent to Dr. Ochsner, who never acknowledged my communications directly, but I soon received his response — human melanoma cells from Buffalo.

I was told that these melanoma cells were from the cancer that had killed my then-hero, U.S. Navy Dr. Tom Dooley, Jan. 18, 1961. He'd written several popular books combining his strong religious and anti-Communist views with commentary about his work as a Catholic medical missionary in Laos and Southeast Asia. His dying statement struck me to the soul: "The cancer went no deeper than my flesh. There

Tom Dooley

Thomas Dooley III (January 17, 1927 — January 18, 1961) was a physician in the United States Navy, who became increasingly famous for his humanitarian and anti-Communist activities in Southeast Asia during the late 1950s when he authored *Deliver Us from Evil* and two other popular anti-Communist books.

In 1959 Dooley returned to the United States for cancer treatment; he died in 1961 from malignant melanoma at the age of 34. He was awarded a Congressional Gold Medal posthumously and President Kennedy cited Dooley's example when he launched the Peace Corps. There were unsuccessful efforts following his death to have him canonized as a Roman Catholic saint.
— Wikipedia

was no cancer in my spirit." Dr. Moore knew how much it meant to me to be able to work with this line of cells. They were ID coded because efforts were being made to make Tom Dooley a Saint in the Catholic Church, and the New York doctors who harvested Dooley's melanoma didn't want anybody 'worshipping' a cancer cell line. (It would be another two years before I learned that Tom Dooley was a CIA asset who had indulged in homosexual activities, from another famous Catholic who was also a homosexual: David W. Ferrie.)

I started growing these melanoma cancer cells in my lab and spent more and more hours there. I also continued to send Dr. Ochsner monthly reports throughout the fall, as he instructed, though he never responded with questions or comments about them.

My college classmates wondered why I was allowed to keep such late hours, as it was uncommon in such a strict Catholic girls school. But I did have a social life and was able to go on road trips to Notre Dame football games to meet boys. And I landed a part in a school play, where the daily rehearsals gave me some recreational fun. I also got a part-time job working as a switchboard operator at the school's rectory. Meanwhile, mid-term exams came and went.

As I explained earlier, the suffering and sorrow that I had witnessed at Roswell Park had a profound emotional effect upon me, and it had merged my desire to fight cancer with my desire to serve God. My current situation posed the question: who was I really working for: Dr. Ochsner, or God?

I yearned for a peace that I did not have. I resented being ordered around by officious doctors who were treated like gods by their staffs, and who sometimes did play God with human lives. Further, I resented the way they sat around and drank wine and plotted how they could use me to get grant money by moving me hither-and-yon. Was this what I'd worked so hard to attain? Was I just a pawn in the "Great Cancer Research Machine"?

Becoming a Sister of St. Francis offered an alternative. It would give me the opportunity to serve God, fight cancer, and prepare me for broader service to humanity, such as being a doctor to the poor and sick in Africa.[13]

After a lot of prayer, I took the leap of faith and went to Sister Veronica, the Director of Admissions, who had become my confidante. We prayed together, and then we talked. Sister assured me that I could join her Order and still pursue pre-med studies and cancer research after that. Amazingly, they had missionaries in Africa, as well. I think her crowning statement was that this Order's home convent was located in Mishawaka, a suburb of South Bend, Indiana. When I grew old, I could retire in the city of my birth! It was, I felt, providential: I made my decision.

She accepted my request and immediately ordered me to lower the hem of my skirt and stop wearing shorts and slacks. The next thing she did was insist that I take daily baths! I already took showers each evening because I worked in cancer laboratories and that was part of basic daily hygiene, but now she required that I bathe in a tub every night. And, I mean, she checked on me nightly! But I supposed that taking baths would please God, or if He didn't care, at least it would please Sister Veronica.

The plan was for me to enter the Order of St. Francis in February of the next year. I didn't tell anyone except Marilyn. She had similar dreams for her life, and we decided that we would enter the order together on the same day, Feb. 2, 1962. I felt I had a new ally in my quest. Together, we would use our brains and industry to reduce the suffering in this world.

On October 19, 1961, I went to Terre Haute, Indiana, accompanied by several sisters from the Order of St. Francis. We travelled to Indiana State College for the fall meeting of the Indiana Academy of Science. One of these kindly and intelligent nuns was a doctor, and two were highly-trained medical technologists (or maybe it was the other way around). They came to co-sponsor my presentation because I was a minor. There I delivered a paper on melanogenesis (melanoma cancer growth) for peer review to the Committee on Bacteriology[14] and to members of the informal organization that had originally invited me — "The Indiana Biological Association." The title of the paper ("Studies on the Increase in Vitro of Mitotic Activity and Melanogenesis in the RPMI HA #5 (7113) Strain Melano") summarized both the work I'd done at Roswell Park with melanoma, and, as the abstract indicated, recent success in getting this human-derived melanoma, which had been grown in hamster "volunteers," to become more deadly.[15]

The paper was accepted and the abstract was published in the 1961 Proceedings of the Indiana Academy of Science on page 71. It was my first science paper to be accepted for publication in a peer-reviewed journal. For that, I was happy: a perfected version of the paper was scheduled to be sent to the Academy at the end of the month.[16] But bigger targets loomed.

The next step in my cancer research project was for me to try to transfer the SV40 monkey virus to human melanoma cells to see what the result of their interaction would be. The monkey kidney cells laden with SV40 would be arriving in about a week. Then there was a pause in my schedule, and I had a moment to ponder my family in Florida. What would my mother and father say?

At first I kept my decision to become a nun secret from my family. It was, after all, my life. Yes, I was headstrong, but my parents were too, as well as opinionated and determined to control my life. The fact that my entire college education would be paid for with grants that I had

---

Proceedings of the Indiana Academy of Science, 1961, p. 71

This abstract of an article was written by Judyth Vary under the direction of her supervisor of research at St. Francis College. It was published in the Indiana Academy of Science in 1962. It deals with preparations for the enhancement of melanoma cancer growth in a strain of modified hamster cells from Roswell Park (as the RP in the RPMI HA #5 indicates) at St. Francis College in 1961.

BACTERIOLOGY

Chairman: GORDON MALLETT, Eli Lilly

GORDON MALLETT, Eli Lilly and Indiana University, was elected chairman for 1962

ABSTRACTS

Studies on the Increase *in vitro* **of Mitotic Activity and Melangenesis in the RPMI HA # 5 (7113) Strain Melano.** JUDYTH VARY and SISTER M. CLARE FRANCIS, St. Francis College.—A 73rd generation un-pigmented melanoma, derived from a metastatic lesion in a human host and cultured in the Syrian hamster, was used in attempts to accelerate the proliferation of the melanoma *in vitro*, employing assays of the basic media #213 against controls of 213, Puck's, Shu, and ELH media. Several hundred variations of twelve amino acid concentrations, in correlation with fetal calf serum percentages of 2%, 5%, and 10% were tested. Although results are inconclusive at this date, indications suggest that specific concentrations of phenylalanine, alanine, and tryptophane influence from a slight to substantial extent the increase in mitotic activity of the melanoma. In some instances melanogenesis was increased to the point that some cells seemed to contain melanin in amounts noticeable under low microscopic powers. Tests with the *dopa* reaction revealed an increase in melanogenic activity in some cases.

The factors influencing accentuated mitosis and melonagenesis may provide a key in the control of this deadly cancer, since the absence or loss of such factors may reciprocally influence the proliferation and metastatic activity of this melanoma in an adverse manner. An area of future endeavor includes testing the influence of Ehrlich-derived ascites DNA; stock RNA; insulin; etc.

earned myself would have impressed most parents; but to my father, it was just further evidence that I was no longer under his control. What would he say when he heard that I had a *new* father and his name was God? After agonizing over it, I decided to write and tell them about my plans.

As soon as my father read my letter, he called me on the phone. He was furious. "They've brainwashed you!" he seethed. "They just want you to work for them for free! And you didn't have the guts to tell them to go to hell, did you?"

He claimed that my life was no longer my own, that I was being controlled by others. He attempted to twist this into a character deficit on my part, saying I did not have the courage to choose for myself. But I knew I *was* choosing for myself and that's what he hated. He wasn't in control!

We argued bitterly on the phone. "You were created by God with a body that shows you're supposed to get married," Dad went on. "Think! You could be the wife of a successful doctor! And have children!"

"I'd never carry babies when I could carry clipboards!" I replied, trying to stand up to him. "And besides, you and mama told me your-selves that I can't have babies, so why marry?"

Frustrated by his lack of power over me, my father stated in blunt language that I did not have his permission to become a nun. He commanded me to withdraw my application to the Order of St. Francis. To that I had just one answer: "No! You can't make me!"

That's when Dad hung up on me. I knew my family would be horrified that I had defied him, had "talked back" to him. It was something never done in our family. We had been taught to respect our parents and to obey them, even if they stood before us in a drunken stupor.

I walked back to my dorm room feeling determined and victorious. I had stood my ground against my father's rude interference in my personal life. Flinging open the door, I saw my sweet, funny roommate Marilyn sitting on the floor by her bed, motionless. Her normal sparkle was gone. She was staring at the floor. A terrible foreboding swept over me. "Marilyn, what's the matter?" I asked, my voice trembling. As I sat down next to her, she looked up at me with tears in her eyes.

Friday, October 6, 1961

Word From Judy

Mrs. C. R. Watkins, chairman Manatee Unit American Cancer Society, reports she has received a letter from Judy Vary, Manatee County's young scientist, who is continuing her work with cancer research at St. Francis College in Fort Wayne, Ind.

Judy said she is presenting a paper for the Indiana Biological Association on "melanogenesis." She is doing special research on some of the aspects of melanoma, sometimes called "black death," which caused the death of the late Dr. Tom Dooley. Judy was assigned to do research on this subject, along with her studies at St. Francis, by Roswell Park Memorial Cancer Research center in Buffalo, N.Y., where she worked this past summer. The American Cancer Society has provided the equipment.

"I have cervical cancer," she said flatly.

The simple sentence hit me like a ton of bricks. I was devastated. Cancer's ugly face had burst into my personal life again. And this time it was someone young and beautiful, in the prime of her life; someone with great dreams and goals. How many times would this happen to people close to me, and why? More than ever, I realized how fragile life is. I asked her if she was still going to enter the Order. Yes, she would. It was up to God to decide what would happen to her. I told her that I would be right beside her on that day.

On October 28 I had received the SV40 virus-laden cells, and was looking forward to transiting the virus into hamster cells, then into live mice, to see what would happen. And my HA melanoma strain would hopefully soon be infected with the same mysterious virus. On October 29, my cancer cell lines and all those other goodies were tucked in for the night in nice, warm plastic flasks. Nothing would need attention for 48 hours, so I had time to concentrate on my part in the school play which would open on Nov. 1 - All Saints Day.

That evening I headed to my part-time job where I worked at the switchboard to earn pocket money. It was late, and I sat at my station rehearsing my lines for the play and watching the clock. I only had about 15 minutes left on my shift. Suddenly, the door opened and in walked my father.

"Daddy!" I exclaimed.

"Judy, you're coming with us," he commanded.

"But I'm not finished with my shift!" I protested.

"I don't care about that. Let's go," he said as he grabbed me by the arm. Through the window, I saw my mother standing by the car, with Aunt Elsie and her son Ronnie sitting in the back seat.

"What are you all doing here?" I demanded.

"We're taking you home."

"You can't do that. I'm in the middle of a semester. I'm doing research and I have a part in a play that opens in two days. I can't leave!"

"You are a minor, and I am your parent. I have legal control over you and your whereabouts. You don't have my permission to be here. And if you don't come with us, I will have you arrested as a runaway and returned to Florida in hand-cuffs."

With that he made me get in the car, saying they had already been to my dorm room and gotten my clothes. Without further ado, he started the car and immediately drove us off into the night back to Bradenton, Florida.

I protested furiously as he drove off and appealed to the others to help me. They would only say that my father was my father, and it was his decision to make.

"You're ruining my life!" I said with venom. "Why are you doing this?"

"You brought it on yourself, Judy," my father said, breaking into an obviously rehearsed speech. "We're not going to lose you to a convent while you are still a minor. You are too young to make those kinds of decisions for yourself. We have to protect you." Then my father mocked my protests by saying I was not acting like the quiet little nun I said I wanted to be, and ended with "Where is your respect for your elders?"

The long hours of driving through darkness were torture for me. I could not believe my own family had kidnapped me, and that they had the legal right to do it! I had been betrayed by the very people I should have been able to trust. I was angry and bitter, and I started to feel real hatred for the first time in my life.

It wasn't until we finally arrived back in Bradenton that I realized the clothes they had grabbed from my dorm room belonged to my buxom, overweight roommate. My entire wardrobe was still in Indiana! All I had to wear were a bunch of baggy clothes that were way too big. My father told me I didn't need more clothes because I would not be going anywhere.

Once inside the house, my father marched into my room and removed the telephone so I couldn't call anyone. He told me that if I left our property without his permission, he would have me arrested as a runaway. Then he fixed himself a drink.

The next day Sister Veronica called our house, pleading with my father to allow me to finish the semester, but to no avail. I begged him to let me go back. Was it really necessary to derail my education and ruin my career, just to "save" me from the nunnery? "I'm not concerned about that," Dad answered. "All a girl needs in this life is a high school education and a good body. Don't tell me how 'important' education is to you. In a few years, you'll forget all about it. Your hormones will make that decision for you."

I ground my teeth with the anger I had been taught to always re-
press. Where was God? Where was God's power? How could God let
this happen to me? How could He allow cancer to destroy all my loved
ones and then, when I offered my very life to Him, let my parents have
their way instead? Ever since I was that small child in the hospital with
the nuns, my greatest fear had been that I might one day lose my cherished faith. Now, I teetered on the brink.

Isolated, mocked, and feeling helpless, I remained in my room, tear-
fully pleading with a silent God who was failing me. Dad didn't help
matters by giving me a stack of anti-Catholic literature. "Read it and
weep," he said. I knew Dad had only converted to Catholicism in order
to be accepted by my mother's Hungarian family. Reading those anti-
Catholic books and pamphlets ripped my soul.

That's when I lost my faith not only in God, but in the very idea of
religion itself. Who was I, then? Just the result of an egg and a sperm
that collided in a womb? I was left staring at the rude outline of barbaric life itself: animal eating animal; humans bombing humans, bodies eating themselves. I felt forsaken, burned alive like Joan of Arc.
Nature stood before me, "red in tooth and claw."

Was I merely a piece of flesh waiting to be eaten? Were we all merely
a bundle of chemical reactions to be reduced to scientific analysis?
Was life itself just a Darwinian game that would eventually decide
who was "fittest"? Life without faith was life without purpose. Did the
power to kill equate to the *right* to kill? The specter of life without
love, without faith, and without a higher purpose stood before me. It
was a terrifyingly lonely experience: a thunderous vision that made me
ache inside. Suicide might end my pain, but it would not answer my
questions. Having my faith stripped away from me was the spiritual
equivalent of rape, and my family didn't even seem to care.

---

1. See sidebar on page 49 about Roswell Park Cancer Institute.
2. Ludwig Gross, BH, Mar 22 or so , 1961.
3. The Friend Virus is a strain of leukemia virus infecting mice and rats that was identified by
    Charlotte Friend in 1956. The virus infects immunocompetent adult mice and is a well-
    established model for studying genetic resistance to infection by an immunosuppressive
    retrovirus. The Friend virus has been used for both immunotherapy and vaccines. It is a
    retrovirus which has single stranded RNA as its nucleic acid, instead of the more common
    double stranded DNA. Officially, its classification is: Group VI (ssRNA-RT), Family: Retroviridae,
    Genus: Gammaretrovirus, Species: Murine leukemia virus, which means it is from the same
    Group and Family as SIV, HIV-1, and HIV-2, but from a different Genus and Species. Retrieved
    from http://en.wikipedia.org/wiki/Friend_virus. A related article is "Immunity to retroviral
    infection: The Friend virus model" The most famous retrovirus is HIV-1.
4. Lab mice should have exercise wheels, a few simple toys, a little variety in the diet, to relieve

stress and boredom. Research results can then be more reliable, because stressed, sedentary mice and other lab mammals have less healthy blood chemistry than unstressed, non-sedentary ones.

5. "Research, Inc.."

6. A rumor spread that I had been dismissed that final week from the program due to violating the housing regulations, but in fact I continued on in Dr. Moore's lab and with Dr. Grace.

7. St. Francis had a fine premed and medical training program run by some outstanding medically trained nuns, some of whom also worked at local hospitals, while others did medical research. Still others cared for the sick in Africa.

8. One about the onset of melanoma (skin cancer), a second on the techniques of handling monkey viruses safely, and a third on developing a medium for "advanced tissue cultures." (These were code words for "cancerous human cells.")

9. I continued my relationship with Dr. Reyniers and his research (including using radiation) into cancer-causing viruses influenced me greatly. I also felt I had a little impact on him as well, as we discussed these subjects for hours at a time.

10. Because I'd been accepted at Purdue University, Dr. Diehl had begun to set up contacts for me there. Then came the conference at Dr. Moore's home, where I persuaded Moore and Diehl to let me go to St. Francis for two years. Dr. Diehl then contacted Dr. Fuller — a new graduate from Purdue and highly recommended — asking him to facilitate matters for me at the hospital where he now held a high position.

11. I should point out that Eli Lilly was the first company to synthetically produce the psychoactive drug known as LSD.

12. I knew that the polio vaccine had been contaminated and that some people had been injected with it.   At this time, I assumed that surely the rest of the contaminated vaccines had been removed from distribution after this "error" had occurred. That assumption proved to be incorrect, as I would later learn in New Orleans.

13. I had a latent fear about my poor vision and the predictions that it would get worse in time. If my vision problems worsened, I could no longer work with microscopes.

14. An unofficial group of scientists who vetted me for the National Science Foundation grants.

15. "HA" indicates that the melanoma under study was grown in the body of a hamster. However, the ID number of the melanoma being studied in the hamsters showed it was of human origin.

16. My parents removed me from St. Francis so quickly that the paper was left behind. But the abstract was published anyway, in anticipation that, of course, the paper to which it referred would soon be submitted. It never was. Further, when I entered the University of Florida, the threat that my parents might interfere meant that I did not dare ask to work with such precious materials again until I was permanently out of their reach.

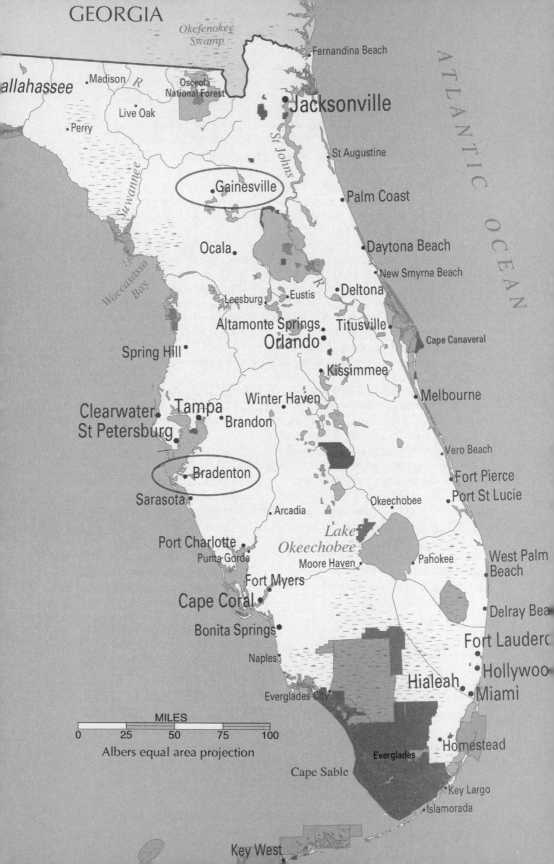

— Chapter 5 —

Breaking Away

By January 1962, my world had crumbled. My dream of getting an elite education to prepare me for my ultimate goal of finding a cure for cancer had been shattered.

Only 18, in Florida I was still a minor and therefore subject to parental control.[1] My father demanded that I live in his house on Snead Island, outside of Bradenton and comply with the "rules of the house." If I tried to leave, I would be arrested and returned to my parents in handcuffs. I had no car. There was no bus service where we lived. My father disconnected the phone line in my room and forbade me to make long distance calls. He was determined to cut me off from my connections up north. I was basically under house arrest and isolated on remote Snead Island. For weeks, my only relief from this confinement was to accompany my father to his office and do his tedious clerical work. (I didn't even know how to type.) He paid me one dollar per day, so I would have money to buy lunch, which he watched me eat. Are we under control yet?

I was miserable. When I complained to my mother, she said that she was powerless to stop my father. She simply had too much at risk to voice any objection. And my younger sister was essentially in the same situation I was.

But there were still some people in my life that my father did not control, particularly on my mother's side of the family. Her half-sister, Aunt Elsie, and my Grandpa lived nearby and were well aware of the problems in our house.

I had always been very close to Aunt Elsie. She was born during an earlier marriage, so was older than my mother. Aunt Elsie was a veteran parent who understood the games of marriage and parenting as well as anyone. She had successfully raised her three sons, but she never had a daughter. Due to the attention and affection I received from her since childhood, I felt that Aunt Elsie loved me as the daughter she never had.

Aunt Elsie and Uncle Emery were "snowbirds" who spent their winters in St. Petersburg. On some Sundays, she drove over the Skyway to attend Mass with our family. But when my father refused to allow Elsie to take me anywhere — even to Mass — and told her that he also planned to keep my sister out of college, and close to home, she became concerned. Observing that I was locked in my room whenever my father couldn't keep an eye on me, she quietly made it clear to my mother, who was terrified to interfere, that she wanted to help. But how? I needed something just short of a miracle to dislodge myself from the grasp of my father, plus a boat-load of resources to get my education back on track.

Complicating matters further was the fact that it was now late January. The colleges had all started their spring semesters and classes had been in session for nearly a month. Unless something happened immediately, I would have to wait until fall term to be admitted. All this would have to happen without proper applications and past all deadlines. Who would have the power to pick up the phone, tell a college to admit me immediately, and inform them that they were to provide me with a full scholarship? There was only one person I could think of who had that kind of power and might be willing to help: Florida's U.S. Senator George Smathers.

Senator Smathers had made it clear to me the year before that he wanted me to go to his alma mater, the University of Florida, and it was well known that he had been funneling large amounts of money into UF for new buildings, libraries and a new teaching hospital. This was the kind of influence I would need to fix my situation, but would the senator still be willing after I had turned down his offer the year before? And how could I reach him when I could not even use the phone in my own house? Aunt Elsie had offered to help, but how could I ask my little old Auntie to call the powerful U.S. Senator and get past his protective staff? I needed an intermediary, someone with the strength and confidence to call the Senator's office, navigate past his staff, and who knew about Smathers' interest in me. The answer was Col. Doyle.

I asked Aunt Elsie to call Col. Doyle, and tell him that I was "desperate to return to college immediately." Amazingly, it worked. Senator Smathers promptly picked up the phone and got me admitted to the University of Florida through the back door. Aunt Elsie got a call from Col. Doyle, and it was done. But we had to move fast, as they were expecting me soon. Of course, all of this had to happen without my father's knowledge, right under his nose.

Grandpa stepped in and used his influence on my mother to convince her to let me go, and pledged her to secrecy.

But how would I get there? What about money? And what would I wear? Virtually my entire wardrobe had been abandoned at St. Francis. My blessed grandfather took out a personal loan at the bank, picked me up in Elsie's car and took me out shopping.

We stopped at Sharp's Pharmacy in Bradenton so I could buy some personal items. It had been our favorite place to meet for a chocolate soda when I was in high school but, today, Grandpa said he didn't want one. He stayed in the car while I went in to shop. When I came back, Grandpa took my hand and looked at me with his faded blue eyes. He reminded me that Grandma had died in 1956 of cancer, and that he was proud of my work.

"Judy," he said, "you have to keep going in cancer research."

Why was he saying this now? Was it because I had mentioned that Sharp's Pharmacy was located in the same building where I had given my mice radiation during high school? Or was he trying to tell me something else? Then I heard him sigh. After the sigh, he went into one of his coughing spasms. Grandpa had been exposed to mustard gas in World War I and his lungs had been permanently damaged. He had chronic emphysema and I was used to his coughing, but this time I heard something different: the telltale wheezing sound that I had been taught to recognize at Roswell Park. It was at this moment that I realized my dear grandfather had lung cancer. Must I lose yet another family member to this plague? "No!" I cried, hugging him. "Please — no!"

University of Florida campus

Jesse Whiting

Jesse Whiting was Judyth's maternal grandfather. Born in Indiana in 1890, he became a professional baseball player in his teens and played on minor league teams in the Midwest, northwest U.S. and Canada. In 1917, when the United States declared war on Germany, he enlisted in the U.S. Army and fought on the frontlines in France with the 347th Machine Gun Battalion. After being wounded twice in action, he was poisoned with Mustard Gas which damaged his lungs. After hospitalization in France, he was returned to the United States to be honorably discharged in 1919. The damage to his lungs prevented him from returning to baseball and plagued him throughout his life. He lived in Bradenton when Judyth was a senior in high school and was instrumental in getting her into the University of Florida in 1962. He died of lung cancer complications in March 1965.

Jesse Whiting in 1960 with Judyth's prize-winning Magnesium exhibit.

"Don't worry," Grandpa said, "I'm tough. It's just in one lung — and I've got two of those puppies! If I end up losing the fight, just remember, I've been separated too long from your grandmother." Tears filled our eyes as we held each other tight. Grimly, I promised to do my best to continue my cancer research.

After shopping, we met Auntie Elsie, who had purchased a bedspread, lamp and other things for my dorm room. Then we skipped town, heading for Gainesville and UF in Elsie's car.[2] It was early February 1962.

Upon my arrival at the University, I checked in with the Dean of Women who promptly slipped me into the computer system as easily as if she were correcting a typo. The Dean was Miss Marna Brady, a Ph.D. who had spent the first 15 years of her career teaching at the college level up East. During World War II, Dr. Brady interrupted her university career to join the U.S. Marine Corps Women's Auxiliary and rose to the rank of major. After the war, she became the first Dean of Women when UF went co-ed.[3] By the time we met, Dean Brady had already spoken to St. Francis College and heard about my sudden removal in the middle of the night by my parents. She expressed her sympathy and concluded our short meeting by earnestly saying: "Come see me if you run into trouble with your parents."

So I started attending classes, which were already in their fifth week. I had to work hard to catch up, but I was happy to be there. I was back in a good college and had decent clothes to wear. My dream of finding a cure for cancer was still alive, and part of the deal was that I would be working in a well-equipped laboratory on campus doing research on the chemistry of cancerous human blood. My instructions from Senator Smathers included sending monthly research reports to Dr. Ochsner in New Orleans, which made it clear to me that he had been involved somehow in Senator Smather's decision to intervene under such extreme circumstances.[3]

I enrolled in the normal freshman curriculum, but I also audited two additional premed classes.

I started working in the laboratory at once, which was euphemistically called the Nutrition Lab. Because both my grandparents suffered from cancers that were well-developed before they were discovered, I wanted to create a diagnostic test to detect rapidly growing cancers. I eventually got permission to tag human cancer cells with radioisotopes. By injecting such cells into the bloodstreams of mice, I hoped to track how long they stayed alive, where they went, and where they died. Such foreign cells wouldn't live long in mice, so these tests were very time-sensitive.[4] One of my goals was to develop a blood sedimentation test which would identify the presence of cancerous activity in the human body. The other was the use of radioactive isotopes to track metastasis as the cancer spread to other parts of the body. The combination of the two would provide a simple clinical test to establish if the person had cancer, and to prove whether that cancer had metastasized or not. Because I was still a minor and not legally allowed to conduct this type of research, I was asked to keep my age and activities secret. To further complicate matters, the radioactive portions of my research required that I have access to rooms in the nuclear engineering building where minors were not even allowed. In essence, I had become two people: just another freshman co-ed who was of little interest to anyone other than boys, and a scientist quietly conducting stealthy cancer research after-hours in the university's laboratories.

My late arrival guaranteed that I was housed in the seediest dorm on campus. It was called "Grove Hall." But it was miles better than being stuck on Snead Island with my father. As in high school, I quickly became involved in campus life, became editor of the dorm paper, the *Grove Groan*, got elected to the Honor Council, and joined the Women's Intramural Sports Team.

No more fasting and prayers for me! Life was good again. The days flew by and the pace increased. I struggled to catch up in my classes and managed to get by on just a few hours of sleep, trying to keep up with my new premed friends who seemed to live on coffee and Dexedrine. I gradually began wearing shorts, lipstick and tight sweaters buttoned down the back, like most of the coeds. There were far more men on campus than women, and my social life began blooming. I was 18 years old, and my figure was practically perfect. Surrounded by popular female friends, and being "the new girl," I quickly attracted the attention of a number of boys and started dating right away. If I didn't have my faith anymore, at least I had boys!

Back at home, my father was furious that I'd vanished. Piquing his anger was an exchange we'd had before I left in which I bluntly told him that if I ever got free, I was determined to lose my virginity. These were strong words from a girl in a strict Catholic household to say to her father, but I was trying to get back at him for ruining my life at St. Francis. As a result, he stormed around the house fuming over the image of me prowling the college campus trying to lose my virginity.

He tried to make my efforts to receive a decent education look vain by accusing me of chasing the fictitious pot of gold at the end of the rainbow; as if becoming a cancer researcher would somehow interfere with my ability to earn a decent living. He even wrote a letter to me, articulating his numerous frustrations and objections, along with a rare bit of praise: "Put you on a horse, and you'll ride like a pro. Put you among nuns, and you'll become a saint. Put you in a lab, and you'll be a scientist. Put you in a college with a lot of boys, and you'll be the Campus Queen."

My father decided to take action. He knew I was still technically a minor, and quickly decided to use this authority. First, he cleaned out the money from my bank account in Bradenton that Grandpa had given me.[5] Then he called me at school to demand my return. When I refused to answer his calls, he called the police in Gainesville and told them I had run away. He instructed them to arrest and hold me.

Dean Marna Brady

Marna Brady became the first Dean of Women at the University of Florida in 1948 and remained in that position until 1966. Originally from Ohio, she received a B.S. degree from the University of Cincinnati in 1925 and taught there for two years. In 1928 she earned a MA degree from Columbia University in 1928 and spent the next ten years teaching at Bryn Mawr College, followed by five years at Wheaton College in Massachusetts. In 1943, she joined the U.S. Marine Corps Women's Reserve, advancing from the rank of Private to Major. She returned to Columbia University and got her Doctorate in Education in 1948 and immediately became Dean of Women at the University of Florida, shortly after it became coeducational in 1947. After retiring as Dean in 1966 Brady remained an associate professor until 1970. She died in 1984.

My distraught mother overheard everything, and as soon as Dad left for work, she called Aunt Elsie, afraid to contact the university herself because the long-distance call record would tell Dad what she had done. Aunt Elsie immediately called me – just in time. I ran to Dean Brady's office, arriving breathless with the police only minutes behind. Dean Brady immediately locked her office door, just as the police entered the building, saying that would slow them down. Then there was the knock: "Police. Open up."

"Do you have a warrant?" she bellowed through the door.

"No," they admitted.

"Well, I am not going to open the door until you do."

The cops left and Dean Brady went to work. It was easy to see why she held her position as Dean of Women. She promptly prepared a "writ of emancipation" for me. This is a legal document that would change my legal status from minor to adult. Usually, it requires a signature from one of the parents, but one could "self-emancipate" if you could prove you were self-supporting. I signed Dean Brady's documents, and they were notarized by someone on her staff. Next, she prepared the paperwork showing I had three part-time jobs on campus, to prove I was self-supporting. She made no mention of my grant monies, to eliminate the possibility that my father might seize them as he had done with my bank account.

When the police returned with their warrant, she showed them the documents and argued that I could not now be detained as a minor. The police scratched their heads and went back to the judge who had issued the warrant. For the next several hours, I sat in Brady's office, awaiting the judge's decision. To pass the time I reviewed her family genealogy books. It turned out we both had distant relatives from Rensselauer County, New York. Finally, the police returned to confirm that the warrant had been withdrawn. My father's attack had been repelled. From then on, Dean Brady remained my firm ally, and I her grateful friend.[6]

I had already begun my work in earnest at several laboratories, officially working as a lab assistant, but with access to everything I needed for my assigned projects. This was the real reason I had been allowed into the system under such extraordinary circumstances. Most of my work was done in the nutrition lab, but I also had keys to several others, including the botany lab.

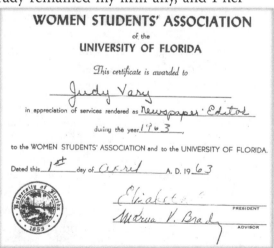

I saw very little of the professors who oversaw my "official" work in the nutrition lab, and they knew only that grants and equipment came along with me. The bottom line was that I was allowed to "putter around" in their labs after hours, once my required work on their projects had been done. They also understood, but would have been hesitant to acknowledge, that I had access to a couple of other labs in the medical center, though they never knew the full extent of what I was doing. And since I was an 18-year old coed, it would have been reasonable to conclude that it could not have been much.

The use of radiation in research involving human cells is considered dangerous and was highly regulated by licenses from the Atomic Energy Commission. Various departments at UF individually petitioned the AEC for its coveted permission. It was not only a time-consuming process, but it put UF in competition for licenses with other universities. Without licenses, there would be no research, and without research there would be no funding. The result was a combination of red tape and an unhealthy competition for favor.

By the early 1960s, UF was set to receive an avalanche of funding for scientific and medical research, thanks mostly to the influence of Florida's powerful political delegation, especially UF's own Senator Smathers.[7] But the complex AEC licensing process was frustrating their efforts. They turned to those Florida politicians, such as Senator Smathers, who cared the most about university growth in the sciences in an era when NASA's space program brought huge revenues and employment to the state. The idea was that the AEC would issue a master license to the university, which would issue sub-licenses to its various departments and be responsible for oversight. Technically, the AEC still issued the final licenses, but the real decisions as to which research got licensed would be made at the university level. It was a matter of patriotism to support such efforts, and the AEC agreed to allow the University of Florida to establish its own special committee to streamline the red tape problem and monitor research involving radioactive isotopes and human cells.[8] It was called the Committee for the Human Use of Radio-isotopes, or CHUR, for short.

Coincidentally, all of this came about the same month I arrived at UF. And in order to facilitate the generous grants, CHUR was quick to relax the restrictive AEC standards, for the "greater good." Applications for licenses for the "broad human use" of radiation were suddenly expedited. Thus I was able to pursue my work under an umbrella of various licenses issued to several professors, in whose labs I worked during this year of rapid expansion. While they knew what I was doing for them individually, none of them had any real knowledge of my other work.

I was at the peak of my physical attractiveness, and due to some good looks, my natural ability to get along with the opposite sex, and my unrestrained joy at having escaped months of tyrannical isolation, I welcomed the attentions of a rather large group of smart young male suitors.

One such suitor was a graduate engineering student from Iran. What I knew about him may have been shallow, but it was very important at the time: His father owned oil wells, and he drove a red Ferrari! We dated many times. When he asked me to convert to Islam so we could marry, I declined his offer, wondering how many wives he would eventually accumulate.

If this Persian prince attracted me, so did a handsome German student who almost won my heart. I remember one day when he took me riding on his motorcycle, and drove up to a plate-glass window where we could view our reflections.

"Look how good we look together, my darling!" he said.

The semester ended with no victors, and I was not about to go home, so I continued to study at UF during the summer session of 1962.

In June 1962, I took a world history class and there I met a young man named Robert Baker. I challenged him with some Russian phrases, and he countered with ancient Greek. I was charmed. Robert wanted to be a writer. Tall with dark wavy hair, deep blue eyes and a strong quiet personality, Robert possessed the requisite combination of good looks, brains and self-confidence that qualified him for my attention. He gladly entered the clutch of beaus who were making my days so happy.

My German boyfriend, impelled to send a love letter after spotting me at Robert's side in the Campus Club, added that I shouldn't be afraid of his wrath. "There is no need to fear me," he wrote, knowing that I indeed did fear another suitor.[9] This was an upperclassman from India who was studying nuclear physics. Armed with a compulsive personality, his affection turned to obsession, and he became so possessive that when he spotted me with another man, he would come up to me and say, "I *keel* you!"[10]

Despite this international cadre of prospective mates, all of whom were basically looking for a loose American girl to conquer, my Catholic upbringing prevailed. I still wanted to save myself for my future husband. Admittedly, this stands in sharp contrast to the amount of time I intentionally spent being pursued by the opposite sex. But I had a strategy that worked, at least for a while. I protected my virginity by playing my boyfriends off against each other. I frequently walked around campus with three or four guys at a time, all of them "guarding" me from the other. Over the next several weeks, Robert drove the others away, one by one, with his dominating behavior.

The last to surrender was a young Jewish boy named Don who stubbornly refused to give up my companionship. I was very fond of the slightly built young man, who visited me day and night for weeks. Don was passionate about life, and it was from him that I learned a man doesn't have to have a big body to have a big heart. But Robert became my choice, or, more precisely, I became his. Perhaps he was just the last man standing in this Darwinian competition. Whatever the reason, by mid-summer of 1962, Robert and I were "going steady."

But UF was not paying my tuition so I could flirt with boys. I was there because they knew I could work in profitable laboratories and conduct sophisticated research that few college students knew how to do.

Thanks to my training at Roswell Park, I knew a large number of advanced lab routines, so I was able to spend many hours helping in various UF laboratories whenever a substitute was needed.

Robert remained oblivious to my work. Unlike my other friends, he never even asked why I spent so much time at the Medical Center and in the basement of the Engineering Building where he would come to meet me. His disinterest in my personal life was actually a relief. Nor did he ask me what my life goals were, so I never told him. He towered over me both physically (by 10 inches) and psychologically; and he was cute, too. I felt safe at his elbow, and that he would defend me like a Doberman should the situation ever arise.

Robert's parents, however, were growing suspicious of his romantic activities, because he had obviously moved away from a long steady relationship with his previous girlfriend, the daughter of an important business associate of theirs whom they hoped he would marry. So his parents decided to visit him in Gainesville to investigate. Something like, "Daddy has business in town. Let us take you and your lady friend out to dinner."

At the same time, my own father was looking for an opportunity to re-open channels of communication with me after the calamity in Dean Brady's office. He heard that a ham radio operators' convention was being held in Gainesville, and used it as an excuse to inject himself into my life.[11] So the forces of parental intervention collided one night at a dinner table in a nice restaurant in Gainesville. Robert and I felt obliged to attend, and make nice with both sets of our unwelcome and self-invited parents.

My father assumed that Robert had taken my virginity, though he did not ask me any direct questions to determine if it were true. In fact my virginity was doing just fine, thank you, but I wasn't about to explain that to him. Let him think what he wanted and drive himself mad, if he must!

Things were tense from the beginning, particularly between my father and Robert. As dinner progressed, things got worse. Robert's mother was obviously a blue-blooded snob who looked down on my family. When my father attempted to impress her with his social contacts in the entertainment industry, Robert's mother rolled her eyes. My father's contempt for "that stuck-up Protestant bitch" turned to hatred. I watched the meltdown with cold resignation.

My mother, who was a shade more diplomatic than my father, saw a tactical opportunity to extort an agreement out of me to return home for a visit before the next semester started. It would have been very awkward to refuse such an invitation in front of Robert's parents, so I accepted. In fact, her invitation was little more than a plot to sabotage my relationship with Robert on her home court and in her own way.

The following week I decided to make the visit home because I missed my sister, who would soon graduate from high school, and was worried about my sick grandpa. Robert said he'd drive down to pick me up if I got trapped on Snead Island again. At first, things went well. I visited my grandfather in the hospital, and he was feeling better. I was also pleased to see that my aunt Elsie's son, Ronnie, was living with my parents while he attended college. That relieved my concerns about Lynda: Ronnie knew how to defuse family squabbles and would protect her. He even worked after school with Lynda at Morrison's cafeteria, so she had some income and wasn't going to be isolated as I had been.

But things got tense that brief weekend when my mother informed me that she had set up a date with a nice young Catholic man, who'd been my boyfriend when I was thirteen. Even taller than Robert, he was now in medical school. If I married him, my mother said, I'd be the wife of a doctor in Winter Park. Surely the perfect match!

I felt obliged to honor her request so I went on the date, but in the end, as we stood together watching a fiery red Florida sunset I told him: "Sorry, it's too late."

My heart belonged to Robert.

That Sunday night I was supposed to catch the bus to return to Gainesville, but my father had started drinking and began to accuse me of being morally depraved. When my sister tried to intervene he slapped her so hard that I took Lynda's hand and hurried her to her room, Dad following close behind. I shut the door and locked it, but he unlocked it in an instant and stood there yelling. "Forget about going to the bus station!" he shouted.

Finally, he left. At that time, I noticed a small scar on my sister's forehead. "How did you get that scar?" I asked her.

"Oh," she answered, "I just hit my head in the swimming pool."

No way did I believe that: I knew her too well. She just didn't want me worrying about her. The mark of the slap on Lynda's face had turned an ugly red. Dad had gone outside to his boat so now Mama knocked on the door, offering to take me to the bus station. I told her I'd just call a cab, but she sadly admitted that Dad had torn all the telephones out of the walls, so I couldn't call anybody! That's when I realized how sick my father was becoming.[12] We had to sneak out of the house while

Dad was with his boat, and I managed to get on the bus in time, vowing never to return.

In September 1962, Gainesville hummed with the rhythm of a new school year about to begin. There was excitement in the air, and football games to attend, though for me, they lacked the excitement I had known at Manatee High School. But I was glad to be away again from my former life in Bradenton.

Grove Hall was being torn down, so we were removed to Yulee Hall. There I became the editor of its big dorm newspaper: *Yuleevents.* My

friend Diane and I also won medals that semester for being members of the best Intramural Women's team on campus, scoring tops in basketball, volleyball, and so on.

That year, the University of Florida adopted the new Trimester System, which divided the school year into three equal instructional periods instead of two long semesters and a short Summer Session: Fall 1962 was 1st Trimester of the 1962-63 school year. The Trimester System is a better system for many reasons, and most universities eventually switched over to it. At the time, though, that made UF out of

Judyth in Grove Hall with her Egyptian mural painting and friend Diane Butterfield.

synch with other schools, and this caused problems in terms of planning summer jobs and scholarship grants.

Once settled in my new dorm and snugly back in Robert's arms, and with a job at the Craft Shop earning pin money, I plunged again into my studies and cancer research. Curiously, though Robert would observe me and my friend, Kathy Santi,[13] working hard in our premed classes — and he carried all those heavy science books for me when we met at Shands Hospital — he never asked what I planned to do with my life. His silence I took for great depth of thought rather than thoughtlessness, for his taciturnity, his chess-playing, his well-written short stories and his plans to become a writer had impressed me. But my science-oriented world influenced him more deeply than he would ever admit: soon Robert was blazing A's through science and geology courses. After I encouraged him to visit the computer center, he was hooked, his truly great talents in mathematics awakened within him.

And meanwhile, the Cold War had started heating up again. In October, the U.S. Government announced that the Russians were moving offensive nuclear missiles into Cuba, less than 100 miles off the coast of Florida! On October 23, 1962, President Kennedy signed an order quarantining Cuba, to stop the arrival of Russian ships loaded with more missiles. A shiver rippled through the campus. Then the Cubans used a Russian surface-to-air missile to shoot down an American U-2 spy plane in Cuban airspace.[14] The tensions increased dramatically and the world drifted closer to the edge of nuclear annihilation. What would be next? 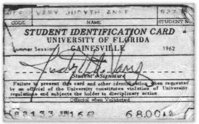 Would America attack Cuba in retaliation? Would Castro launch his nuclear missiles at us? Would we all die before midterms?

I couldn't help but remember my Cuban friend Tony López Fresquet and his passionate hatred for Fidel Castro. I sought out and found new anti-Castro friends drinking coffee in the Commons where they gathered to share their bitter frustrations. But Robert ignored my new friends. He thought I was interested in other cultures and languages because my roommate was an anthropologist. Nor did he see why I should be so excited about politics. "The world was here yesterday, it's here today, and it will be here tomorrow," he said. "Your worry or mine will never change a thing."

One night at a football game, my Cuban friends in the section next to ours held an anti-Castro protest. I rose from my seat to join in, but Robert continued to sit quietly. "I stay out of everything," he said calmly. "I just like to watch."

I enjoyed all the petting and smooching, but by December, 1962, Robert's patience was ending. I still refused to sleep with him, despite his relentless advances for nearly six months, for my Catholic upbringing trumped my amorous desires. After yet another fruitless expedition without success, Robert dropped me off at the dorm and said, "I'm not coming back until you grow up."

I just let him go, figuring that if he really wanted me, he would be back. But after waiting two miserable weeks for his return I sought advice from some girl friends. They encouraged me to let him have his way.

So I called Robert, and simply said, "I give up. You win."

He said, "I'll be right over."

Like everyone else, I still remember that fateful day. My friends Kathy, Diane and Mickey cheered me on as I ran out of the dormitory to embrace Robert. He promptly picked me up and carried me away to his blue Ford coupe. It was not long before I kissed my virginity goodbye. Truly emancipated! Or so I thought.

January and February were a delightful time for me, as indicated by the frilly layout of the Valentine's Day edition of my dorm's newspaper. As a result of my new night-time hobby, I had to resign from Honor Council for repeatedly breaking curfew. Then, in the early spring of

1963, despite all my precautions and the fact that I had been told I was incapable of having children, I became pregnant. I was shocked.

What if my parents found out? What if Ochsner and Smathers found out?

Even Robert's deep-keeled calm was shaken. He vanished for several days to think over his options. Abortion was out of the question, a legacy of my Catholic upbringing. Then the problem was solved. I suffered a miscarriage. I made it to the school's infirmary with so much blood dripping down my legs that there was no way to hide my condition. Since I was obviously not married, the staff quickly deduced that I had lost an "illegitimate" conception, a big taboo back in 1963. I collapsed into a hospital bed and did my best to rest and recover my health.

A couple of days later, Robert strolled into my room. The staff could scarcely believe that the fellow responsible for my condition dared show his face. The fact that he did so in such a nonchalant manner galled them even more. In contrast, my friend Don visited me with deference and empathy. His honest face was scarlet the whole time he stood at my bedside, even though he was not the one responsible for my pregnancy.

Robert returned, ignoring the conspicuous stares and whispers. He took my limp hand and whispered to me, "I've decided I don't want to take this kind of risk again."

Huh? What did he mean? Was he going to leave me? Or have a vasectomy? I was bewildered and remained silent.

"I don't want to lose you," he said. "So I've decided to marry you."

I was still weak from the miscarriage, so I simply looked at him blankly.

Later, I began thinking about his "proposal" and realized that Robert had not asked me to marry him. He had simply informed me we would be married. How romantic! No diamond, no flowers, no sunset, and no bended knee. To receive such an "offer" in that time and place stunned me. I did not know how to feel. I was numb from it all.

My stay in the infirmary was longer than I expected. I missed classes, assignments, lab work and an important interview for a summer position. When I finally recovered my strength enough to return to classes, I left the Infirmary and headed to the Nutrition Lab. As I raced to catch up on my classwork, I finished up my blood sedimentation research, which developed a titration model able to provide statistically significant

evidence of live cancer cells in the human body. Simply said, I did not have time to sit around the Craft Shop earning petty cash. So, by the time the school year ended I was broke.

I also missed important interviews that had been scheduled for summer job positions I had applied for. It was the end of March, 1963.

UF was now firmly on a trimester system, but its grant schedule had not yet adapted to it. Of particular concern to me was that my scholarships were set up for only two payouts a year, so I needed summer income.

I had already applied for summer lab internships in three different states and expected to be accepted, so I did not make plans at UF. But due to my miscarriage I missed required phone interviews, and lost out.

Facing a summer without study or income I telephoned Smathers' office, hoping he would be willing to sponsor me for a summer internship at Miami University. But the senator was out of town, so I explained to a sympathetic female aide about how my miscarriage had affected my summer plans, and made my request. She said she'd see what she could do. Several hours later I received a call, not from Senator Smathers' office but from Dr. Ochsner 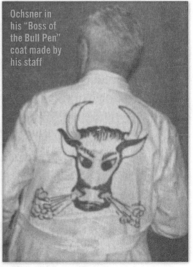 himself. I was thrilled to hear his voice and figured he was calling to help me, but soon he had me cowering.

Ochsner in his "Boss of the Bull Pen" coat made by his staff

"What is the matter with you?" he thundered.

"First, you wanted to be a nun. The stupidest thing in the world!"

I humbly agreed. It had been stupid. But Ochsner wasn't finished.

"The next thing I know," he went on, "after all the pains we took to rescue you from your own parents, you get pregnant and have a miscarriage!"

I sadly admitted that this was so.

"Judy!" Ochsner roared, "Will you please make up your mind?"

I said that I was sorry and asked for his forgiveness. Mollified, Dr. Ochsner revealed that his star cancer specialist was interested in having me work in her lab as an intern for the summer. Would I like to come to New Orleans and work with Dr. Mary Sherman?

I had heard of Dr. Sherman through my study of cancer research. She directed the bone pathology laboratory at Ochsner Clinic, which helped put them on the map as a respected medical center. She also wrote brilliant articles that influenced the debate about the fundamental nature of cancer, and was considered one of the foremost cancer researchers in America.

"She's a good steady woman," Ochsner explained. "Just what you need to guide you." He told me that he had shown Dr. Sherman some of the reports I continued to send him, and she was interested in my blood sedimentation research. She also needed a lab assistant familiar with handling the carcinogenic SV-40 virus and fast-growing cancers. She would like me to work in her lab this summer, should I decide to come to New Orleans instead of Miami.

Dr. Ochsner suddenly changed subjects and asked me how I felt about Fidel Castro. I assured him that I thought Castro was a dreadful Communist dictator whose behavior was criminal, and who should be removed from power, by force if necessary. "Good girl," he chimed in with amusement and approval.

Then Dr. Ochsner sweetened the pot, making his offer irresistible. If I came and worked with Mary Sherman for the summer, I could skip the rest of my undergraduate education and enter Tulane Medical School in the fall. Tulane accepted undergrad students only on rare occasions, he cautioned, but he stressed he had influence there. What an offer!

Next Dr. Ochsner put the cherry on top. He reminded me that Mary Sherman was from the University of Chicago and he would see to it that she used her influence there to get me into the UC medical school the following spring, should I still desire to go. He had me, hook, line and sinker. I gratefully accepted his offer and promised heaven and earth in return.

Then, with the air of a man covering a few routine details, he said my tuition to Medical School would be paid, my room and board would be covered and a stipend would be provided to cover other expenses. The good Dr. said he would send me a one-way bus ticket to New Orleans, and that I would stay at a YWCA where my rent would be taken care of as it had been in Buffalo. Then Dr. Ochsner said, "I'll see you the second week in May!" and abruptly hung up.

Uh-oh! The second week in May was almost a month away.

UF was on the trimester system, but Tulane was obviously not. My school year had already ended. How was I going to survive in the meantime? I was already almost completely broke, and I was about to lose my dorm room because I wasn't registered for the summer.

Normally, a student who lived in Florida would simply have gone home for a summer break, but my disastrous home life had passed far beyond such simple solutions. The idea of being a guest in my father's house repulsed me. We had gone our separate ways, and with good reason. I just couldn't go home. I needed a game plan. Most of my friends were already out of town, and Robert lived in a boarding house that didn't allow girlfriends. I thought about calling Dr. Ochsner back, but he had called long distance from Washington, D.C. I didn't even know where he was.

Suddenly, I realized that I could have my cake and eat it too, if I could lure Robert to a university in New Orleans. Their petroleum geology schools were superior to anything in Florida at the time. We'd have time to marry and have a honeymoon before I started my summer work for Dr. Sherman.

I took Robert to the university's library and showed him a New Orleans newspaper full of ads from petroleum companies pleading for summer help, and saw to it that he wrote some of the addresses down.

I told him that I would probably be working in a medical lab in New Orleans, but held back the idea of starting medical school in the fall.[15] I didn't want him to think I was leaving him. Robert had only one trimester left at Gainesville before graduation. If we married, we would only have to live apart for about four months. Given his disposition I was concerned that he might not marry me under those circumstances so I wanted him to see New Orleans first, get to know their superior geology departments, and then decide for himself.

I did tell Robert I was out of money and would not be returning to UF. Though he drooped when I told him I would be leaving UF, he also understood my problems with my family. He said, quietly, "I still want to marry you."

"Honey, I don't want to push you," I told him. "But you haven't mentioned any particular time for us to get married... and I can't stay any longer."

What I didn't mention was my disappointment that Robert hadn't purchased an engagement ring, but I did not dare bring it up.

Maybe he just couldn't afford it.

Knowing I couldn't bring up the ring gracefully, I told Robert that if he didn't marry me I couldn't get birth control pills. He would just have to use condoms, because I wasn't going to risk another traumatic episode in an infirmary. If anything could inspire Robert to marry it was the specter of having to use condoms. Only married couples could obtain birth control pills in 1963. At least in Florida, bachelors had to take their showers wearing a raincoat. The decision was now up to him.

On April 16, 1963, I heard the words I longed for: Robert said he would apply for a job in New Orleans and come there to marry me. At last!

As he held me in his arms and kissed me I heard him say, "I love you," for the first time. Robert was a man of few words, but these were the magic ones.

"But first, I have to go home to Fort Walton Beach," he told me, sucking the air from my romantic balloon. "My folks need me at their office. But I'll convince them that going to Louisiana means a money-making career in geoscience, instead of starvation as a writer." Robert smiled. "That should do the trick."

Tensions were still high over the girlfriend issue and he dared not mention me to his parents, since they still felt I had somehow derailed him from fulfilling their dreams. "We'll have to figure out how to stay in contact," he told me. Meanwhile, I could go on to New Orleans alone. He would join me when he could.

A courier service delivered the bus ticket to my dorm box and I now held in my hand the ability to try a little life on my own before having to report to Dr. Sherman for a summer of disciplined science and research. I savored the thought that this would include my right to take a husband if I so chose. If the conditions were right, and if he showed up.

After I told Robert that the campus cafeterias had closed and I would need to find another place to eat, he decided to drive me to the bus station so I could begin free housing at the "Y." The cheapskate!

He dropped me off at the bus station on his way to a beer bust at Lake Wauberg celebrating the trimester's early end. He did invite me to come with him, but due to my solemn oath against drinking alcohol I declined. As I waited to board the bus, Robert warmed me with kisses and gave me fourteen little pink pages. On each page were the words "I love you," in different script styles.

"Tear them off one by one, once a day" he said, "I'll be there before you look at the last one."

As I waved goodbye to Robert, my eyes misted with tears. A whole new life was twenty-four hours away! What if he got cold feet and didn't show? What if I changed my mind? Either way, I still had a future in New Orleans. If Robert did come, I would then confide much more about my plans. I'd tell him I would be staying in New Orleans to start medical school in the fall, and not returning to Gainesville. If he really cared, he could work all summer with me in New Orleans, get interviews at the fine grad schools there, make the contacts he would need, and together, we could start building ourselves a little love nest.

Then he would return to Florida, remain loyal and faithful for one more trimester, graduate, and return to his loving wife in New Orleans. Both of us would then be properly positioned to embark on our glittering new careers: me, the insightful cancer researcher, and he, the well-compensated geologist.

Meanwhile, I would enjoy the history and romance of America's most exotic city. The same famous doctor who had quietly shepherded my career for the past few years would be there directing and protecting me with his gruff, fatherly concern. I held his commitment in my hand, in the form of a prepaid bus ticket. Plus I had $42.00 in cash, for emergencies. I had it all worked out.

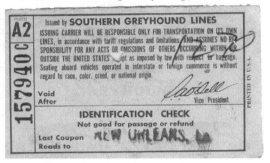

What could go wrong?

---

1. Today, the age of majority is 18, but in the 1960s, you were legally considered a child until the age of 21, except that you could join the military, if you chose.

2. Gainesville is located in the central part of northern Florida, halfway between Miami and Atlanta, Ga., about 130 miles southwest of Jacksonville.

3. Monthly reports were sent religiously to Dr. Ochsner from the fall of 1961 through spring, 1963, though I never received any feedback.

4. Dr. Moore was my inspiration for this idea: he was the world pioneer in detecting cancer cells in vivo using fluorescence and radioisotopes, via his virtual invention of scintigraphy, the science of tracking the distribution of radioactive tracer substances in body tissues. He reported the basics relating to this science, using radio-fluorescence, at the 4th annual Science Writer's Seminar that I had attended in Florida in 1961.

5. I later learned that my Grandpa's college loan money was used to buy my mother a mink cape and a set of golf clubs. I had significant funds that were left behind at St. Francis, too, but I never saw a dime of it and assume my father confiscated the money from that account as well.

6. But the combination of my late registration and these legal maneuvers created a technical problem for me. A new student number had to be generated for me in the computer to replace my original number which was needed to pay my dorm bills, get my meals, and pay for my books. The confusion as to my identity in the U of F record system continued for years. The good news was it was guaranteed that I'd pass every subject, so I didn't have to attend classes regularly. The down side was that at the end of the semester the computer awarded me randomly generated grades. I received an A, two Bs, a C and a D. This resulted in an average GPA, but the D was in chemistry! Grrr! The computer generated a second set of similar trash the next semester, too, before I could straighten some of it out with petitions. Despite those unimpressive grades, I continued with a full scholarship and was awarded a letter of recognition for 'outstanding' scholarship (see Appendix) for what I accomplished

behind the scenes. My premed classes were not on the "official record" either, since those classes were closed before I'd even arrived, but I was told this would last only one year. My records became so jumbled that eventually I was blessed with two identical degrees. But I was told the computer problem didn't matter, because the people who really mattered would take good care of me.

7. Florida was blessed with legendary Congressmen such as Claude Pepper, Robert Sikes and Wilbur Mills and led by Senior Senator George Smathers. Smathers helped secure Senate support for Kennedy's proposal to ban nuclear bomb tests in the atmosphere (Ref: interview with Harold Brown, Director of Research Engineering, Dept. of Defense: 1963 Partial test ban treaty, JFK Doc. #5, 6/26/1964, p.38)

8. I have referred to this as the "window of opportunity" in various interviews. CHUR only existed for two years, and was shut down.

9. My editors decided that his letter should not be reprinted in this book. Steve was a fine fellow, though. I think he returned to Germany.

10. Once, my former boyfriend from India pretended to offer reconciliation to Robert by inviting us to dine at his sparsely-furnished apartment (we sat on the floor to eat there). Sneakily, he laced Robert's food with so much cayenne pepper that he nearly choked on it. Robert's face turned red and he started perspiring, but Robert stoically ate every bite, too proud to admit that the conspicuously over-spiced food bothered him. Mine, however, had not been spiced in the same manner. .

11. My father had been a licensed ham radio operator since childhood. Besides having been an electrical engineer who had run the technical end of a television station, he wrote a column, "CALLING C-Q" that ran in the *South Bend Tribune* in his high school years. Two of his call letter IDs were W8AUG and K4KDM.

12. My father's leg kept him in agony: he had become a man I no longer recognized. About a decade later, his leg was finally amputated at the knee. For the next few years, Dad was his old self again, free of pain, sober, and willing to forgive me. He earned commendations when a hurricane hit Florida in 1972, using his ham radio operator skills to keep police radio contacts going where floods had stranded elderly people, despite his amputated leg and the possibility that he could have drowned. I began to be proud of him again. But then an infection from his amputation created blood poisoning. It began destroying his mitral heart valve, and Daddy died of a heart attack on my birthday — May 15, 1977, just as we had finally forgiven each other and tried to make up for the past.

13. Kathy Santi would become a respected and admired doctor.

14. On October 27, 1962 Cuba shot down an American military plane (U-2), which brought us dangerously close to war. On October 17, Cuba was discovered to be readying missiles armed with nuclear warheads — and they were aimed at the major cities of America. It would only take a few minutes for them to hit the Capitol. October 18-29, 1962, the famed Thirteen Days of the Cuban Missile Crisis brought the world nearly to the brink. Nuclear war was a real possibility between Russia and the USA: being only 90 miles from Cuba, Florida would have been annihilated if Castro shot missiles carrying nuclear bombs at us. I remember seeing tanks rolling down the highway toward the Florida Keys. I showed Robert where the University's underground computer facility was at this time, in case we had more than a minute to take cover.

15. Robert's mother regularly drove up to Ochsner Clinic for therapy on her arm (a recurring rotator cuff injury in her shoulder), and sometimes took her ailing mother (Nonnie) there, too, so I didn't specifically mention Ochsner Clinic to Robert, in case he might accidentally reveal my whereabouts to someone who might tell his mother, or my parents. I only told Robert I was going to take a Civil service exam so I could get a permanent job in New Orleans "in a lab or clinic." In fact, I was advised to take the Civil service Exam when I filled out my application papers so that I could "do lab work, if necessary" at the U.S. Public Health Service facility. Edward T. Haslam has uncovered information about this facility and goes into some

detail about the clandestine work that went on there in 1963 in his book *Dr. Mary's Monkey*.

Here is an excerpt from the letter I wrote to Robert a week after my arrival, mentioning the Civil Service exam:

The all-important *first* birth control pill was taped to the letter after we got married! Note name "Raleigh" (Raleigh Rourke, Robert's friend). Also note auto accident of the stripper's fiancé mentioned in second-last line…

Sunday

My Honey:

I'm writing this as small as I can so that it'll only be a page. Raleigh probably doesn't write a book. When you come, bring as many good references as you can — you'll need them! Perhaps I have checked into the "Y" as planned, but it is pretty bad there; in fact, it is a filthy hole. The YWCA is a brand-new castle, however, and very beautiful. Honey, I miss you so much. I have already checked on several jobs, but nearly every decent one requires references, or residency here for at least four mos., or giving of home address, and so on. So I have applied to take a civil service exam, just in case nothing else works out. Rent is due at the "Y" on Thursday and I'll be out of money by then (that is, money to pay rent with) so I hope by then you'll have sent some by money order. I'm in a room with four other girls, and I keep everything locked up tight as they are a bit untrustworthy (no fault of their own, they just have to take what they can get – dog-eat-dog – poor girls!). Consequently it is difficult to keep well-dressed, especially out of a suitcase. So far I've managed fairly well. This city is shocking. Here is the new race of men — no dreamers allowed. One of the girls I was talking to said, "Honey, get out of this dump. You don't belong here. You will have it..." Of course, I didn't tell her why I'm here, but this is a girl who is exceedingly unhappy. She told me she came down here to get married, and he got killed coming here in an auto accident. Both of us cried. She didn't understand, of course, but

Looking down Bourbon Street
from the front door of the 500 Club, early 1960s

— Chapter 6 —

New Orleans

Friday, April 19, 1963

The Greyhound bus pulled out of familiar Gainesville and headed to exotic New Orleans. In less than three weeks, I'd be working under the famous Dr. Alton Ochsner, Sr., and with Dr. Mary Sherman, one of the most respected women in American medicine. Then in September, I'd start medical school without even finishing undergraduate school.

As the bus roared down the highway, I watched the scenery roll by and tried to ignore my nagging doubts. The image of Robert waving goodbye returned to my thoughts again and again. He wasn't concerned about my trip. He was sure I would manage somehow. I tried to believe it. I had not told anyone about our plans to marry. My name was poisonous to his parents, as his was to mine.

As I thought about Robert, I pondered how opposites attract. It was as if love were ultimately a collision of forces like magnetic fields, or chemical reactions. Robert and I were very different. Yes, we both liked writing short stories and having sex, but that's where our similarities ended. I was emotional, creative and made a point of exploring new possibilities. Money was a secondary issue to me. Robert was steady, focused, and determined to get rich, partly by not spending what he earned. And for some reason, Robert's tenacity assured that he always got what he went after. I guess I was just one of the things he went after. What was it about domineering men that attracted me? Perhaps their self-confidence made me feel secure.

Pensacola and Mobile passed by my window through the afternoon and into sunset. As we entered Mississippi, twilight blanketed the landscape. Biloxi swished by in a blur lights. Then solid darkness settled in as we rolled down an alley of tall pine trees which ended suddenly at the Louisiana state line. Finally, New Orleans glowed in the distance

and slowly emerged from the night. It was late when we arrived and I was tired, but my curious eyes were wide open.

I saw beautiful European-style buildings, antique streetlamps and garish neon signs. When the bus finally stopped in downtown New Orleans, and I got out, I suddenly felt very alone. Nobody was expecting me yet, and I didn't know how to get to the YWCA.

The bus station was my first look at the seedy underbelly of the city. Men's eyes tracked me like radar as I walked through the station to the office, where I got directions to the YWCA. I was told it was "just down the street," so I picked up my bags and headed out the door.

As I began to walk down the poorly lit streets of downtown New Orleans, I realized I was being followed. Not good. Time for Plan B. I quickly returned to the bus station, hailed a cab, and got in. Despite the late hour, the city was full of noise. There were police sirens and what sounded like gunfire. The cabbie told me the new District Attorney was busy cleaning up the city. He called him "Big Jim."' What I had heard, he suggested, was probably one of Big Jim's raids.

The YWCA was not far and we reached it quickly. I was surprised

YWCA at 130 S. Claiborn Ave.

to find it somewhat dilapidated inside, unlike the clean, well-run YWCA in Buffalo. Dr. Ochsner had told me he would pay for my room, but when I inquired at the desk, I discovered my name wasn't on their list. Though I had told nobody at Ochsner Clinic that I was coming three weeks early, I was miffed that no room had been reserved for me. How naïve can you get? It was about 5:00 a.m. — way too early to call anybody — so I rented a bed in the cheapest room available.

When I unlocked the door, I was surprised to discover there were already three women inhabiting the room. They looked up eagerly when I opened the door, but when they saw me they seemed disappointed, and somberly let me in. They were anxiously awaiting their fourth room-mate who was late returning from work, and I was not her.

There were five narrow beds in the small, dingy room, but only one closet. The room was a mess. Bras and panties hung drying in an open window in full view of the street. Coffee boiled away in a battered pan sitting on a hot plate. Everything was far below the standard I was used to, but I kept these thoughts to myself. At least my bed was clean and neatly made, as if it had just been placed there.

I introduced myself and began hanging my clothes in the empty closet, wondering why a closet in a room with four women was empty. Then they told me that if I hung up my clothes, the cleaning ladies would steal them. The two younger girls were attractive, but they looked tired. They had been in New Orleans for a few weeks, and both worked at night. The older girl was heavy-set and worked days as a waitress. So the younger girls regularly paid her 25 cents to keep watch on their belongings while they worked at night. "Things get took even if you sleep right on top of them, honey," the waitress told me. I under-stood her warning and quickly gave the gentle extortionist a quarter. I didn't want to wind up with nothing appropriate to wear when it was time to go to dinner with the doctors!

The waitress said she worked at a Royal Castle on Airline Drive near the airport. I was familiar with Royal Castles, since we had them in Florida. They were fast-food joints that served cheap hamburg-ers, fries, coffee, and breakfast with fresh-squeezed orange juice. The waitress said they always needed help for the morning rush, in case I needed a job.

Thinking that this dumpling could not possibly appreciate the ab surdity of offering such a menial job to "the Great Cancer Researcher," I politely declined, but asked her to tell me about it just to be sociable. My new friend told me she got up before dawn and put on her uniform in time to catch a bus at 6 a.m. and ride for nearly an hour to the out-skirts of town, for the privilege of serving greasy food all day for a dol-lar an hour. Minus the deductions for food, uniforms, insurance, and taxes, she brought home almost seven dollars a day!

I wasn't tempted.

As I changed into my nightgown, one of the other girls extended yet another job opportunity. "You sure have the boobs!" she piped. "Why don't you come work with me? We need more strippers!" (I was so na-ïve that I wasn't even sure if the term "boobs" meant breasts or buns, but I was sure it did not mean brains.)

She assured me that stripping paid a lot better than slinging burg-ers. The idea was both flattering and amusing, but when it came to nudity, I was hopelessly modest. I may have thought of myself as a free thinker and sexually liberated but, in fact, I was a shy girl, with the right lower part of my abdomen a mass of scars.

The third girl was by far the best looking. A dark blonde with an attractive figure, she said she was going to Bunny School and would be working as a cocktail waitress at the Playboy Club in the French Quarter. When she had finished repairing a rip in her costume, she

suggested I try it on so she could inspect her work. We didn't do this in the lab! It fit perfectly. She told me they were look-ing for more recruits and showed me the newspaper ad.

Being a Playboy Bunny was better than being a stripper, she counseled, because the club had rules that protected the girls. She was promised there would be no "man-handling" at the Playboy Club. I ad-mit that this, combined with the fact that I would wear what was basically a one-piece bathing suit that covered my scars, made it somewhat more attractive than the stripping idea.

The girls were still anxiously waiting for their missing friend Carol to show up. It was now 8:00 A.M. and I went downstairs to call Och-sner's Clinic. It was then I learned that nobody was expecting me for another two weeks. Dr. Ochsner was in Washington on his way to Central America. Dr. Sherman was also out of town. I still had to fill out some formal application papers, which Ochsner and Sherman had promised to sign when they returned. But until then no funds would be released. And until the forms were signed I couldn't even get tem-porary work at the Clinic, or at any other hospital or lab in town. I suddenly realized that I was really on my own.

After counting my remaining cash I began to panic. Forget about genteel dinners in nice restaurants with the doctors. I'd have to pay my own way until my sponsors returned, and I didn't have enough money to do that. I wasn't about to beg for help from my sick grandfather, and asking my father was out of the question. And my fiancé, had warned me not to call his house, but had said he would send me some money when he could spare it.

It was now about 8:30 and I was so tired I could have slept on a bed of nails. Just as I collapsed on my bed, the missing girl stumbled into the room clutching newspapers to her body! Breathless and frightened, she struggled to embrace the other girls who ran to greet her. I opened my eyes in time to see her drop the newspapers in exchange for a bathrobe, only to see that she was wearing nothing but a g-string and pasties.

Pretty and with a striking figure, she had fled from her strip club after receiving a tip that the police were about to raid the joint.

Being under age and fearing arrest, she ran out the back door when she heard sirens. She grabbed somebody's raincoat, but dropped it in panic when someone yelled at her. All but naked, she gathered up some newspapers to cover herself and hid in a telephone booth until daylight. Then she crept from hiding place to hiding place, until she reached the YWCA.

The Royal Castle waitress announced that she needed a few hours of sleep before she had to leave for work. It was Saturday, and she worked the afternoon shift on weekends. Equally exhausted, the Playboy bunny soon followed. I should have been sleeping, too, but I couldn't resist listening to Carol's detailed account of her unusual adventures to the other stripper. My "educational horizons" were expanding dramatically.

The girls at the club had told Carol the police were actually only interested in pestering Jada, the club's headline act and Carol's mentor at the Sho-Bar on Bourbon Street, one of several clubs controlled by New Orleans Mafia Boss Carlos Marcello. As Carol's tale unfolded, I learned a man called Jack Ruby was in town trying to steal Jada for his Carousel nightclub in Dallas. But Jada was in love and

Jack Ruby in front of his Carousel Club

refused to leave her boyfriend, who managed the Sho-Bar. So this Jack Ruby fellow was using his local Mafia contacts to encourage police raids on Jada, to drive her out of New Orleans. I guess "banned in New Orleans" would have been good publicity for a stripper in Dallas!

As Carol explained it Jack Ruby's boss was the powerful Godfather of New Orleans, Carlos Marcello. Ruby handled Marcello's interests in Dallas, including cop-fixing. Marcello was described as "a marvelous gentleman" who "only rarely cheated on his wife." Marcello would buy a nightclub, gas station, restaurant or hotel and "sell" it for a pittance to a "friend." The new "owner" would hand over most of the profits to Marcello, if he wished to keep his health. The Sho-Bar was supposed to be independent of this corrupt system, but Carol said that was a joke.

Carlos Marcello

True, this talk was hearsay, but she spoke knowledgeably, as I soaked up every word. What Jack Ruby wanted Jack Ruby got, Carol explained. The girls said Jada should be grateful nobody beat her up for resisting her transfer to Dallas. They said fame had gone to Jada's head. She didn't realize that, like City Hall, you can't fight organized crime.

Both Jada and her lover had been arrested at the Sho-Bar two days earlier: Jada for performing an "obscene" dance and he for permitting it. The Sho-Bar hadn't been open but two consecutive nights when the police returned for an encore — only this time, everybody was on the alert and, like Carol, had escaped (barely!). Still, Carol hoped that Jada would put in a good word for her with Ruby. Maybe he would hire her away from her purgatory in New Orleans as well. The rumor was that despite his notoriously aggressive behavior Ruby was a generous man, who treated his girls well. He bought fancy clothes for them and took care of their abortions and penicillin shots. A few girls even got sent up to the big league in Las Vegas. Of course, they had to sleep with him to get ahead. (Reportedly, he was "bisexual.") Such is the price of success in that world. The girls, seeing I was a babe in the woods, introduced me carefully to their New Orleans, full of people who got drunk, loved music, and sometimes went to jail.

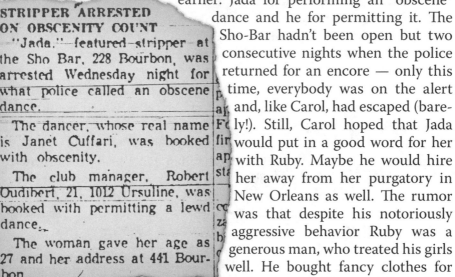

STRIPPER ARRESTED
ON OBSCENITY COUNT

"Jada," featured stripper at the Sho Bar, 228 Bourbon, was arrested Wednesday night for what police called an obscene dance.

The dancer, whose real name is Janet Cuffari, was booked with obscenity.

The club manager, Robert Oudibert, 21, 1012 Ursuline, was booked with permitting a lewd dance.

The woman gave her age as 27 and her address at 441 Bourbon.

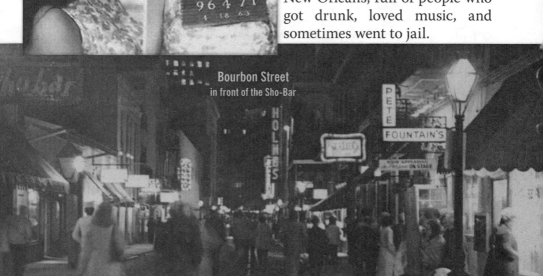

Bourbon Street
in front of the Sho-Bar

These two women lived in a world I had never seen. And I was impressed to learn that they had dreams of their own: to marry a man with a big house who didn't cheat on them — too much — or to become the mistress of a rich man who was married to a woman who did not fulfill him.

Both had been led into their current profession by difficult circumstances. The 16-year-old had been raped by several football players after a game and became pregnant. Her father said it was her fault for being a cheerleader, and for drinking that night. After her dad paid for her abortion he drove his daughter a hundred miles to New Orleans, handed her a hundred one-dollar bills, and left her on the street.

The other girl had an even sadder story: she and her fiancé had planned on starting a new life in New Orleans. She came to town first while he finished up his job. Two weeks earlier, on his way to join her, he was killed in an auto accident. He had his life savings on him in cash, but when she identified his body at the morgue, the money was missing. Desperate and broke, she had gotten herself trapped into a bad contract at the strip joint.

Chills went down my spine when I heard her story. Robert, too, had a long drive to reach me.

Morning was now advanced, so I called Ochsner's Clinic again and pleaded for assistance. When I made the mistake of telling them how much money I had, they told me to buy a bus ticket and go back home until Dr. Ochsner was ready for me, which I estimated to be May 6th. Gloomily, I said thanks and hung up. I looked around the stairwell where the pay phone was. There was no Nobel Prize winner offering to pay my bills, no obscurely named account to pay my rent. I finally saw the ugly reality of money. The same one my new roommates lived with daily. But I was determined to stay in New Orleans. After all, the plan was for Robert to come and marry me. Then everything would be fine. And, despite the temporary setbacks, the taste of freedom was sweet.

As reality sank in, "the Great Cancer Researcher" decided to follow her new friend to the Royal Castle, just to see what it was like. I was offered a waitress job right on the spot, and started work the next morning.

Most of my work experience up to that point had been in sterile laboratories with precise routines and high sensitivity to the invisible dangers of viruses and bacteria. We worked slowly and carefully and even used black lights to illuminate microbes unseen by the naked eye, especially those lurking in cracks and crevices. The idea of using the same filthy cloth to wipe down counters between customers alarmed me. We were just spreading the bacteria around, and in my mind's eye

I could see the little buggers! When I stopped to rinse my cloth, I was admonished for wasting time. Hurry! Hurry! Hurry!

The customers were mostly working-class males in a hurry to eat and get going so they wouldn't be late for work. It seemed like they all needed attention at the same time. In my haste, I burned myself, cut myself, and confused customer orders. Despite my frantic pace I was much slower than anyone else, and resigned myself to the probability that I wouldn't make the grade. At the end of the shift I was relieved when the boss said, "For some reason the customers like you, so I won't fire you." Thanks.

When I got my first paycheck, I was surprised how proud of it I was. It was enough money to buy a pretty linen dress for my wedding day and a see-through nightie for my wedding night. I even bought a second-hand wedding band at a pawn shop. Robert had made it clear that rings weren't on his list: another reason to wonder if he would really show up or not. The ring was too big for my finger, but it was genuine 14K gold, or so they said. After those purchases there was still enough left to pay my rent at the Y, if I dined exclusively on soup and sandwiches until the next payday. For the first time in ages I had no lab work to do, no journals to read, no reports to write and no classes to attend. Free at last!

Monday, April 22, 1963

Two days later I located the central post office, which was near the library. There I found that Robert's first letter had arrived. In it, he instructed me to place a newspaper ad in the Personals section of the local newspaper using "JARYO" as a code, so he would know I had arrived safely. I'm not sure where he came up with JARYO as a code word, or why he wanted me to place an ad. Why hadn't he simply called? I

New Orleans Civic Center and U.S. Post Office, early 1960s

knew he was at his parent's house in Ft. Walton Beach, but he could have called me from a pay phone. Of course that meant spending money, which he hated to do. He also told me to put his "traveling friend" Raleigh Rourke's name and return address on the letter I was to write to him, so his parents (who received all the mail) wouldn't guess I was writing to him. "And remember, no perfume on the letter!" he had warned. "My mother would really wonder what was wrong with Raleigh." On April 24, a second letter arrived from Robert containing a $5 bill. Not much considering my circumstances, but from a miser like him it was some proof of love. I was thrilled and read his tender words that discussed our secrets:

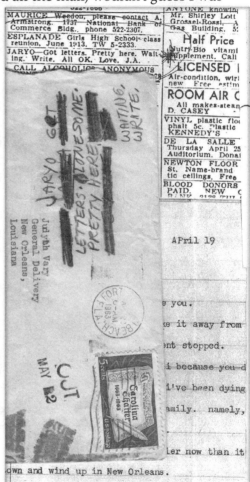

> *I've been dying to tell everyone that there's about to be someone coming into the family. Namely, judy, judy, JUDY! I haven't told, of course, but I still think about it … I'll be so glad when these 11 days are gone. The post office will close soon, so:*
> *love, love, love, Robert xxxxxxX*

I read those words over and over, and looked forward to more letters filled with words of love. For the next four days in a row, I returned to the post office filled with anticipation and left empty with disappointment. Robert, who had promised to write daily, wrote nothing. My impatience was exquisite and growing. I had been to the post office so often that the clerk knew me on sight. By this time the JARYO ad was out and I bought a newspaper, just to imagine Robert reading it back in Florida. I even put a lipstick kiss on the ad, and carried it around with me as a love token.

A portion of Robert's letter is shown under this envelope on which I wrote my "Jaryo" ad, showing Robert mentioning the original 11 day wait. The "out" indicates when the letter, postmarked April 22, would have been returned had I not picked it up.

Friday, April 26, 1963

On the fourth day I made the long bus trip once again to Royal Castle for another two-hour dose of stress and chaos. On the return trip, a woman plunked herself down beside me. She was skinny with long white hair. She wore a yellow flowered dress, sandals made from slices of auto tire and a string of dried chicken feet around her neck. Her fingernails curled like claws in different directions, and she smelled like something had died. I wanted to move away, but was afraid it would hurt her feelings.

When I got off the bus, I noticed two people standing nearby on the sidewalk — a tall, skinny black man talking quietly to a short, fat white woman. How nice, I thought. Colored people and white people getting along here in the heart of the South. There is reason for hope! Suddenly the black man backed away, almost knocking me down. Then he began to run. The woman chased after him, waving a whiskey bottle above her head and screaming curses at him. Then she threw the bottle. It bounced off the man's back and exploded on the sidewalk. The shattering glass almost hit me.

I was starting to experience culture shock, which I had thought was only encountered while traveling in the Third World. It was a scary feeling. *If Robert were here*, I thought, *I would feel safe again.*

Back at the YWCA I changed into a dress and high heels for a visit to Ochsner Clinic, and headed for the post office once again, carrying the letter I'd been writing over the past several days. At the post office, I finished the letter at a side counter, addressed it, then got into the line where General Delivery service was offered. Under my arm was a rolled-up newspaper with the "Jaryo" ad with its red lipstick kiss circling the ad — because Robert's eyes had read those very same words by now! Having been up since 5:00 A.M., I felt wilted. I was only vaguely aware of a man standing in line behind me.

When it was my turn at the counter I asked the clerk if a letter for "Judy Vary" had arrived from Fort Walton Beach, Florida, from Robert A. Baker. The postman checked but found nothing. Still hopeful, I inquired, "Would you please see if a letter for a "'Mr. Rourke' might be there, from Robert A. Baker?" But the clerk said that only Mr. Rourke would be allowed to pick up Mr. Rourke's mail, not Judy Vary.

"Do you have any ID with you?" the clerk asked. I got out my Royal Castle pay stub. "You can call Royal Castle about who I am," I said.

"No, ma'am," the postman said. "Can't do that. I'd need something that says Mr. Rourke will let you pick up his mail for him."

Remembering I had Robert's first letter with me, I opened my purse and rummaged around until I found it. "How many letters come here to General Delivery from Fort Walton Beach?" I asked. "And look, right here," as I waggled the letter under the clerk's nose, "It says I should put Mr. Rourke's name on the envelope."

The clerk agreed to look for something from "Rourke." As I waited I turned and glanced up at the young man standing in line behind me. He offered a friendly smile. How clean-cut he looked! The clerk returned to tell me that there was nothing for Mr. Rourke either. Disappointed, I sighed and bought a stamp. Distracted by the feelings that swamped me, I handed the letter to the postman, and as I did, the newspaper under my arm fell to the floor. The young man behind me picked up the newspaper, glanced at the lipstick-kiss, then handed it to me. As I took it, I gave him my prettiest smile.

"Karashaw, Tovarisch," I said to him (Loosely, "Thanks, Comrade." in Russian). I had frequently used my limited Russian as an ice-breaker at college. It was fun, and since most Americans were not familiar with the sound of Russian, it generally started a conversation. It also gave me an excuse to keep up my Russian skills so they wouldn't slip away, but I admit there was more going on. I was mad at Robert for not writing. Consequently I was flirting with this clean-cut young man. Yes, there are other men in the world, and I'm not married yet!

I was shocked when the young man leaned close to me and said, in perfect Russian, "It's not good to speak Russian in New Orleans."

"But I like to speak Russian," I protested in Russian, as politely as I could. As I turned to leave the building, the young man said, "Please! Wait!" — once more in Russian.

"Okay," I said to him in English, unable to recall the Russian phrase. The young man went to the counter and inquired about a letter for Lee H. Oswald.

When we left together, he at first tried to indulge me by speaking only Russian, but his fluency was far more advanced than mine. So we settled into English.

"You must be new in town. I just got into town myself," he said after he offered to walk me home. "I was born in New Orleans and lived here as a child, but I've been away for nearly ten years. I'm staying at the YMCA right now, until my family gets into town."

I asked him where he learned to speak Russian so well, and he explained that he had lived there for several years.

Lee Oswald, June 1962, leaving Minsk, Russia, en route to USA.

I told him about my interest in all things Russian, and how I read Russian literature and listened to Russian music, like Rimsky-Korsakov. Russia was tops on the list of countries I wished to visit. I told Lee how my family called me "Juduffski."

He confirmed his interest in Russia's classical culture and asked me if I had read Dostoevsky's *The Idiot*. It was one of my favorites, and I had written a poem about Prince Myshkin, the title character. I recited it for him. As soon as I finished, he translated it for me into melodious Russian. I was impressed. Not only did he know the language, he knew the culture.

"I notice that you have no southern accent," he remarked. Nor did he, I observed back. That's when I noticed a thick wedding band on his right hand and remembered that both Russians and Hungarians wore their wedding rings on their right hands.

Curious as usual, I observed him as we walked. Lee Oswald was slender, but well built; the type of man who would never get fat. He had intense, blue-gray eyes and fine wavy brown hair, with a precise way of carrying himself. As he turned toward me again, I saw the neckline of a clean white undershirt under his worn, but spotless, khaki shirt which created a sort of military air about him.[2]

His posture was erect, his head held high. He took his place on the curbside to shield me from the traffic like a gentleman. When my hand touched his accidentally, he moved slightly away. What a sweetheart, I thought, and what a nice contrast to other men.

"So what does the 'H' in your name stand for?" I asked.

"Henry," he joked. "Hogan. Herkimer. Horace. Guess," he teased.

"Hoover," I replied with bluster.

"That would be even worse!" he laughed. "My middle name is Harvey. I don't particularly like it. My Russian friends called me Alek, because Lee sounded weird to them. And half the time, when I wrote it people misread it as "Henry," so I started using "H." I have calculated that will save me many hours during my life by avoiding writing Harvey."

We continued to walk. After several blocks, I began to question my shoe selection. Who invented high heels in the first place, and why would an otherwise intelligent woman wear them? Finally, we found a bench in a shaded area near the YWCA and sat down. I noticed a U.S. Marine Corps ring on his left hand. "Well, you're a Marine, as well as married," I commented.

"You're so observant," Mr. Oswald replied.

"I am terrible at remembering faces," I admitted. "And I get lost going around a corner, but I am good at noticing odd little things that other people don't."

"I won't forget *your* face, because you look like my wife. Are you married?" he asked.

"Almost. In a few days, if he comes. And if I still want to marry him," I said, still miffed about not getting a letter.

"If he comes? If you still want to marry him?" he mocked.

"I love Robert." I insisted. "But if he doesn't show up, I'll survive."

"Love — unto the death!" he responded with grand sarcasm.

I got his point. His directness was penetrating, but his wit was disarming. I wanted him to know more about me. So I told him I was in New Orleans to do cancer research. Dr. Ochsner himself had invited me, but I would be working with Dr. Mary Sherman, who ran a cancer laboratory at his hospital. I also said this to show Mr. Oswald that I had important contacts in town, just in case he wasn't as nice as he seemed. He surprised me once again by saying that his friend Dr. Ferrie had mentioned Dr. Sherman's name just the night before. "She's famous," I said proudly, while calculating the mathematical odds of Lee's hearing her name only yesterday, after being out of town for nearly a decade.

Then Lee demonstrated some of his own powers of observation. He said he had noticed the Royal Castle check stub when we were in at the post office. "So why is a cancer researcher working as a waitress in a fast-food restaurant?" he queried.[3]

It was a fair question, so I answered it by explaining my predicament. We sat on the park bench and continued to talk for the next hour. We discussed a variety of subjects from literature to politics. We had both read Aldous Huxley's utopian nightmare in *Brave New World* and Lee contrasted it to George Orwell's dark view of the future in *1984*. I was surprised at how well read he was, and how adroitly he navigated the maze of political theory. We even discussed Bertrand Russell, the British mathematician who became a vocal anti-war activist, championed nuclear disarmament, criticized Germany for its fascism, the Soviet Union for its totalitarianism and America for its international military adventures. I told Lee I had received a telegram from Russell, and that my father had torn it up because he considered him a Communist.[4]

Lee Oswald voiced his surprise at my Socialist ideals, which he gently juxtaposed to my anti-Communist attitudes. We were now in his territory. He was the only person I had ever spoken to who had actually lived in a Communist country. It was a subject he could articulate skillfully and without prejudice. I admired the clarity of his responses and how carefully he offered me new ideas. Frankly, I was amazed at how one hour of sitting on a park bench in New Orleans had suddenly opened my eyes to the river of thoughts flowing around the world. I had never had this sort of conversation with Robert or anyone else. I pondered the irony of this chance encounter at a post office where I was desperately awaiting a letter from my fiancé, then suddenly became fascinated by a total stranger who happened to be standing in line behind me!

As he spoke, I got a good look at his blue-gray eyes. A shame he's married, I thought, then realized what I was thinking and my Catholic upbringing kicked in. Guilt swelled up within me.

Lee must have sensed my sudden mood shift, because he said: "My wife is in Texas because, unfortunately, we are not getting along very well right now." His sorrowful words rang true. I did not think he was trying to tell me that he might be available for romance if I was interested. It was more like a friend sharing a burden.

Then Lee suddenly changed subjects and asked me if I played chess.[5] Yes I did, and considered myself quite good at it. Lee said he had never met an American girl who liked chess, wrote poetry, loved Russian literature, and had even learned to speak some Russian.

"I'd like to play you at chess sometime," he proposed, adding, "Dr. Ferrie has a chess set we can use. He's involved in cancer research himself," he remarked. "I think you two should meet." Lee ended by saying he would definitely call Dr. Ferrie right away and stood up to leave. He went over to pick up a shirt and told me that, if I needed help with anything, I could leave a message for him at the YMCA.

As we parted, Lee gave me a squeeze of the arm, a boyish smile, and then walked away. I just stood there daydreaming. I loved the way he talked and walked. And those eyes! And how he spoke Russian. The way he let me be myself. I tried to look away as he walked confidently down the street. I didn't want to be too obvious.

No, no, no, Judy! I told myself. You are supposed to be in love with

Brent House, 1960

Robert Allison Baker, III. Remember? I snapped back to reality. Angry at myself for indulging in such an extended flirtation, I went upstairs to rest awhile. There I re-read Robert's two letters to remind me who I really loved. An hour later, I was on my way to Ochsner's Clinic to fill out application papers for my summer internship.

I listed YWCA as housing choice, because Ochsner Clinic was in the middle of nowhere.

The last thing I wanted was a room at Brent House, the hotel on Och-sner's campus with nothing but bland, expensive hospital food to eat. The YWCA was close to cheap restaurants, movie theatres, universi-ties and libraries ... and for additional educational experiences I had strippers for roommates!

That night, one of my roommates invited me to her club in the French Quarter to watch her act. I went to the dressing room to help with her hair, costume, and make-up. I was surrounded by girls ap-plying pasties to their nipples and putting on G-strings. The smell of hair-spray, make-up and perfume filled the air.

My friend was part of a three-girl dance routine most of the night. Bright stage lights darkened the audience and made their performance seem more theatrical than sexy. Finally she performed her solo act. As I watched from back-stage, the whole scene struck me as a strange barbaric ritual. The idea of a beautiful young woman taking off her clothes to entertain a group of anonymous drunken men whistling and shouting at her, was really off my chart. It was clearly "the other side of life" that I had not witnessed before. And the reason for her to do all of this was, of course, the money. She made a lot of cash that night, but had to give half of it to her "sponsor." I calculated that she made as much in a week as I could make working full time at Royal Castle for a month. But hers was a tough life and it was taking its toll by turning her brassy.

Finally the long, tangled day ended and we returned to the Y. As I lay in my bed waiting for sleep to overtake me I pondered the events. New Orleans was, indeed, a new experience. What to make of this mysterious Mr. Oswald? What an interesting man! So how does such

Early 1960s
Ochsner Clinic

a well-read intellectual emerge from this decadent French colony, speaking fluent Russian? And why was he returning to this corrupt sin-sick city with his young family after years of international travel?

Inside the Sho-Bar, early 1960s

1. "Big Jim" was the widely used nickname for District Attorney Jim Garrison, due to his 6'6" size. He made his reputation as a tough-on-crime enforcer.

2. That summer, Lee completely wore out his khaki shirt and pants. Instead of throwing them away, he put them into a doghouse where a mother dog had newborn puppies!

3. Later, Lee told me he never would have spoken to me about some of his 'private business' — the clandestine side of things — but he thought I was also involved. Items such as "Rourke," "Robert A. Baker," the "Jaryo" code in the newspaper, my working at that particular Royal Castle (the dead drop where Bobby Kennedy's men left spy information about Marcello in his next-door office at Town and County) and my later mention of Eglin AFB. All of this made Lee believe I knew more than I did, and gave him, he said, the confidence to tell me things he later learned I should not have been told. Some people have told me Lee was sent deliberately — and I see no conflict with the fact that Lee may not have been told much about me — which in this case worked in my favor, as I learned much about Lee that he freely confessed he would not have told me, had he known how out of the loop I actually was.

4. My father received several telegrams congratulating me after my high school cancer research story went national. Two of them were exceptional: one was from the actor and TV star Arthur Godfrey, who himself had lung cancer. Godfrey had the Damon Runyon Cancer organization send me funds. My father was so excited about that telegram that he called all our relatives about it. The other extraordinary one was from Bertrand Russell, which irritated my father because Russell, he said, was a Communist. He tore that telegram to pieces. Later, my father gave me a book by Russell, *Why I Am Not a Christian*, while I was held incommunicado on Snead Island under his authority. The book made a deep impact on me: I was an atheist for the next seven years.

5. "When I was about fourteen, I lived here in New Orleans," said Lee, "I knew an old man called Alexei, who taught me how to play chess." It was Alexei who kindled Lee's desire to live in Russia. My own interest in chess had also been sparked by an elderly Russian, who taught me the game when I was a child at the Lake Maggiore Youth Center when we lived in St. Petersburg, Florida.

Sho Bar
Sho Bar
NO MINIMUM
NO COVER
Appearing NITELY...
Champagne Girl
Continuous ENTERTAINMENT
NO COVER
Champag
CLUB
Hotsy Totsy
RL SHOWS
St. Cyr
DODGE
20H635

Carlos Marcello in his Town & Country Motel office

New Orleans
Civic Center

Royal Castle
Town & Country Motel

Ochsner Clinic
& Hospital

TOWN
AND
COUNTRY
MOTEL

— CHAPTER 7 —

THE FAVOR

Saturday, April 27, 1963

The next morning at 6:00 A.M. I boarded the bus in downtown New Orleans and headed to the Royal Castle half way out to the airport in Jefferson Parish. Soon, the now-familiar onslaught of men demanding breakfast began and I was taking orders, flipping burgers, scrambling eggs and squeezing oranges for a gallery of gulping Adam's apples.

These were laborers who needed their breakfast fast, before heading out for a day of exhausting work, like building roads or laying brick. They were basically good men who worked hard. Their voices were loud and bold. They flirted with me and called me "honey," "babe," and "sweetie." They forgave my unimpressive waitress skills and left tips anyway, mostly because they liked how I looked in that uniform and little apron. But the pace was frantic and the work exhausting.

Racing to keep up with the orders, I suddenly burned myself. Forcing myself to keep smiling despite the sudden and unexpected pain, I looked up to see Lee Oswald coming through the door. Had he come this far just to see me? Yes! I gave him a quick wave. He smiled, and got in line until a seat opened up at the counter. I made sure I was the one who took his order.

Lee was better dressed today, wearing tight black pants and a white shirt, with a brown tie. He looked quite handsome, sitting there with his quizzical smile and discerning eyes. He ordered a glass of fresh orange juice. As he watched me press the oranges against the spinner of the electric juicer, it nicked my thumb. With my thumb bleeding, as I handed him the juice, he said, "I'll have to drink it all, because you shed your blood making it."

It was an odd thing to say, but he said it in a grave voice that conveyed a dramatic sense of purpose. I couldn't imagine Robert or any of the other boys that I had known saying anything so valiant. With each out-of-the-ordinary thing Lee Oswald did, he became a little more intriguing. Then he took a paperback book from his pants pocket and started reading silently. As I hurried on with my tasks, I wondered what he was reading.

When I returned to see if he wanted anything else, Lee ordered a full breakfast with eggs, coffee, and toast. As I scribbled the order on my pad, I stole a glance at the title of his book: *The Prose and Poetry of Pushkin.* I was familiar with Alexander Pushkin, because he is the most famous of all Russian writers.

Alexander Pushkin

Considered to be the founder of modern Russian literature and Russia's greatest poet, Alexander Pushkin was born in Moscow in 1799 at the height of the Russian Empire. His innovative style of storytelling mixed drama with romance and satire, and he is known for introducing vernacular speech into poems and plays. By the 1820s, he became the radical voice of social reform, causing the government to exile him to southern Russia where he wrote *Boris Godunov*, which became his most famous play. Having achieved considerable literary success, he married in 1831, and he and his wife became regulars at court in Saint Petersburg. Angered by scandalous rumors that his wife was having an affair, Pushkin challenged her alleged lover to a duel in 1837. Pushkin was fatally wounded as a result and died two days later. His political views influenced generations of Russian rebels.

I was first introduced to Pushkin in the introductory Russian course during high school, and had read various translations of his richly textured prose work ever since. I discovered his perplexing poetry in that wonderful library at St. Francis. In time, Pushkin came to be my favorite Russian author. I found some satisfaction in the fact that Lee was reading an author I liked so much. Another shared interest. My mind was still reeling from our expansive conversation on the park bench the day before.

Lost in my daydream, I suddenly heard my boss yelling at me through the chatter: "Jump to it, Judy! You've got customers waiting!" I snapped back to reality and rushed to serve the other customers. Lee kept reading, as if nothing had happened.

As the breakfast crowd thinned out, Lee moved to a table and continued to read. I wiped off the counter, then the tables, cautiously moving in Lee's direction so as not attract my boss's attention.

When I reached his table I noticed that he had turned his glass upside down to indicate he had finished every drop of his orange juice, fulfilling his promise. I asked him what he was reading. He responded by reading these lines from Pushkin in a dramatic tone:

> *Once more a prey to doing nothing*
> *His spirit sick with futile rage,*
> *He sat down with the worthy purpose*
> *Of mastering wisdom's heritage.*

"It sounds better in Russian," he said simply. "I love reading more than anything, – except for making love," in a voice devoid of mischief.

The way he said it sounded so natural that I was not offended. Then I noticed another customer, so I slid away and tended to his needs. When my shift was over, I clocked out and changed clothes. Though it was only two hours, I was always stressed and drained. Seeing that Lee was still buried in Pushkin, I quietly sat down beside him, waiting in silence until he looked up.

"I don't know how the others do it," I told him, "but I can't take much more of this job, even though I need the money to rent a room for Robert and me."

Lee slowly put his book away. "Well, I contacted Dr. Ferrie," he said. "He wants you to join him for lunch today. Maybe he can help. It'll be a late lunch, because he was up all night."

"I'm grateful," I said. "My thumb can't take much more from that juice machine!"

Lee smiled. "You mean you don't want that juice machine to take much more from your thumb!" I smiled as I pondered his wry sense of humor.

"I'm looking for a temporary job, myself," he said. "Maybe I can find a better one for you, too, until our real jobs come into play." I knew what my "real job" was, but what was his "real job" going to be? Did he have something that had been pre-arranged as well?

Then he said that his uncle had offered him work, but he preferred not to get tangled up with Marcello's people.

"Marcello!" I said. "Everywhere I go, I hear that name!"

Lee didn't respond.

"Another thing I am hearing wherever I go is talk against Castro. There is as much anti-Castro sentiment here as in Florida. Maybe more."

Lee asked me what I had heard about Castro, and I told him about my own anti-Castro feelings and how my Cuban friend Tony Lopez-Fresquet had influenced them. Lee displayed interest and asked me questions about Tony and his family. So many questions, in fact, that I wondered if he was pumping me for information. Still sensitive to Tony's security issues, I changed the subject and started talking about my Hungarian grandmother and her family. At the mention of Hungary, Lee quickly recalled the Hungarian Revolution of 1956. He was a teenager when Soviet tanks rolled in to crush the Hungarian Freedom Fighters. Lee said he admired them as heroes and lamented that he did not speak any Hungarian, so I taught him some words and phrases that I had learned from my family. Lee had a good ear, and after only slight corrections, repeated the phrases perfectly. I was impressed, because Hungarian is a very difficult non-European language, related only to Finnish.

"Now tell me about your family," I urged him. "That's only fair."

He did so laconically. Lee said his mother was connected to the Mafia through various boyfriends over the years, one of which was Marcello's driver (and bodyguard). She had also worked for a law firm that represented Marcello. Her sister Lillian had married Charles Murret, who had been with Marcello for years. In the early days, "Dutz," as everybody called him, had been a boxer and union enforcer on the docks and had moved up in Marcello's ranks. Now Dutz helped handle Marcello's money, mostly from various gambling operations.

"I had to make a choice early on," Lee told me. "Whether I was going to be one of Marcello's soldiers, or be another kind of soldier and join the Marine Corps, like my brother. Either the world can be an influence on you," he went on, "or you can be an influence on the world. I chose to stay out of Marcello's world."

"Besides," he continued, "I come from a military family. Both my brothers served. I originally wanted to join the Air Force to become a pilot," he added, "so I joined the Civil Air Patrol. But due to this," he said, tapping his left ear, "I couldn't qualify. So I joined the Marines instead."

Chronic infections in his left ear had damaged Lee's hearing, leading to a painful operation called a mastoidectomy. In fact, he was hospitalized at the same age I was. Recalling how my protracted illness affected my religious views, I asked Lee if he was religious.

He shook his head. "No, there are so many religions out there that claim they have the only God-given truth," he said, "so I concluded that God must not be a good communicator. Therefore," he said, "I am not responsible."

Wow. I realized that Lee was an intellectual disguised in common clothes, so I probed further. "Are you an atheist?" I asked.

"Are you?" he shot back.

I lapsed into silence.

"I'm nearly one." he continued. "Perhaps I am a reluctant atheist. I hope there is somebody watching over things, but I doubt it. Look at the condition of the world. We seem to be on our own in this life."

We discussed the God problem for nearly an hour, with a mixture of anxiety and venom. The specter of Nazi concentration camps was only eighteen years in the past, and the Nuremberg trials had painted a clear portrait of those horrible atrocities. How could God forsake humanity like that? I told Lee about my own bitter disappointment with religion, having offered my life up to God, only to have my parents kidnap me from St. Francis and almost wreck my college career.

Upon hearing that I had wanted to become a nun, Lee said, "You and Dr. Ferrie have that in common. He's actually a priest who can't

get ordained because he is a homosexual. It broke his heart." Ferrie
had wanted nothing more than to serve God as a priest, Lee added,
but he could not keep his hands off teenage boys. Despite this, Ferrie
insisted that God existed. "He has strong arguments," Lee warned me.
"He almost makes you believe."

"It's time to warn you about his appearance," Lee went on. Ferrie
had lost almost all the hair on his body, and the little that was left on
his head made him look like a clown.[1] He wore cheap wigs and put on
fake eyebrows to keep dust and dander out of his eyes, which is necessary for flying or using a microscope, and he did both.[2] Lee told me to
ignore these superficial things and look for the great mind underneath.

Ferrie was brilliant, Lee assured me – and in addition to his consid-
erable talents, he was a courageous man. His work in the fight against
Communism was appreciated by both "government people," and the
Mafia.[3]

I knew about Dr. Ochsner's own anti-Castro feelings, so it was easy
for me to accept the idea that Dr. Ferrie would be anti-Castro as well,
since he was working on a project with Dr. Sherman.

Dr. Ferrie's mixture of medicine and politics explained his relationship with government people easily enough, but I was fascinated by
the idea that Ferrie also worked with the Mob. This was the first time
I had encountered the idea that the Mafia and the U.S. Government
might be working together against Castro.[4]

Lee said he had asked around about affordable rooms for me. He
was looking for something in a safe area that would not require references or a security deposit. He'd be happy to take me to see some
of them if I wanted. So, I decided to spend the day with Lee Oswald,
looking for a place to live. We caught a bus back into town.

As the day progressed, I noticed that every time I turned my head to
look at Lee, he was also turning to look at me. Our eyes met constantly
in a fascinating rhythm. We naturally clicked. Unlike the alert regard
I had for Robert, as if a balancing act had to be performed to keep him
happy, I felt comfortable at once with Lee. I felt my attraction to this
former Marine growing. With him at my side, I felt safe in this ominous city. But I did not allow myself to dwell on these feelings. I was
engaged to Robert and anxiously awaited a letter from him about our
marriage plans.

Back in town, Lee and I first went to the post office, where a letter
from Robert was waiting. When I opened the envelope I found a $20
money order that I could use to make a down-payment on our room.
With my spirits lifted, I began to read the letter. It was then that I realized Robert was going to be a day late. My spirits sank. We had planned
on getting married on May 1st — May Day! The Rites of Spring! But in

order to reach that target, we'd now have to get married the same day he arrived. Robert also hinted that he might be shipped out of town to work offshore in the oil industry. I should prepare myself for that inconvenience, he counseled. Lee sensed my disappointment and suggested that we walk to Canal Street to get my mind off these matters.

As we window-shopped, we were surrounded by the bustle of tourists and streetcars. Each upscale window held elegant treasures and sophisticated fashions. My eyes were wide with wonder at all I surveyed. Gold lettering on one of these windows read "Se habla Espanol" to invite the tourists from Central and South America into the store, and assure them that their staff was ready to serve them in their own language. Suddenly, I thought of my Cuban friend Tony. Still curious about Lee's long list of questions about Tony's family, I asked Lee what he knew about Cuba. "I know a little bit," he replied, as we sat down on a bench,

"I wonder if you know as much about Cuba as I do," I said boldly. Lee closed his eyes, passed his hand over his forehead like a conjurer, and began rattling off the names of every city and town on the island. He began at one end of Cuba and ended at the other. His recitation was methodical and thorough. I listened, transfixed.

Then he ticked off the names of Cuba's cabinet members, politicians and generals. When he started reciting a list of all the mountains and rivers, I was overwhelmed.

"Stop!" I insisted. "How in the world do you know all of that?"

"I was ordered to memorize it," he smiled. "Since I returned from Russia, I've spent a lot of Saturdays with Cuban maps. I've always loved maps, anyway, so it wasn't such an arduous task." He said he could get around in Cuba with his eyes closed, though he needed to work on his Spanish.

"Are you going to be involved in trying to kill Castro?" I asked, for rumors about U.S. assassination plots had been a constant piece of chatter among my anti-Castro friends.

"No, I'm going there to give him a medal," he replied. "What do you think?"

I realized that I was looking at a man willing to risk his life to get Castro. He had already penetrated one Communist country, and was now preparing to infiltrate a second one – a dangerous and forbidden country the American government was punishing with blockades and quarantines. I was thoroughly impressed, and felt privileged to know someone with such courage. Lee was starting to take on heroic proportions for me, like the scientist and WW II spy Dr. Canute Michaelson who had inspired me in high school. It was impossible for me to hide my admiration.

Lee took my admiration and careful silences for knowledge of the intelligence community that, frankly, I didn't have. He seemed to believe I was also part of these clandestine circles. But I wasn't. Or, more accurately, I just didn't know it yet.

Next, Lee made a collect call to Dallas from a pay phone. I could overhear his side of the conversation from where I sat on the bench. After another call or two, Lee obtained an address, and we boarded the St. Charles streetcar. It was my very first ride on a New Orleans

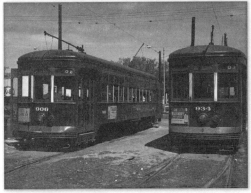

streetcar, and the experience thrilled me. The varnished wooden seats and brass trim spoke of timeless elegance, and the open windows provided a refreshing breeze. The antique carriage produced its own symphony of sounds and rocked rhythmically as the steel wheels rumbled down the tracks. The swirling sound of its electric engine swelled each time it started and was punctuated by the familiar pattern of bells, brakes, and doors each time it stopped, with an ever-changing gallery of passengers getting off and on.

Inside a 1960s St. Charles Avenue streetcar

Dr. Sherman's Apartment Building

Loyola

Tulane

Zemurray Mansion

Lee sat close to me and showed me the landmarks, as we headed uptown on St. Charles Avenue. Victorian mansions, lush parks, and fancy restaurants lined this amazing street. Lee pointed out Dr. Sherman's apartment building near the corner of Louisiana Avenue as we passed. For the first time since my arrival in New Orleans, I was enjoying the city in daylight. I chattered away in delight at all of the interesting sights and sounds.[5]

As we passed the Gothic cathedral at Loyola University, our conversation turned briefly to religion again, discovering that most of our family members were Catholics. Next came Tulane University, which was studded with stone buildings that reminded me of that wonderful Romanesque castle I had enjoyed at St. Francis. Next door to Tulane was Audubon Place, where the wealthiest of New Orleans live. At its entrance stood a white-columned mansion built by Sam "The Banana Man" Zemurry who amassed his fortune as president of the United Fruit Company. Never had I seen such an opulent residence.[6]

Several blocks later, we got off the streetcar. Across the street stood a stately home with gables and grand columns. Flanked by moss-draped oak trees and emanating dignity, this charming Southern mansion was now a boarding house. The generous wooden porch welcomed us to a front door that sparkled with cut glass as we approached. Lee rang the bell as I peered through the jewel-like glass door into the foyer where a brilliant chandelier blazed. Near the staircase at the far end of the hall was a red love seat fringed with gold. There a beautifully dressed lady sat with an equally well-dressed gentleman. I saw them reach for each other and kiss. What a romantic place!

I wondered if I could afford to rent such grandeur. Then, a red-haired woman well past her prime came plodding down the hall in a rumpled dress and slippers, and opened the door. This was Mrs. Webber.

Lee introduced me as "Mrs. Baker," adding, "Mr. P sent us." That was what she needed to know. She invited us inside.

"There's nothing left but the parlor," she said coldly. "You'll have to use the bathroom down the hall. But I'll let you use the fridge and stove in my kitchen."

Then she looked me over carefully and peered at my hand. "Where's your ring?" she demanded in an irritated voice. I had forgotten to put it on, but I had it in my purse. I dug it out and showed it to her, commenting on how loose it was. The old bag softened her tone and said, "You must be starving, poor thing!"

"You, too," she said to Lee. "Come on in. Have a ham sandwich."

It was not yet noon, and a ham sandwich seemed like unusual breakfast fare, but Mrs. Webber said she was out of eggs. When she also offered us tea, Lee and I asked if she had any milk, almost in the same voice. We looked at each other with surprise. Yes, we were both milk drinkers! It was a small, silly thing, but typically precious to people who discover a soul mate.

Mrs. Webber said her parlor rented for $30 a month. I was surprised because this was cheaper than my dormitory room at the YWCA. Not only was it a private room, it had a rosewood wardrobe for my clothes. Mrs. Webber said she would have her handyman move her mother's old-fashioned bed into the room right away. The parlor doors were pulled together and locked, so I couldn't see inside. But I was thrilled to be in such a beautiful house, and handed the old lady my $20 money order, asking if it would do until my husband arrived.

"I want all of it now," she replied, "or it ain't no deal."

"Mrs. Baker," Lee interrupted. "Are you going to rent the parlor sight unseen?"

"I trust your recommendation," I told him. Lee hesitated, and then reached into his pants pocket, bringing out an old brown wallet. "I always carry a ten dollar bill for emergencies," he said. "This looks like one." He paid her and off we went.

New Orleans YWCA, early 1960s

Lee turned out to have plenty of change in his pockets, so we could continue to use the city's fine public transit system. We went back to the YWCA and got some of my things.

When we returned to the boarding house I was able to inspect the former parlor, which would be my bedroom. The view was delightful. Through the tall floor-length windows I could see the streetcars as they rolled past under the majestic old oaks. Behind them were more Victorian mansions across the street. The azaleas were in bloom and their pink flowers added bright colors to the scene. What an interesting landscape! I thought about how much I would like to paint it. And it was just outside the window.

Lee pointed out other amenities in the room. There was an oriental rug lying on the hardwood floor. The walls were paneled to waist level in dark wood, and crowned with beautiful molding. Above the molding was European wallpaper depicting a hunting scene, complete with stags and thoroughbred horses. The bed was a magnificent antique, fit for a prince and his consort. Carved from mahogany and draped with a satin bedspread and silk quilts that carried the faint scent of lavender, the bed rose so high I had to climb onto it from a stool. The romance was overwhelming.

Mrs. Webber handed me a generic skeleton key. It did not make me feel safe, and I said as much to her. She dismissed my concerns by saying that nobody would know if I didn't tell them. Lee then asked how late the front door was kept unlocked. Instead of answering him, the old witch concluded that his motives were suspicious, and asked me if I was cheating on my husband!

Lee stiffened with resentment at the question.

"Mr. Oswald is a dear friend of mine," I snapped. "We have to meet a doctor friend for lunch and get some groceries. He's helping me." Mrs. Webber mumbled something under her breath about no hanky-panky being allowed in her house.

"I just kicked out a woman who was sunbathing on my front porch swing, naked as a jaybird," she said. "As for keys, you don't need a key to the front door. Just ring the bell, and I'll let you in."

"That's ridiculous," Lee protested. "Give her a key, or give her back her money."

After fumbling around, Mrs. Webber pulled a key from deep between her pendulous breasts, complaining it was the last one she had.

Now that I'd rented a room, I needed to get the rest of my things from the YWCA, so we headed back in that direction. As we waited for the streetcar, Lee asked why I was so silent. "You called me 'Mrs. Baker,'" I said. "And I lied, too. I feel miserable."

Lee frowned as he considered my comment. "Juduffki," he said, "sometimes it's necessary. I hate lying, but some lies are beneficial," he said as the streetcar came to our stop. Lee took my hand and helped me onto the streetcar. Once seated, he added, "I've had to tell lots of lies, because the truth could have hurt somebody. I do regret one thing, though. I no longer feel bad afterwards."

I pondered his enigmatic comment as the streetcar rolled down St. Charles Avenue, but said nothing about it.

Midday - Saturday, April 27, 1963

As we moved things from the 'Y' over to Mrs. Webbers' place, Lee mentioned that he could borrow his cousin's car and show me the city. He also hoped to locate his father's grave, and in the process, I would get to see a typical New Orleans cemetery. Lee waited in the hall and made phone calls as I changed clothes and prettied up. Anticipating meeting Dr. Ferrie, I wanted to look my best, so I put my hair up and donned a classy gray-brown sheath that fit like a glove.

When I emerged from my room, Lee announced that his plans had changed. His uncle (Dutz Murret) needed a favor, so we would have to take our tour of the city tomorrow, but I could come along with him if I liked, adding that he would enjoy my company. Then he cautioned me. "It's something connected to Marcello. You don't have to come along, if it makes you feel uncomfortable."

It was a fair warning, but it enticed me. Yes, I had heard that he was a Mafia don. But this might be an adventure! It would certainly expand my horizons, just as living at the YWCA had. Besides, we were still scheduled to have lunch with Dr. Ferrie later in the day, and I did not want to miss that. So I went for it.

We boarded a streetcar and transferred to a bus, which took us to his uncle's house in Lakeview just off Canal Boulevard near City Park. On the way Lee said he didn't want his aunt and uncle to see me, since they'd soon learn of his rocky marriage and might jump to conclusions, so he wanted me to wait outside.[7] As we rode, Lee talked about his efforts to locate his father's grave. His mother had taken him to the grave site once, but he was too young to remember much detail. His Oswald relatives certainly knew where it was, but they were upset that Lee's name (and consequently theirs) had been plastered all over the newspapers announcing his so-called defection to the Soviet Union. Therefore, Lee was now estranged from most of the Oswald clan, and they might not be willing to help him find the grave.

But the Murrets were different. They were connected to his mother's family. For them family trumped politics, and Lee was family. Lee said that he had lived with the Murrets as a child when his mother was having financial problems. Now that Lee had returned to New Orleans, the Murrets had invited him to move in with them again until he could find an apartment for himself and his family.

When we reached the Murrets' neighborhood, we got off the bus and walked a block or two. As we approached their house, he sat me down on the steps in front of a neighbor's place, where I waited and watched the children play. They did all of the wonderful things that kids do: pulling wagons, riding bikes, playing tag, and throwing balls. The trees were green, and the gardens were bursting with the flowers of Spring. It was a happy April day in a family neighborhood, full of the simple joys of life.

When Lee came out of his uncle's house he was all business, and said we had to go the Town and Country Motel, which was a long bus ride away. We returned to the bus stop, caught the next one, and rode out to the motel. Along the way Lee pointed out some of the landmarks. "If there's time after our lunch with Dr. Ferrie, we'll visit this old aunt of mine. She might tell me where my father's grave is." Then Lee showed me a list of addresses and phone numbers of relatives that his uncle had given him. "The two underlined ones might talk to me," Lee told me. The others hated him for his "defection" to Russia.

Lee said his defection had been front-page news, and was broadcast around the world. Even his half-brother heard about it on Armed Forces radio when he was stationed in Japan. But now Lee, "the defector" was back in the U.S., walking around a free man. There was obviously something fishy here. I knew the rules of loyalty and patriotism. Had Lee really defected, he would never have been

Fort Worth Defector Confirms Red Beliefs

SUN NOV 15 1959

BY ALINE MOSBY.

MOSCOW, Nov. 14 (UPI). — Lee Oswald, still sporting the chop-top haircut he wore in the U. S. Marines, said Saturday that when he left America to seek citizenship in Russia "it was like getting out of prison."

But his dream of achieving Soviet citizenship in exchange for the U. S. citizenship he renounced went aglimmering. The 20-year-old Texan from Fort Worth said Soviet authorities would not grant him citizenship although t h e y said he could live in Russia freely as a resident alien.

"Imperialism" and lack of money while a child were his main reasons for turning his back on his native land, he said.

A slender, well-groomed youth, he carefully thought out his phrases before speaking in an interview at a Moscow hotel.

He had announced on Oct. 31 that he had renounced his U. S. citizenship and was seeking Soviet citizenship "for purely political reasons."

He said he told the U. S. embassy he was a devoted believer in communism and had read books on the subject since he was 15. Memories of a poverty-stricken childhood played a part in his decision, he said. His father, he said, died before he was born.

"I saw my mother always as a worker, always with less than

we could use," he said. He insisted his childhood was happy, despite poverty. He admitted his mother "would not understand" why he had fled to Russia.

"In the Marine Corps I observed the American military in foreign countries, what Russians would call military imperialism," he said.

"I was with occupation forces in Japan and occupation of a country is imperialistic," he said.

"I would not want to live in the United States and be either a worker exploited by capitalists or a capitalist exploiting workers or become unemployed.

"I could not be happy living under capitalism."

He said Karl Marx' work "Das Kapital" set him on the road to communism, and he began to read all he could find about it.

Oswald joined the Marine Corps at 17. During his hitch he learned to be a specialist in radar and electronics.

"I saved my money—$1,600—to come to the Soviet Union and thought of nothing else," he said.

Many things bothered him in the United States, he said—race discrimination, "harsh" treatment of "underdog" Communists and "hate."

Ft. Worth Telegram Nov. 15, 1959

allowed to return, and if he had, he would have been arrested and imprisoned or forced to leave again.[8]

As we rode, Lee told me that one of his childhood heroes was Herbert Philbrick, an FBI agent who infiltrated the Communist Party and wrote a book about his experiences, entitled *I Led Three Lives*.

Herbert Philbrick

Herbert Philbrick was an advertising executive who infiltrated the American Communist Party on behalf of the FBI in the 1940s. He wrote about these experiences in his 1952 book *I Led Three Lives: Citizen, 'Communist', Counterspy* which became a best seller, and soon became the basis for both a radio series (1952-54) and a television show (1953-56). Herbert Philbrick personally narrated each episode and served as a technical consultant, and the scripts for all 117 episodes were approved by J. Edgar Hoover and the FBI. Most of the plots had very little to do with the actual events of Philbrick's life and frequently involved international intrigue in which Philbrick never participated.

Lee Oswald was 14 years old and living in New York when the series began. It became his favorite show.

In 1963 Philbrick presented officials in INCA – the anti-Red organization headed by Dr. Alton Ochsner – an anti-Communist film prior to becoming an advisor to INCA. Lee told Judyth he met Philbrick there, but was dismayed because Philbrick acted as if Hoover was "Jesus Christ."

A 1950s TV series loosely based on Philbrick's book became Lee's favorite program. It inspired him to become a spy. It was then I realized that Lee's so-called defection had to have been some type of intelligence assignment. He had really been an American spy behind the Iron Curtain.

I realized that spying behind the Iron Curtain at the height of the Cold War would take a tremendous amount of courage. Getting caught could have dreadful consequences. I had always admired the work that spies did. Now I realized I was actually talking to a real one!

Thinking about Lee's rejection by the Oswald side of his family, I tried to comfort him by telling him about Dr. Canute Michaelson, who came to my school years before in Bradenton. His experience was eerily similar to Lee's. During World War II, Michaelson had pretended to be a Nazi in order to infiltrate their ranks and report their secrets to the Resistance. His family was not aware that he was undercover, and only saw his pro-Nazi activities. Many of them turned against him and accused him of being a traitor. When they finally learned the truth they realized both his bravery and his loyalty, and welcomed him back into the family.

"Did you know that Dr. Canute Michaelson became my shining hero?" I said, in hopes of showing him how his fortunes might change one day.

Lee said nothing, but smiled at me, indicating that he knew he had my respect. As I took his hand, I could almost see the weight lift from him. He needed someone to believe in him, to see past the charade he had to live every day.

"But your aunt and uncle are being way too friendly, Lee," I ventured after thinking the matter over. "My guess is that they understand your true character."

Lee then told me about his cousin Marilyn. She was the Murrets' daughter and Lee's playmate as a child. She left New Orleans to see the world just as Lee had, and had also lived overseas. Lee said she understood him better than others, and perhaps that influenced her parents.

We finally arrived at the Town and Country Motel, which was next to the Royal Castle. We went into the lounge. Lee told me the place really hopped at night, but it was early afternoon at the moment, and almost deserted. I could hear the clinking of glasses being washed and a radio playing quietly in the background. We sat down at one of the tables and waited

silently until a busboy came to our table and poured water. Lee then asked to see the manager. As the young man left the table, he winked at me. "I should have told you this is a pick-up joint," Lee whispered, frowning. "I'm ashamed to have brought you here. This is one of Marcello's places. It seems that every time I come to New Orleans I'm asked to run errands to places like this."[9]

"But you want to please your uncle, don't you?" I offered.

"I owe him," he said firmly. "So I have to help out sometimes."

As we waited at the table, Lee explained that his father had died a few months before he was born.[10] When he was a child, his mother struggled with financial problems so severe that she sent Lee to live with her sister Lillian and her husband Dutz Murret.[11] Uncle Dutz and Aunt Lillian had cared for Lee along with their own houseful of children while he was too small to go to an orphanage, where his brothers had been placed.

"My mother had a bad hand dealt to her," he explained. "She went through three husbands and lost everything, but she wouldn't ask her husband's side of the family for help no matter what it cost us. She was too proud, even when the insurance money ran out. That was a big mistake."

Years of hardship turned Lee's mother bitter. She looked old before her time. Lee felt sorry for her, and he believed his very existence was partially responsible for her misery. He took part-time jobs as a teenager to help out and sent her money while he was in the Marines.[12] "My brothers left home as soon as they could. So did I. And that was fine with her."

A waiter finally came to our table with menus, but Lee shook his head "No" and said, "I just want to see Mr. P." The waiter withdrew without comment, and Lee continued talking about his mother. He said that when he was stranded in

Marguerite, 1957

Marguerite Francis Claverie was born in New Orleans in 1907. About two years after she married New Orleans Stevedore Edward John Pic, she became pregnant, and Pic left her because he did not want any children. She and Pic were divorced, but Pic sent support money for their son John Edward.

In 1933 Marguerite married Robert Edward Lee Oswald, an insurance agent. Their first child, Robert, was born in 1934. In August 1939, Mrs. Oswald's husband died of a coronary thrombosis; two months later, on Oct. 18, she gave birth to her third child, Lee Harvey Oswald. Marguerite recalls that "other kids teased Lee because he was so bright. He learned to read by himself before he went to school. He was always wanting to know about important things."

In 1945 she married an industrial engineer from Boston, Edwin A. Ekdahl, and moved to Fort Worth. They kept Lee with them, and sent the two older boys to a Mississippi military academy. Lee lived at home and developed a warm attachment to Ekdahl, occasionally accompanying his mother and stepfather on business trips around the country. Lee started school in Benbrook, Tex., but in the fall of 1946, after a separation from Ekdahl, due to his infidelity, Marguerite reentered Lee in the first grade in Covington, Louisiana.

In 1948 Ekdahl filed for divorce, charging that Marguerite nagged him constantly about money, hit and scratched him, threw a bottle and a cookie jar at him, and once nearly crowned him with a vase.

the USSR she had written letters to important people in the U.S. Government, asking them to let Lee back in.

The U.S. State Department lent him enough money for the family to take a train from Russia through Europe. They spent a day of rest in a bed-and-breakfast in Rotterdam, Holland before they boarded a luxury ocean liner to New York, after which they flew to Texas. The trip was fast, but had to be made as comfortable as possible, he said, because their baby daughter, June, was so very young. "I paid that loan off, every penny," he told me proudly. But think of it. A so-called "defector" getting a loan from his government to return to the U.S.![13]

At first, they lived with his mother while Lee worked to repay the loan and save money for an apartment. But it was simply impossible to stay on good terms with his mother, he explained, because she was both intrusive and manipulative.

"That is one thing I like about Robert," I told Lee. "He doesn't stick his nose into my life. In fact, he's never met most of my friends."

"Are you sure this man loves you?" Lee asked.

"I'm sure," I answered, trying to convince myself. "Even though he never says so," I admitted reluctantly.

"He never tells you he loves you?" Lee asked incredulously.

"Well, he wrote it," I answered. Then I dug through my purse and produced the little booklet of pink sheets stapled together that said "I LOVE YOU." "See? He gave me these."

"That's cute," Lee said. "Where did he find pink paper?"

"His parents have a real estate business, and their signs are pink and black. They use pink paper at their office," I told him. "Now it's my turn to ask you something. I'm curious. What exactly does your uncle do for Mr. Marcello?"

"I know you're curious," Lee replied, with a quick grin, "but I can't tell you. Use your imagination." We talked a while longer, then Lee said, "Here comes Mr. P. He's the manager. I have to talk to him, so be very quiet."

The middle-aged Italian man came over to our table and sat down. He had an air of importance to him. Maybe it's the way the Mafiosi

Maple Ridge Dr.

Site of
●
Town & Country Motel
1425 Airline Dr.

Site of

Royal Castle
1401 Airline Dr.

←— to Airport

Airline Drive - Hwy 61

2 miles to downtown New Orlea

carry themselves. If you experience it, you can recognize it. They like to feel powerful and respected. Lee and Mr. P. talked quietly for a minute. I took Lee's instructions seriously and kept my eyes down. Since I was looking down, and I could see under the table, I noticed Mr. P. pull a wad of rolled-up bills from his pants pocket. He passed the money to Lee under the table, talking the entire time, as if nothing was going on. Then he gave me a hard look and smiled.

"Does she need a job?" he asked. "We could use her here."

"She's got a job," Lee answered, somewhat testily. "And she's not that kind."

"I meant nothing, Lee, I meant nothing," Mr. P protested and got up from his seat. "Be sure you tell Dutz hello for me."

"Let's go," Lee said, not even bothering to look at the money he thrust into his pocket.

"We're not going to eat anything?" I asked anxiously. I was famished, and it would be hours before our lunch with Dr. Ferrie. "I wouldn't feed my dog here," Lee growled.

As we walked out, Lee put his hand on the back of my neck to guide me. While not politically correct by today's standards, this domineering practice was used by many men at the time, including my own fiancé. I welcomed it as a sign that Lee was willing to take charge. He had also defended my honor after the manager's thinly veiled suggestion that I might be an asset to Marcello's motel, increasing my confidence in him.

As we rode the buses back toward Dutz's house, Lee surprised me. Despite his prior statement that he wasn't going to tell me what his uncle did he now released some information, as if his confidence had increased in me as well. He said there was no reason I shouldn't know that Dutz kept "books" for Marcello, involving betting at horse races, casinos and so on, and that a cash transfer had become necessary.

We arrived back at the Murrets' home. Once again, Lee had me wait outside, where kids were still playing. Then Lee emerged at a quick pace. As soon as he reached me, he smiled and said, "Dutz gave me two hundred dollars for helping him out, so you can forget about the ten I lent you."

I told him he'd get the $10 back, anyway. My intention was sincere, but I had no idea how tight my future budget was going to be when Robert got control.

We left Dutz's house, got on another bus and headed to a restaurant called the Kopper Kitchen, where we were to meet Dr. Ferrie.

As we entered the restaurant, I could hear my stomach rumble. Dr. Ferrie was not there yet, so we sat down at a booth, and Lee urged me to go ahead and order anything I wanted, because Ferrie was paying.

Great! I went overboard, ordering a hamburger, fries and coke, and a hot fudge sundae for dessert. I was then a bit embarrassed when Lee merely ordered a bowl of soup and a glass of milk.

"I think Dave might have cancer, himself," Lee said, referring to Dr. Ferrie. "Maybe that's why he's working with Dr. Sherman." Ferrie's cancer experiments had begun years earlier in a lab he set up in a big house out by the airport. Ferrie sometimes used himself as a guinea pig, and told Lee that he blamed his embarrassing hair loss on the chemicals he was using in his experiments.

"Dr. Ferrie might let you do some research of your own with his cancer specimens," Lee said. "He might even pay you to help keep his lab going."

"Does he need an assistant?" I asked.

"Very much so," Lee replied. "They've requested help."

I had to admit that slaving away at Royal Castle for a dollar an hour had lost its charm, and the thought of getting paid to do laboratory work was appealing.

"Well, that could be me," I said, "but I'll be in Mary Sherman's bone lab at Ochsner's clinic."

"Maybe you're supposed to be working in both places," Lee said. "He's very busy, and he has to travel a lot, soon. Not only for us, but also for Marcello."

The "us" made me realize that somehow Lee was involved in Ferrie's research project.

Lee watched with concern as I downed my big "free meal"—topped by the hot fudge sundae.

"That stuff isn't good for you," he told me. "You should watch what you put in your body."

"I know you're right," I answered, "I usually do better — honest!"

"I used to smoke and drink," he said, "but then I decided to respect the only body I'd ever have."

Dr. Ferrie finally arrived.[14] He was wearing an airline captain's cap and jacket, with shabby trousers and scuffed shoes. The combination was odd. His appearance was as unusual as Lee said it would be. His eyebrows looked painted on with a grease pencil and had fuzz on them.

David Ferrie

His movements were jumpy, and his eyes bugged out — a telltale sign of either an overactive thyroid or too much thyroid medication.[15] Here was a man who could not enter a room unnoticed.

Dr. Ferrie seated himself with the authority of a military man. I found his intensity intriguing. I noticed he was wear-

ing a ring made from an Eastern Airlines pin. So Dr. Ferrie
was also Captain Ferrie.

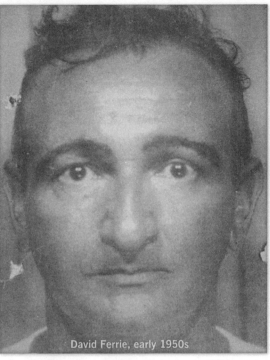

David Ferrie, early 1950s

Lee introduced me as "Miss
Judy Vary," and Ferrie immediately made a joke about our
similar-sounding names: Ferrie and Vary. Despite his odd
appearance, there was a charm
about him, and we warmed
to each other quickly. As his
mental acuity began to unfold,
I noticed his appearance less
and his words more. He asked
about my medical training and
plans for the future. I replied
using lots of medical terminology to establish my credentials.
Soon, Dr. Ferrie was satisfied
that I indeed knew my way
around a medical lab. "I'd be happy to get any equipment or supplies
you might need," he said, "since I hear you'll be staying in town for
awhile. I have connections." Having heard from Lee that Dr. Ferrie
knew Dr. Sherman, I replied that I planned to enter Tulane Medical
School in the fall.

"Maybe I could help out on weekends, for some extra money?" I offered. We continued to talk about my science work. When I told him
about my magnesium project, Dr. Ferrie asked if I knew organic chemistry. "With my eyes closed," I told him.

"I'm familiar with a big lab in Gainesville," he went on. "We sometimes order exotic chemicals from them. Peninsular ChemResearch
is the name. Your best chemistry professors run the place. When we
need stuff we can't get anywhere else, PenChem makes it for us," he
said with an enigmatic smile. "If you do go back to Gainesville, I can
get you a good job there."

Ferrie excused himself for a moment and went out to his car. He
returned with a big Fisher Scientific catalog and some others for medical supplies. "Take these catalogs, and after you see what we're doing,
circle anything you want, and I'll order it," he said.

He then looked around to see who might hear him, and began talking about Dr. Sherman, whom he referred to as "Dr. Mary" to keep
her last name out of the conversation. "Of course," he went on, "the
work Dr. Mary and I do is confidential, because we are investigating

cancer with drugs that are not available in the United States. We have them brought in from Mexico, if you understand what I mean. So you shouldn't talk about what we're doing at the Clinic or anywhere else." I promised I would be careful with the information.

Then Dr. Ferrie explained that their cancer project was getting results faster than typical research projects, because they did not have to do all the paperwork, and all of this was under the direction of the great man himself, Dr. Alton Ochsner.[16]

Dr. Ochsner again. So he was involved in this, too. Dr. Ferrie said Dr. Ochsner knew how to get things done.

He had access to anything needed and avoided red tape by bringing in some of the materials himself from Latin America. Ferrie described Ochsner's Latin American connections in more detail, saying that he was the on-call physician for many Latin American leaders. He kept their secrets and got rewarded in return, including big donations to his Clinic. As a result, Ochsner had his own unregulated flow of funds and supplies for every possible kind of cancer research, with no oversight. "We're using various chemicals, in combination with radiation, to see what happens with fast-growing cancers," Ferrie said. "We're using it to mutate monkey viruses, too."

Mutating monkey viruses! Radiation! Fast growing cancers!

"That's exactly what I've been trained to handle," I commented, noting how conveniently my skill set just happened to match their research.

"I was told you were," Dr. Ferrie said, without explaining how he came by that particular piece of information, but I figured it had to be Dr. Ochsner.

Lee and I got into Dr. Ferrie's old car and he drove us to the YWCA, where I spent about twenty minutes getting the last few things I had left behind, and said goodbye to the girls. I emerged to find Lee at a pay phone making calls, and Ferrie nowhere to be seen. When Lee was finished, he said Ferrie had gone to get some provisions and that we would meet him back at his apartment.

We rode a bus to Louisiana Avenue Parkway. As we walked along a

Back of David Ferrie's Apartment

service road behind the houses, Lee told me that Ferrie had a better life in the past, but since he had lost his job with Eastern Airlines, his fortunes had declined. We finally reached Ferrie's house and entered through a back door, which led to a staircase that took us to the second floor. This was the entrance that Ferrie's friends always used. Now barefoot and dressed in casual clothes, he met us at the screen door. He was busy cleaning up his kitchen for a party to be held the next night. It was a spectacular mess.

Ferrie showed us around his apartment, which was full of his mother's old-fashioned furniture, plus a hodgepodge of junk reminiscent of a garage sale. The lab, such as it was, resided on utility carts located to the side of the large kitchen. There was distilled water, propane gas, and a fume vent. Several cages of mice and rats sat on the counter beside the sink.[17] There was denatured alcohol and acetone for clean up.

Ferrie explained that most of the mice were kept nearby, where they lived under standardized conditions. They were brought over for the experiments with other equipment, which came and went. Except for the microscopes and some test tubes, the true nature of the place would be unnoticed by untrained eyes. The mini-centrifuge, for example, was a sophisticated little piece of equipment, but to the layman it was just a small metal globe with some holes in it. The blender was a normal kitchen item, and would not be seen as a device for macerating excised tumors. The refrigerator held a collection of mouse tumors that looked vaguely like hamburger meat. Upon seeing it, I decided that I would not be eating anything stored in Ferrie's refrigerator.

Ferrie assured me that I would be safe working with him because he was a homosexual, who was only interested in young men. Lee had forewarned me of Ferrie's homosexuality, but I was caught off-guard with his openness about it. My respect for Ferrie had plummeted since the restaurant, and I soon started calling him 'Dave' instead of Dr. Ferrie.

The tumors should have gone to Dr. Sherman's today, Dave explained. He would have dropped them off at her apartment himself, but he did not like to be seen there. He pointed out that I could be used as a courier for the harvested tumors, since I could pass as a medical student visiting Dr. Sherman.

I was asked to exercise caution, and avoid being seen by outsiders whenever possible, since gossip in New Orleans had a tendency to assume a sexual motive for just about everything, and secretive comings and goings might lead to rumors that Dr. Sherman was conducting a lesbian affair with a medical student. Ferrie told me that Dr. Mary Sherman was not a lesbian. She was a widow who had never gotten over the death of her husband.[18] Being single and a professional, she was careful about appearances in this gossipy city.

Dave generously offered us dinner. I declined, noting that we had just had lunch at the restaurant. Ferrie then treated us to a discussion of philosophy. He began gently by saying that people tended to look at things in two ways, through a telescope or through a microscope;

meaning that what they saw was colored by their own problems. They rarely saw things as they were in "the natural landscape."

For the next several hours, Ferrie plowed through centuries of moral and political philosophy, reciting classic passages from memory as he went. He articulated the thoughts of the great 17th Century British philosopher Thomas Hobbes and his Social Contract, quoting from his masterpiece *Leviathan*, and juxtaposed it with the observations of Huxley, Sartre and Plato.[19] "Overregulating humanity," he said, " — and it will keep happening, for economic reasons — is just as destructive as nature's lack of any regulation. The end is the same: human life becomes lonely, poor, nasty, brutish, and short."

Then he moved on to his favorite arena, religion, and started instructing us on the works of the great religious philosopher, Thomas Aquinas. Dave constantly dropped names and quotes of the world's great thinkers into the conversation to bolster his case. He challenged us on everything.

Astounded by his breadth of knowledge, I started taking notes. Ferrie mixed a generous portion of his powerful observations about God and the universe into the brew. Lee and I tried to challenge him, tried to match wits with this prodigious brain, but Ferrie, pacing back and forth smoking cigarettes and drinking beer, kept sinking our ships. Why, he snarled, were Lee and I toying with atheism?

What arrogance, to declare there was no God when we understand so little!

"It's idiotic to be an atheist!" he proclaimed. "Look at what we have learned in just a hundred years," he said. "We've now pierced the heavens with rockets and discovered DNA. What if we keep on going for a million years like that? How dare we declare there is no God, when we ourselves might be considered gods by our ancient ancestors?"

Dave continued to rant and pace back and forth through an increasingly thick cloud of cigarette smoke, consuming bottle after bottle of beer, and oscillating between piety and profanity. By midnight, his tone sank to confession, saying that he had tried to be a father to Lee, years earlier. Instead, he had almost destroyed the boy. When Dave left the room to go to the bathroom, I asked Lee what this was about.

"It was the world's hardest way to become close friends," Lee said solemnly.

"What happened?" I asked.

"I'll let him tell you about it," Lee said with resignation. "It's going to come out anyway, because he's drunk. It happened a long time ago, and I know he feels guilty about it."

I concluded that Ferrie must have accosted Lee when he was young.

Lee stared at the table. "It was the hardest fight I ever put up in my life," he said sadly.

Alarm bells were going off in my head. "You're frightening me! I want to go home — now! Before he comes back."

"You're safe with me," Lee said, looking straight into my eyes. "Trust me now." I looked around to see if the windows were open. Would people hear me if I screamed? Then I looked at Lee again and saw tears running down his face.

"Don't you feel that there is something wonderful developing between us? Don't you know that I would never let anybody hurt you?" he whispered.

I took a deep breath and nodded. It was true. I might have been naïve about many things, but I'd had plenty of experience with boys telling me lies. I knew Lee wasn't lying to me; a man with tears in his eyes! I felt a surge of concern and affection.

David Ferrie's piano & typewriter

Dave re-entered the room. He sat down and plunked a few sorrowful chords on his piano.

"Go ahead and tell her about it," Lee said.

Dave turned to me and began to tell his tortuous tale in sorry detail. Lee and some other boys had been invited to Dave's house after a Civil Air Patrol meeting. Dave was the squadron's Commander. Curious as ever, Lee had gone upstairs to see Dave's laboratory. When the other cadets left, Dave went upstairs, where he found Lee. As Dave entered the lab, he locked the door.

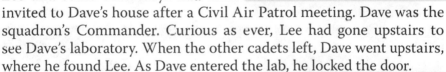
Captain David Ferrie

When Lee saw that, he assumed the worst. Dave said his only intention was to talk to Lee about his fatherless situation, but Lee had bitter experiences in a detention facility in New York, which taught him the worst of lessons about people.[20] As Ferrie approached, Lee decided to arm himself and broke the windowpane with his elbow. Dave tried to convince Lee that he was not there to hurt him, but Lee did not believe him and picked up a shard of the broken

David Ferrie & Lee Oswald at a Civil Air Patrol picnic

glass to use as a knife. As Ferrie closed in, Lee jabbed the glass knife at Ferrie. Ferrie was furious over the combination of disrespect and aggression from one of his cadets and decided to teach Lee a lesson. A brutal fight ensued, and Lee got the worst of it. But Lee kept getting up, until a last blow to his mouth nearly knocked him out.

Despite his denial of bad intentions, Dave suddenly realized he was having an erection. He had never raped anybody. Would this be the first time? Filled with shame, Ferrie came to his senses and remembered that Lee's uncle was in the Mob. As he saw blood coming from Lee's mouth Dave suddenly had visions of his body being cut into little pieces. He began apologizing, and begged Lee not to tell on him. He helped Lee up, washed his face off, and saw a loose front tooth. There was also a big cut in Lee's gum, which was bleeding profusely. It needed a stitch. Ferrie explained what he had to do, and when Lee took the stitch stoically without flinching, Ferrie cursed himself for what he'd done. He told Lee that the tooth was probably going to be okay, but if it fell out, he was to immerse it in milk and go at once to a dentist, who could re-implant it. Dave pushed a twenty-dollar bill into Lee's pocket to cover dental fees, then handed him ten dollars for ice cream to ease his pain. Dave said he felt like the lowest form of life, and once again he begged Lee not to tell on him.

"I'm no snitch," Lee told him. "But I never want to see your ugly face again."

Close-ups from the Civil Air Patrol picnic photo

Dave took Lee home wondering what he would tell his mother, who was out having dinner with one of Marcello's men. Since she wasn't home and Lee had no key, he had to leave the boy sitting on the porch. That made Dave feel even worse. "Ma just thought I'd been in another fight," Lee told him later.

Lee stopped going to meetings until he heard that Ferrie was no longer active in the CAP, then joined a unit far from Ferrie's house. In the summer of 1955, Lee went to their two-week-long summer camp. As luck would have it, Ferrie was a guest lecturer at the camp. Dave immediately thanked Lee profusely for not telling on him. Lee realized that Ferrie was never going to lay a hand on him again.[21]

It was now close to dawn, and Dave drove Lee and me home. He invited us to attend his party on Sunday night, dangling the fact that Dr. Sherman would be there as bait. I was anxious to meet Dr. Sherman, so despite my concerns about Dave I reluctantly agreed. When we reached my boarding house, Lee walked me to the door and invited me to see the city with him after lunch the next day. I agreed. I caught a few hours sleep to prepare for another busy day in my new amazing life. But I was beginning to wonder what I was getting myself into.

---

1. Alopecia is a medical condition where the hair falls out for no discernible reason. It may create circles of lost hair on the scalp, or extend to affect the entire body.
2. Lee didn't mention Ferrie's activities at this time, just that dust and dander had to be kept out of his eyes, but I would soon learn that Ferrie was also a pilot.

3. For convenience, I use the word "Mafia" in this book. Lee actually used the Mafia's name for themselves — Cosa Nostra — when he referenced the Mob.

4. I have been criticized for not speaking out until 1999 about all I knew. But if I had attempted to tell the world that the CIA and Mafia worked together to try to kill Castro before July, 1975, I would not have been believed. It was only after the Church Committee exposed these matters in 1975 that I could even dare bring up such a matter. Even so, the CIA did not acknowledge the deadly alliance between the CIA and the Mafia to kill Castro until 21 June, 2007 when "The Family Jewels" of the CIA proved that mobster Johnny Roselli had been recruited for the purpose by the CIA. It was not until May, 9, 1973, that CIA director Schlesinger commissioned the "family jewels" compilation that provided an official record for this activity. CIA Records have only recently emerged, as well, that not a few, but hundreds of plots to kill Castro existed — by almost every means imaginable – and that these attempts did not stop in 1962, as once claimed, but continued at least through 1963.

5. I saved that ticket, in memory of that day of fun with Lee, and the ticket from April 28, as well. The fact that I saved streetcar tickets with dates on them before Robert even arrived in New Orleans helps provide circumstantial evidence of my growing affection for Lee. The ticket stub on page 145 shows that Lee and I got on the streetcar at 9:00 AM (it is cut at the 9:00 AM line) on Sunday, April 28. We got off to an early start!

6. Sam Zemurray. Today the home is used as the residence for the President of Tulane University.

7. Lee's aunt said Lee stayed only 3-5 days at the Murret's home. People have asked why Lee did not move in at once upon his arrival in New Orleans. At this time, Lee discussed with Dutz when he might be able to move in with them. Dutz' daughter, Lee's cousin Marilyn, was already temporarily living with the Murrets, so Lee offered to stay at the "Y" a few more days before moving in. To help pay the YMCA bill and other expenses, Dutz gave Lee $200 after he ran the errand, described in WC documents as a 'loan.' It was actually a gift. Lee later called from the bus station to have his possessions picked up there by car: he had kept everything in lockers a the bus station, rather than dragging them over to the YMCA.

8. Lee mentioned several actions he took in the USSR for the U.S. government:

    (1) He was instrumental in getting information about the U-2 spy plane into Russian hands. This was allowed because the Corolla satellite system was put into commission, and the CIA did not want Eisenhower, whose health and mental acuity, they claimed, meant he might be bested by the Soviet leader, to hold a summit with Russian Premiere Nikita Khrushchev. Downing the U2 stopped the summit. (2) Lee, as a 'radar man" (his term) was supposed to obtain information about the quality of radar installations that the Soviets were shipping to Cuba. He found this aspect of the assignment almost impossible because he was shipped to "White Russia" (Belarus) — Minsk. (3) He "believed" he saved somebody's life in Moscow who had been suspected of being a double agent, convincing the Soviets that this person was not involved. (4) He sent information about the radio and TV factory, where he worked, which also made other electronic components, on to the U.S. in some manner. He was in touch with at least two other agents: one was a doctor. Another agent was contacted through attending the performances (movies, I believe) of Пиковая дама, Pikovaya dama (The Queen of Spades). He would use the same libretto of Пиковая дама, Pikovaya dama in Mexico City to make a contact there, though I know no other details. Lee told me that movie theaters were where he made contacts, with a marked libretto left under a certain seat. Sometimes he sat next to an informant in the theater. i have often considered this when reading that Lee moved from seat to seat and sat next to people, including even a pregnant woman, in the Texas theater, on Nov. 22, obviously, to me, seeking a contact. But instead, he was surrounded by the Dallas police. I believe he was betrayed in that theater so he could be captured.

9. Lee's statement "every time I come to New Orleans" was in contrast to his earlier comment that he had not been in New Orleans in a decade. Lee was beginning to confide in me: he told me that he had been to Florida as well. Witness Anna Lewis and her husband David both stated they had seen Lee in New Orleans in the Fall of 1962. Lee's whereabouts on Oct. 8 and 10, 1962, were unknown. He was separated at that time from his wife, Marina. It is a short

plane trip between Dallas and New Orleans: I know Lee had access to such transportation a number of times in 1963.

10. On August 19, 1939, Robert Edward Lee Oswald died suddenly of a heart attack. Two months later, on October 18, 1939, Lee Harvey Oswald was born.

11. Charles (Dutz) Murret was born in New Orleans in 1901. In his youth he was a boxer but later worked as a steamship clerk. His wife, Lillian Murret, was the sister of Marguerite Oswald, the mother of Lee Harvey Oswald. When Oswald was a child he lived with the Murret family. Oswald returned to the Murret home after returning from the Soviet Union in 1962. In the Warren Commission Report, Murret was portrayed as a steamship clerk. However, the House Select Committee on Assassinations discovered that Murret was an illegal bookmaker. Murret was also an associate of Sam Saia, one of the leaders of organized crime in New Orleans. Saia was also a close friend of Carlos Marcello. Another of Murret's associates, Nofio Pecora, was linked to Jack Ruby. According to an FBI informant in 1979 Marcello admitted having known both Murret and Lee Harvey Oswald. Charles (Dutz) Murret died in 1964 – a bad year for witnesses.

12. Lee also told me he gave Marina a parakeet once to keep her company and bought her an expensive coat so that she would have something nice to wear in winter.

13. The fact that the U.S. Government lent Lee Oswald money to return to the U.S. gives credence that he was not a real defector.

14. For a detailed biography on Ferrie, see *Dr. Mary's Monkey* by Edward T. Haslam.

15. This condition is called exophthalmia, and I had been trained to recognize it in a premed course.

16. A 1957 photo shows Dr. Alton Ochsner in an Air Force jet. His close friend, General Claire Chennault of the CIA's China Flying Tigers, got Ochsner into planes, too (Chennault died of cancer in Ochsner's Touro Infirmary in New Orleans). As advisor to the Air Force Surgeon General, Ochsner flew to Washington weekly for years, and traveled worldwide inspecting medical facilities for several Surgeon Generals.

17. Later, we kept mice in Dave's dining room.

18. There is some reason to believe that Thomas Sherman had not died, but had, in fact, deserted her. Whatever the actual facts, Mary Sherman's public posture was that of a widow.

19. I only knew about Aldous Huxley's writings at the time, but (probably from Dave Ferrie's religious rants) Lee was also familiar with Thomas Huxley, who promoted Darwin's theory of evolution.

20. Lee inferred to me that he had been beaten and sexually assaulted at the City of New York facility where he had been sent for skipping school.

21. Later, Ferrie recommended Lee to contacts in the Marines as a candidate for intelligence training as a spy – Lee's great dream. All he had to do was survive Marine boot camp. In the end, Lee received two years of specialized training, including Russian lessons and spy craft. He would eventually be sent behind the Iron Curtain at the height of the Cold War at the age of 19.

David Ferrie's airline captain hat
on his living room table

— CHAPTER 8 —

THE PARTY

Sunday, April 28, 1963

The next morning, I worked my two-hour shift at Royal Castle and returned to the boarding house on St. Charles Ave. Lee arrived by mid-morning as we had planned. First he wanted to locate his father's grave, then show me the sights of his city. His Uncle Dutz had given him the names of a few relatives who might be willing to help him find the grave. One was an elderly aunt. We caught a streetcar and transferred to a bus. As we rode, Lee pointed to a street and said, "My cousin's visiting over there. I can use his car later today to show you around the city."

"Why can't we use it now?" I asked.

"They need it to go to Mass, but later, it'll be okay."

"Are you going to buy a car?" I continued.

"On my income? Cars are handy," he continued, "but if I owned a car, how could I play the role of the unhappy American worker who can't get ahead? What would be my motive for wanting to go to Cuba? Most Cubans in Uncle Fidel's 'Worker's Paradise' don't have cars."

"Well, it could be a long time before you're sent into Cuba."

"Maybe a year or so," he agreed. "But there are other reasons. For example, my driver's license. I had to stash it away." Lee explained he had been warned that the Texas Highway Patrol had tagged his driver's license as "belonging to a known Communist."

"They could stop me for going through a red light," he said, "Then one call could give them that information. They could arrest me on some trumped-up charge. Maybe even beat me up. So there are no cars in my life for now."

We arrived in the neighborhood where his elderly aunt lived. As we approached her home, Lee thought it best for me to wait a few houses away. "If she blows up at me," he said, "at least she won't blow up at you, too."

After half an hour, Lee came out. I could tell by the expression on his face that the meeting had not been pleasant. She had been soured by the news of his defection, but after scolding him she grudgingly gave Lee information concerning his father's gravesite.

We got back on the bus and went to pick up the car. I thought to myself, "At least one of his cousins still likes him." By now, I knew his relatives shouldn't be seeing me, so I waited beside the car, while Lee got the keys. Then we got in the car and drove off to find the cemetery. As he drove, Lee talked about his aunt's bitter rejection.[1] "It's the price I have to pay," he told me, "but that doesn't mean I have to like it," ending with "I hope someday my children will know the truth about me."

Lee stared straight ahead as he revealed more about his difficult childhood. His father died two months before he was born. When the insurance money ran out, his brother Robert and his half-brother, John Pic, were taken to the Lutheran Bethlehem orphanage in New Orleans. Lee, at first too young to go there, was sent to stay with his Aunt Lil and Uncle Dutz Murret until he was three years old. Then Marguerite placed Lee with his brothers in the

Lee Oswald at two years old

Five years old

Three years old

Seven years old

orphanage "to keep the boys together," visiting them only on weekends. "My aunt and uncle cried when I left. So did I," Lee admitted.

For the next three years, Lee's brother, Robert, took care of his little brother there, not always happy about the responsibility. In 1945, when Lee's mother married an industrial engineer named Edwin Ekdahl, Lee and his brothers were brought home from the orphanage. The family moved to Fort Worth, Texas, and Robert and John were sent off to a military boarding school. Lee traveled with his mother and her new husband, who treated Lee as a son. There were several years of stability, but then Marguerite divorced her third and final husband for infidelity.

After that, Lee's brothers left home as soon as they could, joining the military, while Lee and his mother continued "to move a lot."

My heart ached when I heard his tale. I reached over and stroked his arm.

"Don't feel sorry for me," he said stoically.

Marguerite & Lee on vacation in Arizona

Ten years old

Edwin Ekdahl and Marguerite on their marriage day

We reached the cemetery, and wandered through a fascinating maze looking for his father's grave. New Orleans is home to some of the most interesting cemeteries in the world. These Cities of the Dead are filled with marble statues and ornate elevated vaults, reminiscent of the cemeteries in Paris. The reason for this was recently demonstrated by Hurricane Katrina.

As Lee searched for his father's grave, he talked about sad moments from his past. There were a lot of them. Though usually thrifty with his words, Lee talked freely that day, as he unveiled the emotional wreckage of his youth. Hearing his stories stirred emotions within me and called to mind the problems I had experienced with my own family. This was another common ground between us.

As Lee and I discussed these matters of the heart, I started to recognize how much I was missing in my relationship with Robert. I found it curious that I shared more things with this man I had just met than I did with Robert, whom I had dated for months. For example, Lee agonized over religious questions just as I did, but Robert was indifferent to such "impractical" matters. Lee recited poetry and loved to sing, just as I did. We even sang duets together as we rode the buses around the city. Robert didn't even like to hear me sing, preferring that I listen to him play the guitar. Robert smoked cigarettes and went out drinking with his friends. I hated both smoking and drinking, just as Lee did. With each similarity we discovered, I felt closer to Lee. Finally, I confided in Lee that I was having second thoughts about marrying Robert. I was particularly disturbed that he had broken his promise to write to me every day.

"I guess he hasn't called, either, because it's so expensive," I sighed, realizing that I was making excuses for Robert's neglect. My talk of marriage caused Lee to bring up the subject of his wife Marina who was still in Texas, living with Mrs. Paine.

Ruth Paine & Marina Oswald

"Marina was supposed to call by now. I worry about her because she's pregnant. She could call me from Mrs. Paine's house, if only she would. I've been worried sick."

"Well, could you call her?" I said hopefully.

"I'm not supposed to," he replied crisply. "I'm supposed to be the callous creep who hit her, then left, and who's out of money." Huh? I was amazed that the role he was playing for his assignment was so deeply tangled in his personal life. Frankly, it was a disturbing thought. But I was more concerned about hearing the word "hit."

"Did you say you *hit* her?" I asked, digging for more.

Lee avoided my question by saying, "We're really estranged."

After a pause, he added: "We're working on a permanent arrangement, so I can go on with my life without worrying about her. Mrs. Paine will arrange everything this summer. She speaks Russian, and she's in the middle of her own divorce."

Suddenly, my warning lights went on. He had dodged my question about hitting his wife! Was this young man that I had only known for a few days really a wife-beater? Nobody even knew that I was with him in this strange town. And we were in a cemetery with no one around. I considered asking him to take me back to the boarding house, but decided to wait until he found his father's grave.

I found a cement bench and sat down silently. He continued to search  unsuccessfully. Finally, Lee went to the office to ask for help. There they checked their records and found the location of the grave. A caretaker emerged from the office and led him to it. I watched from my bench as Lee cleaned off some debris from the stone to read the name. He stood for several minutes; then sank to his knees. After a while, he came and brought me to the humble site.

I stood respectfully while Lee knelt down again and put both hands on his father's grave. He remained in this position, with his head lowered, for several minutes. "Well, Dad," he said as he got up, "rest in peace."

We got back in the car and Lee said the orphanage where he lived in his youth was nearby, and that he wanted to see it. I was still leery, but it was a hard request to refuse. We arrived and sat down on a bench looking at the stately old orphanage, a monument to Lee's first-hand knowledge of life with a dead father and a desolate mother.

Lee turned the conversation back to his wife Marina. He said Marina had repeatedly been unfaithful to him since the early days of their marriage. "It almost destroyed me when she cheated on me the first time," he admitted. "But she did it as easily as drinking a bottle of beer."

Lee told me how their relationship began back in the Soviet Union and described it as a marriage of convenience. Lee had feared deportation, and needed to marry a Russian girl to stay in the country. Marina, on the other hand, wanted to marry an American man so she could go to America. But Marina's infidelity had turned Lee bitter and hardened him towards her. In return, she began criticizing him in her matchless way.

"I thought I was past caring about people anymore," he told me. But then, the birth of their daughter June changed everything for Lee.

June Oswald

"I was a daddy!" he said. The feelings that his daughter June awakened in Lee were intense. It no longer mattered to him that Marina's love was shallow.

Lee went on to explain that since coming to America, he and Marina had discussed getting divorced many times, but she was worried that she would be deported back to Russia. Lee was consequently concerned that his daughter June might be deported with her. So Lee and Marina decided she should get pregnant again, in hopes that having an American-born baby would help establish her as the mother of an American citizen, and protect her from deportation.

"She knows she's just being used now, so I deserve to suffer her tongue. But think of what I have had to live with!"

"But you said that you hit her," I said, not letting the subject rest. "And once a man hits a woman, he'll do it again."

"If I told you all that she did, you'd understand. You'd see why I lost my temper."

Lee then described insults so cruel I will not repeat them here. As a result, Lee hated both what she had become and what he was becoming. He had once been a kinder, more considerate lover. While he was a Marine Lee was stationed in Japan, where he had an affair with a delicate Japanese girl trained in the art of Geisha. His next assignment forced him to abandon her. He told me she had always spoken kindly to him but, "Marina has the tongue of a snake, and when she starts mocking me..."

The way Lee said the word 'mocking' made me recall my Russian instructor saying, "Mere English can't crush a soul, or destroy one's self image the way that Russian can."[2]

I told Lee that I had heard how harsh Russian words could be. He gave me a look of appreciation. Seeing signs of understanding, he admitted that he'd lost his temper and hit his wife, not once, but several times! Perhaps a dozen, if the truth be known. "I even beat her up a couple of times." The words fell from his mouth slowly, his head low. His voice was solemn. Ashamed.

I was stunned. He *is* a wife beater, I thought in my horror.

I stiffened with repulsion, and my mind flashed back to my father's violence.

"I don't want to hear another word!" I shuddered. "You disgust me!"

He accepted my comment in silence. There was nothing for him to say. Robert may have been neglectful, but he wasn't a wife-beater.

Ironically, while I feared Lee for his violence, after hearing his confession I respected him for his honesty.

After a rather long pause, Lee humbly asked me to let him continue to show me New Orleans. My attitude had not softened much, but I felt I had made my protest known, and I did want to see the city.

Lee drove us to the French Quarter, where we walked around Jackson Square and looked at the artists' paintings hanging on the fence. There we saw the majestic St. Louis Cathedral, flanked by the historic Cabildo buildings which hold much of the city's colorful history. We walked down Pirate's Alley and window-shopped our way down Royal Street's antique stores and fine art galleries. When we got to Bourbon Street, Lee pointed out a restaurant where he'd swept floors and washed dishes as a teenager. "It was my first lucrative job, working for my uncle's friends," he joked, explaining that he spent the money he made on comic books and playing pool. Lee noted that he wasn't much richer today, though he did have enough change for buses and hoped to have enough money for a trip to the zoo.

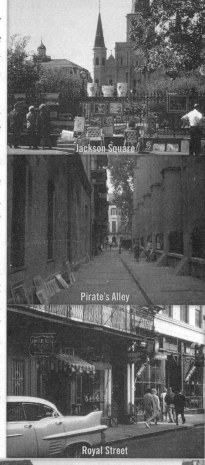

Jackson Square

Pirate's Alley

Royal Street

Corner of Bourbon & Bienville
looking toward Canal Street

I brought up my own love of animals. I told him how difficult it was for me to slaughter the mice for my cancer research, and that the mouse tumors in Dave's refrigerator clued me in that I would probably soon be engaged in that kind of thing again.

Next, we drove uptown to Audubon Park where we visited the Seal Pool, which was free. There we watched seals swim and sun themselves on a little island in the center of their pool. Lee noticed the infected condition of one of the seals' eyes. He commented that more national parks needed to be set up so wild animals didn't have to be confined like this and swim in their own excrement. Despite my anger about how Lee treated Marina, his sensitive comments about the animals once again began to soften my feelings about him, so I asked Lee if he would beat a fawn or a deer.

"Animals don't make fun of your manhood," he replied.

Still, Lee told me that there were some quiet days between him and Marina, mostly centered on little June, who had become the most important person in Lee's life. Seeing the affection in Lee's eyes as he spoke softly of his daughter had its effect upon me.

There were children in the park that day. I noticed how easily they interacted with us. I loved little children, just as Lee did. And you could see that the children sensed it. Lee then said he would welcome half a dozen children if he had a loving wife, and would like to adopt some orphans on top of that. I told him I felt exactly the same way.

Audubon Park Zoo, early 1960s

This forged a truce between us that began to overcome my anger about his domestic violence.

We were both planning to attend Dave's party that night, but I needed to get some sleep first, so Lee dropped me off at the boarding house and gave me a brotherly kiss on the cheek. Remembering Robert's imminent arrival, I said "You'll be able to meet my fiancé soon," wondering how they would get along. Lee smiled and headed to the Murrets' house for Sunday dinner, while I went inside, lay down on the bed, and fell asleep.

A loud tapping on my window woke me up. It was Lee. He had brought some groceries from a deli. I put the perishables in Mrs. Webber's refrigerator, and then we sat together on the porch swing and ate oranges. Long shadows on the lawn foretold the sunset. My attempt to peel my orange was unsuccessful. Lee put his right arm around my neck, and, holding my orange with his right hand he began peeling it with his left. The peel came off in one long, unbroken curl. OK, he was showing off to charm a girl, but I was impressed.

Just then Mrs. Webber came clip-clopping down the hall in her slippers, threw open the front door, and stared at us with a fierce scowl.

"You're practically naked!" she yelled at me. "Put your legs together!"

"What's your problem, woman?" Lee snapped, as he jumped up off the swing. "She's wearing shorts. You're the one that's half-naked." He pointed at the woman's big breasts, overflowing the seam of her low-cut dress. Mrs. Webber stiffened, threw her red-haired head back with scorn, and stormed off, slamming the door behind her. Lee and I looked at each other and laughed.

"What a harpy!" I said, standing up because I was so embarrassed by her insinuations.

"I am used to harpies in my life," Lee commented. "My mother and my wife are both experts in that department." I fell into silent thought, saying to myself: "Oh, Lee! Why did you have to tell me that you beat your wife?"

Lee studied my silence. "Are you really going to go through with your marriage?"

I closed my eyes, wondering what to answer, when he suddenly kissed me. And it was not in a brotherly way!

"I want so much to hold you in my arms!" he said, as I pushed him away.

"We've known each other less than three days!" I protested.

"Don't marry that man!" Lee said heatedly. "If he loved you, he would have called. He would have written every day, just to keep your heart from aching."

Lee was right. Robert was neglecting me.

"Please," Lee whispered. "Think! Take more time. If he treats you this way now, how will he treat you after you're married? I'm falling in love with you, Juduffki!"

I turned my back to Lee, close to tears.

"I'm going to divorce Marina," he confessed. "Everybody knows that."

"Just because of you," I told him, "I might not have married Robert. But then you had to tell me you beat your wife!"

"Because I care for you!" he answered. "I didn't want to hide it from you. It would have been wrong for me to do that."

I fell silent as I considered which was more insane: to marry a man whose arrival I no longer anticipated with my former passion, or to become involved with a wife-beater I had just met?

I changed tactics and dug into Lee's head as deeply as I could, by reminding him that he had babies he wanted to keep. I tried to pin him with responsibility, but I suddenly realized that I had emotions of my own which needed to be aired. I admitted that I cared about him, but his confession about beating his wife had shaken me. If he only knew how much I hated my own father for that kind of behavior!

"Now I'm afraid of you. You could hurt me! My own father did it, when he drank. I wish I could believe you can change." Tears sprang from my eyes, as Lee embraced me anxiously.

"Well then," he said, "I'll prove that I can. As time goes by, you'll see. As my love grows stronger for you, so will my proof," he said with a voice that trembled. "For as long as it takes."

Lee & Marina Oswald
Marriage Day, April 30, 1961

"What proof are you planning?" I asked in an incredulous voice.

"This is my promise to you," he answered. "I will never lay a hand on Marina again. I will do this to prove how much your affection means to me."

Lee's promise was a relief to me, and I planned on holding him to it.

"You know, you didn't give yourself much time before falling in love," I commented. "How long did you know Marina before you fell in love with her?"

Lee confessed that it had been mere days. They married after knowing each other only six weeks.

"See?" I said. "Your love is good for six weeks. Or six months."

"There were other circumstances," Lee insisted. "I can't tell you more," he said softly. "I'm sorry. I'm a fool."

He sat down gloomily on the swing and began to rock slowly. I was still standing and looked down on him. I finally sat next to him.

I blurted out: "I've never, ever been attracted to anyone as I am to you!"

"It is the same for me."

"I love Robert, but I never feel comfortable with him. It's like I always have to think about how to behave with him to make him happy. I never feel natural with him."

"But when you are with me," Lee said, "it's the way it should be, isn't it?"

"You know it is," I answered. My emotions were raging. "This is driving me mad!" I said. "Kiss me! And then go away!" Lee then gave me two slow kisses, with a tenderness I had never experienced before. Then, he backed away. "After you're married, I won't be able to kiss you anymore."

He stood for a moment as if he was going to leave. Then he rushed forward, dropped to his knees and pressed his face against my stomach. As I held his head in my hands, I felt dizzy. Was I being worshipped? Right here on the porch? Then Lee straightened himself up, collected his thoughts, sighed, and backed away. He trained his blue-gray eyes upon me as if he was looking directly into my heart: "Maybe we could be brother and sister," he concluded with a shrug.

"I never had a brother," I answered, pondering the absurdity of his comment. Then I started to cry, and stamped my foot at him. "Go away! You're torturing me!"

He agreed to go, but asked me if I would still go with him to Dave's party. Because I wanted to see Dr. Sherman, I nodded my agreement. He said he'd be back in about an hour to get me and then he walked away.

"Lee," I whispered to myself. "Can you really change?"

As I got ready for the party, I thought about how my father had repeatedly promised never to hit my mother again. He meant it when he said it, and he was good to his word when he was sober. My common sense screamed at me: Forget Lee Oswald and marry Robert Baker. I knew I would never be worshipped or adored, but at least I would not be beaten.

When Lee returned, he brought a newspaper. "Look!" he said, turning the pages, "The beaches are open!" He showed me the article. I read that several beaches described as "free of pollution" were now open "on a limited and controlled basis."

"That's the way they let you know that these are segregated beaches," Lee told me. African Americans (still "Negroes" back then) were only allowed to swim at Lincoln Beach, which Lee told me was inferior and run down.

"If I asked you to swim with me at Lincoln Beach with the Negroes, would you go with me? Yes, or no?"

"Of course!" I answered. "I'm not prejudiced."

"That's my girl," Lee said, his eyes shining. "Well, then, would you go swimming with me at a nudist colony?"

"Swim by yourself, Bub," I replied. "Clothing is how we protect ourselves from prying eyes." To point out the absurdity of his comment, I recalled a sci-fi story about sexless women, all of whom lived nude, except for elderly women who dressed in black robes to hide their physical infirmities.

"*The Last Man*," Lee interrupted.

"You mean the story by Mary Shelley?" I interjected.

"No. I mean the one about the last real man, kept in a cage. The sexless women stared at him, and at his gonads. But one girl really cared. And she was the only fertile woman left in the world. Am I right?"

I was amazed. "Nobody knows that story!" I exclaimed. "I read it in a Pocket Book edition that Mama had. But the last few pages were missing."

"Ah! So how much did you miss?" Lee queried with objectivity.

"They ran away together with a mob chasing after them," I replied.

"Ah! So that's all you know!" Lee said, smiling, "Yes, they ran away, with half the planet after them! How interesting..."

"Tell me!" I demanded. "How did it end?"

"Hmmm...!" Lee replied, with a Cheshire Cat smile.

"Please," I begged, "how did it end? Did they become the next Adam and Eve?"

"Hmmmm!"

I hit his chest with a mock flurry of fists. I have never hit to hurt anybody but bullies in my life, and I'm sure Lee was amused, but he flatly refused to tell me the end of the story. I even offered to go to bed with him. It was a hollow promise, but my proposition made it all the easier for him to laugh.

Lee had returned the car to his cousin, since I had nixed plans to drive around with him after Dave's party was over. Now we were on our way by streetcar and bus, sitting quietly together as we traveled. I wanted very much to meet Dr. Sherman, who was slated to make an appearance at the party, but I was still feeling uncertain about Lee. He pulled a book from his jacket pocket and began reading. Curious, I slid closer to see what it was.

The book was an old science fiction anthology. "Oh my gosh!" I said, grabbing his arm. "Is it possible that *The Last Man* is in there?"

Lee smiled and looked into the table of contents, keeping the pages hidden from me.

"Oh, come on!" I tried again. "Did they make it?"

Lee smiled, and folded his arms, hiding the book. "I'm not going to tell you."

"Fiend!" I cried, pounding his chest again with more mock fury.

"Ah, stop! " Lee said. "You're hurting me! You're hurting the book!"

We both laughed, because I had scarcely touched him. Even as we got off the bus, I was still imploring him.

"At least, tell me the author's name. I've forgotten it!"

"Only if you make a promise," Lee said, "that you will never lay a hand on me again! You've hit me twice in one hour, and here you complain about me being a wife-beater! Only when I'm sure you'll keep your promise, will I tell you the ending."

"Oh, no!" I answered.

"Oh, yes! " Lee said.

"You are a very wicked man," I declared, "because I am certain to beat you up again. So then I will never know the ending."

"Monster!" he quailed.

We walked arm-in-arm up to Dave's apartment. The upstairs porch was brightly lit, with rock and roll music announcing the party. Competing with it was the sound of many loud voices. A number of older cars were parked in the street. I saw two men sitting in one of the cars, kissing. Lee noticed them, too.

David Ferrie's apartment building

"Be prepared," he said. "There will be some unusual people here."

"I'm beginning to notice," I confirmed.

"Dave has to cultivate a variety of contacts," Lee explained. "You can't have an information network in this city without running into some of these characters."

"I'm glad you're with me," I said, as we walked around to the back door, climbed the stairs and navigated around a pair of boys who were smoking pot and smooching.

As we entered Dave's kitchen, Lee said, "I say, to each his own. It's a human right to have sex, whatever way you wish, so long as it doesn't hurt anybody. Is that offensive to you?"

"No, no," I answered. "But my preferences are totally traditional."

"Have you explored other options?" Lee countered.

"Not interested," I assured him. "I am happy with the male variety, thank you very much."

"As for me," Lee said, "I observed that the original blueprint was successful. Men and women were built to fit together like a puzzle. But if that doesn't work for somebody, let them do whatever pleases them. I used to tear pictures of pretty women from comic books and catalogs, and take them to bed with me," he confided, smiling. "I just never had the tendency to tear out pictures of good looking men and fantasize about them. So I guess I'm not gay."

The apartment was filled with people. Dave had put the paraphernalia out of sight, so no one would guess he had a lab in his kitchen.

David Ferrie's kitchen

We grabbed some goodies, then moved to greet Dave, who stood between the crowded dining room and the kitchen, chain smoking. He was talking earnestly with some young white males who looked like students. The air was thick with smoke, mingling the sweet aroma of marijuana and illegal Cuban cigars with cigarette tobacco.

Dave introduced us as "friends" to several people, but the music was so loud I could hardly understand a word. Most of the guests were fit looking adult males, mostly Cuban and Mexican, some with their girlfriends in tow.

I managed to ask Dave where his lab animals were.

"I don't want anybody messing with my mice," he said. "They've been moved for the night. "

"Is Dr. Sherman here yet?" I asked, having no idea what she looked like.

"Not yet," Dave replied, "but she'll be here soon. Meanwhile, enjoy yourself. And remember, I'll be taking you two home tonight."

Lee and I had fun dancing to a couple of rock 'n' roll songs and then took time to rest. I noticed a pair of thin, nervous looking men dressed in black suits. Lee said David Ferrie called them "Martin and Lewis," a nickname that referred to the comedian Jerry Lewis and his singing pal, Dean Martin.

"They look like they're from the FBI," I commented.

David Lewis

Jack Martin

"They should," Lee answered. "They work for Guy Banister, and he was a big FBI hotshot. They're probably here to pick up information for Banister."

Lee introduced me to the strange pair. Both apparently had wives who were not present. As Jack Martin continued to drink, he became increasingly obnoxious and started flirting with some of the gay men. David Lewis ignored him and got out one of Ferrie's chess sets. I didn't want to play because Dr. Sherman might arrive at any moment. So I sat in a corner with a book and kept an eye on the party while Lee played Lewis.

The party was still in full swing when Dr. Sherman arrived. You couldn't miss her. She was by far the best-dressed person in the room. She was a professional, middle-aged woman with attractive features. Her hair was pulled back severely in a French twist.

Dave Ferrie brought me over to her. She was speaking fluent Spanish to two dark men.

"Mary, this is Miss Vary," Dave said. "She's been anxious to meet you."

"I'm sorry, but I can't talk to her now," she told him, without looking at me.

"Dr. Sherman," I interjected, "Has Dr. Ochsner spoken to you about me yet?"

"I can't talk to you now!" she repeated, sharply. "Please excuse me."

She then turned around and resumed talking to the two men in Spanish, as if I were not even there. She led them onto the porch, leaving Dave looking perplexed.

My insecurities swelled. Why didn't Dr. Sherman want to talk to me? "Is she upset with me about something?" I asked Dave.

"Let it go, for now," Dave said. "She must have her reasons."

I felt crushed. "Can I go in your bedroom, and just read until she leaves?" I asked.

"I wouldn't recommend going in there," Dave said. "Just go back to your corner, if you want to read. Nobody will bother you."

I curled up with my book again. I thought about asking Lee to take me home, but I didn't. Dr. Sherman did not stay long. As she prepared to leave, I saw her open the refrigerator and remove the container of mouse tumors. Were they the real reason she had come to the party?

After a while, Lee approached with the chess set and invited me to play. As we started to play, we tuned out the rollicking party in the background. Since Lee had walloped David Lewis in their chess game, he stopped by from time to time to see how our game was progressing. David Lewis worked several part-time jobs, mostly handling luggage, but his passions were politics, chess, and classical music. These were interests he shared with Lee. He said that his wife Anna was a waitress at Thompson's Restaurant on St. Charles Avenue, and he invited Lee and me to stop by the restaurant for a free piece of pie. In the same breath, he warned us not to mention anything about his working for Guy Banister to Anna, because he'd told her he had quit.

When David Lewis was out of the room, Lee told me about some of Lewis' and Martin's other activities, one of which was driving voters around during elections, so they could cast multiple votes for well-paying candidates. Further, Dave Ferrie thought little of Jack Martin and called him "Jackass Martin" behind his back, but tolerated him because he was an artist, who could create fake documents. Fake documents? Voters shunted around to corrupt city elections! My concern about the kind of characters Dr. Ferrie had at this party was deepening as the night progressed.

Lee had stopped our chess game for awhile to talk to some Cuban exiles, so I sat and read my book and listened to the conversations in the background. Then I heard David Ferrie say, "That S.O.B. Kennedy needs to keep being careless and riding in open cars, so he can get his head shot off!" Then Ferrie started cursing President Kennedy for the Bay of Pigs deaths. I looked across the room into Lee's eyes questioningly. He came over to me and said quietly, "Later, Juduffki. He'll explain later."

Things started getting pretty crazy. Ferrie physically ejected Jack Martin from the party, calling him a drunk and telling him to go home. Around two A.M. the police arrived and ordered Ferrie to shut the party down. The music suddenly stopped, and people left. The place was a wreck. Ferrie looked at his disheveled apartment and muttered that he wasn't going to have another party for a long time.

"Let them trash somebody else's place for a change!" he said, kicking the debris. I asked Dave to drive us home, but Dave said he didn't want to just yet. Instead, he began to explain that he was having some problems keeping the get-Castro project under wraps.

Dave said he caught Jack Martin browbeating Dr. Sherman, trying to get info out of her. So he ordered Martin to go home and forget about ever coming back. When Martin said he had a right to talk to anybody he wanted, Dave grabbed him by the ear and led him down the stairs with David Lewis following. "You'll be sorry you ever humiliated me!" Martin yelled, embellishing his threat with considerable foul language.

"Martin is losing his mind," Dave said. "He used to be good. We worked well together. Then a project fell through, and Martin said it was my fault! Lewis doesn't drink, so he's okay. But whatever Lewis finds out, he has to tell Martin. He's become Martin's eyes, ears, nose and throat because Jack-Ass can't think for himself anymore."

Perhaps Dr. Sherman behaved as she did because of the presence of "Jack-Ass Martin," Ferrie opined, adding that Martin probably thought Dr. Sherman's presence meant big money was coming into Dave's pockets, and wanted to get in on the deal.[3]

As far as Dave Ferrie was concerned, their friendship was now over. Dave suggested that it was probably Martin who called the police, since he had thrown loud parties at this location before, with no complaints.[4]

Dave now clarified that I was needed in his lab whenever I wasn't working for Dr. Sherman. I told him my time would be limited, because Robert would soon be moving in with me. I apologized for not telling anybody about my impending marriage, and hoped it wouldn't complicate things. Secretly, I was glad to have an excuse to wriggle out of working with Dave. He and his friends were indeed a suspicious bunch.

"You still don't seem to understand how serious this is," Dave protested. "We have to get Castro soon, or it will be too late. If we don't kill him soon, everything will be lost." This comment made me all the more suspicious. Why was Dave trying so hard to impress me with the importance of his project? What did that have to do with my work on his project? Had I missed something? I finally told him that I had heard him say he hoped Kennedy would get shot in the head. Dave almost wilted. "I'll explain," he said, "*if* you agree to help us."

But I was having deep reservations about Dr. David Ferrie and his cancer research project. He was a blatantly suspicious character, who had made subversive remarks against President Kennedy, and claimed that he was ordered to kill Fidel Castro. This, in combination with the wild nature of the party, Dr. Sherman's refusal to speak to me, Dave's drunkenness and the assortment of shady characters made me want to run in the opposite direction. So I put him off, saying I couldn't make any decisions until I talked to Dr. Ochsner.

"That's fine with me," Ferrie said. "After all, Ochsner's the boss."

Dave then offered to drive us home, but Lee, seeing Dave was too tipsy to drive safely, declined the offer. Lee called a cab, and we went outside to wait for it. I said I didn't believe Ferrie's project was secretly sponsored by the CIA. I thought it was all a dream in his messed up head. Lee said soothingly, "Dave might sound like he is exaggerating, but he's not. I don't know all the details yet," he went on, "but if Ferrie says it's that important, it is."

I informed Lee that I wasn't all that impressed with *him*, either. As far as I knew Lee could be a spy for the wrong side, right along with this so-called "Dr. Ferrie," and I wouldn't agree to anything until I met with Dr. Ochsner later the next week.

"It'll be too late by then," Lee said, "to get you into the proper position."

"What proper position?" I asked. "I don't even know if Dr. Sherman will accept me into her lab now." I was frightened at the thought.

Soon we arrived at the boarding house, but the hour was very late. Mrs. Webber, whose schedule seemed to include staying up all night and sleeping until noon, would surely notice.

"There's no law against attending a party," Lee said firmly, escorting me up the steps. "You have the right to come and go as you please. But I can't leave you upset like this. What can I do?"

"I don't know," I told him. "I need proof that Dr. Ferrie isn't lying and that Dr. Sherman isn't going to dump me; and that I'm not getting into the wrong crowd."

As Lee stood there, I searched for my key. As I did so, I saw the same girl sitting on the same red love seat in the hall, just as I had on our first day here. But this time she was with a different man.

"I have an idea," Lee said. "You need proof that Dr. Ferrie is legitimate and that we really are working on a government-sanctioned project to get Castro. You're upset because of how Dr. Sherman behaved, and you need assurances. Correct?"

"For the millionth time, yes," I said, continuing to hunt for the house key.

"I have a solution to your problem. You should meet Guy Banister. He was the head of the FBI's Chicago office and can verify the legitimacy of our project. Would that make you feel better?"

"I would very much like to meet Mr. Banister," I admitted.

"Then you must play a bit of a role," Lee said. "We don't want you seen there, so we need to disguise you as my wife. Nobody in Banister's office has seen her so far. I can fix your hair into a ponytail, like Marina. We can take off your makeup. You can wear her clothes."

"You have her clothes?"

"A box or so," he said. "I'll look through them."

"Do you ever sleep?" I wondered aloud.

"Let me see..." Lee said, looking me over. "You're the same size, same height, same hair color, same blue eyes. And you can speak a little Russian. But you must never smile showing your teeth." He looked me over from head to feet and added, "You don't look exactly like her, of course, but it's close enough, since they've never laid eyes on her."

I reminded Lee that it was late, and in a few hours I had to return to Royal Castle. But at noon or so, we could meet and go visit this Mr. Banister.

Lee said he would arrange it and told me to meet him at the lunch counter at Woolworth's on Canal Street at noon. I was relieved to finally say good night to Lee and went inside. What a day! I was getting

Corner of Canal & St. Charles

involved with a strange — possibly even violent — group of people. All of this was troubling to me, and I did not feel safe anymore.

---

1. Some have argued that Lee did not know how to drive. That is simply wrong. He drove well and often, albeit apparently without a driver's license.

PEOPLE WHO HAD KNOWLEDGE THAT LEE COULD DRIVE

Cliff Shasteen	Joyce Bostic
Leonard Hutchinson	Inez Laake
Fred Moore	Gayle Scott
Malcolm Price	Peggy Smith
Floyd Guy Davis	Mrs. Ernie Isaacs
Gertrude Hunter	Margaret Budreau
Edith Whitworth	Clifford Wormser
Red Pope	FBI Agent Bob Barrett
Leo Sepulveda	DPD Captain Westbrook
Sonny Stewart	Edward Brand
Robert Janca	Garland Slack
Robert Roy	William J. Chesher
Al Bogard	Howard Price
W.M. Hannie	Sterling Wood
Mrs. Lee Bozarth	Dr. Homer Wood
Aletha Frair	Randy Sundy

OFFICE OF THE DISTRICT ATTORNEY
STATE OF LOUISIANA
PARISH OF ORLEANS
DATE: February 14, 1968

STATEMENT OF: ALETHA FRAIR

RESIDING AT: 8001 Benson
New Orleans, LA
Phone - 242-2126
S T A T E M E N T
My name is ALETHA FRAIR (MRS. JOHN FRAIR). I live at:
8001 Benson
New Orleans, La.
Phone - 242-2126

> I worked for the Department of Public Safety in Austin, Texas from the early part of October 1963, through the early part of December 1963. While I was employed at the Department of Public Safety I worked in the License Records Department. This department was responsible for the IBM computer records of all drivers licenses in the state of Texas.

> My husband, JOHN, was working for the United Press International during November of 1963 and on November 22, 1963 he was in Uvalde, Texas, covering the birthday of ex-Vice President JOHN NANCE GARNER.

I did not go to work on the 22 of November, 1963, but the following event occurred (sic) the week after the assassination of President KENNEDY.

During the week following the murder of LEE HARVEY OSWALD, on either Wednesday the 27th, or Tuesday the 28th of November, 1963 the Texas driver's license issued to LEE HARVEY OSWALD came into my division.

The record (IBM card) on OSWALD was pulled from the files. Several other employees (5 or 6) of the Department saw the driver's license which was dirty and worn as though it had been carried in a billfold. The license was the talk of the office that day since everyone knew who OSWALD was, and the reason his driver's license records were being pulled from the active file was the fact that he had been killed.

In October of 1966 my husband and I moved to New Orleans and in June of 1967 my husband went to work for WWL-TV, Channel 4.

I, ALETHA FRAIR, hereby affirm that all of the above statement is true to the best of my knowledge.

Signed February 14, 1968.

(Signature of Aletha Frair)

(Signature of witness Gary Sanders)

(Signature of witness Jody Duek)

2. To illustrate this point, my Russian professor utilized ego-ripping words and made explosive gestures while correcting the errors of his students. His ferocity intimidated me and made me afraid to speak in his class.

3. Jack Martin's original name was apparently "Jack Suggs." Others called him "Jack S. Martin," which Dave Ferrie conflated to "Jack-Ass Martin."

4. Martin was the individual shown in Oliver Stone's movie, *JFK*, pistol-whipped by Guy Banister on the night of the assassination, which sent him to the hospital with head injuries. A publicity-hungry Jack S. Martin would call the police on November 23, 1963, naming Ferrie as an accomplice to Oswald in JFK's murder.

The Newman Building
544 Camp Street
New Orleans,
early 1960s

Federal Offices

Entrance to
Guy Banister's
office 100 ft. down
Lafayette St.

Mancuso's
Restaurant

544 Camp St.
entrance

— CHAPTER 9 —

THE TARGET

Monday, April 29, 1963

After a few hours of restless sleep, I took a bus to Royal Castle, where I once again plunged into the hectic morning rush. I was surprised when Lee walked in, since we had agreed to meet later in the day at Woolworth's on Canal Street. He sat down and ordered breakfast. As I served him, Lee said that the previous morning his Uncle Dutz had moved his stuff by car from the bus station lockers to the Murret's garage: Lee was now living with the Murrets. Dutz had also given him the car to use today, which is why Lee could meet me so early. We had wheels for the day! After my shift ended, we headed back to town.

On the way, he said he wanted to buy some second-hand clothes for me like Marina would wear. I would have "my own set of Marina clothes, whenever I needed them." That way, she would not be puzzled about missing clothes. *Whenever I needed them?* Would I have to meet even more people, at other times, pretending to be Lee's wife? Whoa! But a sense of adventure had risen in me. I was being brought into Lee's clandestine world! We stopped at the Salvation Army store, and Lee bought me a skirt and blouse. He was going for the Russian peasant look of that period, which was very plain. I put the clothes on, and they fit fine. In the car, Lee brushed my hair and put it into a ponytail. He said that my hair was finer in texture than Marina's, but it was the same color and length.

He wanted to pass me off as Marina in Banister's office, so Banister's staff would not know I existed. It was, after all, a private detective agency, full of nosy and observant people. All of this sneakiness was adventurous to me. It was real-life theatre: undercover work with an actual spy who had worked behind the Iron Curtain. I felt like we were playing Boris and Natasha from the Rocky & Bullwinkle shows, but I still needed answers to my questions.[1]

Lee then drove us downtown. Hoping for a letter, I asked Lee to stop at the post office. There happened to be two letters: one was from Indiana — probably the birth certificate I'd ordered, so I could prove I was of marriageable age — and the other was from Robert. I opened that one immediately.

But as I read Robert's words, my joy subsided: he would be coming without any money. Well, there would be no honeymoon, then. He also told me to get a job. That made me bristle. So! Robert still didn't know I had a job! I had only been allowed to send a single letter to him, and he knew he was supposed to call last week to see if I was OK. It was a call I hated to miss, but I'd left my new address at the "Y," as well as the message that I had a job. It took only one day for Robert's letters to reach me, so clearly, he'd failed me. Anger burned in my breast: I could have been dead, and he wouldn't have known! I shoved both letters in my purse, too upset to even look at the other one.

We got back in the car and Lee drove us to Lafayette Square, located in the 600 block of St. Charles Avenue near the old federal courthouse. He pulled over and let me off on Camp Street, telling me to wait there while he parked the car. He came back on foot in a few minutes and then walked me around the corner to Mr. Banister's office.

Inside, the air was musty from old air conditioners, and the décor reminded me of an out-dated attorney's office. I saw several people who looked like secretaries working at their desks. Swinging doors guarded the entrance to the file room, providing some privacy for people han-

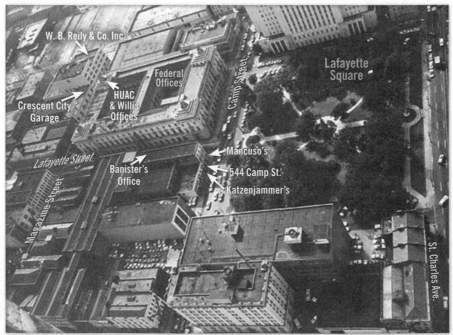

dling the confidential files. A door which led to Guy Banister's office was clearly marked with his name. It was closed.

Delphine Roberts, Banister's Secretary

We approached the middle-aged secretary, and Lee introduced us by saying "Mr. and Mrs. Oswald are here to see Mr. Banister." The secretary greeted us in a friendly manner and made a comment to me, but I kept my head down, as Lee had directed, and softly said something back in Russian. "Mrs. Oswald doesn't speak any English," Lee explained to the secretary, "so she can't really talk to you." The secretary kept talking to me anyway, as women often do. This annoyed Lee, so he stressed the point again by saying, "I am sorry, but Mrs. Oswald *does not* speak English."

After a few minutes, Mr. Banister came out and invited us into his private office. Once inside, I saw even more file cabinets and piles of papers stacked on the floor. Mr. Banister was alert and businesslike, with a commanding presence. "So, this is Mrs. Oswald, is it?" he said, as he shook my hand. Then he smiled at Lee, as he closed the door. Banister's sly smile made me realize that he already knew I wasn't really Mrs. Oswald.

"I understand you needed to meet me," he said sternly. I was now standing face to face with a man who was supposed to allay my fears and instill trust in me. His craggy visage was framed by a square jaw and wavy grey hair. His eyes glared with authority that was almost arrogant. And one could not help but notice that he was wearing a shoulder holster which held a large silver pistol. This man was armed and wanted those around him to know it. I was almost speechless, but managed to acknowledge his comment, as my eyes studied the room.

Guy Banister

The walls were covered with certificates and awards from his years in the FBI, alerting his visitors to his former greatness. Noting my interest, he gestured to one of the documents to make sure I knew that he had been in charge of 500 FBI agents in the Chicago region. Pointing to another frame he explained that he was a Red Raider, an elite group that uncovered communists, traitors, and radicals who were out to destroy the Land of the Free. He practically quivered with enthusiasm as he told me about his ability to find subversives, no matter how hard they tried to elude him.

Lee gave me a nod to let me know it was time to tell Mr. Banister why I was there. So I explained to Banister that I had misgivings after hearing Dave Ferrie and his Cuban friends talk about killing both Castro and Kennedy. I needed to know if the project that I had been asked to work on was really a secret project for the American government.

Mr. Banister assured me it was, and added that Ferrie would often float ideas like that to measure the Cubans' reactions. It was part of his job as an undercover agent working within the Cuban exile community. He said they were working on a get-Castro project, and that summaries of Ferrie's cancer research reports were photocopied on the Xerox machine in his office before being sent on to Georgia.[2] Banister said I was needed for this special medical project, and then urged Lee to take me upstairs, gesturing to the room above his head.

The only access to this inner chamber was a staircase along one wall. The stairs were newly installed and the wall had not yet been sheetrocked, leaving the wooden studs exposed. He said these stairs would soon be concealed behind a normal-looking wall of sheetrock, so people wouldn't know they were there. Not even Banister's own staff had access to the room above without passing through his private office.

We climbed upstairs, where there were even more filing cabinets. These were Banister's "high treasures." He proudly explained that these were the secret files that David Ferrie had been helping him with. Information was his business, Banister boasted, and these files were the really important ones. There, in his secret upstairs room, Guy Banister told me Lee Oswald was also working with him, and was being groomed to do his part to save Cuba from Communism.

With these comments, my concerns about Lee and Ferrie's loyalties and Ferrie's outlandish claims about Kennedy and Castro were put to rest. Mr. Banister had shown me that both men were engaged in real anti-Castro and anti-subversive projects, albeit secret ones, which were sponsored by the U.S. government.[3] That was good enough for me. I thanked Mr. Banister for his time, and Lee and I left his office.

Once we were back in the car, I asked Lee what in those files was so important. Lee explained Banister's situation to me. After leaving the FBI, Banister had come to New Orleans to be the Deputy Chief of Police, supposedly to root out corruption. His stay was brief. There was an incident which led to Banister's dismissal from the NOPD. Lee suggested that Banister may have been framed. But being publicly fired disgraced this proud man, who was determined to get his revenge. In response, he started a private investigation agency and hired spies to gather incriminating information on the New Orleans police and the city's politicians, concerning their connections to the Mafia. He updated his secret files constantly to chronicle the deep and persistent state of corruption.

Ironically, Banister was being paid for these efforts by Carlos Marcello's attorney.[4] But, Lee cautioned, despite Banister's moralistic veneer, he was now drinking too much and had taken one of his secretaries as a mistress, both of which made him vulnerable. Lee said Dave Ferrie was concerned about Banister's drinking, as it increasingly loosened his lips about their secret operations.

At last, I understood how Dave could work for the former head of Chicago's FBI and Carlos Marcello at the same time, despite the apparent conflict of allegiance.

"And you finally understand that I am really a good guy," Lee concluded triumphantly.

We were still in the downtown area, and Lee wanted us to check in with two employment agencies. We did so quickly and then, since we still had his uncle's car, Lee suggested we go to Pontchartrain Beach, the amusement park on the shores of Lake Pontchartrain that had just opened for the year. I was quite ready for some fun, and my trust in Lee was re-established, so I agreed.

While Lee drove, I decided to open the letter from Indiana. It was indeed my birth certificate, but to my surprise, it didn't read "Judyth Anne Vary." Instead, it read only 'Female Infant Vary.' You can imagine my surprise. My name was not on my birth certificate! I had seen it before when my mother registered me for school. It had my full name on it.[5] Why didn't this one?

My immediate concern was that I was about to get married and would need to present the certificate. I could hear the words "Do you Female Infant Vary solemnly swear to take this man..." I wondered if it would even be accepted. I also needed to get a Social Security card for my job. Would the Social Security office accept it?[6]

"Don't worry," Lee said, "We'll solve that problem for you," and suggested that it was probably due to a clerical error. But later, Lee would

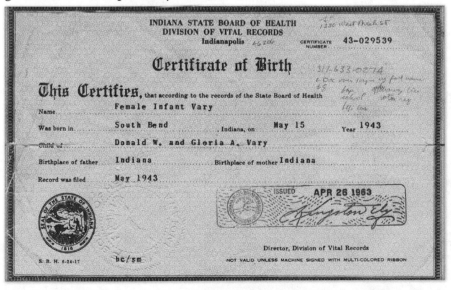

tell me that just such matters — the birth certificate — the code name "Jaryo" that was marked in the newspaper I'd dropped, and my using the name "Rourke" (He knew a CIA asset named Rorke, and heard me say the name to the postal clerk) — all had worked together to convince him of my involvement in some kind of secret agency. This is why he now felt comfortable telling me that he would be getting a "cover job" shortly at a company near Banister's office. He suggested that I might be able to get a job there too, and reminded me that I'd make enough money to be financially independent from Robert, just in case my marriage crashed.

We had reached Pontchartrain Beach, and Lee parked the car. While the amusement park was indeed open, there weren't many people around. Lee said it was busier at night. We walked on the beach for a while to enjoy the waves, but didn't go swimming. Frankly, the dark brackish lake did not look nearly as appealing to me as the blue-green waters of Florida's beaches. I wasn't dressed to swim anyway, so we went on to the amusement park.

The atmosphere in the amusement park was that of a carnival, complete with brightly painted scenes on walls and bright lights. We walked from one end of the park to the other. As we did Lee talked

to the staff, acting like he knew some of them. How, I can't say. I was busy watching children laughing on the kiddy rides and vendors spinning cotton candy.

At one end of the park there was a house of mirrors, which made you look as fat or thin as you desired. At the other there was an incredible roller-coaster, called The Zephyr. Officially it wasn't open yet that day, but Lee persuaded the crew to let us ride on one of their test runs. We were the only people on the entire roller-coaster. What a rush! Seeing how we laughed and screamed, the crew let us ride again for free. It was like having the amusement park reserved just for us.

By now we were hungry for more than cotton candy. Lee knew where we could get a real meal, at a covered pavilion where the park's personnel were busy eating lunch. After lunch, we spotted a shooting gallery with air rifles. The proprietor was still cleaning up and had not yet opened for business. Knowing how to get things done in New Orleans, Lee quietly offered the man a small bribe, which he quickly accepted. After carefully looking over the guns available, Lee chose one and started firing without hesitation. He hit every target, won a Kewpie Doll, and gave it to me. He then explained that the sights of the rifles in the shooting gallery were deliberately misaligned to make people miss the target. But if you knew this, you could work around it and hit everything.

Lee then told me that he had been shooting since he was a child, when he hunted squirrels. But knowing he would be trained to infiltrate the Soviet Union, he made a point of scoring poorly on his marksmanship tests in the Marines. If the Soviets got hold of his records, they wouldn't suspect him of being a sniper who might be entering their country to pick off somebody important.

After a wonderful day, Lee dropped me off at the place I was now calling "The Mansion." He said he had dinner plans at the Murrets, and that he would meet me at Royal Castle in the morning. We kissed before parting. A surge of passion hit me, and I immediately felt guilty. One part of me still loved Robert. The other part of me was still mad at him, so I was kissing Lee to strike back. I realized that my tangled emotions were a sign that I was deeply uncertain of Robert's love. Why would I risk marrying a man when I was uncertain of both my love for him and of his love of me? I decided to tell Robert that our marriage plans were off.

That night, I was left to myself in my romantic new home. As I looked around, I was shocked to see an *eye* at the keyhole. Mrs. Webber! That nosy old bat! I stuffed it with paper. Then I locked the sliding doors and went to sleep.

Tuesday, April 30, 1963

The next morning I headed to the Royal Castle for my morning shift. Lee arrived as expected and after eating he made some calls on the pay phone. I noticed that he was on the phone longer than usual. When I got off work, Lee said he'd been talking to Dave Ferrie. I knew not to ask questions; Lee would tell me what I needed to know in time.

Now that I'd met Guy Banister, Lee wanted me to visit Ferrie again. The good news, he added, was that Dave had spoken to Dr. Sherman about her aloofness. Everything was OK. He guaranteed that Dr. Sherman would meet me soon, and that she still wanted me to work with her. Apparently, she did not want to talk to me at the party because she knew that almost everybody there was homosexual, and she was afraid if people saw her talking to a young female they might conclude she was interested in me for non-scientific reasons. She had only gone to the party to retrieve the tumors in the refrigerator before they got too old.

Dave relayed that I could work both in her bone lab and at his place on alternate afternoons, as nobody would be in his apartment until he got home from work. Lee assured me that all of the hours I spent in Dave's kitchen lab would count toward my internship in Dr. Sherman's lab. My taking over Dave's lab work would release him to concentrate on his other duties with the anti-Castro cause. Finally Lee said that I would be taken to meet with Dr. Ochsner in a few days, and that he would personally advise me about what I was expected to accomplish.

The news from Dr. Sherman relieved me immensely. Back in town we went to the A-1 Employment Agency, where Lee and I both registered, just in case I needed to prove to Robert that I was job hunting. I had not yet decided how much to confide to Robert. I held secrets both *with* him and *from* him. I hadn't even decided if our marriage really was off. The heart of a young woman can be a tangled mess. Mine sure was. What was I going to do? Lee hoped that I would follow his advice and not marry Robert, and Dr. Ochsner knew nothing of my wedding plans.

We got on another bus heading uptown. Lee scooped up an abandoned newspaper and opened it to the horoscope section, entitled "Moon Messages For You." Lee said he read it regularly. In response, I dismissed horoscopes as nonsense, but I did glance at the passage, and it caught my fancy: "Today's Moon rays agitate high-strung individuals," I read aloud. "Many contrasting opinions are expressed. In love -life, excitement and passion builds to a crescendo. Temper sentiment with common sense. Emotional people pull situations askew."

"That's you!" Lee proclaimed.

"I suppose so," I agreed. "After all, I'm supposed to get married tomorrow."

"He is indeed the lucky one," Lee commented.

"Apparently you're to be invited to our wedding," I said, teasing him about his interest in the horoscope. "It says here under Libra, 'attend a social event.' We'll need a witness, you know."

"I don't want to be there when you make your mistake," Lee said sadly, avoiding my eyes.

We got off the bus at Tulane University where Lee said he had to meet Banister for "some work." He walked me to Tulane's library, which I explored while Lee and Banister went to a student meeting. The battle over integration was still front page news in 1963, and Banister was a staunch segregationist. From his Far Right perspective, integration was just a manifestation of Communism in America. The purpose of his visit to Tulane was to ferret out student radicals that might promote integration over the summer. His tactic was to lure students into a discussion, in which they would identify themselves as pro-active liberals who supported de-segregation. Banister was too old to be a convincing participant in a student debate, so he needed someone younger like Lee to play the part of a "student" who would challenge them to argue by presenting a Far Right perspective.

When they were finished, Lee picked me up from the library. He was clearly disgusted. Several of the students had proclaimed they were Socialists or Marxists, and Banister had gotten their names. He would be reporting them to the House Committee on Un-American Activities (HUAC), the FBI, and to university officials to brand them as radical left-wing student agitators.[7] These students could be expelled as a consequence, and their lives and careers ruined as a result of Banister's intrusion. Lee said that Banister had planned more meetings at Tulane and Loyola, and at the University of New Orleans on the lake front, and that he wanted Lee's help with them.[8] Banister's obsession with racial issues grieved Lee, but he looked forward to a more appealing Banister project: a training film for anti-Castro guerillas.

We stopped for some oyster stew near Tulane, then headed to Dave's place on the Claiborne bus. As we rode, Lee explained that he had told Marina he would be moving in with the Murrets, and he was worried she might call there. So, if anybody from Texas called, he had asked the Murrets to say he would be moving in soon. That way, Marina wouldn't be a burden by coming before he got their apartment. As for me, I had stopped wondering if Robert would call.

We arrived at Dave's place, which was still a mess. I noticed that several cages of mice were back. The disarray of the apartment brought back fresh memories of his raucous party. Dave had a hangover and was drinking tomato juice from a lab flask. I wondered what else was in the flask. Furthermore, I was still angry about Dave's rambunctious behavior at the party. While Mr. Banister's assurances may have explained Dave's comments about Kennedy, I now had fresh concerns over Banister's own conduct, since he was obviously willing to ruin the lives of idealistic students just because he disagreed with them. Where was our freedom of speech amongst these zealous patriots? I was loaded for bear and ready to give Dave a good "talking to."

"Thank you for giving me another chance," Dave said contritely. "There's a hell of a lot I need to explain."

I took aim. "I need to know more about you, Dave," I told him. "I don't care if you sleep with tangerines!"

"With tangerines?" Dave repeated. "With tangerines?"

David Ferrie's living room
as it was at the time of his death
on February 22, 1967

I blushed. "I only mean that's not what upsets me," I stammered. "Whether you're gay or whatever, I don't care about that."

"If she works for you," Lee broke in, "she has to feel safe from your friends."

"I haven't worked with a murderous warrior before," I added coyly. "They were always people who went home at night to a wife, a kid and a dog."

"I'm not a murderous warrior," Dave objected.

"That's how you were describing yourself at the party," I reminded him. "I could hear you carrying on about how you hated Kennedy, that you hoped he rode in an open car until somebody shot him. Bragging you were going to kill Castro. Bragging about your other exploits where people got killed." Once I felt that I had made my point, I paused to hear his response.

"I'll explain," Dave said, pulling up chairs to his dining room table. "And after I do," he said, lighting a cigarette, "I believe you'll accept the task of taking over the lab. It will solve a lot of problems. It's possible that your work here could benefit America."

I had suddenly gone from working for him to running the whole lab! I became more interested in his proposition. We sat down. Dave continued: "If I was known to love the president and sing 'Hail to The Chief,' how many Cubans do you think would have shown up at my party? One? Two?" He drew a deep drag on his cigarette. "I'm a private investigator, among my other talents," he declared. "Through these blokes, I have my hand right on the nuts of the Cuban exile community, even though I haven't been part of their absurd and foolish suicide missions for quite a while."

He then described how the local anti-Castro leaders had kicked him out of a leadership position in the struggle to regain Cuba, because his homosexual activities were reported in the papers.[9]

"What hypocrites!" he insisted. "Those so-called homophobes didn't expel their own gay members. Just me. And after all I had done for them!"

Nevertheless Dave explained, he still held parties to attract the anti-Castroites, and listen to them talk of murdering Kennedy for his treachery in the Bay of Pigs invasion.

"That is, if he ever dared show his butt in Miami again," he said.

At this point I reminded Dave that I was a lady, and that he should clean up his vocabulary. "I know you're capable of speaking foully in a variety of languages," I said. "I now challenge you to express yourself in the manner of Milton, Blake, and Thomas More."

"Good God, girl," Dave said, "why are you such a prude?"

"Weren't you going to be a priest at one time?" Lee broke in. "In 1961, she wanted to enter a convent." Dave stared past us toward an

David Ferrie at St. Mary Jesuit Seminary, Cleveland, Ohio

old statue of the Virgin Mary. When he spoke again, his voice was softer. "That's all I wished," he finally said. "And in my own way, it's still all I want."

"I only wish you to be the gentleman you can be," I persisted. "You want me to respect you," I said. "Don't I deserve a little respect, too?"[10]

"I was already well known as hating Kennedy's shit concerning the Bay of Pigs," Dave continued. "I let them know I wanted to strangle that SOB with my bare hands for betraying us." With that, I got up to leave.

"Damn it!" he said. "I'm sorry!" He asked me to sit down, and then started pacing the room. "At the time, I meant it. I really wanted Kennedy to die. But truth is, he's my Catholic brother and my Commander in Chief. And most importantly, I now know who really betrayed us at the Bay of Pigs. It wasn't JFK."

Dave said he had been invited to some secret sessions where he was asked to provide input about any crazy Cuban plans to murder JFK. "I tell Marcello all their plans," he said, proudly. "That puts me in tight with the Mob. So long as I still seem to be one hundred percent on their side," he added, "I will continue to be in the know."

"What about telling the CIA?" I ventured.

"At this point," he said, "I trust nobody I know in the Agency. The CIA and the Mob are bed-buddies, which means no protection for the (Commander-in-) Chief (Kennedy) from the Mob. There's no telling if this talk has reached higher levels or not. The CIA is no friend of JFK. He fired their precious Allen Dulles and wrecked General Cabell's career. Then there's General Walker. The Kennedys canned him and had him straitjacketed in a nuthouse for awhile."

Dave shifted the conversation back to our project. Castro was the target, not Kennedy. Dave then said there were several other underground labs already set up to help, so nothing I might want would be lacking. Everything was organized through Dr. Sherman and Dr. Ochsner. Sherman was a widow, had no close friends outside the research community, and traveled a lot to conventions and Latin America, so her lab was used to dealing with her frequent comings and goings.

I was useful because I was almost untraceable, since I wasn't a doctor yet. Who would believe that a 19-year old college undergraduate, and a *girl* at that, would be involved in such an activity? I

General Edwin Walker

General Edwin Walker was an outspoken American military general from Texas who denounced communism, liberalism and integration. In the early 1960s he championed segregation and instigated anti-Civil Rights incidents. Walker fought in southern Europe during World War II and later in Korea, but in 1961 JFK relieved him of his command in Germany for distributing racist, right-wing literature to his soldiers.

Walker, a vocal member of the John Birch Society, unsuccessfully ran for Governor of Texas in 1962 with financial help from the anti-JFK right-wing oil millionaires H.L. Hunt and Clint Murchison. Later that year, in Oxford, Mississippi, he led segregationists against the integration of the University of Mississippi, where he gave a speech comparing the Supreme Court to the anti-Christ. A violent 15-hour riot resulted: he was arrested, and charged with insurrection against the United States. Held for a week in jail, and then released, his return to Dallas was greeted by an admiring crowd.

On April 10, 1963, a metal-jacketed bullet (not the same brand of bullet that was fired from the rifle supposedly owned by Oswald on Nov. 22) plowed through a window in Walker's study, slightly wounding him. For the next seven months, the police had no evidence or suspects in the case, but within hours of his arrest on Nov. 22,1963, Lee Oswald was accused of the crime. Oswald's wife (under sequestering and questioning) and Ruth Paine (who provided much other damning evidence against Oswald) both said he told them he fired the rifle into Walker's home. Some believe Walker was somehow involved in planning the JFK assassination. In the 1970s Walker was disgraced after his arrest in public rest rooms in Dallas, and charged with public lewdness. He died of lung cancer in 1993.

had a unique opportunity and a grand chance to be of service to my country. I sat there and dissected what he was saying. Dave sensed my calculations, and realized that I had not yet bought in. So he tried more rational inducements. He said I would still get credited for my internship, since the work would be close to what I would be doing in Dr. Sherman's lab. But if I worked in his lab, rather than Sherman's, the records wouldn't need to be laundered, hundreds of control animals wouldn't have to be killed, and, more importantly, the whole project would go faster.

Dave said that I would have the whole place to myself in the afternoons. I just needed to clean up each day before he got home from work, because friends who were not privy to these matters might drop in. Time, he said, was running out. The project, he finally admitted, was part of an effort to kill Castro. Doing so would focus the entire Cuban community on regaining Cuba, and they would abandon their crazy dreams of revenge on Kennedy. The project had been in existence for a year, but had been foundering lately. I could save the day, since I was an untraceable asset with the rare training needed for the final phases.

Now I knew that the goal of Dave's research was to murder Fidel Castro. Gulp! And they wanted me to help. All of my knowledge and training had suddenly been perverted into making a biological weapon. What would Grandpa say? What would Mrs. Watkins say? My head started to spin as the stark truth finally sank in: Dr. Ochsner, who had inspired my dreams for years, was in charge of a project to use cancer to murder the head of a foreign government. I realized that, given what I now knew, I was involved in the secret whether I worked in Dave's kitchen, or for Sherman in her lab at Ochsner's Clinic.

Dave sensed my stress. "Don't worry," he said. "Nobody will harm you if you decide not to join us. You can go into Dr. Mary's lab and take it easy. But we need you here." We both sank into silence while Lee watched.

After a while Dave showed me a newspaper article published a month earlier on Dr. Ochsner's move of his clinic to its huge new home next to the existing hospital on Jefferson Highway.[11] A photo showed a long line of trucks that shuttled back and forth for days with equipment, animals, and supplies.

"This is when the ring of clandestine labs was set up," Dave said. In the confusion, a truckload of microscopes, lab equipment, cages, chemicals, cancer cell strains and pedigree mice somehow lost its way. This is where all

Founders and financiers of original Ochsner Clinic see it demolished

The Ochsner Clinic & Hospital in 1963 showing new additions in foreground.

of the equipment for the labs had come from, leaving no paper trail. They were never reported as stolen. They just disappeared, and nobody ever missed them.

Those wealthy oilmen from Texas, Dave said, had contributed millions, in both visible and invisible funds, to help build Ochsner's impressive new facilities. In exchange, Ochsner's medical — and political — cooperation with them was solid. Dr. O also shared attitudes with the "Oil Barons" about anti-Communism, racism and taking things into one's own hands in order to "save democracy."

"I know you probably think of him as God," Dave said, "But Ochsner is naïve when it comes to dealing with these slick Texas millionaires, the CIA and the Mob. They've got him wrapped up for Christmas, right where they want him. They drink together, hunt together, play golf together, gamble together and decide what's best for the country together."

Dave continued to explain the players. Lyndon Johnson was so close to Clint Murchison that they said each other's names in their sleep.[12] And former Vice President Richard Nixon was another one of Ochsner's friends. Despite what the public thought of him, Nixon would do anything to become president. He was in line for the job behind his power-hungry ally, LBJ. The dimensions of this sinister network began to take shape in my mind. Acquiring presidential power was not about the lofty idealistic goals that peppered their speeches and television ads, but an imperative forged of money, nerve, and connections. And organized crime was obviously part of those connections. The Mob could even trump the FBI, since "Madame Hoover is Clyde Tolson's missus."

"He is what?" I protested. "*The* J. Edgar Hoover?

"Also known as 'Mrs.' Hoover," Dave said, smiling. "All the 'fairies'

Clint Murchison, Jr.

Clinton Murchison, Jr. (1923-1987) was a well-known Texas business man who inherited a fortune in real estate, construction, railroads, publishing and oil. In the 1940s, the Murchisons became close friends with J. Edgar Hoover, the Director of the FBI, who invested in Murchison oil interests.

In 1955, a Senate committee discovered connections between Murchison and well-known Mafia figures like Vito Genovese and Carlos Marcello. Murchison was fiercely anti-Communist, became a member of the John Birch Society, funded the infamous anti-Communist campaign of Senator Joe McCarthy, and held extreme right-wing political views. Dr. Alton Ochsner made many trips to Murchison's ranches in Texas and Mexico, and Ochsner's official biography, *Surgeon of the South*, notes that Murchison annually gave Ochsner a Cadillac, helped Ochsner obtain cheap land for his hospital, and generously helped finance his new hospital.

The evening before the JFK assassination, witnesses say Murchison hosted a high-level gathering at his home in Dallas (with H.L. Hunt, J. Edgar Hoover, Richard Nixon, Lyndon B. Johnson, Clyde Tolson, and John J. McCloy) which led to speculation that Murchison was involved in the assassination of President Kennedy. Eventually, Murchison's business fortunes soured, and in 1985 he filed for bankruptcy.

know this," adding a wink to punctuate his disclosure. "So does the Mob. They have photos of Hoover and his lover, so they know he will cooperate with anything the Mob decides to do about the Kennedy brothers. He also knows that JFK wants to force him to retire. That means the FBI is all fucked up."

I was shocked. Not by his profanity, but because he was saying that our national bulwark against crime, the mighty FBI, had been corrupted. The scales were cascading from my eyes.

Dave went on to explain that two big events would eat up his free time in the months to come. First, Carlos Marcello had asked him to be part of his team to fight off Bobby Kennedy's efforts to deport him.

J. Edgar Hoover & Clyde Tolson

The Boss wanted Dave to attend that trial and counsel him. Secondly, Dave had his own problems to attend to. Eastern Airlines had fired him after he was arrested in an outrageous incident involving a teenage boy and an airplane. So Dave had to go to Miami for hearings in hopes they would re-instate him as a pilot.

Both events would require research, meetings, written briefs, and trips. These would stretch him thin. I told Dave I needed time to think about this, as well as to consider whether to proceed with my upcoming marriage. And there was one more problem. This was all sounding really dangerous. So I was blunt.

"Who is going to protect us?" I asked, "What if Castro finds out about the project and decides to have us killed?"

"This isn't the movies," Dave said. "Castro can't kill everybody. Lee, here, is part of our protection. He's going to help root out anybody who's pro-Castro in this town. It was one of his jobs, so don't feel guilty about it. As for the rest of it, just keep your mouth shut."

I glanced at Lee, and realized that after nearly three years behind the Iron Curtain, he had returned unharmed by either side. That took brains and courage. It also took connections. One look at that calm face gave me the assurance I needed: Lee Oswald was indeed my protector. My bodyguard.

Lee and I had spent all Tuesday night and the early hours of Wednesday morning at Dave's. As the conversation rambled from politics to philosophy to science, we explored Dave's astonishing mind, which shone like a diamond inside a lump of coal. This great brain was trapped in a quagmire of human foibles. What a waste!

We returned to the Mansion just before dawn. I was tired, but exhilarated by all that I had heard. Knowing I needed to get some sleep, since Robert would be arriving later that morning, Lee quickly kissed me goodbye; it was short but so sweet. "I won't be able to kiss you, after you're married," he said again.[13]

True enough. I'd never dream of it! But as he departed, with that military way of walking he had (his back ramrod straight, his feet always straight ahead), I found myself pondering his kiss. Then I suddenly realized that my thoughts were as off-limits as Lee's kiss should have been: I was supposed to get married today! And here I'd not even thought about inviting Carol or any of my newfound friends (what would Robert think of them, anyway?). I didn't have an extra penny to get my hair fixed, we'd use the second-hand gold band I'd purchased at a pawnshop, and there would be no flowers, no music. It was a sorry situation, and far from "romantic." I had to remind myself that birth control pills were, at least, a pretty pink.

1. Boris and Natasha were the male-female Russian spy team characters on the *Rocky and His Friends* and later *The Bullwinkle Show* cartoon television shows.

2. Today photocopy machines are in every office, and even in many homes, but in 1963 they were both rare and expensive. Virtually all were made by the Xerox Corporation, which held the patents on the technology. The few machines that existed in hospitals and medical school were closely guarded by the secretarial staffs to make sure each copy was properly logged and accounted for. Many times this had to do with federal grant money connected to research. Personal use was seriously frowned on, and official use left a paper trail. The ability to access a photocopy machine at Banister's office meant that copies could be made for off-the-books projects without leaving a paper trail.

3. J. Edgar Hoover's phone logs were made available to researchers as a result of the JFK Assassination Records Act of 1992, after Oliver Stone's *JFK* movie. They show that Hoover was communicating regularly with Guy Banister during the summer of 1963. If this was not an official U.S. Government project, it at least involved officials of the U.S. Government. To ponder that such corruption may have penetrated the federal government at such a high level is disturbing, but it explains the involvement of people like Banister and Hoover. Either it was "official" as I was told, or I was lied to by corrupt officials who used their status as cover for darker purposes. Whatever the reality was, I agreed to work on the project believing that it was a clandestine project sponsored by the U.S. Government for the benefit and safety of America.

4. G. Wray Gill was an attorney who represented Carlos Marcello. The FBI Interviewed Gill on November 27, 1963, and the results of that interview were published in Warren Commission Document 75 pp. 219-221. Gill advised the FBI that he had known David W. Ferrie since about 1961, when he represented Ferrie in a criminal matter in Jefferson Parish, Louisiana and in a grievance with Eastern Air Lines following his dismissal from that company. Guy Banister served as a character witness for Ferrie in this latter matter. Following these events, Gill hired Ferrie as an investigator. At the time, Gill's office was at 1705 Pere Marquette Building, named after a famous Jesuit priest. The building was owned by the Jesuits. Gill later moved his office to the Richards Building, which was also owned by the Jesuits.

5. In 1954, my parents obtained birth certificates for me and my sister, anticipating a move from Indiana. These had our full names on them. We eventually enrolled in public schools in Florida.

6. My social security number shows that it was issued in Louisiana, and my personal SS records go back only to 1963.

7. In 1963 the Chairman of HUAC was Congressman Edwin Willis, whose offices were located in the Federal Building next to Banister's office.

8. The University of New Orleans is part of the Louisiana State University system. From its inception in 1956 it was called LSUNO. In 1974, its name was changed to the University of New Orleans.

9. Dave did not bother to mention that these homosexual activities involved an under-age boy and that he had been arrested for them.

10. That conversation was a turning point in our relationship. After that day, Dave behaved differently in my presence. He curbed his excessive cursing and began revealing to me some of his personal religious activities, which were bizarre remnants of the life he had yearned to lead.

11. The new clinic's land was provided through a deal masterminded by Ochsner's wealthy Texas Oil Baron friend, Clint Murchison, an enemy of both Castro and Kennedy.

12. Lyndon Johnson was famous for "bringing home the bacon" — getting federal tax dollars for pet projects for his friends in Texas. He was the visible head of Texas politics, but the real power was always the money in the back room where people like Murchison sat. Long-time observation shows that powerful people, rather than run for office, find it easier to own those who do.

13. Lee taught me to walk with my feet "straight ahead"—just as he did— giving me such a variety of good reasons that I agreed to do so. I have continued to walk that way ever since.

Robert & Judyth pre-marriage

— Chapter 10 —

May Day!

Wednesday, May 1, 1963

It was finally May Day, the day Robert and I planned to get married, so I had arranged to take the next two days off from work. At 8:00 A.M. the alarm sounded. I struggled to emerge from a much-needed sleep to prepare for Robert's arrival. By 10:00, I was waiting anxiously on the front porch, wearing the bone-white linen dress I'd bought in the French Quarter, my hair up in a twist, with pearls around my neck. I wanted Robert to see that his girl was already dressed for the wedding. Robert's blue Ford pulled up in front of the boarding house about 10:02 A.M.

As he got out, I could see that he was dressed in khaki shorts, a plaid shirt and flip-flops. I couldn't help but laugh as I thought about what our wedding photo might look like: The Princess and the Pauper. But that smile! That face! I called out his name, and my man came rushing up the steps. He took me into his arms and swung me in a circle. I relished the familiar smell of his aftershave as he kissed me.

"Let's get married!" he declared and kissed me again. I was thrilled. I had almost forgotten how tall, how well built, how take-charge he was.

"We have a noxious old bat for a landlady," I told him. "She thinks we're already married, so..." Robert laughed, and went back to his car to get his bags, his guitar case, and his typewriter, which he lugged up the stairs and into my bedroom. Then we got in his car and headed downtown to the Courthouse to get married. As he drove, I considered the little talk I'd planned — about all my second thoughts — but now my head was spinning with excitement and I didn't know where to begin. I wondered why he hadn't dressed better for our wedding. Ah, well. He probably wasn't planning on keeping his clothes on that long anyway!

As Robert parked his car near the courthouse, I pointed out a sign to him that indicated the parking space was "private." But Robert was unconcerned about something as trivial as parking restrictions, and dismissed my worries. He was on a mission.

"We're only going in to buy a marriage license," he said. "It won't take five minutes." We entered the courthouse, filled out some paper-work and handed it to the clerk, saying we wanted to get married today. When the clerk told us there was a two-day waiting pe-riod for marriages in Louisiana, Robert exploded in anger.

"What?" he raged. "In a back-ward state like this? You're jok-ing!" But nobody was joking. It was hard for me to believe that Robert, the hot-shot scholar with the reputation for thoroughness, had not bothered to look up the laws for marriage in the State of Louisiana. I said as much to him. Not to be out-done in his moment of pique, he snapped back that he couldn't believe I hadn't looked up the regulations either, given my stratospheric IQ.

Robert had simply assumed that Louisiana was a primitive, redneck state that allowed cousins or anybody else to marry each other when-ever they wanted. But his caricature was wrong. Louisiana operated under the Napoleonic Code, which was far more sophisticated than Robert imagined. It wasn't a big deal to me. Who cared when the pa-perwork got done? Waiting two days wasn't a big problem — we had each other!

"But I only have one day left to marry you," he said. "After that, I have to start working." Now I understood. We wouldn't have a free day to celebrate until the weekend.

Robert calculated his options for a moment, then told the clerk that he wasn't going to buy the license. Taking my hand, he turned on his heel and walked me outside. What was going on? Had he decided not to get married? When I reminded him that I would not sleep with him unless he used a condom, he dropped my hand and stomped on ahead of me toward the car.

Just then, we saw blinking lights – the dusty blue Ford was being towed away! We ran after the tow truck, screaming for them to stop, but it was useless. Off it went, disappearing into the traffic as Robert stood there helpless and seething. For the next hour, we walked in gloom; finally we reached the "car pound" where Robert paid the $7.50 fine and marked "Paid under protest" on the release form, though "Paid with contempt" would have been a better description of his actions.

"Let's go to the library, so we can look up marriage laws for nearby states," he growled. There we found that only Alabama had no waiting period. Robert had located his backward state that didn't care who married who or when, as long as they were both the same color.

We would head east in the morning to Mobile, about four hours away. Robert calculated that if we started at dawn we could drive there, come back the same day, and avoid paying a motel bill. My so-called wedding day had not worked out well. When we chose May 1st, it was due to my Catholic roots: on May Day, a little girl was crowned "Queen of the May" with flowers in the church. I yearned to think of myself as still sweet and innocent, though I was marrying outside the Church.

I wanted very much to talk about everything going on in my life, but Robert wasn't interested. He was frustrated and tired from his long drive into New Orleans. We sat stiffly in the car as he drove back to the boarding house I called, "The Mansion."

"What went on in Fort Walton while you were there?" I finally asked.

"Nothing," he replied. "All I did was type stuff in my parent's office."

"Well," I pursued, "did they catch on to us?"

"No," he said.

"Did they figure out that the letter from Raleigh Rourke was actually from a girl?" I continued, hoping that I could find some common success that might soften his mood.

"No, but you shouldn't have used such cute stationery," he scolded. "They might have thought Rourke was queer!"

Hearing that, I decided it was time to stop beating around the bush and tell Robert that I wanted to stay in New Orleans and go to medical school at Tulane in the fall. Maybe he would change his mind about marrying me, but I knew it was the right thing to do. I decided to approach the subject obliquely.

"Can I tell you something I've been thinking about? " I ventured. "Something that's on my mind?"

"Did you find a job?" he interrupted.

"Well, yes, but..."

"I'll bet you thought I wasn't going to come."

"I needed to hear from you more," I managed to say. Still, Robert seemed ready to marry me, so I repeated, "I really do need to tell you how I feel about something."

"You were upset because I came late. Right?"

"Well, yes, but it's more than that. I'll just say this: I've made some contacts. If you don't want to marry me, I'll be okay, even if you go back to Florida."

"I said I'd show up," he answered, stroking my face. "Tomorrow, you'll be legal!"

I was so glad to see his happy shift in mood that I temporarily stopped promoting my plans and started worrying about his hands, one of which was no longer on the steering wheel! Grabbing his right hand firmly I said, "I need to tell you something."

Robert replied that there was only one thing he really needed at the moment, and that I was about to provide it. There would be plenty of time to talk later. After all, we had our whole lives to talk. He parked in front of The Mansion, and we crept quietly into my boudoir. Robert paused only long enough to close the blinds, which were too high for me to reach. Once they came down, we went to bed, but I did not get much sleep.

Morning - Thursday, May 2, 1963 –

I awoke early in the morning and watched Robert's face as he slept. How had he avoided any intimate conversation? We'd been apart twelve days. Not very long for him, he claimed. But it had seemed a century to me. For him, it was first things first. It's time to make whoopee! What could possibly be more important than having sex? Marriage meant access to birth control pills, safe sex, and Robert's protection and companionship in a rough, tough city. Dear God, I felt I needed him so! Surely I must love him. And I wanted those birth controls pills fast.

After several nudges, Robert awoke, and we headed to Mobile, Alabama. All I remember of Mobile was the Bankhead tunnel under  the river, which we had to traverse because the courthouse was on the other side. Once at the courthouse, we purchased the marriage license in short order. They were satisfied with my U. of Florida ID. I breathed a sigh of relief, because it meant that I would not have to explain that my name wasn't really "Female Infant Vary." Anybody old enough to be a college student was old enough to get married in Alabama. Then we went around the corner to the Marrying Man, who inspected the license and saw a blank space.

"What's your mother's maiden name?" he asked Robert. My fiancé was a superb mathematician and writer, but his memory about people and events was terrible. He said he couldn't remember because he hadn't known her back then. The marriage ceremony was performed anyway with a yawning clerk acting as witness. The words rushed by too quickly for me to even understand. I brought out the wedding band and asked Robert to put it on my finger when the official paused. When he did, we were pronounced "man and wife." It was the least romantic ceremony imaginable. As I stood there, I wondered if I would have gone through with all of this, if Lee had not told me he had beaten Marina. However, he had, and I was now Mrs. Robert Allison Baker, III.

Afternoon - Thursday, May 2, 1963

We stopped at an Italian restaurant to eat. For our wedding feast, he ordered the restaurant's best spaghetti-and-meatball dinner, but nothing to drink and no dessert.

"We have to be careful until my first paycheck comes in," he said. After dinner, we stopped at Providence Hospital for the state-required blood test, necessary before we could pick up birth control pills. Next we stopped at a pharmacy and bought the all-important pills, and started the long drive back to New Orleans. As the hours wore on, Robert's moodiness returned. What could be wrong now? Hoping to soften him, I snuggled against him, only to feel him draw back. I sat up, worried and alert. Robert was always quiet, but now he was too quiet. A frown crept over his features as he drove, staring at the highway. What was the matter? I started to put my arm around my new husband.

"Don't touch me!" he said, pushing my arm away.

"What's wrong?" I demanded.

"My parents will cut me off financially when they find out that we eloped. You'll have to get a job," he said bluntly.

"Dr. Ferrie offered to set me up with a job at PenChem in Gainesville," I said, hoping to please him. "I could work there and continue to go to school."

"You'll need to work full time in order to support us."

"But what about you? We could get by on two part-time incomes."

"I'll be in graduate school and will need to make good grades. I can't work and do that. You'll need to support both of us."

"But what about my grades?"

"Your schooling could wait," he concluded emphatically.

I turned and stared out the window at the endless row of tall pine trees that lined the dark highway. They looked like the bars of a prison cell. In the silence, my heart ached, and I began to tremble with anxiety: What had I done?

Night - Thursday, May 2, 1963

When we finally returned to The Mansion in New Orleans, it was late, but there were so many cars we had to park a block away. Not long after we entered our room, Mrs. Webber knocked on the door and questioned whether Robert was really my husband. After all, she'd seen me with Lee many times and made her own sinful assumptions about our relationship. But I held up my hand for her to see the wedding band, while Robert waved our marriage certificate at her.

Then the old bag wagged her bony finger at Robert and said: "Your wife is a lousy cheat! She's been runnin' around with another man behind your back!" I gulped. But then she topped her claim with an even wilder accusation, saying I had been sunbathing naked on the front porch to attract a little business my way.

Robert laughed at her and closed the door in her face. He knew how modest I was about nudity and automatically regarded her exhibitionist claim as preposterous.

Giving me a quick kiss on the forehead, he said, "That's for all the wicked things you might have done with other men while I was gone!" I felt a surge of guilt, and decided not to explain about Lee Oswald until a better time.

This was our wedding night. There were no flowers, nor even a photo. We didn't even have a souvenir postcard of Mobile. It was the most meager honeymoon possible.

As my husband bathed down the hall I started thinking. Robert and I had previously enjoyed campus movies and plays. Maybe we couldn't have a honeymoon, but surely we could have a night out tomorrow after work. Thanks to my friends at the YWCA I knew some nice places in the French Quarter where we could celebrate cheaply. When Robert returned to our room, I told him I had to leave for work at Royal Castle in less than six hours. "I hope you can drive me over," I told him. "I'm working extra hours today, so we'll get a bigger paycheck Saturday. Then we can go to the beach, or have fun in the French Quarter."

Robert agreed to drive me there, but then he said something shocking.

"Don't cash that Saturday check," he said. "Send it to me, instead."

All of a sudden, alarm bells went off.

"What do you mean by 'send you my paycheck?'"

"I'll explain later," my new husband said. "Right now, first things first!"

"But I have to get up soon — and I'm tired!"

I took a birdie bath, hoping Robert would fall asleep. No such luck. That man was inspired by my very breathing. Finally, he allowed me to get a bit of sleep.

Morning - Friday, May 3, 1963

The alarm went off. The physical and emotional stress of the last few days had taken its toll. I was so exhausted that Robert helped get me dressed, which was a switch, and then he drove me to work. I entered

Royal Castle, dazed and blanched. I was in no condition to work. Robert climbed into the back seat of the car and slept as I tried to handle the demanding breakfast crowd. It was a disaster. I was a zombie. Walking like a wounded soldier, I dropped things and spilled coffee. My condition was impossible to conceal and my performance was indefensible. It no longer mattered how much the customers liked me. After six hours, the inevitable happened: the manager fired me.

Too tired to care, I stumbled back to the car and collapsed inside, but Robert had spent the last six hours stretched out sleeping on the back seat. He was ready the minute we got home to prove he was one of the great marathon lovers of all time. I begged for mercy, but then he broke the news.

"I have to get in as much lovin' as I can," Robert said, pleadingly, "because our days together are going to be few and far between."

"W-what are you talking about?" I managed to stammer.

"I'm going to be in the Gulf of Mexico for ten or twenty days at a time," he said, dressing me in the baby doll see-through nightie I'd purchased for our honeymoon. "I'll only have two or three days off between hitches. That's why we have to get in as much lovin' as we can. Like right now!" He began kissing and caressing my tired body.

"I'm not going to worry about you," he added, "because you've got yourself a nice hidey-hole here, and a job to cover your expenses. You'll do fine without me, just as you said. And every time I'm back I'll be just as horny as I am now!"

Afternoon - Friday, May 3, 1963

"I have to drive to Houma at 3:00 P.M. to sign on with the crew," he muttered. "By Monday night I'll be on a quarter boat doing seismic exploration." Then he confided that he was replacing a man who had both hands blown off by a charge of dynamite. But the pay was good, and there was free room and board as well.

As Robert continued to indulge in his impressive manly pursuits on my benumbed body, my brain managed to function enough to formulate one thought clearly: "What possessed me to get married?" Then I fell asleep briefly, waking to see him finish packing. I was too tired to move, but my tangled thoughts were still active. It took awhile, but Robert finally noticed that I wasn't speaking to him.

"You're mad now, but you'll miss me when I'm gone," he said. "You'll feel different later." I was still silent.

"Finances have to come first," he added. "We have to have enough money to pay for my last semester at school. That's the goal. Now – please — give me just a little more lovin'," Robert begged, "before I have to go!" I wearily wondered how much it would cost to get a civil marriage annulled. My feet were sore, so I mentioned that I needed new walking shoes, telling Robert I would not be able to work another day in high heels (my flattie shoes were worn out). Instead, Robert handed me three dollars for bus fare and meals, adding "You have to make this last. Remember — don't cash your next paycheck. Send it to me. I might need it for car repairs."

I was still in a state of disbelief. Robert was not going to be in New Orleans. I was tired and sore, I had no job, and a hellion for a landlady. Just then, we caught her looking through the keyhole again, so I opened Robert's umbrella and hung it open over the lock, making my new husband laugh. Then he was kissing me passionately again, as I considered the pantry of excuses that women offer men to avoid just saying "No."

Robert finally got up and started taking things to the car. He would be gone at least ten days on a quarterboat owned by Evangeline Exploration. But he refused to reveal the name, location or phone number of the ship's owners. "I don't want you spending any money coming over to see me," he said. "Don't worry," he added. "I'll write."

At the last minute, Robert put his guitar on the bed and told me to keep it for him because the salt air offshore could ruin it. He kissed me goodbye and left me sad, exhausted and lying there in my black baby doll see-through nightie, and my almost-there panties with a big red rose sewn on the front! Too tired to take off my honeymoon attire, I closed the guitar case with my bare foot, and fell into a deep dreamy sleep. It was long overdue.

Night - Friday, May 3, 1963

In my dreams, I floated gently above the beautiful bed in a Victorian mansion in which I was sleeping. Then suddenly, I woke to the sound of men yelling and women screaming. Police sirens pierced the night at point-blank range. Car doors slammed. It was midnight, and my room was pitch black. Shouting, crying and cursing resonated through the walls. The house was being raided by police! So much for Mrs. Webber's posturing about morality. I had rented a room in a brothel!

"Judy," I told myself "You're on your own. You've got to do something fast!" As I climbed out of bed I realized I was still wearing the black nightie, and nothing else. It was hardly the way I wanted to greet the vice-squad. I yanked off the negligée, stuffed it into a suitcase and trying to look collegiate threw on a shirt, pants and shoes as fast as I could.

I wanted to get out of there as soon as possible before I got swept up in the mass arrest. The sounds of heavy footsteps shook the building as the police stormed through the foyer and up the stairs. I frantically packed my two suitcases in the dark and hoped that the police would keep heading to the upstairs bedrooms and bypass my darkened ground-floor parlor. I quietly loaded my books and Robert's typewriter into a cardboard box.

Peering out the curtains to plan my escape, I saw four patrol cars crowding the curb in front of the house with their lights flashing. A girl clad in a feather boa and handcuffs was being man-handled down the front stairs. Above me, I could hear the sounds of the police as they systematically invaded room after room searching for sinners. Several more handcuffed girls were brought out of the building with bed sheets thrown over them. Some cursed as they passed my door. Others wept. Finally, I saw several men escorted out with uniformed policemen at their elbows.

Men! What about the men in *my* life? Lee Oswald had booked me into this whorehouse and Robert Baker had abandoned me here! And I had really only wound up here in the first place because my father beat the women in his family. Thanks a lot guys. I could have strangled all three of them.

The problem was they weren't there, the vice squad was, and my options were quickly narrowing. Think! What can I do to show them I am not one of the good-time girls? Wait, I just got married. Where is my license? I had just started frantically digging through my suitcase, when I heard a thunderous banging on the door. There it was! I grabbed my certificate in one hand and flipped on the overhead lights with the other, flooding the room with bright light, just as a uniformed policeman burst in.

He was a huge man, overweight and red-faced with excitement, towering over me like a bridge. "You!" he yelled at me, as he put his hand on his gun. "What's your name?" I froze and stared at him.

"M-Mrs. Robert Allison Baker, the Third," I stammered in a crackly voice on the edge of hysteria. The policeman laughed cruelly and said that was the most ridiculous excuse for a name he'd heard all night.

"I just got married. Here's my certificate," I said, waving the paper at him.

"So where's your husband?" he queried with cop logic and in a cop voice.

"He works offshore. He just left a couple of hours ago," I countered.

Then Mrs. Webber entered the room with her hands on her hips, demanding attention. "She's cheating on her husband, I tell ya'. You ought to haul her away with the others. Besides, she's been lying around naked on my front porch trying to drum up business."

"Shut up!" The police officer told Mrs. Webber with impatient contempt.

"All right," he said turning to me. "I get it. You're clean. But you're going to have to leave. We're closing this place down, so get your things together and get the hell out of here now."

"Please don't swear at me," I mumbled. "I'm not used to it." The officer seemed to understand that I was a good girl after all. Seeing that I was caught in this trap by accident, he helped me carry my two suitcases, my box of books and Robert's guitar case down the stairs and out to the sidewalk. At least I wasn't being arrested and thrown in a paddy wagon with a bunch of whores, but what to do now?

As I stood on the sidewalk with the neighbors who'd gathered for the spectacle, I pondered my situation. I clutched my purse close to my body to make sure I hung onto the three-and-a-half dollars I had left. I decided I'd better get out of there before someone changed their mind about arresting me. Within the last 24 hours I had lost my job, my room, my food, and my new husband had come and gone. I began walking away with no clear destination, lugging my possessions as I went.

Early A.M. before dawn - Saturday, May 4, 1963

Slowly I dragged myself and my belongings down the narrow sidewalks of St. Charles Ave. The uneven concrete paths were hopelessly broken by the massive roots of ancient oak trees erupting from the earth. Their branches towered overhead and entwined with each other.

As the commotion of the raid disappeared into the distance, silence set in. The streets were empty. The leaves were still. Everywhere I looked were black shadows full of unknown dangers. What was next for me? Did I need to be beaten and raped to complete my initiation

into this strange city? I began to tremble with fear. Will the next bush or snarled tree be the one that the assailant springs from? Suddenly a cat leapt from the darkness and ran across my path with a growl. I shrieked and stumbled, falling to the sidewalk and scraping my knee. I rolled over and sat up on the sidewalk, digging the pieces of stone and dirt out of my knee. I started to cry. Forget about "Adventures in New Orleans"! I was alone, afraid, angry and miserable. I had never felt so vulnerable in my entire life. I needed a plan, and realized that panicking would not help my situation. It's time to focus, Judy!

I had heard about a 24-hour restaurant when I was at Dave Ferrie's party. That skinny little man named David Lewis said it was on St. Charles Avenue and that his wife worked the night shift on weekends. He had invited Lee to bring me there for some free pie. It was called Thompson's. And it was somewhere down these streetcar tracks. If I could just reach Thompson's, I could stay there until morning and then call Lee, since he was the only person I knew how to contact at that point. And I figured he owed me "big time," for getting me into this mess.

I thought about calling Lee immediately, demanding action. Maybe he could borrow his uncle's car and come get me. Maybe I could get curb-side service. But I hadn't seen a single pay phone in the residential neighborhood I trudged through. And what would the Murrets think of a strange young woman calling Lee in the middle of the night?

Dragging my possessions down St. Charles Avenue was slow going, frustrating and painful. Then I saw a streetcar coming down the track. I hadn't imagined that they ran all night. When I saw it, I galloped clumsily towards the next stop, burdened with two suitcases, a box of books and a guitar, but I couldn't reach it in time. The driver rolled past without even seeing me. I figured it would be at least an hour until another came along.

I continued on, pushing the box of books with my foot. Finally, the bottom broke. My frustration blossomed into anger. Robert! You clod! Why did you leave me here alone? And that devil of a landlady! I even thought about saying a prayer, but if there was a God, I didn't want to give him the satisfaction. Instead, I struggled on through the dark silence for what seemed forever, denouncing the people whose ignorance, selfishness and incompetence had conspired to confound me, while I denied my own part in creating this mess. Suddenly, a flash of hope! I saw the sign for St. George's Episcopal Church just ahead, on my side of the street. Next to the church was the rectory, where the pastor and his family lived. A light was on in one of the windows, and I saw a silhouette moving across it. Somebody was still awake!

With tears in my eyes, I knocked on the door. It slowly opened to reveal a small minister, with his wife behind him. She inspected me silently, then reached out and took the typewriter that weighed me down. I got about three steps inside before I collapsed on their floor and began to sob, heaping my fears and frustrations on this quiet couple. They listened patiently and consoled me, then fixed up a couch with sheets and a blanket, so I could get some rest. In the morning, everything would surely look better.

Saturday, May 4, 1963

Some time the next morning they woke me with a modest breakfast, just to get me started. I learned that the pastor had been up late writing a funeral sermon, and he believed God wanted me to listen to

some of it. The sermon was about Providence, and why we should trust in God. But right then I had no reason to trust anybody, so the sermon didn't reach me, though I promised to re-examine the reasons for my disbelief. By now, this kind couple had learned how I'd been evicted from my room during a police raid and that my husband was out of town, having "accidentally" neglected to leave his phone number. I anxiously showed them my marriage certificate, which finally convinced them of what I'd been through. At this moment, the pastor told me to call him "Father Bill," like everyone else.

Father Bill then mulled over what to do with me. Given my limited options, I suggested we call Lee. I gave Father Bill the Murrets' phone number and asked him to make the call on my behalf, since it would be awkward for a strange woman to call a married man asking for help. He did, and once he explained the situation Lee said he would be right there. My rescuer arrived by streetcar shortly before noon.

He was mortified to hear what had happened to me. "I was told the place was a haven for girls from out of town who needed a safe place to stay, not a den for prostitutes!" Lee said apologetically.

Certainly Mrs. Webber's posturing about morality had given both of us the impression that she would not tolerate any impropriety in her establishment. As nosy as the old bird was, she must have known what was going on within her domain. But what to make of her crazy comments about my "trying to attract business?" Was it an attempt to take my money, and get rid of me? Anyway, I had other problems to deal with.

St. Charles Street seen from inside church gates

Lee made such a good impression on Father Bill and his wife that they invited us to stay for lunch. We accepted their offer and as we ate, Lee talked sensibly about religion and politics, skillfully navigating those touchy issues so as not to offend anyone. They assumed he was just a college student.

Then Father Bill excused himself, saying he had to prepare for a funeral later in the day. He retired to his study and left Lee to make phone calls in order to find me a place to live. After several attempts, someone called back. It was an elderly woman who had known Lee since he was a child. Now she was a widow. She had converted the front half of her modest wood-frame house into an apartment and was willing to rent it to a nice couple. The address was 1032 Marengo Street.

Mrs. Richardson, Father Bill's wife, said that Marengo Street was close by. It crossed St. Charles about five blocks from their church, and the neighborhood in that direction was "acceptable." I was encouraged. Mrs. Richardson then drove us down St. Charles Avenue, turned toward the river at Marengo Street, and stopped on the curb after several blocks.

As we rode, Lee explained several benefits of this location. First, it was not far from Dr. Sherman's apartment, perhaps even within walking distance. Second, it was less than two blocks from Magazine Street with convenient access to its bus, which went to the Central Business District and the French Quarter. I was just glad I would have a safe place to sleep.

The moment we arrived at 1032 Marengo, a little old lady came out to greet us. She immediately gave Lee a big hug, like she was welcoming home a long-lost son. She then scolded him lovingly for having been gone too long. He told her he intended to visit her soon and often, since he would be living nearby on Magazine Street.

The little old lady was Susie Hanover. Susie's late husband Billy Hanover had once been a stevedore on the docks of New Orleans.[1] Apparently her husband knew Lee's uncle Dutz Murret and his friend Carlos Marcello from the early days when the three worked together on the docks. By now, I was resigned to the fact that everybody I met in New Orleans had some kind of connection with Carlos Marcello.

My new home was small and bright, with a big bedroom, a living room and hall, and a big bathroom with no bathtub. The bathtub was smack in the middle of Susie's kitchen. This was an old house and, long ago, water was heated on the stove and poured into the tub. Now, an overhead pipe diverted water from the ceiling into a showerhead aimed straight down. A shower curtain provided privacy. I told Lee I wasn't concerned about the location of the tub. It would be fine.

Lee apologized again for the events at Mrs. Webber's boarding house, promising "I'll get your money back." Meanwhile, Lee gave Susie twenty dollars as partial payment on the rent. I also had no food, nor any money to buy it. Lee assured me he would take care of that, too, and that I should not worry. "I'm not going to let you go through any more hell," he told me. "Now it's my turn to watch out for you." I wondered if he really meant it.

1032 Marengo was a sunny, cheerful little cottage, and it felt a whole lot more like home than that big stuffy mansion with the crazy landlady. Susie was as sweet as can be and lived in the back half of the building. My portion had the front porch and the front door. There was also an entry on the side which led either back to Susie's or forward to my place, depending on which way you turned. Susie and I shared access to the kitchen, the bathtub, and the phone. Susie also had a dog named "Collie" who immediately accepted Lee and me as family, but alertly protected her from strangers.

It was time for me to settle into my new home. As I unpacked, Lee got some groceries. But when he returned he left promptly, saying he had to do some things for Dave and Banister, and would call me later.

Evening, Saturday, May 4, 1963

Lee called and said Dave had asked him to handle some lab orders. He was unfamiliar with the terminology and wanted to tap my medical expertise to make sure he was marking off the right items. While his call was all business, he did take the opportunity to mention how helpful it would be if I would finally decide to run Dave's lab. I told Lee that Robert was going to be gone for weeks at a time, and everything was different now.

"What?" he guffawed, then commented that I was going to have some lonely nights ahead of me, adding that his own wife and child would be arriving soon.

"Get some sleep," he concluded. "I'll check on you later."

The apartment was small and had a very pretty bed, with hand-sewn quilts and carved wooden bedposts. There were two tall windows in the bedroom, which made the room sunny and bright.

Between the late night sessions at Dave Ferrie's and Robert's persistent demands, my sleep had been erratic for days and I felt sick. So I slept, as Lee suggested. Meanwhile, Susie made a big pot of homemade soup. Finally, I took a nice, long bath. Robert Baker seemed to be a million miles away. Well, fine! Life was starting to look appealing again, even though he wasn't in it.

Lee returned later that evening. He had picked up a discarded newspaper on the bus and offered to read to me about the raids that had been going on all over town. We sat together on the edge of the bed and went through the newspaper, looking for information on the raid at the Mansion. However, there had been several raids and only one story mentioned St. Charles, listing a different address. For some reason, the raid at my house had not been reported. At least, not in the articles.

"The reporters were probably spread too thin last night," Lee commented, noting that he had picked up some gossip about the raids from the Murrets, since they knew some of the people involved.

As I ironed some clothes on Susie's breakfast table, Lee gave me his take. The raids were just a sham. The police regularly put on a big show for the benefit of the public, but nothing much ever came of it. The same brothels and strip joints would re-open soon afterwards, and the money flow never stopped.

Only the girls suffered, by getting into debt to their lawyers or "boyfriends" who sprung them from jail. Things would return to normal, if what went on in New Orleans could ever be called "normal." As I ironed, Lee noticed that my strength was fading. Ever since my miscarriage I lacked stamina. Hearing my tired sigh, Lee got up. "You've been standing long enough," he said. He took the iron from me, and finished my clothes with precision. It's 'women's work' to most men, but Marines are trained to take care of their own uniforms.

When he was finished, he sat beside me on the edge of the bed and read to me as I rested. First, he read an article in which District Attorney Jim Garrison called Cuba's leader Fidel Castro a 'Soviet pawn.' Then he found an article entitled "Prober's Work Nets Arrests: Collegiate-Looking Undercover Man Scores." We read the article twice.

"Here's the answer!" Lee declared. "This is how I can get the attention I need."

Lee explained that he needed to be able to enter Cuba; therefore later in the summer he needed to appear to be pro-Castro. Banister was running him as an anti-Castro/anti-Communist conservative. How would he change his image 180 degrees? He would need publicity to make the switch and convince people that he was really pro-Castro. Lee read the article out loud:

PROBER'S WORK NETS ARRESTS

Collegiate-Looking Undercover Man Scores

The collegiate-looking son of a wealthy Scarsdale, N.Y., advertising executive is the undercover officer who made 145 illegal purchases for the police narcotic division.

He is John H. Phillips, a 23-year-old, clean cut young man, who looks like he could be on a senior debating team or an executive trainee on Wall Street.

For 21 months, he investigated illegal traffic in narcotics, barbiturates and amphetamines in New Orleans and nearby parishes.

He got into a fight at 6 a.m. one day on Bourbon St. to try to prove he was on the wrong side of the law—

BEATEN BY THREE

He won that one, but was badly beaten in February by three men, one of whom he was in-

"The collegiate-looking son of a wealthy Scarsdale, New York, advertising executive is the undercover officer who made 145 illegal purchases for the police narcotics division. He is John H. Phillips...a 23-year old, clean-cut young man..."

Lee broke off, and smiled. "I'm also twenty-three," he said. "And I'm clean-cut, too." He then resumed reading the rest of the article aloud:

"... For 21 months, he investigated illegal traffic in narcotics, barbiturates, and amphetamines in New Orleans and nearby parishes. He got into a fight at 6 a.m. one day on Bourbon St. to try to prove he was on the wrong side of the law..."

Lee chimed in his approval, insisting that this was the way to proceed. He and Banister were making plans to lure pro-Castroites to places where their names could be recorded and photos made: they planned to hand out pro-Castro pamphlets in highly public places, making sure photos would be taken by the TV media, which would be pre-warned.

"If I can create a pro-Castro 'incident' with TV cameras there," Lee said, smiling, "I'll make a good impression." It seemed like a good idea to me, too, until Lee read on: "Beaten by Three... [Phillips] won that [fight], but was badly beaten in February by three men..."

I broke in. "Oh, no, Lee! Don't even consider it!"

"Oh, I'd make sure they would secretly be my friends, don't worry!" Lee said. "I don't want to get 'badly beaten.' Maybe just a punch in the nose. That would do."[2]

Suddenly I realized how much I cared about this man sitting next to me. I did not want to see any harm come to him. I was married to Robert, who cared mostly about money and a good time in bed. I was just a necessary component for half of that equation. And he wanted to make me go back to Gainesville to support him through graduate school so he could sit around and study, instead of continuing my own education in New Orleans. My bitterness and frustrations were easy for Lee to see.

"Did you tell him about your plans to go to Tulane Medical School?" Lee asked quietly with a puzzled look.

"No, I didn't get a chance to tell him. He cut off the conversation as soon as I mentioned the possibility of getting a job at PenChem in Gainesville."

Lee smiled. "You mean, you didn't tell him anything about Ochsner?"

"No," I said. "He thinks I'm still working at Royal Castle. A̶
concerns him is that I have a job. And now he's gone, for ten days a̶
least." I let my exasperation show in my voice and in my crossed arms.
"He made me so mad I stopped speaking to him."

"So, he's without a clue about everything that's happened?" Lee
asked carefully. I sensed that Lee was referring to issues involving David Ferrie, Guy Banister and the get-Castro project.

"Yes, and unless he asks directly," I said firmly, "I've decided never
to volunteer a word about it. He's going to get a taste of the same medicine he gave me. He deserves it."

"That's good news," Lee said, realizing that the choice of slaving for
Robert or pursuing my medical career was no contest. Moreover, Lee
saw that I was finally angry enough to make my own decisions instead
of listening to Robert.

"So you might consider taking a cover job with me, at Reily's?" Lee
ventured. That's how Lee was going to provide income for his family
which he could account for, so he could do his clandestine work with
no questions asked.

"I might," I replied calmly and with a smile. With that, I finally
threw in the towel: "It looks like Dave Ferrie might get his wish after
all." And with that sentence, I agreed to participate in the Ferrie-Sher-
man-Ochsner plan to develop a biological weapon to kill Fidel Castro.
I had bought in. The die was cast.

Lee told me that tomorrow, after Mass, he had to have lunch with
the Murrets, but he would come over as soon as he could. Then he
encouraged me to get more rest and left.

----

1. Susie's grand-daughter told me that her grandfather went on to become a merchant marine
   and a ship captain. That he knew Lee's uncle and Marcello was clear to me, but his relationship
   with them may have been personal and not business. I have no reason to assume that Billy
   Hanover was part of the Mafia.

2. I would always remember this remark, made to me on May 4, because three months later, on
   August 9th, three anti-Castro Cubans, among them Carlos Bringuier, would accost Lee in a
   staged fight – inspired by this very news article.

PERIOD ENDING	HOURS	RATE	GROSS EARNED	F.I.C.A.	FEDERAL INCOME TAX	STATE INCOME TAX	FOOD	UNIFORMS	HOSPITAL INSURANCE	ADVANCES	TOTAL DEDUCTED	MISC.	NET PAY
163 24	100	14.00	.53	.30		.30					1 13		12.87
	EARNINGS	*				DEDUCTIONS							

DETACH BEFORE DEPOSITING   ROYAL CASTLE SYSTEM, INC. – NEW ORLEANS, LOUISIANA

Stub from my last Royal Castle paycheck.
I worked mornings, an average of 2-3 hours/day at one dollar per hour.

NOTE: Locations are circa 1963

Ochsner Clinic & Hospital

Town & Country Mot...
Royal Castle

Dr. Ochsner's House

Crippled Children's Hospital

U.S. Public Health Service Hospital

Judyth's "Mansion" Apt.

Tulane U.

Loyola U.

Palmer Park

Ferries's Mouse House

Judyth's Apt.

Lee Oswald's Apt.

Ferries's Apt.

Dr. Mary's Apt.

Tulane Medical School

City Center

Rev. Jim's

Teen Oswald Home

Banister's Office

Intl. Trade Mart

Sho-Bar

YWCA

Charity Hospital

INCA

500 Club

Royal Orleans Hotel

Reily Coffee

Customs House

MISSISSIPPI

CHAPTER 11

THE PROJECT

Sunday, May 5, 1963

Awakening next morning, I lay half-dreaming in the pretty new bed at 1032 Marengo St., musing how events of the past week had turned everything upside-down. Though Lee Oswald had led me to The Mansion and its miserable outcome, he had also stepped forward and made up for it by finding this little cottage and paying a third of the rent. Surely the rush of affection I felt, just thinking of him, was due not only to his generosity, but also because I felt abandoned by Robert, who had not only hidden the news that he'd be living apart from me, but also had refused to tell me how to contact him. The scrap of paper that represented our marriage was just a birth control pill generator. As Lee had said, when I first met him: "Love — unto the death!" didn't seem to apply to Robert A. Baker, III.

I got up and got dressed. Susie said a "housewarming gift" had arrived from somebody in Marcello's family. It was a big loop of sausage and a medium-sized wheel of cheese — enough food for a week.

Before long, Lee arrived and escorted me to David Ferrie's apartment. We caught the bus on Louisiana Avenue and quickly plunged into an impoverished black neighborhood. At the far end of Louisiana Avenue was Claiborne Avenue, where a branch split off to the left, becoming a smaller street named Louisiana Avenue Parkway.[1] This is where David Ferrie lived. Its close proximity to a ghetto was rather alarming to me, but side-by-side opulence and squalor is one of the things that give New Orleans its unique personality.

Today, Lee and I met with Dave Ferrie to go over the "Project," as he called it. Dave explained that the makeshift lab in his apartment was actually part of a sophisticated network of laboratories strung across uptown New Orleans, each with different equipment and performing a different function, but all united by a common goal: to develop a cancer weapon and kill Fidel Castro.

The configuration of these labs was basically a circular process which repeated itself over and over. With each lap around the loop of laboratories, the cancer-causing viruses would become more aggressive, and more deadly. Originally, these viruses came from monkeys, but they had been enhanced with radiation. The virus we were most concerned with was SV40, the infamous carcinogenic virus that had contaminated the polio vaccines of the 1950s. But the science of the day was not terribly precise, and cross-infection between species was common in the monkey labs. So it was impossible to know if we were working with SV40 only, or a collection of viruses.

We assumed there were probably other viruses traveling with it, but whether it was SV40 or SV37 or SIV did not really matter to us. What mattered was whether it produced cancer quickly. For our project, these cancer-causing viruses had been transferred to mice because they were more economical than monkeys, and the viruses thrived just as easily, which is why mice are so widely used in medical research.

This loop included a large colony of thousands of mice kept in a house near Dave Ferrie's apartment. I called it "the Mouse House." People connected to the Project handled the daily care and feeding of the mice, and bred them to replace the population which was constantly being consumed. Several times each week, fifty or so live mice would be selected based upon the apparent size of their tumors. These mice  had tumors so large that they were visible to the naked eye. They would be placed in a cardboard box and quietly brought through the back door of Dave's house for processing. Once in Dave's kitchen, we would kill the mice with ether and harvest their tumors. Harvesting meant cutting their bodies open and excising the largest tumors. The tumors were then weighed, and their weights recorded in a journal. The odor was terrible.

The largest of the harvested tumors — the most aggressive cancers — had a destiny. We first cut very thin slices from these tumors and examined them under a microscope. We had to be sure what kind of tumor we had, in each case. Bits of the "best" tumors were selected for individual treatment: each specimen was macerated, strained, mixed with RPMI medium, then poured into a carefully labeled test-tube. These were placed in Dave's table centrifuge, and spun. Most cancer cells went to the bottom. The liquid on top was poured into a big flask, then more RPMI medium, with fetal calf serum, and sometimes other materials, was added to each test tube. These were the beginnings of tissue cultures, to be grown elsewhere. The test tubes were then placed

Alley access to Ferrie's back door

David Ferrie's Apartment
3330 Louisana Ave. Parkway

Louisiana Ave. Parkway

Ferrie's "Mouse House"
3225 Louisana Ave. Parkway

in a rack in a warm, insulated box. The rest of the tumors, from which these cultures had been started, along with the liquids in the big flask, were poured into Dave's cooled-down Waring blender (container was chilled in the refrigerator). The result was a "soup" you'd never want for dinner. Filtering the "soup" created a "cell-free" filtrate labeled to correspond to the tissue cultures and slides. The liquid, full of cancer causing viruses, was placed into a cooler with ice. The tissue cultures and the cell-free filtrate were now ready for the next lab. We called this "The Product."

The next lab was in Dr. Sherman's apartment, where she would examine the slides under a microscope. There, the world-famed oncologist and surgeon selected the most promising examples and took them to another lab on Prytania Street, where she used a more powerful microscope to examine the cells in exquisite detail.[2] I never went to the Prytania Street lab myself, but I was told that it had an electron microscope.

Once Dr. Sherman had determined which samples showed the most promise, she would take them to yet another lab in uptown New Orleans, where the carcinogenic viruses would be exposed to high-voltage radiation, in hopes of mutating them. You can't predict whether the genetic damage done to the virus will make it stronger or weaker, so it is an imprecise step. But once these newly enhanced viruses are allowed to "work," the question answers itself. The stronger ones quickly become cancerous, and the weaker ones do not.

Our goal was to find aggressive cancers that produced fast-growing tumors. So these mutated monkey viruses were put into tissue cultures to establish themselves, and the most aggressive of these cancers were brought back to the Mouse House to be injected into newborn 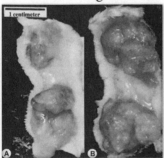 mice, whose immature immune system was incapable of fighting off the cancer. There, a new generation of tumors grew quickly. These mice remained in the Mouse House until their tumors were large enough to be harvested. Then batches of them were brought across the street to Dave's apartment where "The Process" started all over again, making the cancers more aggressive with each generation. It was an endless loop.

Precisely what these mutated monkey viruses had become after exposure to the radiation, nobody knew. All that mattered was whether they produced cancer. But the Project had gotten bogged down because the cancers were not transferring successfully back into primates. And if they did not work in primates, they probably wouldn't work on humans, like Fidel Castro.

The other problem was that the new cancers were getting dang ous to handle, and somebody with specialized training had to take over at David Ferrie's lab, for everybody's safety. That's where I came in. The training I had received at Roswell Park Cancer Institute, and the melanoma experiments I had quietly conducted for Dr. Ochsner at St. Francis and at UF, gave me the right credentials. My innocent teenage girl pose made me an ideal candidate for this secret cancer work.

Another part of the job was based on my speed-reading skills. I would read and digest cutting-edge cancer research, and pass the most promising ideas and methods on to Drs. Ochsner and Sherman with my comments. They would then decide which of my recommendations to implement. To get me started, Dave handed me a foot-high stack of papers, and more kept coming on a regular basis. Keeping up with the constant storm of material occupied many of my "idle hours."

As I read these documents, I was not surprised to see that Ochsner's friends, including Drs. Moore, Grace, Mirand, and others at Roswell Park, were working on related subjects. There were also papers from colleagues at Sloan-Kettering, M.D. Anderson, and the University of Chicago, as well as a few papers from Japan and Germany. Most of these articles were culled from conferences and journals, but some were unpublished.

Lee's part in this effort was also important. Besides helping me get set up in an apartment and a cover job, he told me that he was with the anti-Castro Cuban community in part to determine which medical contacts could be trusted in Cuba.[3] The plan was for Lee to infiltrate Cuba and deliver the bioweapon to friendly doctors. To that end, he needed to learn how to keep the tissues alive during transport to Mexico, and then on to Cuba.

Nothing about the Project, its people, methods, or materials was to be written down. So Lee would have to learn the medical jargon and techniques from me over the next few months, memorize the technical information needed to use the weapon, and transfer that information to others orally. In addition, he had to perform other duties for Guy Banister, as well as pretending to have a job, so he was quite busy most of the time.

Dave and I talked about my schedule. I would come to Dave's apartment on Wednesdays, Thursdays and Fridays. As long as I left before Dave got home from work, I would not run into anybody. Mice would come and go, but since they were all identical (white with red eyes) who would notice that they were actually different batches? Dave said that he dreaded writing the reports, so I told him to bring it on, noting that I had nothing else to do at night.

"I don't have a TV set," I explained. "Not even a radio. Since Lee will be busy at night with his family, and Robert isn't going to be around, I'm free to write reports."

Tired from all he'd been going through the last few days, Lee had been sleeping on the couch while Dave briefed me on the Project. Just then Lee got up, yawned, and sat down at the table with Dave and me.

"No TV or radio, huh?" he said to me. "So, what would you like to do today? Besides make love to me?"

"Gee, that's a hard question!" I replied. "Why would I want to do anything else? How about horseback riding? It's been a year."

"I like horses, too," Lee said. "Let's do it."

Dave told Lee where two different stables were located, noting they were fairly expensive.

"Well, then, we'll only go riding one hour," Lee told him. "After that, we'll just play chess." He got up and snatched a board from one of Dave's cluttered shelves. "Do you have an extra set of chess pieces?" he asked, folding the board under his arm.

"I have Robert's medieval chess set," I offered.

Dave, who didn't want us to leave, said "They ride the horses into the ground on the weekends. Why don't you go in the middle of the week, when they won't be tired?"

Reluctantly, we sat down again.

"Do you know why the queen is the major playing piece in chess?" Dave asked. "Why isn't it the king, as one would expect?" These were the kind of intriguing questions Dave would throw at us, out of nowhere. He then went into a long explanation about the Indian and Persian origins of the game. Suddenly, he stopped short.

"Chess!" he said, looking at Lee "That's the key! They're using chess terms in our code names. As if we're in a colossal chess game."

Lee raised an eyebrow. "I have to think about that," he said. "In Russia," he commented, "my keys involved a queen, three cards, and an opera's libretto."

Lee said he had been required to memorize an entire opera by Tchaikovsky called *The Queen of Spades* (*Pikova Dama* in Russian), based on a short story by Pushkin. Lee liked the opera very much, but had grown indifferent after having to memorize it for contact purposes. I had never heard of it, so Lee promised to read the original Pushkin to me from a little gray book he had, to help me appreciate the libretto. I'll never forget that little gray book; Lee read to me from it on several occasions.[4]

That evening, the last we would spend all night at Dave's house, Lee and I sat, spellbound, as Ferrie's encyclopedic knowledge once again captivated us.

After an hour or so of philosophical lecture, Dave showed us how to fetch his two young Cuban helpers by phone. They arrived within minutes, bringing in a new batch of mice. These boys were poor, and knew little English, but they were diligent and dedicated. Miguel and Carlos also did lab cleanup work, such as autoclaving, cleaning flasks, and incinerating mice. Usually only one came, but this first time, we met both. After caging the mice, Dave said, "Watch this demonstration of hypnosis." He gestured toward the boys: within seconds, both collapsed onto the couch, in a trancelike state. Dave admitted he took advantage of them sexually when they were hypnotized, but also when they were not; they seemed to enjoy Dave's company.

Under hypnosis, the older boy, Carlos, went immediately into a snoring sleep. Miguel was told to stand up, and I thought he was awake, but he obeyed Dave's order to steal a dollar bill from my purse right in front of me. It was the last dollar I had, so I was anxious to get it back. Dave told Miguel I couldn't see the dollar, and amazingly, the boy behaved as if this was true, denying he had taken a thing while waving the bill up and down.

"He'd walk right off a fifty-story building if I told him to," Dave said. "But people resist bad suggestions unless they're really brainwashed."

After the boys left, I declared that weak minds might be hypnotized like that, but not strong ones. Dave laughed, saying it was easier to hypnotize smart people, because 70% of them would agree to turn off the more rational left side of the brain. The smarter and more creative the subject, he said, the greater the chance they'd allow their right brain to take control, making hypnosis easier.

Dave then asked permission to hypnotize us, with interesting re sults. Dave worked awhile with Lee, but was unable to get him to cooperate. Finally, in frustration, he commented, "Why don't you trust me?"

Lee laughed, reminding Dave that perhaps he still had some deep inner fears of Dave, so he would always resist hypnosis from him. Dave said Lee's imagination was deficient and that was the reason he wasn't "going under." I disagreed. I had read a science fiction story that Lee had been writing at my apartment, and it clearly displayed his creativity and imagination.

I then offered to allow Dave to hypnotize me. "Go ahead, Captain," I told him, seating myself before him. "Have fun."

What Dave didn't know is that my sister Lynda and I had practiced hypnosis on each other for years. I knew the drill. For some minutes, Dave struggled to take me down. Once he thought I was under his control, he ordered me to do a few absurd tasks, such as to rub the top of my head. I complied.

"See?" Dave told Lee. "Women's minds are more flexible, they are more receptive to suggestions, because they are more verbally oriented. Now watch this," Dave said, "and don't jump on me when I do it."

"Be nice to her!" Lee said, uneasily, seeing that Dave had brought out a large hatpin.

"I only wish to demonstrate that, in this state, she can feel no pain," Dave said. "J," he said to me gently, "I am going to stick this needle into your arm, but you damned well will not feel it. Hold out your left arm, please."

Oh, brother! I extended my left arm and Dave pushed the hatpin into my flesh like he was giving me an injection. Having been poked a thousand times during my long stay in the hospital, I had learned to tolerate the pain of needles. I didn't move.

"See?" Dave said, triumphantly. "Why don't they use this for childbirth? Think how this could help women. Do not move," he told me. Taking up a Polaroid camera, Dave snapped a picture of the thing in my arm. But I'd had enough. As soon as he lowered the camera, I said, "I thought you weren't going to use 'damn' in my presence anymore!" With that, I pulled out the hatpin and rubbed the sore spot on my arm,

"Damn!" Dave repeated, oblivious to the irony of his comment. As Lee realized what I had done, he began to smile.

"Why be so violent?" I complained, finding some alcohol and cotton. "You didn't even swab my arm first. I could get tetanus from that old needle."

I explained that I not only had prior experience resisting hypnosis,

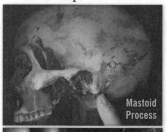

Mastoid Process

I'd gone through months of round-the-clock intravenous feedings, penicillin shots, blood tests and spinal taps, so that I'd learned to ignore the pain of needles long ago. "But if you had tickled me with a feather, I wouldn't have been able to keep a straight face," I admitted.

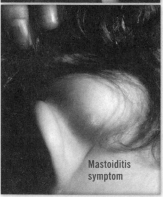

Mastoiditis symptom

Lee then recounted his own horrific hospital experience from his youth, when he endured an operation on the mastoid process — a part of the skull that juts down behind the ear. Infections in bone are extremely painful, and in the 1940s operations to cut away the infected bone resulted in agony for days. Such experiences stay with children, and help them understand suffering in a way others cannot.

Dave was defeated. His attempts to hypnotize us had failed. Trying to regain some of his former stature, Dave said he wanted to show us something special and brought out a black light. He invited us to follow him into the bathroom. He closed the door, turned off the overhead light, and switched on the ultraviolet lamp. There we saw the germs, mold, microscopic flora and fauna thriving in Dave's filthy bathroom. All of it splashing to life in hideous color.

"I can get any hospital closed down for unsanitary conditions," Dave said. "Just take a black light and go in with sanitation inspectors. They use the same bucket of dirty water over and over, and just spread the germs around."

I was horrified to see rivers of yellow stains flowing in the toilet, with splotches of orange bacteria on the toilet seat. I immediately resolved never to sit on Dave's toilet again. From then on, Lee and I avoided Dave's bathroom as much as possible.

"You think this is bad?" Dave crowed. "You should see what's on a public toilet seat. They think Howard Hughes is nuts because he takes Kleenex everywhere to handle doorknobs. But he knows what regular light won't show you. He saw all this stuff with a black light."

Dave continued to expound on the benefits of ultra-violet light, saying that it could kill anthrax, tuberculosis, even the black mold that stubbornly plagues ships and 'sick' houses. "People don't know how to kill black mold, and some die from it," he said. "But if they kill that stuff with acetone or mineral spirits, then they can use a black light every few weeks to finish off any new stuff that shows up. I use this lamp to kill whatever crud the mice are bringing in here," he said. "I do have my housekeeping standards." Lee and I looked at each other and smiled: we had never noticed any!

We returned to the table and Dave brought out a variety of things for us to view under the black light. He presented a horse tooth, fossils, seashells, and rock samples, like fluorite and uranium. Dave also brought out three rings: an aquamarine ring that he said belonged to his mother, a small ruby ring that glowed purple under the light, and one carved with an ugly mythological creature.

"This is my priestly ring," he said. "I use it for black magic. And Satanic rituals."

"Are you serious?" I said, taking up the exotic ring.

"Of course not," Dave replied. "When I say a Mass, and sometimes I do say a Mass, it isn't a Black Mass. I'm not a son of Satan, so I wouldn't wear that thing. I love God. But I use things like this to penetrate religious cults. I can go into certain places around here with that ring on, and they think I'm one of them."

Dave said he knew about every religion on earth and had witnessed the rites of Voodoo and Santeria.[5] In fact, his interest in hypnotism came from observing religious oddities, like speaking in tongues, chanting, and rosary prayers, which had essentially the same result. They hypnotized the participants to make their minds more pliable. The drugs used in Voodoo were of particular interest to him. Eventually, Dave said, he was asked to participate in a study of hypnosis secretly conducted at Tulane by the CIA.

Dave said he made friends with some of the professors at Tulane by bringing in young test subjects they could experiment on, and that he even taught a couple of classes for Dr. Heath, who was working with the CIA on a secret program investigating mind control.

The CIA, Dave explained, was intrigued by the legends of zombies. Under the influence of drugs, these people became slaves without a will. "I became a consultant," he said. "At first it was with Voodoo drugs. Later, it was hypnosis."

Then Dave showed us a large, olive-colored metal container with a lock on it. As he opened the box, he said that if we ever heard he committed suicide, not to believe it, because he was a Catholic. When I told him I felt the same way, Lee remarked that the right to commit suicide should be an individual decision, but Ferrie snapped back and they began arguing about suicide.

"What's in the box?" I asked.

After extracting a promise from us never to describe its contents while he lived, Dave showed us. There was his will, some letters, photos, religious cards and post cards.

At the bottom was a fat brown file wrapped with a black cord knotted in front. Dave opened this file. Inside, the pages were stamped TOP SECRET. Because of my position at the table, I could only see the pages upside down. They were held at the top with fold-over spindles going through two holes. All the pages were stamped and signed. These were MK-ULTRA files. With the files was a report, also stamped and signed, that Dave pointed to proudly. His name was not on the report – just a number.

"This is based on my dissertation about hypnosis and retinitis," Dave confided. "What a crock! My 'dissertation' to get my 'doctorate' was a cover for my real work: logging responses of the size of the pupil in our hypnosis experiments."

He added that the size of the pupil could tell a lot about what a person was really thinking, and would even indicate if they were really hypnotized. Dave said he had helped the CIA link pupil size-changes to truth-telling

"I shouldn't have told you to close your eyes so much," Dave said to me. "I should have looked at your pupil sizes, and checked their responses."

"Why didn't you do that, Dave?" Lee asked.

Dave shook his head. "I find myself avoiding looking directly into people's eyes much anymore, ever since my hair started falling out." Dave's mood suddenly changed with this admission. He abruptly carried the box back to his room, and then got himself a beer. Despite the late hour, he had more to tell us about mind control and the experiments on people, frequently without their knowledge. Yes, American citizens were being used as guinea pigs by their own government.

"They tell people the program is shut down now," Dave said, "but that's not so. It just has a different name. These things never die. It's an iron-clad law that it takes more energy to stop a government program than to start one. This one's self-perpetuating."[6]

I sat down at the piano and started to play, as the two men talked and drank beer. Lee had been down some mind-twisting avenues himself: he had been taught passive non-resistance techniques to avoid releasing information, and through severe, stressful training, had learned how to resist harsh interrogations. He was prepared for capture and torture when he entered Russia. Visions of what Tony Lopez-Fresquet had told me came before my eyes. I better understood what a big chance Lee took when he entered the Soviet Union. The Soviets were aware of the existence of a CIA training center at Atsugi, hidden in former Japanese bunkers. They would surely suspect Lee of being a spy. So how did he manage to survive?

Lee Oswald, USMC

When Dave went to the bathroom, Lee handed me his beer can. "See how much I drank!" he said, smiling. "I saw how you looked at me," he went on. "You were thinking about your father. Beer doesn't taste half bad, you know. But I rarely actually drink it. I gave the stuff up."

The can was almost full. I would never have guessed!

Then Lee told me how he got himself thrown into the brig by pouring beer over a Marine sergeant's head. He said the act was a necessary part of his cover to prove his "hatred" of the Marines.

Lee said he'd believed the odds of his leaving Russia alive were about 50/50. And, if he did make it out, his own boss might have him arrested. Lee said his name was "Jesus," letting the irony speak for itself.[7]

"He'd wonder how I survived," he told me. "Maybe wonder if I became a traitor."

Lee said he had carefully planned everything, though, to prove he wasn't a turncoat.

Lee and I were tired and wanted to leave. We both needed sleep before another challenging day, but Dave said he had one more piece of instruction to give us. David Lewis, he explained, had been recruited to help Lee. We should, therefore, cultivate a social friendship with David Lewis and his wife Anna, so they could meet without Jack Martin getting involved.

Lewis had agreed to this and would be paid for his services, provided Jack Martin was kept in the dark.[8] David Lewis' role was to get information about Cubans arriving on buses from Mexico and pass it on to Lee, so he could hunt down potential Pro-Castro infiltrators coming into the United States. For this reason, David's temporary job handling luggage at the Trailways bus station was expanded.

"More Cuban refugees use Trailways than Greyhound to get here, because it's the cheaper of the two bus lines," Dave explained. "And infiltrators like to pose as just another poor refugee seeking asylum."

Dave said the real refugees brought all the possessions they could cram in their suitcases. Those who came with half-empty suitcases probably intended to return to Cuba, bearing American goods that had become scarce since the near-total embargo imposed by Kennedy in 1962.

"Car parts, you name it," Dave said. "That's how they make money behind the blockade. Those guys are probably harmless, but some might be pro-Castro spies."

David Lewis would get names from tags and tickets, and provide general descriptions of all Cubans he discovered with underweight baggage.

"By the way, Marcello will also be getting our information," Dave said. "In some cases, Marcello will take care of some of these characters himself, for his good friend, Santo Trafficante." Dave hastened to say that Marcello rarely killed these people. He preferred to ruin their reputations so they'd return to Cuba in disgrace. One method was to have a cooperative police officer plant drugs on the suspicious Cuban, arrest him for drug possession, jail him awhile, have him beaten up, and then deport him.

Dave said we would soon meet his illustrious friend, Mr. Lambert, who had worked with Dr. Ochsner for years on his Latin American dealings. Lambert would make use of the information that Ochsner secretly learned from Latin American leaders who sought his services as their emergency physician.

"There is no man in the United States with closer ties to both Latin American leaders and the CIA than Ochsner," Dave said. "He's the go-between, the doctor for all those big names the CIA wants to control. Dr. O's a tough bird," Dave added, "but he's naïve as a kid about what he's gotten himself into. Still, he's feisty, always ready to pass information back and forth for the CIA."

As for himself, Dave warned us clearly: "If anybody ever asks you if I have anything to do with anti-Castro matters anymore, the answer is always "No." If anybody asks you if I have ever been associated with the CIA, the answer is always "No." You can say I help out the FBI from time to time. That's okay. But to my boys, and everybody else, I'm just a sex fiend, a drinking buddy, and a pilot. Let's keep it that way. As far as my friends know, these mice are the same white mice, day in, day out, for some nutty project of my own."

Dave said he would make concessions so that I would feel safe doing my work in his apartment. First, he said he wasn't going to have any more parties for a couple of months, so we could get the project on a faster track. Secondly, his new room-mate would only be there on weekends, and when college classes ended, he would "go home to Mama." And then Dave reminded me that if my husband ever showed up again, he should never know about my connection to Dave's apartment. "Robert's sure to return," I said bitterly. "He'll show up eventually, because he can't go without his lovin' too long." Robert still had not written. I could have been dead and buried by now!

By now, I knew what Robert's priorities would be after several weeks at sea. As his new wife and "lovey-dovey," the sequence of events was all too predictable. "But this time," I told Lee and Dave, "If he won't let me have any rest, I'm going to dump a bag of ice cubes on the hottest part of his anatomy. Maybe then he'll cool off enough so we can actually talk!" They both laughed.

When Lee took me home, it was shortly before dawn. Collie barked a few times as we arrived. Susie hushed her. When I realized that we had woken her up, I told Susie I was sorry. She explained that she had spent years rising at an ungodly hour and feeding her husband a solid breakfast before he went to work on the docks. We sat at the kitchen table as she served us a breakfast of ham, eggs, and fresh squeezed orange juice. Lee closed his eyes as he finished, leaning back and smiling happily. He was in heaven. Susie beamed. "I have no one to cook for anymore," she said, adding that her children rarely came to her house since she had started renting out the front.

"I'm glad to rent to a girl," she added. "The last two were men, and they didn't pay me."

"If this girl doesn't pay, let me know," Lee told her. "I'll send a hit-man over."

"Very funny!" I replied. "I see you need another beating!"

"I see you're never going to find out if Adam and Eve got away!" Lee replied, grinning. It was now morning, and we were exhausted.

"I wonder if Robert sent a letter," I mumbled, so sleepy that Lee and Susie guided me to my bed, where I collapsed, too tired to undress.

"I'm leaving now," I heard Lee tell Susie. "But I might be back. I'm going to try to intercept the mail at Mrs. Webber's place around 10:00. If he wrote, it will ease her mind."

"Why don't you just stay, Lee?" Susie suggested. "You can sleep on my couch until it's time to check the mail." He admitted it would be good to sleep and headed for the couch.

I was drifting off. Almost asleep, I noticed that Susie was taking off my shoes. "Can I do the dishes for you? " I offered in a dreamy voice.

"Goodness, no, child," she answered. "Sleep now!"

"Do you know why we were out so late, Susie?" I asked her.

Susie paused. "I learned a long time ago not to ask what Bill had to do to get along with the people here in New Orleans," she finally answered.

"This isn't about Carlos Marcello and his people," I told her. "Lee is a very brave man ... trying to help our country. He is working for our government ... but because he is also connected to Marcello through his uncle Dutz, he can go places and find out things that regular agents can't."

"Oh! I hope you don't get hurt!" Susie said.

"I'm not out there risking my neck like Lee is," I mumbled. "I just do lab stuff. But I sure owe a lot to him, for finding this lovely place. And I owe a lot to you." I gave Susie's hand a squeeze and said, "Thanks for letting me stay here."

"You can stay as long as you want," Susie answered, leaning down and kissing me on my forehead. "Now go to sleep, honey," she whispered. "I'll wake Lee when it's time."

Monday , May 6, 1963

The next morning I heard a tap-tap-tap that was now becoming familiar. Lee was standing there with a big smile on his face, holding four flower pots full of begonias. I let him in.

"Good morning, Juduffki," he said cheerily. "I decided you needed these." He went to the window, which stared at a bleak wooden wall of the house next door.

"This will help brighten things up," Lee said, putting the plants on the window sill. Then he stepped back to admire the pink and red blossoms.

"They're beautiful, Lee."

"I also brought you a radio," he said, opening a sack and removing a little radio. After he showed me which stations played which types of music, I asked him if Robert had written.

"Go get ready," he said, avoiding my question. "We have to go to the employment agency."

I looked at the clock. It was almost ten. I quickly put on a red plaid dress and high heels. Lee said I looked nice, but advised me to take some casual clothes along, too.

"Did you see if Robert sent a letter? " I asked again.

Lee said he had, but there was still nothing. I withered a little more inside.

As we boarded the Magazine Street Bus, I told Lee, "I don't understand it. He wrote me every day the two weeks we were separated last summer."

"He's on a boat. Maybe the mail was delayed," Lee said soothingly. "Let's go sit in the back."

"Why?" I asked.

"See all the Negroes? They are required to sit in the back of the bus," Lee explained. "I don't want to sit up front, when they can't."

Lee hadn't mentioned this before, since the buses we had been on were almost empty, but the Magazine Street Bus always had a lot of riders, and from then on we made a point of going all the way to the back. In time people began to save us a seat. We had the satisfaction of making our own little statement in racially tense New Orleans.

In 1963, there were still signs everywhere proclaiming 'white' and 'colored' for water fountains, parks, rest rooms, and so on. At the end

of that year the signs finally came down. Though laws were on the books forbidding seating discrimination on the buses, the social reality still forced even a poor worn-out black cleaning lady to shuffle her weary way to the back. That was wrong. I soon felt as strongly about it as Lee.

We could not march with Martin Luther King, but we could do this much. And we did. I never hesitated to support Lee in all such gestures.

We arrived at the A-1 Employment office shortly before noon and practiced typing.

"I have to pretend to seek work in order to get my unemployment checks from Texas," Lee told me. "For example, I have to agree to go to interviews, but I rarely actually go."

Lee said he needed the unemployment checks to account for his economic survival before his job started in New Orleans. He had to have some visible source of funds, or it might look suspicious.

"On Thursday, this will be over," Lee said optimistically. He would go for a final "interview" at Reily's, and then he would be hired. The outcome was a foregone conclusion, he explained. The process was really a sham. It just had to look real. Then he once again inquired if I would go to work at Reily's with him.

"I'm still in a quandary about it," I told him "I'd like to talk to Dr. Ochsner first, but it looks like I'm being pushed in that direction whether I like it or not." Lee then showed me the newspaper classified ad that he was responding to, as well as the ad for the job I could get.

"It says here they are looking for two clerk-typists. That's not me," I protested.

"That was before they heard about you," Lee explained. He said he had called Mr. Reily this morning to find out how to fix that.

"Two weeks ago, Mr. Monaghan, the Vice President, lost his executive secretary," Lee explained. "They decided it was safest to hire two part-time clerk-typists to take her place, because they didn't have anybody they could trust except Monaghan to handle my cover."

"But I'm a lousy typist," I objected.

"The beauty of the job is you really don't have to type much," Lee explained. "They only decided to hire two clerk-typists so they wouldn't catch on to me."

"And I would supply you with protection, instead of this Mr. Monaghan?" I asked, without understanding the dimensions of the commitment.

"You'd help a lot, just by clocking me in and out," he said. "So I won't get fired for too many absences and late arrivals. I have to be there at least three months. As Monaghan's secretary, you'd have access to the time cards. You could also help to reject the background security checks of anybody Personnel tries to hire to take my place, until it's time for my termination."

"You'll be terminated?"

"I have to look like a failure," Lee reminded me. "Why else would I hate America and want to go live in Cuba?" Lee said softly. "Besides, I can't work on the training film if I'm still cleaning out roasters at Reily's in mid-July."

"Cleaning out what?"

"Roasters. They roast coffee beans at Reily's. At least, until their new factory opens. I'll be doing all kinds of odd jobs, too," Lee said. "Oil machinery, replace lights, help with packing. Whatever. But we'll be together every day, if we both work there," Lee added. "We'd ride to work together on the bus. We'd ride home together every night. For weeks."

I admitted that was an inducement, but still felt my incompetence would show at once. I'd never get away with it.

"Ah, but this is no ordinary secretarial position," Lee said. "Most afternoons you'll be able to work at Dave's lab and, because Monaghan is a former FBI man, it will all be safe."

"An FBI man?"

"He's been brought in to protect not only me, but a few others who also have cover jobs there," Lee said. "He's the first Vice President Reily Coffee's ever had who wasn't a Reily. It's all part of INCA's big push against Castro."

"What's INCA?" I asked.

"That's The Information Council for the Americas," Lee explained. "It's Dr. Ochsner's anti-Communist propaganda arm, used by the CIA."

Lee told me that INCA taped anti-Communist and anti-Castro programs, shipping them to hundreds of Latin American radio stations on a regular basis. Ochsner and Dr. Sherman made trips to Latin America frequently, providing and gathering even more information, which was shuttled through INCA to the CIA. Originally, Lee hadn't wanted to work for Reily, to give him time to be in the training film; but then he learned that the Reily brothers were major supporters of INCA, and INCA used Reily's private offices for secret meetings with advisors linked to the CIA and FBI. When Lee learned that his hero, Herbert Philbrick, was coming to a meeting that summer at Reily's as an advisor, he requested a position there in order to meet Philbrick. That meant getting more deeply involved in Ochsner's get-Castro project. But Lee's dream to meet the real legend behind the TV show *I Led Three Lives* could now come true.

After we finished our A-1 typing tests and interviews, I followed Lee to another employment agency, getting a good look at Reily's modern,

air-conditioned building at 640 Magazine Street on the way. Lee pointed out that Reily's was convenient to Banister's office, just a block and a half away around the corner. After phone calls to Monaghan, Dave Ferrie, and Dr. Sherman, Lee sat down with me at Mancuso's, a coffee shop located in Banister's building, and told me what he'd found out. First, Ochsner confirmed that he would interview both of us on Wednesday.

"He hopes you'll agree to work at Reily's," Lee told me. "He said you'll need to go to the library to learn how to read Standard & Poor's credit rating books, and so on, but not to worry, you'll still be doing your lab work."

There would be errands, visits to the courthouse, background reports to analyze, credit risks to check on, and paychecks with problems to be issued on time.

"Is that all?" I asked sarcastically, feeling overwhelmed.

"That's all I remember," Lee said.

"When in heaven's name will I have time to be in a lab?" I asked.

"You'll always clock in at Reily's," Lee said, "and you'll clock out there, too. But you'll be doing lab work three afternoons a week. Monaghan will cover for you."

The word from Ochsner was that if I didn't want to do this, I could still enter an internship with Dr. Mary, right at the Clinic, living rent-free in Brent House. Otherwise, Robert's earnings would have to cover an apartment in town, and transportation costs. He would hate that, of course, but if I accepted the internship and moved over to Brent House on Ochsner's campus, we would not be living together at all.

"I guess Robert and I can always go back to making love in his Ford," I said.

"He'll have to live at the YMCA when he comes to town," Lee said. "It's no life for a married man. I know from experience."

"He has it coming to him!" I said. "And if he says, 'Let's pack up and go back to Gainesville,' I'll say 'Guess what? I've got a scholarship to medical school, and I'm staying. It'll be your turn to wait for letters.'"

Lee saw how bitter I was. "Maybe you should get your marriage annulled," he suggested.

"Maybe I will," I replied.

---

1. Claiborne Avenue was named after Gov. John Claiborne, the first governor of Louisiana. Generations later, the Claiborne family remained active in Louisiana politics. Lindy Claiborne married U.S. Congressman Hale Boggs who became Majority Whip of the House and sat on LBJ's "Warren Commission." After Hale Boggs died in a plane crash in Alaska, his wife Lindy took his place in Congress. After she retired from the House, she was appointed the U.S. Ambassador to the Vatican. Hale and Lindy Boggs had a daughter named Cokie, who became a CBS Correspondent in Italy, before becoming a political news analyst on National Public Radio. Today she is better known by her married name, Cokie Roberts.

2. The original location of Ochsner's clinic was on Prytania Street. I don't know for sure if that is where this lab was housed, but if there is an official investigation into this subject, it could be worth looking into.

3. Ochsner had a solid list of trusted Cuban medical contacts, as he and his staff had trained doctors from Cuba for decades, and many of them were furious with Castro's decision to have all future doctors trained in the Soviet Union, which cut them and their protégés off from a long and illustrious association with Ochsner's Clinic.

4. Veteran researcher Mary Ferrell was astonished when I told her, in the presence of witnesses, about the book. She was unable to conceal her amazement, stating that the unique gray book I described to her — of an unusual size, with floppy gray covers, and printed in Russian — was the only one of its kind that she had ever seen. She knew that it had belonged to Lee Oswald in 1963, because on a New Year's evening in the 1970s, Ruth Paine had brought it out to show her and Ferrell's husband, Buck. The gray book was a treasure the police hadn't confiscated when they searched the Paines' house looking for Lee's possessions.

5. Santeria is a religion of African origin which is practiced in the Caribbean islands. Basically, it involves humans working with spirits. While it has some similarities to voodoo, the difference is that voodoo is much more involved with drugs and poisons.

6. Researcher Greg Parker helps confirm Dave's remarks with records such as this: "To quote from extant MK-ULTRA documents, "The security considerations applying to xxxxxxxx were found to be significantly different from those governing manipulation of human behavior. a) Many xxxxx external projects in support of the xxxxxxxxxxxx are being funded and managed securely outside the MK-ULTRA mechanism." (July 26, 1963 memo from JS Eaman, Inspector General, Director, CIA)." (Internet Post #133 05-28-2004)

7. One of Lee's CIA handlers when he went to the USSR was James Jesus Angleton, the famous spymaster who planned the CIA's most complex missions. His telltale quote is worth considering: "It is inconceivable that a secret intelligence arm of the government has to comply with all the overt orders of the government."

8. We used "Sam Spade" as a code name for David Lewis that summer. I did not use it in the narrative to avoid confusing the reader.

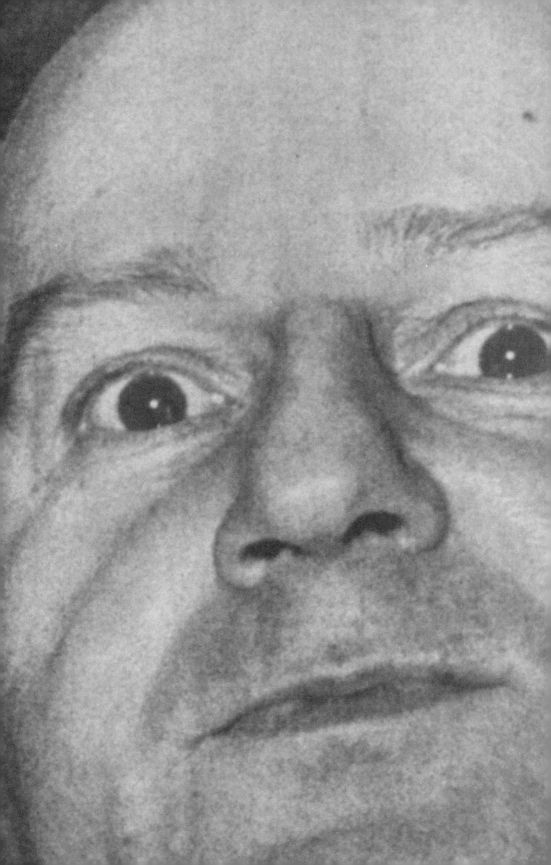

— Chapter 12 —

Sparky

When Lee finally came for me, he said we would have to put off horseback riding because we had been invited to meet an important out-of-town guest at Dave's. I was wearing riding slacks, but Lee said I was dressed well enough and didn't need to change. We went to the Fairgrounds instead, arriving before the gates closed. After we watched the horses exercise on the track we were allowed into the stables, which surprised me.

"Sure we can come in here," Lee said. "I just say the magic words. You can guess who runs these racetracks," inferring that this was yet another Marcello operation.

Lee said that as a kid, sometimes when he was skipping school, he used to visit these stables to pet the horses. Lee had picked up a handful of sugar cubes in the lounge area, which we fed to the horses. Lee showed me the grave of a legendary horse known as Black Gold.[1] He was the most famous horse from New Orleans, and his heroic story put a lump in my throat. After winning the Kentucky Derby  in 1924, Black Gold was retired to stud, but proved infertile. After several years he returned to the racetrack, never to win again. In his final race he broke a leg in the homestretch, and hobbled across the finish line on three legs before collapsing. He was put to sleep right there on the track, and buried in the infield near the sixteenth post. As a horse-lover who'd read every horse story I could find since childhood, just to stand there was a privilege. Then we headed back to Dave's, arriving around sunset.

"We practically live in this place," I complained to Lee as we climbed the back stairs. "We should have stopped to eat something," I added.

"Worry not," Lee said. "Tonight we get to eat at a fancy restaurant."

Lee said he didn't know which one yet, but we were sure to like it, because the people who were paying the tab had expensive tastes.

As we entered Dave's living room, we saw him sitting quietly in a chair. He was wearing priest's vestments, and praying softly in Latin from a breviary —a black prayer book used by priests and monks. When he finished, he stood up and walked to the table to pick up a ring. It was then I noticed that it was the same ugly carved ring that he had shown me the other night. "I thought you didn't wear that ring, Dave," I said.

"Oh, I had to wear it yesterday," Dave said regretfully. "But I took it off to say Mass. It's sacrilegious to wear it during Mass, you know." I raised my eyebrows at the thought of David saying Mass. "Yes, I said a Mass this afternoon," he confirmed thoughtfully. "For my parents. They were so proud to offer a son up to God. The least I can do is pray for them."

He walked slowly into the other room holding his prayer book against his chest, his religious robes flowing gently as he walked. "What a tragedy!" I thought. Never had I seen such a strange, sad, solitary figure. I did not know if his parents were alive or dead, but I could see how their memory weighed on Dave.

Dave changed clothes and returned confidently, wearing black pants and a dark shirt with his full wig firmly in place. He looked quite presentable and started straightening up the place for his guest. We told him of our experience at the fairgrounds and seeing Black Gold's grave. Dave knew Black Gold's history and agreed that he was a noble horse who deserved the respect that was given him. Then our conversation meandered to other animals we had known.[2] I mentioned my dog Sparky, a fuzzy little lapdog with a perverse nature. Sparky had a bladder control problem and used to jump up on my bed late at night, begging me to let him out.

Judyth & Sparky

"If I didn't get up in time, "I told them, "The consequences would be 'Vary' wet!"

When I was eight years old I was asked by the nuns to read my best short story to a school assembly, so I selected one appropriate for the event. But once there I saw how bored the parents and nuns looked, so I decided at the last minute to liven up the crowd. I read my Sparky story instead.

"When Sparky was angry at me," I read to the assembly, "He just couldn't control himself! And so, tonight in the dark, a nasty odor hit my nostrils. I could feel the hot wetness soaking into my blanket, and jumped up. Sparky had done it again!"

The nuns turned pale. The parents gasped. My mom and dad shrank into their seats. As the blood drained from my head and my temperature skyrocketed, I realized that I had misjudged my audience. I had embarrassed my parents and shocked everyone. But things definitely livened up!

Dave and Lee laughed, admitting they couldn't top that one. Dave checked his watch, noting that his guest would arrive any minute. I went into Dave's bathroom to freshen up. When I returned, I could see that Lee and Dave had conspired to play some kind of joke on me.

"We've decided to tell you more about one of our illustrious visitors," Lee said.

"We have to! " Dave broke in. "He's got the same name as your dog, Sparky."

"He's another dog who can't control himself," Lee said. "And he knows how to train the ladies, too!" Dave and Lee started laughing. I had no idea what they were talking about, but I was glad Dave had shaken off his gloom and was his old jovial self again.

Dave continued his modest efforts to clean up his apartment. I was surprised to learn that he actually had a vacuum cleaner! He mentioned that Jack S. Martin had reappeared, demanding to know what was going on with David Lewis and accusing Dave of betraying him, after all they had gone through together.

"We didn't *go through* anything together," Dave said. "It's all in his head. He needs to go back and get some more shock treatments."

"He had shock treatments?" I asked.

"Doesn't it show?" Dave asked, putting away the vacuum cleaner. "He hasn't been through anything, but they do have ways to make you talk, without leaving a mark."

"Cattle prods," Lee said.

"Or they put a wet suit on you," Dave said. "Tie you up, cover your eyes, ears and mouth with tape, and suspend you in a tub of warm water. The lights are off, you can't see a thing. There's no sound, no way to know if you're up or down. Total sensory deprivation. Days seem to go by, even though it's only about 24 hours. Suddenly, you're lowered underwater. Water rushes in your nose. You're drowning. They pull you out and give you artificial respiration, and then you're cleaned up, dressed and returned to your prison cell. Not a mark on you. Then they threaten you with another day in the tub, and you always talk. If you finally contract pneumonia and die, it gets listed as death by natural causes."

What horror! These men do this to each other? I felt weak just thinking about it.

Lee said, "The Russians interrogated me. That's when I dropped out of sight. They made me stand for a couple of days. If I moved, they hit me."

"Stop it!" I said, covering my ears. I fell to the couch and started to cry. "What's the matter with people?" I stammered through my tears. "Why did they do that to you?"

"Honey, I'm sorry," Lee said, sitting down beside me and stroking my hair. "You're so innocent," he murmured, shaking his head.

"I'm sorry, J," Dave said, bringing me a cup of water. "I didn't mean to be so graphic. It's just that people don't know what happens to political prisoners. People are no more humane today than in past centuries. They just hide it better."

"If it's any consolation, my personal discomfort didn't last too long," Lee said, wiping my eyes with his handkerchief. "I pretended not to know a single word of Russian. I acted so entirely stupid that the Russians finally gave up. They concluded that I was an idiot. I was very young, after all, and because of all the Communist quotes I gave them, they decided I really was just a harmless kid steeped in Marxism. They even apologized for hurting me. After I promised not say anything about it I got a nice apartment. They knew they could trust me," Lee said.

"How did they know that?" I asked.

"They told me that if I mentioned being interrogated, I could be treated very badly upon my return to the United States," Lee said, "They would want to know if I had caved in, and had become a turncoat. Of course I didn't tell. And I urge you never to speak of it."

"Well, I won't," I agreed.

Dave brought in a little dish of cheese and crackers and put it on the coffee table, along with some beer nuts and candy, but neither Lee nor I were in the mood to eat after these sobering revelations. I leaned against Lee and closed my eyes. I could feel his heart beating in his chest.

As we talked more about his Russian experience, Lee said he had learned first-hand that people are the same everywhere. It's the power structures under which people exist

Lee Oswald with comrades in Soviet Union

that make them adversaries. He felt there was hope for America, however. Before coming to New Orleans he had stood in Dallas with a sign around his neck proclaiming "VIVA CASTRO." He got away with it. True, a Red Squad could have beaten him up or killed him or he might have been arrested. But it didn't happen.

"In Russia, had I worn a "VIVA KENNEDY" sign around my neck, I would have gone to prison," Lee assured me. "But of course," he went on, "the sign was just a ploy."

"Just as you're going to do again," I commented. "Here in New Orleans."

"Have you ever read *The Scarlet Pimpernel*?" Lee asked suddenly.

"Baroness Orczy's books?" I asked.

"Then you have!" he said, quite pleased. "Good."

"Sir Percival Blakeney. He fooled the French spies so brilliantly.... I love Percy," I said, looking up at Lee. "An incredible man."

"I was the Scarlet Pimpernel!" Lee said proudly. "And I still play 'the demmed fool.' Just as Percy did."

"You've been *playing* Sir Percy?"

"Yes. I present myself as a worthless fool. If necessary, even stupid. He is my model."

"So this goes beyond job interviews? You let people think you're stupid?"

I saw Lee flush. A hard knot of pride tightened in his jaw.

"When I must," he finally said, avoiding my eyes. "I pretended I couldn't shoot, and then I 'accidentally' shot myself in the arm."

The Scarlet Pimpernel to the Rescue
Illustration from the book

Lee rolled up his sleeve revealing a thin scar, along with a depression, in the bony part of his left elbow. I hadn't noticed it before because it was hard to see with his arm straight.

"As you know, I'm actually a good shot," Lee boasted.

"Shooting cardboard ducks at Pontchartrain Beach doesn't count," I countered.

"I can get us some revolvers," Lee said, "We'll go shoot at real birds, if you'd like."

"I'd love to!"

"You would?" Lee looked surprised.

"Sure," I told him, "just as long as we don't kill anything."

Lee groaned. "I knew it was too good to be true."

"If you're starving, go ahead and kill them," I said. "Otherwise, why take them out of somebody else's mouth?"

Those were the right words to say to a man from Louisiana, where poor country folks hunted deer, ducks and alligators for their meat. Otherwise, there would only be cornbread and greens. Lee was raised in a state where squirrel and possum were often in the slow-cooked stew on the back burner.

Dave came over asking if we wanted something to drink, but we declined. I noticed that Dave was practicing some shadow-boxing moves, letting off tension, as we waited for his important guests to arrive.

"Do you know martial arts?" I asked. Dave and Lee smiled at each other.

"We both do," Lee said.

"So do I!" I announced.

"Oh, really?" Dave said. "Come here—"

I jumped up and stood before him, using one of the stances I'd been taught by one of my UF boyfriends. Though I knew enough karate for self-protection on the streets, Dave had no trouble flipping me to the floor after only one or two fakes.

"I know more than you do," Dave said, softly and menacingly.

"You sure do," I agreed. "No need to convince me further!" I returned to the couch with my pride hurt and rubbing my derriere. I focused again on Lee. Here was a man who acted out the role of the Scarlet Pimpernel in deadly earnest, and I was sitting next to him. I thought of that little poem he recites in his foppish public pose:

> They seek him here, they seek him there.
> Those Frenchies seek him everywhere.
> Is he in Heaven, or is he in Hell?
> That Demmed, elusive Pimpernel!

"Did you ever rescue anybody?" I asked.

Photo taken Jan. 1960 at Minsk Radio Plant

"I believe so," Lee replied.

"Sir Percival Blakeney, Baronet," I mused. "He pretended he knew no French, when he was a master of the language. He concealed his powers. Nobody guessed."

"I pretended to know almost no Russian when I arrived in Moscow," Lee said. "Which was also, as you know, not quite the case." Lee made a rather bitter laugh. "I was determined to rescue my own aristocrats from Madame Guillotine. But so far, I haven't found many to rescue."

"Is there a book you haven't read, Lee?" I asked him.

"Of course. But just give me time."

I asked Lee to help me with some Russian phrases, and as we were working together Dave, who had been bouncing out to the porch every few minutes, suddenly announced, "Hot damn! Here they come! That's Carlos Marcello's car!"

Dave was so excited that I expected to see a black stretch-limo pulling up. Instead, I got a glimpse of an ordinary two-tone Chevy sedan as it entered Dave's driveway on the side of the house, and disappeared behind the building.

"That is the Godfather's car?" I said in disbelief.

"Little Man is a wise man," Dave said. "Remember, to the Feds, he's just a poor tomato company guy. But he comes up with the goods when he needs to show off." Dave fluffed up a flattened cushion on a chair. "He knows how to go all out. Chauffeur, bitches to serve drinks in the limo, the whole fucking crock of shit."

"Clean up the English, Dave," Lee said, putting his arm around me.

"Oops," said the man who, an hour earlier, had impressed me with his show of piety.

Dave and Lee then hurried down the back stairs. When they returned, there was only one man with them. He was the same height as Lee and Dave.

"J," Dave said, "I would like you to meet Mr. Sparky Rubenstein, a man who definitely reminds us of your dog."

"He's asking for a brass-knuckle sandwich," Sparky said, smiling. "Happy to make your acquaintance," he said with charm.

Standing before me was a well-built, well-dressed man whose face beamed with friendliness and self-confidence. He kissed my hand. "So, how do you like New Orleans?" he asked in a mid-western accent that was unique to the Chicago area. I gave him a polite answer, asked him if he was from Chicago, and how did he like life in Louisiana?

"It's been a while since I lived in Chicago," he answered, taking off his hat. "You guessed that part right. But I'm from Texas now. Excuse me for a moment," Sparky said. "I have to get something from the car. Almost forgot." With that Sparky set his hat on the table and went back outside, followed by Dave. Lee stayed with me.

"He's going bald," I commented.

"So am I," Lee said. "It's hereditary."

"I've read that the more testosterone a man has, the more chance he'll go bald," I said soothingly. "I guess you must be oozing with testosterone."

"Naturally."

"Is this guy allowed to know about the lab?" I queried.

"He brings money to help finance it," Lee said.

"What happened to everybody else who was supposed to come?"

Sparky returned, carrying a steel barbell with blue weights attached. I saw how strong he was. Behind him came Dave, puffing along with more. Sparky was carrying twice the weight, but wasn't out of breath.

"I can't use these things up here, Sparky," Dave protested. "It'll crack the ceiling under us if I drop it," Dave added, coughing from his exertion.

"Let's put them out on the porch, then," Sparky said.

Dave continued to cough.

"You got to stop the smoking, Dave," Sparky counseled. "You got to pass your physical every year. How you gonna' do that, smoking like you do and eating the junk you eat?"

Dave scowled. "I take vitamins," he said lamely.

"Are you using the blender I gave you to make carrot juice?"

"He's using it to liquefy cancerous tumors," I piped up helpfully. "The stuff in the refrigerator that sort of looks like carrot juice and cherries is actually chopped up tumors. Just a warning."

Sparky's eyes traversed my body quickly, as he smiled.

"You look pretty strong yourself," he commented. "Nicely developed arms and legs, and other stuff," he added.

"I was in an acrobatic act with my sister," I replied. "Back flips, cart-wheels, hand-stands, all that stuff," I offered.

Sparky Rubenstein's Early Life

Jacob "Sparky" Rubenstein was born in Chicago in 1911 into a large family that had recently emigrated from Poland. Jacob caused trouble at school and earned the nickname "Sparky" for his quick temper. At age eleven Sparky was sent for psychiatric treatment and assigned to a foster home. His mother was eventually admitted to a mental hospital, and his father was arrested for assault.

After leaving school in 1927 Jacob did various odd jobs and is said to have worked for mobster Al Capone, the boss of the Chicago underworld at the time. He also spent time in Los Angeles and San Francisco, eventually returning to Chicago where he worked for the Scrap Iron and Junk Handlers Union.

From 1943 to 1946, Rubenstein served in the United States Army Air Forces, got into fights over comments about his being Jewish, and rose to the rank of private first class.

In 1947, after moving to Dallas to manage a night-club for his sister, he was arrested by the Bureau of Narcotics, though he was eventually released without being charged. The sheriff claimed that he had been sent to Dallas by criminals in Chicago to manage illegal gambling activities. This is also the time that FBI documents indicate he was doing work for Richard Nixon. Jacob changed his name at that time to Jack Ruby and remained in Dallas where he owned several nightclubs, some of which failed.

In 1959 Ruby visited Cuba at the invitation of Dallas nightclub owner, Lewis McWillie, supervisor of gambling activities at the Tropicana Hotel in Havana. Back in the U.S., Ruby was in regular contact with associates of Carlos Marcello and Santos Trafficante in 1963.

"Can you show me something?" Sparky replied.

I was still wearing slacks so I stood on my hands and then completed the flip, landing on my feet.

"That's pretty good," Sparky said. "You're in good shape."

"Thank you," I said. "It looks like you're in good shape, yourself."

"I am!" Sparky said proudly. "I can do handstands, too. I'll show you."

Sparky took off his suit jacket and tossed it on the couch. Then he stood on his hands, raising his legs high into the air with his tie hanging down. He then began walking around the room on his hands with his feet curved over his head. There was no doubt that he was in splendid condition.

Then he balanced himself on just one hand: "Dave, bet you can't do this."

As he did, the contents of his pockets cascaded out of his pants. Coins, keys, brass knuckles, business cards, an address book, and a large roll of money secured by a rubber band fell to the floor.

Sparky's face grew red as he came down hard. Lee said, "By the way, remember that place you recommended for girls new in town?"

"What place?" Sparky asked as he reloaded his pockets.

"Over on St. Charles, near Carrollton. The place where you said young girls and couples were always welcome."

"O God! That was a joke, Lee! You didn't take me seriously?"

"Yes, I did," Lee said, folding his arms. "And J, here, was kicked out of the place when they raided it on Friday night."

"You're kidding!" Sparky laughed. Then he sat down on the couch next to Lee and me. "They raided it?"

"They all went downtown, except J," Lee said. "But she lost her thirty dollars for the room. Landlady refused to give it back. Same for her food."

"I'll speak to her," Sparky said, with an edge of menace to his voice that raised goose bumps on my arms. He pulled out the roll of bills from his hip pocket, peeled off a fifty and handed it to me. "Here, baby," he said. "That'll take care of the thirty dollars. I'm really sorry."

I'd lived so many days on the edge of being completely broke that the fifty dollar bill seemed like a reprieve from Hell.

"Now I can pay Susie," I said.

"No, don't do that," Lee cautioned. "How would you explain that to Robert? You'll have to wait for a Reily paycheck, or move over to Brent House. Talk to Dr. O first."

"I thought you understood my jokes by now, Lee," Sparky mused. "You've known me long enough." Turning to me Sparky said, "I've known Lee ever since he was a little boy."

Sparky explained that, when he was first getting set up as Marcello's "helper" in Dallas, he went to some family parties in New Orleans hosted by Marcello that were attended by Lee's mother, aunt and uncle. He remembered Lee playing with other children at a couple of these get-togethers, and over a period of years talked to Lee's uncle often, especially about boxing. When Lee and his mother moved to Fort Worth, Lee's uncle asked Sparky to keep an eye on the boy, who had worked for Marcello from time to time as a gopher. "Watch over my boy Lee," Dutz Murret had told him.

"Those jobs for Marcello were employment records I didn't keep," Lee said, opening my purse and putting the fifty dollar bill inside. "Couldn't use any of those for job references."

Sparky said he had tried to interest Lee in working for Marcello at a time when he needed more men in the Dallas organization, but Lee had already made up his mind to be a military man, following in his brothers' footsteps.

Dave joined the conversation and added that he kept his promise to Lee and recommended him for intelligence training. "I did it because he knows how to keep his mouth shut," Dave said.

I was concerned that Dave revealed this freely, right in front of Sparky, and shot a frown in Dave's direction.

"It's okay, J," Dave said. "Sparky cares about Lee like a son. And he's a patriot, like Ochsner. The arms of the government have been wrapped around Lady Cosa Nostra in this dance for a long time now."

"My goal was always the Marines," Lee said. "Either the world can be an influence on you, or you can be an influence on the world," he recited once again. "I chose to serve my country."

"Are you still so naïve?" Dave asked.

Lee said stubbornly, "I'm under no delusions. I choose to serve, anyway."

"Leave him alone!" Sparky snapped at Dave. Then he turned to Lee and said gratefully, "I'm glad somebody still cares about this damned country."

Dave apologized, to soothe Sparky, then asked him, "How did you get that car?"

"Well, I flew in for a change," Sparky said. "Sammy met me at the airport. I can keep it for the night."

"Where is everybody else?" Lee asked.

"They should be here any minute," Sparky answered.

Sure enough, a few minutes later, a cab dropped off three men in front of Dave's house. Sparky and

Dave went down to greet them, while Lee and I watched from the porch.

"That's Mr. Gaudet, who writes propaganda for the CIA," Lee said, pointing him out. "Ochsner pays him to write an anti-Communist magazine that's sent out all over Latin America. That one's Sergio Smith. He's from Houston. He flies in every once in awhile, so you'll see him again. Used to be a big shot before he got kicked out of the overt anti-Castro movement here along with Dave, a couple of years ago. But that makes both of them useful in the anti-Castro underground." The third man was a heavyset Latino whom Lee did not know.

"Mr. Smith's mustache reminds me of my father," I commented, noting that Sergio was heavier than my father. "But he's got to be a Cuban or something. Is his name really Mr. Smith?"

"It really is," Lee replied. Dave came back in and announced that we were all going out to eat.

"Oh, wow!" I said, when we reached the car, "I get to sit in the Godfather's car! I get to put my little rear end down on the same upholstery the Godfather does!"

"You little doodle-head," Lee said affectionately, "I don't think so."

"Darn!" I complained. As the men filled the car, I realized that the only place left for me to sit was on Lee's lap.

"Actually, I'm rather glad that your little rear end has nowhere else to go," Lee said, making everybody in the car laugh.

"She's an acrobat!" Sparky told everybody.

"She knows martial arts, too!" Dave said, and everybody laughed again, as we headed to the French Quarter. Then the men started talking. Lee had warned me to keep quiet and play dumb, which I did. Lee was silent, too, and contributed nothing to their conversation. The men dis-

Sergio Arcacha-Smith

Sergio Arcacha-Smith was a Cuban exile who was active in several anti-Castro groups in New Orleans, Miami, Tampa and Houston in the early 1960s. He was associated with David Ferrie and Guy Banister and introduced Ferrie to Carlos Bringuier, Carlos Quiroga and Jack Martin. According to an FBI report Carlos Marcello offered Arcacha-Smith money around the time of the Bay of Pigs invasion in return for gambling concessions in post-invasion Cuba. While living in New Orleans he served as the New Orleans delegate to Frente Revolucionario Democratico and established the Cuban Democratic Liberation Front with David Ferrie, but was later thrown out of that group for mismanagement of their money. He was suspected of being involved in several arms deals, though he was never arrested.

Born in Havana and educated at a Texas college, Arcacha-Smith served briefly as Cuba's consul in Bombay, India during the Batista regime, and later became assistant manager of a hotel in Caracas, Venezuela (1954-57). After several years in New York City and Miami, he returned to Cuba briefly after Fidel Castro gained power and then went into exile in 1960, living primarily in New Orleans where he was active in anti-Castro groups and had an office at 544 Camp Street. He was granted political asylum in the U.S. in 1962.

In 1963 he moved to Texas and became friends with right-wingers like Edwin Walker and oilman H.L. Hunt.

In 1967 Jim Garrison considered Arcacha-Smith a person of interest in his JFK investigation and tried to have him extradited from Texas for questioning.

cussed their business as if we were not even there. I again thought
about what Lee had said about the Scarlet Pimpernel, and felt that I
was playing my own minor part in his charade.

When we reached Antoine's Restaurant on Rue St. Louis in the
French Quarter, Marcello's car was recognized immediately. When we
got out, we were treated like royalty. Antoine's was perhaps the finest
old restaurant in New Orleans.

As we entered, I hung on to Lee's arm. It was like we had plunged
into *Gone with the Wind*. Here was a timeless sophistication rarely
seen in modern-day America. Tuxedoed waiters hovered quietly
around tables cloaked in white linen and stacked with beautiful crystal. The chandeliers blazed, as the ceiling fans turned majestically.
Quiet music played gently in the background and mingled with the
tender clinking of wine glasses. Civil conversation and exquisitely
polite manners were everywhere. I hoped Dave Ferrie would conduct
himself properly.

I soon discovered that my concerns about Dave's behavior were un-
necessary, as he was indeed capable of playing the role of the perfect
gentleman when he needed to. As the only woman at the table, I was
treated extremely politely by all. (I could get used to this!) When I
ordered a "Roy Rogers" (coke with grenadine) instead of wine, several
eyebrows went up at the table and lips smirked. Lee didn't want me left

Antoine's Restaurant

Since Antoine's served its first meal in 1840, it has been a bastion of French Creole cuisine
and an island of grand tradition seated at the heart of old New Orleans society, with many
of its 15 unique dining rooms named after the city's oldest Mardi Gras krewes. It is located
on Rue Saint Louis deep in the French Quarter.

out, so he ordered the same. The food was fabulous. It was, indeed, one of the finest meals I've ever eaten, perhaps *the* finest. We had:

Crab cakes, a small cup of seafood gumbo, and a hearts-of-palm salad as appetizers. Then they brought us *Chair de crabes au gratin* (Lump crabmeat in a cream sauce sprinkled with a light cheese and French bread-crumb mixture baked and browned in a casserole), followed by Filet Toronado (a petit filet mignon crowned with Bernaise sauce), and for dessert, a delicate portion of bread pudding, set atop a cinnamon custard pudding impregnated with raisins and crested with a buttery rum sauce, sprinkled with roasted pecans. Yummy!

When we finished, we got back into Marcello's car, drove a few blocks and parked on Dauphine Street. The six of us walked along the dark narrow street, beneath fanciful wrought-iron balconies and past stucco walls punctuated by quaint articulated doorways that guarded lush private courtyards. Dave, Sparky, Sergio and the heavyset Cuban walked in front, with Lee and me trailing. I hung on to Lee's arm, as we strolled through a prior century.

We were headed to Clay Shaw's home at 1313 Dauphine. As we walked, Lee explained that Clay Shaw was a very important person in New Orleans. He was one of the directors of the International Trade Mart, and a close friend of Dr. Alton Ochsner's. His renovations of neglected historic buildings in the French Quarter were an inspiration to the community. His own house and adjoining stable (ex-slave quarters) had been transformed into elegant modern residences cloaked in their original charm. I said that I was interested in meeting him, but Lee cautioned me.

1313 Dauphine Street

"Maybe not tonight. These men have been drinking," he warned. "Listen to how they're talking before you decide to go in there."

I had been too lost in my own enchanted world to notice what the men were saying. When I tuned in to the conversation, I realized that Lee was right. They had turned to telling crude homosexual jokes, and their intent in visiting Mr. Shaw seemed to be for more than business purposes.

"I see what you mean," I said to Lee quietly.

When we reached 1313 Dauphine, they rang the bell. A servant came to the door and invited our group in. As he did, I got a glimpse of Shaw's beautiful courtyard and elegantly lit European fountain. Lee tapped Dave on the shoulder and told him that, under the circumstances, he and I would prefer to meet Mr. Shaw some other time. Sparky overheard Lee's comment and handed him the keys to Marcello's car, saying "Have a good time. Just come back by midnight and wait for us in the car. Besides, she'll finally get a chance to sit on the upholstery."

 We quickly said our goodbyes and strolled through the French Quarter, stopping at Preservation Hall to hear some traditional New Orleans jazz, and seeing the many sights. We continued our walk down Bourbon to Canal Street where we stopped at the Saenger movie theatre and saw a movie poster announcing that *Dr. No* (the first James Bond movie) was "Coming Soon."[3] Lee and I discussed the movie and realized we both enjoyed the James Bond novels, and were interested in seeing this new film. We wanted to see it together but that would be more difficult now, because Lee's wife would soon arrive and he would have fewer evenings to spend with me. But we vowed that, one way or the other, we would see *Dr. No* together.

It was quite late, and Lee decided it was time to take me home. He stopped at a store-front to buy us two cokes with chocolate syrup (my favorite way to have a coke) and we began walking back to Dauphine Street where the car was parked. The streets were almost deserted. If Lee had not been with me, the dark corners and alleyways would have frightened me. We were content to stroll along in relative silence.

As we turned onto Dauphine Street, Lee said: "It's time we got off the streets. Let's go make your dream come true, and put your bottom down in the Godfather's car."

We had just passed 1313 Dauphine and were headed to the car parked at the end of the block. Suddenly, a man jumped out of the shadows. Holding a knife at Lee's throat, he demanded, "Your wallet! Hand it over!"

We froze. Our assailant was a huge blonde fellow wearing a sailor's suit. He was over six feet tall and weighed about two-hundred and fifty pounds, with big, throbbing veins in his neck. He had obviously hyped himself up to do this, and Lee wasn't going to argue with him. Lee slowly reached into his back pocket.

"I want your purse, too, girlie!" the sailor said. "Hurry up!"

"You don't want her purse," Lee countered.

"Shut up!" the robber snapped, as Lee slowly offered his wallet at about the sailor's belt level. As he did, a switchblade suddenly sprang out from underneath Lee's wallet, its silver blade gleaming in the darkness.

Furious at the sight of the blade, the sailor snarled, "Throw that damned wallet on the ground, or I'll cut your face!" as he moved his knife toward Lee's head.

"You may cut my face," Lee said, in slow, icy words, "but not before I get your balls." With that, Lee made a vicious jab at the man's crotch. The man jumped back and turned, cursing Lee as he ran.

Lee immediately grabbed me by the hand, and we sprinted to the car. We all but threw ourselves inside, and Lee locked the door behind us. We sat in the stillness, out of breath and hearts pounding from adrenalin. The silence of the car was conspicuous and comforting. I even forgot it was Marcello's car. It could have been a popsicle truck. Then Lee stuck the key in the ignition and turned on the engine.

"We should get out of here in a hurry," Lee said, "just in case the creep returns with a friend."

"You saved us! " I told Lee, throwing my arms around him in gratitude. I took his head in my hands and began kissing him, grateful for what he had done. He flushed with embarrassment. Then I noticed that he was trembling from head to foot.

"You're shaking!" I said, grabbing his hands, which were cold. I held them in mine.

"It's a reaction, because I was afraid," Lee said. "It will pass."

After a few minutes, he stopped shaking and relaxed.

"You're not a coward if you feel afraid," he said. "Everyone feels afraid when confronted with danger. You are a coward only if you don't overcome your fear when necessary."

And then Lee kissed me for real. Like a girl wants to be kissed. Eventually he drove me home and then returned Marcello's car to Sparky.

---

1. Black Gold, the famous race horse of the 1920s, who won the Kentucky Derby in 1924, was elected to the U.S. Racing Hall of Fame in 1969.

2. For example, Father Rose, who was our parish priest in Niles, Michigan, owned a big Irish setter whose stupidity was only matched by my parents' Dalmatian.

3. *Dr. No*, the movie, was released on May 8, 1963.

— Chapter 13 —

Charity

Tuesday, May 7, 1963

This was the day we were finally supposed to meet with Dr. Ochsner. "Don't pretty up for Ochsner," he'd said. "We'll be seeing him at Charity Hospital."

That was where the poor went to get free medical treatment. Lee suggested that I dress down and wear comfortable clothes, so I wouldn't look out of place.

As I changed clothes, to pass the time, Lee looked at my portfolio of drawings and short stories. While I brushed my hair, Lee finished reading my story, "Hospital Zone."

"This is good," he said, adding softly, "I want to be a writer."

"I think you'd be a good one, too," I told him. "All my science talk derailed Robert from being a writer, to geology," I mourned. "Now he's out on a quarterboat somewhere."

"Well, you're influencing me to be a writer," Lee rejoined, "so now, it's even." Lee called Dr. Ochsner's office to pin down exactly when we were to meet him at Charity Hospital. He was told Ochsner had finished surgery, had finished making his rounds, and was meeting with staff before a quick lunch. Then he'd leave his hospital to drive over to Charity. He should arrive by 2:30 p.m. We might have to wait an hour after that, because Ochsner donated his time at Charity, offering his services free of charge to the desperately poor. Some of the more interesting cases would receive free care at Ochsner's Clinic.

I was impressed. Ochsner got more done in a single day than most people could in a week. I later learned he also flew to Washington almost weekly, working on his research papers or reading medical journals en route. Duties in Washington finished, he'd fly back the same night, sleeping on the plane and arriving ready to conduct surgery at sunrise. That same week might find him in Venezuela, or at a medical conference in California. Or perhaps he would take off a day or two to play cards, or to hunt at a ranch with his Oil Baron buddies in Texas,

Impression by . . .

Dr. Alton Ochsner, world famed surgeon and President of both the Alton Ochsner Medical Foundation and the Information Council of the Americas (INCA), who was perhaps the only listener who knew of Oswald's defection before the debate.

Close-up from the back cover of the vinyl LP pictured above, *OSWALD – SELF-PORTRAIT in RED*, published in 1964 by INCA (more in Chapter 22).

raising funds for the Clinic. Ochsner also attended meetings for INCA, the Trade Mart, and International House (he was its CEO!), but he'd be operating on people every morning, or thundering imperatives into the ears of terrified medical students. He visited recovering patients with his staff. On some weekends, Ochsner took his turn at night duty for emergency operations — the same as any other surgeon on his staff. My admiration for Ochsner was boundless.

We then began to discuss how to find a way to account for Sparky's fifty-dollar donation. As I started to tell Lee that Robert had still not contacted me after all this time, I suddenly felt overwhelmed and burst into tears. Lee soon learned that I was crying myself to sleep every night over that man. He then made a few calls on Susie's phone, after which we took the Magazine bus downtown. A few more blocks of walking, and we were in front of a modest storefront, where numerous souvenirs, piñatas, Mardi Gras masks and other oddities were on display in the cluttered windows. This was 545 South Rampart Street. If you turned your back to the windows, and looked carefully, you could spot Reily Coffee Company way down to the right, on Magazine Street. A large sign overhead said "Rev. James Novelty Shop." A smaller sign read: "Novelty and Religious items."

Reverend James' Novelty Shop, known locally as Rev. Jim's, was both a souvenir shop and a gateway to a storehouse of the grotesque and beautiful, where shiny alligators ten feet tall, lifesize carousel horses, and colorfully painted dragons, devils, and dinosaurs were created for Mardi Gras floats, carnivals, and shop windows. There was a long table in the store, where people were busy lettering souvenirs with the words "New Orleans." The shelves and counters overflowed with rubber masks, wigs, African drums, Indian headdresses, costumes full of sequins, costume jewelry, and feathers. One section was stacked with bibles, framed religious poems, and statues of the Good Shepherd.

This was the retail end of an unusual industry — a charitable enterprise creating work for poor artists, musicians and transients who needed to make a little honest money to get by. The lady in charge was a member of Reverend Jim's church, and she was an artist. She welcomed Lee and showed us around. Behind Reverend Jim's and the building next door was the warehouse where Mardi Gras floats were stored. Its cement floors were littered with sawdust and fluffy lumps of papier-mâché, with molds of all kinds.

There was a separate room full of critters ready to paint. We filled out papers testifying to financial need, read a Bible tract, and signed a promise to stay sober and drug free. We could work up to four hours a day at minimum wage, if our work was neat and satisfactory.

We started painting "New Orleans" over and over, on ceramic alligators, maracas, and salt & pepper-shaker sets. But soon, Lee was taken from the table. He had painted, in a very neat hand, "*Wen* Orleans" on several pieces.[1] I asked to go with him when he was sent, with paint and brushes, to the papier-mâché warehouse to add colorful eyes and rosy mouths to some trolls. Altogether, Lee and I spent three hours painting trolls, dwarves and carousel horses. Then, realizing we could be late for Charity Hospital, we claimed our reward: five dollars and change!

"I told you to trust me!" Lee said, as we emerged, blinking, from the land of wombats and wizards into the bright sunlight of a busy city. But he immediately stopped in front of an African-American newspaper office nearby. "I have to talk to somebody here," he said. "But you go on. Just head toward Reily's," he said, turning me in that direction. A few minutes later, Lee caught up with me.

"I have to go to Banister's right away," he said. "But I called about Ochsner again. We've got an hour before we have to show up at Charity. The doctor's running late."

I wondered who had the busier schedule — Lee Oswald or Alton Ochsner! Soon we reached Banister's building. I sat on the steps of the Camp Street entrance while Lee walked around the corner and entered through the Lafayette Street entrance. The doors were all propped open to catch the breeze, so from where I sat I could see into Mancuso's Restaurant, where David Lewis and Jack Martin were sitting drinking coffee. As they were about to leave, David Lewis spotted me and came over. He invited me and Lee to meet his wife at Thompson's

Restaurant, which was around the corner. He said that he was grateful for the Trailways work arranged for him, and needed to discuss some of the details with Lee. As he left, I told Lewis that I would give Lee the message. While I continued to wait, I saw several Cubans walking toward Banister's office. A few minutes later, David Ferrie hurried past. I called out to him and he gave me a quick wave.

"I'm late!" he shouted. "Talk to you later!"

After fifteen minutes Lee appeared, and we boarded the street-car and headed uptown. "Is this the way to Charity Hospital?" I asked.

"No," said Lee. "Our meeting with Ochsner has been called off for today. He's in emergency surgery. We'll have to see him tomorrow." We were now on our way to Palmer Park, a pleasant, quiet place where we could play chess, unobserved. Nearly across the street was an eatery called Lee's Coffee Shop. He wanted us to eat there, because it said 'Lee.' His ultimate goal, just for fun, was to take me every place named 'Lee' in New Orleans. We played chess for over an hour, without resolution to the game, so Lee folded the board after memorizing the setup, and we went to get something to eat.

While we waited for our food, I gave Lee the message from David Lewis, which he said was good news. He called Thompson's restaurant to arrange our date with David. Lee's Coffee Shop served a mixture of good Chinese and American food: we eventually ate there a dozen times.

Wednesday, May 8, 1963

Lee had been invited over for breakfast, and I invited Susie to join us. I made palacsinta: Hungarian crêpes, the way my grandmother taught me.[2] We ended up discussing the Hungarian Revolution, and I learned that Lee, too, had listened on short-wave radio to the pleas of the Hungarian rebels as they begged for America to come to their aid. Lee had admired the courage of the Hungarians ever since.

He asked many questions about Hungarian culture before we moved to my living-room couch to finish the chess game. Lee won: I had forgotten my strategy, but it was clear that he had not. At about 10 A.M., the mail arrived. As Collie tore after the postman, Susie brought me a letter. Robert had written, after five long days. It touchingly revealed that he didn't care what my Catholic parents might think about our elopement:

> *"...we'll have to live with each other, not with them, so let's tend to ourselves, our own happiness. If they wanted us, it would be different. I knew who my mother-in-law and father-in-law*

would be before I married you, so let me take the responsibility for it."

This manliness on Robert's part warmed the cockles of my heart. Feelings of love swelled in my soul. But his next words reminded me how very much I was on my own:

"I hope you haven't given up writing stories. Coarse as it may seem, take advantage of my absence. I'll be back as sure as the sun will rise. Meanwhile you have a life to live without me, a secondary life, but a life not dead. There are three of us now, you, me and Us. It's too late to write anymore now. The mail boat leaves early in the morning. I love you, I love you, I love you. Robert"

So, a letter took just one day to reach me, once the mail boat picked it up.

"I feel so guilty," I told Lee, in Susie's presence. "Is it possible to be in love with two men at the same time?"

Susie and I had discussed everything Lee had done for me, along with his miserable marriage, and the insensitive conduct of my brand-new husband. Now she spoke up.

"Follow your heart," she told me. "In your heart, you already know the answers to all your questions, honey."

I looked at Lee helplessly. His wife would be arriving in a few days. And Robert would return "as sure as the sun will rise." I had married him both for love and to get birth control pills. And though we were newlyweds, he left me alone for weeks at a time. I thought, "If that's how he treats me now, how will he treat me after the novelty has worn off?" Lee observed that the date showed Robert wrote the letter before he knew I'd moved, but the address on the envelope was my new one.[3] He hadn't mentioned anything about it.

"It would have been nice if he asked 'what happened?' or 'Are you okay?'" Lee said. Susie then pointed out other peculiarities, which I hadn't noticed.

"He didn't ask for your phone number, and he didn't say when he'd be back."

Astonished, I searched through the letter. It began, "My darling Judy," and then began describing the quarterboat, what the work routine was, and the situation with my parents. Susie was right. There was still no mention of how to reach him in an emergency, and not a word about when he might be back; just the admonition that I must get along without him. Still, I defended him, since he'd finally written!

"Good Lord, girl," Susie said, "You were only married three days when he wrote this. You're supposed to be his sweetheart."

"He is adjusting himself to his new surroundings," Lee offered.

"Poppycock!" Susie said, taking back the letter. "If he had time to write the new address on the envelope, he had time to ask questions."

"He'll ask, soon enough," I predicted.

"Sure, he will," Susie said, "when he wants to get back between the covers with you. As for me, I hope he stays out there all year. I don't want to meet him."

"Neither do I," said Lee.

"Darn!" I told him, "and here I was going to use you to make him jealous!"

"I'm afraid I would punch him in the nose," Lee said.

"Well, so much for all of us being buddies," I said. "Scratch that one."

Lee said he had more work to do for Banister, and left. I went into my room and starting reading research papers in preparation for my meeting with Dr. Ochsner. As I read, I thought about the people in my world. So much had happened in the five days Robert had been gone! And how many days would it be before he returned? Who knew what would happen next? As I pondered Susie's comments about Robert's letter, I decided not to volunteer any information about how I was feeling, or how I spent my time. If Robert wanted to know, he should ask. If he cared about me, he would. Until then, I knew I couldn't count on him.

The other people in my life didn't look much better. Dr. Sherman had not bothered to contact me since that awkward incident at Dave's party. And Dr. Ochsner was only now making time to see me. How could I count on them? Dave Ferrie was friendly, but without Lee at my side, I couldn't trust him either. Susie was elderly, and I didn't want to load her down with my problems. The only person in the whole equation that I felt I could trust with everything was Lee. Loyal. Steady. Reliable. He had never let me down. Deep inside, I felt he never would.

As I thought about Lee, I realized how close we had become. Too close to be just friends. I thought about the way he kissed me in the car after he rescued me from that knife-wielding sailor. Lee probably could have seduced me that night. We both knew that. But he didn't. If I wasn't married, we might have already become lovers. But I was not going to let that happen simply because he saved me from a mugger. Nor would it be because he found me a place to live when I had no-where else to go. I had to know that I had his respect. Anything based upon my desperate situation, or upon Lee coming to my rescue, would be a false foundation for love, a shallow romance. Lee didn't want us to become lovers on such a basis either. In fact, he had not even kissed me since that delicious night in Marcello's car. If we became lovers, it would have to come from a position of mutual respect, based on strength. We both felt that way.

Wednesday, May 8, 1963

We got on the Magazine bus heading downtown to Canal Street. From there, we would transfer to another bus to reach Charity Hospital for our appointment with Dr. Ochsner. As usual, in our effort to make a silent statement supporting the rights of blacks to sit in the front of the bus, or wherever they liked, we moved to the back bench of the bus and sat amongst the black passengers. I had my research papers in a big canvas bag on my lap. In the back corner seat of the bus sat a heavy-set black woman wearing a cotton dress that hung on her large frame like a flour sack. Her eyes were closed, and she swayed from side to side as the bus lumbered along. Her arms were wrapped around a paper bag on her lap. We noticed a heavy odor around her. The other passengers noticed it too, and quietly moved away from her.

Then Lee nudged me with his elbow and used his eyes to point to the woman's feet. Blood was dripping down her legs and pooling around her shoes. Lee was sitting just one seat away from her, and tapped her on the arm. She opened her weary eyes and looked painfully at Lee. Her face glistened with sweat and her mouth was locked in a sad frown.

"Ma'am," Lee said. "We're on our way to a hospital. We would be happy to help you see a doctor there."

The woman shook her head solemnly and looked away without answering. I wondered if it was because Lee was a white man, and she was embarrassed about the blood. Perhaps she was on her way to see a doctor and would be getting off the bus soon, so we waited, saying nothing. She turned her head to the wall and leaned against the side of the bus, still holding onto the thick paper bag. "What's in the bag?" I wondered. She rode all the way to Canal Street, the end of the line, and people filed out the back door. The woman slowly forced herself to her feet and made her way to the back door, leaving a trail of blood as she went. Lee signaled for me to follow him, as he stayed close behind her.

As she stepped off the bus and onto the sidewalk, her blood-soaked shoe slipped, and down she went, on her hands and knees, dropping the bag as she fell. The dark bottom of the paper bag ripped open, and a small stillborn baby and placenta spilled from the sack. Somebody screamed at the sight.

Lee immediately sprang into action, hailing a cab. As I knelt down to help the woman, she desperately tried to scoop the dead baby back into the torn sack. "Billy! Billy!" she cried. Between the sobs, she mumbled that her husband was a sailor who was out to sea, and her mother and sister were at work, so she was all alone. She'd called a doctor, and he told her to bring the dead baby and placenta to the hospital, but she had forgotten how to get there. "Oh, Billy!"

"We're taking you to Charity Hospital," I told her. Blood was now all over the sidewalk. When the driver saw all the blood, he didn't want to let the woman in his taxi. Lee told the driver bluntly that if he did not help she would die. Before the cabbie could offer any more resistance, I quickly spread my research papers out to cover the seat of the taxi and sat her down on them. At this point, he had no choice. Fortunately, the hospital was not far. Soon, we reached the emergency entrance.

Lee helped the weak and wobbly woman get out of the car, as the cabbie grabbed a wheelchair. I transferred the blood-soaked paper bag (and the dead baby) into my canvas bag. Lee and the cabbie maneuvered the woman into the wheelchair and placed the canvas bag on her lap. The ER staff came out promptly, and Lee told them she had lost her baby. Without another word, the medical staff whisked the woman inside. I retrieved my bloody research papers from the back of the taxi and threw them in the trash. Lee said "What do we owe you?" to the cabbie. By now he realized there was a dead baby in the bag, so he refused to accept any money for his services.

Lee and I looked at each other blankly. Our emotions were drained. Both of us had blood on our hands and arms: we needed to wash up before meeting Dr. Ochsner. As we entered the hospital, the medical staff took one look at us and assumed that we had been fighting, so we had to calm them down and explained that we had just helped an injured woman get to the emergency room. We then cleaned ourselves up as best we could in the disappointingly dirty rest rooms. When we were done, we went to the registration desk and said we were there to see Dr. Ochsner.

Then Lee told me we couldn't sit together because it might be remembered. The good news was that we would not have to wait long. Lee said that he would see Dr. Ochsner first by himself, then after a few other patients, I would follow, so nobody in the waiting room would connect us. It was easy to see that Charity Hospital's clinic was overwhelmed by an avalanche of the poor, mostly blacks and latinos, in need of medical service. Lee's precautions seemed ridiculous. But, I resolved to play it his way. Okay, we'll play James Bond, I thought to myself, as I sat down on the wooden bench alone. I soon realized there were no white couples in the room. There were few whites at all. Lee was right, we'd have stood out like ticks on a dog's ear.

Charity Hospital, New Orleans, La.

Charity Hospital had been a bold move into public health in the 1930s. It was the brainchild of populist Governor Huey Long, and the 1,700 bed hospital was the state-of-the-art facility in its day, providing Louisiana's poor with free health care for the first time. The gleam of the old polished wood and the faded overhead lamps gave me a glimpse of its previous glory days, but now the floors were dirty, and the waiting was endless. After half an hour, someone came out to get Lee and escorted him down the hall. He was gone about forty-five minutes. After he came out, he stopped to drink at the water fountain and then seated himself where I could see him. Fifteen minutes later, a nurse came out and asked me to follow her. She led me to a small conference room with a frosted glass door with no name on it. Inside sat Dr. Alton Ochsner, Sr.

"Won't you sit down, Miss Vary?" Dr. Ochsner said politely.

Distinguished, mustachioed, and self-confident, power shot from this man's eyes like little electrical charges. It was like being seated before an emperor. Nobody sassed Ochsner. Nobody stood in his way. He commanded everything around him in a relaxed manner that indicated he knew there would be no resistance to anything he ordered.

"Have you caught up with the literature?" he asked.

"Yes, sir."

"We're having reports flown in from both coasts even before they're published. Every new strain of lymphoma in the country can be in our hands within days. Breeder mice are being ordered from different sources to avoid suspicion. If you need anything, let me know."

I noticed that Dr. Ochsner avoided mentioning anything about my working in Dr. Sherman's lab. Was Dr. Ochsner ordering me to run Dave Ferrie's clandestine lab without even discussing the matter with me?

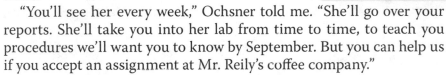

"My internship...?" I queried gently.

"Of course you're going to Tulane in the fall," Ochsner said. "I wouldn't have asked you to come to New Orleans otherwise."

"Will I still be working with Dr. Sherman?" I asked.

"You'll see her every week," Ochsner told me. "She'll go over your reports. She'll take you into her lab from time to time, to teach you procedures we'll want you to know by September. But you can help us if you accept an assignment at Mr. Reily's coffee company."

"How would my talents be useful at a coffee company?" I asked.

"Your presence there will cut out two girls who could present problems for Mr. Monaghan," Ochsner explained. "He has to have someone there every morning, and he needs you to cover for Mr. Oswald's absences."

Ochsner then explained that Lee would also be working on the Project by transporting chemicals, equipment and specimens to several locations. Nobody would suspect that Lee had anything to do with a project involving cancer research, he pointed out. Ochsner said Lee's offer to work at Reily and to courier materials had already been accepted, but that he would also be involved in another aspect of the project, slated for later in the year.

My position at Reily would be salaried, so that my time out of the office would not be recorded and Reily would, in effect, be paying for my hours spent on cancer work. The same was true for Lee's position.

This arrangement meant that I would receive more money than the stipend he had originally planned for me, Ochsner explained, and I would be able to live comfortably. Mr. Monaghan would see to it that I received a week of training at Reily, so I shouldn't be afraid to tackle the tasks involved.

"I want you to remember that Mr. Oswald will be there to help you," he stressed. "Mr. Oswald will have additional duties unrelated to his job at Reily's, just as you will, but you can commandeer his courier services any time you need them during his work day."

I pointed out to Dr. Ochsner that he was not giving me a choice about working in Dr. Sherman's lab or at Reily.

"You managed, once again, to get yourself into some trouble," he said firmly, "by somehow nosing yourself into the wrong side of this project."

Ochsner looked sternly at me for a moment, but then gently added, "I will overlook it, however, since I didn't know your schedule had changed, and I wasn't available to direct your course."

"I also got married," I blurted out, before adding "You'd find out soon enough, anyway."

"Do you need birth control pills?" he asked as if he had already guessed my motive. I was very relieved that he wasn't angry.

"Yes," I said simply.

"As far as your husband knows, you're only a secretary at Reily."

"I doubt he'll know where I'm working," I said. "He'll be out of town a lot."

"Write nothing about cancer research on any forms you fill out at Reily."

"How can I justify being hired, without any prior experience in the field?" I asked. "I flunked my typing test at A-1 Employment."

"Make up something," he told me.

"No, I won't do that," I answered, stubbornly.

"Damn it!" Ochsner complained. "Have you no prior office experience whatsoever?"

"Well, my dad had me running his business for him for a few months, after he fired his accountant. I did bookkeeping and answered the phone. He did the typing."

"Write that down," Ochsner said. "Don't mention you can't type. Do you have any idea what creative lying is?"

"Mr. Oswald is certainly good at it," I said. "But I won't do it."

"Foolishness!" Ochsner huffed. "On the other hand, I suppose I can take everything you say and write as plain and straightforward fact, then?"

"You can be certain of it," I answered.

"Well, that's worth something."

"To understand the project, I need to read the prior reports," I told him.

"They're destroyed immediately after statistics are pulled from them," Ochsner replied. "However, Dr. Sherman keeps a log. Talk to her about that."

Ochsner grabbed a notepad from the desk and wrote a prescription for birth control pills, telling me to take the prescription to the hospital's pharmacy. He also gave me a voucher for enough free pills to last the rest of the year.

"Take vitamin C daily and an aspirin every other day with those things," he warned me. "The high hormone doses in those pills can cause blood clots. I don't want to lose you due to a blood clot."

"All right, I'll do that, Dr. Ochsner," I told him. "But I still don't understand why you want me in Dave Ferrie's lab. I think I could do more for the project in a real lab. The set-up at Ferrie's has some problems."

"That's precisely why I need you to be in charge of Ferrie's part of the project," Ochsner said. "You know how to work under primitive conditions. In addition, besides your capacity to run it without supervision, you're the fastest reader I've ever seen, and we need some ideas. You're an unconventional thinker. I want your input. We've reached an impasse, and we need your serendipity."

With that, Ochsner handed me a briefcase filled with a thick stack of research articles.

"What's the problem?" I asked.

"Cross-species transfer," Ochsner said. "And there's another problem. We can inject a mouse with half-a-million cancer cells, but ten minutes later, the mouse has sifted all the cells out of its circulatory system. Only if we inject the mouse with over a million cells, do we get cell survival. If we injected a human with a dose of cells on the same scale, he'd have to take a pint of injections." Ochsner then dropped the magic words. "Nobody could get away with injecting Fidel Castro with a pint of anything."

With that, Ochsner concluded our meeting, and I left. Back in the waiting room, Lee was nowhere to be seen. I surmised he might be in the bathroom and waited a bit. Soon a nurse came over to me and told me Mr. Oswald was waiting outside the building. When I found him, Lee and I started comparing notes on Ochsner as we walked to Canal Street. Lee said that he had been questioned closely as to his right-wing sympathies, but knowing Ochsner's leanings, had offered some of his creative lies by praising Banister's work in ferreting out radical students.

"I also told him, and this part is true, that I wished to mimic Herbert Philbrick's ideas about pamphleteering," Lee said. "I brought up Philbrick, of course, in the hope that Ochsner would allow me to meet him when he comes to Reily's for the INCA meeting."

"Did it work?" I asked.

"I think so," Lee replied. "I told him I was willing to do curbside leafleting to smoke out pro-Castroites here in New Orleans, and that both Banister and Dave thought this would be fine, after the students leave for the summer. I also showed Ochsner the newspaper article about Phillips, who was beaten by three men, and suggested since INCA had media connections that the more publicity my leafleting activities generate the more easily I can get into Cuba, if necessary."

"Did he agree?"

"He's going to think about it. I also volunteered to take the serum to Cuba, if they can't find anybody else. I'm a radar man. Nobody would ever suspect I had anything to do with a biological weapon."

We walked in silence for a few minutes, while I ruminated on the courage contained in these statements. If Lee was caught inside Cuba, and the nature of the materials were discovered, he'd be tortured and executed.

"We need to turn this day around. Let's go see Lee Circle, and then pick up a few more dollars at Rev. Jim's so we can eat Chinese tonight," he said, taking charge of my briefcase.

We had gone around Lee Circle a number of times on the streetcar, but this time we walked around the park to see the sights. Lee pointed out the statue of Robert E. Lee and proudly reminded me that he was named after the famous Confederate general. Then he pointed to an unremarkable new building and explained how it sat on the site of the old Carnegie Library, a spectacular building graced with Greek columns and magnificent appointments. Lee said this library had been one of his favorite haunts as a teenager.

"They tore down a beautiful building, constructed to last for centuries, " Lee said angrily, "in a crooked money-making deal." Lee added that other historic buildings were also being torn down all along St. Charles Avenue so that cheap, modern structures could be built. All this because bribe money was going into corrupt pockets. "Anything to make another crooked dollar!"

As we continued to walk, Lee was plunged deep in memories. I again noted how he walked with his feet straight ahead at all times. Everything about Lee was straight, I mused — except for his 'creative lies.'

"Oswald! Is that you?" someone suddenly shouted.

Lee looked up and noticed a thin young white man coming around the monument, carrying a Polaroid camera.

"Thornley!" Lee answered.

"What are you doing here?" Thornley replied, breaking into a rambling lope. Reaching Lee, he grabbed his shoulders in a warm masculine greeting.

Kerry Thornley was a fellow Marine with whom Lee had served at El Toro Marine Base in California. Both wanted to become writers and see the world. Thornley said he lived nearby and invited Lee to play some pool with him, but Lee declined, saying he was going to take me out to eat. Thornley suddenly took our picture with his Polaroid, as Lee protested. When the picture scrolled out of the camera, Lee took it, watched it develop, and then tore it to pieces.

"Hey, what did you do that for?" Thornley asked. "I just wanted to give you and your wife a picture."

"This isn't my wife," Lee said.

"You're not? " Thornley asked. I shook my head.

"We just found out we've been hired by the same company," Lee said, "So we're going out to celebrate. My wife won't be here for a few days — and the same for her husband."

"Are you sure that's all there is to it?" Thornley asked, grinning.

"Tell you what," Lee said. "Go ahead, take another picture."

"I can't." Thornley said in a disgruntled voice. "That was the last one in the camera."

Lee drew out a tiny camera from his shirt pocket. "Well, I have a miniature camera with me. I'll show you how to work it, and then you can take another picture of us with that. Okay?"

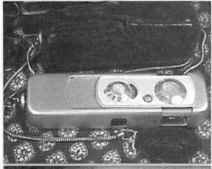

It was silver, in a dark leather case with a chain hanging from it.

Very cool," Thornley said, taking it from Lee and inspecting it. "You kept it!" It was a Minox--a tiny spy camera.

"You know I like photography," Lee responded. "With this little baby, I can take pictures anywhere, and carry it in my pocket, unlike your Polaroid."

Lee quickly showed Thornley how to use the camera, and Thornley snapped our picture (If I only had that photo!). Then Lee took one of Thornley.

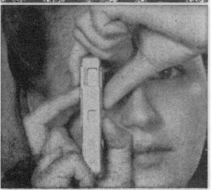

"I develop 'em myself," Lee said. "I'll bring you a print. Just tell me where you live." The two talked awhile longer, then Lee and I continued to Reverend Jim's, where we worked another two hours.

With what we'd made the day before, we had enough money to pay for a good meal at the House of Lee, a Chinese restaurant owned by Harry Lee's family. Lee knew Harry because he worked part-time with Lee's friend David Lewis at the bus station to help support his big family. Harry Lee was there that night, and greeted us warmly. He insisted that we eat for free and saw to it that we were treated like celebrities.[4]

Harry Lee was Sheriff of Jefferson Parish, Louisiana for 27 years, from 1979 until his death in 2007. Born in the back room of his family's Chinese laundry in New Orleans in 1932, he grew up working with his family's Chinese restaurants. Lee attended LSU and joined the Air Force in the 1950s. In 1959 he returned to Louisiana and worked in his father's restaurants, the most famous of which was the House of Lee, which opened in 1961. Soon Lee met Congressman Hale Boggs, who became his political mentor and for the next six years Lee moonlighted as Boggs' driver whenever the Congressman was in Louisiana. In 1964 Lee was elected president of the New Orleans Chapter of the Louisiana Restaurant Association and presided over the peaceful racial integration of New Orleans restaurants in compliance with the Civil Rights Act of 1964.

After graduating from Loyola Law School in 1967, Lee practiced law until Congressman Boggs helped him get appointed first magistrate for the U.S. District Court in New Orleans in 1971.

In 1972 Boggs invited him to travel to the People's Republic of China with the Congressional Delegation led by Boggs and Representative Gerald Ford. (Both Boggs and Ford served on LBJ's Warren Commission, and Boggs was killed in a plane crash after they returned from China). Publicly known as a zealous crime fighter, Lee was a political insider and had close contacts with Louisiana Governor Edwin Edwards. He also maintained close contact with Congressman Boggs' family after his death.

In 1975 he became chief attorney for Jefferson Parish, Louisiana, and in 1979 was elected Sheriff. He immediately gave deputies raises and computerized the Sheriff's Office. His popularity was confirmed by six re-elections despite many turbulent conflicts with the local media. Lee developed prostate cancer in 2007 and died of leukemia later that same year.

When Lee finally took me home, it was long past dark. We had once again been through a day filled with unexpected stress. Yet, in the end, we emerged relaxed and content with each other. We lingered on the front porch saying our long goodnight, as Collie came out from under the house and rested against our legs. Lee reminded me to meet him at 1:00 P.M. at Walgreen's prior to our Reily interviews, so he could tell me how to mask the fact that we were pre-hired. I leaned against him, thinking of all we had been through.

"I just want to hug you, Lee," I finally said. "Nothing personal."

He laughed, and said okay. I then kissed his cheek. That made me very happy, so I kissed him on the mouth.

"Now I'll be suffering all night because of you!" Lee said. "Heartless wench!"

"I can't help it," I replied. "You said it was OK to hug you."

"Hug, not kiss! Bad Juduffki! How will I sleep? How will I rest? Now it's my turn," he said. "You have it coming to you."

Lee reached for me and kissed me. The song, "Then He Kissed Me" came out later in 1963, and thereafter, whenever I thought of that kiss the song would roar through my head: He kissed me in a way I'd never been kissed before... in a way I wanted to be kissed forever more!

We broke away, our hearts pounding. "How are we going to handle this?" I asked.

"Slap me," he suggested.

"I could never slap you," I said. "I love you. Besides, then I'd never find out how the Adam and Eve story ended."

"To make you happy is all I want anymore," he said, his eyes cast down.

"Oh, Lee," I answered, " ... that's all I want; to make you happy, too!"

He bent down and whispered, "But do you really love me, Juduffki?"

I was silent a moment, then whispered, "Yes."

"Then I'm content," he said. "I have to go now."

He stroked my hair gently. Then he turned and walked away without looking back. I continued to pet Collie, wondering what in the world would happen next?

---

1. Lee's Aunt Lillian Murret told the WC she did not know that Lee had visited his father's grave on Sunday. As I reported, Lee talked to his uncle about that. Soon after that statement, Lillian also mentions Lee trying to get a job "lettering" at "Rampart Street."

   Of course, Lee didn't give away our work periods there, but may have had to explain his first contact with Rev. James:

   From WC. Vol. VIII, pg. 46:

   "Now what he didn't tell me was that on Sunday he must have gone to the cemetery where his father was buried... anyway, Lee looked in the paper and finally he found this job – I don't know where it was, but it was up on Rampart Street, and they wanted someone to letter."

   Mr. Jenner: To letter?

   Mrs. Murret: To do lettering work, yes, and so he called this man and the man said to come on out, so he went on out there to see about this job. First, while he was waiting for the appointment time, he sat down and tried to letter, and well, it was a little sad, because he couldn't letter as well as my next door neighbor's 6-year-old child, but I didn't say anything, so when he got back he said, "Well, I didn't get the job." He said, "They want someone who can letter, and I don't know how to do that."

   In fact, Lee didn't want anyone to know that we went to Rev. Jim's to make pin money (and would do so late in the summer, as well). Later, he would say he had worked at an address on Rampart at one time.

2. One researcher said a person had reported that Lee had been born into a Hungarian family and thereby knew both Hungarian and Russian fluently from childhood. Anyone who had spent time with Lee knew how hard he practiced his Russian. His ability to pick up language orally was rapid and excellent—probably a compensation for his dyslexia, which made him an excellent listener, but he did not know Hungarian. I have lost most of my knowledge of Hungarian over the years, but fifty years earlier, I knew some spoken Hungarian. Lee knew none.

3. At the library, Lee and I found the address of Evangeline Seismic, and I called them on Susie's phone to locate Robert. They passed on my new address to Robert.

4. Harry Lee was interviewed before his death concerning whether he knew Lee Oswald. He claimed it was his brother, not he, who had known Oswald. Nevertheless, it was Harry, not his brother, who was so gracious to us that night.

RED SCISSORS
Coupons
SAVE COUPONS
PACKED IN
LUZIANNE COFFEE
LUZIANNE TEA
NET WEIGHT
ONE POUND
LUZIAN
REG. U.S. PAT. OFF.
West Bend
PERCOLATOR
$5.95 ONLY
with $6.00 gift certificate inside
COFFEE AND CHICO
WM. B. REILY & COMPANY,
NEW ORLEANS, U.S.A.

CHAPTER 14

COVER JOBS

Thursday, May 9, 1963

The day of our interviews at Reily's finally arrived. I had read research papers deep into the night, then tossed and turned until dawn, alternately daydreaming about Lee and then feeling guilty about Robert. I loved both men, and that was highly troubling. How could I have fallen in love with Lee Oswald only a week after my marriage?

I finally fell asleep, to wake with sunlight high overhead. Oh, no! I had no alarm clock, and my watch had been left behind at the Mansion, so I went into Susie's kitchen to see what time it was. It was 12:30 already! I was at least half an hour away from Walgreen's. At 1:15, I reached Walgreen's out of breath, and sure enough, Lee was waiting at the counter, reading the newspaper over a cup of coffee. Late arrivals irritated Robert: he would have frowned. But Lee smiled. "You're right on time!" he said cheerily.

"How can that possibly be?" I asked.

Lee said that he knew I didn't have an alarm clock, so he simply added half an hour to my schedule, just to be on the safe side. I pondered how considerately he had adjusted his schedule without grandstanding or making me lose face, as Robert would have done.

Lee had met his mother's friend Myrtle Evans to go apartment hunting before 8 A.M. Myrtle managed apartments herself, so she was a logical choice. As was true for so much of Lee's world, things were not as they seemed. Lee already knew which apartment he would rent and how much he would pay for it. Just as Lee predicted, he was finally able to maneuver her to 4905 Magazine Street, where he spotted the "For Rent" sign. "Now it's official," Lee said, as he held up the keys.[1]

Lee noted that I would need an alarm clock for my new job, so he gave me a dollar to buy one, and we headed for the A-1 Employment Agency.[2] As we approached A-1, Lee said that we still had an hour before our appointment, so we slipped into Reverend Jim's for an hour, to earn a little more pocket change. As we painted ghouls in Reverend Jim's warehouse, Lee said we shouldn't be seen going to Reily together, so he would go over first, and then call me when it was time for my interview.

"We'll start working at Standard Coffee tomorrow and stay there for a week, while you learn the ropes and launder my records," Lee said, explaining that Standard Coffee was a subsidiary of Reily. "Then we'll transfer over to Reily's."

Launder his records? Why would he need his records laundered and why would I be the one to do it? I held these thoughts to myself, figuring that Lee would tell me when I needed to know.

When it was time, we went to A-1's office. Lee asked if there were any job openings for him, but the woman said she had nothing. Then he asked her about me, and she said there were no job prospects for me, either, but she promised to make some calls. Lee thanked her, and then asked if it would be okay if I practiced typing while he went to the interview. He said he would either call me if he got the job, or come back to get me. That way, he could check to see if A-1 had found any new prospects for him. I smiled to myself about Lee's creative lying. He already knew he had the job, so this little ruse was to reinforce his cover story with one more person along the way.

As I practiced typing, I pondered how our list of coincidences kept growing. I had already noticed this person who I "accidently met" in the Post Office already knew someone who was working with Dr. Sherman. I now realized that Lee already knew Dr. Ochsner, which struck me as unusual for a poor kid from New Orleans, who had been out of the country for the last six years. And both Lee and Dr. Ochsner wanted me to take the job at Reily's to help cover for Lee's absences and launder his records. Tomorrow, we would both start working at the Standard Coffee Company, and in a week, we would both transfer over to Reily's.

I started thinking about how things had worked out. Lee had gotten us apartments within walking distance of each other. We would be working at the same place, which meant that we would ride the same bus to and from work. Then I realized that everyone involved in the project (Sherman, Ferrie, Ochsner, Lee and me) lived surprisingly close to each other, and to the string of secret laboratories.[3] Even the Mansion had been in the same area. I wondered why they wanted me to think all this was accidental. Why not just tell me it was pre-arranged?

After a half-hour, Lee called. The A-1 lady handed me the phone, and stood so she could listen.

"Hello?" I said into the receiver.

"You can come over now," Lee told me. "Your interview will be at four."

"Okay," I said. "Can you remind me again how to get there?"

As usual, I was afraid I'd make a wrong turn and get lost, so I scribbled down the directions. But as I returned the phone, the A-1 lady said, "I know where you're going, and why. Those clerk jobs at Reily's are listed with us. If you're hired, you owe us a week's pay. You realize that, don't you? "

"You told me you had no jobs for me!" I protested. "If I do get a job there, you have nothing to do with it."

"Let me tell you something, Mrs. Baker," she snapped. "You were told to go to Reily's, using this telephone. We keep phone records of every call just for that reason. That call probably came from a Reily telephone, so we can prove you were here today. If you get the job, you'll pay, or we'll see you in court."

"Like heck I'll pay!" I answered, grabbing up my briefcase and going out the door. Unfortunately, I left the directions behind and had to go back to retrieve them. Feeling as ridiculous as Lucille Ball in *I Love Lucy*, I scooped the note off the vixen's desk and walked out again in a huff. Thanks to Lee's directions, I eventually found Reily's main building at 640 Magazine Street. There I was introduced to Al Prechter, a genial older gentleman of a highly conservative bent. Mr. Prechter explained that Lee had gone, so that we would not be seen together. He was concerned that I could only type fifteen words a minute, but I told him I had been practicing and was now up to nineteen. Mr. Prechter sighed, then had me fill out forms. I embellished my duties at my father's office, avoiding any mention of cancer research, per Dr. Ochsner's instructions.

"You'll start tomorrow," he told me. "You've been hired by Standard Coffee Company, for one week. Then we'll move you over to William B. Reily Coffee Company. Please report to Personnel at 8:00 tomorrow morning, here. You'll get your time card, punch in, and then proceed to 725 Magazine. You'll meet Mr. Oswald there at that time."

I went out to the bus stop, where Lee joined me.

"I should have told you more about why we're working at Standard for the first week," Lee said, as we walked. "Remember what I said about laundering records? You'll be purifying my past with plenty of creative lies," Lee said with a smile. "Creative lying" had become an ongoing joke between us.

"How will I do that?" I asked.

"Reily orders background checks on new people," Lee explained. "The only time they don't is if they transfer over from Standard. Since both order background checks, it would be redundant for Reily's to order another one."

"So your background check will be ordered by Standard?" I wondered out loud.

"Yes, and guess who will be writing it?" he teased.

Lee explained that they did not want Retail Credit (the company that did the background reports) to investigate him. Imagine what they would find! 1). Lee was in the newspapers four years ago as a defector to Russia. 2). Lee was in the newspapers less than a year ago as a returning defector from Russia. 3). Lee had a Russian wife, and a baby born in Russia. 4). Lee had supposedly been fired from his last job. 5). He had an undesirable discharge from the Marines. 6). He hadn't been in town long enough for any friends or neighbors to provide reliable information about his spending and living habits. And, if they investigated me, they would find out about my cancer research, which Dr. Ochsner did not want the people at Reily's to know about. So we would both transfer over from Standard Coffee with laundered background reports, another 'coincidence.' Key people at Reily's obviously knew about this charade, but for the rest of the staff, our records needed doctoring.[4]

"You'll be clocking me out for a full work-day, whether I'm there or not," he explained. "You'll have to calculate it."

"Won't somebody notice if you're late?" I asked. "I was told that if I'm five minutes late, I'll be docked. Are you going to be immune?"

"I don't have to be on time," Lee said. "But you have to. Monaghan's phone starts ringing at eight. You're not only his credit, payroll, and shipment examiner; you're also his floor secretary in the Finance Department. I'm just doing maintenance work. Besides, if Personnel finds a problem with my time card, guess where they'll take the problem?"

"To me?" I said incredulously.

"That's right," he confirmed.

One great advantage to his job at Reily's was that he might be working on any of five floors. "It's good to have a job like that," Lee said, explaining that it would help him slip away unnoticed. "You have to be gone long enough to be missed, then they have to hunt for you, and no-

body is sure when they saw you last."[5]

"Since we're rich now," Lee said, referring humorously to the pittance we'd earned at Reverend Jim's, "let's get some target practice."

But I was dressed for a job interview, not for target practice. So we went to a thrift store to get me some sneakers and cut-off shorts.[6]

Lee told me our next stop was Banister's building, which was only about a block away. Once we got there, Lee found the janitor, who lived in the building. He unlocked the door for us at the top of the stairs, and Lee and I went to the third floor. No one was there, but the room was filled with war materiel, enough to supply a garrison. Strewn across the dusty and neglected wooden floor were bedrolls, tents, poles and stakes, machetes, axes, and bayonets. There were heaps of canteens, piles of blankets, mosquito netting, and wooden boxes full of rifles and ammunition, and more rifles stacked against the wall. Boxes of Sterno and Army surplus rations were heaped beside the blankets. The musty smell of mildew filled the air. The ceiling was painted a creamy green color, with splotches of brown where water leaks had made it sag. Dust particles floated in a beam of light from the late afternoon sun. We reached a table in the corner with several cardboard boxes containing smaller firearms and a clipboard. We were alone.

I told Lee that I needed to change into my shorts, so he should turn around to give me some privacy. As he did, I wondered if all his espionage training had given him eyes in the back of his head.

Lee busied himself with the handguns and did not turn around. He selected a long-barreled .38 caliber Smith & Wesson revolver. The gun was shiny and appeared to be in excellent condition. It had a leather holster and belt. "This is mine," he said proudly.[7]

544 Camp Street front entrance   Lafayette St. entrance to Banister's office

After writing his initials on the clipboard, Lee handed me a .22 target pistol and showed me a small .22 caliber Derringer which he owned.[8] This, too, appeared to be in good condition.[9] Lee said he kept his firearms here, and not in his home, for two reasons.

"First" he said, "I'm afraid Marina might shoot me, if she got angry enough." Lee's smile informed me he wasn't really serious. Then he told me the real reason. "Junie can walk now, and I don't want Junie getting into my guns, and maybe hurting herself."[10]

Lee put the weapons in a small green canvas case, and we headed for a levee on the lakefront, where we rigged up some targets to practice on. I witnessed what a good shot Lee was with his .38, and he observed that I was a fair shot with the little .22.

It was time for supper, so we headed to Thompson's Restaurant, where we met with David and Anna Lewis and ate dinner, complete with the promised free pie for dessert. When Anna got off her shift at 7 P.M., we contributed babysitting money, allowing her and David to

join us on a walk through The French Quarter. As we strolled down Bourbon Street, we enjoyed the music as it flowed into the streets and mingled with the cool night breeze from the river. In the 400 block, we reached The 500 Club. Anna told us this was Carlos Marcello's favorite haunt when he came to town, and that he had an office on the second floor with a one-way mirror to watch for police while he conducted his business.[11]

View of the Vieux Carré from the second floor balcony of The 500 Club

We talked about going inside, but concluded it was too expensive, so we kept walking. David and Lee started talking about eliminating Castro, but the night was too romantic to dwell on the subject for long.[12]

We reached Jackson Square and sat down in a park overlooking the Mississippi River watching the horse-drawn carriages, occupied by lovers, trot past.[13] David began to kiss his wife, so Lee and I moved to another bench to give them some space. Lee brought out his transistor radio, setting it on top of his green canvas case. He put his arm around me. I leaned close to him, and let the romantic spell of New Orleans take us away. Then the radio began to play "Let It Be Me" by the Everly Brothers: "I bless the day I found you ... I want to stay around you ... and so I beg you ... let it be me ... "[14] I began to see how far into love I was falling.

Friday, May 10, 1963

This would be our first day working for Reily Coffee Company.[15] Once again, I made breakfast for Lee and Susie. At 7:20 A.M. Lee and I caught the bus at the corner of Marengo St. and headed for Reily's. I had hoped to sit with Lee, but he directed me to another seat with his eyes. He

William I. Monaghan

W.J. Monaghan — Bill Monaghan served in the FBI for three years during World War II (1942-1945) and was assigned as Special Agent # 005074. He left the FBI and returned to New Orleans where he found work at the Standard Fruit Company, a New Orleans based shipping company that primarily imported bananas from Central America; Monaghan was their head of security.

In 1961, Monaghan joined forces with Dr. Alton Ochsner and Ed Butler to form INCA, a political action organization to fight communism in the Americas. INCA core members were local businessmen and citizens who shared their anti-Communist mission, including WDSU owner Edgar Stern, ITM General Manager Clay Shaw, Eustis Reily of the Reily Coffee Company, and Robert Rainold, President of the Former Special Agents of the FBI.

By 1963 Monaghan worked at the Reily Coffee Company where he became the VP of Finance and managed their Standard Coffee division. On May 10, 1963, both Judy Vary Baker and Lee Harvey Oswald were hired by Standard Coffee Company, and then transferred to the Reily Coffee Company one week later. Baker continued to work as Monaghan's secretary for the summer.

After the JFK assassination, Monaghan provided the FBI with a list of Lee Oswald's clock-in and clock-out times, as well as his actual time cards which bore Judyth's initial, and later testified briefly to the Warren Commission. The WC published the list, but not Oswald's time cards. Monaghan claimed he did not know Oswald, and never mentioned that he hired his own secretary, Judyth Vary Baker, on the same day.

Soon Monaghan left Reily Coffee and became Executive Director for the Metropolitan Crime Commission (MCC), a private civic organization formed to monitor crime levels in New Orleans. In 1967, he was summoned before the Orleans Parish Grand Jury to explain a letter that the MCC had sent to the Louisiana State Attorney General criticizing the conduct of Orleans Parish District Attorney Jim Garrison, who had just begun his investigation into the assassination of President Kennedy. The leadership of the MCC was populated with many familiar names, including Dr. Alton Ochsner, H. Eustis Reily, Robert R. Rainold, and Warren C. de Brueys, an FBI agent associated with Lee Oswald in New Orleans. Monaghan served on the MCC board for many years and became Chairman of the MCC Board in 1997.

later told me that we were posing as new hires who didn't yet know each other. So for now, we had to treat each other as strangers. When we reached Reily's, about ten people got off with us, proving that his concerns were well founded. After getting our time cards and punching in, we walked down the street to Reily's Standard Coffee office, where William I. Monaghan met us.

Mr. Monaghan was dressed in a good dark suit with regulation tie and crisp starched white shirt, and stood a couple of inches taller than Lee. He was a powerfully built, middle-aged man with well-groomed dark hair and a craggy handsome face that reminded me of Broderick Crawford.[16] In other words, Mr. Monaghan looked and acted every inch the Fed. A man of few words, and usually all business, he seemed almost a clone of Guy Banister in the way he thought and organized himself. He possessed a dignity of spirit, distaste for wasting time, and a sense of self-importance that made an indelible impression. I had little prior experience with anyone associated with the FBI, but after meeting Banister and Monaghan, I no longer wondered why these agents used so many informants. From their slicked-back hair to the shiny black shoes, they were unmistakable G-men.

Lee departed to Reily's to learn how to grease machines, and Mr. Monaghan took me to the courthouse, where he showed me how to look up delinquent liquor and tobacco permits, taxes owed, bankruptcy data, and pending lawsuits, to help assess an account's creditworthiness. Reily's bought coffee cans, raw coffee and tea, trucks, boxes, and many other items. They sold coffee and tea, of course, but also trucked certain items, such as mayonnaise and soap products, for other companies. Grocery chains, restaurants, and mom-and-pop food stores received the products. Reily's factory equipment was sometimes used to package products for other companies, as well.

Getting their money was always the most important thing. Reily's wouldn't send a teaspoon of coffee on credit if the business was shaky. I was shown their copies of Standard & Poor's, the credit rating books which were kept in their office. The financial health of Reily's customers was never taken for granted, and every one of them got checked regularly.

Mr. Monaghan invited me to have lunch with him in a supervisor's cubicle. As we ate sandwiches, he had me taste samples of Reily's various products, like Luzianne coffees and tea, so I would understand what products the salesmen were selling. After lunch, he introduced me to three salesmen-in-training, later informing me that one of them would be selected to take over a lucrative route. As Mr. Monaghan went over their resumes, he showed me how to analyze the "Character and Financial Report" generated by Retail Credit for each salesman. One was divorced, and Monaghan said if there had been any other black marks against the man, he would not be hired, because divorce was considered evidence of a potential problem. Another had a drunk-driving conviction. That alone was sufficient to make sure he was gone.

"I expect you to produce a believable and unremarkable report on Mr. Oswald," Monaghan told me. He then asked if I could take shorthand. I said "No," but suggested that I was good at speed writing.

Knowing better, Monaghan scowled. "Luckily for you," he said, "I've noticed you have something going for you. "

"What is that, sir?" I asked.

"You have good legs," he replied. "Otherwise, I'd send you back." It was hard to decipher where his humor ended and his hormones started. From that day on, I couldn't help but notice that Mr. Monaghan spent a considerable amount of time looking at my legs. Other than that, he behaved like a gentleman. At 4:30, I clocked Lee out for the first time. My instructions were to go to the front of the line and say, "I'm Mr. Monaghan's secretary, excuse me, please." I was then able to clock Lee out without waiting.[17] Anyone more than five minutes late got docked 20 cents (unless your name was Lee Oswald). You got docked more if you were ten minutes late. Obviously, since Lee clocked in 45 to 90 minutes late on multiple occasions, his paycheck would have reflected this, had he been on an hourly wage, but it didn't.

The first day passed, and Lee and I pretended we were recent acquaintances when we rode the bus back to his apartment. He wanted to clean it up before Marina and Junie arrived. This was also a dry run to see how long the trip would take, and how many employees from Reily's would be on the bus. Again, about ten Reily employees got on the bus with us, and not all got off before we reached Lee's stop, so we didn't get to talk much. Once off the bus, I mentioned the problem to Lee.

"I've thought about that," Lee said, as we entered his apartment. "We can ride all the way down to Audubon Park, and have a nice visit. Then we can take a bus headed back toward town. There will be no employees on that bus, and we can sit together."

It was a brilliant idea, worth the pocket change. So from then on, when we didn't have to go elsewhere, we'd grab an extra hour by going straight from Reily's, passing our apartments, and getting off at the park. There we spent as much time together as we could, and then caught the bus back. Lee would get off first, at Upperline, and I'd get off one or two stops later at Marengo.

4907 Magazine Street   4905 Magazine Street

Lee's apartment at 4905 Magazine St. had a nice screen porch where Junie could play safely.[18] The side yard was rich with colorful flowers, ferns, and strawberries. As we entered from the side porch, I saw a large, almost empty living room with bare wood floors that needed a good mopping. The bathroom was wallpapered and mostly clean, but the tub needed a good scrub. The linoleum floor around the new gas stove was starting to curl, so we flattened it by lifting the stove and pushing the linoleum under it. As we did, roaches ran out. The refrigerator was clean and looked new, but the freezer was iced up.

"This is a nice apartment, Lee, but we have to clean it up," I said noting the roach droppings on the counter.[19] Lee said the double bed was clean, and he would spend the night there.

"Let me help you fix things up," I suggested.

"Well," Lee said slowly, "I could use some help."

Lee brought out cleaning supplies from under the sink, and he knew where a broom and mop were stored in a side closet, as if he had stayed here before. While Lee mopped floors, I defrosted the refrigerator and scrubbed the sink and bathtub.

The kitchen fan didn't work, so Lee opened the windows and door, to dry the place out. There were several boxes, and a couple of seabags that he had brought over earlier.[20] From one of the boxes he removed a plaid blanket, which protected some cameras and lenses, filters, and other paraphernalia useful in photography. I also saw bottles of hypo and acetic acid for developing film, carefully wrapped in brown paper.[21] It all looked quite professional.

He shook out the blanket and laid it on the bed. "I made sure to bring that blanket," he said. "It's Junie's favorite, and I was afraid Marina would forget it." Looking down at the pillowless bed, Lee said, "Well, that's all I need to spend the night here."

I commented that there wasn't much furniture, and noted that the bed had only a sheet-covered mattress, but no pillow or bedspread.

"It's only for five months," Lee said. "Then Marina goes back, to have her baby."

Lee's almost complete lack of interest in Marina's comfort concerned me.

"The less comfortable and more boring it is for her, the easier it will be to leave me," Lee explained. I tried to understand how someone who had treated me with such affection and gentleness could feel so hostile toward his own wife. "No matter what she may tell others," he said with a voice full of grief, "she knows that I know what she did." With that, he dropped the subject and refused to say another word about it.

While I wiped down the cupboards, Lee went to the store and returned with a brand-new garbage can. I tried to remove the label from the can, but it ripped, leaving half of the label on the trashcan. "It doesn't matter," Lee said, "it's just a garbage can."

Lee placed it outside on the curb near some others, and we put some trash in it.

We finished cleaning up and walked toward my apartment, checking the route.

Halfway home there was a Catholic school and a playground with a large sign that said, "BINGO TONITE" in snap-on letters. We sat on a bench near the sign.

"Why don't you go home and change into your new shorts?" Lee said, seeing how dirty my skirt had become. "Then come back with your typewriter. I'll wait for you."

"Why not come get it yourself?" I said, thinking how heavy it was. I knew Lee wanted to finish his first draft of his science-fiction story, "Her Way" before Marina showed up, but why should I drag the typewriter over to him?

"I don't want to be seen walking with you to your apartment in the daytime," Lee explained. "But if you bring the typewriter this far, I'll carry it the rest of the way to my place. I have another reason," he said. "I want to see if you can find your way back."

I had surprisingly little trouble finding my way back: the hardest part was carrying the typewriter. As I approached, Lee took it, saying "You remembered how to get back because I made you carry that thing. A mind works hard to avoid work." He was right. Seeing I was tired, Lee had me wait on the bench while he took the typewriter to his apartment. As I waited, I noticed Lee had changed the Bingo sign to read "I Binge Not." Before long, he was back, carrying the green canvas bag. But something had upset him.

"What's the matter, Lee?" I asked. "What's bothering you?"

"Well," he replied, "when I got there with the typewriter, the garbage can was gone."

"What? It wasn't out there an hour!"

Lee said he should have painted his name on the can and that he knew better.[22]

It was a beautiful afternoon so Lee bounced back, saying we should go to Lake Pontchartrain. We took the bus out to the amusement park and walked east to an isolated stretch of Lakeshore Drive, near Franklin Ave. Lee said this was the back fence of the Army and Navy training centers, so there were no houses or people around. We were inside the city limits, but Lee pulled out his pistol. There were seagulls flying over the dark waves as the sky turned to sunset. Then Lee spotted some mallard ducks which were paired off for spring nesting.

"Quiet!" Lee cautioned. He knelt down slowly, and put a cotton wad in his right ear. "Aha!" he said, taking aim, "duck for dinner!"

"Please, Lee," I said. "Have mercy!"

"Oh, ye of little faith!" he said. "Just watch."

He took aim at a drake about a hundred feet away.

He fired the first shot, and the duck scrambled into the air in confusion, as a couple of tail feathers fell from it. At the sound of the shot, all the ducks took flight, but Lee fired a second round, sending a few more feathers flying. Lee checked his revolver, putting bullets into empty chambers. "I wouldn't really hurt those ducks, Juduffki," he said. "They're in love, and about to make baby ducks. I only kill when I'm hungry, and then I only kill bachelor ducks, and old maid ducks."

Lee filled a row of beer cans with sand for me to shoot at from fifty feet. I hit them all, which pleased Lee very much. When we were done, Lee quickly and carefully cleaned the guns and returned them to the bag. We then walked along the seawall toward the amusement park, until we came to an area where we could see blue crabs scuttling across the shallow bottom. Lee told me to never keep a crab wearing an 'apron,' referring to the fuzzy material on the front of a female crab where she guards her thousands of little eggs. Protecting the mother assures there will be plenty of crabs in the future. "That's why crabs should be checked after they are netted," he said. Lee said he hated to buy crabs caught commercially because they didn't throw back mother crabs. He preferred to catch them himself.

It was twilight, and the lights of Pontchartrain Beach amusement park were now on. We went on most of the rides, including "The Whip" and the "Tilt-a-Whirl." Then, when Lee approached the shooting gallery, the proprietor recognized him and quickly closed up. At the end of the night, having dined on cotton candy and sausage sticks, we headed home. It was a wonderful evening, and when we got back to 1032 Marengo, we did not want it to end. "If I never live another day," Lee said, "and even if I never have the exquisite pleasure

of sleeping with you…" I stopped him from saying more, taking his head between my hands, and slowly kissing him, with a degree of passion I didn't know I possessed. We held each other tight, feeling our hearts pulsing against each other. Our desire was so strong, we could hardly breathe. Lee's strong arms sheltered me. New Orleans had turned from a city of fear and loneliness to a glittering treasure chest, full of the jewels of romance. The only problem was that we felt like pirates stealing the jewels.

Saturday, May 11, 1963

At dawn next morning, Lee tapped at my window. I jumped up to let him in. He had returned with the typewriter and two copies of his science fiction story, "Her Way." The top copy was white. The bottom was a carbon copy, exploiting the pink paper that came from my parents-in-laws´ real estate office.

"It's finished!" Lee announced. "I worked on it all night. I used a dictionary," he finished, almost apologetically. "Most of the words should be spelled correctly."

I saw he was anxious for me to read it. I'd sat beside him through most of the writing of this story, but had no idea what the ending was going to be like. Wrapped in my robe, I read it as Lee paced back and forth, waiting for my reaction. I realized that Lee had writing talent indeed, and knew how to tie up the loose ends of a story. However, I had never read so many bizarre and alien ideas, words, and descriptions.[23]

"I can't figure out why the spaceship is trapped and can't escape the depredations of the Phoenix, if Alt and the "feely" are really from an advanced civilization," I finally said. "But otherwise, I'm impressed. "

"I'll fix it," Lee said at once, nervously. "Anything else?"

"It's a unique style all your own. And you've made up words I've never seen before."

"That's probably because I can't spell," Lee said, looking miserable.

"No, no, these are really original and interesting words," I replied. "They add to the story all the way. I'm fascinated by them."

Lee had read some of my poetry and short stories, mostly well after midnight while lying in bed at his uncle's house. He had expressed respect for my writing. Now it was my turn to encourage him.

"Don't show it to anybody," Lee said. "But fix anything you like."

"By the way," he added, "you're supposed to meet Dr. Sherman for lunch at noon today, at her apartment." This was the first I had heard anything about lunch with Dr. Sherman! I set aside Lee's story, a little miffed. "Why am I the last to know these things?" I complained.

"My love," Lee said, stroking my hair, "I was supposed to tell you last night, but you scrambled my brains when you kissed me."

I buried my head against his chest, as he put his arms around me.

"I won't be able to be with you like this for days," Lee said. "I'm going to hate that. But I promise to be here in eight minutes if you need help for any reason. If there's an emergency, just call this number." Lee handed me Mr. Garner's phone number. He was the apartment manager's husband, and he drove a cab. It would not seem unusual to call him, as long as it was at a decent hour. All I had to do was say I was trying to reach Reily's new janitor, and Mr. Garner would pass the message on to Lee.[24]

He kissed me goodbye and said he'd see me Monday morning on the bus. I sighed as Lee left, and pondered the dilemma of my love life. Marina was coming, and I was now the "other woman." It was getting harder to stay faithful to my husband. I even wrote a poem about my romantic quandary.

I solemnly watered the four begonias sitting in my window, and studied their pretty blossoms. I was writing to Robert, but he wasn't replying. The nights were long and lonely. What was Robert doing right now?

---

1. The evening before, when we returned by the Magazine bus to my neighborhood, we got off near Lee's apartment-to-be. At that time, Lee asked the property manager there, Mrs. Garner, to place a 'To Let" sign outside. Then he walked me home.

2. It was a brass Baby Ben wind-up alarm clock that I had noticed in the display window at Woolworth. I used that clock for the next 20 years.

3. Explained in Edward T. Haslam's book, *Dr. Mary's Monkey*. Years before he knew of my existence, Haslam drew a circle on a map of a portion of New Orleans in his first book about the secret labs, showing that Lee, Dr. Mary Sherman, Ochsner, and Ferrie all lived inside its perimeter — not knowing that my apartment at 1032 Marengo was also within that circle.

4. Such a report would make it impossible for the highly conservative Reily Coffee Company, which prided itself on hiring only fine citizens, to openly hire Lee Harvey Oswald. They would never touch a former Marine with an undesirable discharge, let alone a former defector to Russia. And they would report such a person to the FBI, the CIA, and HUAC. William Reily was a charter member of INCA, and fiercely anti-Communist.

    I knew that HUAC (The House Un-American Activities Committee) was renowned for witch hunts against actual and supposed Communists, sometimes ruining the lives of innocent people in the process. In 1963, HUAC still followed the imperatives of McCarthyism, including tracking and reporting defectors with the help of the CIA. I own copies of correspondence between HUAC's Chairman, Louisiana Rep. Edwin Willis, and Francis J. MacNamara of the CIA, written in 1963, about how to use a brand new Russian defector for propaganda purposes. Willis' office was located right across the street from Reily's. Willis had been informed about Lee's true role, so Lee had nothing to fear from HUAC, because Willis was (conveniently) named Chair of HUAC in May, making him privy to the CIA's secret use of Lee. So when Lee later passed out Pro-Castro pamphlets almost under Willis' nose – and got arrested for it – HUAC looked the other way, until publicity on TV and radio forced them into minimal action.

Mr. Monaghan sent me to Willis' office several times that summer, with sealed envelopes. It has been suggested that Willis may have been bribed, or simply given away information, such as forewarnings about Lee's activities. The proximity of Reily's to Chairman Willis' office, and his leadership of HUAC, went unnoticed by researchers for decades until I broke my silence.

5. Since Lee was on salary, most of his Reily checks were for exactly $53.72, despite his many late clock-ins and absences for hours at a time. Lee also received substantial pay from what was most likely the CIA. I saw the contents (cash) of one of his envelopes. Lee stashed unused funds in an account for Marina and his children, in case something happened to him. He spent no government-issued funds for personal pleasure, which is why he enjoyed earning a bit with me at Reverend Jim's.

6. I also bought Lee a brown, long-sleeved shirt to thank him for all of his help. A two-for-one sale, I got Robert one, too (size 'large'), reflecting my divided love.

7. The hand-gun that Lee showed me that day in New Orleans was certainly not the same weapon supposedly wrestled from him inside the Texas Theater in Dallas on the afternoon of November 22. Lee had shown me a pistol with a 4 to 6 inch barrel, but the Texas Theater pistol had a 2 inch barrel, often called a "snub nose." Unfortunately, they attempted to use that same gun to argue that Lee had killed a Dallas police office named J. D. Tippitt. The central problem with their argument was pointed out long ago by JFK researchers: The evidence found at the scene of Officer Tippitt's murder indicated that he was shot with a semi-automatic pistol, not a revolver. In the same breath, they claimed Lee was carrying a revolver when they arrested him. This single piece of evidence could have exonerated Lee from any involvement in Officer Tippitt's slaying. But since Lee was murdered before his trial, this never hit the headlines.

8. Under a column where I saw the word "Hidell," (it was not the first time, and would not be the last, I'd see that name, I also saw another word that looked like "Nagy" or "Nagel.")

9. Lee never mentioned a rifle, and I never saw a rifle.

10. June Lee Oswald was 14 months old and becoming an active toddler. She would soon be arriving with her mother from Texas. Marina Oswald originally testified to police that she never saw Lee with a rifle at their Magazine Street apartment. But later she told The Warren Commission that she frequently saw Lee dry firing his rifle on the porch. Then, later, during the Clay Shaw hearings, she said she was unable to recognize Lee's rifle. Marina was an intelligent woman whose choreographed memory lapses made it difficult to use her as a trusted witness against her deceased husband.

11. At the time, Marcello was fighting Bobby Kennedy's deportation order and was not even supposed to enter Orleans Parish, but he did anyway. All three times I saw him, he had an attorney or two with him, in case a Fed might try to arrest him for crossing the line. The attorneys would, no doubt, swear Carlos was on his way to a funeral, a wedding, or had to visit a dying relative in the hospital – whatever excuse seemed plausible.

12. Witness Anna Lewis said that at one point David Lewis asked Lee if they were planning to shoot Castro. Lee answered, "No. We've got that taken care of." Anna dismissed these comments as mere talk.

13. The carriages were actually drawn by mules, but they were such finely-bred animals that everybody called them "horses."

14. From that moment, "Let It Be Me" by the Everly Brothers' became our song. To this very day, if I hear it played without warning, the first chords make me break into tears.

15. Officially known as the Wm. B. Reily & Company, Inc., this company produced Luzianne Coffee, Standard Coffee, and other products.

16. Broderick Crawford was a film and television star from the 1930s through the early-1960s. He is best known for his role as Dan Matthews in the late 1950s TV show, "Highway Patrol."

17. This is why evening (but not morning) stamped times on Lee's time cards, as listed in the Warren Commission volumes, are so consistent. The long line of forty or fifty employees, all wanting to leave, meant some had to wait up to eight minutes. The clock-stamping process took ten seconds (move forward, scan to find your card, pull your card, position it correctly, get it stamped, return it to the right slot, move forward). Only six or seven people, then, could get their time-cards stamped in one minute. In the morning, everybody tried to arrive five minutes early to avoid a possible late clock-in.

18. Mix-Ups: The 4905-4907 Mix-Up, and the Reily Coffee Co.-Leon Israel Coffee Co. Mix-Up. Though Lee and his family would be living at 4905, Lee had set up 4907 Magazine Street as his 'real' address. Interestingly, Lee had the utilities turned on at 4907 – not at 4905 (the utilities were already on). But why? In fact, Lee would use 4907 as a "fake residence." Most researchers didn't notice that 4907 wasn't Lee's true address, for he placed '4907' on flyers and wrote '4907' almost anywhere an address was required. And all of Lee's mail went to 4907 – not to 4905 (Lee had his reasons, as we shall see). The power went on – the lights gleamed – the pilot to the gas oven was lit – but it was all at the WRONG apartment – 4907 Magazine Street – as of May 9, 1963. Lee also had a key to 4907, which I discovered on May 11. Lee gave his work address as – "Leon Israel Coffee Company' (instead of Reily), at 300 Magazine (not Reily's 640 Magazine)," CIA asset Patricia Johnson McMillan wrote an "official version" biography called Marina & Lee, based on lengthy interviews and years of research carefully crafted to create a picture of Lee Oswald that scarcely resembled him, but fit well the portrait of a cruel weirdo with sex problems. Concerning the fake address he gave the landlady, she wrote: "The landlady was Mrs. Jesse Garner, and Lee gave her a month's rent and an application for utilities along with a $5 deposit. But then he told another of his funny, pointless lies. He said he worked for the Leon Israel Company of 300 Magazine Street. The company existed, but it was not the company that hired him." (p. 389) But this wasn't 'another of his funny, pointless lies. Lee didn't want the 'landlady' (actually, Garner was the building manager) to give Marina the address to Reily's, just in case Marina – sure to smell coffee on his clothing – might ride the bus over there and spot Lee and me together. It is known that she visited Leon Israel Coffee Company seeking Lee there. So it was as simple as that. Before this, McMillan admits, Lee always told Marina exactly where he was working – but not this time. In fact, many of Lee's true activities in New Orleans – where the assassination plot was first hatched – were obscured by Lee himself, because he was playing a part, à la the Scarlet Pimpernel.

19. Roaches and mold are the bane of New Orleans. People wouldn't eat in a New Orleans restaurant if they could see the insect life that takes over once the lights go off. The only place I've ever lived where roaches were worse than New Orleans was Saltillo, Mexico.

20. Lee had kept his seabags, luggage and boxes at a bus station locker, then moved them to the Murret's garage. When Marina and Junie arrived, brought by Ruth Paine from Texas, his Uncle Dutz and his cousin John moved the rest of the Oswald belongings to the 4905 apartment by car. Lee ended up spending this night at the Murrets again, I later learned, anticipating a phone call from Marina.

21. Today I know the twin-sized blanket was supposed to have held the killer Mannlicher-Carcano rifle for an unknown period of time in Ruth Paine's garage in Irving, Texas. There was no rifle in the blanket on May 10, 1963.

22. A week later, while on the bus, we saw a new garbage can with the partially torn label on it about three houses down. Somebody had painted their initials on it, but there was no doubt that this was Lee's garbage can. Lee later told me that he would sneak out in the middle of the night and place his garbage in that can.

23. Lee would type a final, brilliant draft of "Her Way" later that summer, after he met Clay Shaw and added the character Crawley.

24. The first two letters of "janitor" are "J A" (as in Judyth Anne, the first two initials of my name): this told Lee that I was the caller.

Dr. Mary Sherman,
first woman physician on the staff of
Ochsner Clinic & Hospital, 1953.

CHAPTER 15

DR. MARY

Saturday, May 11, 1963

Today was the day I would finally get to talk to the famous Dr. Mary Sherman. Using Lee as the messenger, she had invited me to have lunch in her apartment at noon. Dr. Sherman lived in the Patio Apartments on St. Charles Avenue near the corner of Louisiana Ave. It was so close that I could have walked there from my place on Marengo Street, but I preferred the refreshing streetcar ride. I entered her complex exactly at noon, and located her apartment at the far end of the elegant courtyard up one flight of stairs. At the end of the courtyard was a small patio, lush with plants and flowers in bloom, I stopped by the stairs and looked up. I saw the "J" on the door of her apartment and knew at once I wouldn't have any problem remembering which was hers.

As I approached the door it opened, and Dr. Sherman stepped out to greet me with a gracious smile. "Judy, we've been expecting you!" she said in a warm, friendly voice. Dr. Sherman was dressed attractively in a peach-colored suit with her hair up in a French twist. She took me by the hand and guided me into her spotless home.

In the front room, lunch was already set out on a table decorated with fancy glasses and fresh flowers. Much to my surprise, there was a

Dr. Mary Sherman

Dr. Mary Sherman was one of the most respected women in American Medicine. Born in Illinois in 1913, she studied in Europe and spoke several languages. In 1934, she then entered the University of Chicago Medical School and became friends with classmate Sarah Stewart, who later discovered the first cancer-causing virus.

Mary married Thomas Sherman, who paid for her medical education. But Thomas was an alcoholic, and their marriage was a disaster. Whether Thomas committed suicide or abandoned Mary is unclear, but she claimed to be a widow.

Throughout the 1940's, Mary continued at the University of Chicago, where she was trained as an Orthopedic Surgeon, and eventually became the Chairman of the Pathology Committee of the American Academy of Orthopedic Surgeons. Her main interest was cancer, and she published many medical articles in the field. While in Chicago, she was close to the legendary physicist Enrico Fermi, famous for the first sustained nuclear reaction, which paved the way for both nuclear power and the atomic bomb. Mary became an expert in the medical uses of radiation and wrote numerous articles on that subject. In 1953 Mary moved to New Orleans, where she became an Associate Professor at Tulane Medical School and a partner in the Ochsner Clinic. There she set up a laboratory, now named in her honor.

On July 21, 1964, hours before the Warren Commission began their investigation into Lee Oswald's activities in New Orleans, Dr. Sherman was murdered. Her body was found naked in her apartment, her right arm and thorax had been burned completely off, but the rest of her body was not burned in the same manner. There were seven stab wounds to her body, one of which penetrated her heart and caused her death. In October 1967 Jim Garrison revealed that his investigation into the JFK Assassination had connected Mary Sherman to David Ferrie and hi-lighted their private cancer experiments with mice. She is the subject of the book *Dr. Mary's Monkey*, by Edward T. Haslam.

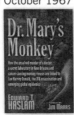

man sitting at the table smoking a cigarette. It was David Ferrie.

Dr. Sherman offered me a seat and presented me with a plate of finger sandwiches. Her soothing manner was entirely different from the stern woman who had cut me off so abruptly at Dave's party. Today she was so hospitable that I soon let go of the humiliation of that earlier experience. When I addressed her as Dr. Sherman, she invited me to call her Dr. Mary instead. We had fruit compote, pastries, salad, and a conversation like none I had ever heard before.

Dave and Dr. Mary had been chatting about the conquest of Mount Everest, but the conversation quickly shifted to medicine. Both Dave and Dr. Mary began describing chilling experiments on human brains being conducted at Tulane by Dr. Robert Heath. Heath's most recent exploits were described in the newspaper on Friday. I had not seen the article they were referring to.

Dave said, "Listen to this, J. 'Dr. Heath Tells New Technique. Electrical Impulses Sent Deep Into Brain... [a patient]... had tiny wires implanted into precise spots in his brain. The wires were attached to a self-stimulator box, which was equipped at a push of a button to deliver a tiny, electrical impulse to the brain...'" Dave paused to let what he was reading sink in. "I wonder how many brains Heath went through before he had success with these two?

How long did it take to find those 'precise spots' in their brains with his hot little wires?"

"Dr. Ochsner would never do such a thing," Dr. Mary said, pouring me some tea.

"It sounds like science fiction," Dave said. "Who knows what kind of mind control could be exerted over a brain, twenty or thirty years from now?"

"I doubt John Q. Public will ever have a clue," Dr. Mary replied. "They certainly have no idea they were getting cancer-causing monkey viruses in their polio vaccines," she added bitterly. Seeing my expression of shock, Dr. Mary went on to explain that she and a few others had privately protested the marketing of the SV40-contaminated polio vaccine, but to no avail. The government continued to allow the distribution of millions of doses of the contaminated vaccine in America and abroad.

She said she was told that the new batches of the vaccine would be free of the cancerous virus, but privately she doubted it, noting that the huge stockpile of vaccines she knew were contaminated had not been recalled. To recall them would damage the public's confidence, she explained.

I was speechless. Were they telling me that a new wave of cancer was about to wash over the world?

"The government is hiding these facts from the people," Dave said, "so they won't panic and refuse to take vaccines. But is it right? Don't people have the right to be told the contaminant causes cancer in a variety of animals? Instead, they show you pictures in the newspaper of fashion models sipping the stuff, to make people feel it's safe."

My mind raced. It was 1963. They had been distributing contaminated polio vaccines since 1955. For eight years! Over a hundred million doses! Even I had received it! A blood-curdling chill came over me. Their words seared into my soul.[1] The scale of the

Cancer-causing Monkey Virus

In 1957 Sarah Stewart, MD, PhD of the National Cancer Institute and Bernice Eddy, MD, PhD of the National Institute of Health discovered SE Polyoma, a cancer-causing virus present in their laboratory animals. It was soon cataloged as Simian Virus 40 (SV40), and it's origin traced to monkeys. Studies around the world soon confirmed SV40 as a cancer-causing agent.

Upon the discovery that SV40 was present in both of the polio vaccines produced from Rhesus monkey kidney cells, a new federal law passed in 1961 mandated future vaccines should not contain this virus. However, this law did not require that SV40 contaminated vaccine stocks already produced be destroyed, so distribution of the tainted vaccine continued until 1963. Bottom line: the Boston Globe estimated that 198 million Americans were inoculated with SV40-contaminated vaccines between 1955 and 1963. Some critics have alleged that SV40 remained in the polio vaccines until the 1990s. Recent biopsies of tumors found SV40 in a variety of soft-tissue cancers, although the American government continued to dispute its causal role.

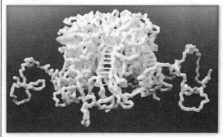

accusation confounded me. The thought of a cynical bureaucracy that put its own reputation over the fate of millions of innocent people settled into me like a poison.

Dr. Mary said she'd received threatening phone calls, so she gave up protesting publicly. Instead, she and Dr. Ochsner started working privately on ways to fix the problem. Together, they tackled the world of cancer-causing monkey viruses to see if they could figure out how to defuse them. For the past two years, they had been subjecting these monkey viruses to radiation in order to alter them into a benign form.

"We're not quite sure what we have on our hands, now," Dr. Mary said. "Our work altering the simian viruses led to the development of some rare and potent cancer strains that seem facilitated by their presence."

I had brought along the research papers Dr. Ochsner had given me, having spent the last several hours frantically reading as many as I could to prepare for this lunchtime meeting. I had read enough to participate in the discussion, and to comprehend these revelations, but nothing could prepare me for what I was about to hear.

"As you know," Dr. Mary said, "we've been working for some time on a project."

"I heard you hit a stone wall," I commented. "Dr. Ochsner told me," I said, thinking I knew where she was going with her comments.

"But we may have hit upon a viable means to eliminate Fidel Castro, by what will appear to be wholly natural causes," she said.

"No more poison pills, bazookas, or exploding cigars," Dave said. "The Beard is on to all that. Everything's been tried." Dave lit a new cigarette before his other cigarette was finished. "We worked together," he went on. "All of us. The anti-Castro people. The CIA. Cosa Nostra. The best mercenaries in the world, but he's defied the odds. Do you understand?" I nodded cautiously.

"We became a machine ready to kill troublemakers who threatened American interests anywhere in the world. It was supposed to be able to wipe out Fidel," Dave said as he studied his cigarette, then took another deep drag. "The problem is that a certain man says he will dismantle our machine if it doesn't obey him. This man is the most dangerous threat to America of all. He is soft on Communism. He refuses to go to war. He lets his baby brother go after the Mob, and errant generals. He plans to retire Hoover and wants to tax "Big Oil." He thinks he can get away with it, because he's the Commander-in-Chief."

I caught my breath, and glanced at Dr. Sherman as she began taking dishes from the table. The frown on her face told me they were deadly serious. Dave cleared his throat and coughed. "They'll execute him,"

Dave said, "reminding future Presidents who really controls this country ... those who rise to the top will gain everything they ever hoped for, and look the other way."

Dave's hands trembled as he spoke. His nerves were as raw as his voice.

"If Castro dies first, we think the man's life might be spared."

"How?" I asked, as the weight of his comments began to sink in.

"If Castro dies, they'll start jockeying for power over Cuba," Dave said. "It will divide the coalition that is forming. It may save the man's life."

"Where ... how did you get this information?" I pursued

"You're very young," Dr. Sherman said. "But you have to trust us, just as we have to trust you. If we were really with them, you wouldn't be privy to this information. These people have the motive, the means, and the opportunity. They will seem innocent as doves. But they're deadly as vipers."

"What about Dr. Ochsner?" I asked.

"I don't know," Dr. Sherman said. "I can't tell. Perhaps..."

"He's an unknown element," Dave broke in. "But we know he's friends with the moneybags. He thinks Mary and I hate 'the man,' just as he does."

"Would he go so far as to— " I started to ask.

"I think he might aid others," Dr. Sherman said. "Perhaps without even knowing it. He functions as a go-between. His interest was originally to bring down Castro, because he's anti-Communist to the core. But he's remarkably naïve."

Dr. Sherman explained that in the past, Cuban medical students came to the Ochsner Clinic to train. Now Castro was sending Cuba's medical students to Russia. Ochsner resented this rejection. Some of those medical students realized that studying with Ochsner could have made them rich and famous, so they were bitter about Castro's denying them that right. Some of them were bitter enough to help kill Castro. Dr. Sherman's comments called to mind Tony's similar degree of hatred.

"The clock is ticking," Dave said. "It's going to require a lot of hard work if we're going to succeed where all the others have failed."

"We believe we have something," Dr. Sherman said. "But we want to see what you make of it," soliciting my opinion and gently stroking my ego with her words. "Dr. Ochsner says you have serendipity."

"Yes," I replied. "He told me that."

"It's a rare compliment," Dr. Sherman went on. "You induced lung cancer in mice faster than had ever been done before, under miserable lab conditions." Dr. Sherman reached over and took my hand, squeezing it warmly. "That's what Ochsner likes about you. Your serendipity. And we know you're a patriot. That's why you're here."

"This is lung cancer we're talking about," Dave said as he began smoking his third cigarette in five minutes. "Your specialty."

"That's what they wanted me to work with, ever since Roswell Park," I admitted.

"You're untraceable," Dave continued. "With no degree, nobody will suspect you, because you're working at Reily's, and you're practically a kid."

"We have only until October," Dr. Sherman said.

"Maybe until the end of October," Dave amended, as he snubbed out his half-smoked cigarette.

"You can still choose not to participate," Dr. Sherman told me.

"Yeah, we'll just send you over to Tulane to see Dr. Heath. A few days in his tender care, and you'll never even remember this conversation took place," Dave said.

"You're not funny!" Sherman snapped at Dave, seeing my face. "Of course, nothing will happen to you, Judy. Dr. Ferrie and I are the visible ones, not you."

"Hell, I was joking," Dave said.

"She is so young," Dr. Sherman said reproachfully. "You frightened her."

"I'm sorry, J." he said. "What are you, nineteen?"

"I will be twenty, on the 15th," I said softly.

Dr. Mary saw that I was trembling. She poured me a little glass of cordial and offered it to me, saying that it would relax me, but I declined to drink it.

"All I came here for was to have an internship with you, Dr. Sherman," I said, adding that I still wanted to go to Tulane Medical School in the fall.

"Don't worry, you'll be there," Dr. Sherman said. "Dr. Ochsner said he'll sponsor you. That's set in stone." She paused. "We will not mention this again, at any time …. Take all the time you want to decide," she added as she gently grasped one of my hands. "If you say no, I'll just have you work in my lab at the clinic three afternoons a week. That way, you can fulfill the terms of your internship, while still working at Reily's."

Dave got up and started pacing the floor. "You got onto the wrong side of this project by accident," he said. "It was a matter of bad communication and timing. Ochsner always intended to have you involved, but it was supposed to be unwitting."

"I wish it was unwitting," I said.

"You can always let me hypnotize you," Dave offered, trying to find some humor in the situation.

"No, thanks," I said.

Gloom settled into the room. I noticed a large pastel painting hanging over Dr. Sherman's mantel depicting a series of dramatic scenes, such as a bull being killed with a sword, and a woman being stabbed by a Roman soldier. The whole painting was about brutality and death. *"What have I gotten myself into?"* I thought to myself.

"I want to think about this for awhile," I said.

"Take your time, Judy," Dr. Sherman replied. She got up and went over to the kitchen counter where two microscopes sat next to a rack holding probably sixty test tubes, turning slowly under a light. I recognized this round rack from my work in the lab. Each test tube held a clear pink liquid in which cancer cells were growing. A motor rotated the rack, shaking the tubes slightly as they turned. Every three days or so, the fluid had to be replaced. About once a week, the cells were loosened from the glass and transferred to new test tubes, so they wouldn't choke each other to death.

"I have something to show you. Before you say 'Yes' or 'No,' I want you to inspect these first," Dr. Sherman said, as she motioned for me to sit down on a stool at the counter. Then she handed me a stack of glass slides to view under the microscope. Each slide was carefully labeled, and they were in sequential order. The age of the cells was indicated by hours and minutes, and clearly displayed so one could see how fast they were growing. I looked at several slides. What I saw was familiar. These were normal cancer cells.

Then Dr. Mary gave me a second set of slides to inspect. I looked carefully, first at one slide, then another ... and another ... I couldn't believe what I was seeing

"I've never seen anything like this," I finally said aloud, as I continued to recheck the ages of the cells at various stages, and saw how rapidly they were dividing. "These are monsters!"

"They are, aren't they?" Dr. Mary said.

It wasn't their size that got my attention. It was their aggressive growth rate. These lung cancer cells were phenomenal. I had never seen such a fast and furious rate of division. The scientist inside me suddenly woke up. I began to get excited.

"I need to see all the log books and reports. Whatever statistics you have."

"I'll get them," Dr. Sherman answered, knowing that the hook was in.

"Somebody bring me a note pad," I said, not looking up from the microscope. "I assume you have electron microscope studies on these things, right? Do you have photos?"

"We have them," Dr. Sherman confirmed.

Dear God! I thought to myself, I am looking at the most deadly lung cancer cells in history. Here, on somebody's kitchen counter. Who would ever believe me?

"Well, J," Dave said, "now what?"

Just then the phone rang. Dr. Sherman answered it and handed me the phone. It was Lee. He said he was at a grocery store and was in a hurry.

"They've arrived safely," he said, referring to his family. "All is well. I'm picking up groceries now. They're waiting for me in the car."

"You sound happy," I said. "I'm glad."

"Well, I am happy to see her, I can't deny it," Lee said. "So far, she's been nice to me, and my aunt and uncle already like her."

I was not prepared for his next statement.

"But I feel like I'll be cheating on you, if I sleep with her," he said. "I'm calling to tell you that."

"I'll have the same problem when Robert comes back in town," I said, turning my back to Dave and Dr. Mary, hoping they couldn't hear me. "How will I be able to say no to him? He's my husband. Besides, I still love him. It's just not the kind of love I have for you."

"I feel the same," Lee said.

"Just don't hit her anymore!" I reminded him. "You said it would prove you loved me."

"OK, just let me come over sometimes, if she riles me too much," he said. "I have to go now." With that, he hung up.

"Was that Lee?" Dave asked.

I nodded, then blurted out, "We're falling in love, and we're both married."

Dr. Sherman turned suddenly, her eyes laced with some inner pain. "Who do you love more, your husband, or Lee?" she asked.

"I think I've already said too much," I answered.

"Whatever you do," Dr. Sherman advised, "Don't stay with a man simply because you feel obliged to do so. He might turn out to be an albatross around your neck."

"She speaks from experience, J," Dave said.

"Getting married was the worst mistake I ever made in my life," Dr. Sherman said. "It ruined my life. I hope it doesn't ruin yours."

"Probably the stupidest thing you ever did was marry Robert Baker," Dave said.

His criticism did not sit well with me, nor did Dr. Mary's advice.

"I wish to remind you both that I came here two weeks early," I said. "It's easy for you to give me advice now, after the fact. But where were you when I had to pay my rent? He came and married me," I said hotly.

"And Dr. Sherman, you walked away from me when I tried to talk to you at the party. That hurt."

Mary Sherman sat down on her couch, and motioned for me to sit with her.

"I'm sorry, Judy," she said. "I meant to get in touch with you about that. I should have called you immediately. But I had to go out of town the next day. And then it slipped my mind."

"Well, I have to divorce him," I said.

Dave suddenly changed his position."Don't divorce Robert yet," he advised. "There are advantages to having the name Baker."

"The name 'Vary' is rare," Dr. Sherman added. "People can look it up and discover your past, and your experience with cancer research. They might figure out who you are and why you are here. But nobody has heard of Judyth Baker. You're protected by his name."

"Hey!" Dave said, smiling, "Dr. Ferrie, Dr. Mary, and Dr. Vary! How about that? But seriously, J," he went on, "keep your 'Vary' name as low profile as you can. Among us, you're J. Vary, but in the big, bad world out there, you're Mrs. Baker, just a secretary at Reily Coffee Company. It's really a fortuitous thing. Stay married to the guy. At least until your work here is done."

With that, Dr. Sherman handed me a key to her apartment and a note card with her maid's schedule on it, saying that it would be best to avoid running into her. I went back home to see Susie and her dog Collie, hoping for some normalcy in my life, which was getting stranger by the day.

Sunday, May 12, 1963

On Sunday morning, I rested in bed, reviewing all the events and people in my life. Finally I got up, and stared at the stack of medical reports that I had to read. Just then Susie knocked on my door, saying she had made me breakfast. I told her to come in.

"I get worried about you," Susie said, setting down the little tray. I thanked her and gratefully began to nibble on some toast. I told Susie that Lee had promised not to hit Marina again, but might need a place to calm down if they had a fight.

"I suppose it would be the Christian thing to do," Susie said. "Why not make an extra key, and give it to him?"

I gave Susie a hug. "You're too good to be true!" I told her.

"My Bill knew Lee's uncle Dutz a long time," Susie said. "They worked the docks together before he went to sea. Dutz was always good to Bill, and Lee's his nephew. It pleases me to help him out, if I can."

Susie then asked if I'd like to go to church with her, but I declined. I spent the day reading medical reports.

Monday, May 13, 1963

I got dressed and headed for the Magazine Street bus. When I got on, Lee was sitting in the back reading the newspaper. I sat in the seat directly ahead of him, but did not turn around to talk.

When we got off at Reily's, Lee said, "I'll be over to help you with the background report after lunch." He gave me a look, and then we clocked in. Lee walked to the right, into the production side of the Reily building, and I went back outside, heading to the Standard Coffee office across the street, where I was soon joined by Mr. Monaghan.

"Time to go over to Congressman Willis' office," he said. "After that, we'll visit the Retail Credit company and go over some of their files, so when you meet with Oswald, you'll know what to do."

Monaghan and I walked about a block and entered a stone building with thick columns and interesting statues at the roof's pinnacles. Inside, building materials and boxes cluttered the marble halls.

"They're renovating the building," Monaghan said. "The attorneys and courts are all moving. Today you'll meet Willis' secretary. Then, whenever I send you over here, she'll know who you are."

Willis' secretary had been with him for years. From her loyal perspective, there was no greater patriot than Congressman Willis. She proudly showed me a stack of letters from constituents and political

friends, encouraging Willis to keep fighting Communism and to never give up the battle. I could not help noticing that some letters also condemned President Kennedy and his policies. Others attacked Kennedy for firing racist Army General Edwin Walker. Another favorite topic was a call-to-arms to 'Impeach Earl Warren,' the liberal Chief Justice of the Supreme Court. Willis' secretary was quite pleased that her boss was about to head the House Committee on Un-American Activities.

"He's in Washington right now," she said, "but he'll fly in next week. He goes back and forth, you know."

"Ask Mr. Willis to call me with respect to a young man we have recently hired," Monaghan told the secretary. Apparently Monaghan wanted Willis to know who Lee really was.

After leaving Willis' office, Monaghan stopped in the hall to describe the task before us. We had to get some blank report forms from Retail Credit. These would be necessary to create Lee's bogus background report. It wouldn't be easy, because Retail Credit executed tight control over anything with their logo on it as a matter of professional integrity. We arrived at their office at about 9:30 A.M., and Monaghan introduced me to the supervisor, Mr. Henry Desmare, who gave me his card. Desmare was in charge of three or four men, who were frantically working the telephones. Desmare said his investigators spent considerable time on the phone, but sometimes they visited character references in person. While his underlings investigated unremarkable and conventional individuals, Desmare and another supervisor handled the background investigations of important people, such as executives. Those reports were more expensive, and thoroughly detailed.

> **Congressman Willis**
>
> Edwin E. Willis was born in 1904 in Louisiana and, after practicing law in New Orleans for several years, was elected to the Louisiana State Senate in 1948. Less than a year later Willis, a Democrat, was elected to the United States House of Representatives where he served until 1969. During his tenure, Congressman Willis served as Chairman of the House Un-American Activities Committee (HUAC) from 1963 until 1969. He died in 1972.

Desmare treated Monaghan with great respect, mostly due to commercial interest. The Vice President of Wm. B. Reily & Co. Inc. represented an important account. Monaghan wasted no time requesting access to Desmare's extensive files, and said he had the name of a candidate who could replace one who hadn't passed muster, due to a drunken driving charge. The new applicant's former boss had mentioned a favorable report from Retail Credit, and Monaghan wanted to save Standard Coffee an employment agency fee. This was classic Monaghan manipulation.

Mr. Desmare had no choice but to allow Monaghan access to his files, because he couldn't risk irritating an important client over such a small request. Desmare knew that Reily was building a big new factory for producing instant coffee and roasting beans. They would be hiring many new employees by the end of the year, and that meant lots of background reports from Retail Credit. Monaghan eventually found a carbon copy of the report in question, and the three of us sat down at one of the empty desks to review it together. Monaghan and Desmare explained how I should interpret what I saw.

Once Monaghan had Desmare's complete cooperation, he handed him my Reily job application, and basically told him to hire me. They asked me a few simple questions and typed up my "background report" right there, as I stood in Retail Credit's office with Reily's VP watching them.

"We're going to be doing a lot of hiring soon, so I'd like Mrs. Baker to see some negative reports," Monaghan said. "All we have in our files are reports for people we hired, which are, of course, not negative."

Mr. Desmare had no problem with that, he said, as long as I pledged confidentiality. Once I did, he pulled out a stack of carbon copies of old reports prepared for Reily's.

While Monaghan and Desmare intermittently discussed Reily's new contract, I was asked to type examples of negative comments on a couple of blank report forms, which Monaghan insisted he needed for his secretarial training manual. Monaghan commented that Reily's would probably continue its relationship with Retail Credit, as he was pleased with the quality of its reports to date. They talked for about an hour, until Mr. Desmare noticed how much trouble I had typing the sample reports.

"The carbon keeps getting wrinkled," I said lamely. "How in the world do you line up this onion-skin paper, so it doesn't slip?"

"You'll have to retype that more neatly later," Monaghan said, as he scooped up a few empty report forms.

"I'll have her work on this at our office," he said to Desmare as he prepared to leave.

"I would prefer you didn't take any of those," Mr. Desmare objected. "They're company forms."

"I know," Monaghan said. "But I want her to type up some anonymous examples to put in our training manual. If the manual had some negative examples in it, I wouldn't have had to waste my time bringing her over here."

Monaghan had pinned Desmare. He really could not object further. Out we went with their precious forms in our grubby paws. We now had what we needed to create a report to turn "defector Lee" into a model citizen, so he could pass Mr. Reily's muster.

"You got them! I am so impressed, sir," I told Monaghan, as we headed back to Magazine Street.

"Of course I got them," he replied. "I get everything I want."

When we returned to Standard Coffee's office, Monaghan searched for a typewriter with a typeface that matched Retail Credit's typewriter. He found one in Reily's main office, and had it brought over to ours. I started to realize how careful this "former" FBI agent could be.

Working with Monaghan was like working with a police sergeant. He would stand at his desk like a bird of prey, staring at the rows of women working on billing records, and watching to see if anyone shrank from their duties for the slightest moment.

Monaghan knew I would only be at Reily's temporarily, so he didn't bother to give me a real desk. He told me I could sit at his desk when he wasn't there, but when he was, I had to move over to a little extension desk that adjoined his. I called this my "half-desk." As a consolation prize, Monaghan gave me a nice nameplate to display on his fine, dark-walnut desk when he wasn't there.

As the summer progressed, Monaghan was gone more and more often. I was not privy to what he was doing during these absences, and sometimes the workload was very heavy. I came to realize that his employment at Reily's was as much of an arrangement as were Lee's and mine. Monaghan was the first non-family Vice President that Wm. B. Reily Coffee Company had ever had.

Lee walked in just as Monaghan was leaving, and in a few minutes we were out the door to have lunch together. I told Lee about my morning, and he told me about his.

"It sounds like you're going to be busy," I said.

"Today, yes," Lee told me. "And tomorrow afternoon I have to go to Baton Rouge on business. You'll have to clock me out at five o'clock."

"But I get off work at 4:30," I protested. "Do I have to wait until 5:00 to clock you out?"

"Most mornings I'm going to be coming in about 8:30," Lee said, "because I usually have a meeting somewhere else first. I could even show up later than 8:30."

I gloomily realized I would have to be at work from 8:00 A.M. until however long it took Lee to accrue his eight hours. If Lee was to be clocked out at five every day, I'd be putting in two-and-a-half extra hours a week. Lee explained there were advantages in this arrangement.

"You'll be at Dave's, and at Dr. Sherman's apartment two or three afternoons a week," he reminded me. "Sometimes I'll help you there. You'll be out of Reily's at least ten hours a week."

"You forget that the real rat race, or should I say 'mouse race,' will be going on at Dave's," I reminded him. "And then I'll have a lot of work to do at night back at my place. Writing reports. Reading papers. Studying photos."

"That reminds me," Lee said, taking out his address book. "I need to sketch a layout of your apartment." He found a page with room for the sketch and turned his address book upside-down. "That makes it a bit harder for others to recognize," he said, as he sketched. "I always assume this book might be read at any time by someone else."

Finishing the sketch, he said, "All right, here's your porch, the door, and the living room. There's the window that's not blocked by your bed. Here's the big bathroom with no bathtub yet, and here's where the hotplate and counter is, where you still don't have a kitchen." Lee had

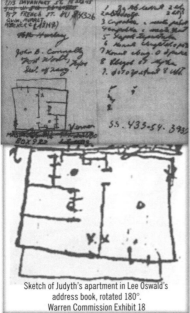

Sketch of Judyth's apartment in Lee Oswald's
address book, rotated 180°.
Warren Commission Exhibit 18

drawn an indentation there. He added lines showing the back entry and a step that led into Susie's kitchen. "Now, where will you be hiding your lab papers and notes?" he asked.

I understood. If Robert ever saw those materials, he might wonder about them.

"Susie said I can give you a key," I told him. We decided that it would be placed on a high ledge near the utility box, near the door to Susie's kitchen. I could store the microscope box on a high shelf in the living room, and the papers on a book-case in the bedroom, under my folded clothes.[2] "If anything happens to you, we will need to remove things right away," Lee said. "We don't want Robert seeing any of this."

If anything happened to me?

Lee put an X on the proper places.[3] "I remember some overhead lights," he commented. As I pointed them out, he drew some little circles. I asked why he wanted to know. "It could save time at night," Lee said. "Those lights have wall switches."

I finally got the courage to ask how it went with Marina.

"She was nice to me," Lee said simply. "We're trying to get along. Ruth Paine is already being a pain, though." (From then on, Lee always called her "The Pain.")

Lee said he believed Ruth wanted Marina to divorce him. "She acts like a lesbian," he said. "But maybe I'm reading too much into it."

"How did she get involved with Marina?" I asked.

"She was selected to babysit Marina and Junie for me. But she's not to be trusted, or her corrupt friends."

"But Lee," I protested, "You are living like a Spartan, posing as a person unable to thrive in this country, and later, you're planning to pose as a friend to Castro, in an anti-Castro town. Did Marina agree to that life?"

"She was happy enough in Russia with an apartment to ourselves. She was content with just a few things." Lee said. "But now it's different. Now she wants everything. A car, a house, new furniture. She will have it, or else," he said. "I can't provide her those things and still look like a financial failure. I never cared about any of that in the first place. We are completely incompatible."

"I know," I answered. "But what are you going to do?"

"The Pain is going to stay in town until Tuesday," Lee said. "After she leaves, I'll try to reason with Marina. I'll give her little things she wants, within my means, to make her comfortable. If only she'll be patient. Otherwise," he said, with sudden heat, "back to Russia with her. Let her see if anybody there will give her a better life than I did!"

Seeing it was time to change the subject, I told Lee I still had no letter from Robert. "My birthday is Wednesday," I added. "I'll no longer be a teenager! But I think he's forgotten."

"Well, I'll make sure you won't be forgotten, but I can't help you celebrate on Wednesday," Lee said. "I'll have to be with my wife. It will be only the second night without Ruth. I need to spend time with Marina, because she thought I forgot our wedding anniversary. It couldn't be helped," he added, apologetically.

Lee leaned over and gave me a tender kiss. "No sadness about your birthday, now, Juduffki," he said. "You'll soon see what I'm arranging for us. We're going to have our own chance for happiness. You don't care if it's Spartan, do you?"

"My dear Scarlet Pimpernel," I said, " If we can be together, let it be in Antarctica, for all I care."

We finished our lunch and returned to the Standard offices, where we sat down to look over what I'd typed on Lee's fake background report.

"I used 757 French Street, your aunt and uncle's address, as your residence."

"That's just fine," Lee said. "Nobody will care." He looked over the form, and began to smile. "Hmmmm! We can have some fun with this," he said. "Let's make Lee H. Oswald a successful capitalist pig. Happy. Content. Perfect and prospering, with a loving wife and child."

"OK," I said. "Here goes!" *(See the credit report form on page 294.)*

Wednesday, May 15, 1963

It was my 20th birthday. I was no longer a teenager! Would my husband Robert even remember?[4] On the bus, Lee was in a glum mood. He confided that he'd "done everything this morning."

"I changed the baby, made coffee, fed the baby. I fixed my own lunch, washed out a diaper and, as usual, Marina wouldn't get out of bed."

"She's pregnant. Maybe she didn't feel well."

"She was okay," Lee asserted. "But Junie was crying, because I had to leave. Marina just stayed in bed, and let her cry!"

He said he placed Junie next to Marina, but she kept begging for him to stay.

"Make sure Marina goes to bed really early," I suggested. "Then she'll wake up earlier."

"Fat chance of that," he answered. Then I shoved a letter into Lee's hands.

"Look at my birthday present from A-1," I whispered, so bus riders couldn't hear.

Inside was a demand for my first paycheck.

"It isn't fair!" I said. "Susie needs her rent money on time next month, but now, I won't have enough. We've been eating breakfast there every day, too. And her electric bill is due."

"Well," Lee said, taking the letter, "I can handle this. Since I can't be with you tonight to help you celebrate, at least I can go to A-1, and talk to them."

"Oh, thank you!" I put my hand on Lee's, and he slid a little closer to me. Our eyes met, then we looked away.

I finished the phony background report on Lee, dated it May 16, and placed the original in the manila folder, for Lee's transfer from Standard Coffee to Reily's on Thursday.[5] I worked on improving my typing speed, and learning protocol and procedures from the vice president's secretary's manual. It was tedious, and lunchtime couldn't come soon enough. Lee made life more interesting with some good news.

"I found out that Banister's secretaries never doubted you were Marina. Especially after you mumbled some Russian. So let's practice it some more. Even though Marina's in town now, we can find ways to be together and do things, because you can still pose as her. She's not really showing yet."

Turning the subject away from Marina, I asked if he'd found a chance to deal with A-1.

"First I went to the state employment agency," Lee said. "I pretended I still didn't have a job, so they gave me an appointment card. Then I went over to A-1 and showed them the card. That made them think I was still job hunting. Our friend, 'Miss-Ogynist,' found a photo job for me to check out. I almost thought about responding," Lee said, smiling. "I have to clean out the roasters Friday, and I hear it's not as much fun as photography."

"Not nearly so much," I agreed.

"After she gave me the referral," he said, "I showed her your letter, and told her I was upset. How dare she agree that I could make a call to you, then charge you a week's wages?"

"Did she get mad?"

"Yes, but I told her this would be the last time me or my friends would ever darken A-1's door, if she didn't at least cut your fee in half."

Lee handed me an envelope. "Look at this."

I opened it, and saw a bill for 35% of the original amount.

"You did it, my darlink!" I said, with a fake Russian accent.

"She wrote out new terms," Lee said. "Just one payment, then it's over. And it won't be due until after you're paid, on the 24th."

That evening, Lee and I rode the Magazine Bus all the way to Audubon Park, where Lee let off steam about his marital problems. He told me Ruth Paine hadn't been gone an hour before he and Marina had an argument over how to discipline Junie. Their toddler was getting into everything. Lee and I both believed that children could be disciplined without violence, while Marina slapped Junie to correct her. "The first thing I said when she slapped Junie was, 'I hope you go back to Russia!'" Lee admitted.

"Change your pattern," I said. "It's pure habit. Instead of yelling at her, do something else. Walk out, if you have to. You can choose to change."

As we rambled through the park together enjoying the spring flowers, Lee felt his spirits rising. By the time we got on the bus and rode back, he was planning to take his wife to the zoo. "I'll take her crabbing too," he said. "I'll get her away from the baby for a day. Maybe she'll have fun, if we go by ourselves."

It sounded good to me. We kissed quickly just before Lee got off the bus, and the driver gave us a wink.[6] I got off at Marengo, and walked slowly toward my apartment. I entered through the kitchen to say hello to Susie and Collie. Had Robert remembered my birthday? After having some dumplings and milk, I finally checked the mailbox. Yes! There was a letter. It read:

"My Darling Judy,

This is the back of a seismic record & the pen I'm writing with is the one I use to number seismic bumps with...Breakfast is 5-5:30 and supper is 4-4:30 P.M., or maybe an hour or 2 hours later. After that, there's just time to shower & relax enough to sleep. I haven't figured out how the workday can be so long & so short at the same time. Today the boss has gone ashore, so I get a chance to write. The French they speak around here is terrible.... "

I found Susie and proudly read my love letter to her. But Susie again observed that Robert didn't ask how I was, or why I had moved to a new place. Nor did he tell me when he was coming back.

"The work is really rough. It amounts to 6 hrs/day if I go out on the boat and 4 hrs/day if I stay here. The rest of it is eat, sleep & read. (There's an extra 3 hrs on the boat because it takes that long to get out & back). Then again, the first day I started work, the boat

to take us to the quarter boat (here) broke down, and the work day was noon 'til 8:00.

He wasn't being overworked, that's for sure! Well, at least he had written. That was worth something, I told myself, though he'd obviously forgotten my birthday. I had research papers to read, so there wasn't time to mope.

There was absolutely nothing romantic about the letter. In fact, it could have been written to a man, except it ended with my favorite words, "Love, Bob." In my emotionally tangled mind, I weighed the factors. Robert's influence in my life was shrinking, but coveting Lee's attention wasn't fair to Marina. She, too, was a stranger in a strange land. She, too, needed Lee's love and care. And many men who have an affair return to their wives after their fling. There was no safe haven.

Since Robert didn't mention receiving the letter I'd sent, I was afraid to direct another one to the beer and bait store. I'd have to wait for his return. Susie went to the deli and brought back a slice of carrot cake with a little candle on top. I wondered, as I blew out the candle, how my family in Florida was doing. They would have given me a birthday party. Homesick and sad, I felt guilty, but I sure didn't want my parents to know I had ignored their advice and eloped, only to find myself left alone.

Thursday, May 16, 1963

Back at work, one day before our transfer from Standard Coffee to Reily Coffee, I handed the finished background report on Lee to Monaghan, who then took me to Reily's. I learned who the salesmen were, saw their client lists, and accessed maps to trace their sales routes across the various states. After that, Monaghan escorted me into the attached five-story building where Lee and many others labored.

It was a factory workplace filled with machinery. Here were the hard-working employees, some of them Cuban girls with kerchiefs tied over their hair so it wouldn't get caught in the machinery. Supervisors hovered around them, working as hard as their underlings. The thumping of rollers and motors filled my ears as the packing lines and conveyor belts moved rows of coffee cans and boxes of tea along. There was no air conditioning, and though it was only May, it was uncomfortably warm. Each floor was full of machinery, sacks of products and stacks of supplies. Coffee dust floated everywhere. I saw Lee moving through this haze, adjusting a belt here, squirting some oil there. He spotted me looking at him.

"Mr. Oswald!" Monaghan called out, raising his voice over the noise of the machines. "Please come over here!" Lee went over and stood before Monaghan as if he were a soldier. His hands were dirty, and there was grease on his shirt.

"Yes, sir?" he said.

"I've been advised that you have satisfactorily passed your training sessions," Monaghan told Lee, making sure his main supervisor, Emmet Barbe, heard everything.

"Tomorrow morning, you'll clock in and go to the Standard offices, prior to your permanent transfer to Reily's. Mrs. Baker will meet you at that time. She will personally carry your Standard files over to Reily's, and will adjust your time card and records to reflect that transfer, so your paycheck can be issued tomorrow without any delays."

"Thank you, Mr. Monaghan," Lee said.

"Congratulations!" Mr. Barbe chimed in.

Lee then excused himself, and left the area to go to another floor, while I was introduced to the supervisors in charge of the packing and shipping areas. They needed to know who I was because it would oc-

casionally be necessary for me to stop a shipment, change an order at the last minute, or add a special order to help fill a truck.

After more training at Monaghan's desk, including how to use a dict-aphone, he asked me to reproduce a business letter. I created two decent samples before lunch. Monaghan reviewed the letters and was pleased, despite the fact that it had taken me almost an hour to type them.

"God help us if you had a dozen letters to type. You'd be here until midnight. I hope the doctor's project will be finished before I lose patience with you," he finished.

Miffed, I stood up for myself, telling Monaghan that "losing patience" with me was disrespectful. No secretary could handle the research and lab work I had agreed to conduct. From that moment, Monaghan treated me more thoughtfully.

From his remark about "the doctor's project," I was certain Monaghan knew about its existence, but I don't think he knew any significant details.

Just before lunch, Dave Ferrie called and told me it was time to make a dry run to his apartment, to calculate the time it took to get there and back. I would have to return by 4:30 to clock myself out and stay on Reily's premises until Lee's time card hit eight hours, rounded to the nearest half hour.

Since Lee hadn't been on the bus this morning, I was worried I'd have to wait longer than usual, but in fact Lee had barely missed the bus and Mr. Garner drove him to town in his cab without charge. He clocked in only a few minutes later than usual. At lunchtime, I tried the test run. It took less than half an hour to get to Dave's apartment via streetcar and bus.

Dave's place was quiet as a tomb, but the odor of mice struck me at once. It didn't take long to set everything up and get the routines going. I noticed there were more mice now. From the logs, I knew Dave would be slaughtering this batch tonight. As I went over Dave's surprisingly well-organized logs, I recognized where we were in the cell-culture cycle and cooked up a new batch of medium, acutely aware that I was using the last of the fetal calf serum. Lee called just as I finished refreshing the cell cultures.

"Just wanted to see if everything's okay," he said. "Is there anything you need?"

"We need fetal calf serum right away," I answered. Lee asked me to spell it, and I did so. "I'm making a list and checking it twice," he said.

"Okay," I replied. Suddenly, Lee hung up. I realized it must have been necessary to break the connection quickly, because he didn't say goodbye. I made copies of the new log entries and left for Dr. Sherman's apartment. It took only ten minutes to get there from Dave's, because I caught a bus right away. Okay, I thought: that's the deadline bus. I have to hit that one right!

At Dr. Sherman's apartment, the gardener noticed my arrival, so I stopped in the courtyard to chat with him. I showed him my key and told him I was interning with Dr. Sherman on an independent study, and that once or twice a week I had to drop off materials at her apartment, fill in her logbook, and use her microscopes to finish my reports. I was surprised when the gardener said Dr. Sherman had already told him I would be dropping by from time to time.

Dr. Sherman's apartment was in perfect order. Of course, she didn't have to put up with cages full of cancerous mice. After my duties, I caught a bus back to Reily's, arriving there about 4:20. I had not taken time to eat lunch, so I was starving. I stopped at the Crescent City Garage next door, and spotted a vending machine that held a single row of cookies and crackers. I bought a small packet of Lorna Doones (my favorites) and went back to Reily to clock Lee out.

At five o'clock, I waited at the bus stop, hoping Lee would show up and ride home with me, but he didn't, and I boarded the bus for home. I arrived tired and sad. The house was empty. Susie had gone to visit her children. Even Collie was gone. Robert was in the Gulf, and Lee was with Marina. I was lonely. I missed my sister, my Grandpa, my parents, and my friends back in Florida. I crawled into bed and crashed.

---

1. There had already been deaths and crippling from a previous faulty batch of the Salk Vaccine. Dr. Ochsner's own grandson had died from a bad dose of it, and Ochsner's granddaughter had been stricken with polio due to another. The new oral vaccine had to be advertised as safer, even though it might cause cancer. Otherwise, all kinds of vaccines might be distrusted by the public.

2. The house was photographed in Jan. 2000 with Messrs. Shackelford, Platzman, and Riehl, with Anna Lewis and myself present, and was essentially the same, except the bathroom was finished, and closets had been added (everything was renovated by 2003, with even the front door moved to center: the house had been purchased, we were told, by a doctor from London).

3. Lee Oswald drew a sketch of my apartment and put it in his address book. What a shock, when I saw this page, after all those years! I thought that surely, that page would have been destroyed, as other pages are missing. Note two x's where research materials were kept. Note single x on side of house (back right) where key was kept. Note that Lee started the sketch upside down, with the porch then, running out of space, he had to squash the back a bit. The owner's daughter verified to three witnesses present with me that the tub was originally in the kitchen. Bathroom in front apartment was unfinished in 1963. I didn't know Lee's address book had been preserved until later, when researchers told me, therefore *60 Minutes* never got this important piece of evidence. Lee's address book is found in the Warren Commission documents.

4. On Robert's birthday, I made certain that he got royal treatment: a blow-up ducky with a plaid bottom, a new shirt, and a pizza supper. We drank grape juice from two silver cups Robert brought with him. "Only the woman I will marry will drink with me from these cups," he said. Such moments spin romantic dreams.

5. Monaghan would later slip the carbon copy (slightly different, but who cared?) into Retail Credit's files. That way, if Lee had to change jobs later, he could use the background report on file at Retail Credit to serve as evidence of his 'fine' character.

6. The bus driver got to know us well. We later learned *he* was having an affair!

STANDARD COFFEE COMPANY, INC.
NEW ORLEANS, LA.
STATEMENT OF EARNINGS, EXPENSES AND DEDUCTIONS

EXPENSE	D E D U C T I O N S									NET AMT.	DA
	7.80									38.20	
EXPENSE	FED. W/H & F.I.C.A. TAX	OTHER W/H TAX	CASH BOND	S. UNEMP	SHORTAGES	INS. OR HOSP.	UNITED FUND	MISC.		NET AMT.	DA

DETACH BEFORE DEPOSITING

RETAIN THIS RECORD

NC	NORTH CAROLINA TAX
SC	SOUTH CAROLINA TAX
LU	LOUISVILLE TAX
DC	WASH., D.C. TAX
MD	MARYLAND TAX

IT IS A STATEMENT OF WAGES, EXPENSES, TAX AND MISCELLANEOUS DEDUCTIONS AND IS YOUR PERMANENT RECEIPT FOR TAXES WITHHELD

EMPLOYEE'S STATEMENT OF EARNINGS AND DEDUCTIONS

DATE	HOURS WORKED	EARNINGS				TOTAL EARNINGS THIS PERIOD	EXPENSES	FEDERAL O. A. B.	INCOME TAX	DEDUCTIO MISCELLANEOUS	
		SALARY	COMM. OVERTIME							AMOUNT	ITEM
MAY 24 62		46.00				46.00		1.67	8.40		

DETACH THIS STUB BEFORE CASHING. KEEP THIS RECORD. IT IS A STATEMENT OF YOUR EARNINGS AND TAX DEDUCTIONS AS REPORTED TO THE FEDERAL AND STATE GOVERNMENTS UNDER THE SOCIAL SECURITY LAW, AND IS A BASIS OF ANY CLAIMS FOR UNEMPLOYMENT INSURANCE AND PENSION.

Judyth's first Reily paycheck stubs

WM. B. REILY & COMPANY, INC.
NEW ORLEANS, U.S.A.

EMPLOYEE'S STATEMENT OF EARNINGS AND DEDUCTIONS

DATE	HOURS WORKED	EARNINGS				TOTAL EARNINGS THIS PERIOD	EXPENSES	FEDERAL O. A. B.	INCOME TAX	DEDUCTI MISCELLANEOUS	
		SALARY	COMM. OVERTIME							AMOUNT	ITEM
MAY 31 63		46.00				46.00		1.67	8.40		

DETACH THIS STUB BEFORE CASHING. KEEP THIS RECORD. IT IS A STATEMENT OF YOUR EARNINGS AND TAX DEDUCTIONS AS REPORTED TO THE FEDERAL AND STATE GOVERNMENTS UNDER THE SOCIAL SECURITY LAW, AND IS A BASIS OF ANY CLAIMS FOR UNEMPLOYMENT INSURANCE AND PENSION.

WM. B. REILY & COMPANY, INC.
NEW ORLEANS, U.S.A.

EMPLOYEE'S STATEMENT OF EARNINGS AND DEDUCTIONS

DATE	HOURS WORKED	EARNINGS				TOTAL EARNINGS THIS PERIOD	EXPENSES	FEDERAL O. A. B.	INCOME TAX	MISCELLANE AMOUNT
		SALARY	COMM. OVERTIME							
JUN 7 63		46.00				46.00		1.67	8.40	

Wm. B. Reily & Co. Coffee Inc. where Judyth worked with Lee Oswald, viewed from corner of Magazine & Girod

— CHAPTER 16 —

THE OFFICE

My new alarm clock went off. I got up, got dressed and headed for the Magazine Street bus, hoping Lee would be on it. He wasn't. Disappointed that I had to ride to work alone, I thought about how important Lee had become to me in such a short time. But working at Reily's and the arrival of Marina made it more difficult to spend time with him. I arrived, clocked in, and walked over to Standard Coffee's office, hoping to find Lee there, but he wasn't. About 9:15, Lee arrived. When we saw each other, it was like magic: we couldn't stay in the office pretending neutrality, so we retreated to a private area where we held each other tight.

"I've missed you so much!" I managed to say.

"Hush, Juduffki!" he answered, kissing me again and again. I rested my head against his chest, listening to his heart race. Finally, I said, "I hope you've kept your promise about Marina, because I can't go on, if you ..."

"I'm keeping my promise!" he answered. "I'm not going to break it. She's okay."

"I have begun to dream about you," I said.

"I know. We meet each other in our dreams."

His statement startled me, because my dreams of Lee last night had been so vivid I felt it was a real meeting of our spirits. Could it be that somehow our subconscious minds had really reached out to each other? Lee slipped a tiny, crystalline plastic heart into my hand. "I made this for you on a lathe they have in the machine shop," he said. "When you look at it, remember, you can see right through it. My love for you, I want it to be transparent, hiding nothing."

I saw that Lee's thumb had a bandage and mentioned it.

"Oh, I over-polished my thumb a bit when I was polishing your heart," Lee said with charm. He got another kiss. Then I told him we could enjoy an extra long lunch break together every Friday, because on Mondays and Tuesdays weekend order problems and emergencies always piled up, leaving no time for lunch. This meant we could have that long lunch today! Then I reminded Lee that Robert was returning Sunday, and would stay until Tuesday morning.

"If he asks what I'm doing, I will tell him everything," I warned Lee. "Even about us. If things in our marriage don't improve, I'll divorce him."

"On the other hand," Lee said, "as long as you are a newlywed, it would seem improbable that you and I might be having an affair. Have you thought about that?"

"We're not sleeping together, Lee," I said soberly. "We're not cheating on them."

"Yes, we are," Lee said. "Just as it says in the Bible, we're committing adultery in our hearts. The only difference is that we haven't committed it in bed … yet."

"But I can't lie to him."

"You don't have to lie," Lee said. "You already said, 'if he asks'… If he doesn't ask, he doesn't deserve to know."

"If he finds out about you, he'll be very angry and hurt."

"Tell him we didn't mean it to happen. You were kicked out of your room, all alone. He didn't concern himself with you, or call."

"I think he'll walk out on me if I do that."

"Well, I won't abandon you, if he does. Besides, would you really notice any significant change in your life if he walked out? He wouldn't hit you, would he?"

"No, he'd just leave."

"Well, then," Lee said, "Leave it in his hands. If he asks, tell him the truth. If he doesn't ask, he doesn't deserve to know."

"I could hardly stand it this morning on the bus without you."

"I'm still having problems getting away from the baby. I'll make it up to you."

Lee took a look at my big, self-winding Benrus wristwatch which my father had given me off his own wrist as we said goodbye on my departure to St. Francis, saying I needed an accurate watch for my experiments.

"Nice watch," Lee said. "I have a Benrus too, but I can't stand wearing the thing unless I really need it. Speaking of time, it's time to transfer my records over to Reily's."

We found Monaghan, who put our personnel files in his briefcase and walked us over to Reily's for our official transfer.[1]

At Reily's Lee was introduced to the Personnel director's secretary in the presence of clerks and secretaries in the huge office room, none of whom paused in their labors. Monaghan told her that I, too, would officially transfer over from Standard today. She told him my check had already been cut by Standard, but Lee's check would be issued by Reily's that afternoon. We were pleased to hear this, because it put some distance between us in the paper trail. Both of our files were accepted without inspection.

Thus Reily's, famed for its strong right-wing stance and strict hiring practices, successfully added a notorious defector, disgraced Marine, known pro-Castro sympathizer and purported Communist to its employee roster.[2] Nobody noticed a thing.

When we rode the bus late that afternoon down to Audubon Park, we again sat in the back. Several white people looked at us with hate in their eyes. This was the first time I'd experienced such looks, but Lee had been putting up with it for a long time.[3]

That evening, we discussed segregation and the racial situation in New Orleans. Lee whole-heartedly supported equal education for blacks, and he loved black children. He was also fond of the jazz heritage in New Orleans. Lee despised "hate groups," and did not hide his feelings about them. I naturally agreed with him.

"I am willing to fight for racial equality, and would die fighting for it if necessary," he said.

"I do not care a whit about money, power, or if we'd ever have a car or a nickel in our lives, Lee," I told him. "People, and their rights, have to come first."

"You and my friend George are the same," Lee said, referring to George de Mohrenschildt. "He told me I needed to get back to the survival stage, to get in touch with the important things of life again. I agreed, and told George I wanted to go walking through the jungles just as he had done with his wife. But how can I? Marina is not that kind of woman. But you would walk through the jungles with me, wouldn't you?" he asked, as he stroked my hair with his bandaged thumb.

"I would like nothing better, Lee," I responded, as if in a dream.

Lee said he had a birthday surprise for me, which I'd get next week after a Friday dinner at Thompson's restaurant with the Lewises. The bus had reached Upperline, and Lee got off. Marina was waiting at the stop wearing pedal pushers with a scarf tied around her head and holding their daughter June by the hand. When Junie saw her father, she raised her little hands for him to pick her up. As  Lee bent down to pick up Junie, Marina reached into Lee's back pocket and removed his wallet. I could hardly believe my eyes.

Photo of Marina Oswald that Lee kept in his wallet

Once home, I told Susie all I had seen and done, and then showed her my un-cashed paycheck. "You'll soon get your rent money!" I told her. "Robert said we'd have a bank account by Monday."

I was grateful that Susie was so patient about the rent but couldn't bring myself to eat any of her food that night, because her refrigerator was almost empty. I'd had a good lunch at Thompson's, and that would do for today. Susie went to watch TV and I plunged into my stack of medical research reports, but soon fell asleep. The next thing I knew, Collie was whining at the door. I woke up and yawned. It was 8:00 P.M., and dark.

I got up and looked out the front porch window. On the sidewalk in front of the house, I could see Lee pacing back and forth. He must have seen me sleeping, and didn't want to wake me up. I opened the front door, and he quickly came in without saying anything. We went into my bedroom, where Lee sat in the chair, and I sat on my bed with Collie beside me.

"What a surprise!" I said. "What happened?"

"I'm here," he said, "because we had a fight."

"Did you...?"

"No. There was yelling, I am sorry to say, but that's all. I took your advice. I walked out."

Lee had my sympathetic ear, and poured out his story.

"She burned the potatoes," he said. "When I complained, she said it was all I deserved. So I told her, "Go back to Russia to your boyfriends, and see if they'll put up with you." Then she said she'd rather have sex with a German shepherd than have me touch her."

"Oh, that was harsh," I said. "I'm sorry. But think about it. The woman burned the potatoes. You complained. She insulted you, and once more, you told her to go back to Russia. Isn't that a big punishment for burning potatoes, Lee?"

He stood up, walked over to the fireplace mantel, and stared at the alarm clock.

"I peeled the demmed potatoes for her!" he said, defensively.

"What would you do if I burned your potatoes?" I asked.

"You're a good cook, you wouldn't."

"You made her feel worthless by telling her to go back to Russia for the umpteenth time, so she attacked your manhood. Also for the umpteenth time."

"It's true," Lee mused. "That's what's been happening."

"You know why she does it, so let it be," I said. "Every time she attacks your manhood, remind yourself she's pregnant with your second child. You're a Darwinian success, Lee! I can assure you, you're a handsome man. I can hardly keep my hands off you!"

The transformation in Lee as I spoke these words was remarkable. He suddenly relaxed and returned to his chair.

"I've had no desire for material things," Lee said. "And I've observed you are the same. I wish to live above the demands of the rat race and the gray flannel suit. I want peace. But I let her get to me."

"I know how gentle you can be when you interact with dogs and children," I said. "But then, they're no threat to your pride and feelings. The task is to dare to love somebody who is capable of hurting you, and trusting that they won't step over that invisible line."

"It's too late for Marina and me," Lee said. "She doesn't just step over the invisible line. She has built her house on the other side of it."

"But I am not Marina," I told him. "We're building on something else here. I feel it. Trust. Faith. I feel betrayed by Robert, so it helps me understand how Marina hurts you. But I have to forgive him. If I don't, it will eat me alive. And you have to forgive her, too."

"Forgiveness!" Lee muttered. "We're not kids anymore!"

"It's the key," I repeated. "Forgiveness can take the place of what you felt when you first loved her. Forgiveness refuses to hit back."

"I didn't hit her," he said proudly. "I succeeded in controlling myself."

"Did you ever hit your Japanese lover?" I asked. "You say you loved her. It concerns me, because you abandoned her."

After a long pause, Lee shook his head. "I don't know what happened to her," he admitted. "I was very young. I thought I would get back to her someday. But it was impossible."

Lee flushed, as if ashamed. Then he covered his face with both hands, in silence. I suddenly saw a tear fall from between his fingers, so I got up and put my arms around him.

"I loved her!" he said, getting himself under control. "They made me leave her!"

I hugged him, as he wiped his eyes. "She was so good to me. And I let her go."

"Did you ever hit her?" I asked.

"No, no," he answered. "I did not know it was possible for me to hit a woman, until I had to live with Marina."

"You had to live with Marina?"

"Yes, yes, I had to. I can't say any more than that."

Collie came over and put her head in Lee's lap. He absently petted her. "It's true," he said. "She has hurt me to the core. At one time, I was fearless in love."

"If you were fearless once, you can be that way again."

My words were having impact. Suddenly, Lee stood up, went down the hall and down the step into Susie's kitchen, calling Susie's name. Susie was hard of hearing, so he knocked at her door and called her again. "Susie! We're going to go out for a while. We'll be getting some beignets. (Pronounced ben-yays) Can I bring some back for you?"

"Oh, I'd love some!" Susie replied. I happily began brushing my hair out, and put on some lipstick. Then Lee came back, and with his finger, slowly and gently wiped away the lipstick.

"Your lips are perfect the way they are," he said. "Remember, I had a surprise for your birthday? Well, it turns out that tonight is just as good as next week. Come on, Juduffki. I want to woo you."

Oh, dear, I thought to myself, I wonder what he has in store for me? But as Lee guided me out the door, it was my turn to relax. Lee was my comforter and my protector, and I trusted him. Under the night sky we went walking toward St. Charles Avenue, where we boarded a streetcar and traveled to the French Quarter, stopping for a meal of oysters, shrimp jambalaya and crabs. It was delicious.

"They say the world's food gets worse the further you get from here," Lee said as we walked to Jackson Square.

"Here, here!" Lee called out, stopping a horse-drawn carriage.

"No, it's so expensive — !" I protested, but Lee picked me up and put me in the seat. The carriage started up, with its gentle rocking motion, the clip-clop of the hooves and the chiming of the bells on the horse's collar. And the driver was kind to the animal. We passed fountains, brightly lit shops and fancy restaurants. We heard music come and go, as we passed night clubs. Lee put his arm around me, and leaned his head against mine. We leaned back to watch the wrought-iron balconies and the sky above. The stars were mingled with low clouds that gently passed.

"Happy birthday, my love," Lee said.

As our idyllic tour of the French Quarter came to an end, the carriage brought us back to Jackson Square, where we went to the Café Du Monde, one of the world's most charming coffee shops. Lee or-

dered us each a cup of their silky smooth signature coffee, café au lait, and an order of beignets.

Lee purchased two more sacks of beignets to go. One for Susie, and one for my breakfast. Arm in arm, we headed back to 1032 Marengo and sat on the porch steps, silently enjoying each other's company. It was now midnight. Then Lee drew a small white box from his pocket and handed it to me.

"It's your present," he said. "I got it for you on your birthday."

I opened the box, and saw a necklace made of faceted black beads, carved from real jet. They glittered in the streetlamp.

"It's exquisite, Lee!"

"They are like the jet buttons in Kate Seredy's book, *The Good Master*," Lee said.

I had recommended the book to Lee, but did not know he had read it.

"Then you've already read the book?"

"Of course," Lee said as he took up the necklace and fastened it around my neck. The necklace was heavy, and the jet beads glistened. "They suit your Hungarian skin. You and I have the same spirit," he said, placing his hands on my shoulders. "That's why we've been dreaming of each other."

"Yes," I said, "We are going mad with love for each other."

"But I know you. If we were living under repression in Hungary, we'd both be freedom fighters. We'd be the ones to pull down the big statues and throw Molotov cocktails at the machine guns. That's why I want you to have these jet beads."

Lee was right. I'd fight for freedom. Lee and I were the same.

Sunday, May 19, 1963

It was late Sunday afternoon, and Robert's return from offshore was imminent. About two weeks earlier Lee and I had gone to the library and found the telephone number for Evangeline Seismic, and I'd called the company, asking them to give Robert my new address. Later, we knew that he had gotten it because it was on the letter he'd sent. Now I was ready to tell him all about the raid, and everything else. I wanted him to know how drastically my life had changed in the seventeen days he'd been absent. Anxious and worried, I dressed to the nines for him, with upswept hair, pearls and makeup.

It was a beautiful spring evening in New Orleans. I thought about the opportunities the evening held. We could go out for supper and enjoy the city's wonderful cuisine, walk around the French Quarter together, and have some real conversation that our separation had denied us. If things worked out, I would tell him everything. Confide in him. Set things straight. We could renew our relationship in total honesty, and respect each other's needs. What a great night it could be!

Robert knocked, and I rushed to open the door. One look at him was all it took. I melted and forgave all. He looked so handsome, dressed in his khaki pants and shirt from his ROTC days. His dark hair had grown long and curly. He threw his arms around me, and I could smell the salty sweat of the sea on him. "Oh, you kid!" he said, looking down and kissing me. I had come to accept that this was his way of saying, "I love you."

He released me long enough to throw Susie's dog out the front door. She landed with a yelp, and a pang went through my heart. That was no way to treat my innocent friend! Nevertheless, as he closed the door and locked it, I shyly put my arms out toward him and he led me to the couch, where he pulled my shoes and nylons off, throwing them across the room. I protested.

"Shhhhh!" he said, kissing me. "We'll talk later. Right now, there's only one thing that matters. You — and me!"

He laughed, believing I was embarrassed because it was still daytime. He carried me to our bedroom and lowered the blinds. He was amused by my modesty and found my resistance entertaining. "Come on, 'switch-heart,'" he said. "I need my lovin' — and so do you."

His physical needs rolled over my emotional needs once again. There was no quiet dinner, no stroll through Jackson Square, no heart-to-heart conversation, and not much sleep. It was another all-night sex session where he got everything he wanted, and as much as he wanted too. In the morning I gathered myself together and headed to work while he slept in exhausted bliss.

Monday, May 20, 1963

As I waited for the bus, I was anxious to find out how things had gone for Lee with Marina. As I climbed on the bus, I saw Lee sitting in the back. This was our second week of riding the bus to work together, so the driver and the regulars had all seen both of us get off at Reily's each day. We felt it was now safe to sit next to each other, as if we were co-workers who had become friends. So I headed to the back of the bus and sat down next to Lee. He began by asking me if I had a chance to talk to Robert.

"I never had a chance to tell him a thing," I said. "He finally fell asleep. And he's still asleep!"

"Marina's still asleep, too," Lee said in a down voice, adding that he had played with their baby June longer than usual last night to tire her out so her mother could sleep in. It worked. A small victory, and he was able to leave without June screaming for him to stay.

I thought about him and Marina, and wondered how they had gotten along. Frankly, I was wondering if they had sex. I told Lee that Susie had suggested we introduce Robert to Marina and let nature take its course. I thought it was an extremely clever idea. Lee just sat quietly and did not respond. I had hoped for at least a smile.

"As for sex," I whispered, to make sure he was listening, "I'm exhausted. The man should have a harem!"

"He sounds like a formidable lover," Lee said flatly. "I doubt I could compete."

"There's more to love than what happens in bed!" I blurted out before realizing that I was talking a bit too loudly. "I just hope I can get a decent night's sleep," I added, returning to my whisper.

Lee reminded me about my plan to dump a bag of ice cubes on Robert's privates to cool him off long enough to talk. I laughed and told him I had the bag of ice, but had forgotten about it. I thanked him for reminding me. The plan had fresh appeal for me now!

Mondays were always hectic at Reily's, when an avalanche of new queries landed on Monaghan's desk. There would be nearly a hundred items demanding immediate attention: Inquiries from billing clerks, new customer orders, unusual, sometimes unreadable hand-written orders. Was there enough product for a certain big order? What about an order for a discontinued product, or a poor credit risk hoping for a new start? Could we ship a certain product to Germany?

All of these had to be dealt with on top of my normal workload as Monaghan's secretary. This included handling both his financial documents and his field correspondence, as well as approving (or rejecting) the Finance-Character Background Reports for new Reily employees. The salesmen's questions could be answered on the phone, but the finance-related letters had to be typed. I also handled queries arising from unusual time cards, expense advances for salesmen and paycheck disputes.

On Tuesday, we'd get even more. Then the pace slowed, so I could leave Reily's at noon to do lab work the rest of the week.[4]

That Monday, Lee finished at 5:00. As we boarded the bus, he asked me to ride with him all the way to Audubon Park, even though I'd told him I was dead tired and just wanted to go home.

"But we have to train them not to expect us until 6 or 6:30," Lee countered. "Otherwise, we'll lose this time together." He was right, of course. We spent half an hour at Audubon Park, saw the seals, and then headed back.

When I got home, Robert informed me his goal for the next day was to open a bank account. Then he said it was time for us to go straight to bed.

"Relax!" he told me. He began to softly strum his guitar, knowing its soothing effect. I closed my eyes and let exhaustion spread over me. As I rested, Robert told me that he had bought some sandwiches from the deli. They had been there for an hour, Robert said a bit testily. Where had I been? Weren't working hours from 8 to 5?

I said I had to work late and thanked him for getting the sandwiches, because I had no time to eat lunch. Robert knew I took my lunch to work, so he checked my purse to make sure my little bag of food was still uneaten. It was, so he moved on to the next topic. He complained that by receiving a salary, I would not get extra money for overtime.

As we ate, Robert got out the bank papers for me to sign. The name was already filled in: Judyth A. Baker. Ferrie had told me to use "Mrs. Robert A. Baker, III" to keep the paper trail more obscure, but I couldn't explain that to Robert. So I signed 'Judyth Baker' on the form, but I would insist on signing all checks "Mrs. R. A. Baker, III." The bank didn't like it, but they finally accepted it. (see Appendix)

"Can we go out tonight?" I asked. "Maybe just walk around the neighborhood together? I know where we can get some ice cream,"

"First," Robert told me, "you're tired. Second, it costs money to go out." Then he complained that while the apartment was nice, it cost twice as much as the room I'd formerly rented for only $30.00.

"But that was a whorehouse, Robert!"

"We still don't have a private bathtub," he said. "I've calculated our budget again," he went on. "You can see for yourself how much more expenses we have. And if the car breaks down, we're up a creek."

We'd have to live on my paycheck alone, he said, and put everything he made straight into the bank just to make sure we'd be okay. He had cashed a personal check from our new account for $25 when he was at the bank. He put $10 into my purse and kept $15 for himself. This would have to cover my meals, transportation and all other needs until he returned again, whenever that would be. Robert, however, would be living on a boat with free room and board. Why did he need so much money? I should have confronted him, but before I could figure out how to broach the subject, Robert told me he needed his breakfast at 5:00 A.M., before he had to leave for work in Houma at 6:00.

Then he cajoled me into yet another exercise session in bed. Much as I liked sex, this was overkill: after it was over I got up and sat quietly on the edge of the bed, hoping he'd fall asleep. I looked at him lying there looking cute and harmless, wondering when I could lie down again in safety.

Then I heard him mumble, "Who knows how long it'll be, before I'm back?"

"You did ask how long your next hitch will be, didn't you?"

"Oh," he said, yawning, "I forgot. It just didn't pop into my head."

To my silence he added, "By the way, I'm thirsty. How about fixing me some iced tea? By then, I think I'll have another surprise waiting for you!"

Another surprise? I got up slowly and went into Susie's darkened kitchen, where I slowly mixed two glasses of instant iced tea. Maybe he'd fall asleep. But just in case, I got the bag of ice out of the freezer and set it next to the bed when I returned. After he had his iced tea, Robert was indeed ready for more whoopee the moment I got in bed. So at the right time, I grabbed the bag of ice and emptied it on his "love machine." His response was immediate: "Hey! What the hell!"

"I needed your attention," I said. "I'm informing you that you've had enough lovin' for tonight, and I'm going to get some sleep!"

I laid down with my back to him and smiled, wondering what Susie had heard in the other end of the house.

Tuesday, May 21, 1963

The next morning, Robert prepared to leave for another stint on the Gulf. He lugged a seabag in from his car, full of dirty clothes. He told me to do his laundry and buy some spray starch for his shirts so when

I ironed them, they would be crisp and nice. He was too grouchy to even say 'please.' He did try to motivate me, however, by saying that the other men on the quarterboat envied the fact that he had his own "little woman" to do his laundry and iron his shirts for him.

Robert was still upset about his icy surprise. Feeling refreshed and confident after a few hours of good sound sleep, I could hardly hide my laughter.

"That wasn't funny! I hope you grow up!" Robert growled.

"You need to grow up, too, and quit holding grudges," I replied.

"If you ever do that to me again, I'll never forgive you!"

"Fine. Besides, you should be called 'Rat' instead of Robert."

"And why in hell would you do that?" he said, seeing that I was flying the flag of open rebellion.

"Thanks for asking — at last!" I said, hurt feelings bringing tears to my eyes. "First of all, we've been married three weeks, but you only wrote twice!" I wiped my tears angrily. "I was forced to move in the middle of the night, and — thank God! — found shelter at a rector's house! You never bothered to ask about what happened, or how I got this apartment, or how I got my job."

"I'm sure 'God' had nothing to do with it," he answered, as he picked up his car keys.

"Don't you want to know how I managed to move here, with so little money?"

"Well," he replied, "I assumed the rector at the church helped you."

"Wouldn't you like to know more?"

"Do you know what time it is?" he answered. "It'll have to wait. I have to leave."

"You never once asked in your letters how I was! You didn't call! And now you can't even tell me when you're coming home again?" I started to cry again. "And you forgot my birthday!"

"Damn!" he said. "I'm sorry! When was your birthday?"

"Wednesday. A week ago."

Robert frowned. "Well, you have a right to call me 'Rat,'" he said apologetically. "I need to be more thoughtful." As he stood in the doorway, ready to leave, he insisted that I go see Mrs. Webber and make her refund the rent money. Then Robert left, taking my house key with him!

When I realized I couldn't lock my door I went to Susie, who was always up early. She reminded me of the extra key up on the ledge outside, but we were both too short to reach it, so we pulled a stepladder out from under the house, and retrieved the key.

I headed to work and got on the bus. Lee was in his spot in the back. Only then did I realize how little I had been able to tell Robert. I told

Lee that Robert had taken my key, and he said that he would get another copy made for me later in the day.

With the early-week crunch over, I took myself over to Dave's lab and Mary Sherman's apartment on Wednesday, Thursday and Friday to continue our work on the Project. When I was finished, as per instructions from Dr. Mary, I wrapped the specimens in newspaper to insulate them and dropped them in a car parked near Eli Lilly on my way back to Reily's. That was usually Lee's job, but this week I did it. Once the Product was dropped off a driver would get into the car and whisk it away for another round of radiation, presumably at the U.S. Public Health Service Hospital. My evening hours were spent writing reports, reading research papers and catching up on work I could do at home for Reily's.

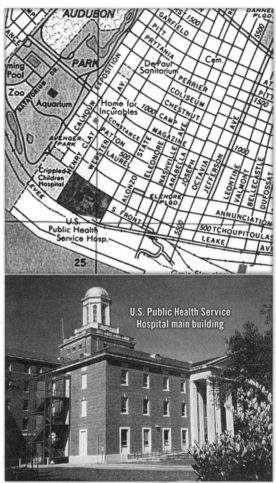

U.S. Public Health Service Hospital main building

Monday, May 27, 1963

Around lunchtime, Lee showed up and obtained permission from Monaghan for us to leave the building for two hours. The last time Lee had pulled this stunt, he told Monaghan we had to go see "a film about clandestine matters." The film was, in fact, *Dr. No*, which we finally got to see together.

I had no idea what Lee had up his sleeve because it was not a Friday, when things were more relaxed at Reily's. It was a Monday, the busiest day in the Reily work week. So what was Lee up to? Once we were out of the building, Lee explained that he needed me to buy a money order for him.

"You now have a bank account," he said. "So, I'd like you to take out $30 and buy me an American Express money order. Don't worry. I'll pay you back right away. I have to rent an office for the FPCC, and I don't want a clerk remembering my face, in the event that the FBI ends up nosing around. As long as you don't put your name on the thing, and you're never photographed with me, you'll be safe."

My anti-Castro friends had told me that the FPCC (Fair Play for Cuba Committee) was a pro-Castro organization, so I pelted Lee with questions about his rationale.

"It's a ploy," Lee explained, as we walked. "We're out to shut down the FPCC. They're not on the list of subversive organizations yet. But HUAC wants to put them there." Lee explained that by joining their organization and then overtly acting like a Communist Castro supporter, he'd give HUAC a reason to ban the organization as subversive. "To do it right I need to rent an office, though we'll never hold a meeting there."

"Why rent an office at all, then?" I asked him.

"It's needed to get started," he answered. A money order receipt number would 'prove' to FPCC headquarters that a donation was used to pay the rent, should a representative come to New Orleans after the office closed down: Lee didn't intend to have it open more than a month. Both the janitor and Sam Newman (the owner of Banister's building) knew Lee was actually Banister's man, so there would be no long-term lease to sign.

"The only problem," I replied, "Is my A-1 check. I have to pay them $17.44 today." Lee's face clouded over. He had forgotten about that, and my bank account was perilously low. We calculated that a $30 money order would put me in the hole if Robert wrote any checks I didn't know about. Lee then asked if I had money in my purse.

"Lee Oswald, you're a genius!" I answered. There was indeed money, and many other things, in my purse! I'd been stashing nickels and dimes in there for weeks. And I still had $14 left over from Sparky's $50. Robert had just given me $10 for lunches and bus rides. As I hunted, I pulled out tissues, various lipsticks, a hairbrush, a plastic horse and fifteen mouse pins, much to Lee's amusement.

By the time I finished my search, I even found some money left from Reverend Jim's. All totaled I located $31.00 in bills and change, and gave it all to Lee. He took the money, counted it, and said it was enough. Then he handed it back to me. I would have to go into the American Express office alone and purchase a $30 money order. "Just don't write your name on it, and leave the recipient line blank. You don't want to have to explain who 'Mr. Sam Newman' is to Robert," he advised.

Lee then told me that he would be able to pay me back tomorrow after he cashed his unemployment check from Texas.[5] My straight-arrow Catholic upbringing sprang to the fore. "But you're working. Isn't it dishonest to get unemployment checks when you're working?"

"Was it honest for my boss to tell people I was fired at my last job, when I did good work there?" Lee asked. "It was all part of the plan," he said.

"But how did you get the State of Texas to … ?"

Lee smiled and put his finger against my lips. "I can't tell you," he said slowly, letting each word fall with its own weight in four beats. "But I can guarantee that the money isn't coming from Uncle Fidel."

I gave up trying to follow the players, techniques, and motives in Lee's complex covert world, and bought the American Express money order.[6] In return he bought us hamburgers and Dr. Peppers, which we quickly ate before I returned to Reily's.

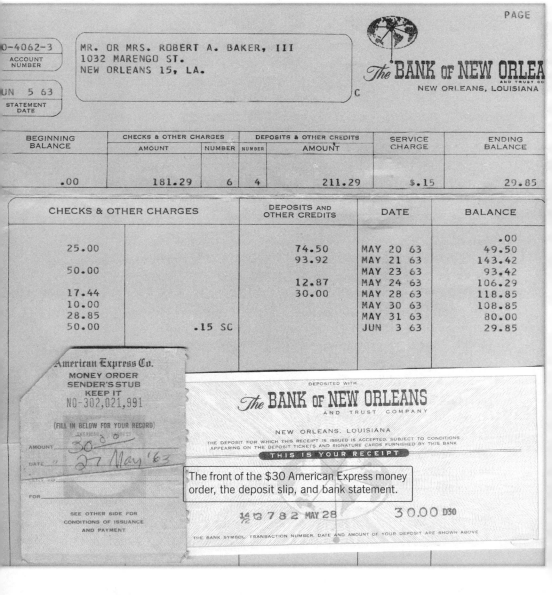

The front of the $30 American Express money order, the deposit slip, and bank statement.

Tuesday, May 28, 1963

The next day, as I toiled away at Monaghan's desk, Lee arrived, bringing me a banana, $33 in cash, an envelope from my bank, and a deposit slip for me to sign.

"You need to put $30 in the bank right away," he said. "You're skating too close to the edge."

"But how will I explain it to Robert?" I whispered,

"Easy," Lee said. "Just tell him you cleaned out your purse!"

He was right, that's all I needed to say! Robert would never object to my giving him every penny I had. I kept the American Express receipt in a safe place, just in case Lee ever needed it to 'prove' the money was donated.

CONDITIONS OF ISSUANCE AND PAYMENT

The sender of the money order bearing Serial Number on this stub assumes responsibility for the insertion of the date of purchase, payee's name, and sender's name and address on the face of the money order, legibly and IN INK. Sender authorizes the Company to pay the money order to the order of the payee whose name appears thereon at the time of presentation for payment. If the money order is lost or destroyed the owner should surrender this stub and execute the company's refund agreement.

Back of the $30 money order.

I deposited the money during the lunch break, which turned out to be vital because the balance on the next statement was $29.85, thanks to Robert's unbudgeted expenditures.[7]

I was clocking out at five, then working another hour or more at my desk, waiting for Lee's clock-out time to roll around. This staying late every night was noticed by the clerks, helping to cover the fact that I was absent Wednesday through Friday from 11:30 to 4:30. Since I worked through lunch on Mondays and Tuesdays, too, the impression was that I worked a full 40-hour week.

That day I had assumed that Lee would clock out at 6:30, as he had been doing recently. But he surprised me. He had clocked in an hour early, so we could leave an hour earlier. He said this was my reward for helping out with the money order. He then handed me a library card and asked me to pick out books for us to read together.

Lee and I rode the bus up Magazine Street to Audubon Park an hour ahead of schedule because Lee had clocked out early. As the bus stopped in front of Lee's apartment, we saw Kerry Thornley sprint up to the porch, open the screen door and enter without knocking, as if he owned the place. To Lee, the situation was self-evident: Thornley was fooling around with his wife. Lee exploded in jealousy and started to get off the bus to confront Thornley, but I grabbed him.

"Think!" I whispered. "You now know something about Thornley that he doesn't know you know. That can give you an advantage." Lee remained seated, but he was fuming with anger. You could see it in his eyes.

The bus started up again, but I was afraid Lee would get off at the next stop. I only had a few blocks to talk sense into him.

"If you go in there with blood in your eye, you'll upset your little girl, and somebody may call the police," I whispered, "Do you want the police coming to 4905? Will your family be safe during your pro-Castro stunts, if the police know you live at 4905?"

Lee frowned, squeezed his hands together, and calmed himself. "I'll get to the bottom of this," he said.

"Please stay with me," I said. "That way, you'll be coming home at the expected time. If he is still there, maybe he has nothing to hide."[8]

It was now the end of May, and the Project's weekly cycle of slaughter-harvest-irradiate-and-reinject mice was fully operational.

On Wednesdays we sacrificed the mice, harvested the tumors, weighed them and prepared their tissues for processing on Thursday. The mouse carcasses were then picked up by the Cuban boys from David Ferrie's Mouse House for disposal.

On Thursday, the remnants were minced, and cultures created:

The Process: The cancerous cells were started in a Roswell Park 1640- type solution + 10% Fetal Calf Serum (FCS). The recovered cells would be centrifuged in the little tabletop centrifuge, the pellets then placed in fresh medium plus FCS, The cells would now start to attach to the glass of the test tubes, where, bathed in RPMI medium, they began to grow. We also used plastic stackable mini-flasks for cultures, insulated at 37° C. The cultures would be examined on Friday for cell density and morphology. Cell cultures only remained with Dave or Dr. Mary one to two days. Back-ups were kept longer in case the cultures sent out might become contaminated and need replacement. A pH indicator (Phenol Red) was added to tell us when waste product build-up in the test tubes required a change of medium, turning from bright pink to yellow as wastes made it more acidic.

Cell density determinations were made at 10 X with an ocular grid. The cell density was plotted on a log scale vs. length of culture time.

On Fridays, I generally delivered the Product to Dr. Sherman's apartment, but sometimes Lee would deliver it to the U.S. Public Health Service Hospital or the Prytania Street lab, depending on where Dr. Sherman was that day. When Lee was not available, I left it in the aforementioned car. On a few occasions, I even went directly to Ochsner's Clinic to pick up hard-to-get materials such as neonatal umbilical cord serum and ascites fluid. A few times I had to go to Hugh Evans' lab on Camp Street to get chemicals that we needed.

I was becoming overworked and stressed out. My typical day started before 6:00 a.m., and ended around midnight. The final task of my nightly routine was always to hide the lab reports and research papers, in the unlikely event that Robert showed up unannounced.

I had a few short meetings with Dr. Sherman at her apartment, at which time she reviewed our progress. An occasional night at Dave Ferrie's also entered my schedule for several weeks.

Dr. Ochsner wanted to speed up the Project. He called me at Reily's several times to ask for ideas.[9] I offered him several. One recommendation was that we try the transfer from mice to monkeys again, but this time the monkeys should be exposed to radiation beforehand to suppress their immune systems. Ochsner liked the idea and noted that they had concentrated their radiation efforts on tissue cultures, not living hosts. I was surprised they had not done this earlier, since I had told them back in 1961 that I had used this method to develop cancer in mice more rapidly. So I recommended irradiating the monkeys to expedite things, and Dr. Ochsner agreed. Then I went back to resolving the pile of credit problems on Monaghan's desk.

---

1. I clocked Lee in as a Reily employee at 9:57 A.M. His clock-in record for that date, therefore, shows two entries: one at 8:25 A.M., and the other at 9:57 A.M. Now you know why.

2. The Dallas police had reported seeing Lee Oswald distributing pro-Castro handbills in Dallas shortly before he came to New Orleans. A background check with the Dallas police would have uncovered that event. Of course, that check was never actually made, despite the fact that I placed the initials of Retail Credit's supervisor, Mr. Desmare, at the bottom of the report — the only set of initials I felt comfortable using, as I did not know the initials of anyone else currently working at Retail Credit — but I did have Desmare's business card. Some contend that Desmare simply did a "boiler-plate" "fake" investigation and thereby accuse Retail Credit's supervisor, Henry Coe Desmare, of cheating Reily on background investigations, and being a lying slacker. Desmare, of course, was confused when shown the report six months later, saying he 'must' have written it, because the FBI said so. However, there were so many blatant errors and lapses in the background report that it was obviously bogus. The report was made for "Account No. 6605, which is the number for Standard Coffee Company, New Orleans" (FBI, WCE 1141 (22 WCH 145-146). Researchers did not know that Lee worked for Standard Coffee for that week with me, until I spoke out about it in 1999.

3. Lee's friend in Dallas, George de Mohrenschildt, wrote in his book about Lee, called *I Am a Patsy!*: "Kennedy's efforts to alleviate and to end segregation were also admired by Lee, who was sincerely and profoundly committed to a complete integration of Blacks ...."

4. Other employees didn't notice my absences much, because on Mondays and Tuesdays I never left my desk for lunch, and of course, was always 'at work' at my desk when they left at the end of the day, since I had to stay late to clock Lee out — almost always after everyone was already gone. This gave the impression that I was putting in full work days, and even overtime, despite my absences three afternoons a week. Since the clerks knew I had to go to the courthouse, give reports to Reily's corporate secretaries upstairs, or visit the Standard Coffee office from time to time, my absences those afternoons were not considered extraordinary. It was poor

Monaghan who had to take over much of those extraneous duties the clerks and personnel thought I was handling. No wonder I saw so little of him!

5. It had already been arranged for Lee to get unemployment checks from Texas, even while he worked at Reily's — a handy source of emergency money that could account for his being able to take care of his family if he had to leave Reily's early. Similarly, any "FPCC" donations, conveniently unaccounted for, (since Lee was both the treasurer and secretary) could be thought of as a source of funds as well. I learned all of this when Lee said he would pay me from his unemployment warrant, first thing in the morning, so I could cover my A-1 check.

6. Anyone who has followed my New Orleans history so far knows I had absolutely no need, desire, or time to buy a $30 American Express money order on May 27, when I needed money for A-1, only to put it right back into the bank the very next day. I had an excuse to put the money in my purse into the bank the next day, should Robert ask me about it (he kept close track of all our expenditures). I'd tell him I didn't know if he was cashing any checks, and wanted to make sure we'd have enough. He never knew about the money order, of course.

7. Robert had his own checkbook and actually wrote some checks during this same time period. Robert's reckless spending would have overdrawn our account and one of his checks would have bounced, had I not put $30 in the bank when I did.

   Bank statement shows precariously low balance. Note AmEx money order sender's stub, in my youthful handwriting, for $30, dated May 27. Recipient's area is blank (did not want a paper trail to me). Note my $30 bank deposit the next day, May 28, when Lee repaid me with cash. Note, also: $30 deposit slip dated May 28. Why would someone buy a $30 dollar money order, which required paying a fee, only to put that $30 right back in the bank the next day? And why kiss a receipt?

8. We believed Marina and Kerry Thornley were having an affair, though Thornley always denied it. His denials were so eloquent that Lee gave him a second chance and arranged for Thornley to pick up the pro-Castro flyers Lee had printed. All was well for another week, until the apartment manager said she saw Thornley with Marina. Lee then told Thornley to leave town, or make an appointment with a plastic surgeon. Neighbors testified to the Warren Commission that Thornley was there so often they were unsure as to which one (Lee or Thornley) was really Marina's husband. Jim Garrison's investigation confirmed the same point.

9. Dr. Ochsner knew that I answered Monaghan's phone at Reily's when I was there. So he called and asked for Monaghan. Even if Monaghan himself answered, Ochsner knew Monaghan was in the loop, so he could ask him to have me call him back without a loss of confidentiality. He called me three times that summer using this method.

CHAPTER 17

THE 500 CLUB

Friday, May 31, 1963

Lee and I met Dave Ferrie at Charity Hospital at noon. This time we did not have to wait. As soon as we registered (using only our initials as advised), we were sent to the same room in which we had met with Dr. Ochsner. This time Dave was waiting for us, seated in the same chair that Ochsner had used and conjuring up an air of importance.

I wondered why we were meeting him in Charity Hospital instead of at his house. Perhaps he had just finished meeting with Ochsner? In any event Dave gave us fresh medical reports, which had been flown in from New York, and then informed us that Ochsner had approved our proposed transfer of cancer from mice to monkeys. It was an expensive step, but time was running out. Dave said we had about a month to succeed. Since we would be killing a large number of very expensive monkeys in the process, replacements were ordered from Africa. They were slated to arrive at the primate lab before researchers on other projects beginning in the autumn would wonder what happened to their monkeys.

Dave also gave us a copy of his new schedule, which was getting full. It included flying to Toronto for Dr. Sherman.

Dave had told us that an important arms shipment was expected from Venezuela. "The crux of the matter is simple," he said. "The shipment has to get through. If it's confiscated, people will be murdered in retribution. It will come in one of three sister ships. We'll know which one, when it's time."

"We must protect this shipment," Dave explained. "The problem is some of the stevedores and dock workers are spies. Some are pro-Castro, some are FBI informants. Both will tell the FBI, if they suspect a thing. Hoover loves to see JFK get blamed every time he orchestrates another crackdown on an anti-Castro project."

"Marcello will cooperate because he backs the anti-Castroites here," Lee explained to me.

"I've already talked to Marcello," Dave added. "We might not be able to disable all the spies, so we also have to figure out how to protect the shipment from being recognized."

"What will the cargo look like?" I asked.

"Well," Dave said, "The rifles will probably be packed in unmarked crates, or maybe in barrels."

"Not good," I told them, intrigued by the problem. "Part of protecting something from discovery is to make it look like something else entirely."

I suggested using crates marked as furniture, which would actually have rifles slipped in with an unassembled table, or with two nested chairs.

After removing the rifles, the tables could be assembled — or the nested chairs stacked — to fill the crates, and nothing would seem amiss.

"Good idea," Dave said. "I'll get our friend Shaw to help us out with this one," referring to Clay Shaw. "He can tell us if we can get stuff like that boxed and shipped in from Caracas."

Delta's Three Sister Ships

Delta's three identical ships, the *Del Norte*, *Del Sud* and *Del Mar* were a common sight along the New Orleans waterfront in 1963. The Sisters shuttled between New Orleans and the east coast of South America for over 20 years. Traveling as far south as Argentina, these 495 ft. passenger-cargo ships crossed the Equator in air-conditioned comfort. Considered state-of-the-art luxury transportation, they helped re-establish U.S. trade to South America after World War II. Delta Steamship Lines, Inc. was owned by The Mississippi Shipping Company of New Orleans.

Elsewhere in this book, Judyth describes how she helped Lee Oswald and his associates smuggle a shipment of rifles into New Orleans from South America for the anti-Castro Cubans to use in their raids against Fidel Castro. Oswald helped unload the rifles off a ship which he called "one of the three sisters" after it arrived from Venezuela, its last stop on its South America route. Judyth suggested hiding the rifles in a furniture crate with two chairs that were inverted and stacked on top of each other, and Clay Shaw arranged for the rifles to be packed in this manner and shipped from Argentina. Once in New Orleans, the rifle boxes were removed from the furniture crate, the chairs were unstacked and then placed side-by-side in the same crate, occupying the same cubic dimensions as the chairs and rifles had. Carlos Marcello used his influence on the docks to enable Oswald and Ferrie to retrieve the rifles from the ship without detection. The rifles were given to Guy Banister who supplied weapons to the anti-Castro Cubans being trained in New Orleans. The furniture continued to its final destination without the rifles.

Importing rifles into the U.S. is unusual, since the U.S. is the world's largest gun producer. The likely reason to smuggle in foreign made rifles is to prevent any weapons captured from being traced back to a U.S. source. It gives a covert operation, such as illegal anti-Castro raids on Cuba, plausible deniability.

As an Executive Director at the International Trade Mart, Clay Shaw was at the center of the international trade community in New Orleans. Shaw's mentors, Ted Brent and Lloyd Cobb, had deep connections to both Ochsner and the CIA. Connections between Dr. Ochsner and Ted Brent were so strong that Brent left the fortune he had amassed during his lifetime to Ochsner Clinic upon his death. The hotel on the campus of Ochsner Clinic is named Brent House, in his honor.

Clay Shaw

The CIA's presence in New Orleans was as blatant as it was logical.[1] Shaw and his business associates who traveled abroad cooperated with the CIA's information gathering as a patriotic duty. They would fill out reports for the CIA on people they met and matters they observed. Some spent far more time gathering information than others, and the line between a mere "domestic contact" and a spy could get fuzzy.

Shaw had a history of cooperating with Dr. Ochsner's anti-Castro efforts. His friendship with Dave Ferrie was based on their mutual interest in the homosexual scene in New Orleans. Shaw was described to me as a devoted patriot and CIA asset.

Ted Brent

International House was the Trade Mart's formal link to Dr. Ochsner. He and Shaw had run International House together for years, tracking the numerous international business deals and arrangements created through dinners, meetings and secret deals at "IH." Dr. Ochsner certainly got around. Shaw had been released as IH's acting director just last year. Naturally, a spy and informant ring thrived there.

Leaving Charity Hospital, Lee and I headed to Louisiana Avenue Parkway to finish the week's lab work. There, Lee began learning procedures to keep cell cultures alive. When finished, we returned to Reily's, where I picked up my paycheck and punched out. Since Lee had clocked in very late that morning I would have had to wait two more hours to clock him out, so he suggested that we get something to eat and then come back to clock him out.

"Don't worry," Lee said. "I have a key to Reily's, and we can get back in." Lee cashed his paycheck at Martin's Restaurant, and then we went on to Thompson's where Anna Lewis cheered us up with her down-to-earth jokes. David Lewis was there, too, so after dinner the four of us walked to Preservation Hall to enjoy some New Orleans jazz.

Then, we remembered that Lee hadn't punched out yet! We hurried back to Reily's, Lee unlocked the door, and we went in. He clocked out at 7:32 P.M.

"Luckily for you," I told Lee, "I am the one who will have to resolve your late clock-out when Payroll starts screaming."

"What are you going to tell them?" Lee asked.

"I'll say I was working late. You called and said you forgot to clock out."

"That will work," he confirmed.

"Another lie!" I said wistfully. "I hate having to lie all the time."

Clay Shaw and Dr. Alton Ochsner

"Think about what Dave told us today," Lee said. "Sometimes there's no choice. A lie can sometimes save a life."

Despite how late it was, I stopped and bought some needed groceries, knowing I was going to be too busy on Saturday because Dr. Mary had invited me to tour the Crippled Children's Hospital with her.

The moment I got off the Magazine bus, I spotted Robert's blue Ford sitting in the driveway. I was glad that I had a sack of groceries, since it would help explain my lateness. I was in no mood to argue with Robert, nor could I tell him what I was really doing at this point. I doubted he would even ask. I quickly stuffed the research papers I had with me between some colorful brochures from the Crippled Children's Hospital, and entered the apartment quietly.

Robert's blue and white duffel bag was sitting just inside the door, filled with dirty clothes. I wondered if Robert had returned so soon because he needed his laundry done. I could see him lying in the bed. His army boots and ROTC pants were on the floor. Groceries in arms, I tiptoed through the back door into Susie's kitchen, where she was humming to herself as she removed an apple pie from the oven. She offered me some tea, as I unloaded the groceries.

After a while, I went in to Robert who, of course, wanted the usual *happy hour* in bed. I decided to trade affection for information and began to negotiate.

Clay Shaw

Clay Shaw was a New Orleans business man who worked at the center of the New Orleans trade community. In 1963, he was General Manager of the International Trade Mart, when it served as the backdrop for one of Lee Oswald's leafletting activities. Shaw was swept into the media spotlight on March 1, 1967 when he was arrested and charged with conspiring to murder President Kennedy by District Attorney Jim Garrison, who had identified him as "Clay Bertrand," a mysterious character which witnesses had seen with Lee Oswald in the months before the JFK assassination. Shaw denied knowing Lee Oswald and was acquitted on March 1, 1969.

It was not until 1993, when the JFK Records Act released classified testimony from the House Select Committee on Assassinations taken over fifteen years earlier, that it was learned that law enforcement officers in Clinton, Louisiana had identified Shaw as the driver of the car that Lee Oswald emerged from during a voter registration drive in August 1963.

Shaw had been a major in the Army during WW II, and after the war, helped Lloyd Cobb and Ted Brent start the International Trade Mart to facilitate trade. Through these circles, Shaw knew Dr. Alton Ochsner. Shaw was also known locally for his efforts to preserve buildings in New Orleans' historic French Quarter, and for his social activities.

In 1979, Richard Helms, former director of the CIA, testified under oath that Clay Shaw was one of many contacts of the CIA's Domestic Contact Service who provided information from travels abroad. Shaw died of lung cancer in 1974 at the age of 61.

"How long will the next hitch be?" I demanded.

"I have no idea!" he answered. "They keep changing the schedule on me."

"How come they know the schedule at the office over in Lafayette?"

"Weather happens," he said. "Problems come up. You're mad over nothing."

"You need to write and to call! I'm your wife! I need to know you care!" I almost blurted out that I was struggling hard not to sleep with another man and that I needed love in ways other than sexual, which Lee was providing, but I came to my senses in time.

"Do you realize you never say 'I love you'?" I said, starting to cry. "I tell you I love you, but you never say it back. I have feelings!"

"I might be gone twenty-one days, next time out," Robert retorted. "They're trying to finish early. That's why I came home for a day. And you're wasting all the time we could have had together by fighting. So how do you feel about that?"

We stopped talking again as Robert busied himself checking my expenditures. He broke the silence by observing that I had lost weight and told me to be careful to eat enough. As soon as those words of concern were out of his mouth he reminded me not to buy anything frivolous, such as dresses or shoes.

Then he played a song on his guitar and began purring like a lazy lion. He turned on the radio Lee had given me and found some relaxing music. Then came kisses. My body responded, but this time a part of me held back. When it was over, we had sandwiches he had brought from the deli. Susie had offered us some of her apple pie, which we enjoyed.

Robert hadn't mentioned receiving any of my letters and still did not say "I love you" to me. My sadness deepened as I ironed his shirts. I felt like a pit stop in his routine.

"We've been married almost a month," I told him, "and we still have no photos of us together."

"Why did I come?" he replied. "I might as well go back right away." He took the shirts I had ironed out to his car. When he came back inside, he said his parents had a camera in Fort Walton Beach and that he'd be taking me to see them soon. "We'll take a picture then."

"I'll call you next Sunday," he said. Then he left, forgetting his shaving brush and lather cup. I thanked the God I no longer believed in that Robert had stayed only one night! Then I fell asleep.

Saturday, June 1, 1963

Early next morning, I baked some brownies and packed them with Robert's shaving equipment in a little box with a note that read "Look

for mold before eating!" I mailed the package at the post off.
his address at Pip's Place, then continued to the Crippled Childr.
Hospital where I met Dr. Mary.

She took me around to see the patients. There were children in iron lungs, in traction and others with bone pain so extreme I had to leave their bedside to get control of my emotions. Some were still recuperating from surgery which Dr. Sherman had performed. She handed out little stuffed animals and candy suckers laced with aspirin.

Dr. Mary explained that several of the children in the polio ward had actually been crippled by the faulty polio vaccine. This was another reason Dr. Sherman was discreetly engaged in polio vaccine research, and why she was so interested in the cancer-causing virus that had contaminated the polio vaccines. Dr. Ochsner's horrific experience with the flawed polio vaccine that had killed his grandson and crippled his granddaughter put these two colleagues on the same page. Both were aware of the SV40 contaminants still present in millions of doses of the vaccine, and both doctors realized its potential to cause an epidemic of cancer in the future.

THE TIMES-PICAYUNE, NEW ORLEAN

Physicians Offer Sugar Lump Toast

WITH CUPS LIFTED to the success of the Sabin Oral polio vaccine campaign are these three New Orleans physicians. From left are Dr. Philip H. Jones, Dr. William River- bark and Dr. Thomas E. Furlow Jr. The were among volunteers handling assignment Sunday at KO-Polio headquarters, 1060 Charles.

For professional and political reasons both were publicly silent as the pro-vaccine propaganda machine churned out fresh publicity aimed at the unsuspecting citizenry.[2] They quietly searched for a solution. Perhaps a benign strain of SV40 could be used as the basis for a vaccine. But as the political landscape changed, their well-intentioned covert medical project had gotten tangled up with the fanaticism and "patriotism" of the moment, and been perverted into a biological weapon to kill Fidel Castro. We had to live with the knowledge that our government was withholding the truth about the safety of the new polio vaccine. Because I had been raised to trust my government, the shock to my young, patriotic soul was devastating.

Tuesday, June 4, 1963

Lee had a meeting with David Ferrie at Banister's, so he once again clocked in late. There, strategies were discussed to protect the upcoming arms shipment. When the meeting broke up Dave gave Lee a card to access Tulane's medical library, so I could research some things related to our cancer work. Lee told me to go to Tulane's medical library immediately after work and have the librarian call Dr. Ochsner's office right away, so they could verify that my name had been added to the list of those who used the card. "Ochsner said you could use Dave's access card until you're issued your own card, in the fall," Lee said.

That afternoon, Mr. Monaghan agreed to clock me and Lee out, so we could meet at 4:30 near Eli Lilly.

We arrived at Tulane's medical library and presented the card to the librarian. As we waited for the librarian to call Ochsner's office, Lee and I sat together at a table by ourselves and talked. He was worried about Marina's pregnancy. She had fainted during a walk. He dreaded the idea of her waiting for hours at Charity Hospital, so he had cared for her assiduously all weekend, keeping her in bed as much as possible. In the middle of this humane concern for the health of his pregnant wife, he said, "I now tell her every day that she should go back to Russia,"

"But Lee," I protested, "I thought you were going to stop doing that to her. And here she's been fainting!"

"I know," he replied. "It looks mean. But I need her to think she has a choice between being happy without me in Texas, and being happy without me in the Soviet Union. I've already started processing things with the Russian Embassy. She'll be able to return to Russia if she really wants to. She won't be safe here, unless I take extraordinary precautions. I keep telling her to go back to Russia, because it will also help develop my pro-Castro image."

"Because, if you send her back to Russia without divorcing her, it means you still love Russia and Cuba. Is that it?" I offered, trying to follow the game.

"Precisely," Lee replied. "If it's known I want her and my baby to go back, that proves I prefer Mother Russia as the place to raise my children. That looks good for my Cuban credentials, and it makes it safer for Marina to go back. I don't want anybody there to pick on her for having lived in this country. It has to seem as if she wished to return."

"But in actuality, she'll choose Texas, won't she?" I ventured.

"Yes. And that will be good, because I can readily pop in and see my babies if they're in Texas. Here, there's nobody to help but Marcello, and my aunt and uncle, especially if I end up in jail, or prison over this."

"Jail? Prison?" I asked, taking his hand. "Could it come to that?"

"Anything can happen with the New Orleans police," Lee said. "Somebody might draw a gun on me. An incident could happen. They could plant a gun on me, or drugs, and try to send me up the river. Because I'll be acting like Fidel's best friend. That means dangers for my family, if they stay."

There was so much Lee did not dare tell Marina. It made him feel guilty, because she was pregnant.[3]

Lee said "The Pain" (Ruth) was planning a long vacation, which would delay Marina's return to Irving. That was okay, he added, because he wanted to be with Junie as much as possible before his more dangerous work started. At this time, Lee didn't know that Ruth Paine's vacation would be extended so long that it would create problems for him and concern for Marina's safety.

I was then called to the desk. The librarian said she had called the Ochsner Clinic, and that I would be issued a temporary pass for the summer. The first few times I used it I also had to show the original card, but after that the Tulane librarians recognized me. I kept the card in my purse and eventually forgot it was there.

When Lee and I returned to Reily's, Lee spent an hour oiling the roasting machinery. I clocked him out. By now it was both dark and hot in the closed-up factory area. Lee came out covered with sweat, heading to the bathroom on the first floor by the canteen to wash up.

We got on the bus, which was almost empty, and Lee, exhausted, rested his head in my lap. When I got home, I found Susie crying. "What's the matter, Susie?" I asked. By now, she meant a lot to me. "Pope John has died!" she grieved. "It was stomach cancer!" I was thunderstruck. So many people were dying of cancer! I thought of my grandpa, and full of worry decided to risk calling him. He told me he was in remission, and not to worry. He also promised he wouldn't tell my parents where I was. The Pope's death reminded me that instead of striving to cure cancer, I was creating a bioweapon from cancerous materials! How could such a devout young Catholic girl stray so far from her path? I was disgusted with myself. Sick to my stomach, I collapsed among the pillows and wept. For the first time, I feared that I might never again be involved in curing cancer. How could things have gone so wrong, so quickly?

June 5, 1963 — Wednesday

The two hardest days at Reily were finished for the week. Today the hard work was at Ferrie's. Dr. Ochsner wanted us to speed up the project, so he doubled the number of mice we had to kill. Instead of fifty, I had to slaughter one hundred weanling mice, eviscerate them, then salvage and weigh the largest tumors. Lee had business elsewhere, so I was on my own. It was disgusting work, and it took me longer than usual to clean up. I returned late to Reily's. There Lee met me with a book under his arm: *The Huey Long Murder Case,* by Hermann Deutsch.

Lee was interested in the Huey Long case because Dr. Ochsner had known the accused assassin, Dr. Carl Weiss.[4] But did Weiss deserve all the shame and blame he had received? Lee decided he'd visit a few bars to see if some of the old-timers remembered details about the murder.

Carlos "The Little Man" Marcello

Carlos Marcello was best-known as the head of the Mafia in New Orleans. Born Calogero Minacore in 1910 in Tunisia to Sicilian parents, he adopted the name Carlos Marcello when his family moved to Metairie, Louisiana. At 19 he was arrested in New Orleans for bank robbery, but the charges dropped. At 20 he was convicted of assault-and-robbery and sent to prison for 5 years. At 25, he was back on the streets.

In 1938 Marcello was arrested in New York for the sale of more than 23 pounds of illegal drugs, and served 10 months in prison. Afterwards he associated with Frank Costello, the leader of the Mafia in New York.

By the late 1940s, Marcello had taken control of Louisiana's gambling network and joined forces with Meyer Lansky to buy some of the biggest casinos in the New Orleans area, making him the undisputed leader of the New Orleans Mob. He was to hold this position for the next 30 years.

In March of 1959 Marcello appeared before the Senate Committee investigating organized crime, facing Robert F. Kennedy as chief counsel to the committee and his brother, Senator John F. Kennedy, as a member of the committee. Marcello repeatedly invoked the fifth amendment, refusing to answer any questions relating to his background, activities, and associates.

After becoming president, JFK appointed his brother as U.S. Attorney General, and the two men initiated a war on organized crime. By the spring of 1961, the Attorney General had Marcello arrested and forcibly removed to Guatemala.

But it didn't take long for Marcello to return to the U.S., with vengeance in his heart. Undercover informants reported that Marcello made several threats against John F. Kennedy. He told Edward Becker that "a dog will continue to bite you if you cut off its tail. Whereas if you cut off the dog's head, it would cease to cause you trouble." Becker reported that Marcello "clearly stated that he was going to arrange to have President Kennedy murdered in some way." Marcello told another informant that he would need to take out "insurance" for the assassination by "setting up a nut to take the blame."

The summer before Kennedy was assassinated, Jack Ruby visited New Orleans to meet with Marcello and another Mafia don, Santos Trafficante, about a problem he was having with the American Guild of Variety Artists. This was the same summer Judyth Vary and Lee Harvey Oswald resided in New Orleans.

On Nov. 22, 1963, at the moment of the JFK assassination, Marcello was sitting in a courtroom in New Orleans with David Ferrie at his side awaiting a verdict concerning Bobby Kennedy's attempts to deport him permanently. Shortly after hearing the news of the assassination, Marcello was acquitted and headed to a party to celebrate his victory.

After the assassination, J. Edgar Hoover's FBI investigated Marcello and concluded he was not "a significant organized crime figure" but rather "a tomato salesman and real estate investor." The Warren Commission then concluded there was no direct link between Jack Ruby and Marcello.

In 1966 Marcello was arrested in New York and, after a long drawn out legal battle, was convicted for assault. He served less than six months of a two-year sentence.

In 1981 G. Robert Blakey, chief counsel to the House Select Committee on Assassinations, published *The Plot to Kill the President,* in which he argued *Continued next page...*

Lee eventually learned from old-timers that Weiss was shot at least fifty times, rather than the thirty-two reported. The old-timers said bullets removed from Huey Long didn't match Weiss' smaller caliber revolver. Two decades after the assassination they described Weiss as a decent man, a good doctor. Lee said Weiss was "probably a patsy," explaining that "patsy" was a slang term for an innocent man forced to take the blame for a guilty one.[5]

Thursday, June 6, 1963

I clocked out at five, and went back to Monaghan's desk. Then the phone rang. It was Dave Ferrie. "No lab work for you tonight, bright eyes," he said. "I've taken care of it for you. And guess why?"

"Because you're a kind, sweet, wonderful, sensitive man," I said. "No, seriously, why are you being so good to me?"

Carlos Marcello, *continued* that Marcello organized the JFK assassination, as did author John H. Davis in 1989 in his book *Mafia Kingfish: Carlos Marcello and the Assassination of John F. Kennedy.*

In January 1992, the New York Post claimed Marcello, Jimmy Hoffa and Santos Trafficante were all involved in the assassination of JFK. Trafficante's lawyer, Frank Ragano, was quoted as saying that at the beginning of 1963 Hoffa had told him to take a message to Trafficante and Marcello concerning a plan to kill Kennedy. When he later met with the men at the Royal Orleans Hotel, Ragano told them: "You won't believe what Hoffa wants me to tell you. Jimmy wants you to kill the president." He reported that both men gave the impression that they intended to carry out this order.

In his autobiography, *Mob Lawyer*, Frank Ragano related that in July, 1963, he was once again sent to New Orleans by Hoffa to meet Marcello and Santos Trafficante concerning plans to kill JFK. When Kennedy was killed Hoffa apparently said to Ragano: "I told you you could do it. I'll never forget what Carlos and Santos did for me." He added: "This means Bobby is out as Attorney General." Marcello later told Ragano: "When you see Jimmy, you tell him he owes me and he owes me big."

Carlos Marcello died March 3, 1993.

"Call Susie Hanover and make sure your hubby's not in town," Dave answered, "because if he's not, you're going out!"

"I am?"

"Indeed you are. Remember that Sparky fellow who walked around my place on his hands?"

"How could I forget?"

"He's going to foot the bill for all of us, including you, me, Lee, and the Lewises over at The 500 Club. But we have to be there by 7:00."

"What about Marina?"

"That's Lee's problem," Dave said. "Not ours. He has to attend. Marcello's going to be there."

When I met Lee at Thompson's Restaurant, he had just finished talking to Marina on the phone. He was still concerned about her fainting. I asked him how it went. "Oh, she's feeling all right, so far. I'll just stay for an hour or two. I told her I had to work late. But I promised to bring her a treat." Lee asked Anna to wrap up two slices of pecan pie for him to take home.

Lee gave me the pie slices to carry in my semi-bottomless purse. Anna got off fifteen minutes early and went to freshen up. As soon as David arrived, away we went to 441 Bourbon Street. The 500 Club! I couldn't wait to see it. We arrived at seven o'clock as instructed. Sparky came to our table, giving us special attention and chatting. He sat with us until Carlos Marcello arrived surrounded by several large companions.[6] Sparky went over to greet them. Then, a tall silver-haired gentleman entered with another man and a woman. They sat down with the Marcello group, but were hard to see because of the way the tables were lined up.

"The one who just came in, that's Clay Shaw, the managing director of the Trade Mart," Lee whispered. "He's the one building the new trade center and can get things set up in Caracas. We can trust him."

"Do you know anybody else over there?" I asked.

"Yes. That's a railroad guy," Lee said. "And that's a railroad guy, too. Over there, next to Shaw, is a guy from Terry Smith Stevedoring. I think that's his wife with him. And next to him, that's Hugh Ward. He's a pilot, and Banister's partner. Dave and I have worked with him. Next to him, I don't know. I think he's a bodyguard. The other guys are Marcello's brothers, Sammy and Pete."

"Why are they meeting here, at a night club?" I asked.

"I suppose, because Marcello wants it this way."

"But why are we here?"

"Because, sometime tonight, they'll get around to talking about the Venezuelan matter."

As we waited for dinner to begin, I took a sheet of note paper from my purse, full of notes on one side from a Dave Ferrie lecture, to jot down some of Lee's remarks about married life in Russia. I also sketched a small black horse and, a little later, impressed by some dancing girls that came out to perform, I began to draw one of them. That's when Sparky noticed I was sketching something and came over to investigate. After looking at my sketch, he returned with a poster and turned it over with the blank side up.

"Can you draw me a black stallion?" he asked. Impressed by Lee's story of the famous horse Black Gold's remarkable history, I began to draw at once. As I worked on it, the waiters would stop by to look. Sparky checked on my progress at one point, then sent the waiter to bring the drawing over to his table when I was finished. He showed it to Marcello, apparently to prove that I had not sketched the people attending his private meeting. Soon, I was asked to draw a cat, then a dog, which kept me busy through most of the meal. Sparky had each drawing shown to Marcello when it was completed. Meanwhile, the place filled with people and smoke. Lee, David Lewis and I had Dr. Peppers while everybody else was drinking alcohol. The music got louder as the plates of food came and went. Marcello also made a point of smiling at Anna Lewis several times during our meal.

Sparky finally signaled Lee to go over to Marcello's table. I saw him sit down next to Clay Shaw. I could not hear the conversation, but Lee later told me they discussed how to handle the Venezuelan arms shipment, which would soon be on its way. The music was exciting, the food was rich, the stage show was titillating for the guys, but Lee said he didn't want to leave Marina alone any longer, so we had to leave. That was fine with me.

We said goodnight to David and Anna. When we stepped outside, we were escorted to a Cadillac and driven home in style. It was about ten o'clock when we reached my apartment. I handed Lee the pecan pie slices to take home to Marina.

This night was a pivotal event for Lee and me: we never again had to pay for anything at Marcello-connected restaurants in the French Quarter. Naturally, that meant we enjoyed some free meals at the 500 Club. In hindsight, this should have triggered concern. Lee was being compensated "on the arm" by the Mafia boss himself. But at the time, nothing was normal in my world.

If the CIA and the FBI were in with the Mob, I certainly couldn't stop them; and if it meant that Lee and I could eat for free in nice restaurants, so be it.

Friday, June 7, 1963

On Friday, Lee clocked out at 5:30 and we finally got to spend some private time with each other. We had so much to talk about. As we strolled along the shops at Canal, Lee spotted a black Japanese-style blouse, bought it, and had me put it on in the dressing room.[7] Then we sipped sodas at Walgreen's, and he had me practice some Japanese phrases he had learned while stationed in Japan.

Back on the bus, Lee worked on my hair to make me look like Marina. Then we went to Mother's, a restaurant not far from Reily's, where I spoke Russian and impersonated Marina. Everybody there thought I was Mr. Oswald's Russian wife who had no English. Lee ordered two classic New Orleans sandwiches called Po' Boys — one for me and one for Marina. Then we got on the bus. On the way home, Lee explained that he would be busy during the afternoons next week and would not be able to ride home with me on the bus. We would not be able to have our private time together in the park, but he would see me on the bus in the mornings, and "in his dreams."

So I focused on the Project, burying myself in reading research papers and writing reports. I also met with Dr. Sherman, who reviewed my work.

A one-page letter from Robert arrived. Yes, he had gotten the brownies, and he enclosed his paycheck to deposit in our account. The letter was from Hopedale, a hamlet with a couple of docks and a gas station on a bayou in the remote marshes of southeast Louisiana. Boats refueled and picked up people and supplies there. Dr. Mary helped me find it on the map.

A few days later, another letter from Robert arrived. This one was seven pages long. Two letters in one week! Maybe it was the brownies! Robert said that bad weather had delayed their Evangeline Seismic activities and he did not expect to be home for another twenty days.

Robert ended his letter with advice about money and a directive to eat more. But it was Lee who brought me bread and milk twice a week and made sure I ate well, and for free, in Marcello's restaurants.[8]

Monday, June 10, 1963

On the morning bus, Lee told me that Marina was still not feeling well. He was frustrated that he was unable to get prenatal care at Charity Hospital. If he took her to a private clinic, he would have a problem explaining where a "poor working man" came up with that much money. For the first time, I saw Lee really fret about the health care available to the poor. He consoled himself that Ruth Paine had arranged for Marina to deliver her baby at a clinic in Grand Prairie, Texas, which was an excellent facility. And he reminded himself that the birth of

Junie had been easy and quick. Still, Marina wasn't feeling well and needed to see a doctor.

"Nobody should be denied medical care," he said. "It's a basic human right! Just as the right to own a house. The people in this country are serfs and slaves," he went on, heatedly. "If they don't pay taxes on the house they think they own, they can be evicted. So who really owns their house? The government! They might as well live in Russia. And hell, if they get sick and are new in town, they can drop dead. Nobody cares. We're living in a world as barbaric as ancient Rome!"

"Maybe Rome had some things better," I offered, noting Rome had heated floors and trained doctors two thousand years ago. That led to Lee's taking out the book, *Everyday Life in Ancient Rome*, from the library for us to study.

About the same time, Lee created a fake health card for himself so

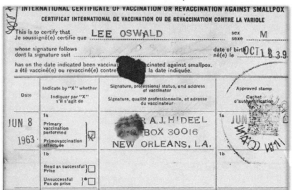

he'd have vaccination 'proof' — necessary for travel to backward countries. His vaccinations were up-to-date, thanks to Dr. Ochsner, but he couldn't put that name on his health card. Instead, he used the fake name "Dr. A.J. Hideel." There was that name again! I'd seen it on the third floor at Banister's, and a variation on a fake FPCC membership card Lee carried. "Hidell," Lee told me, was a 'project name' used on fake ID's to access certain funds. Further, he said he was not the only person using the name.

In June 1963 racial tensions were flaring all across the South. The integration of the school systems and the universities was a major battle ground in this struggle. The segregationists, like the White Citizens Council, somehow equated integration with Communism, and rejected it with Cold War certainty, arguing that segregation was part of the natural order of things. Dr. Martin Luther King and the NAACP staged protests and called for equal access to all public institutions as a fundament legal right.

Both sides claimed the moral high ground, and the outcome of the struggle was still uncertain. The local segregationists were led by the White Citizens Council of Greater New Orleans, with 25,000 members. Violence flared at Civil Rights marches in Birmingham and Selma, Alabama. Footage of white police beating black protesters and carrying them off to jail was broadcast on a daily basis. When the courts began ordering integration of school systems and universities, the new laws were met with stiff resistance. The situation was so volatile that President Kennedy called out the National Guard to occupy and forcibly integrate the University of Alabama. Lee applauded Kennedy's courage for doing so: though I'd been prejudiced against JFK by my anti-Castro friends, Lee was making me a believer.

Alabama's Governor George Wallace and General Edwin Walker incited riots with their speeches. The Klu Klux Klan (KKK) burned crosses to intimidate black leaders and black churches were bombed. When prominent NAACP leader Medgar Evers was murdered in Jackson, Mississippi, Lee and I decided to avoid problems and sat in the front of the bus the next few days.

By the end of the week Marina was feeling better, and she had visitors. Ruth Paine wrote to Mrs. Ruth Kloepfer, a fellow Quaker who lived in New Orleans, ostensibly asking her to check on Marina and June. Mrs. Kloepfer just happened to be married to a Tulane professor, Dr. Henry Warner Kloepfer, and they would just happen to move from Pine Street to Louisiana Avenue Parkway — close to David Ferrie — not long afterwards. The first visit to 4905 Magazine involved only Mrs. Kloepfer and her daughters. Marina was unaware that Dr. Kloepfer was a geneticist at Tulane Medical School, who was involved in the Project. Dr. Kloepfer's name, address and phone numbers were later found in Lee's address book.

Friday, June 14, 1963

Lee was finally able to join me for our evening rendezvous at Audubon Park. He told me that he had ordered both *The Militant* and *The Daily Worker* to be delivered to his "faux address" at 4907 Magazine Street to bolster his leftist image. When I admitted that I didn't know the difference between the two publications, Lee was surprised. "With all you know about Russian culture and literature!"

"I read Dostoyevsky, Gogol, and Tolstoy, not Marx, Engels, and Lenin. I haven't read any Communist publications," I countered.

"I can't have a decent conversation with you about what I'm doing, until you get some basic understanding of Communism," Lee stressed. "And that starts with understanding the difference between Marxist and Marxist-Leninist philosophies." He put his arm around me, and drew me close. "You do know the difference between the KKK and the ACLU, I presume?"

"That's easy. One has its initials all the same, and the other has its initials all different," I said, facetiously. "But seriously, I don't know the difference between a Marxist and a Marxist-Leninist."

"Do you care about the difference?" he inquired.

"I do now, Lee," I replied.

"Castro betrayed Marxism," Lee said. "He's a Marxist-Leninist."

"So which one will you be posing as? A Marxist, or a Leninist?"

"I'll let you decide," Lee said, "after I give you some stuff to read. By the way, I'm going to be handing out pro-Castro flyers Sunday next to the aircraft carrier USS *Wasp*. The sailors on the *Wasp* will be coming back after a night on the town. I'll try to give them flyers. We'll see who takes one. Those are the ones we'll be interested in. Of course, I hope they don't knock my teeth out.

"Oh, stop!" I said. "Why must you take on such risks? Haven't we had enough problems with sailors?" I reached out to him, took his head between my hands, and kissed him.

"Ah, my little mouse," he answered, kissing me back, "I'll be all right. There will be someone with a camera taking photos, and others to support me."

"Why don't you do it on Saturday, when there will be a lot of people there?"

"Why, then I might really get hurt," Lee replied. "The docks are crowded on Saturdays. No, it's best on Sunday. We've been spreading rumors that a pro-Castro nut is going to be hanging around the *Wasp* on Sunday. Now, who would be interested in that?"

"Your fanatic anti-Castroites? And pro-Castro spies?"

"Precisely," Lee said. "Sir Percy Blakeney, at your service, putting on yet another disguise." Lee made a mock bow. Then he sighed. "I've been to a lot of taverns, strip joints and bars these last few days. It was tiresome getting picked on, just because I ordered milk."

"Milk?" I said. "What is this, with milk?"

"Oh, I order milk, or lemonade, and you should see them carry on about it," Lee said. "I get a kick out of it. I got the idea from Hopalong Cassidy."

"I remember," I said "Good ol' Hoppy. What was the name of his horse?"

"Topper," Lee said. "So anyway, they're saying to themselves, 'what is it with this guy who orders milk?' And they're saying, 'What does he mean, some pro-Castro nut is gonna be at the Dumaine Wharf this Sunday?'"

Lee smiled. "Our local patriots will be upset. They'll try to stop me, or call the police. Little do they know we'll be looking to see who else is around, like the stevedore who stands and watches too long. The one who starts talking to somebody, then takes a flyer."

"And then?"

"They'll fire the suspicious ones," Lee said. As he drew me close to him, he said, "You smell so fragrant."

"I've been working in a coffee company," I told him.

"I've been in so many gay bars the last couple of weeks," Lee said, "I've almost forgotten I'm straight. Surely you can help out a poor fellow, who's almost lost his way...? "

"Do you need more girl kisses?"

"Many, many more."

After I straightened him out a little, we talked about the Venezuelan project. "This is fascinating to me," I said. "So you believe you'll catch the pro-Castro stevedores this way?"

"There's no telling if we'll get them all on Sunday," he said. "But there's more we'll be doing between now and when the shipment arrives. In particular, we've taken up your idea about disguising the cargo."

"Did you follow through on that?"

"You'll see."

I was excited to hear they had adopted my idea, although I didn't think I would ever put "rifle smuggling" on my resumé.

Saturday, June 15, 1963

Lee came over a little before noon with his daughter Junie. He said Marina wasn't letting him near her, so he wanted another kiss to remind him what grown-up girls were like. He handed me a little blue bottle of "Evening in Paris" perfume, which I'd told him I wore in grade school. I was charmed, and Lee got his kiss.

Sunday, June 16, 1963

Sunday was USS WASP Day.[9] I was worried sick for Lee's safety. The thought of him being mauled by a bunch of drunken sailors was more than I could bear. Finally, Dave Ferrie called Susie to say the event was over and that Lee was okay. Lee later told me that his activity was reported to the Port police, and to the FBI, which downplayed it.[10] The fact that the FBI did not interview Lee about trying to hand pro-Communist literature to U.S. Navy personnel, next to an aircraft carrier, was a dead giveaway that he and the FBI were already well acquainted.

1. How close was the CIA to its New Orleans business contacts? A Congressmen from New Orleans prepared the CIA's budget for Congressional approval. Former CIA Deputy Director Gen. Charles Cabell, whom Kennedy fired after the Bay of Pigs debacle and (whose brother, Earle Cabell was Mayor of Dallas when Kennedy died there in November) came to New Orleans in 1963 to talk to the trade community about political developments in Cuba and Latin America. What else he talked about there might be worth knowing.

2. Such were the political pressures that Ochsner and Sherman had to keep silent, even when the product they both knew was contaminated with the cancer-causing monkey virus was being advertised by New Orleans doctors they respected as 100% safe, as this local *Times-Picayune* photo from May, 1963 proves: "K-O Polio!" The physicians aren't drinking it, but a model is.

3. In the book *Marina and Lee*, McMillan wrote:

    "Sometimes he went a whole day without speaking, and then spent the next day making it up to her. He would take her and Junie to the park, do the laundry, and mop the floor. He would even hang up the wash, while Marina leaned out the window and shouted directions, and Junie waved at her "Papa." He often told Marina how much he had missed her...But Marina was anxious. She was afraid that Lee was nice to her because he would soon be getting rid of her."(p. 402)

    Note that sentence "He often told Marina how much he had missed her." That sentence in the "official" book gives a hint that sometimes Lee was out of town for a day or two — something Marina never admitted. Yet he certainly was.

4. Looking into the case deeply, we came to believe that Weiss was deliberately set up. He was known to be hostile to the Governor, and was approaching Long when one of Long's skittish bodyguards opened fire, mortally wounding Long instead of Weiss. Turning their gunfire on the doctor, they then covered up Huey Long's unplanned murder.

5. Weiss's fate pre-figured Lee's, with the official fairy tale of a "lone-nut assassin" and fall guy, who is conveniently too dead to defend himself.

6. Marcello became a major player in gambling and illegal rackets during the 1940s. In 1947, his boss was deported to Sicily, leaving Marcello the undisputed leader of the Mafia in New Orleans for the next 30 years. In the 1950s, his influence expanded to Dallas, Texas. In 1959, Carlos Marcello appeared before Bobby Kennedy's Senate Committee and said, "I don't know nuttin about that Mafia thing," and refused to answer most questions. On April 4, 1961 U.S. Attorney General Robert Kennedy arrested and forcibly removed Marcello to Guatemala. But through his considerable influence with American political figures, Marcello returned to the U.S. in spite of having no passport. In his book *Mafia Kingfish,* author John Davis claimed that Marcello organized the 1963 assassination of President Kennedy. Marcello died on March 3,

1993 after an early release from prison where he was said to have confessed his involvement in the JFK assassination.

7.   I still own that blouse and keep it as a reminder of my days with Lee.

8.   Time to add those trips up: Marina: ~2 per week. Add Lee's 'several' (at least 3) trips for bread and milk. Total so far: 5 trips per week. But Lee also comes with Marina for 'larger purchases.' We must assume some 5 visits to the grocery store every week. And the store is closed on Sundays. In other words, groceries are being purchased almost every day the store is open. Marina, all by herself, is reported spending 'about' $10/ week ($90/week in today's funds) – a generous sum for three. But Lee is also 'buying bread and milk … alone several times a week.' Lee also goes to the store with Marina for 'larger purchases.' Why so much bread and milk? Answer: there was a secret milk-lover in Lee's life who often ran out of bread and milk!

9.   I later learned that New Orleans District Attorney Jim Garrison had wondered why Lee handed out leaflets at the dock site of the U.S.S. WASP in mid-June, when his FPCC chapter wouldn't be known or publicized again until mid-July. Wrote Garrison:

"…in New Orleans, in the summer of 1963, Lee Harvey Oswald was engaged in bizarre activities which made it appear ostensibly that he was connected with a Cuban organization, although… there was no such organization in New Orleans. …on June 16th… he distributed "Fair Play for Cuba Committee" leaflets on the Dumaine Street Wharf … at the docking site of the … U.S.S. Wasp. Upon request of the commanding officer of the Wasp, Officer Girod Ray of the Harbor Police… [told] him… to stop passing out leaflets and leave the wharf area. At this time, Officer Ray confiscated two pieces of the literature…One … was a leaflet, yellow in color with black print, entitled "Hands Off Cuba!"

10. The New Orleans FBI office did go through the motions of asking Dallas FBI about Lee after the USS Wasp incident.

Lee Harvey Oswald's Passport Photo, June 1963

CHAPTER 18

THE PASSPORT

Monday, June 17, 1963

I headed to work as usual, but this was one of those days when Lee did not wish us to be seen together going to Reily's. He had been leafleting at the Dumaine Street wharf, and he was sunburned.

About 2:00 P.M., when I was away from my desk, Lee came by and left a banana and a book. When I returned I was hungry, and was happy to see the banana. I ate it gratefully, but when I saw the title of the book, *What We Must Know About Communism*, I slipped it under the desk beside my purse. In 1963, any book about Communism was better left unseen, particularly if you were working at a place like Reily's.[1]

Lee rode with me on the bus on the way home that evening.

"You don't know enough about Communism," he told me. "We can't have a decent conversation about politics until you've read that book."

There was something else on Lee's mind; something that was troubling him. When we got to Audubon Park we fed the ducks with Lee's lunch sandwich, which he had been too upset to eat.

"We need to talk," he said. My warning lights flashed on. I could feel his tension as we sat down on a park bench, but I said nothing. Finally, Lee took my hand, and I heard that tiny 'clink' of his wedding band hitting mine.[2] I instantly felt guilty, so I told Lee I was feeling bad about it. "It reminds me that I'm married," I said. "And I'm having problems with that."

"I'm having problems in the same department," Lee said,

Lee had finally kicked Kerry Thornley out of town; but that same night Marina resisted his advances, saying she preferred a former lover named Anatoly. Angrily, Lee had sex with Marina anyway.

Lee Oswald and Anatoly
in Russia

"I didn't hurt her. I wasn't mean, but I didn't respect her," he said. "Now I'm sorry."

I was moved that Lee confessed his sins concerning Marina with such frankness. But I was very disappointed at this new revelation.

"So you have kept your promise not to beat her. But it's okay to force yourself on her! That doesn't count?"

"She keeps talking about other men!" Lee said, miserably. "It makes me furious. I was afraid to tell you. Will you be afraid of me, now?"

"Of course it scares me, Lee," I said. "You acted like a cave man. As for Marina, she's five months pregnant. She's carrying your baby, isn't she? "

"Of this, I am certain," he answered.

"It's not Thornley's baby, or Anatoly's baby," I said. "So let her talk."

"I'm disgusted with myself," he said. "At one time, I was serene. I did not let anything get to me...." Lee closed his eyes. "Now, if she says something, at once, we play the old game. I tell her to shut up. She tells me I'm not a real man."

"But you said that before you married Marina, you had always been gentle with women. Did you lie to me about that?"

"No, no."

"Remember, then, when we make love for the first time," I said softly, "that I'm the woman you'll marry after Marina. A different woman."

"Women always think they can change a man," Lee answered, "but usually, they can't. It's the man who decides to change. Well, I can decide to be the man I want to be. And I'll do it. For you."

Lee's challenge was to do no harm, to make a safe haven for June, and to forgive Marina. His reward would be my respect, increasing trust, and growing love. As he struggled to meet these goals, I saw Lee grow before my eyes.[3]

Though I could speak wisely to Lee, when it came to forgiving Robert for his neglectful ways I wasn't so evolved.

Meanwhile, the get-Castro project was taking shape, and it consumed most of our free time. On June 19, we heard that monkeys had been ordered from Africa, set to arrive by the end of August.[4]

Tulane Monkeys Arriving Today

Some 8,000 pounds of live monkeys will arrive at 7:40 a. m. Sunday at New Orleans International Airport on a chartered flight from Portland, Ore.

Ken McKinsey of United Airlines said the animals, "at least a couple of hundred of them, will be used by the Tulane University Medical School primate center in Covington.

This article appeared in the *Times-Picayune* on Sunday, August 25, 1963, on an inner page. No fanfare was wanted. With expected arrival at 7:40 a.m., by the time anyone read the paper, the monkeys would be out of sight. There were 8,000 pounds of them.

Friday, June 21, 1963

On Friday afternoon I had extra work to do in Dave's lab, so I was there later than usual. Dave arrived while I was still there, and made some phone calls. Then he told me I could go with him out to the airport, if I'd finished my reports. I asked him why and he said only, "It's a surprise." Dave helped me clean up my work space and put the files in order. Miguel came and took away the mouse carcasses, and I worked on report summaries. Dave then drove me to Dr. Sherman's apartment. I took the reports up to apartment "J". When I returned to Dave's car he was under the hood, cursing. It was just a stuck carbure-

Downtown New Orleans

Lakefront Airport

tor, but Dave grumbled that he deserved a better vehicle for all the work he was doing for everybody.

Just before sunset, we reached the Lakefront Airport. Dave parked his car and helped me out politely. He went to a shed, picked up some things, and took a clipboard over to an office while I waited by the car, slapping mosquitoes.

Dave returned and led me across the tarmac to some hangars. Next to them I saw several small planes. The plane of interest was silver, with a long stripe down its side. It had an oversized cargo-release door, and an extra fuel tank.

Members of New Orleans Cuban Revolutionary Council

Someone was inside the plane curled up on the seat, sleeping. It was Lee. Then two other men arrived. One looked like a Cuban. The other introduced himself as Mr. Lambert.

It was Clay Shaw. I remembered him from the 500

Club, but I kept mum. I was beginning to get the hang of things. What a good little spy was I!

Dave was going to fly these men to Toronto. Lee got up, stretched, and shook hands with the two men. He walked over to me.

Julian Buznedo with David Ferrie and his airplane

Dave pointed to us and said to Lambert, "Those two are in love, you know." I blushed, Lee coughed and Lambert laughed. "There's no need to feel embarrassed," he said. "After all, love's what makes the world go 'round."

"In their case," said Dave, "it's going 'round and 'round!"

We thanked Dave for letting us have some time together, then stood watching the plane as it taxied for the take-off. Suddenly, it screeched to a halt, and Dave jumped from the plane and came running toward us.

"Lee, can you do me a big favor?" he asked. "Will you come along and help me fly this thing? You'll be back by tomorrow afternoon," he promised. "I'm tired," he added. "I'm afraid I'll fall asleep at the controls."

Dave said Lee could sleep in the plane after reaching Toronto, so he'd be alert for the trip back. With a shrug Lee agreed, and Dave handed me some money for a cab. Alone and envious I watched the plane take off, then went to the airport office, called a cab and went home.[5] Such sudden demands on Lee's time and energy occurred all summer. How he managed to stay so cool and collected was beyond me.

A little after midnight, Collie began to bark. I woke to hear the front door open, and Robert shush the dog. The journals, the logbook! I jumped out of bed and hid them in the 'X' spot, under my folded clothes, as quickly as I could. Even so, hearing his voice sent a thrill through me. He *was* a hunk, and he was my hunk. Into the bedroom he walked, wearing his big, heavy army boots, and tight blue jeans. For once I was rested, my hair damp from a bath. I held out my arms, and he came into them.

Once Robert was finished 'getting into port,' he informed me of our other plans. We were going to Ft. Walton Beach to see his family. It was time to tell them our news!

After the quick tumble in bed, I found myself hustled into the car with only enough time to scribble a note to Susie, who was gone for the weekend and had expected me to take care of the dog. Robert had put her outside as usual when he had arrived, but now he said there was no time to call her back and feed her. "It's only two days," he said. "The dog won't die." But I loved Collie. What if something happened to her, out all night in the dark?

Sullen and grumpy, I sat in the blue Ford as Robert drove. "There's a chance the folks will be very angry," he warned me.

There's a chance that I will be very angry, too, I thought to myself.

Robert hadn't given a hint that we were going to spend the weekend in Florida, until he told me it was time to leave! Nor did he ask if I had any plans or obligations. He just hurried me into the car. I barely had a chance to dress. I hoped Lee would come over after he returned from Toronto, see the note in Susie's screen door, and feed Collie. I prayed she wouldn't get run over.

"Don't say I never take you anywhere," Robert said grimly.

The trip was tense and silent: Robert was worried about being disinherited, and I was feeling very guilty about being in love with Lee. Once more, I didn't try to open his eyes.

When we arrived in Fort Walton, Robert parked the Ford on the side of his parents' big real estate office and vanished inside. I waited anxiously in the car. How would they react to our elopement?

Finally, Robert brought out his parents. Robert A. Baker, Jr., ruddy-faced and white-haired, offered me his hand — and a check for $700 (worth ten times that in today's funds). It was our wedding gift! Robert immediately pocketed it. Mrs. RAB, Jr., noted that I wasn't wearing any nylons, but surmised that my skin was "tan enough" that I didn't need them, though ladies here *did* wear nylons, and we would have to go shopping for "more appropriate clothing" before I could meet her friends, who were "all ladies."

Thus it was that I was transported from an implausible life in New Orleans to squeaky-white Ft. Walton Beach, Florida, to become the captive of Robert's micro-managing mother. Tall, silver-haired, and rigid, she considered herself both sophisticated and socially prominent. What was I? A Hungarian peasant girl, who had seduced her unwitting son! Determined to dress me "sensibly," she took us downtown and purchased a black dress — "respectable for work" — two "leisure dresses to go with your swarthy skin," and a hideous flannel nightgown.

Robert was having fun with his brother and old school friends, while I faced gauntlets of prim matrons interested in whether my belly was distended (Did he have to marry her?). The whole weekend was surreal, and Mrs. Baker's treatment of me in private was hostile. When we finally returned to New Orleans early Monday morning, I was exhausted — but Robert wasn't. He had only a few hours left before going back out to the Gulf, and he was determined to make the most of the little time remaining.

Monday, June 24, 1963

At 7 a.m., Robert finally let me get dressed for work. I stood staring into the mirror at the dark circles under my eyes. My hands were shaking. I was wearing the new black dress, my black high heels and had a black purse. It was early summer, but I was dressed for a funeral. Robert helped me into the car and drove me to work. It was the first and only time he came near Reily's the entire summer.

I sat down at Monaghan's desk, in a daze. I could hardly focus my eyes. In a few minutes, a Monday morning work load landed on my desk. I wondered how I would make it through the day.

At about 1 o'clock, Lee came with hot, black coffee.

"I called Susie," he said. "It seems you haven't had any sleep."

"Oh, Lee!" I said. "I'm afraid I'm going to get sick. I'm so tired!"

"I can't stand here long. It will attract attention."

"I love him, but he hurt my feelings so!"

"I can't ride home with you tonight. Can you make it okay, without me?"

"I know you'd be there if you could," I told him, staring at the pile of credit problems. When I looked back, he was already gone.

I normally did not drink coffee, but the caffeine helped me make it to 4:30. Afraid I'd fall asleep before clocking Lee out, I went downstairs to the canteen and walked around and around, to stay awake. At exactly 5:30, I stamped Lee's time card. At 5:45, I got on the bus.

I stood up, holding unsteadily to the pole as the bus lurched along. Because the driver knew I was a regular he called out "Marengo!" when we reached my street.

I opened the front door, and walked in. I went down the hall around the corner and gasped with amazement.

There was the bed, carefully made, the pretty quilts turned down. A box of chocolates rested on the pillow. There were balloons tied to the bedposts, with a sign suspended between them on yarn. "Welcome back!" was written on it, in colored crayon. There were roses on the little table that I used as a desk. Rose petals dotted the floor. Lee was there, by the window.

"Go get undressed," he said, smiling. "I'll wait."

Oh, no. I thought to myself. He wants to make love, today, of all days?

We hadn't yet slept together and I wished I had more strength. As I undressed, Lee talked quietly to Susie in the kitchen. I pointedly put on my new Granny nightgown, crawled under the covers, and, having eaten so little all day, opened the box of chocolates.

"You can come in now!" I called, ready for the terrible moment.

In came Susie, Collie, and Lee. Susie kissed me on the cheek, Collie whined and Lee sat at the foot of my bed. Then Susie left, discreetly taking Collie with her and closing the door. Lee moved from the bed and knelt by the bookshelves: there was a portable record player on the floor. He turned on the record player, picked up the needle, and gently set it down. It was the Everly Brothers:

> *I bless the day I found you,*
> *I want to stay around you,*
> *And so I beg you,*
> *Let it be me."*

"You were gone all weekend," Lee said, quietly. "I missed you!"

"Come here, Lee," I said to him. "I give up. I can't say no to you."

"I don't want you to say, 'I give up,'" Lee replied. But I saw that he was taking off his clothes. "I already knew you wouldn't say no to me."

He got into bed with me, and began stroking my body.

"I love you, Juduffki," he said. "But I'm not here to take you. I'm here to show you that I will never unite with you, unless you want me."

"But I do want you, Lee," I told him. "I want you more, all the time."

"Shhhhh," he said. He took off my nightgown with great care, folding it and placing it at the foot of the bed. Now our bodies rested close together, naked in the bed. I waited, as he began to rock me gently. Then, as he held me in his arms, I fell asleep. It was dark when he woke me.

"I have to go home now," he said. "In case you are wondering, not a thing happened that would have embarrassed you. Only, your whole body knows you are cherished. You won't get sick now." He got out of bed, and bent over and kissed me. Then he dressed in the darkness.

"Good night, Lady Blakeney," he said. "Until tomorrow."

He closed my bedroom door and let himself out through Susie's kitchen. I could hear his footsteps going down the driveway and heard him return the key to its place on the window sill. I reached for the alarm clock, to wind it. It was already wound, and the alarm set. *Oh, my sweetheart*, I said to myself. *You've won... You've won!*

Though I slept all night I was still exhausted, so Lee asked me to get examined by a doctor. But there wasn't time in my schedule to see one, so I dragged myself to work again. Lee contacted Dave, and at about 10:00 A.M., Monaghan told me I had a day of sick leave. He said to see a doctor, and take the rest of the day off. A taxi showed up, compliments of Dr. Mary, and drove me to Charity Hospital.

The doctor immediately did a blood test, and said I was suffering from anemia. I felt so stupid, because I used to do my own blood tests and knew I was a borderline case. I was given a B-12 shot, ordered to eat more red meat, and to take iron. Lee was waiting for me when I emerged from the hospital, and I told him I had anemia.

"Maybe that's what's the matter with Marina," he said, as we got into the taxi. "I'll have to bring more meat home." He added, "Would you feel up to meeting somebody? He's a friend of mine. Dr. Mary says we can keep the taxi for a while, so don't worry."

We stopped near the Customs House. I waited while Lee went in-

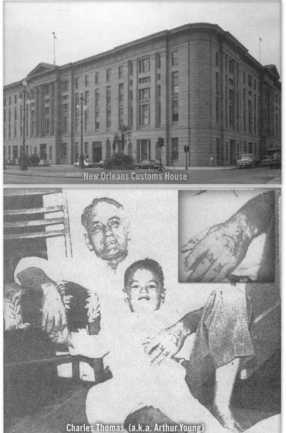

New Orleans Customs House

Charles Thomas, (a.k.a. Arthur Young)

side. He soon returned, accompanied by a gentleman with silvery hair. Lee then helped me out of the taxi, introducing me. "This is J," he said. "She knows all about this, so I wanted her to shake your hand." Turning to me, Lee said, "I would like you to meet Arthur Young, who expedited my passport for me."

As we shook hands, I was startled to see that this distinguished looking gentleman had tattoos on his fingers. Mr. Young, smiling, said that he had "hurried the process along" before anyone looked too closely into Lee's past. He had also hurried along a number of other applications at the same time, so Lee's would not stand out. Had Young not done so, Lee would have had difficulty getting a new passport and might have had to rely on a fake one. It was always better to have the real thing, Mr. Young opined. Lee's old one, filled with stamps from the USSR, could have given him problems if he used it again.

It turned out that the taxi was not just for me: Mr. Young had to return at once to Miami, and he needed the taxi to get to the airport.

As he helped me into the taxi, I noticed again the unusual finger tattoos. Though he spoke perfect Spanish to the Latino taxi driver, to us
he spoke English with a German accent. When I asked Young if he was
an American citizen, he said he was that and more, because he was
married to a Native American, a Chitimacha Indian.

Lee and Mr. Young were obviously friends, and as we headed toward Reily's the two men
talked quietly about old
times. Young commented
that he first met Lee a decade earlier when he was
working with Customs at the
border between Canada and
the U.S. at Niagara Falls. Lee
had been playing hooky from
school and had hitch-hiked
all the way from the Bronx,
itching to cross the border
so he could say he'd been off
American soil.

Young at New York - Canada border Customs

Lee was about thirteen at the time and Young, impressed with Lee's
zest for adventure, told the boy he could cross over for the day. He
wouldn't tell. Young did ask for Lee's name, address and a phone number where his mother could be reached in case he didn't return, but
Lee was afraid he'd call the authorities. Young promised he would not
do that, reminding Lee that he *was* "the authorities," in charge of the
border station. Lee gave him the information, crossed the border, and
returned by dusk. Some time later, Young contacted Lee in New York
and they ate lunch together.

At that time, Lee confided his dream to become a spy and Young,
impressed, gave Lee the names of persons who might be interested
in developing his interests in New York. But not long after, Lee was
arrested for truancy and sent to Youth House, where he was brutal-
ized. Young intervened to get Lee out, but soon after moved to Florida.
Now they had met again, with great pleasure. Young and his wife had
been living in Miami, and he had continued working with Customs on
a clandestine basis. He was now affiliated with the CIA's anti-Castro
movement.

I was able to speak with Young for nearly half an hour before I was
let off at my apartment. By then, I realized that Arthur Young was not
his real name.

Lee later confided that his friend's real name was "Thomas," though
I did not know if that was his first name, or his last![6]

"He's a good guy, like me," Lee later assured me.[7]

Lee's passport application was made on June 24th. This was the height of the Cold War and, though Lee boldly indicated that he planned to visit Cuba and the Soviet Union, he received it on June 25th, only 24 hours later.[7]

That evening, Lee stopped by to see how I was doing. Susie had gone out to buy me a steak. "She's been so good to me," I told Lee. I was lying on the bed, across the pillows, and he bent over and kissed me.

"Well, here it is," he said, showing me his passport.

"Are you impressed?" he asked. Indeed I was. He told me I needed a passport as well, but I protested that something had gone crazy with my birth certificate. The one I had recently ordered said 'female infant' Vary, instead of my full name. Lee said a fake ID would be supplied for me, perhaps using a different name. "Welcome to my world," said Lee. "You should see all the names on file that belong to me. And all the places I'm supposed to have been at the same time."

"I can understand, to some extent," I replied. "I was two people, myself, at UF. It made it easier to do unauthorized research. So who are you, really?"

"I'm the real me," Lee said. "And I'm in love with the real you."

Dr. Ochsner had once again tried to speed up our research by increasing the number of mice to be processed to two hundred per week.

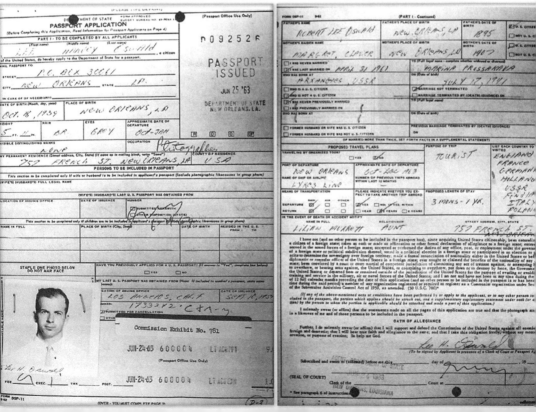

Ferrie had hoped I would feel well enough to handle the mice, but Lee objected, saying I was sick and needed to rest. He volunteered to do the dirty work in my place. "You stay put at Reily's!" he commanded. "I'll do the mice, and Dave will pick you up for the technical part later."[8]

On June 26, 1963, Lee anesthetized and killed 200 mice suffering from huge cancerous lumps. The mice were sliced open from stem to stern, and the tumors cut out.

At the end of the day I arrived at Dave's later than usual, as directed. Lee looked green. I inspected the tumors, and when we were finished, Dave said he would start the new cultures the next day at the Prytania lab instead of his place, because his boyfriend was coming over for a day or two.

Thursday, June 27, 1963

I was feeling better and ate a minute-steak for breakfast. Monaghan was pleased that I put in a full day's work. I even managed to type a few letters at a decent speed. Just as I was about to clock him out, Lee phoned.

"No more 6:30 clock-outs," he said, and asked me to meet him at the 500 Club.

"I have a special reason for taking you there today," he added.

At the club, Lee told me the arms shipment from Venezuela was supposed to arrive the next day. We'd then know if the efforts to trap pro-Castroites and keep the FBI's informants off-track had paid off.

But I could see that more than tomorrow's challenges weighed on Lee's shoulders.

"Lee, what's the matter?" I asked.

Lee avoided my question, saying I could order anything I wanted, but his appetite was still off, because of the mice.

"Please eat, my sweetheart," I urged him. Then, he hit me between the eyes.

"Don't call me sweetheart!" he said, not looking at me. "We have to talk. Now."

In his eyes, I saw a look of despair. I took his hand, but felt him stiffen.

"After calling you," he said slowly, "I began to think about things."

"What do you mean?"

"Where you and I are going!" he blurted out. "What this means. I love little Junie," he said slowly. "I know I will also love the baby to come, and how much they both will need me." Lee sighed deeply. Life was precious, he said. Killing so many innocent animals had made him think about how helpless his own children were. I couldn't speak. I knew the guilt he spoke of.

"I have to make a final decision, but I don't want to hurt you."

"If you can say those words to me, Lee, then you've already made your decision." I pulled my hands away.

"I could lose Junie forever, if I'm not careful," he said. "I've thought about this. I don't think I can handle that." Tears stood in his eyes, and he got up abruptly. "I'll be right back," he said. "I have to go to the toilet."

I watched him walk away, thinking that he felt forced to make a choice between his family and me. I realized that Lee's affections must run deep.

He'd always said he'd be transparent. I thought of the little plastic heart Lee had given me. How he must dread losing contact with Junie, and their unborn child. Lee and Marina were getting along better now: perhaps their marriage would succeed. Perhaps I was now the element that was causing Lee distress.

I began to cry, then grabbed a napkin, found a pen, and wrote:

> *I have no right to interfere with the hope you have for a happy life with your family. Forgive me for bringing you this grief. Do what is right.*
> *Love, J.*

I took my little plastic horse out of my purse that I had carried with me since I was five years old in the hospital. I wrapped the napkin around it, and laid it on the table in front of Lee's dish.

I hurried from the club and went home, where I fell into bed, tossing and turning under the covers, sleepless and heartsick.

I never learned what happened on the evening of June 27. Lee never spoke of it to me, but according to one of Marina's biographers:

> *Lee was sitting in the dark... staring down at the floor. Marina put her arms around him, stroked his head, and could feel him shaking with sobs.*
> *"Why are you crying?" she asked. Then, "Cry away. It'll be better that way." Marina held him for about a quarter of an hour and he told her between sobs that he was lost.*
> *He didn't know what he ought to do. Then he said suddenly, "Would you like me to come to Russia, too?"*[9]

Friday, June 28, 1963

I almost didn't go to work, such was my mood. But I knew I would have to cover for Lee because the Venezuelan shipment was coming in. That was more important than my feelings, or his.

Lee was not on the bus that morning, and Personnel started searching for him after lunch.

Monaghan and I had to concoct an excuse for him: Lee had been sent over to the new coffee plant, to work as an oiler for a crane operator. Mr. Prechter was forced to promise, however, that he'd find a replacement for Lee. Prechter met with Monaghan in his glassed-in cubicle, which blocked out typewriter noise for his private conversations and phone calls. Before long Monaghan came out of his cubicle, with Prechter in tow. He glanced at a fist-full of applications, and then handed them to me.

"I don't care what he's doing for God and Country," Prechter told Monaghan. "I can't make up any more excuses for him." He said that every time he turned around, Lee was missing. He was either sitting over at the garage reading, or had just arrived "from some damned errand you people have sent him on." If he got one more complaint from the production people in the back, it was "Goodbye" for Lee. Nobody at Reily's believed Lee was just hiding in a corner somewhere. He had been gone too often and for too long.

At 4:30, I clocked myself out and returned to my desk to catch up with the last of the credit problems. At 5:30 I clocked Lee out. As I handled his time card, I noticed that he had clocked in after 9:00 a.m., for the first time in three weeks. Had last night been as rough for Lee as it had been for me? He obviously had a slow start this morning.

I knew the arms shipment from Venezuela was scheduled for today. Romance or not, I was worried and wanted to know what happened. Did my disguise work? Was Lee safe? I stood at the bus stop and worried. Suddenly, Dave Ferrie drove up and honked to get my attention. I got in his car and saw a thin, good-looking young man seated there. Dave introduced me: his name was Layton Martens.[10] Then Dave drove us to the Trade Mart's warehouses on the river.

Layton Martens

"Hot damn!" Dave said, weaving in and out of traffic with immense skill. "We did so damned good today!" He was so excited he repeated his last sentence in all the languages he knew.

I asked where Lee was, and Dave laughed. "You'll find out," he said.

"It's okay, I understand," I said disappointedly.

"Just wanted you to see what we did," Dave said. "It was pure genius." (Referring to my idea to hide the rifles in furniture crates.)

Then Dave and Layton started discussing how they could mark some of the weapons to make them seem to have come in from Cuba.

Dave, realizing I had no perspective on what they were talking about, clarified things: the donors were rich, anonymous oilmen who could purchase weapons anywhere, anytime, to further their causes, and if that meant planting weapons with falsified markings on them to make Castro or any other "Commie bastards" look bad, all the better. They were also financing training camps to get Castro, as well as to remove any leaders in Latin America viewed as threats. "They want their Cuba back," Dave said. He turned his head and gave me a smile, continuing to steer like a race car driver through the traffic.

"It seems to me that too many people are in the know on this," I said, uncomfortably. "I don't think that will work."

"So, who's going to talk, J?" Dave said. "Me, or Lee? Will Marcello? We all have too much to lose. That includes you. You're getting a ride today because Lee is up to his eyeballs in bananas at this very moment. And it's your fault," he said, once again reaching for humor.

"How could bananas be my fault?" I asked Dave. He laughed again.

"We took your advice and were very creative. We took the furniture idea all the way. It made a really good disguise for the shipment," he said. "So yeah, it's your fault."

Dave pulled over to the curb and let "Layton Martens" out of the car. It was the only time I ever saw the man. Dave continued to the docks where mixed cargo for the Venezuelan ship had been unloaded, and parked as close as he could get. We got out of the car and walked to the warehouse. As we walked, Dave told me to hold tight to my

purse. Laborers, sailors, longshoremen and stevedores had finished their work for the day and were now leaving. Dave said the docks were the battlefield of every port city. The unions ruled and headed the fight to stop the Communists from taking over.

I was surprised. "There are Communists out here?"

"There's everything out here," Dave said. "Organized crime, labor unions, stockholders, Communists, Castroites, anti-Castroites...." He waved his hand over the whole panorama of cranes, tractors, dollies, forklifts, trucks and elevators. The surrealistic landscape went on for miles. Cargo was stacked high in boxes, barrels and bales. Here, much of America was fed, clothed and traded. New Orleans was one of America's major ports, Dave told me. And its docks were controlled by the mob. Lee's uncle Dutz got his start there. The unions kept things going 'the right way.'

We now entered one of the Trade Mart warehouses. Dave said it was Mr. Shaw who had been so instrumental in helping rain to fall on Castro's parade. Inside one room, fifty boxes were stacked and marked in Spanish. Their labels said they contained hardwood chairs suitable for dining. Other boxes contained the tables.

Dave encouraged me to inspect one of the boxes that contained chairs. I saw two chairs packed together, side-by-side. A thick felt pad

protected the legs from rubbing against the crate. I saw nothing out of the ordinary.

"What am I looking at?" I asked.

"Where the rifles were," Dave said, smiling.

Dave explained that the rifles had been shipped in the boxes with the chairs. Originally packed four chairs to a box, two chairs had been removed to make room for the rifles. The two remaining chairs were nested together. When the rifles were removed, one of the two chairs was inverted, so that they sat next to each other, using up twice the space. Then the cartons were resealed. My smuggling idea had worked.

And what was Lee's job? And why did Dave talk about bananas? Most of the rifles removed from the cartons were placed in the bottom of big crates with bunches of bananas placed on top. The crates were then loaded into a truck, along with regular fruit crates, and hauled away "to Cuban markets." But what to do with the fruit left behind? There were heaps of it, but Lee had worked out a plan. He and a few others were selling the fruit dirt cheap to the big ships along the docks. They gave away what they couldn't sell quickly.[11]

That night, Lee called at about ten from a pay phone near his house.

"Just to let you know," he said, "we're not going to run out of bananas for lunch anytime soon."[12] His voice was soft and gentle. He said he had called to see if I was OK.

"I'm as well as can be expected," I told him. "I have only one thing to say. Yes, your little girl and unborn baby have to come first. They are hostages of fortune. But please!" I said, sobbing, "Don't come over any more! I can't bear the pain!"

Lee protested. I caught my breath and said, "No, Lee! This has to end. Now! I only want you to remember one thing. If you ever feel like hitting Marina again, remind yourself that I fell in love with a great man. To me, you'll always be my shining hero."

When I was finished, there was only silence. He had hung up. Distracted by my roaring emotions, I could not work on my lab reports, nor could I sleep.

Saturday, June 29, 1963

In the morning, I received a letter from Robert. With all my heart I tried to look at things from his viewpoint, but it was difficult.

> *"June, a Thursday Ma Chere Judy, Lovey-dovey, don't write me anymore! Monday at latest I should be off...."*

I calculated: Robert would probably be home by July 3rd, then. That made sense, because the 4th was a national holiday. At the end, aware he had failed me once again, he signed "Rat."

It was a time of huge racial turmoil, but Robert rarely mentioned national events. His letters reflected little outside his immediate mini-universe, which he tried the best he could to share with me. I contrasted in my mind how Lee and I agonized about how to do more to support the civil rights of Negroes everywhere. There he was again — Lee on my mind! My thoughts then focused on President Kennedy,

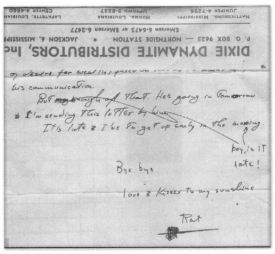

who had courageously submitted a Civil Rights bill which Lee and I fervently hoped would become law. But now, three young civil rights workers had just gone missing. We feared they had been murdered (they were.)

Almost a thousand actions were mounted in over a hundred southern cities, resulting in over twenty thousand arrests.

Robert rarely mentioned national events. His letters reflected little outside his immediate radius. Locked into his own mini-universe, I know he did the best he could to share it with me. Aware he had failed me many times, he signed this letter "Rat." I was all the more blue: I'd married a man who could write, "...the lowest form of life in the state of Louisiana is, of course, the Nigger." He meant it as a joke, but there was no humor in what was happening at Birmingham, in Jackson, Mississippi, or in the bombed Baptist church.

I had given my affection and love. Lee was seemingly withdrawing from my life, but the man who married me had never quite entered it. I lay on my bed, and pounded my pillow. Desiring something — anything — to reduce the misery, I turned on the radio. Little Peggy March's song was playing. It just made everything worse:

I love him! I love him! I love him!
And where he goes
I'll follow, I'll follow, I'll follow!

But Robert hadn't wanted me to follow him. As for Lee... I stared over at the begonias placed near the bed, just because they reminded me of him. I looked upon the roses, still fresh in their containers. I would have to throw them out before Robert returned. Tears sprang to my eyes. I knew Robert would not buy me roses. Lee had told me how Marina had cheated on him, just a day before he had filled her room with blue cornflowers. He had such a romantic heart, but she knew how to crush it by bringing up her other lovers. I fell into a dreamless sleep, to waken a few hours later when I heard that familiar tapping at my window. I sure knew who that was. "Go away!" I called, my head buried in a pillow. The tapping continued. I threw the pillow at the window.

Collie was whining. I could hear Lee's voice. "Now, Collie, I saw you chasing Mr. Cat up the tree. You know you shouldn't. Now I shall have to get him down."

Lee had an endearing habit of calling animals he did not know "Mr. Cat" or "Mr. Dog" or "Mr. Squirrel." It was our little joke. It had started when I began calling Monaghan "Mr. M." Curious, I betook myself to the window, to see what was going on. My pillow under my chin, I looked through the crocheted curtains. Lee took Collie around the back and put her in the house on Susie's side. Now he was carrying the stepladder. I watched him go across the street and lean it against a tree. After a few minutes, he brought down a squalling tomcat, and let it go. He was coming back with the ladder so I retreated to my bed, putting the pillow over my head. I just wanted him to go away! There it was again, the tapping....

"Please, Juduffki..." I heard him say.

"Go back to your family!" I shouted. "Don't do this to me! You're killing me!" I began to cry again. There had been so many tears lately. He was carrying the ladder again: I could hear him walking along the gravel and concrete. Then I remembered. Oh, no, he has a key! I got under the bed, taking the pillow with me.

In he came: I could see his scuffed shoes as he stood there, from my position underneath the bed on that cool wooden floor. There were dust bunnies all around me. Yuck! I held my breath, keeping as quiet as I could. Then he said, "If you wish to persist, and stay under the bed, may I hand you a quilt?"

"Please, Lee..." I whispered. "I can't take the pain of seeing you. I know you belong to her. Go home." He got down on his knees and peered at me. "Well," he said, "I planned to go down on my knees to you today, anyway. I just didn't think you'd be way down here when I did it."

I told him not to tease me like that. He said it would be quite a while before he could straighten everything out, but in the end, he believed he could. Then he whispered, looking into my eyes as I lay curled up under the bed: "Please, Juduffki. Let it be me in your life." I could not reply. Tears were again rolling down my cheeks. When I wiped them away, a dust bunny clung to my nose. I knew I looked ridiculous.

"Judyth, my love," he said, "Will you marry me?"

I lost my breath.

"It's you I love and want," he said. "I tried with all my might to send you out of my heart. I even told Marina I would go back to Russia with her. But I can't do it. I'll find a way to see my babies, if I can't get custody of them."

He reached down. "I want you to take my hand," he said. I didn't move.

"I'll wait, then," he said, "if you want to stay under the bed. I know I hurt you." When I still didn't speak, he added, sadly, "I just want you to say something besides 'go away'! Anything."

From the depths of my soul, all the love I felt began to pour from my heart. Lee was back! Lee was asking me to marry him! So I told him the truth.

"Lee," I said with adoration, "you are still my shining hero."

I saw his face change, the anxiety fall away, the pain in his eyes change to happiness. I let him help me out from under the bed. We smiled shyly at each other as I dusted myself off.

"I only want to hear you say 'yes,'" he persisted. "Say you'll marry me, as soon as we can get Robert and Marina out of the picture. Then I'll go home, if you wish."

I looked into his eyes. "Ask me again," I said.

"I'm perfectly aware that Baker never asked you to marry him," Lee replied. "So I will ask you a hundred times, if only you will say yes just once. Will you?"

"Ask me again."

He knelt down. "Please give me the inimitable pleasure," he said, "of your hand in marriage." He took off his wedding band and laid it on the floor. "The day will come," he said, "when I will come to you, without this wedding ring."

I told him I would consent, but that it was all so sudden. I felt overwhelmed.

"I'm not finished trying to overwhelm you," he said. "I've dreamed to show you my love, as I dreamed from the start," he said. "But only if you are ready."

"Come ...!" I said, sitting down on the bed and starting to unbutton my blouse.

"No — I want a fresh bed for us!" he insisted. "Besides, you still haven't said yes. So — will you marry me?"

"Ninety-eight to go!" I said, smiling.

"Put on your nice brown dress," he said. As I dressed, and then hunted for my purse, he went out to talk to Susie. I was surprised to see him return with her car keys. "I'm going to go kiss that woman!" I told Lee.

"How easily you are kissing everybody but me!" he said, for I had not even touched him yet. I got dressed and put my hair up, but he shook his head. He took the pins out of my hair.

"I want it long and free," he said. I placed the emerald studs my sister had given me on my sixteenth birthday in my ears. Lee guided me to Susie's car. We went to the Roosevelt Hotel. There, Lee brought in the best the hotel had to offer — a glorious feast, with music and flowers. He put on the Everly Brothers' song "Let It Be Me."

He kept asking me to marry him, over and over. He asked me in the car. He asked me standing on a chair, standing on one foot, and standing on his head. He asked me ninety-nine times, and I counted every one. Then he picked me up in his arms, like he was carrying me across a threshold, and placed me on the beautiful bed. As his body hovered lovingly over mine, and our lips met, we melted into each other's embrace. How tenderly, how slowly, we loved! "Will you marry me, my beloved?" he asked, for the hundredth time. As I exploded with a joy I didn't know could exist, I told the man I would love forever, *Yes!*

1   So what was Lee reading, these months in New Orleans? The Warren Commission looked into it. How they reported it was another matter. For example, Ferrell's chronology for this date noted that: Oswald returns "Conflict" to the library and checks out "Soviet Potential", "What We Must Know About Communism" and "This is My Philosophy". (WC Vol 22, p. 82)

"Conflict" sounds a bit sinister. In fact, the Warren Commission didn't show the whole title of this, or several other books, which helped disguise the true nature of his reading, and in some cases, downplayed the intellectual quality of his reading choices. This is important, for in every way, Lee's true identity and character have been subtly masked. I here attempt to set some of Lee's reading records straight, for these little tricks in the record even tended to downplay Lee's patriotism, instead suggesting that violence, mental instability, and hatred of America colored his reading choices. Details of his reading, such as full titles, which might have dispelled such notions, were lacking. For example, the book title described only as Conflict turns out to be: *Conflict: The History of the Korean War, 1950-53*.

This is My Philosophy turns out to be: *This Is My Philosophy — Twenty of the World's Outstanding Thinkers Reveal the Deepest Meanings They Have Found in Life* (with essays by Oppenheimer, Schweitzer, Huxley, Sartre, Jung, etc). It is not light reading.

Soviet Potential looks like a book touting communism, but is actually a scholarly work on the geography and natural resources of Russia, and how politics affected land use. The last of the books listed is indeed 'all about' communism — a book I feared to be seen on my desk, because of its title. But decide for yourself if the book was pro-communist. Here are two typical quote from it:

"…the Communists … will not be able, however, to lead from strength once the outside world becomes clear about the fact that freedom's best ally is the normal human being's wish to lead a normal life.… certain matters … are at stake in the cold war…the principle of liberty under law, respect for the integrity and uniqueness of the individual…the right to apply moral judgments, not merely political judgments …." The FBI's J. Edgar Hoover praised the book.

In 1959, Hoover wrote this to the Overstreet husband-and-wife team who authored the book: "I do hope that your fine book *What We Must Know About Communism* will enjoy excellent sales and wide reading … We need more and more people like yourselves who will devote their nationally recognized academic talents to the exposure and ultimate defeat of the menace of world communism."

What We Must Know About Communism is also another bit of evidence for my presence in Lee's life in New Orleans, for Lee, himself, had been reading dozens of books written by Marx, Lenin, and their compatriots, for a decade. He had lived in the USSR nearly three years, leaving there less than a year ago. He'd worked in a Soviet-run factory. He'd made Russian friends and enjoyed affairs with Russian girls. He married a Russian woman. In other words, Lee had no use for such a book — and Marina wouldn't be interested in reading it, even if she could read that much English. But what about me?

2.   Lee's was on his right hand, in eastern European style, while mine hung loosely on the ring finger, left hand.

3.   Mary Ferrell reported to me and witness Debbee Reynolds in 2000 that researcher David Lifton told her that "surprisingly, for some unknown reason, Lee Oswald never laid a hand on Marina again after she moved from Texas to join him in New Orleans," though he had done so on a number of occasions prior to May, 1963.

4.   Tulane's National Primate Research Center was founded in 1962, perhaps the best source for research monkeys in the world. After our project destroyed dozens of monkeys supplied by Tulane that summer, replacements arrived August 25th.

5.   This was one of several times I know Lee made an overnight trip by plane. Technically, he had been home this particular evening, but then he walked out, and didn't show up until late the following afternoon. Those who say Marina's word should be trusted — that Lee was 'always'

home "right after work" — must remember that Lee's clock-outs varied between 4:30 and 7:30. And Lee clocked out many times at 6:30! If they fought, he had no set hour for returning at night. Marina was used to his occasional absences: she always had some grocery money so she'd never run short of necessities (and more).

6. I hunted for witnesses in Louisiana in 1999-2001, afraid they might all be dead, but eventually found Charles Thomas' family. It was my description of his German accent, his tattooed fingers, and the fact that he had been an important Customs agent at Niagara Falls that allowed me to locate them, through correspondence and face-to-face interviews with his amazed granddaughter, Kelly. Her family lived on the Chitimacha reservation. Thomas' family affirmed that Charles, now dead, had used the pseudonym of Arthur Young and had lived in the Miami area in 1963. The handwriting on the photo is by Young's grand-daughter, not only a well-educated college English instructor, but also a valued friend.

    There are more photos. I was given copies of photos of Charles from the Niagara Falls Customs station, from New York, Miami, and Louisiana. Family members were aware that Charles had connections with anti-Castro Cubans, some of them associated with the Mafia, and at first were afraid to affirm that, but I stressed that in 1963, the Mafia and CIA were working together to try to kill Fidel Castro. I was then supplied photos showing Young's association with Miami-based Cubans and their associates. Thomas had also received retirement payments from a mysterious government agency fund, a source of great pride to him.

6. This comment was in response to something David Lewis said later: that Young had dined with Marcello's lawyers.

7. As the stamped section indicates, even though New Orleans was a Port of Call, with many immigration problems requiring careful reviews of passport applications. Recall that Lee was "a returned defector," married to a Russian — and Lee's application hints that Marina and he would split. For example, Lee did not give Marina's name as the one to contact "in event of death or accident." Instead, he named his Aunt Lillian Murret. For his 'permanent' address, Lee didn't mention Magazine St. Instead, he gave his aunt's 757 French St. address, for the arrangement between Marina and Lee, including their present address, was not to last.

8. Lee went through with the slaughter. What effect did it have on him? I quote from McMillan's book. She implies that Lee's symptoms (see below) were because of mental instability without offering any concrete reason for his behavior. In fact, Lee and I were dealing with a project that gave us nightmares. In the first sentence after mentioning that Lee obtained his passport, coinciding with our first big mouse killing, McMillan next describes Lee having nightmares:

    "...Lee was having trouble in his sleep again — the first time since February. One night he cried, yet when he woke up he could not remember what his dream had been about. He started having nosebleeds... and one night toward the very end of June he had four anxiety attacks during which he shook from head to foot at intervals of half an hour and never woke up." (p. 417)

    Because I loved Lee, reading this sentence (even in 1999) caused me to say out loud, "She didn't wake him up?" What caring wife, witnessing her husband suffering in his sleep, from not one, but four anxiety attacks, would not have wakened him, would not have tried to comfort him? I then understood what a hard heart Marina had toward Lee, if McMillan told the truth. Then — a harsh assessment from McMillan — "Just as in the period when he was making up his mind to shoot General Walker," the CIA affiliate wrote, "these attacks appear to have presaged a decision that was causing him pain." McMillan tries to convince the reader that Lee is about to make yet another horrific decision — perhaps involving 'another' murderous attempt on somebody — such as President Kennedy — and says this is giving him nightmares.

    McMillan inadvertently gives some proof as to what Lee did with us there, for she mentions nose bleeds. Most adults do not suffer from nose bleeds, but some of us who worked in laboratories in the 1960s did, for volatile chemicals such as isopropyl alcohol and acetone were used liberally to cleanse dangerous areas, the fumes of which dried out mucous membranes, making us prone to nosebleeds. My family remembers my nosebleeds when in high school, while working with my mice. Such nosebleeds no doubt contributed to my anemic state.

9. Quote from *Marina and Lee* by Priscilla McMillan-Johnson.

10. I believed Layton would remember me, despite the briefness of our acquaintance, and therefore tried to find him after speaking out. I finally located him, through a musician who knew both him and musician/Marcello bouncer and possible hitman, witness Mac McCullough. Layton was still living, and in fine health, in Louisiana, with a band of his own. I called him, and we arranged to meet on Saturday, March 25. But Martens suddenly died of a heart attack (age 57) exactly one week before our meeting, on March 18, 2000.

11. Would there be a trace of this operation, even after all this time, because of the odd nature of Lee 'selling fruit'? In fact, a trace remains: a respected independent investigator has plodded the streets of New Orleans for years, kindly providing information to me, and several others. "Cal" sent us the results of what he was able to learn about Lee, the docks, and selling fruit. He warned us that informants who requested anonymity could not be trusted. However, in this case, the informant's name was freely given.

12. By purchasing fruit and selling it to ships along the docks, Lee set up a temporary reputation as a 'fruit seller.' So, when it was time to be rid of the bananas and oranges removed from the crates to hide the rifles, Lee and others were ready, and nobody noticed. This is probably how I ended up with bananas at lunch time! As for visiting "the old Men's Mission on Esplanade" recall that Lee had asked "old men" about the slain doctor Weiss in the Huey Long murder case.

Concerning the car, in the same report, a time would come when Lee would try to obtain a late model car for our use for a drive to Jackson, Louisiana at the end of August. I found it remarkable that a trace of Lee's attempt to find a better car, rather than the old one we were forced to use, has perhaps survived the years.

THE GARAGE

Next door to Reily's was the Crescent City Garage.[1] Though privately owned, it was where the FBI, CIA, Secret Service and other government agencies parked their vehicles, since it was directly across the street from the federal court house and convenient to the various government offices clustered around Lafayette Park.[2] Its location was very important to Lee Oswald for several reasons.

First, Lee frequently needed to slip out of Reily's for his various covert activities, unnoticed by the staff. But the windows of the Reily offices looked out onto Camp Street, Capedeville Street and Magazine Street, so their staff could easily observe pedestrians on these sidewalks. It was simply not possible for Lee to slip out of customer or employee entrances unnoticed.

But Reily's coffee and tea products were loaded onto trucks for delivery from a dock at the rear of the warehouse. Here large doors opened onto the alley behind Reily's and the Crescent City Garage. Trucks came and went all day, backing up to the loading docks and blocking the view of the alley. When Lee needed to leave quietly, he would slip out through the door by the loading docks, cross the alley behind the trucks, and enter the Crescent City Garage.

Normally, Lee would simply walk through the rear entrance to their service area, sometimes stopping to greet the garage's manager, then exiting through the garage's front entrance on Magazine Street unseen by anyone at Reily's. The nearest street to the right was Lafayette Street where Guy Banister's office entrance was located. To facilitate this secret route Lee cultivated a friendship with Adrian Alba, one of the owners of the garage, so his presence would not seem unusual to the employees. To this end, Lee spent some extra time at the garage, reading magazines, sometimes eating lunch there, and talking with Adrian about the man's favorite subjects — hunting and guns.[3]

Another benefit of this garage was that Lee was able to communicate easily with members of the local intelligence community, since

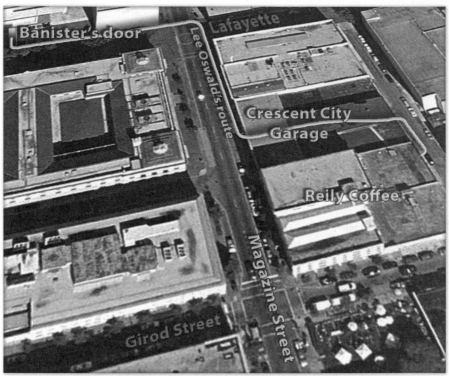

they parked their cars there. Lee could deliver and receive intelligence information without being noticed. On "First Fridays" Lee's visits with Adrian would be longer, since he had to wait for his CIA paymaster to show up and get his car. Then Lee would go outside on the sidewalk where his paymaster would pull his car to the curb and hand him an envelope. Adrian Alba reported seeing Lee do this and Lee showed me one of these envelopes, which was full of crisp new $20 bills.[4]

During the month of June 1963, Lee ran his faux office of the Fair Play for Cuba Committee (FPCC) out of Guy Banister's building. He had received an authentic FPCC membership card and bought a rubber stamp kit, pamphlets, flyers and membership cards for his fake organization.[5] So Lee was both gone from Reily's and in and out of the Crescent City Garage frequently.[6] It was during this same month that Lee told me Robert Kennedy instructed Guy Banister to hold a meeting in his office with an important anti-Castro group. Banister then positioned Lee so he could view (and perhaps photograph) each member as they entered Banister's office, presumably so he would be able to recognize them in the future.

By late June, Lee was at a watershed in his personal life. We were falling deeply in love but Lee struggled with his inner turmoil each night, oscillating between the poles of love and loyalty. Trying to preserve their family, he initially chose loyalty and told Marina that he would return to Russia with her. She was delighted, and Lee wrote to the Soviet Embassy (in Russian) requesting entrance visas.[7] Then Lee changed his mind completely. He was ready to leave Marina for good and start a new life with me. We would divorce our current mates and go live somewhere remote, like Mexico. Lee wrote the Soviet Embassy again (this time in English) asking that Marina's visa be rushed through, with his own to be considered separately, enabling him to send Marina back by herself.[8] He also told Marina of his desire to go to Cuba, to help prepare her for his upcoming trip to Mexico City.

Lee and I started planning our life together and discussed our options after this New Orleans chapter finally came to a close. We talked about where we would live and how we would earn a living. Lee told me more about his friend, George.[9] George was in charge of Lee's stowed-away money and could help us, making sure that a large sum would be given to Marina and the children after we disappeared. Some of it was Company pay, accrued while Lee was a spy in the USSR. George de Mohrenschildt was one of Lee's immediate handlers, a sophisticated Soviet-born petroleum geologist who was from bona fide Russian aristocracy which had been displaced by the Communist Revolution. He still held the title of Baron. George was now in Haiti representing the interests of Dallas oil magnate Clint Murchison, which caused Lee some concern, but George was a romantic character whose recent trek with his wife through Mexico and Central America fueled Lee's desire to follow in his footsteps.[10]

George de Mohrenschildt

George de Mohrenschildt, one of the most mercurial figures of JFK assassination lore, befriended Lee Harvey Oswald in Texas about a year before the assassination, at a time when he worked for Texas oilman Clint Murchison. A Russian emigrant who was born into an aristocratic family in Tsarist Russia and entitled to be called "Baron," he ran in high social circles and was friends with George H.W. Bush (later 41st President of the U.S.) whom he called "Poppy" and with Jacqueline Bouvier (later known as Jackie Kennedy, wife of President Kennedy) who called him Uncle George.

While still a young boy, his wealthy family fell victim to Russia's Communist Revolution. In the 1920s, when his father was arrested by the Bolsheviks, they fled Russia and escaped to Poland, grounding his strong anti-Communist sentiments in his personal history and loss of fortunes.

George was well-educated in Europe in the 1930s, and received the equivalent of a doctorate in international business. In the late 1930s, he emigrated to the United States where he was placed under FBI surveillance as a possible German spy - a rumor which followed him around for many years and which he repeatedly tried to dispel.

During WWII, George's brother worked for the U.S. Office of Strategic Services (OSS) and later for the CIA's Radio Free Europe during the Cold War. George, however, received a master's degree in petroleum geology from the University of Continued...

George de Mohrenschildt, *continued from prev. page*   Texas in 1945 and settled in Dallas, Texas where he did oil exploration work for Clint Murchison and other oil companies. He became a U.S. citizen in 1949 and married four times.

De Mohrenschildt met Lee Harvey Oswald and his Russian wife Marina in the summer of 1962 in Fort Worth, Texas. Concerned about rumors of Oswald's defection, he consulted with the CIA's Dallas office which said that it would be "safe" for him to assist the Oswalds. He and Oswald became friends and, by most accounts, he treated Oswald with respect and described his Russian as excellent. After the assassination, de Mohrenschildt testified to the Warren Commission and minimized their relationship. His different accounts of Oswald at different times raises questions.

Before the assassination, in June 1963, de Mohrenschildt moved to Haiti to plot out the location of geological resources on the island and to negotiate access to these resources with Haitian dictator Papa Doc Duvalier for Clint Murchison. He lived there during the JFK assassination and returned to live in the Dallas area in 1967 when Jim Garrison was investigating the JFK assassination. Garrison reports frequent phone calls with de Mohrenschildt about Lee Oswald.

A decade later, in 1976, Congress decided to investigate the JFK assassination. At the time de Mohrenschildt felt the U.S. government was harassing him because of his involvement with the Oswald case, so he wrote a letter to his Texas oil buddy George "Poppy" Bush, who was then Director of the Central Intelligence Agency, asking for relief. Bush wrote back, "I hope this letter has been of some comfort to you, George, although I realize I am unable to answer your question completely."

In March 1977, George de Mohrenschildt died while waiting to testify before the House Select Committee on Assassinations. His death was ruled a suicide. Needless to say, due to the timing of his death, suspicions continue to circulate.

Wednesday, July 3, 1963

Our cover jobs at Reily's continued to obscure our activities at Dave's primitive lab, where we strove to meet our new directive to process 200 mouse pups at a time. Dave and Lee had conspired to save me, again, from the nastiest part of the work, so today Lee left Reily's well ahead of me. But when I arrived, they were struggling with a time problem. Our mice were suffocated in a standard Bell jar, with ether-soaked cotton wads, but it could handle only ten pups at a time. Then Dave found a big glass cake cover, and the problem was solved. Sealed at the bottom with petroleum jelly, it became a large, efficient gas chamber.

At least it put the little critters out of their misery quickly and quietly. But the act of slaughtering, then slicing open these helpless mice, literally made him ill. Lee even vomited after he finished pulling out the guts and tumors, and then continued burping from an upset stomach.

The Fourth of July was the next day, and Robert had said that he would be coming home for the holiday. As usual, he did not say when he would arrive, so we worked as fast as we could. I was afraid Robert would get to Marengo Street before me and be full of questions about where I had been.

Lee suggested I should stop on the way home for groceries, as the stores would be closed on the Fourth, and use the grocery shopping as an excuse for my late arrival. We continued our work at Dave's without any breaks, knowing that Monaghan would clock us both out so we would not have to return to Reily's. When we were finally finished, I headed home, arriving with my armload of groceries at about 7:30. I was relieved to see that there was no blue Ford in the driveway. I still had time to hide my materials and bathe. I took a full bath in the tub in the kitchen and tried to wash off the cancer odor as best I could. I was sure Lee was doing the same. We both took evening baths, rather than morning showers, to remove the noxious odors of the cancerous mice.[11]

Robert finally arrived with the usual load of dirty laundry, and hungry for his "lovin'." Sad because there were no flowers, no gifts, and so little was said, I nevertheless yielded to his needs, partly out of shame. Disconcerted at my own duplicity, I was astonished that Mother Nature was absolutely no help in resisting. He had been my first lover and I responded, though my heart belonged to Lee.[12]

Thursday, July 4, 1963

I got up to make breakfast as Robert slept in. Dave Ferrie called to tell me the tissue cultures had been delivered to the Prytania Street lab, where an unlucky soul would spend his or her Fourth of July holiday dealing with "The Problem." Dave was more talkative than usual, and went on to say that he had to go back to Miami next week to deal with his Eastern Air Lines troubles. We would stop further mouse slaughters until July 12th. By then, we should have the results of the experiments on the marmoset monkeys which had already been inoculated. But before Miami, Dave was going to fly to Illinois where an ancient but primitive branch of the Catholic church had accepted his seminary credentials.[13] He proudly said that he would assist in offering a Mass and that he hoped to get ordained, at last.

"Good luck, Dave," I said as he hung up, wondering to myself why it would be important for such a brilliant man to be ordained by a conspicuously bogus church.[14]

I resumed making breakfast for Robert and served him breakfast in bed. As he munched on French toast and scrambled eggs, I asked if we could go somewhere together.

"I have to leave tomorrow, while you're at work," he protested. "That only gives us twenty-two hours together. Besides, I'm too horny to do anything else," he added, pinning me with "unless you'd like to go over our new budget."

Choosing sex over budgets, I spent the day making sure Robert wasn't "horny" anymore. By mid-afternoon, Robert finally conceded that he needed a break. I put on makeup, braided my hair, and put in my brown contact lenses.

By 4:00 p.m., we boarded a streetcar together for only the second time, and headed to the French Quarter. As we strolled through the historic streets enjoying the sights, Robert navigated us to Pat O'Brien's where he wished to sample one of their famous Hurricanes, the rum drink for which O'Brien's was renowned.[15] Entering through an ancient brick tunnel, we soon found ourselves in a lush tropical paradise.

The moment we were seated, a waiter appeared. Robert promptly ordered two Hurricanes before I had a chance to remind him that I didn't drink, but the waiter was gone before he could do a thing. So when the Hurricanes arrived, Robert bit the bullet and drank both of them. I got to watch.

"If I buy another drink we'll blow our budget. We've seen enough," he said. "Let's go home, before we get tempted to buy something else."

That was the first and last of the French Quarter I saw with Robert — a good thing, too, since Lee and I went there so frequently. As we rode the streetcar back up Saint Charles, Robert told me he wanted to go to The Mansion so he could try to get our rent money back from Mrs. Webber. As I waited outside, I could hear them arguing. Then Robert appeared, holding a check aloft in victory.

"She gave it all back!" he announced proudly.

"No, she gave you a check," I amended, figuring that Mrs. Webber had given him a bum check just to get him out of the house. I couldn't believe he fell for it. We boarded the streetcar and stopped at the bank on the way home to deposit the check. Robert instructed me to call in the morning to see if the check was good.

We arrived home at dark and sat reading for a while. Suddenly Robert looked up from his book and suggested we go see the fireworks. Fabulous! We jumped in his car, but soon ended up stuck in a massive traffic jam on top of the Mississippi River bridge. Robert sat there, quietly cursing, ordering those cars to move! When they didn't, he became angry at me. "See?" he said. "I told you we should have stayed home." Whose idea was this? Robert seemed to miss the point that the

400 foot Mississippi River Bridge was probably the best place to see the aerial fireworks (that is probably why the traffic wasn't moving). Everyone else was enjoying the fireworks while Robert was fussing.

Friday, July 5, 1963

Robert was gone again, pleased with freshly ironed shirts and a good breakfast. As for me, I looked forward to a long Friday lunch with Lee after hard work at Monaghan's desk. We first went to Banister's building, though Lee's Fair Play for Cuba Committee "office" was now closed down. He still had his 2nd floor keys, though, since his dark room was now complete. Pro-Castro posters and flyers decorated its windowless walls. Noting my interest in the posters, Lee said, "I took the rest of that junk home, to impress anybody who might show up

Some of Lee Oswald's printed material

there just how much I love my Uncle Fidel."[16] We didn't stay there long and soon headed to the Prytania Street lab where I picked up the Project's log books which Dave had dropped off for me. I also inspected the cell cultures and gave them to Lee to courier to the U. S. Public Health Service lab for Dr. Mary. Lee headed uptown to meet Dr. Mary, and I returned to Reily's. The July 4th holiday had meant less mail than usual, giving me time to type some letters for Mr. Monaghan. But it was hard to concentrate: Lee and I had planned a tryst for that evening!

After clocking out, I went downstairs and waited restlessly until it was time to clock Lee out. Then I returned to the big room where I paced, waiting for Lee to return. The last Reily's employee was gone, but the lights still blazed. I was lonely and nervous. Finally Lee appeared and took me in his arms. At last! We were love-struck, like two little birds![17]

Lee turned off the main light switch and, in the semi-darkness, we retreated to the privacy of Monaghan's cubicle. As we embraced, Lee said he had learned a lot from the geisha he'd loved in Japan, as his hands touched me ever so lightly, entrancing me. I found myself drawn into a tide of passion, my mind and body caught in Lee's slow love that swept so tenderly over me. "I thought I had lost these powers," Lee whispered, "but you have brought them back. I have at last returned to that kind of giving."

I felt myself transported to an exotic, romantic world. I loved the smell of the coffee and oil on him. His legs were as hard as steel. His hands were beautiful. His thoughts were one with mine. All too soon, it was time for us to leave Monaghan's cubicle. As we made ourselves more presentable, Lee said, "There won't be much more of this, here at Reily's. Barbe has had to stop pretending that he doesn't know where I am. My time here is obviously drawing to a close."[18]

"I suppose after you leave, you'll be doing the leafleting again?" I said in a voice that failed to hide my fear for his safety. Lee avoided answering, as he so often did, bending down to pick up some keys that had fallen from his pocket.

"Here, I have a surprise for you," he said showing me the keys. "It's in Alba's garage. And it's ours, for the next few hours." We then went out the back to the garage next door. Lee unlocked the door to the garage with one of the keys. As we entered, I noticed the heat. It had to be over a hundred degrees in there.

"Wow, it's hot in here," I observed.

"Well, in a few minutes we'll be out riding, enjoying the breeze," Lee said, as he led me to a red van. We got in the van, but the engine wouldn't start. Lee got out to look under the hood. There he discovered a problem with the van's solenoid.

"It's shot, I can't fix it,' " he said, wiping the sweat from his forehead. We looked at each other, realizing we were alone, and that the van had pull-curtains.

"I've got an idea," Lee said, taking my hand and sliding the side door open. Without more ado we slammed the door shut, and tried to make love in a van whose interior got hotter by the second. Not even the heat of our passion could compete with the heat of that hot metal box! Drenched in sweat, we left the garage feeling like utter fools. As we walked toward the French Quarter, looking forward to gulping down as much fluid as we needed to recover, Lee (who never complained) complained.

"Me and my bright ideas!" he said gloomily. "And all because I haven't got two cents to rub together!"

"It's all right, sweetheart," I told him. "Who would have guessed that red vans could be a source of medieval torture?"

"You don't deserve this," he said. "Neither do I. We have a hell of a lot left to do this summer, and we need a safe place to be together."

"There's 1032 Marengo," I reminded him.

"I can't," he replied. "The sheets there are still warm from Robert. The very thought makes me jealous."

I understood how he felt: Robert had confessed that he enjoyed making love to me in the Ford as a sort of revenge, for it once belonged to a former girlfriend who'd ditched him.

"That's two good reasons never to make love to you in a car again," Lee said.

Crescent City Garage   Reily offices

"Well," I answered as we walked, "we still have public rest rooms, university listening rooms, the place behind the Seal Pool at Audubon Park, and — "

Lee burst out laughing. "You silly little Minnie Mouse!" he said affectionately, "and how about that plane? It's got a bench seat."

"Don't think so. Dave has flown it up to Illinois. I guess we're sunk."

"You just wait," Lee said. "By this time tomorrow, I'll have an answer to this."

Despite our rumpled clothes and our hair still in sweaty strands, we walked into The Acme Oyster Bar on Bourbon Street and enjoyed two plates of oysters. I posed as Lee's wife, speaking only Russian. Then we caught the Magazine Bus home.

Back at Marengo Street, there was a letter addressed to me on the side table. Robert had opened it. It was from Robert's mother, and contained an invitation to a ladies-only bridal shower to be held on July 20th, at The Coronado Hotel in Fort Walton Beach. A note accompanied the card expressing regret that only her own female friends were invited, since she felt she would not be able to get along with my mother. She would also feel awkward inviting my sister without inviting my mother, and she did not know any of my friends. She hoped I would understand. I certainly did.

"I am really looking forward to this!" I thought, inspecting the engraved invitation. Who knew if Robert would even be back in time?

Saturday, July 6, 1963

Lee went downtown for a quiet business meeting in the morning, and then spent the rest of the day with his wife and daughter. Susie and Collie were still gone. I hated being alone. So I busied myself by washing clothes by hand in the bathtub, then hanging them out to dry, ironing shirts and skirts, and reading medical reports about dying monkeys.

Sunday, July 7, 1963

Lee called early in the morning to ask if I would like to meet him at the Fur Shop on Canal Street. He didn't have to ask twice. When I arrived, Lee took me by the neck and started walking us across the busy street into the French Quarter.

"I have a surprise for you!" he said.

"Uh-oh," I replied. "I've heard those words before. Not the van again!"

"Not by any means," said he, leading me straight into the handsome lobby of the Monteleone Hotel,

at the time one of the most elegant hotels in the country. Lee had already registered us as "Mr. and Mrs. Robert E. Lee."[19] Lee showed me to our room. As we walked through those hallowed halls, Lee said softly, "Tennessee Williams, Sherwood Anderson, William Faulkner. They all lived here! Masterpieces were written here!"[20]

Our room was, in fact, a grand suite equipped with a record player and a stack of records. A basket of fruit and flowers graced an antique table. A simple white card sat on the table.

"Look at the card," Lee said, as he opened the curtains to reveal a view of the lush courtyard. "Best wishes to the young lovers," I read aloud. "May you enjoy this music as much as I have." It was signed "CLS."

"Who is CLS?" I asked.

"That is Clay LaVerne Shaw," Lee explained.

"But how — ?"

"He felt sorry for us," Lee said, kissing me. "I had to see him Saturday morning at his office. We had business to discuss about using the Trade Mart as a future site for my pro-Castro demonstration. He'd just been updated by Dave about the cancer project, and was pleased by my involvement in it."

"Is that the tall fellow from The 500 Club?" I queried.

"Yes, the same one. He's working night and day right now, trying to lease offices in the new Trade Mart building, but he took time to meet with me. Shaw represents important anti-Castro interests. When he asked about you and me, I described some of our recent adventures. After he finished laughing, he told me to meet him in a few hours at a rather remote location.[21] He was going to get some money from his safe. In return, all he requested from me was an FPCC flyer to keep as a souvenir."

Lee showed me the money. Shaw had given him a thousand dollars, in hundred dollar bills. "He volunteered to make reservations for us." Lee continued, "I will only be asked to call. We'll use different names and different hotels."

"We're playing Boris and Natasha again."

"Well, not quite," Lee said. "He hoped this would be enough to keep us out of the closets in Reily's offices and the INCA van for a while."

Lee said Clay Shaw was both Ochsner's longtime friend and Dave's friend, and that he suspected that Shaw had strong connections to the CIA. Lee also knew that Shaw was fiercely anti-Castro and had cooperated with the *Wasp* project. But Lee also suspected he was a member of the get-Kennedy coalition. Lee considered Shaw to be a wildcard. And the fact that he was now being so generous about our hotel bills made Lee suspicious of him.

But these thoughts passed as we relaxed and turned our attention to each other, which led to an experience with Lee that I would never forget. As I have mentioned, I have two large scars on the right side of my abdomen from operations I had as a child. My body was sleek and strong, but marred. I was embarrassed by my scars, so I went over to close the curtains and darken the room. Lee protested, and opened the curtains.

"Ah, but I want to see you. All of you!"

"No, you don't," I replied, closing the curtains again. "I have a big scar ..."

Lee opened the curtains again.

"You're not going to hide under the covers," Lee said. "What's more beautiful than a young woman, standing in the sunlight?"

"While I believe you are among the most remarkable and handsome of men," I replied, "I am not so blessed among women. I have a major flaw."

"Judy," he said tenderly, "I need to see this scar that concerns you so much. "

"You've already felt it," I said, blushing, as Lee began to undress me.

"I myself once had a dangerous scar," he told me. "It could have been used to trace me wherever I went, so I had it hidden by a very simple procedure."[22]

Lee had discarded all of my clothing by now — and I had finished removing most of his. There I stood, in full view of the window's light, the large, thick scar on the right side of my belly displayed for Lee's scrutiny. He walked around me, looking critically at every part. He laid his hands on my hips, and rotated me.

"My God, you're beautiful," he said.

"You say that to all the women you conquer," I replied, smiling shyly.

"No, no," he answered. "It's true. But I need to look a little longer."

"I think you're taking advantage of me," I complained.

"I hope so. But first, I must find this scar that concerns you so much," he said inspecting me. "I can't understand it," he concluded. "You puzzle me."

I felt his finger tips trace my body, always with a single point of attention that communicated his affection.

"Hmmm!" he said, with an enigmatic smile. "Hmmmmmm!" he said again, stepping back, and looking me over again. Then, he shook his head.

"What scar?" he asked.

I understood, and fell into his arms, knowing I was home at last... Later that afternoon, we discovered the theme music for Lawrence of Arabia on one of phonograph records that Clay Shaw had left for us, and proceeded to have a fantasy fling only starstruck lovers can imagine. We also decided to read Lawrence's *Seven Pillars of Wisdom* together. After a delicious ten hours together, we were forced to return to the wicked world.

Monday, July 8, 1963

Mondays were always busy, so I worked without a break. Lee knew the drill by this point and would not come anywhere near me in the office. However, I got a glimpse of him in the back, on the shipping lines, working with the latest female Cuban exiles recruited by David Lewis. After work, we rode the bus past our apartments and waited for the final Reily personnel to get off the bus. We moved to sit together, and talked.

Lee said he had received a letter from his cousin Eugene Murret who was studying to be a priest. Eugene had invited him to give a lecture on his experiences in Russia.[23] The lecture would be held in Mobile, Alabama, at a Jesuit seminary known as Spring Hill, on Saturday, July 27, 1963. Over 50 young students and several college professors would be attending the day long seminar, which would focus on the issues of Communism and Marxism. Lee would speak in the evening on his experiences while living in the USSR.[24]

The lecture was scheduled to last about an hour and would be followed by questions from the audience.[25] Because the invitation had come from his son, Uncle Dutz was quite supportive of Lee's participation and said he would drive his family there for the event.

Lee said there was far more preparation behind this invitation than met the eye. He began to prepare not only for his lecture, but also to answer important questions behind the scenes.

"Why would the Jesuits be interested in Marxism?" I wondered.

Lee explained the Jesuits' predicament. The Order was traditionally very conservative, but the younger generation of missionaries working in places like Nicaragua preached a radical philosophy, known as Liberation Theology, which supported Castro's Marxist-Leninist ideals.[26] These Central American countries were ruled by right-wing oligarchs who were also fanatically anti-Communist, and loyal Catholics.

On the other hand, Castro's revolution in Cuba was pro-Communist, but anti-Catholic. The Jesuits were in an awkward position. Where should their loyalties lie? Should they promote or resist Marxism in Central and South America?

Lee asked me to help him prepare his lecture, and mentioned that even Marina would be bringing some Russian music along for one of the Russian-speaking Jesuit priests.

When I got home, I found another letter from Robert waiting. It was more advice about money, and tightening our budget. But I had to laugh when he described a scheme that he thought I could use to cheat the transit system out of five cents per day, by trying to use old bus passes. *(See page 395.)*

He also counseled me about finding a dentist, suggesting that Susie Hanover or Mrs. Richardson could help. I was surprised that he had remembered Mrs. Richardson's name. I had not seen her since that day she gave Lee and me a ride from her church to Susie's house, and had only mentioned her to Robert on one occasion.[27]

Wednesday, July 10, 1963

I received an important call at Reily's from a Dr. Bowers, who told me Dr. Ochsner had asked him to relay good news to me. He said that cells isolated from two of the lymphoma strains from the mice had produced dramatic results in the marmoset monkeys. They suf-fered from not one, but two variations of a galloping cancer. We had broken through the barrier between mouse and monkey. Now we could move on to specific types of lung cancers, but would need to keep the mouse cancers going, in case a failure occurred, when we moved from marmoset monkeys to African Green monkeys.

Friday, July 12, 1963

Dave Ferrie was back in town, and it was time to resume the unpleas-ant task of slaughtering mice. Dr. Ochsner had decided to increase the number of mice to be "processed" to 400, finishing the run. It was a daunting task, so Lee came to work a half-hour early so we could get an early start at Dave's. For the first time in five weeks I clocked him out at 5:00, so we could get the work finished at a reasonable hour.
 Lee had been at Dave's for hours killing cancerous mice by the hun-dreds and cutting tumors out of their bodies. It was the height of sum-mer, and the fans couldn't drive out the stench of 400 sick mice.

Dr. Mary arrived to help out. Later, as Dave drove us home, he told us how he had to go back to Miami, and that Marcello's case was now taking a lot of his time. "I haven't even had time to eat," he said. "Not that I want anything after this."

"I knew better than to eat today," Lee said. "I would have puked."

"I didn't eat before coming, either," I said. Dave drove us up to 1032, but I didn't want to get out. Lee suddenly belched and looked pale, like he would be sick.

"You'll be home in a couple of minutes now, sport," Dave said to Lee, who had to put his head out the window to get some fresh air.

"Those baby mice," Dave went on, "were the saddest, most torment-ed little creatures I have ever seen." He shook his head. "To think they fought so hard for their lousy little shreds of life, only to be gassed to death."

"Stop!" I snapped. "Sadist! If you keep it up, I'm going to be in the same state as Lee. And to think we're trying to give Castro the same thing! It's just plain evil, Dave." The pure horror of it had finally hit me.

Dave's grin turned to a scowl.

"Get this straight, chickadee," he snapped. "This is about Kennedy, not Castro. Kennedy is surrounded by his enemies. He can do nothing right in their eyes. And he's gonna' die, unless we can stop it."

Dave threw his cigarette out the car window and lit another one.

"Listen," he went on, "You'd better know what your boy Lee, here, is up against; and me, too. We're risking our lives to get this stuff into Cuba. Yes, we're saying we want to help them take out JFK, and they believe us. If that son-of-a-bitch Castro is eliminated, we might save more than Kennedy. We might save the whole god-damned country from becoming a fascist nation."

"Well put," Lee said. "Excuse me, while I go puke."

I later helped Lee out of the car in front of his apartment, despite the risk of being seen, as he was so sick from vomiting. Then Dave drove me home where I took a long bath trying to wash the horrible smell of cancer off my body.

That night, about midnight, Lee came over, pale and grief-stricken. He looked so sick and dehydrated that I got him a glass of water.

"She told me I was a dirty beast," he said, sitting miserably on the floor. "And it's true! I stink! I couldn't get clean if I sat in the tub all night. When I closed my eyes, all I could see was cancer."

"I understand," I told him. "Not even Castro deserves to die like that."

"Is there any way you can sabotage it?" he asked.

"No. But I'm ashamed. I feel like telling them to go on without me."

"You can't," Lee said. "Something could happen to you."

"I'm not going to work with murderers," I protested. His eyes narrowed into a steely gaze. "All right, I said, "I withdraw that statement."

"We're stuck," Lee observed. "Besides, you must weigh the life of the one against the life of the other." I understood him to mean Kennedy versus Castro.

"If we do that, then we're playing God," I said.

"I'm now going to confide in you," Lee said, as he drank the water. "I am going to trust you. I've done that with no one. I tell you this: They want to assassinate Kennedy in Florida, or Texas. They'll show what happens to somebody who doesn't play their game."

"Dave was right. If Kennedy dies, a new system of government will take over. It will exist to generate profit; mostly by waging wars that will not result in clear victories. It's the old Orwellian idea. Today, we're at war with Oceania. We've always been at war with Oceania. Tomorrow, we're at war with East Asia. We've always been at war with East Asia.

"We can still vote, and choose our leaders." I said.

"If you're black, try to vote in the south!" Lee said heatedly. "And who will you vote for if JFK dies? Your choices will be Lyndon Johnson, Barry Goldwater, or George Wallace. Good God."

I said nothing. The gloom settled in.

"You know," Lee said, getting up, "JFK is slow to wage war. That's a man worth taking risks for."

Lee glanced at my alarm clock. "Someday, I'll have to conform to society and wear a watch like everybody else," he said. "It's my last holdout against western slavery." He straightened his shirt and pulled a comb through his thin, wavy hair. "Well, time to go back and face some more of her music. Maybe I deserve what she calls me. By the way," he went on, "I didn't hit her."

"I'm proud of you. Remember that!"

"Well, she's going to be mad tomorrow, too."

To my inquiring look, he said, "Because I'll be gone all day Sunday, working on the training film. And next weekend, it will be the same."

"But when will we be together again?" I asked. "Robert's job is about to terminate."

"So is mine," Lee said. "And after that, you'll have to leave Reily's, too."

"But it's too soon! I need a paycheck to keep Robert satisfied!"

"You were just there to cover for me. Monaghan can't wait to get a real secretary again," Lee replied frankly. "Still, they should pay you something, so you'll make it until September."

"I hope so," I said. "Maybe we'll be in Mexico by then."

"Look at the bright side," Lee said. "I'll be fired. So will you. We'll go to Reverend Jim's again. And we'll have twice the time to spend together. You'll see. Kiss me quick! I have to go back."

Our jobs were ending, but our dangerous days were just beginning. Lee was concerned about his family's safety and told Banister they needed more protection. Soon Mr. and Mrs. Eric Rogers would be moved into 4907 Magazine, the front portion of Lee's apartment house, to keep an eye on things.[28]

Wednesday, July 17, 1963

At Reily's, I received another complaint that Lee was missing and was required to examine his incomplete work logbook. I located Lee by phone at Dave's: Ochsner had insisted that yet another batch of mice must be processed! On top of his afternoon absence, Lee was late again that morning. Knowing he would be working late at Dave's on the Project, he had spent some extra time with his family.

At about noon, Personnel instructed us to find a replacement for Lee at once. Monaghan and I could no longer put off going through a list of new applicants for Lee's job. We had one ploy left: recommending a man whose background check was incomplete, so he could not be hired immediately. It was all we could do. Lee's cover job at Reily's had to end soon anyway, because he was preparing for public pro-Castro activities which were detrimental to Reily's anti-Communist image.

I hurried to Dave's apartment, where I found Lee and Dr. Mary working with the mouse tumors in the kitchen. But the level of "laboratory precautions" had suddenly increased dramatically. Both Lee and Dr. Mary were wearing surgical masks, hats, plastic aprons and surgical gloves. Dr. Mary's hands were thrust into the portholes of a portable germ-free "clean bench" with an air-pumped filter to prevent airborne contaminants from floating around the kitchen and into our lungs.

Dr. Mary noticed me staring at the equipment.

"The marmosets are dying," she told me somberly. "All of them, including the control group."

I pondered the implications. Our bioweapon had migrated between the two groups of monkeys, presenting the terrifying possibility that our mutated cancer was not only transferable, but actually contagious. We both knew that from this moment on we needed to be concerned about being exposed to a contagious, cancer-causing virus.

For the next hour, I worked with the microscopes, until Dave showed up. As my eyes were tired, I decided to help Lee, whose hands were now thrust inside the clean box's gloves, and leave the microscope work to Dr. Mary. I bent down and kissed his perspiring forehead.

"You shouldn't touch me," he said, through his face mask.

"I'm going to help," I told him, putting on my lab coat. I could see a book in Lee's pocket through the clear plastic apron. "I see you brought along *Profiles in Courage*," I said to Lee, hoping he was finished with it, and I could borrow it from him.

"I'm trying to get my hands on everything I can about 'The Chief,'" Lee answered. "I'll read it tonight. I will also pretend I can't hear Marina when she starts yelling at me for being late again."

As Lee said "Marina," an image of her flashed in my mind. I could almost see her, pregnant and sitting in their apartment with little Junie at her side. I thought about how neglected a woman can feel, and about how Robert had forgotten my birthday.

"Oh, Lee! Didn't you tell me that today was Marina's birthday?" I asked suddenly.

Dave heard my question, and whistled like an in-bound missile. "The ding-dong bells are gonna' ring all over your poor head, boy!" he teased.

Lee suddenly stepped back from the clean box and starting peeling off his apron, lab coat and hat. "I need a shirt!" he said urgently. "This one stinks!" He stood up and hurried past me, going through the back door of the kitchen toward the hall, to wash up.

Dave headed for his bedroom and went down on his hands and knees to search through a heap of clothes on the floor.

"Here, Oswald!" he yelled, holding up a white T-shirt.

"Okay!" Lee replied. Dave tossed him the clean shirt and Lee put it on. He kissed me on the cheek, handed me *Profiles in Courage,* and sprinted down the back stairs with Dave on his heels.

"I'll be right back!" Dave yelled, with his car keys in his hand and his cap on.

"Go, go, go!" Dr. Mary called out, from behind her surgical mask.

Dr. Mary and I continued working for the next several hours, and Dave returned as promised. We finally finished around midnight, and Dr. Mary drove me home. I took *Profiles in Courage* to bed and slept with it, because Lee had given it to me.

Thursday, July 18, 1963

I woke up tired and headed for Reily's, where my fatigue made my work day seem longer and harder than usual. Rumors about Lee were circulating again, and it was clear that the end was near. That afternoon Lee and I got on the bus and moved to the back together. Lee told me his supervisor had pounced on him for being late again. Since Mr. Barbe was nearby, he had to show displeasure too, skewering Lee for putting false entries into his logbook.

When Lee passed my desk, I said, "This is my fault," knowing that killing the mice was my job, not his.

"No," Lee said kindly. "I had a choice."

Monaghan and I knew Personnel was closing in on Lee, so we sent them a memo saying we could have a replacement by next Friday, in hopes of delaying the lynching. Personnel fired back a memo saying that they would take somebody straight from the Birmingham Jail, if that's all we could find. Lee was hounded so much that he was unable to take any breaks, even for lunch. He practically had to ask permission to go to the toilet. He had been scheduled to pick up something from an agent at Alba's garage, but could not get away long enough to do so. When five o'clock finally came, it was a relief for both of us. It had been a stressful day, so Lee called the Monteleone and reserved a room for us.

The moment we reached our suite, we fell into each other's arms. There was nothing either of us wanted more. We ended up, after great delights, simply resting together. After dozing a while, Lee called room service and ordered food. I ordered a nice dinner, but Lee ordered only soup and milk, even though he'd missed lunch.

"How can I eat well," he explained, "when Marina's eating leftovers? I'm no saint," he went on, "but I've been thinking. I've harmed her. I made her pregnant again. Somehow she must now stand up... have the courage and self-confidence to live without me. After I had beaten her black and blue! And then ... I forgot her birthday!" He sighed. "I don't deserve anything better than soup."

"You've changed! You don't hit her anymore," I reminded him. "You've become a better man. You have to forgive yourself."

After we ate, as Lee placed our tray outside the door and came back to the bed, I observed how utterly glorious he looked. There was not an ounce of extra fat on him. "I'm listening," I told him. "Just talk to me."

"Perhaps the man I wanted to be is dead," he said. "Just a memory I can no longer revive."

"That man exists," I replied. "He's a man with much to give."

"Then I will succeed," he said finally. "Let Marina rave on. I'll bear it, because I have you. It won't be too much longer. She's ready to leave."

"Maybe she'll find happiness in her next marriage."

"Just stay by my side. If you do, I know I can be strong."

Lee was quoting from his current favorite popular song, "Exodus," from the movie of the same name. He put on another album, by the Everly Brothers. After a few songs, their ballad "Let It Be Me" filled our ears and our hearts with love. As it played, twilight turned to darkness, and we made love again. I had never experienced such joy as Lee gave me, and I shook from head to foot and started to cry. "What's happening to me, Lee?" I sobbed. "I don't understand!"

Somewhere within, we were striking a mutual chord, powerful, deep and sad. We hung suspended between the present, and eternity.

"We'll die someday!" I finally whispered. "We've been looking at it, at death, for days in the lab. All we have turns to dust, or to words on a page."

"I know!" he answered simply. We were breathing together, our hearts beating at the same pace, in the same rhythm. It was uncanny. I could feel a wave of electricity travel between us. With Robert, as virile as he was, the skin was always between us.

With Lee, somehow, it seemed that we were meeting past the skin, soul to soul. I can't explain it better than that, for it only happened with him, and I have never experienced it again. We were truly one, and we knew it. We held each other, whispering about what we had discovered and lamenting the moments as they passed. We had been given a great gift, one so subtle and elusive that it scared us to think that we might have missed it. It might have slipped through our fingers unnoticed.

"What if I hadn't spoken Russian to you in the post office?" I asked. "What if we had never met?" The enormity of these few words filled the room.

"No, sweet," he said. "I think we would have found each other even if the very universe was folding itself away."

As we sat on the bus, returning home, I dared to ask Lee if this meant he would now truly confide in me about his clandestine adventures. "If I won't tell you," said Lee, "then God Himself is not allowed to know."

"All right," I said. "What agency do you really work for, and who is your most important handler?"

"You little spy!" he said, smiling. "Here's the answer: I'm loaned to the CIA, and must sometimes help the FBI; but who my main handler is, not even God knows the answer to that. Certainly, I don't. I call him 'Mr. B.'"

"As for me," I told him, "I'm just a pair of hands belonging to Ochsner."

"They don't belong to Ochsner anymore," Lee said. "They're mine now."

I asked him if I had a "handler." Lee said, smiling, "Of course you do. It's me." He said I was a lucky woman. "I shall be your protector," he said. "I won't let any of them hurt you."

I asked why would anybody want to hurt me? I was on the 'good' side. Lee explained: if you're no longer useful, you could be thrown out, unless you were educated.

"You're safer than I am," he told me. "Officially, you are supposedly an unwitting asset. A good position to be in." Then Lee snapped his fingers, saying that, in a heartbeat, I could become his very own Marina Oswald. "Once she's back in Russia, who's to say that you are not her? You even have the same bad teeth. If we pulled just one tooth, your dental records would match."

"Her tooth, or my tooth?" I asked, anxiously.

He said that would come later, so not to worry. I should not obey Robert's orders to go to the dentist. I told Lee he seemed to know a lot about changing identities.

"I should," he said, " It happened to me."

"So, do you know your own name?"

"By the grace of God," he said, "I do. But nobody would believe I was me, if they went through my records." The advantage, he said, was that he could appear and disappear as easily as a shadow.

"As you know, I have a bunch of funny records," I put in, "I could even start a second personality."

"The only second personality I want you to start is a baby for us someday," he said. "That is, if you want to."

I told him I would have a dozen, if he'd help change the diapers.

Lee told me he washed Junie's diapers regularly. But if we lived in a place like Samoa, nobody would have to wash any diapers. We could rinse off our babies in the ocean waves.

Lee asked if there was anything he still didn't know about the cancer research project. "Well, you should know about the etiology of the cancer," I told him. "I've never discussed it with you."

"Etiology? What's that mean?"

"Etiology means origins. This is no ordinary cancer, as you know," I reminded him. He agreed.

"It's probably contagious," I went on. That startled him, since Dr. Mary and I had not really discussed this point explicitly in front of him. I told him that the monkey virus, now altered by radiation, had moved spontaneously from the deliberately infected marmoset monkeys to the control animals. With it came the cancer and all the marmoset monkeys were now dying. That's why there were suddenly all the extra precautions in Dave's lab.

"Remind me not to eat or drink anything over at Dave's," Lee said soberly as he pondered the idea of working around a contagious cancer virus.

"But humans are not monkeys," I told him hopefully, trying to change the mood. "It could be quite different for us. At Roswell Park, I think I saw a way to cure cancer. Maybe we can go that direction next. We were studying bacteriophages. These are viruses that attack bacteria. Say you have a staph infection. Say they genetically alter a bacteriophage to target the staph. If they injected it into you, it would not only kill the staph, but it would stay in your system forever, ready to attack the staph again if it ever showed up. Antibiotics, to which bacteria can build up resistance, could go the way of the Model T."

"Would it work for typhoid, or cholera?" Lee asked me.

"Sure, just alter it for the specific bacterial infection," I replied. "Now, if a bacteriophage could be engineered not to touch any cells in your body but cancerous ones, it could eat common cancers like meat-loaf, leaving a bag of pus behind. But I don't think the cancer treatment industry would like that. They'd lose a lot of money. Of course, you'd have to update the bacteriophage from time to time."

"Bacteriophage... " Lee repeated the word.

"We've created a galloping cancer," I went on. "I think a bacteriophage could be altered to take out even these cancer cells. But nobody's going down that road. We're developing this weapon to eliminate a head of state. But what if we get Castro? Will they really just throw this stuff away? " I asked, shivering at the thought.

"It could be used as a weapon of mass destruction, " Lee answered simply.

"Yes," I agreed. "Think how Hitler would have loved this, to use against the Jews in those camps. They could say a plague went through."

"Or to eliminate Negroes in Africa," Lee said with a cold tone in his voice.

The insane enormity of the idea blew my mind. And I had my fingerprints all over it. I almost wished I'd never been born. Lee asked how many people understood the science behind the Project. I told him Ochsner, Sherman, Dave and I surely knew how it was made and that I knew there were some other doctors involved, but once the bioweapon was created, it could be kept frozen for years and used by anyone who had access to it at some point in the future. We sank into deep silence as we contemplated the dimensions of what we had just said. How had my dream to cure cancer gone so wrong?

---

1. 618 Magazine St., New Orleans, LA.
2. The building held legislators' and government offices at that time.
3. Adrian Alba testified to the Warren Commission about Lee's visits, noting that one day he saw an FBI man from Washington pass Lee an envelope which Lee shoved under his shirt and tucked into his pants.
4. Adrian Alba's testimony before the Warren Commission, April 6, 1964:
    Mr. LIEBELER - Did Oswald tell you what kind of work he was doing for Reily Co.?
    Mr. ALBA -...it was obvious that he was in the electrical end of the maintenance end of the factory at W. B. Reily Coffee.
    Mr. LIEBELER - What did he say? Or why do you say it was obvious?
    Mr. ALBA - He was just like the others there in the maintenance and the electrical end, and they would wear the electrician's belt with a bandoleer screwdriver, pliers, and friction tape, et cetera.
    Mr. LIEBELER - Did he wear that?
    Mr. ALBA - Yes, he did.

    Mr. LIEBELER - Did he seem to have an interest in firearms that was abnormal or extremely great, or anything like that?
    Mr. ALBA - None.
    Mr.. LIEBELER - Other than the fact that he was quiet, was there anything about him that struck you as being odd or peculiar?

Mr. ALBA - No.

Mr. LIEBELER - You didn't suspect he was a violent kind of person, or anything like that, the time that you knew him, did you?

Mr. ALBA - I would answer that indeed not.. I had never gotten the impression from Lee Oswald that he was capable of any plot or assassination, or what have you, of that nature.

— — — — — — — — — — — — — — — -

Alba responded to relatively few questions and was dismissed. Re his later statement to the HSCA Report, pp. 193-194, researcher Bill Davy (Let Justice Be Done) observed: "One day Alba recalled observing an FBI agent handing a white envelope to Oswald, who was standing in front of Reily's. Alba watched as Oswald clutched the envelope close to his chest and walked back into Reily's," ...[but] Alba's recollection came several years after the incident and should be regarded with a measure of skepticism.

5. Lee got his FPCC membership card from FPCC President Vincent T. Lee. Lee wanted to be officially connected to the FPCC so that his actions would ultimately discredit them.

6. This building is called the Newman/Neuman Building in assassination records created by those who, in my opinion, wanted Guy Banister's name dissociated from the building that represented "544 Camp Street" on Lee's pro-Castro materials. The building had not only the 544 Camp St. entrance but also Banister's 531 Lafayette Street entrance. In 1963, nobody I knew called this building the Newman Building, for Banister was there already when Sam Newman purchased it. The building was torn down not long after the assassination.

7. Lee requested visas for himself and Marina, but asked that they be considered separately, because he had no plans for them to enter the USSR together. Lee wanted a visa in his role as "dissident." He had no plans to return unless ordered to do so. Further, the Project needed completion, which included pro-Castro activities to establish his pro-Castro credentials in case he might be asked to enter Cuba, possibly carrying the bioweapon.

A request for a visa to Russia helped raise his safety level. He would later be able to request a transit visa through Cuba to Russia as an excuse to enter Cuba. By showing great admiration for Castro, a request for a visa to transit through Cuba would then not seem suspicious: Lee would want to leave Cuba and head for Russia if he was ordered to carry the bioweapon into Cuba. If he was ordered to stay in Cuba, he could explain that, after seeing Cuba, he had decided not to go on to the Soviet Union after all.

In reality, neither scenario was now attractive to Lee. He wanted a new kind of job with the CIA, where he and I could be involved together in Mexico or South America, as inspired by his friend, George de Mohrenschildt's trek through Mexico and Central America, which was CIA-supported. Such future plans meant that Marina needed a separate visa to the USSR so she could proceed, if necessary, without him. However, Marina did not want to return to Russia, either: these visa requests were made to present a united front to the Russians. This helped Lee in his Cuban mission, but it also helped ensure Marina's safety in case Lee's role as a double agent was exposed: she could always claim that she wanted to return to Russia, and could point to the 'separate' requests to prove she was not cooperating with her husband in any of his clandestine activities.

Lee told me that Marina had indeed cooperated with him on many occasions, which I have never seen mentioned. I have mentioned only one such area of cooperation — her using the 4907 Magazine Street address for correspondence between her and Ruth Paine and those in Russia, to avoid any mail coming to the actual address at 4905 Magazine St.

Marina knew more about Lee's clandestine activities than she has ever admitted, for example, never disclosing his trips out of town except inadvertently, such as to a priest once, at Spring Hill Seminary, when she complained that Lee was "gone all the time." The position Marina was in after Lee's death made it dangerous for her to mention any of that. I consider Marina Oswald Porter a courageous woman.

8. On June 24th, Lee's feelings for me were reflected in the fact that he had not listed Marina as 'next of kin' on his passport application. Instead, he'd put his aunt Lillian Murett's name down.

There had been a crisis of doubt after that, but in the end, he was ready to leave Marina for good and start a new life with me. To assure that Marina would not want to go with him to Cuba (which tale would allow him to vanish), Lee may have done what Marina's "official biography," *Marina and Lee*, and her testimony to the Warren Commission, indicated: Lee proposed outrageous ideas about how to get into Cuba, such as hijacking a plane and asking Marina (pregnancy and all) to help him hijack it, placing maps, plane schedules, etc. in plain view. If this actually occurred, any proclivity Marina might have harbored about going with Lee to Cuba (seeing that he was a mental case) was thereby quashed.

9. Fluent in Russian, George called Lee "Harvey Lee" to avoid using "Lee' as a first name, as did most Russians, who thought of 'Lee" as a Chinese word, or perhaps as a nautical term (подветренная сторона). This does not mean that George thought Lee was actually a man called "Harvey" and that "Lee" was yet another person George might have known. Marina also avoided calling Lee by his name and used "Alek" instead — probably for the same reason. That "Lee" was really "Lee" and not "Harvey" is evident when Lee's first daughter's name is shown in full: June Lee Oswald. In Russian tradition, the father's name is the child's middle name.

10. George de Mohrenschildt had even dated Jackie Kennedy's mother. Jackie Bouvier Kennedy called him "Uncle George" when she was young. George also knew Ruth Paine's father. After Lee's death, George betrayed him to the Warren Commission out of fear, but in his last days, he wrote about Lee with affection and respect. Regarding Lee's ability to speak and read Russian, George, who once lived in Minsk, stated "Lee spoke it very well, only with a slight accent." For no reason George could comprehend, Marina would make fun of Lee for the few errors he made speaking Russian. George was one of the few educated people Lee encountered, besides myself, who appreciated Lee's character, intellect and independent ways. A couple of years after finishing his book, the Baron would end up "committing suicide" with a shotgun in his mouth — scant hours before an interview with Gaeton Fonzi, an intrepid HSCA investigator who may have been able to get some truth from de Mohrenschildt.

11. Even Marina's biographer mentions Lee's long baths and an odor. Lee's burps are mentioned in McMillan's book, dedicated to exposing every repulsive thing possible about Lee. But Reily's was an immaculate and conservative company that insisted that their employees had to dress in clean clothing. It was forbidden to come to work unshaven (a day's growth might have been tolerated, but would be noticed and possibly questioned). Lee kept clothes in a locker there and always looked clean and presentable at work — even wearing pants with a crease pressed into them.
    Evening bathing became a habit I would continue, as my family knows, for the rest of my life.

12. When we divorced 24 years later, Robert wrote plaintively that he suspected I never loved him, and that I considered our children more important to me than he was. But I did love him — just in a different way, for he could never replace my murdered sweetheart — a tragic truth..

13. Dave also said that he would visit his brother in Rockford, Illinois on this trip.

14. Dave's efforts to be ordained were sabotaged by Jack Martin, who called the head of the church in question and reported that David Ferrie had been charged with "acts against nature." Apparently, this was Jack Martin's way to get back at Dave Ferrie for his isolation. See "A Bishop in Heart," from *Dr. Mary's Monkey* by Edward T. Haslam.

15. The famous Hurricane drink from Pat O'Briens is basically a rum punch made with fruit juice. Its signature glass is curved like a woman's body with hips and shoulders.

16. The few pro-Castroites who showed up after the *Wasp* leafleting had now been 'fingered.' Lee had turned to publicizing 4907 Magazine as his new 'office' address.

17. Lee had told Marina he was going to see a movie after work. She didn't like going to movies with him because Junie was such a handful (so said Lee), and she had trouble understanding English (so said she, to the Warren Commission). As for Robert, he was long gone again.

18. Emmett Charles Barbe, Jr. was Lee's immediate supervisor. He testified to the Warren Commission on June 15, 1964.

19. This was the only time we borrowed the General's name to conceal our identities.

20. Lee had read one of my Faulkner books, *Light in August*, and had written a comment in it. He was particularly impressed with Joe Christmas, who did not know if he was black or white. It was a good book to read in New Orleans.

21. Lee did not tell me where Shaw met him, and only said that it was "rather remote." Several years later, one of the witnesses in the Garrison trial said that he had seen Shaw and Lee together at the seawall on Lake Pontchartrain. Assuming Vernon Bundy's testimony is accurate, this may have been that day. Bundy, who was black, a drug-user, and a convict, was portrayed as "not credible" by Shaw's attorneys, who noted that there were no other collaborating witnesses.

22. Lee had his mastoidectomy scar hidden by having the skin pulled tight behind his left ear, erasing a depression there, and hiding almost all of the scar.

23. From Mary Ferrell's chronology: July 8, 1963 (Monday) - Gene Murret, Oswald's cousin who is studying for the priesthood, invites Oswald to tell of his Russian experiences at Murret's seminary in Mobile, Alabama, on Saturday, July 27th. (WC Vol 16, p. 334; WC Vol 20, p. 634; WC Vol 25, p. 919)

24. These were all college graduates who were studying for the priesthood. The student priests did not become official priests until they were ordained.

25. The moderator would be Paul Piazza, S.J., a young Jesuit from New Orleans who was about Lee's age. Paul Piazza's father owned a seafood company that supplied New Orleans restaurants, particularly those in the French Quarter. In the late 1960s, he taught at Jesuit High School in New Orleans. Eventually, he left the order and taught at a school in the Washington, DC area.

26. Nicaraguan President (and dictator) Anastasio Somoza complained that the Jesuits said Jesus was a Communist and peace would come to earth when the entire world was Communist. Wrote Anastasio Somoza:

    As far back as 1963, there was guerrilla activity in Nicaragua. ... The rebel Sandinistas ... (were) like a malignant cancer ... (and) those Jesuit priests ... preached Communism... They believe that Jesus Christ was a Communist; and that we will have world peace when all the world is communistic ... A number of these priests came from the United States and Spain ... more dedicated to the Communist cause than the local priests. (Chapter 2 of Somoza's book, *Nicaragua Betrayed*, finished shortly before Somoza was gunned down).

27. RAB letter

28. Eric Rogers testified before the Warren Commission and revealed information that went unnoticed for decades until I spoke out and drew attention to his significance. In spring, 1964, he and his wife still resided at 4907 Magazine St. — and they had been there since mid-July, 1963. Yet the WC published that Lee Oswald left 4907 for Mexico City without paying the utility bill, implying that Lee was an irresponsible deadbeat, even though elsewhere they published the Oswald family address as 4905. Most researchers assumed 4907 was the Oswald residence, citing the utility bills and other documents (often signed by Lee) stating that 4907 was his address. Even some of Lee's pro-Castro material had '4907 Magazine St.' stamped on it. Both Ruth Paine and Marina herself placed '4907' on all New Orleans correspondence — not 4905 — proving they cooperated with Lee's fake address scheme. Until I spoke up and mentioned that Rogers, who was unemployed, had been deliberately hired to live for free at 4907, beginning from the time Lee was fired at Reily's and began broadly advertised pro-Castro activities — and that 4907 was his fake address to protect his family — researchers had ignored Rogers' presence at 4907. Rogers even took all Lee's subversive mail. Testifying that he never spoke to Lee at any time, Rogers nevertheless could not deny that he allowed Lee's Communist publications, etc. to be delivered to his home. In fact, Rogers had been hired to help protect Marina and little June from potential harm from anti-Castroites who might have tried to confront Lee or his family violently. After Lee left in late September, Rogers got a job with a Meal-a-Minute fast food restaurant, which at that time, I was told, provided interim work for FBI informants. It's probably too late to find any record supporting that now, but in 1964, Rogers was paying his own 4907 utility bills.

Monday

My Darling Judy,

Today I was thinking forward to the time when I'll be working in Town and happened across a scheme that might save us bread money. Don't stop reading just because I'm writing about money. If you get a Transfer going and coming on the bus, you can use the Transfers the next day on the St Charles line. Perhaps you should ride one line in the morning and the other in the afternoon. It may not work for one reason or another, like the color of the Transfer, but it might. If we both do it, it'll save a whole dollar per week.

The prospects of my getting a job in Town look pretty rotten right now, but I'll have to wait and see to be sure. It seems that by July all the students have stopped working on quarter boats. That may mean about then they have all gone in Town. Foo!

As for the necessity of my having a job [just in case I have to go out again, not this job but another], I figure that after the rent & the scholar fund, there is left about $12.70 per week out of your salary, perhaps as high as $13.75. This doesn't include such as The Pig or The Kitty or busfare. I know that we can cut down expenses if we stop eating, but the days of wishful financing are over.

Meanwhile:

Be sure to check on Mrs. Ugh's check.

Find a dentist. Maybe Mrs Hanover or Mrs Richardson can help. Get pulled the ones that need it & a couple filled.

Eat well! I won't have my brand new wife undernourished.

Write Mrs. Webbber.

CHAPTER 20

TIGHTROPE

July 19, 1963 Friday

T hat morning, Lee was on the Magazine Street bus with me in time to arrive at Reily's before 8:00 A.M. He knew a supervisor would be waiting to see if he was late. As the bus worked its way down Magazine Street, we discussed the upcoming weekend. I told him Robert had called last night and said to get ready for another trip to Fort Walton, for the bridal shower that his mother was hosting.

Lee planned on spending all day Sunday working on the training film presumably at the camp across the lake, but wanted to take Marina and Junie to the Pontchartrain Beach amusement park to give them a break from the monotony of Magazine Street.

I clocked in shortly before 8:00 A.M., but I needed Lee to run an errand to Eli Lilly's for the Project, so despite his efforts to be on time, he clocked in late again and got chewed out. For the rest of the day, Lee's supervisors were all over him. He couldn't get away for our usual long Friday lunch, but we did manage to meet briefly at the front entrance to Alba's garage, where the vending machine with Lorna Doone cookies was located. We dined on the cookies, then hurried back to Reily's. With things so tense for Lee at the office, I didn't dare go to the lab by myself that day. It was not a typical Friday, and tension was everywhere.[1]

In the middle of the afternoon, I had to stop a big tea order which was about to be shipped to a poor credit risk. Knowing that the trucks had to be loaded by 4:00, I hurried to the shipping and packing area with a stop-order slip. Lee was on the production line packing boxes of tea.[2] As I approached the noisy production line, I noticed a machine dropping green glasses they were packing into big tea cartons. It must have been a special promotion of some kind, because it was a short run, and there weren't many glasses left to pack. They were deep green, with clear crystal bases — perfect for iced tea. I stared longingly at them, but I'd have to buy a carton to get one. As the glasses dropped into the boxes, I told Lee, "They're beautiful. I wish I could afford one!" My comment had an impact on the man who loved me that I would soon regret.

The foreman heard me and said that if I wanted a glass, I needed to buy a carton of tea at the order counter. I went to the counter to see if I could arrange to buy a carton, but I had no cash and the girl at the counter wouldn't let me pay in installments.

I returned to Monaghan's desk, where I soon found another credit risk for the same truckload. This was highly unusual, but of course, I had to return to the factory. When Lee saw me, he slipped me a small note he'd written. It was a fake receipt. "I want you to take a carton of tea!" he told me. "You can use this, if you have to. I know you'll eventually pay for it."

I tried to give it back, but the shipping foreman spotted Lee refusing it. He came over, inspected the note, then threw it to the floor. "So you thought you could fool that guy!" he fumed. "You might be Monaghan's secretary, but in here you have to follow the rules like everybody else!" Turning to Lee, he gave him a shove. "What are you looking at?" he yelled. "Get back to work!"

At the same time, I reached down, snatched the fake receipt from the floor, and hid it. Though outraged by the foreman's reprimand I was in no position to protest his abuse of Lee, who said nothing and returned to work.

Upset that Lee had been shoved, I followed him to the packing line and said, "It's okay, I can do without." But the foreman wanted me out of there.

Rushing over, he snarled, "Why are you still here? Is there anything else you need, besides a free glass?" At that, Lee's eyes narrowed with anger.

"For what she gets paid here," he snapped, "she deserves a damned green glass!" Then he snatched one from a carton moving along the conveyor belt and pressed it into my hands. I was stunned and stood frozen, holding the glass with the foreman staring at me. Before anyone could react, the carton was taped shut automatically. The foreman turned toward

Lee with his hands in fists: my coveting of a simple glass had triggered a disaster!

"But I did buy a carton of tea!" I said desperately, telling a bald-faced lie. "I just forgot to bring my receipt! The man just tried to help me out, before all of the glasses were all gone!" But the foreman knew better. "If you weren't the boss's secretary," he shouted, "I'd have your hide for this!"

"You'd better leave!" called out one of the Cuban girls. I took her advice.

As I did, I heard the machines shutting down, and the foreman cursing at Lee: "What in the hell got into your god-damned, stupid head?" he shouted. "You've ruined the run!" Nobody knew which box was missing its green glass, but the trucks had to leave soon, so they loaded all of the boxes, including the one missing the glass.

Realizing I had to do something to cover up the mess, I hurried to my desk, my heart pounding. Hiding the glass, I went to my favorite clerk, Annette, and borrowed $2.00 from her, and a dollar from another girl, promising to pay them back on Monday.

I went to the mail boy (who I knew liked me) and asked him to help me out. I gave him the $3.00 and asked him to go buy a carton of tea and tell the clerk that it was for himself. When he brought me the tea carton and gave me the receipt, I gave him a quarter. I quickly removed the green glass packed inside and replaced it with the glass that Lee had given me, then hid the carton under Mr. Monaghan's desk. I slipped into the bathroom and deposited the extra glass into the garbage can.

As I returned to my desk, Monaghan burst into the room with his face furrowed. He marched into his cubicle, made a phone call, and quickly headed upstairs to the president's office. Trouble! Then one of the Cuban girls from the packing area came into the office pretending to ask my help with a hard-to-read label, but she was really there to tell me that ruining the run meant Lee would be fired.

At about 4:15, the female supervisor demanded to be shown the glass. I showed her the carton and my receipt, so she allowed me to keep the glass. I hoped that would be the end of it, but in a few minutes, Mr. Barbe, and a second man in a dark suit came to Monaghan's cubicle.

After a few minutes, Barbe and the stranger left and Monaghan came to me. "You purchased that carton of tea, didn't you?" he asked. Wordlessly, unable to speak another lie, I showed Mr. M. the carton and receipt. To my pleading eyes, Monaghan shook his head. "There's nothing I can do," he said. "Your boy is sunk."

One of the Reily brothers now appeared — I don't know which one — it was such a rare event to see a Reily brother on our floor that every toiling clerk actually paused a moment before plunging into yet harder efforts to look busy. Monaghan sighed as they went to his cubicle.

Suddenly, Mr. Barbe brought Lee into the cubicle and Monaghan left, seating himself in his big brown chair at his desk, with me at his side. From our chairs, we could see and hear everything. Barbe now commenced to list Lee's many company crimes to Reily, as Lee stood at attention like a Marine in his dirty, sweat-soaked shirt.[3] We watched helplessly and silently as Lee took that mass of unfair accusations as calmly as he'd taken the shove from the foreman. Both Reily and Barbe knew who Lee was, but they put on a show of humiliating him anyway. This was my fault! And all for a green glass!

Tears welled in my eyes, and guilt washed over me. I swore to myself that I would never again express any desire to Lee without thinking twice. Mr. Reily's senior secretary, an elderly lady who never spoke to me, came to the cubicle with Lee's personnel file, and Barbe handed Lee a pink slip. He said his last paycheck would be mailed to him. Lee stood stoically, never speaking. Told to leave at once, Lee glanced at me and Mr. M. and shrugged. Then he marched out of Wm. B. Reily Coffee Company for the last time, looking straight ahead. I clocked him out. It was 4:30 P.M.[4]

Mr. Monaghan called me into his cubicle. I figured I would be fired next and braced myself. "Frankly," said he, "I wish we could get rid of you today, but that would look suspicious." Then he explained that Ochsner said he wanted me to stay another month because I was "doing a good job in the labs."

Relieved that my job was not in jeopardy for the moment, I turned my thoughts to the upcoming bridal shower in Fort Walton Beach, where I'd be presented to prominent women who were married to successful gentlemen and ensconced in designer homes overlooking private golf courses. Lee's weekend would be very different. He would be helping to make a training film for the anti-Castro insurgents. Now it was time to go home and get ready. Ugh!

Lee was fired after eleven weeks and one day of employment at Wm. B. Reily Coffee Company. But if you know that Lee was really an undercover agent, you can see that his job at Reily's was a cover job, as was mine. But in Lee's case, the discrepancies between his real job and his cover job were blatant. For example, Lee was always late for work, and yet he was never docked for being late like other Reily employees. He was also allowed to work erratic hours, but was paid for a full 40-hour week. He was frequently missing and unable to be located by other employees.

My job looked more real than his, in that I was expected to be on time every morning, to catch Monaghan's early phone calls and to clock both Lee and me out at the end of each day. I had a real work load and was essentially chained to my desk all day on Mondays and Tuesdays, and for half a day the rest of the week. But my real task was in the cancer lab, and Monaghan knew it. When I punched Lee's time cards to cover his absences, I did it with Monaghan's knowledge and consent. Monaghan also did this for both Lee and me on several occasions.

Lee's time cards were so squirrely that they were frequently sent to Monaghan, as VP, to review. Monaghan would hand them to me to resolve. I would write the number 40 on them, indicating that Lee had worked a forty-hour week, and then sign the cards with my initial "J" to approve them.[5]

Monaghan and I had to protect Lee from the suspicions of the other employees and managers. For the most part, we succeeded. Lee was forced to leave his job only one week earlier than was originally planned. He was then ready for the next phase of his assignment.

See Appendix for more on Lee Oswald's time cards and clock-in/out times

The larger question is whether Mr. Reily himself actually knew the details of what was going on in Monaghan's office. We do know that he was patriotic and strongly anti-Communist. We know he was involved in INCA with Dr. Alton Ochsner. But was he aware that Lee and I were helping Ochsner develop a biological weapon? I can't say. One might argue that the fact that Lee and I were eventually both fired meant that he finally figured it out and wanted to distance himself from it, unless that too was a ruse. However it worked upstairs, when the moment finally came, it was awfully unpleasant.

By 5:00 I clocked out for the last time and went outside to catch the bus back to 1032 Marengo, but Lee intercepted me. We walked away from Reily's, so we could talk privately. I was so upset. "I'm the reason you got fired," I confessed to Lee with remorse.

"I had to be fired sometime next week anyway," he replied, "because I have to go to Mobile and talk at Spring Hill about Communism. Reily's couldn't have me doing that while I was on their payroll. Now I'll have more time to be with you."

As we headed home on the next bus, I sat with the big carton of tea on my lap, feeling the weight of the precious treasure inside. Lee got the driver to slow the bus down as we neared Marengo Street, so we could see if Robert's car was in the driveway. The coast was clear, so he stopped the bus, and we jumped out. Lee carried the tea in case Robert happened to arrive while we were still walking.

I said, rather sadly, "They'll all be speculating if I'm pregnant at my bridal shower."

"Why don't you put a pillow in there, and really shock everybody?" Lee joked.

"Lee," I said, "I know you're used to leading three lives, or thirty. But I'd rather tell the truth! Today, for example..."

"Ah," he said, "You're still not used to it, like I am ... false trails, fake records, fake names. It meant nothing to me to create one more fake document."

As we reached the house, we saw that Susie's car was gone. Stunned, we realized that Robert's car could have been parked deeper into the driveway, and we might have been caught! We'd have to remember.

"I'm going to give this tea to Susie," I told Lee, "before Robert sees it."

"But see how complicated things can get?" Lee commented, smiling. "How are you going to account for the $3.00 you spent?"

It was true. Robert watched what I spent to the nickel.[6]

"You might have to lie," Lee pursued. "The little complications of life."

"We should try for higher ethical standards, Lee." I countered.

"Until then," he teased, "you're going to need this." He handed me three dollars to pay back my girl friends at Reily.

"But he'll see my paycheck. He'll know the $3.00 was from somewhere else."

"You can say you got $3.00 cash from selling a drawing."

"But I didn't! Lee, I hate all this deceit. I must divorce him!"

"Not yet," he said. "You first have to go to the party in Florida, and prove you're not pregnant."

"How am I going to deal with this? I don't love him anymore."

"Yes, you do," Lee said. "You still 'love' him, just like I still 'love' her."

"But I don't want to sleep with him anymore!"

"Shhh! Don't tell me that, I won't be able to bear it."

We entered Susie's kitchen, where I hid the $3.00 in her sugar bowl. Then, I carried the tea into my bedroom with Lee following. I removed the green glass from the tea carton so Lee could see how rich its color was in natural light. Lee noticed his fake receipt inside the glass, and I told him I'd rescued it from the floor to avoid more trouble for him. "Fast thinking, Juduffki!" he said, giving me a little kiss to reward me.

Suddenly, we saw the blue Ford turning into the drive. Robert! Unwilling to risk being seen going down the hall and leaving through the front door, Lee pulled the bed aside and exited through the front bedroom window. I closed it behind him, pushed the bed back into place, then hurried into Susie's kitchen, where I hid the glass high in her china cupboard. Just as I finished, Robert burst in, smiling and full of energy. His curly hair that I loved had grown out even more. Never much for words, he dropped his duffle bag on Susie's kitchen floor and kicked the door shut. He was a big, confident man, with a one-track mind.

As I melted in his arms, I began to understand what Lee had said about different kinds of love. I gave up trying to compare the two men, and accepted that I lived in two different worlds. I was Mrs. R. A. Baker III, and Juduffki.

Robert found the box of tea in the bedroom, and demanded to know what it was for. I was afraid to tell him that I bought it for Susie, so I told him I had bought it for his mother, as a "Thank you" present, for arranging such a nice bridal shower. Once again, I was forced to lie.

As Robert drove us to Fort Walton Beach, we argued about money, and Robert fumed about my purchase of the box of tea. Tired of his criticism, I complained about the sad state of our relationship, to which he responded, "Tell my mother about it. Maybe she'll call off the shower."

When we finally arrived at his parents, it was midnight. The Bakers' beautiful home overlooked a bay that sparkled under the stars. His parents met us at the door, dressed in white silk Japanese bath-robes that matched their silver hair. As we entered the house, suddenly a big black cat pounced on my leg, grabbing my ankle. Dropping the box of tea, I tried to pull it off, but its teeth were enmeshed in my nylon stocking. Clawing my leg wildly, the cat fought to get loose, biting me again.

"Help!" I shouted.

"Stop it, Felix!" yelled Robert's father. "Bad boy!" He quickly grabbed the cat, opened a sliding glass door, and threw it into the bushes.

"If you go into the bathroom, my dear," said Mrs. Baker, with abstract calm, "you'll find a nice, clean washcloth, and I'll bring you a band-aid." I went into the guest bath, washed the blood off my leg, and inspected the damage: two purple punctures in my heel, and a pair of deep, four-inch scratches on my leg. I washed the scratches with the washcloth, but it wasn't enough: an untreated cat bite can lead to a dangerous infection. Mrs. Baker returned with a single band-aid.

"Do you have any antibiotic ointment?" I asked hopefully.

"I don't think you'll need ointment for that," she said. "He does it to me all the time."

"If he does that to you all the time, I'm surprised you can walk."

"You seem to have very thin skin," she said coldly, then turned and left. I felt very small and unwelcome in their plush home. And how my foot hurt!

New Bride Is Honored

The new Mrs. Robert A. Baker III is shown receiving a wedding gift from the hostesses of a Shower-Tea given in her honor. The hostesses were (left to right), Mrs. Cass Davenport and Mrs. Ray Davis. The shower was held on July 20 at the Coronado.

Saturday, July 20, 1963

After breakfast, Mrs. Baker took me to the hairdresser, and then to buy a proper dress. I felt like a doll she had decided to play with. The event was held at the Coronado's Reception Hall, with a country club luncheon following. I was the lone "young thing" amongst a gaggle of elderly women with gray hair and double chins, all dripping with diamonds and jewelry.

We wound up with the predictable cache of gifts — Pyrex, designer cookware, stainless flatware, electronic gadgets, linen sheets and silver serving trays. It was so much "loot," as Robert called it, that it took two trips to get it back to his parents' house. Robert made a list as he inventoried his treasure, saying that he would leave most of it there until we moved to Gainesville. I sat on the bed and nursed my swollen foot. Then Robert's father announced they were taking us out to a fancy restaurant for a steak dinner. On the way to the restaurant, Robert handed me a Trailways bus ticket and informed me that I would be returning to New Orleans in the morning. What?

It would get me back in time for work at Reily's on Monday, he informed me. I felt like he was abandoning me. Then he said he would be staying in Fort Walton Beach for a week or so to help out his parents in their office, since their secretary was on vacation. They would drive him to UF to register for the fall, and pay all his fees. "Pretty cool, huh?" he said.

"But why must I leave tomorrow morning? Why not leave on a later bus?"

"Dad wants to try out his new yacht. It's an all-day affair. I checked the schedule, and we wouldn't be back in time for the last bus."

"But what about your job on the quarterboat?" I protested.

"Oh, I forgot to tell you," he said calmly. "It's over. I'll look for a new job when I get back to New Orleans," as if finding a job in New Orleans would be as easy as buying a newspaper.

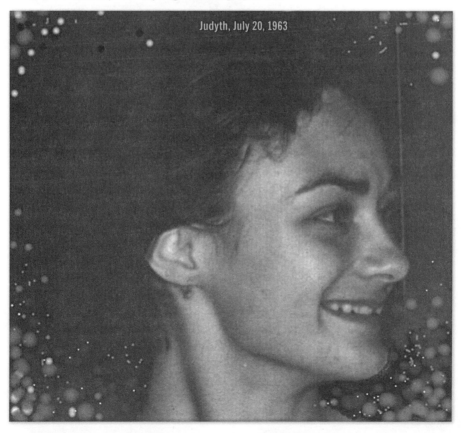
Judyth, July 20, 1963

Sunday, July 21, 1963

Early the next morning, Robert made sure he got one more round of lovin' and then drove us to the bus station. We rode in silence. I was tired, grumpy and sleepy from Robert's endless sexual demands. And he had sent me off without breakfast. Only after boarding the bus did I also realize I was without any money. Robert had me empty my purse's extra change into our piggybank. I was broke. I didn't even have enough to take the Magazine Street bus home.

 At 3:00 P.M., I arrived in downtown New Orleans. I was tired, hungry, and my foot was throbbing from the cat bite. I got my bags and dragged them to the nearest bench, where I rested and examined my aching foot. The cat scratches and the bite on the back of my heel were hot and sore, a clear sign of infection. Not good. Then I dug through my purse, but all I could find were some pennies.

I ran across a collection of photos of friends and family. I hadn't looked at them for a while, so I went through them, wondering where everyone was. I realized that I had no photos of Robert, let alone of Lee. Lonely, I pondered the options: hitchhike, crawl, or hop on one foot? It was only about two miles to my house, so I could walk. If I could remember how to get there! I tried to hype myself up: Come on, Judy! You can do it!

As I prepared to stand up, I realized that somebody was hovering behind me. Then I felt a tap on my shoulder. I turned around and saw David Lewis grinning, with Lee beside him!

"Need a ride?" Lee asked.

"How... ?" I managed to ask.

"David spotted you getting off the bus, and called me," Lee said as he swung my suitcases up off the bench.[7] He explained that he had spent the morning at the training camp shooting his film, and the afternoon processing it in the dark-room in Banister's building.

Lee had advised David to keep an eye on me, but not to say a word — unless I got up to leave — until he got there. I gave David Lewis a grateful hug, then followed Lee to an old car that he had access to for the day, due to his training film project. This was an unusual car called a Kaiser-Frazer, which was discontinued in 1951. It was a roomy and surprisingly luxurious dark green 4-door sedan. I had seen it parked near the Eli Lilly office several times.

"You might want me to take you straight home," Lee said, "if you're too tired. But if you come along with me, you'll get to see Carlos Marcello's plantation."

I said, "Let's go!"

As we rode across the river, I told Lee I hadn't had breakfast or lunch, so he stopped to get me a Dr. Pepper, explaining that there would be a feast once we got to Marcello's. We followed the long road out of town. The landscape was wild and desolate. Green water pooled between towering cypress trees and Spanish moss hung from ancient oaks, adding to the mystery. This was Churchill Farms where, it was said, the Godfather dissolved the bodies of his enemies in tubs of lye, before sliding them into the silent waters of the alligator-infested swamp.

When we arrived, we could see it was actually a working farm, with a barn and tractors, a farmhouse and several outbuildings. This day, dozens of cars were parked willy-nilly in a large unpaved area in front of the barn. Women and children were busy enjoying the feast laid out on picnic tables, while men of all ages paid their respects at the nearby farmhouse. Some stood in clusters outside the buildings. Lee went in the farm house, while I stayed in the car and watched the children play. As they played hide-and-seek in the tall grass beside the barn, I remembered what "Sparky" had told me about seeing Lee at parties when he was just a little boy. I finally understood what he meant. When Lee returned, he moved my luggage over to Dave's car and brought back paper plates loaded with boiled crawfish, potatoes, corn, hush puppies, okra and watermelon.

As I ate this seemingly limitless and delicious gallery of food, I pondered the irony. Robert's decision to send me back to New Orleans by myself was a grave tactical error on his part. It turned out to be a blessing, giving me and Lee extra time together.

As for Marina, Lee had not told her that he was no longer at Reily's, so his days were free while she sat at home thinking her husband was working there.[8] Lee avoided taking her anywhere except to the nearby grocery and the library on Napoleon Avenue.[9] When he needed to be seen out and about with his wife, he had me pose as "Mrs. Oswald."

Monday, July 22, 1963

Lee called me at Reily's and asked me to meet him at 5:00. I was free to leave at 5:00, and climbed into a cab that took me straight to the Roosevelt Hotel, where Lee waited in the lobby. After a delicious meal, we headed upstairs to our elegant room

where Lee had placed a copy of the *Kama Sutra,* the ancient Hindu book about sexual techniques. We decided to try some of those positions. At one point, we even broke a chair. As Lee put it, "The guy from India said it would be fun."

"In the book it looked like it would be fun," I said, as I lay on the floor.

Back in bed and recovering from our adventures, Lee said that he had been even busier since he was dismissed from Reily's. Besides the training film and his normal load of intelligence errands, Lee asked me if I could help him prepare his lecture, which was only five days away. Of course, I agreed.

Tuesday, July 23, 1963

The result of our international sex experiments at the Roosevelt were quite evident on Tuesday when Lee and I met at Thompson's Restaurant, right after work. Frankly, I was in no mood for an encore.

"As much as I love you," I told him. "I'd rather not go anywhere tonight!"

"That's good news," he said. "I can hardly walk."

"I have the same problem," I confirmed.

"The worst part was," Lee said candidly, "when I got home, Marina wanted to make love!"

I had to laugh at the thought, knowing what feats Lee had already performed at the hotel.[10]

"I can't imagine how you were able to rally one more time," I said teasing him.

"It helps because she's cute, all puffed up like that," he replied.

"I have to go to Banister's Building," Lee said. Along the way, he pointed out a man who was striding confidently down the street, well ahead of us. Lee told me to pay attention to the tall figure, who was

dressed in army fatigues. "That's Gerry Patrick," he told me. "He's the guy running Interpen. He's also a big shot in Alpha 66." I was impressed, since my anti-Castro friends in Florida had told me about Alpha 66 and a man named Patrick.[11] As he turned the corner, I got a glimpse of his handsome face and piercing eyes. He had dark, curly hair and a powerful body, but what struck me was his height.

"How tall is he, anyway?" I asked. "Six foot seven?"[12]

"In army boots, maybe," Lee said.

"He doesn't look like a ruthless killer."

"Who told you Gerry was a ruthless killer?" Lee said. "Don't get me wrong. He's had to do things, but he's no psycho. Not that I want you to fall for his charming ways. He's out here for the training camp," he added, "but you might have to talk to him sometime."

"Why would I have to do that?"

"I've been pointing out people you should know," Lee went on, "because things can happen. Situations can come up."[13]

Lee and I reached 1032 Marengo where, after he typed out the last two pages of his science fiction story, "Her Way," Lee brought out his cherished gray-covered book of poetry and short stories by Pushkin. It was all in Russian, which he translated for me in bed where we lay together with our clothes off. Susie was out getting a new battery for her hearing aid, so we had some privacy. Wrapped in a light cocoon of sheets pulled up to our chins, the fan in the window rotating back and forth to cool our faces, Lee read to me from his gray book in fluent, melodious Russian for some time.

Then Susie suddenly knocked on our door. We looked at each other and shrugged. "Come on in, Susie!" I called out. "Just close your eyes!"

"Oh, my goodness!" she said, seeing us wrapped up like that. "Ain't you two the lovebirds, now?"

"We're just reading poetry together," Lee said.

"Oh, dear!" Susie said. "I see! But, what about Robert? When is the Rat due back?"[14]

"He stayed behind in Florida to work for his parents," I answered, "so they'll pay his tuition at college."

Now that she could hear again, I told her about Robert sending me back to New Orleans by myself with no food or money.

"Just more nails in his coffin," Susie commented. "Well, *Gunsmoke* is going to start, so I'll be going."

Lee suddenly sat up.

"It's already 7:30?" he asked.

"Oh, you have fifteen minutes," Susie replied calmly.

"I've got to get home!" Lee said, shooing Susie and Collie out. He then got up to dress.

"I'm working on the film again tomorrow," he said, buttoning his shirt. "And after that, I have to go out of town," he added, putting on his shoes. "Dutz is going to pay for our trip to Spring Hill, so Marina can finally get to see the Gulf, and eat fresh seafood." After a kiss, he added, "Stay where you are, and rest. I'll call tomorrow. If you need anything, let me know. I'll get it for you."

He kissed me again, and left. I thought about the green glass, then about Robert, who had sent me back to New Orleans with so many needs. Lee was so different. He would always try to make me happy, if he possibly could.

Wednesday, July 24, 1963

It was time to do more cancer work. It had rained last night, and the steamy heat of a New Orleans summer day hit me as I left Reily's air-conditioned offices to catch the St. Charles streetcar uptown to Dr. Mary's apartment. There I picked up our medical reports and re-viewed them on the streetcar on my way to Charity Hospital, where I was to meet Dr. Ochsner. This time I had to wait in the lobby until he found time for me, so I continued to re-read the articles. When I finally entered Ochsner's meeting room, he greeted me warmly. I had never seen him so genial.

This meeting was necessary, because it was time to test the Proj-ect's biological weapon on primates. It had worked on the Marmoset monkeys, so it was time to try it on African green monkeys, which were closer to humans but considerably more expensive. These next steps involved the precise work that needed to be done in the monkey laboratory, so others would do that.

I had to discuss the details with Dr. Ochsner. After much of this technical talk, Ochsner said, "By the way, your boy Oswald is going to be a movie star."

"I know he's working on a film," I said cautiously, not knowing how much Ochsner was privy to.

"I don't mean out there," Ochsner said, suggesting that he knew about the training camp. "I mean here in New Or-leans, on TV. Do you have a TV set?"

I assured him that I did not, and he said they had them in the Tulane dorms, where I'd soon be living.

"But go over to Lee's house when we put it on the air," he suggested, "and watch it with his wife. I assume you are friends with her by now." I pondered his comment, but didn't answer. It made me wonder again how much he really knew about Lee's life.

"They don't have a TV set, either," I said. "They're too poor."

"He gets enough money!" Ochsner said stiffly. "Though I am aware he's frugal."

"Sir," I said proudly, "he doesn't spend a dollar of the Project's money unless he has to. He's a patriot of the first order."

"Well, he's all of that," Ochsner agreed. "I don't deny it. I've taken the trouble to look into his records. And I'm thinking about better ways to use his talents."

"He wants to go to college, sir," I said. "Can you help him?"

"Young lady, we want him to stay put for awhile, where he's most useful." Realizing that he was clearly talking about using Lee as a spy, I realized that Ochsner thought of himself as part of the management of that operation, not just a technical resource working for Lee's spymasters.

"So, who am I really working for?" I asked Ochsner bluntly. He shook his head from side to side in dismay and said that I was asking a lot of questions today, as if talking to the wall.

Then, he turned to me and said: "You're working for the foes of Communism." After a short pause, he smiled and added, "I'm not ashamed to say that I would spill every drop of blood I have for my country. And I have always known that you feel the same way."

Ochsner then glanced at his watch, cut me off with a wave of his hand, and handed me a stack of new material to read. "Read these for us, and give us your input as soon as possible. The final step will be with our human volunteer."

"Have you already found one?" I queried.

"You would be surprised," Dr. Ochsner replied, standing up and leading me to the door. "There are many unsung heroes who have bravely stepped forward to accomplish the impossible." Then he added, a little sadly. "There are risks that must be taken for great causes."

"Am I doing all right, sir?" I asked meekly. "It feels strange, not preparing for Tulane yet. I mean, all I've looked at for months now are cancer cells."

"Only two months, and you'll be marching through the doors of Tulane Medical School," Ochsner said confidently. "Are you using Mr. Ferrie's medical library pass?"

"Yes, about once a week."

"Good. Go twice a week, and study there. After you leave Reily's, go every day."

"What will I do for money when Reily's ends?" I asked.

"If you have a problem, ask Mary. She'll lend you money to tide you over," he added tersely.

Dr. Ochsner was obviously finished with our meeting and smoothly slipped back into his charming professional manner, saying "It's been good to see you again." He shook my hand, looked me in the eye, and smiled. Then he told me to hurry with my reports on the new materials, reminding me that they had been flown in from New York, at great expense, just for me to read and distill for everyone. I took the stack of reports and left.

Once outside again, I hobbled to Canal Street on my sore foot. I had meant to ask Dr. Ochsner for antibiotics, but forgot to do so in his overwhelming presence. At last I spotted the Magazine Bus, got aboard, and headed home.

It was now quite dark, and when I got on the bus it was a different driver, who didn't know me. But surely I could recognize my stop, even without Lee. Wrong. We had passed it and I had to ride all the way to Audubon Park, where I caught a bus going back.

Though I asked the driver to call out "Marengo" for me, he forgot, and I ended getting off far beyond my stop. As I walked on my sore foot, my shoe, too tight for my swollen foot, was tearing the big sore open. The sidewalk was so littered with broken glass and trash I couldn't go barefoot. I, who had been so proud because the great Dr. Ochsner craved my opinions, had to face the cold truth: on the streets, I was always getting lost. I was a danger to myself! By the time I reached 1032, humbled completely, my foot was bloody.

Two little boys greeted me at the porch, asking where Lee was. He had often played ball with them and given them piggyback rides. I had played with them, too, but this evening my pain ruled all, and I waved them off. The mail included a postcard saying "Greetings from New Orleans." It was dark, so I hobbled inside to sit down and read it. That's when I got a shock. The card was from Robert! It had been mailed yesterday at 8:00 P.M. from New Orleans!

I was angry and confused. Robert was supposed to be working in his parents' real estate office. He had failed to call to see if I'd arrived

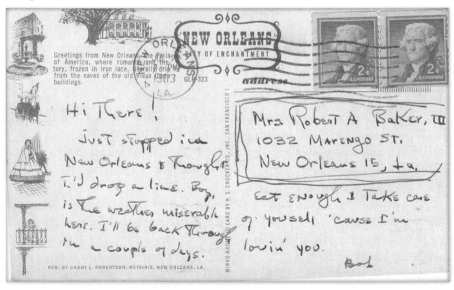

safely — I was used to that — but the postcard said he'd returned and was off somewhere for a few days! Upset, I showed the card to Susie. "Call his parents," she advised. "Maybe they know where he is." So I did, only to be shocked again when Robert answered the phone. He'd just mailed a letter to me, he said, and then he apologized for not calling.[15]

"It would have been decent of you to call," I said bitterly. "But at least, I got a postcard from you. Mailed from here — and postmarked yesterday."[16] Robert coughed, then he said, "I was out partying with the guys for a few days, after they shut down our jobs. We happened to be having a little fun in New Orleans," he went on, "so I wrote you a card. The guys said I'd be stupid to mail it, so I threw it away. I guess somebody found it and mailed it anyway."

"So that's where all the money has been going!" I retorted. "But for us, there's never any time, never any money!"

"I wasn't driving!" he said defensively. "And was I supposed to sit out there in the marsh all summer, and not have a break? Be reasonable — I know you're capable of it."

"And I am capable of cashing a check and buying new shoes, without your permission!"

"You just want to fight, don't you?" he snapped. "If you hadn't bought that ton of tea we didn't need, you'd have enough money for new shoes."

"You know I have a hurt foot. I need new shoes, and I'm getting them!" I ended up slamming the phone down, and in tears started telling Susie what had happened. Then the phone rang.

"It's him!" Susie said. "Don't answer it!" But I did.

It was indeed Robert. "Don't you *ever* hang up on me *again*!" he growled.

Having had quite enough, I did just that.

Thursday, July 25th

One of Reily's salesmen was missing. Monaghan asked me to find him. I looked at his route, started making phone calls, and checked his old expense reports to see where he stayed when he was in that area. Finally, I located him at The Saint Francis Motel. He was quite ill, so Mr. Reily immediately sent a doctor.

My sleuthing pleased Mr. Monaghan, but I was now late for my lab work at Dave Ferrie's apartment. Monaghan agreed to clock me out so I wouldn't have to run back from Dave's at the end of the work day. I left Reily's and headed for Dave's kitchen where I worked with the last of the marmoset tumors. Dave was in the living room editing the film from the training camp that Lee had processed the day before.

Soon Lee arrived with a heavyset Latino man. I stayed in the kitchen and continued working. For all the Latino knew, I was just doing dishes. After a while, Dave closed the blinds and started running the film. Then Lee called to me, saying, "Look, J — there I am!"

I went into the living room to see the film. The first clip I saw showed Lee sitting in a room with a cement floor, demonstrating how to clean and care for firearms.[17] Another scene showed Cubans firing rifles in a maidencane field with Lee walking behind them wearing a cap. When the segment was over, I went back to my lab work and they went back to editing.

From time to time I stuck my head into the living room where I saw other film clips, some with Lee in them. Before Lee left, he came into the kitchen and told me he was heading to the airport. He had to collect some materials for the Project from another city, but would make it back in time to prepare his family to travel to the Russian Seminar at Spring Hill the next day. He kissed me goodbye and promised to call when he could. Then he left with the heavy-set Latino man. When I was finished, I hobbled to the bus stop and headed home.

Friday, July 26, 1963

Just before lunch, I received a long-distance call from Lee. He was still somewhere out of town, and said he couldn't meet me today. I told him it was probably best, because I could hardly walk, and this time it wasn't because of his Hindu gymnastics. My foot had become infected, and (blush!) getting lost recently had made it much worse. "Gee, I didn't notice!" Lee said. "We were so busy with the film."

"I even phoned Robert," I added, "and got the courage to tell him I was going to cash a check for new shoes. When he dared me to, I hung up on him."

"Good for you!" Lee replied. "It's about time you spoke up for yourself. Did you get your shoes?"

"My foot's too sore to walk on — even if I had the time, which I don't."

"I can't help you at the moment," Lee said. "And tomorrow, we're going to Mobile. But you need the shoes now, so I'll send a cab to Reily's when you get off work. Go downtown, make the cab wait, buy your shoes, then get some bread and milk before you go home."

The comment about bread and milk touched me, because Lee had a habit of bringing Susie and me bread and milk on a regular basis.

I protested that the cab would be expensive, but Lee replied that it was Lambert's money, so it was okay.[18]

"I'm in public, but imagine what I wish I could say." With that, Lee hung up.

Meanwhile, Lee's uncle was arranging to take him, his family and assorted relatives to Mobile for his presentation at Spring Hill Seminary.[19]

Saturday, July 27, 1963

Lee would be giving his talk at Spring Hill, so I knew that I wouldn't see him, but I was expecting Robert to return from Fort Walton tonight. That morning I got an urgent phone call from Dave who said he needed help at his apartment keeping some tissue cultures alive, because he could not get back to handle them himself.

I headed to Dave's apartment, being careful because Dave's friends might show up any time. Fortunately, none did. When I was finished refreshing the tissue cultures I called Dr. Mary, who came and picked me up for a working lunch. She looked tired. We talked about the Project, the dying marmoset monkeys and the upcoming injection of the African green monkeys, but we did not mention anything about Lee's trip to Spring Hill.

After lunch, I went back to Marengo Street to do laundry and wait for Robert's return, but he never showed up. I was tired and decided to get some sleep while I could.

Sunday, July 28, 1963

Late Sunday afternoon Robert finally returned from Fort Walton, a day late, not having bothered to call. Trying to make up for his 'Rat' activities, and our fight, Robert took me to the Pontchartrain Beach amusement park, but we didn't go on a single ride because he said they were too expensive. We had an ice cream, then came home again. It was the last time Robert took me anywhere in New Orleans.

Monday, July 29, 1963

On Monday, I quietly got out of bed, leaving Robert asleep, and went to Reily's. When I got to work, I told Mr. Monaghan that my husband was underfoot and needed a job to keep him out of my hair. Monaghan said he could set him up as a commission salesman for Standard Coffee.[20] That would keep him out of the house, pounding the streets. It wasn't much money, but it would be easy duty. All Robert had to do was fill out an application.

Lee called my desk before noon and asked if I could meet him for lunch at Katzenjammer's, a dingy bar so close that no Reily's employee ever wanted to be seen there. I was puzzled, because Lee knew that Monday's were always so busy I rarely even had time to eat. Though he was characteristically calm on the phone, I sensed an edge to Lee's voice I hadn't heard before. Something was obviously bothering him. I told Mr. Monaghan the lunch meeting was important, so he said with a sigh that he would cover for me.

When I arrived at Katzenjammer's, smoke hung in the still air of the dark room and a baseball game was playing on the television set above the bar. Lee greeted me in Russian and called me "Marina" loud enough for others to hear, then quietly explained that Banister frequently had lunch here with his girlfriend, so I would be posing as Marina just in case they came in.[21] When I noted that our food was waiting on the table, Lee said he had ordered it early to save time. He immediately began by reporting on his adventures over the weekend at the Jesuit seminar. The Jesuits were concerned about problems emerging in Nicaragua where their missionaries were preaching Liberation Theology. The Sandinistas were taking up arms against Somoza's repressive government. An insurrection was starting, and the Jesuits were in the middle of it. I knew that Somoza was one of Ochsner's important friends in Central America, so it was obvious what side he would be on.

Lee then said that Bobby Kennedy had sent a Jesuit priest from Georgetown to the conference, and he had asked Lee questions about the training film. This same priest cautioned Lee that there were spies at the conference seeking information about Jesuit activities in Latin America.[22] Both the CIA and the Mafia had asked Lee to advise the Jesuits not to support the Sandinista insurrection. Dr. Ochsner and Banister both wanted Lee to report about any comments the Jesuits might make, so he was, de-facto, one of the "spies" attending the conference. So Lee was walking a dangerous tightrope. I was pleased that Lee was revealing the dimensions of the dangers he was now facing, some of which he was obviously reluctant to tell me about.

After Lee told me about Spring Hill he suddenly said he wanted to spend more time with his daughter Junie, even though he didn't expect her to remember him after he split with Marina. With that sad prediction, he sighed and sank into silence. What was troubling him so? He hadn't even touched his food. I took his hand, hoping that he would talk to me.

"Why such sadness when you spoke about seeing Junie?" I asked.

"I have concerns," he said enigmatically. "Especially for us. I have romantic dreams for us, but I see what is developing..." He paused in mid-sentence and turned his eyes from me. Then he said firmly, and with finality "I'm sorry, but despite my promises, I have to keep some things from you. For your own safety."

"Before you say anything more," I told him, "ask yourself why you would hide anything from me now? What am I to you? Another Marina? Or just like Portia to her Brutus?"

I was referring to the play about the assassination of Julius Caesar by Shakespeare, which Lee and I had discussed, sensitive as we were about the growing dangers to President Kennedy. Brutus puts off confiding in his wife about his plan to help kill Caesar, and she ends up killing herself.

Lee withdrew his hand from mine coldly. He suddenly stood up and glared at me with an anger I had not seen in him before. Then he kicked the chair and walked out. My emotions roared. I was filled with a torrent of inner pain that I had never felt before. "Oh, Lee!" I screamed inside. I bit into my lower lip to distract myself, so I would not follow him. This was not the time to act on impulse.

I was determined to wait at the table and gnawed on my lip to control the turbulence raging inside me. Why had he withdrawn his trust? Why would he not tell me about the dangers he faced? I bit into my lip even harder. Did he think I would betray him? I would die first! Then I tasted blood in my mouth. I didn't care. I was in so much emotional pain, I scarcely noticed.

Suddenly, Lee came back. He quietly slipped into the chair and looked at me. Seeing the blood draining out of my mouth startled him. He said "What have you done to yourself?" and took up a napkin. Carefully, he started blotting the blood off my chin.

"God, Judy, it's still bleeding," Lee said, wetting the blood-spotted napkin in his glass of ice water. I turned my face away from him, rejecting his help.

He dropped the napkin, placed his elbows on the table, and dropped his head in his hands. I heard him hiss through his teeth as he shook his head, his fingers pressed hard against his temples like in a vise. He was in as much emotional pain as I was, but I wasn't doing this to hurt him. My heart suddenly turned to empathy. I reached up and took his wrist. He tried to pull away but I didn't let him. I sought his eyes with mine. When I found them, I saw that they were still filled with anger.

"So you think I would talk!" I said.

"Damn all the women in my life!" he said with quiet venom. "I can't make a scene here, they'll notice. I wish I had never learned to love! It's ripping me apart."

He put some ice cubes into the napkin and gave it to me to nurse my lip myself.

I held the icy napkin against my lip, wondering if I'd have to get a stitch.

"Lucky you didn't have a dagger," he said. "I would've had to take you to the emergency room. God, Judy! All right. I give up."

"No," I mumbled through the napkin, "I don't want you to give up. I'm not trying to win anything. But, I am not your harlot," I concluded, not knowing how he would respond. A long moment of silence passed.

"All right. All right," he said, grasping my point.

Another silent minute labored by, as I pressed the napkin against my bleeding mouth. "I will hide nothing from you. I can't," he said. "But I warn you, you won't like it."

"Let me hold your hand, and then tell me," I said, thinking that I had some inner strength to share with him that would counterbalance what he was about to say.

He looked at me with empty eyes and said, "I think they're going to kill me."

A chill ran down my spine. He said that his efforts to advance in the ranks were being stymied, probably because it was too risky to fully trust a returned fake defector.

"And the more you know," he said, "the more dangerous it will be for you. Past a certain point, I might not be able to protect you. You might even need to denounce me to protect yourself."

"Would they actually risk sending you into Cuba?" I asked.

"Probably not. Not now," he said.

"Because of the lab project?"

"Of course. I know too much. It's not your fault," Lee said. "I was supposed to spy on the project for the CIA, just to keep everybody honest. And then, all the other little things they've had me do, such as these pro-Castro stunts... as if they still want me to prepare to enter Cuba!" Lee laughed bitterly. "What a joke! Both sides would prefer to see me dead first."

"But why?" I pleaded.

"Because I'm not important enough for either side to take a chance on, knowing what I know. If I can't find a way to avoid being expendable soon, then it's over. Now that's the truth. They'll kill me just to get rid of me."

After he let his words sink in, Lee changed the subject from Cuba to Kennedy. He explained that, with Dave Ferrie's help, he'd penetrated to the heart of the groups in New Orleans who were serious about killing Kennedy. Through these contacts, he had discovered an elite circle of even more powerful men, mostly from Texas, composed of politicians, oil magnates, and the military, including CIA officers, whose fanatical patriotism was mixed with monetary ambitions and a lust for power. From their perspective, the country was being held hostage by a President slow to welcome a war which would bring Communism to its knees and reap lucrative benefits for Texas and its power-brokers, such as Lyndon Johnson and others in our government. To them all, Lee Oswald was a pawn to use or to discard as they saw fit. Realizing his fate was in their hands, Lee weighed his options. They didn't look good.

"My concern is this. They want to kill the Chief. And as the only "insider" with a publicly provable motive to shoot him — since I'll look like Castro's agent — they could set me up so easily. I can see it coming."

I put my arms around Lee, trying to comfort him. "I've seen their faces," he went on. "I know names. I know who's behind it. I know about the big group in Texas. But I could prove nothing. I'm snuffed, any way you look at it. So here is where my end begins," he concluded, with a shiver. He buried his face against my hair.

"Can you become indispensable to them?" I asked.

"I'm thinking, I'm thinking!" he answered.

"I'm afraid," I confessed. "Are you?"

"Sure, I'm afraid!" he whispered. "And if I played the Cowardly Lion, and left now, I might survive to tell the tale. But I can't. If I do, Dave will be suspected of bringing in a spy. They might kill him for that. And maybe they'd still find me. As for Dr. Mary, she's been sticking her neck out too far. They might kill her, too. What I need to figure out is how to keep you safe. You, and Junie and Marina." He looked at me with anguish and said regretfully, "I got you into this. I never meant to."

"I asked for it," I said quietly. "But I don't want to lose you!"

"You can't lose me, Juduffki," he answered. "As long as I'm alive, I'm yours."

Better off dead to both sides! What could be done? The power of these people was enormous. With all these terrors rolling through my mind I had to get up and walk back into the world of Wm. B. Reily Coffee Company, leaving Lee sitting there by himself at Katzenjammer's, staring at my blood on the table.

I arrived back at Reily's, still shuddering from Lee's revelations. My mind was in over-drive. I tried to concentrate on my work, but it was difficult. As I waited to clock out, I sat at my desk, and wrote Lee a letter telling him:

Together, today, we live forever. I won't forget!
And I love you forever, dearest beloved, no matter what![23]

I finally understood what it meant to love someone forever, even if death was in our future. Then I got on the bus and went back to 1032 Marengo Street where Robert was waiting for his dinner.

---

1. However, I would have been forced to go to the lab anyway, if our mouse work hadn't been completed there by now. Marmoset work was next, and Dr. Sherman had to bring back the clean bench for that work, which would commence the following week. Lee's necessary errand to Eli Lily's was to make sure a new air compressor for the clean bench was ready and working.

2. Co-worker Mike Kettenring told colleagues that he worked "side by side' next to Lee Harvey Oswald on the production line at Wm. B. Reily Co. (Luzianne Coffee) in 1963. Mike later worked as a news reporter for WDSU-TV, the station owned by INCA's Edgar Stern that sent the crew to film Lee's leafleting. Mike Kettenring later managed three TV stations, and eventually became a Catholic Priest after his wife died. source: http://www.neworleansradiotheatre.org/wdsupersonnellist.html

    An anti-Oswald newsgroup reported Kettenring denied working with Oswald, and that my claim that during summer vacation time, when fewer workers meant even Lee (maintenance) might be asked to help with a production run, was thereby untrue (though that's a non sequitur). But why would those writing a historic record of Kettenring's career in radio and TV make up such a story? Lee's time cards were located in National Archive files with limited access (guarded by the FBI). At my request, Nancy Eldreth persisted, and obtained copies in 2004. I knew I'd written on the cards, but could not recall exactly what, so I wanted copies of the cards. The WC only extracted data from them, failing to publish the cards, most of which have my initial 'J' on them. See these cards, unavailable until 2004, on page 401.

3. Lee, who always looked clean and neat no matter what the circumstances, kept extra shirts and pants in his locker, into which he would change if he had to leave the building for any extended period, so usually, he looked exceptionally well-dressed for his maintenance job at Reily's — but not today.

4. Lee didn't tell Marina he had lost his job until I was forced to leave town September 2nd, to give us even more time together. Marina, early on, told the Warren Commission that Lee worked at Reily's until the end of August (WC Vol. 1, p. 20) — six additional weeks.

5. Lee's time cards were located in National Archive files with limited access (guarded by the FBI). At my request, Nancy Eldreth persisted, and obtained copies in 2004. I knew I'd written on the cards, but could not recall exactly what, so I wanted copies of the cards. The WC only extracted data from them, failing to publish the cards, most of which have my initial 'J' on them. These cards were unavailable until 2004. *See Appendix for more on Lee's time cards.*

    Later, Lee cleaned out his locker and handed me the key to Reily's, which I gave to Monaghan.

6.   In fact, Dave Ferrie had laughed about Robert's scheme to cheat the transit system, giving me a wooden nickel so I'd always "have some change" that Robert couldn't stash away.

7. David Lewis always knew how to contact Lee because he was still regularly informing him about new Cuban refugees coming into town. While he had spotted me at the bus station, as was typical for me, I had failed to notice him while surrounded by others — just as I hadn't noticed Carlos Marcello in the midst of his group as they passed me at the Cathedral.

8. See endnote #4, above.

9. Marina, early on, told the Warren Commission that Lee worked at Reily's until the end of August (WC Vol. 1, p. 20). Lee only pretended to job hunt: unemployment checks were

ostensibly used to care for his family.

10. McMillan now reported that Marina feared Lee didn't find her attractive anymore because of her pregnancy. For the first time, Marina wanted sex more often than Lee did — interesting to me because Lee had promised to never force sex on Marina again. It seems he kept his word.

11. Gerry Patrick is best known today as Gerry Patrick Hemming.

12. I later wrote a book called "Six Foot Seven" basing the adventures of the Hungarian revolutionary hero in the book on Gerry Patrick Hemming's profile. All but a few pages of the book were stolen in 2001. However, I also have correspondence with my literary agent in 1967, Ruth Cantor, mentioning the book which I wrote while living in Saltillo, Mexico

13. Lee said, "Concerning Gerry, just so you'll feel safe around him, if you ever have to deal with him, just remember three things, and you'll get along." Years later, after I told Gerry the three 'secrets,' he finally began confiding in me. I have blind-copy emails from him, sent when he wrote to his Interpen organization.

14. I also told Susie how Robert apparently spent $220 in the past three weeks, on God knows what. I was urged by Susie and Lee to open the bank statement and learn the truth. Though he was spending freely, he would no longer let me write checks without permission, because I'd "overspent" $3.00 on the tea.

15. Bob's July 24th letter mentioned he wouldn't be home until at least Friday, the 26th. He actually arrived late Sunday, the 28th. He enclosed the July 20, 1963 newspaper article from the coffee social with the comment, "the mistakes made by the paper are mistakes given them by my mother." The newspaper article said both Robert and I were English majors, which wasn't true. Bob's 2nd wife wrote newsgroups in 2000, stating Bob told her we lived in Florida by July 20th. She was unaware, I suppose, that I kept thorough records of Bob's absences and working hours as evidence, such as this letter, plus all Reily check stubs, etc., and that Bob had a terrible memory, for he returned to New Orleans, staying more than another month, until September 2nd. However, he did very little work. I have his Standard Coffee receipt showing he worked two weeks in August for them, though he sold nothing (and spent $25.00). He was also unsuccessful working another two weeks for Colliers Encyclopedia. As a computer-specialist and scientist, however, Bob had a brilliant, distinguished career.

16. I still have both the letter from Fort Walton, and the post card.

17. At least two important people (HSCA investigator Bob Tanenbaum and CIA hitman Colonel William Bishop) would view the training film before it vanished from HSCA possession. Tanenbaum stated that it had been found at Georgetown University and ceded to the HSCA.

18. Lee used "Lambert" — probably to avoid using Shaw's name in public.

19. McMillan, who had described Lee as a defeated man retreating from reality a few pages earlier in *Marina & Lee*, now presented him as an over-confident braggart who didn't quail at lecturing a bevy of college graduates at a prestigious Jesuit seminary. In fact, Lee did give talks "all the time" — a statement McMillan repeated to indicate Lee was lying. It was no lie: he'd given short, right-wing lectures to student groups at four different colleges, once or twice a week, for weeks. He had been teaching guerillas how to handle firearms. He led debates about tactics in meetings. He was currently preparing for radio and television events just around the corner, and would soon write a letter about pre-planned media events before he was officially invited to engage in them. Concerning Lee's Spring Hill lecture, McMillan wrote: 'Lee spoke for half an hour' (p. 429), ignoring other reports, and Lee's own hand-written description of a 70-minute speech.

20. I kept one of the Standard Coffee pay-slips Robert got for a week of work, during which he sold nothing whatsoever. His pay was only $3.25! Money remained a problem because Robert had spent hundreds of dollars while away on his Gulf job. I have previously published all of our bank records providing evidence of this.

21. I was told by Lee that Guy Banister was having an affair with his secretary Delphine Roberts.

22. Lee said the spies were working for Aristotle Onassis, a Greek shipping magnate.

23. Full text of letter and photo in Appendix.

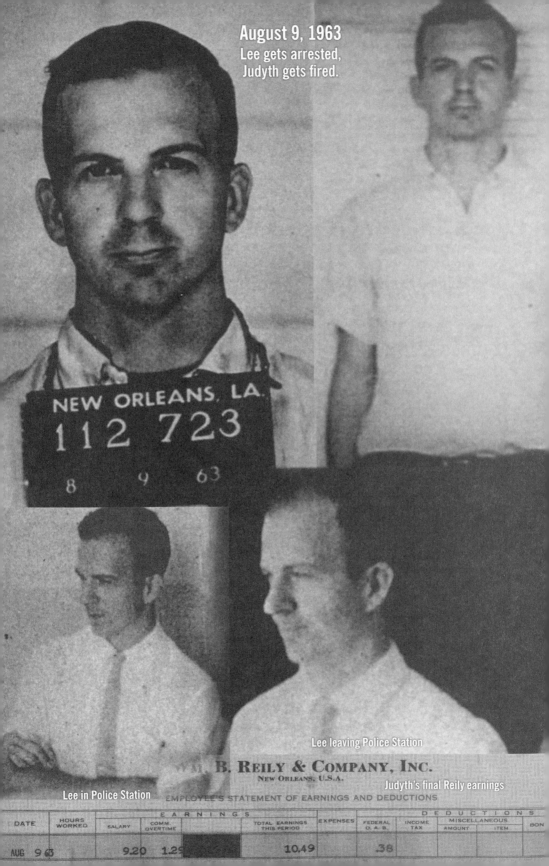

August 9, 1963
Lee gets arrested,
Judyth gets fired.

NEW ORLEANS, LA.
112 723
8 9 63

Lee leaving Police Station

Lee in Police Station

WM. B. REILY & COMPANY, INC.
NEW ORLEANS, U.S.A.

Judyth's final Reily earnings

EMPLOYEE'S STATEMENT OF EARNINGS AND DEDUCTIONS

DATE	HOURS WORKED	EARNINGS					EXPENSES	DEDUCTIONS				
		SALARY	COMM. OVERTIME		TOTAL EARNINGS THIS PERIOD			FEDERAL O. A. B.	INCOME TAX	MISCELLANEOUS		BON
										AMOUNT	ITEM	
AUG 9 63		9.20	1.29			10.49		.38				

Chapter 21

Fired

Monday, July 29, 1963

When I reached 1032 Marengo, about 6:00 p.m., Robert was sitting at his typewriter thinking. As I entered, food was on his mind. "I couldn't find any of our stuff in the refrigerator," he began. "It all seemed to belong to Mrs. Hanover. Are you always eating out? No wonder we've run short of money."

"I buy groceries on Mondays," I said. "That's why the fridge is empty."

"Here, I brought you something, honey," I added. "Red beans and rice. It's traditional on Mondays in New Orleans." I handed him the small grocery sack that held the lunch Annette had given me. He ignored my gift and asked if I'd deposited my paycheck today, adding that he had not found a deposit receipt, and pointing out that this meant I hadn't deposited it on Friday.

I suddenly realized that he had been going through my things. And his comment about the refrigerator made me consider how the combination of his calculating mind, his need for control, his obsession with money and his idle presence meant I had to be really careful about the little details in my life. He was beginning to suspect something was going on that he was not privy to, and that irritated him.

I had many free meals, thanks to both Lee and Dr. Mary, but I couldn't tell Robert about that. The Project was now both secret and dangerous. Robert had to be kept in the dark for everyone's safety.

I told Robert that, yes, I deposited my paycheck, and had kept none of it for myself. Then, he noticed that I was wearing comfortable new shoes.

"So how did you manage to buy those new shoes for yourself?" he demanded.

"I borrowed money from work!" I told him quickly, as I felt the cut in my mouth bleeding again. "I'm getting a raise, it'll cover it.¹ I hurt my mouth. I can't talk anymore!" I said suddenly, as I tasted blood and reached for a paper towel.

Robert's scowl vanished. He got up from his typewriter and came over to me.

"Gee, I should have noticed! What happened?" he said with a mixture of concern and curiosity. I avoided answering his question directly and switched subjects, saying I could not even kiss. "Well," he answered, bending down and kissing me in the small of my back, "As long as your other end is still okay!" in his most adorable voice. Old one-trick Robert! I would have laughed if I could. Then he handed me five dollars and said: "Hope you don't mind going to the store by yourself. I want to finish this short story." I nodded my agreement.

"Be sure to spend it wisely," he instructed me, as he began typing again.

As I picked up my purse, I pondered the absurdity of his telling me to carefully spend five lousy dollars. Compared to Lee's fear of being terminated by professional killers, Robert's self-centered world was amusingly small. I opened the kitchen door to leave.

"Be sure and get Skippy peanut butter!" he called out.

As I closed the door, I juxtaposed the priorities of the two men in my life: One was worried about saving his family from death, and the other wanted peanut butter. At least Robert's problem would be easy to solve.

Tuesday, July 30, 1963

I got on the bus as usual. Lee was waiting for me, so I sat down next to him. The swelling in my lip had increased overnight, and it was really sore, so I had brought a cup of ice to chew on. Consequently, my speech was slow and somewhat slurred. Lee said he was concerned about the swelling and that it might be infected. Then we had the following exchange:

Me: "I gave up on the cut staying shut, so I sewed a couple of stitches in it."

Lee: "Ouch! I know how much that hurt. He should have taken you to a doctor."

Me: "He didn't know. He was writing a short story. I didn't want to interrupt."

Lee: "So you wouldn't interrupt me if I sat there, writing a short story?"

Me: "Kiss you, maybe. You'll be a good writer."

Lee: "Even with my execrable spelling?"

Me: "That's only dyslexia. I just found out about it, in a journal. The brain sees letters upside down or backwards. It has nothing to do with your writing talent. Some famous writers have had the same problems."

Lee: "Really? They punished me for it. It's why I hated school."

Me: "Well, they didn't know about dyslexia, back then. Boys have it more than girls. Especially smart boys. It's a brain wiring problem. For example, Col. Doyle is brilliant, yet he can't smell a thing! Does that mean he's stupid? No, of course not. It's bad wiring! Well, you're not stupid. You just have to work around it. How you conquered Russian, with its weird letters, I don't know."

Lee: "I just kept trying."

He was obviously relieved by my explanation of his problem.

Lee then told me he and Dave had been advised that an FBI raid on the training camp was imminent and he was trying to stay away, so he would not get arrested and be exposed as a militant anti-Castroite. He knew his absences might seem suspicious to the others, so Dave was going to spread plausible excuses. They were forbidden to warn anyone, because they might have to explain how they knew in advance. I was starting to see the daily dangers that an undercover agent had to live with.

I arrived at Reily's and began working on an unusually high pile of credit problems. I tried to avoid phone calls due to my painful swollen lip. After about an hour, Mr. Monaghan showed up and started teasing me about my swollen lip. Then, in a voice loud enough for others to hear, he said I needed to go have it examined.

Once he was sure everyone within ear-shot thought I was going to the doctor, Monaghan pulled me aside and said I needed to go straight to Dave's apartment. They were behind schedule and Dave had spent the night near the training camp, so he had not been able to do any lab work. Monaghan said he would cover my work-load at Reily's. Another blasted emergency!

I took the bus to Dave's apartment, which was supposed to be empty during the week, especially today, since Dave was still at the training camp. At about 9:30, I entered the apartment and heard an unusual sound. I froze and listened. Someone was in the house. The sounds were coming from Dave's bedroom, where the door was partially open. I tiptoed down the hall and looked inside. There, I saw a young man sprawled on Dave's bed amidst a jumble of sheets, magazines, newspapers, clothes and pillows. He was snoring. I figured it was probably Dave's new lover, who was spending more and more time there.

I was not going to be able to grind up monkey tumors in the kitchen without him knowing about it. My larger concern was that he might wake up at any moment, and find me there. With the project getting so dangerous, having someone discover me in Dave's apartment at an odd hour might blow the cover. I quietly gathered up the things I needed to take to Dr. Mary's, and left.

As I rode the Louisiana Avenue bus to Dr. Mary's apartment, I felt my frustrations percolating. My time to do the Project's work was being whittled away on all fronts. I could no longer read and write reports at 1032 because Robert was literally underfoot. Meanwhile I was stretched to the limit working at two demanding jobs and trying to deal with the needs of two very different lovers. And now I was not even able to do the emergency work because Dave's young lover was sleeping in his bed all day!

As soon as I arrived at Dr. Mary's, I wrote her a note to vent my frustrations, complaining about the presence of Dave's lover, then turned my attention to the tissue cultures. There was so much to do that I wondered whether I would be finished in time to get back to Reily's.

Before long, Lee arrived at Mary's apartment carrying a blue duffle bag. He had made an appearance at the training camp early that morning, staying a few hours to make it appear that he was unaware of the raid to come. Now he cleaned himself up in Mary's bathroom and put on a fresh shirt. Soon, Dr. Mary arrived. She had spent the morning performing surgery at the Crippled Children's Hospital, but remembered to bring antibiotics for my mouth, at Lee's request. I took them immediately. Seeing the amount of work, Dr. Mary and Lee pitched in. Around noon we were mostly done, except for a few tasks that Lee wasn't trained to do.

"I'll wait for her, so she won't have to go home by herself," Lee said to Mary.

He then asked me, "Are you feeling better?" hoping the antibiotics were helping. My mouth was still so sore that I was reluctant to speak any more than absolutely necessary, so I mustered a faint smile and fluttered my eyelashes at him. Dr. Mary caught my gesture and laughed.

"There's only one life. You two go on," she said. "I'll finish up."

I called Reily's and took a sick day. Lee and I then took a taxi from Dr. Mary's apartment to The Roosevelt Hotel. It was another wonderful afternoon of love. Lee's tenderness drained all of the tension that had been building up in me, even without kissing my wounded mouth. We talked more about our future together, and fed our dreams. We next took a taxi to a local Piggly Wiggly grocery, to teach me the way, because I had to stop going to Winn-Dixie: Junie now recognized me, due to her trips with Lee to my place. Lee feared she might call out if she saw me at Winn-Dixie. Lee then dropped me off at Magazine and Marengo, and I walked home.

Wednesday, July 31, 1963

I was at work next morning, as usual, when Lee called and said the FBI had raided the training camp across the lake, and that he was safe.[2] I had just finished typing a letter for Mr. M and as I handed it to him, I mentioned the raid.

"I already know," Monaghan said. "Mr. Reily told me." Then looking at my letter, he added "It won't be long now before I have a real secretary again. We're going to try out a new girl in your spot this afternoon." Reily's hadn't wasted any time: they'd placed an order for an ad in the *Times-Picayune* to replace me the moment Lee was fired.

"You know, I'll miss those rich timbres of yours on the Dictaphone," I told him.

"What I do for my country!" Monaghan muttered. "You'll go on to your lab after you show her what's in your desk.³ Then I'll work with her."

We'd tried out a few girls already, but they hadn't matched Mr. M's needs, so a new ad mentioning good pay had been placed in the paper. An attractive woman appeared who seemed bright, was a good typist, took shorthand and had mature phone skills — a real secretary he wouldn't have to cover for. And she didn't have a sore, swollen mouth slurring her speech.

Monaghan told me that my last day at Reily's would be August 16th, so I no longer feigned dedication to his credit investigations. He knew we were in high gear over at the lab, so I would be gone virtually every afternoon. I started training my replacement in the mornings, and worked through lunch so the staff would see me at my desk when they returned from their lunch break. Then I headed to Dave's to work on the Project.

That day, Lee was already there, and I started training him on how to keep the bioweapon alive outside the lab, so it could be transported to Cuba via Mexico City. Several hours later, I returned to Reily's by myself to clock out and then headed to the city library on Tulane Avenue, where I met Lee again to see if we could figure out how to get quickie divorces in Mexico. We discussed thoroughly, for the first time, where we might go and how we would live after Mexico City.

Our whole lives were ahead of us. Lee was only 23, and I was barely 20. We began to dream of a future together. We had high goals, like world peace and equality among all races. We believed in the essential goodness of people. Perhaps we could become a husband-wife team. I'd become a doctor and he would become a social worker or anthropologist, writing science fiction on the side. We'd work among the primitive and deprived people in the Yucatan, or in Central America, and explore ancient ruins. We'd follow Kennedy's Peace Corps ideals and perhaps explore the whole world that way. For the present, Lee needed to remain committed to his mission.[4] Much was at stake. We planned our escape and researched how to get divorced in Mexico.[5]

We roamed through Tulane's wonderful Latin American collection, full of questions. Soon some intriguing books stirred our interest: one was about the ancient Maya, with old photos of a primitive village in the Yucatan, not far from Chichen Itza, which we had already selected as the first Mayan city we wanted to explore. Now Lee asked, again, "Would you really go to a place like that with me? We could live in that village awhile."

"Nothing would thrill me more!" I told him, truly excited at the prospect.

"I need to get in better shape," he told me. "I did get some workouts at the training camp," he added, "but I need to do more. Marina doesn't like the outdoors, so that's made it harder."

"It wouldn't take much to get you in perfect condition," I told him. "Your legs are like steel. I've had problems myself, getting the right kind of exercise."

"What about hunting?" he asked.

"For survival, sure. Besides, I ran wild with my cousins — they hunted a lot."

"So you would be able to cook, in the rough?"

"Be it snake, gator, or frog, I can make it taste like chicken," I told him. "I can render fat from white grubs to grease a skillet if the meat is too lean. Then there are cat-tails. As for ant eggs — "

"I get the picture," Lee said. "How did you learn all that?"

"It started in Girl Scouts. We had a 'survival' campout. I cooked a hamburger meal for our troop on a stove made from a big can. 'Twas a great success, until they learned the hamburger was made out of earthworms."

"So, you wouldn't find a walking tour of Mexico a life threatening experience?" Lee's eyes were shining with hope.

"I'd go today, right now, if I could!" I said.

"God, I thank you!" Lee said, throwing his eyes up to the library's ceiling. "You've sent me the woman of my dreams!"

We started to kiss, but then a librarian came around the corner.

"Does Robert like camping?" Lee asked. "Did he take you places like that?"

"He took me spelunking, scuba diving, and rock hunting. He talked about being a writer, and he played the guitar. But he changed. Now he says he won't have time to do any of those things anymore."

"Why not?"

"He said, 'I do like collecting calcite specimens. As for the guitar, I learned those songs so I'd be able to play them for you. But now that I've got you, I need to concentrate on becoming a millionaire.'"

"Good God!" Lee said. "That's amazing."

"He was angry when he said it," I admitted. "He also said, 'If I hadn't done those things with you, you wouldn't have married me. So I did them.' Then he said, 'We have to give up time-wasting frivolities, because the real world runs on money. You'll be grateful when we're rich.'"

"Well," Lee said, "he'll have a wench on his knee to spend it when he's old."

Lee then asked about fishing, which he loved. I waxed eloquent, for I'd been fishing since I was four years old with parents, uncles, cousins and grandfathers.

"We'd be able to get fat on fish, along the rivers," Lee commented.

"We'd need a good knife or two, and camping equipment." I put in.

On we talked, about getting educated in Mexico, exploring Mayan ruins, and then looking for ways to make the world a better place.

Of particular interest to us was a new book, *The Lost World of Quintana Roo*. We pored over it in Tulane's quiet, august library. Lee told me there was a CIA presence in Merida — and a university there, too. Strictly speaking, Lee never indicated that we would live in Merida, but it was the most well-known city at that time in the Yucatan. Lee and I planned to marry, probably after visiting Chichen-Itza, and stay in a fine hotel. No plans, however, were carved in stone.[6]

Thursday, August 1, 1963

I trained my replacement in the morning, and left Reily's after the lunch break to meet Lee at Mancuso's restaurant. When I arrived Lee was drinking coffee with David Lewis and Jack Martin, so I sat down at a table as far away as I could and waited. When they left I joined Lee, who noted disapprovingly that David Lewis had started smoking.

As we walked out, Lee pointed to a well-dressed young Cuban hurrying down the sidewalk toward Banister's office. This was Carlos Quiroga. Lee considered him a wild card, because Quiroga's father was locked up in one of Castro's prisons and his mother still lived in Cuba. With the kind of family pressure that could be put on him, he could be forced to spy for Castro — even though he proclaimed that he hated the man.

As we walked toward the French Quarter, Lee described what happened during the raid at the training camp. A handful of Cubans and a couple of ultra-rightwing gringos had been rounded up, and the FBI had confiscated arms, ammunition and explosives. Much of the con-

The Raids on the Pontchartrain Training Camps

On August 1, 1963, a headline on the front page of New Orleans's largest newspaper, *The Times-Picayune,* shouted "Cache of Materials for Bombs Seized." The story reported the FBI had raided a house in nearby Lacombe, Louisiana, and had confiscated 2,400 pounds of dynamite, twenty 100-pound aerial bomb casings, appropriate fuses and strikers, plus 50-pounds of the key ingredient needed to turn gasoline into a napalm fire-bomb. All of this happened at a modest pink cottage, nestled in the quiet pines along the north shore of Lake Pontchartrain, halfway between Mandeville and Slidell. The FBI cited vague legal language from the Neutrality Act to justify the raid, but did not mention the word Cuba nor the eleven men that they had arrested that day.

The property turned out to belong to William McLaney, who was financially involved, with his brother Mike, in hotels and casinos in Havana before Castro came to power. Among the eleven men arrested in Lacombe were a known mobster, an arms merchant and mercenary, and nine Cuban exiles, four of whom had previously been caught by U.S. Customs loading an airplane in Florida with bombs destined for targets inside Cuba. All eleven arrested in Lacombe were promptly released by the FBI without being charged and even the fact that they had been detained was covered up by the FBI. (Their identities were eventually discovered when a copy of a list that the FBI had sent to the U.S. Customs office was given to D.A. Jim Garrison during his JFK investigation.)

Seldom mentioned is the second training camp on the adjoining property that was immediately evacuated upon hearing the news of the McClaney raid. This second camp had been set up earlier in the summer to militarily train anti-Castro Cubans, under the direction of soldiers-of-fortune Gerry Patrick Hemming and Frank Sturgis, who directed the military training of anti-Castro Cubans in Guatemala in preparation for the Bay of Pigs invasion. Today, Sturgis is best remembered for his role in the Watergate affair which abruptly ended Richard Nixon's presidency. The trail of all this militant anti-Castro activity on the north shore of Lake Pontchartrain led back to 544 Camp Street. But the owner of the property where the second training camp was located has never been publicly identified. (See *Deadly Secrets* by Warren Hinckle and William Turner, pp. 223-229.)

fiscated material had already found its way back to the third floor of Banister's building, and the FBI had released all of the trainees. Most had quickly fled the state.

Outwardly Banister displayed anger over the camp's raid, but the real anger was in the hearts of the anti-Castro Cubans who saw it as a cruel betrayal by JFK. Instead of helping them retake their homeland as he had promised in Miami following the Bay of Pigs invasion, JFK had ordered the raid of yet another of their training camps. It stoked their hatred of him.

But how did the FBI find the secret training camp? Who gave them the location? Lee told me that he did. He had been instructed to give them a map showing the camp's location. Lee explained the game inside the game. Giving the map to the FBI would prove that Lee was a trusted FBI informant. That would provide him some protection in case a problem with the police developed after he got arrested.

"Arrested?" I asked. "Must you get arrested?"

"I have to," Lee explained. "It's necessary to buff up my pro-Castro image."

He would soon be passing out Fair Play for Cuba flyers and defending Castro's Cuba on radio and TV, to make it safer to courier the bioweapon to Mexico City without suspicion. To disarm anti-Castroite distrust before his pro-Castro campaign began, Lee planned to muddy the waters by making an open show of offering his expertise to them. Of course, after Lee began his pro-Castro activities, the anti-Castroites would be out for blood. They would assume that Lee was probably the one who had betrayed them, but Lee hoped his courage — and obedience — would be noticed, raising his value to his handlers.[7]

"It's a problem, Juduffki," Lee said. "I have to put on my 'Hands Off Cuba' demonstration next week. They won't let me put it off awhile — even though it's practically on top of the raid."

Atop the danger, Lee needed to get arrested through a staged event — that long-planned fake street fight. Then he would pretend he didn't have enough money to post bail, so he would have to spend the night in jail. That would assure newspaper coverage.

Lee said he had arranged for three of his Cuban friends to show up when he handed out "Hands Off Cuba" flyers on Canal Street, and create a commotion by yelling at him, shoving him and stomping on the flyers he was handing out. It was all for show and there was no real danger. If, however, angry anti-Castroites who were not privy to the charade joined in, he could find himself in the hospital instead of jail.

"Why not just put off the demonstration awhile and let things calm down?" I asked hopefully.

"I tried," Lee said. "Originally, they wanted it this week, to look like a protest against the camp. They didn't seem to care that every Cuban in town would want to beat me up."

"So, you got the date changed?"

"I got it delayed until August 9th," he said.

That gave him a week to find somebody else to blame. The problem was that Banister *wanted* Lee to take the blame, since it was more evidence to support his pro-Castro image.[8] Lee finally persuaded Banister that it was too risky, and they should finger someone else. Fortunately, a real pro-Castro spy had infiltrated Banister's operation in New Orleans. His name was Fernando Fernandez.

Lee got several of Banister's informants to help him spread the word about Fernandez, since Dave Ferrie was still out of town. Banister told Lee to convince these informants that he thought Fernandez was part of the anti-Castro team, so he gave him a map; but after the raid he learned that Fernandez was really the FBI's spy. Lee told his comrades he was afraid of being blamed for what Fernandez had done. So the disinformation machinery kicked in, and Lee's team started spreading rumors in the bars across New Orleans.[9]

"We're going to blame this guy," Lee told me. "We'll send out enough threats to scare him back to Miami. Once he's gone, we'll spread new rumors that confirm he left town because he was the FBI informant. That will get me off the hook."

We finally reached the Acme Oyster Bar on Bourbon Street just as the lunch crowd started to filter in, and savored the blast of air conditioning. My mouth was still sore, but oyster stew is nice and soft! We ate quietly and conversed in simple Russian.[10]

A waiter came to our table and told Lee, "The boss wants to see you over at La Louisianne." Without a word, Lee got up and went next door. When he returned, I sensed the tension in his mood.

"I have to go out to the Town and Country Motel," he told me bluntly. "Marcello's people need me to run an errand. I'll meet you at Dave's after that."[11] It was another "favor," as they call it, but I started to see that our free meals weren't so free, after all.

"I don't mind doing it," Lee said. "While I'm out there, I'll talk to Marcello's people about finding this Fernandez character. They'll help us flush him out, so we can finger him."

Once Fernandez learned he was on the hook, he fled New Orleans on August 8th and went back to Miami, where both anti-Castroites and authorities were "alerted" that he was the spy who had infiltrated the training camp.[12]

The "blame game" successfully protected Lee from suspicion just in time. When Lee hit the streets of New Orleans on August 9th with his pro-Castro literature, the buzz amongst the anti-Castro crowd was all about Fernandez being the camp's infiltrator. Today I fretted, hoping Fernandez would get blamed in time.

"Would your three friends defend you?" I asked.

"Well, Bringuier has to play the 'let's pretend' game," Lee said. "He knows who I really am but, of course, he can never tell."

I knew who Carlos Bringuier was by that point.

He ran one of the anti-Castro Cuban groups in town, and wrote blazing letters in the local newspapers about the need for stronger anti-Castro actions in U.S. foreign policy. Lee said the CIA considered Bringuier an asset. He had a stack of anti-Castro picket signs in his store on Canal Street ready to wave in front of the cameras whenever big-shot politicians came to town. Though young, Bringuier was experienced in street demonstrations, the perfect actor to create the aura of real conflict, so Lee recruited him to lead the fake attack.[13] He had also helped Lee spread the rumors about Fernandez.

> ### Carlos Bringuier
>
> Carlos Bringuier was an anti-Castro Cuban in New Orleans in the summer of 1963. He is best known for his involvement in several events with Lee Harvey Oswald that summer. He and Oswald were both arrested following a scuffle between the two men that occurred on a sidewalk on Canal Street on August 9, 1963, an event which called attention to Oswald's handing out "Fair Play for Cuba" flyers.
>
> Later that same month, Bringuier appeared on a WDSU radio show with both Lee Oswald and INCA's Ed Butler, who confronted Oswald on-the-air with his reported defection to Russia. Publically Bringuier and Oswald were political enemies, but this may have been a ruse, since it was later discovered that Oswald had given Bringuier his copy of the U.S. Marine Corps training manual and that Bringuier and Oswald both had offices at 544 Camp Street. It should also be noted that the NOPD officer who arrested Bringuier and Oswald on August 9th later told Jim Garrison's investigators that he felt the Oswald-Bringuier fight was a staged incident.
>
> Bringuier was born in Cuba in 1934 and was educated as a lawyer at the University of Havana. He left Cuba shortly after Castro took power in 1960, residing first in Guatemala, then in Argentina, and finally settling in the United States in February 1961.
>
>
>
> Shortly after Oswald was charged as JFK's assassin, Bringuier was questioned by the FBI and subsequently testified to the Warren Commission. In 1967 Bringuier became of person-of-interest to Jim Garrison's investigation of the JFK assassination.
>
> In 1993 Bringuier wrote a book in Spanish called *Operacion Judas*.

"Nobody will get close enough to hurt me," Lee repeated. "Don't worry!"

Sunday, August 4, 1963

I was in the Catholic playground located about halfway between our apartments when Lee wrote a letter to the FPCC as he sat on a bench there (perhaps that's why the letter is a bit sloppy). He wrote to the FPCC's leader, V. T. Lee, that "Through the efforts of some exile *gusanos* [anti-Castroites, who Lee called 'worms'] a street demonstration was attacked and we were officially cautioned by police. This incident robbed me of what support I had leaving me alone. Nevertheless thousands of circulars were distributed..."

This letter, predicting the long-planned attack, was written five days before Lee's demonstration.[14] Lee had taken Junie for a walk, and I played with her while he wrote the letter, which I later mailed for him.

Friday, August 9, 1963

Lee's staged pro-Castro drama would occur today in the heart of the Central Business District, in the 700 block of Canal Street. On my way to work, Lee gave me some of the flyers he would be handing out and asked me to deliver them to attorney Dean Andrews when he arrived at the demonstration, in case the police confiscated all of Lee's flyers. Lee said he was planning a second demonstration at the Trade Mart later in the month. I looked at the flyers and noticed many of them were not printed properly: the header was too far down the page. I decided to do my part for Lee's cause and make them nicer. During the normal lunch break at Reily's (when few others were around), I trimmed the worst of the flyers using Reily's paper-cutter, and put the colorful trimmings in a trash can near the paper cutter. A few of the flyers were so spoiled they could not be saved, so I threw them away as well.

Since I had apparently worked through the normal lunch break, I took a "late lunch" and headed to Canal Street with the stack of extra flyers about 2:30 P.M. I found Lee wearing a short-sleeved white shirt, brown tie, slacks and sporting a sandwich board about Castro. A doz-

700 block of Canal Street

en people were already standing in a cluster and glaring at
him. I approached Lee, and said,
"I'm so worried for you, honey,"
glancing at the men.

"Well," he answered cheer-
fully, straightening the placards,
"I'm going to be all right. Dave's
back in town, just a few blocks
away, and Carlos will be here
any minute, so don't worry!"[15]

Lee Oswald wearing "VIVA FIDEL" placard on Canal Street

Lee told me to go ahead and give the flyers
to Dean Andrews.[16] Andrews was grossly overweight and always wore sunglasses, so he was an
easily identifiable character. I spotted him approaching from almost a block away.

When he arrived, I could see that his shirt was
soaked with sweat and he appeared ready to have
a stroke. As I approached him, he said that he just
had to see "the fireworks." I handed him the flyers, saying they were from Lee. He took the flyers,
flattened them, and put them in his briefcase.

"Gonna watch?" he asked.

"No," I said nervously.

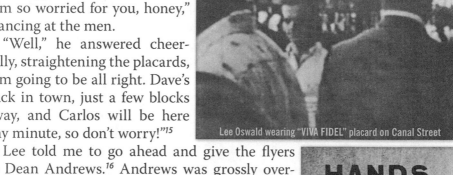

HANDS
OFF
CUBA!

Join the Fair Play for
Cuba Committee

NEW ORLEANS CHARTER
MEMBER BRANCH

Free Literature. Lectures

LOCATION:

L. H. OSWALD
544 CAMP ST.
NEW ORLEANS, LA

EVERYONE WELCOME!

Dean Andrews

Dean Andrews was a colorful attorney in New Orleans who admitted to knowing Lee Oswald in the summer of 1963 and who testified to both the Warren Commission in 1964 and in Jim Garrison's Trial of Clay Shaw in 1967. His statement to the Warren Commission that "Clay Bertrand" contacted him the day after the JFK assassination to go to Dallas and represent Lee Oswald, ultimately led D.A. Jim Garrison to discover that "Clay Bertrand" was actually Clay Shaw, a prominent business man in the New Orleans trade community.

Andrews helped many Cubans with immigration problems and was widely associated with Mafia boss Carlos Marcello, who some call his client. His law office was in the Maison Blanche Building on Canal Street, next door to INCA, which is where Judyth spoke to him and handed him a stack of Lee Oswald's "Hands off Cuba" leaflets on August 9, 1963.

His testimony to the Warren Commission took place in New Orleans on the morning of July 21, 1964, only hours after Dr. Mary Sherman's murder was discovered.

"You're his girlfriend, right?" Dean stated in a voice that was more of a statement than a question. I told him I was married, and so was Lee.

"That makes no difference in this town," Dean Andrews replied, laughing.

At that moment, Carlos Bringuier and two of his friends made their entrance and immediately began heckling Lee to direct everyone's attention. Lee was remaining calm under the hot sun and pretended to ignore them. Then, what had been a disorganized group of bystanders suddenly moved in to surround Lee. He gave me a sidelong glance that meant "get out of here," as the crowd engulfed him.

Being so short, I couldn't see what was happening to him, but I realized Lee would worry about my safety if I stayed, so I began walking

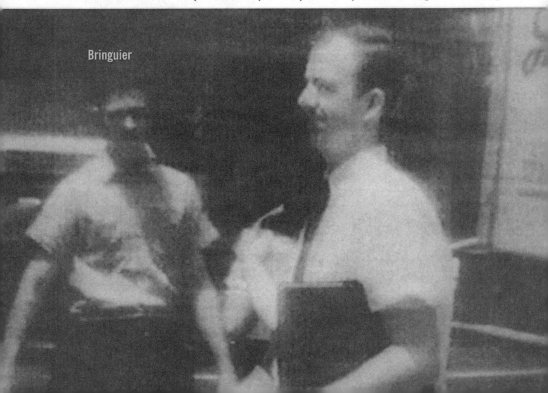

Bringuier

away as fast as I could. I heard the Cubans shouting terrible curses at Lee with voices full of hate and scorn. Suddenly I saw a policeman and waved urgently at him.[17] He came over to see what the problem was. I told him there was some kind of commotion on Canal Street. A big crowd had gathered, and people were screaming at each other. I was worried that somebody might get hurt. The policeman headed to Canal Street, and I hurried back to Reily's. It was all I could do.

I had been working in Dave's lab all week, and this was the first time I had even been in Reily's during the afternoon. As I walked down the aisle, the big room hummed with the clickety-clack of billing clerks working with typewriters and adding machines. It sounded like business as usual, until the typing slowly stopped and the murmuring began. I saw Mr. Monaghan sitting at his desk with Mr. Prechter at his side. Both men were silently staring into the work room as I approached. Monaghan and Prechter together: now, that's a bad combination! My instincts immediately went on alert. As I walked toward Monaghan, I saw the look on his face and realized I was in trouble.

As I reached Monaghan's desk, he simply said "You were seen with him," in a deep vibrating voice that hissed with anger. Then he held up a crumpled yellow "Hands Off Cuba" flyer: "And you left this in the wastebasket. What in hell were you thinking?"

Monaghan stood and motioned for me to follow him into the dreaded glass cubicle. Mr. Prechter followed us in with my personnel file in

Bringuier

Police

Oswald

his hands and closed the door. "I'm asking you to sign this statement which says you have decided to resign," Monaghan said. "They're cutting you a check right now."

"And you're going to be docked for taking all those long lunches," Prechter chimed in spitefully. "You were only supposed to do that on Fridays. Where have you been spending Reily's time?"

"We'll talk about that later, Al," Monaghan said to Prechter. "She's not leaving town or anything. Go get her check."

Prechter walked back to his secretary's desk which was next to our area in the big room. I turned to Monaghan and said, "I'm sorry. I didn't think anybody would notice."

"Judy," Monaghan moaned, "I have trouble equating your famous IQ with the fact that you actually spoke to Oswald in front of some thirty or forty people."

"It was past lunch hour," I protested. "I didn't think anybody from Reily would see me."

"Well, the new secretary and I were out that way, and the little snitch saw you," Monaghan said, removing my things from his desk and placing them on top of the half-desk. Then he ran both hands across his neatly combed dark hair to collect his thoughts. "For your information," he continued, "Mr. Oswald was arrested a few minutes ago. They'll find out he used to work here. Everybody will be talking about it. I have to get rid of you before anyone who saw you with Oswald links you to the company. I have no choice." Then in a soft voice, he said "I have to admit, I'm going to miss you, lousy typist though you are."

As I prepared to leave, I took comfort in the fact that the girl I had been training had already gone for the day and was not there to witness my humiliation. Mr. Prechter returned and handed me a check.

It was for only ten dollars. "What? Where's my pay for this week? What have you done to my paycheck?" I protested angrily.

"Please keep your voice down," Mr. Prechter said condescendingly. Then he told me that I'd been gone all afternoon on Tuesday, Wednesday and Thursday, so my "long lunches" would need to be evaluated. For the moment, my paycheck had been docked, but if the matter was resolved in my favor a final check would be mailed to me. Monaghan listened silently, as I tried to hold back tears of outrage.

"What about my husband?" I blurted out. "What am I supposed to tell him?" Visions of Robert exploding in anger played in my head. What could I do? I could not ask Lee for money. He was in jail. I couldn't tell Robert I was fired, because he would want to return to

Florida; and the Project wasn't finished. If I refused to go with him, he would start following me around town to find out where I was going. Tenacious as he was, he could cause real problems for everyone, including himself. My mood changed from grief to fury. This was madness!

As I turned to leave, my head clerk, Annette, slipped me a photo of herself with her fiancé. She didn't dare say a word. I then walked out of Wm. B. Reily Coffee Co. for the last time, passing a gallery of sad faces that I would never see again. I headed back to 1032 Marengo determined to say nothing to Robert about losing my job.

To Judy,
a real sweet girl,
remember me at Wm. B.
Come to my wedding
when you see my picture
in the paper. Love
Annette

Saturday, August 10, 1963

I awoke on Saturday morning knowing that Lee was still in jail and had spent the night in the hands of the Commie-hating New Orleans police. I was sick with worry that I could not share with my husband.

I knew Lee wanted to spend the night in jail to make sure it was in the newspapers, so he did not post bail. But he did leave $70 with Marina for when he did want to be released. The problem was that he did not want his Russian speaking wife going to the police station to bail out "the Communist," since it would make him even more of a target for the local police. Therefore, he had to find someone else to deliver the money.

On the morning of the demonstration, Lee had gone to the Murret's home to talk to Dutz about picking up the bail money in the event he got arrested, but Dutz was out of town at a Catholic retreat. As for his Aunt Lil, upon arriving at their home, Lee learned that she was in the hospital recovering from an eye operation. Despite his tight schedule Lee immediately went to the hospital to visit her, but did not tell her of his upcoming plans because he did not want to worry her.[18]

So, on Saturday morning, Lee did phone his cousin Joyce Murret and asked her to pick up the bail money from Marina and deliver it to the police station, but she refused. Only then did Lee realize what deep shame his arrest had caused his family. Later, in the middle of Saturday afternoon, an attorney named Emile Bruneau, who was a "business partner" of Lee's uncle Dutz, came to the police station and posted bail. Lee hoped that such an obvious link to the Mafia would go unnoticed, and by-and-large it did.

What was I doing that weekend? Very little, except ironing Robert's clothes and worrying about Lee. Robert was at home lounging about. He read and read, and took me to bed. Between these events, I managed to peruse Susie's newspapers, listened to the radio and watched the local TV news programs for news of Lee. I fretted constantly. I even got Robert to go for a walk, so I could steer him by Lee's apartment, hoping I might get a glimpse of Lee reading on his porch, but Lee wasn't there. I called Dave Ferrie's apartment, but there was no answer. I called Dr. Mary, but she didn't answer either.

I was so tense I couldn't eat. Robert noticed my fidgety state and concluded that I had PMS. I was glad he had a diagnosis that would explain my behavior and satiate his curiosity.

Then, late Saturday afternoon, Lee called Susie to say that he was okay! Susie summoned me with a wave of her hand. She quietly handed me the phone, as Robert continued to read his book about Hitler in the bedroom. Lee said he hadn't had a minute of privacy until now to call. He also said that he heard my job at Reily's was on the rocks, and he did not want me to tell Robert. On Monday morning, I should get up and leave at my normal time, but go to Rev. Jim's Novelty Shop. I could tell Robert later that I had found another job.

"You'll only work at Reverend Jim's one or two hours a day," Lee said, "then we head to Dave's to work on the Project. Between the Reverend and me, we'll make sure you'll bring home enough money to make ends meet, and you'll be able to account for your absences every day." After I agreed, Lee added, "I have to go to court on Monday to pay my fine, so I'll see you at the Reverend's on Tuesday morning!" I was amazed at how cheerful he sounded, given that he had spent the night in jail and was about to appear in court.

Ironically, the loss of my job at Reily's freed me up to work long hours at Dave's lab and still have plenty of time to spend with Lee. Robert's characteristic lack of curiosity about my work helped the situation. He didn't even know where Rev. Jim's was for nearly two weeks, and that was only when I asked him to drop me off on his way to his job at Standard Coffee.

It turned out that Robert preferred lying around our apartment, reading and writing short stories, to pounding the pavements of New Orleans for Standard Coffee in the August heat, which Susie was quite happy to point out to me. But Robert wasn't worried about finances, because I was making enough money to keep us afloat.[19]

Monday, August 12, 1963

I left my apartment at the normal time, but headed to St. Charles Avenue to take the streetcar "to work." My first stop was Dr. Mary's apartment. She had called yesterday, asking if I had a few hours to spare. I expected to be involved in some intricate laboratory procedure at her apartment. Maybe I'd be able to corner her about my internship for

September.[20] I even brought the application forms for the internship with me, so she could sign them.

But when I entered Dr. Sherman's apartment, I saw about a hundred caged mice. They had been there for nearly two weeks, and they were starting to reek. I had been in her apartment during the last two weeks, but I had not seen the mice because she had kept them in her bedroom with the door closed. She said they were backup, so we could revert back to the most recent generation of mouse cancers in case a significant problem arose with the marmosets before the transition to African green monkeys. Since no problem had emerged, and the African green monkeys were developing cancers, as hoped, the mice could now be removed.

This needed to happen immediately. Normally, someone like Dr. Mary would have paid the maintenance man a couple of bucks to help her, but that would have created a witness and possibly raised questions about why she had so many mice in her apartment. So I was "asked" to help, because I was already part of the Project.

We lined the back seat of her car with newspapers to protect the upholstery and started loading the ten cages of mice. As we worked, Dr. Mary said she would be taking them to a new building on Ochsner's campus that was specifically for lab animals. She said that she had delayed moving them there earlier, because such a sudden influx of mice would be noticed. Now there were enough other animals there, and it would be OK. As we quietly carried the cages downstairs to her car I told Dr. Mary I looked forward to entering medical school in the fall, and hoped she would still allow me to work under her in the bone lab.

"Don't worry, I want you," Dr. Sherman told me. "And I've got a grant, so I can afford you."

When we got back inside, I gave her my completed application papers. All she had to do was sign them and turn them in. She set them on the counter and then drove me to Dave Ferrie's apartment, where I went inside alone to retrieve the last of the monkey tissue cultures. Dr. Mary informed me that from this moment on I would focus on blood work of cancer in humans, in anticipation of our tests with the volunteer. Then I asked her to drive me to the Tulane Medical School library. I did not want her to know I was headed to Rev. Jim's, which was close enough that I could easily walk there.[21] As I was about to get out of her car, she turned to me, smiled graciously and took my hand. "I know you've been worried about Lee," she said. "And I have an idea that some divorces are about to occur. Will that interfere with your plans with us?"

"I don't think so," I said as politely as I could, not knowing how much she really knew. "Lee said that he would try to get his people to transfer him and then let him go to college." Lee was, in fact, telling people this myth, but it was to mask our secret plans.

"I hope it works out," she said with a gentle smile and drove away. As I waved to her, I gauged her curious question and pregnant comment.

After checking out some journals I needed to review at the medical library, I finally went to Rev. Jim's. It was as if nothing had changed. It was hot inside the cluttered shop, and a fan helped keep the five or six desperate people who were there to earn their daily bread from melting. The lady in charge recognized me, and she invited me to join the others painting "New Orleans" on dozens of ceramic Gators and Mardi Gras masks. As I did, I wondered about Lee sitting in court and waiting for the judge to sentence him.

Tuesday, August 13, 1963

I spent the morning at Tulane's medical library and, when I was finished, I returned to Rev. Jim's and spent several hours painting "New Orleans" on souvenirs. At about 1:00 P.M., Lee arrived. The lady in charge quickly remembered Lee was the one who painted the words backwards. Realizing we were together, she moved us to another room, a hot, poorly-lit storage room filled with sculptures of gnomes, dragons and other mythological objects. She instructed us to paint the horses for a carousel and then left. Realizing we were alone, Lee and I looked at each other and fell into each other's arms for a long, deep hug we hoped would drain both the stress and the excess love out of each other. It was the first time I had seen him since the demonstration.

When we finished our affectionate embrace, we started painting the papier-mâché horses. Lee told me about all that had happened to him since I had seen him last. On Friday night, the Cubans posted bond and went home. Lee was then interrogated by the police. They pinched his face and ears, and struck him, but Lee stayed cool. He endured the mistreatment without complaint and simply answered their questions.[22] When Lee finally got served the usual jail food, he saw they'd scooped up some dirt and dead roaches, and sprinkled it on top. Lee said, "Ah, Roach à la mode."

This steady, stoic attitude, combined with dark humor, had its effect on both the inmates and the police.[23] The next day Lee asked to speak to the FBI, and an agent showed up and took his report.[24] Lee's cousin had refused to go to his apartment and pick up the bail money he had left with Marina, so Lee had his uncle Dutz's lawyer, Emile Bruneau, post bail, and he was released.

Lee also told me of his decision on Monday to sit with the blacks on their side of the courtroom, while he waited to pay his fine. "They're my black brothers and sisters," he said, "I wanted them to know we were equals."[25]

On Sunday night, his uncle Dutz visited him at his apartment on Magazine Street.[26] Dutz expressed his disappointment that Lee had been arrested and noted Fidel Castro's photo pinned to the wall, chiding Lee in front of Marina. He then told Lee to straighten out his life, get a job, and start taking care of his family. Lee said hearing such criticism from his uncle was a heavy blow for him.

"It almost felt physical," he said. "I had grown up in tough neighborhoods. All around me kids got in trouble, they got arrested. I stayed clean. It was a point of honor. But now — !" Tears welled up in Lee's eyes as he spoke.

Miserable from the tongue-lashing he'd received, Lee then walked with his uncle out to his car, leaving Marina and Junie inside. There, they continued to talk. Afterwards, Lee said that things were "not as they seemed." Dutz turned to him, placed his hands on Lee's shoulders, and said, "I know, son." Lee was stunned.

Lee asked him, "Do you understand what I am really all about?"

Dutz replied, "Do you know how long Marcello and I have been friends? He told me, son." Dutz then put his arms around Lee and hugged him.

"As for your wife," Dutz said. "I don't know what she knows." Then he continued, "I felt if you trusted me enough — sometime, somehow — you would confide in me, and you finally did. So I'm telling you, son — and don't forget it — I've known since you arrived in town what you're about. And I'm proud of you."

Lee told me, "He is the father I never had."

Then Lee showed me a newspaper clipping about his arrest.

His plan had worked. He had gotten the initial press coverage for the media blitz to make him into a pro-Castro sympathizer. He'd already been filmed for the news reel cameras by Ochsner-friendly WDSU-TV, and he was filmed again at court, but because Jim Garrison had returned to town, a lot of footage wasn't used: everyone was afraid Garrison would notice, and Lee might get a long jail sentence instead of a fine, since that action would please the anti-Castroites.

Pamphlet Case Sentence Given

Lee Oswald, 23, 4907 Magazine, Monday was sentenced to pay a fine of $10 or serve 10 days in jail on a charge of disturbing the peace by creating a scene.

Oswald was arrested by First District police at 4:15 p. m. Friday in the 700 block of Canal while he was reportedly distributing pamphlets asking for a "Fair Play for Cuba."

Police were called to the scene when three Cubans reportedly sought to stop Oswald. Municipal charges against the Cubans for disturbing the peace were dropped by the court.

The next demonstration would have to be a quick one, Lee said, before the police showed up. Clay Shaw's associate, Jesse Core, would make sure the TV cameras covered it at the Trade Mart.[27] I volunteered to call yet another TV station, hoping Lee could get on more than one channel before he had to disappear, for it was important to leave before the police could arrest him again. As Dr. Ochsner had told me in our last meeting, "Your boy Oswald is going to be a movie star."

But Lee saw a dark side to all of this. He realized that his reputation in New Orleans would be systematically destroyed. Yes, Dutz knew his little secret, but the rest of Lee's family, friends and associates remained confused and ashamed of his actions. How could he live in New Orleans after this? Was anybody planning a future for him? Was he being made disposable? I think Lee's handlers underestimated him, because he was bitterly aware of these developments. We discussed them.

In the days ahead, Lee and I were busy every day preparing for the final test of the bioweapon on a human. We also had to prepare Lee for his trip to Mexico City where he was to deliver the bioweapon to others for transport into Cuba. But we were also two young people in love, so we cherished our time with each other.

---

1. Lee told me to tell Robert that I was getting a raise, to blunt his objections about buying the shoes. Lee arranged for it, and indeed, the raise is reflected on my last paycheck, which was for a single day of wages, as the rest of the week's wages had to be calculated in a petition, since Personnel wanted to dock me for "late lunches" that Monaghan had allowed me to have without being docked in pay. The settlement was made in full, and was deposited in the bank in New Orleans in the form of an entire week's wages. Because of the raise, the four-day total ended up being slightly more than a week's wages before the raise.
3. I was still having problems with the cat bite on my foot, so the antibiotics helped both.
4. The training camp was in St. Tammany Parish, north of Lake Pontchartrain, near the town of Lacombe. *New Orleans Times Picayune*, August 1, 2, 4, 1963.
5. Mr. Monaghan had been advised that the cancer project was at its most important stage. I don't think he knew much else.
6. A little later, when Lee believed things were going awry, we added hiding time for a year in the Cayman Islands to our basic plans.
7. I had recalled a newspaper article from May 1st, seen in the public library when Robert and I had gone there to look up marriage laws: the glamorous platinum blonde movie star, Jayne Mansfield, divorced weight-lifter Mickey Hargitay — overnight — in Juarez, Mexico. When we visited the Tulane library that week, we looked up the article.
8. Lee's intentions to marry me left a few traces in the record. Lee's Mexican Tourist Card Application form is a good example. Castro had been closing Catholic schools and jailing Catholic priests and nuns in Cuba since 1959. Anyone who wished to enter Cuba to stay, as has been suggested by many as the reason Lee filled out this form, would never place "Catholic" on this form. *(See Appendix.)* Lee was raised by a Lutheran mother and had never been a Catholic.
   Why did he do it? Because I was a Catholic girl. We planned to get a 'Jayne Mansfield' quickie divorce, and then to bribe a "corrupt priest" (one who would not waste time posting banns, or insisting on baptismal certificates) to marry us in Mexico. Lee's application was filled out in early September. A copy was to serve as helpful 'evidence' of Lee's Catholicism.

9. This is why Lee publicly approached Carlos Bringuier at Bringuier's clothing store, (the DRE front for the anti-Castroites in New Orleans), giving Bringuier his beloved *Guidebook for Marines* manual to show Bringuier's DRE friends as 'proof' that Lee wanted to help the anti-Castro cause — yet a few days later, Lee openly handed out pro-Castro literature, to which Bringuier and his two designees responded with a show of violence. The so-called 'fight' that ensued was all on Bringuier's part: Lee

Lee Oswald's *Guidebook for Marines*

did not even respond when he was struck. Lee was upset that his Marine manual had to be sacrificed for this to work: I am upset that Bringuier sold it, instead of giving it back to Marina, knowing he was not supposed to keep it forever. I testify that Bringuier was aware of Lee's true identity, but because he had to play a role, too, he was trapped into denying that he had cooperated with Lee Oswald in a ploy. I hope Mr. Bringuier will someday admit to the truth.

10. Lee originally wanted to hold this demonstration a week later, but Banister told him the staged 'fight' had to be scheduled while District Attorney Jim Garrison was out of town, apparently doing his duty with the National Guard. Banister insisted that Lee's activity, if Garrison were in town, would have incited the D.A. to use the new and untested Communism Control Act against Lee to gain more popularity against a "Communist." But that could uncover the whole ploy. Instead, Banister — the committed racist — wanted Garrison to test the new law against the Southern Conference Educational Fund (SCEF) which openly supported local desegregation and Martin Luther King. Banister got his way: the new law was used as an excuse to raid and ruin the SCEF office in early October, with three arrests, and Garrison right on top of it.

11. Meanwhile, between August 2 and 8, Dave, Banister, Hugh Ward, and Lee worked furiously, with a mandate Banister said would please Bobby Kennedy, to pin down the Pro-Castro agent Fernando Fernandez as the informant on the FBI training camp raid, deflecting anti-Castro anger from JFK by laying the blame on Fernandez. When I first told investigators that Bobby Kennedy was privy to Banister's doings and was involved in some of them, in 1999, they were stunned. I gave leads to researchers, and since 2000, evidence has kept emerging helping to verify my statements (ORINS veteran Jim Phelps called these efforts "Project Freedom").\

12. It was the last time I dared pose as Marina even for a short time, since she was now so obviously pregnant.

13. "Please," I implored in Russian, "What do you have to do with him again?"

    Lee looked around, then moved closer to me. "Sometimes I have to do what Little Man wants," he told me. "But, my darling wife," he said softly, playing with a lock of my hair, "…as I've told you before, 'Either the world can be an influence on you, or you can be an influence on the world.' I decided not to let 'the world' influence me. The world I grew up in. That's why I chose to be self-taught, rather than endure school."

    "When you played hooky?"

    "Big time. But I was caught and incarcerated in New York for my indiscretions. I was a smart ass — the despair of my mother."

    It was the first time I'd heard Lee refer to his mother in a positive way.

    "I thought she could care less, if you got an education."

    "But I wasn't supposed to fail a grade, Juduff. That would have humiliated her. I didn't attend enough days, so I was supposed to be held back. Ma was smart: she used her connections. They gave out fake information so it'd be hard to trace the real me, when we moved here."

    "Why New Orleans? Why didn't you go back to Fort Worth?"

    "It's Yankee to say 'New Orleens,'" Lee corrected me.

"I'm sorry," I said.

"My mother did it to fix my records up," Lee said. "She could get it done here. My uncle had the contacts. But Dutz valued education, so he was mad at me."

At this time, Lee became aware that his mother was dating organized crime members (friends of his uncle) in New Orleans and Covington. Meanwhile, Dutz said Marguerite was getting prematurely gray with worry over him.

"To make me appreciate the value of an education," Lee said, "he set me to work after school doing menial labor." There were errands, sweeping and mopping floors, and washing cars and windows. Years earlier, Dutz had worked himself half to death doing back-breaking work at the docks, until he learned the skills of bookmaking. He wanted none of that for his children, or for his nephew. All the Murret children would attain college educations. Dutz instilled in Lee an ardent desire for the same, telling him, just before Lee moved to Texas with his mother, that he could easily join the Mob in the Dallas area, but he hoped Lee would set his goals higher. The fallout from his work in Marcello's restaurants was that the local Mafia trusted Lee. So today, he had to take something out to Town and Country from La Louisianne.

14. By early September, Fernandez' photo was known to every anti-Castroite of importance, and his spying days in the USA were over:

Ferrell's chronology calls the Pro-Castro spy 'Fernando Fernandez Barcenas.' Fernandez was soon aware he was being watched, and was in trouble. Realizing he might have to flee the U.S., Fernandez alerted the Cuban ambassador to Mexico of his dilemma, possibly considering a flight back to Cuba through Mexico. The M. F. Chronology notes: "Fernandez writes to Carlos Lechuga, the Cuban ambassador to Mexico, that they have to be alert from ...(8/1/63) until August 8." (CD 984a, pp. 2, 11)

Fernandez may have learned that Lee's demonstration was to be held on the 9th, and that Lee was anxious to lay the blame for the raid on him before then. If Fernandez could be forced to flee, he would be unavailable to defend himself against accusations in New Orleans, buying Lee time to convince anti-Castroites that he was truly anti-Castro and supportive of anti-Castro causes, while Fernandez had betrayed everybody. To this end, Lee visited some hot spots in the Cuban refugee community, such as Carlos Bringuier's clothing store (also a front for his anti-Castro activities) and the nearby Habana Bar. Lee and his heavyset Cuban friend (name may have been "Carlos") made sure to be seen and remembered as being compadres. When Lee and his supportive Latino friend visited various bars (the Habana Bar visit survives in the Official Record :WC Vol 11, pp. 343, 356; WC Vol 25, p. 671; WC Vol 26, p. 358), they spread Fernandez' name:

On August 7, 8, or 9, at the Habana Bar Oswald orders a lemonade and his companion orders a tequila. There is some dispute over the price of the tequila. Oswald appears drunk and gets sick around 3:00 a.m. to 4:00 a.m. Orestes Pena describes events. (M.F. Chronology)August 8, 1963 (Thursday) - A Miami publication, "Diario Las Americas," prints a picture on September 4, 1963, of Fernando Fernandez, a pro-Castro spy who infiltrates a secret New Orleans anti-Castro camp. [M.F. Chronology]

15. Later, after Lee's murder closed his mouth forever, Bringuier denounced Lee as a pro-Castro spy, but he never said anything like that in August, 1963.

16. Anthony Summers reported that Lee predicted the Aug. 9th attack in his Aug. 4th FPCC letter in *Conspiracy*, p. 303. What Summers did not mention was that Lee deliberately wrote the FPCC, regarding the attack, and police action, to link the FPCC with his arrest, as all of Lee's mail was regularly opened by the FBI. This gave the FBI fodder to use against the FPCC, as Lee was posing as "a communist." In 1961, David Atlee Phillips had the CIA run a domestic destabilization operation against the FPCC, with the aid of the future Watergate conspirator, James McCord. Later, the FBI infiltrated the FPCC. Ref: John Newman, *Oswald and the CIA* (New York: Carroll and Graf, 1995), pp. 236-244.

17. Lee was referring to Carlos Bringuier, not Carlos Quiroga.

Letter and enclosure from Roy Jacob to William Gurvich dated April 15, 1967 mentions the results of Carlos Quiroga's polygraph. Quiroga lied — answering "No" — to the following questions:

- You have said you were in Lee Oswald's company only on one occasion. Isn't it a fact that you were in Oswald's company on a number of occasions?

- In the late Summer and early Fall of 1963, Lee Oswald is often seen in the company of a stocky, unusually powerful man of Latin descent. Do you think you know the name of this man?

- Is it not a fact that at that time Oswald was in reality a part of an anti-Castro operation?

- According to your own knowledge, did Sergio Arcacha know Lee Oswald?

- Did Guy Banister?

- Did any other persons whom you know of?

- Prior to the assassination of the President, did you ever see any of the guns which were used in the assassination?

The polygraph indicated that Quiroga lied about all these questions. Many others also lied about what they knew about Lee in New Orleans.

18. Carlos Quiroga would later take the flyers to Lee's "office" at 4907 on a pretext.

19. Lee was arrested in the 700 block of Canal Street by two NOPD officers on Aug. 9, 1963. One was Patrolman Frank Hayward who later became a homicide detective for the NOPD and with detective Robert Townsend, investigated Mary Sherman's murder.

20. His visit is on record.

21. There was a bit of fallout: I mentioned hand lettering so much that Robert decided we should create a stack of fancy, hand-lettered Christmas cards to sell to Reverend Jim's store. At night, we began making Christmas cards with hand-lettered parchment inserts that Robert wrote in Greek, copied from a Greek Bible, but we never made enough to sell.

22. I needed the appointment (despite plans for Lee and me to disappear) to make everything seem business as usual until the critical moment.

23. I worried that if she knew about Rev. Jim's, she might offer financial help, and I didn't want her to do that, because by now there was a real chance I'd never show up at Tulane in September. If Lee and I got divorces in Mexico, and stayed there, I didn't want to owe Mary money I might never be able to pay back.

24. Martello's statements to WC.

25. Lt. Martello, who had helped interrogate Lee for the NOPD testified that he would bet his head on a chopping block that Lee didn't kill Kennedy.

26. John Quigley, source.

27. Carlos Bringuier told the Warren Commission about Lee's radical gesture:

    Mr. Bringuier: ... in the court you have two sides, one for the white people and one for the colored people, and ...he sat directly among them in the middle, and that made me to be angry too, because I saw that he was trying to win the colored people for his side... That is one of the things that made me to think that he was a really smart guy and not a nut.

    Bringuier said Lee's sitting with the Negroes was a mere propaganda trick, but Lee's friend, George de Mohrenschildt revealed Lee's true intentions:

    "Lee was indeed all wrapped up in his work, books, his ideas on equality of all people, especially of all races; it was strange indeed for a boy from New Orleans and a Texas poor white family, purely Anglo, to be so profoundly anti-racist. "Segregation in any form, racial, social or economic, is one of the most repulsive facts of American life", he often told me. "I would be willing any time to fight these fascistic segregationists — and to die for my black brothers."

28. The date was Sunday, August 11, 1963.

29. Mention of Jesse Core's role is in D. Chandler's "The Assassin's Trail," *Westword*, November 25-December 1, 1992, p. 15

Lee Oswald at the
WDSU TV studio

CHAPTER 22

ON THE AIR

Wednesday, August 14, 1963

The day started out at Rev. Jim's where Lee met me. We had a lot on our minds in those days. For one thing, we had to figure out how to camouflage the bioweapon for transportation to Mexico City and Cuba in a way that would not be noticed. We spoke to Dave from a pay phone, and he told us to expect a trip out of town, to test the weapon on a human subject. The "volunteer" would be a prisoner from Angola Penitentiary, but he would be transferred to the state mental hospital in Jackson, Louisiana where we could perform our tests in secret.[1]

Then Lee went to Banister's office, where he picked up some unpublished medical articles for me. He also needed to retrieve the flyers that I had given Dean Andrews for safe keeping, since all the others had been ruined or confiscated. Dean Andrews was not about to be seen handing Lee a stack of pro-Castro flyers for his upcoming Trade Mart demonstration, so Carlos Bringuier agreed to send his right-hand man, Carlos Quiroga, to Lee's apartment with the flyers. This was the same nattily dressed Cuban that Lee had told me not to trust. One of the men who ran the training camp drove Quiroga to Lee's apartment with the flyers, but Lee wouldn't let Quiroga leave right away: for over an hour, he probed him, testing his loyalties. "I still don't trust him," Lee told me, "and neither should you."

We headed deep into the French Quarter to the Royal Orleans Hotel, one of several we had come to enjoy.[2] We were anxious to be alone, and wasted no time on formalities. We were madly in love and being together was all that mattered. Later, I told

Royal Orleans Hotel, early 1960s

Lee that I wanted to stroll down Royal Street and see St. Louis Cathedral. As soon as we reached Royal Street, we saw a sign for WDSU-TV studios. The real world closed in on us again with this reminder of Lee's upcoming event at the International Trade Mart this Friday — to be televised by WDSU. He wanted no more arrests, so we had to time everything just right: the TV cameras would film him handing out his "Hands Off Cuba" flyers, then he would leave before the police arrived.

To that end, he asked me to back up Clay Shaw's man by making an anonymous call to WDSU-TV to report the demonstration Lee would soon hold at the International Trade Mart. WDSU had already agreed to send the film crews; they just needed a phone call to pretend they had received a real tip. He also asked me to call WWL-TV and tell them the same thing.[3] Lee didn't think WWL would actually send a crew because they were not part of the deal, but if they did, it would add credibility to his event.

Next we discussed the trip to Jackson, which would give Lee practice transporting the bioweapon in preparation for the trip to Mexico City. He told me that Dave Ferrie and Clay Shaw would drive him up to Jackson to deliver the Package, and that the volunteer would be injected at that time. Several days later, he would drive me up to Jack-

son to see if the bioweapon worked.

Leaving the Royal Orleans, we headed to Jackson Square to walk through the historic streets. It was late afternoon. The weather was beautiful. As we strolled through the historic streets, the St. Louis Cathedral came into view — a magnif-

icent building. Lee began telling me about its ghosts and legends. We were walking under its portico, admiring the colonnades, not noticing the people passing us. Lee was carrying some drawings I'd offered for sale at Reverend Jim's (they bought one), and I was loaded down with the research papers from Banister's office. We then passed a group of men, but I had eyes only for Lee. That was a mistake. A tall man (as tall as Lee) broke from the group and grabbed Lee's sleeve.

"Hey, Oswald!" he demanded. "What's going on?" He was a florid-faced man, impressive in his expensive, pin-striped suit. He oozed brutal power and authority — and he was upset. The group had stopped and turned, and began staring at us. Carlos Marcello was in their midst. The Godfather!

"So, Frank," Lee said, "what's the problem?"

"The problem is your girlfriend, Oswald." Frank then addressed me. "We all want to know, young lady, why you ignored Mr. Marcello, and didn't say a word, or acknowledge him in any way, when he tipped his hat to you."

"He isn't wearing a hat!" I managed to blurt out. I hadn't noticed that Marcello had tipped his non-existent hat at me!

"Don't smart-mouth me!" Frank snapped. "What's the matter with you? Why didn't you show Mr. Marcello some respect?"

"I-I didn't see him!" I stuttered, truly terrified.

"You didn't see him? How could you miss him?"

"I don't know, but I did. I was just looking at Mr. Oswald, sir. Please give Mr. Marcello my apologies — as fast as you can! I'm very sorry. I'm awful at recognizing people!"

"She wouldn't recognize *me*, if she didn't see me every day. She also can't remember where she lives, half the time. For eleven weeks, we rode the bus together, but when I quit riding with her, she didn't know where to get off, and got lost," said Lee, appealing to Frank's sense of humor. "She's an absent-minded professor," Lee went on. "She's good in science and art, but she doesn't notice a thing around her."

"It's true!" I chimed in. "I got lost in my own high school once."

Frank smiled, and returned to Marcello and his men. He began talking to them, adding some dramatic gestures. A minute later, the six or seven men, including Marcello, exploded with laughter. A couple of them laughed so hard they bent over. I wished I could crawl into a hole, but Lee was laughing, too.

"It's okay, honey," he said. "Better they laugh, than stay sore at you."

Then Frank walked back to us. "Miss," he said, "I've just learned that you have a reputation for not being able to find your way out of a paper bag. Mr. Marcello extends to you his own apology for upsetting you, and wants you to know you don't have to worry. Somebody like you is never going to be any problem for us." Frank grinned.[4] "The next time Mr. Marcello passes you on the street, he says he will forgive you if you don't notice him. But how in the hell you can be that blind, deaf and dumb is a mystery to me."[5]

Friday, August 16, 1963

In the morning, when I left 1032 Marengo Street, Robert was still asleep in bed, but this time he had a decent excuse. His new job was selling Collier Encyclopedias, and it required him to work from 2:00 P.M. to 11:00 P.M. This also made his schedule more convenient to my

comings and goings. So out the door I went, and headed for Dr. Mary's apartment where I would meet Lee.

It had been one week since Lee's August 9th arrest on Canal Street and, today, the next scene was to be acted out. The camera crew from WDSU-TV was scheduled to film Lee handing out pro-Castro leaflets in front of the International Trade Mart at 124 Camp Street, where Clay Shaw worked as the General Manager.[6] WDSU-TV was owned by Edgar Sterns, a strident anti-Communist, and founding member of INCA. All of this was planned by Guy Banister and ultimately arranged by Dr. Ochsner. The plan was set. It was time to make it happen.

Lee arrived at Dr. Mary's apartment about 10:00 A.M. I wanted to be there with him, but he was afraid I would be photographed and identified. So I decided to dress up as a Cuban girl to change my appearance. First, I put in my specially tinted contact lenses that made my eyes brown.[7] Then I put on too much make-up and curled my hair like Latinas did back then. I put on a festive looking sun-dress and black high heel shoes to complete the cha-cha look. Lee was amused by my efforts, and thought I could be a "good extra" in the scene to attract attention, but he wanted me to disappear when the TV camera arrived so I would not get captured on film.

Everything worked according to plan. Lee and two paid helpers handed out leaflets. I engaged several Cuban girls in conversation to attract a crowd, discussing America's poor treatment of Cuba. The television crew arrived on cue and I disappeared, heading to Thompson's Restaurant to wait for Lee. Suddenly, David Lewis arrived at Thompson's and said that Lee wanted me to leave right away, because Carlos Quiroga was coming. Knowing that Lee suspected Quiroga of being a Castro spy, I left Thompson's immediately and went home.[8]

As soon as the WDSU camera crew finished filming, Lee shut down the leafleting operation and left the scene before the police showed up. WDSU then interviewed Lee at their studio: his FPCC stunt was to be televised on the 6 o'clock News. Of course, Lee wanted to see it.

Lee invited Marina to bring Junie and go with him to the Murret's house to watch the segment with uncle Dutz on his TV.[9] Lee knew Dutz secretly approved of his covert actions, so he thought it would be OK. But Marina had only heard the scolding that Dutz gave Lee about his getting arrested, so she refused to go. After pleading with her awhile, Lee realized it was too late to go to the Murrets, and there was now a danger that he would not see the broadcast himself.

Thinking Robert might be at my apartment, Lee first went to a store on Magazine Street that had a television, but they would not let him stay to watch it.[10] So Lee ran to Susie's apartment, and seeing that Robert's car was not in the driveway, he burst in, breathless, only moments before the news came on. Susie and I were late, too — we'd barely seated ourselves in front of the TV. I waved Lee in, saying that Robert would not be home for hours. Then the news started. Susie, Lee and I sat there together and watched Lee's first television appearance.[11] (I wish it had been his last.)

Now it was time for Lee to reap the final harvest of publicity from his efforts. Not surprisingly, it all came from WDSU where Dr. Ochsner had greased the skids.

Saturday, August 17, 1963

A WDSU reporter named Bill Stuckey had a radio show called the "Latin Listening Post," which, as the name implies, kept an ear open for any news about Latin America. He was told to contact Lee after the "Hands Off Cuba" leafleting in New Orleans. The next morning, he invited Lee to be a guest on his radio show that same evening. Because I'd nearly missed his TV appearance, Lee told me he would "test" me by inserting a special word into his radio interview with Stuckey. They taped an intelligent but cautious half-hour discussion about U.S. policy towards Cuba, of which about five minutes was broadcast. I heard Lee's special word, though! It was "New Or-leens" — pronounced the "Yankee way" instead of "New Orlins," which Lee had told me was the more proper pronunciation.[12] I was able to prove I'd heard his broadcast, which pleased him very much. For the next broadcast, they recruited two anti-Castro activists. One was Carlos Bringuier. I don't know if they realized he was cooperating with Lee

 to build his pro-Castro image. After all, he was the city's anti-Castro DRE leader. Despite his poor English, he was a passionate speaker. The other was Ed Butler, INCA's co-founder and its current Executive Director. He was a professional anti-Communist who would soon get a job at Tulane.[13] They also backed up Bill Stuckey with the more ex-

Carlos Bringuier   Ed Butler

perienced WDSU reporter, Bill Slatter. That was a lot of talent stacked up against young 23-year-old Lee.

Wednesday, August 21, 1963

Lee appeared on a second show on WDSU Radio. This one was called "Conversation Carte Blanche." It was four against one, with Dr. Ochsner also present in the studio. Lee handled himself well, never getting ruffled and delivering thoughtful, and sometimes evasive, answers. The big surprise during the debate was when INCA's Ed Butler produced a newspaper article and accused Lee of defecting to the Soviet Union. During the tense exchange, Lee pointed out that a defector would not have been allowed to return to the United States, as he obviously had.[14] The recording ends the moment Lee mentions

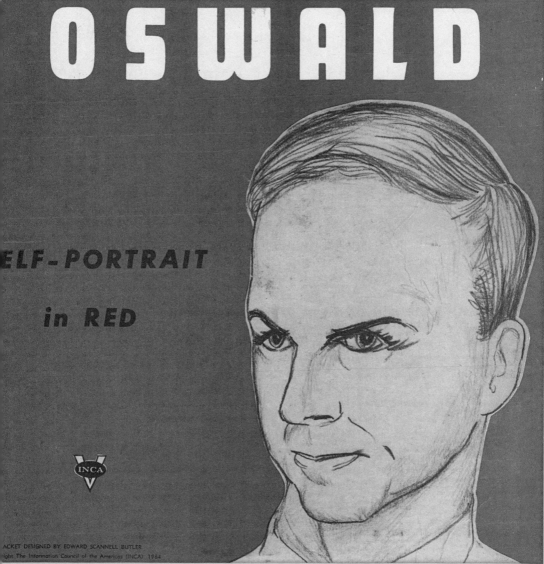

OSWALD

ELF-PORTRAIT

in RED

INCA

ACKET DESIGNED BY EDWARD SCANNELL BUTLER
ight The Information Council of the Americas (INCA) 1964

socialized medicine as a manifestation of Marxism embraced by free democratic countries like Britain.[15] After the show, Stuckey took Lee to Comeaux's bar, a favorite hang-out for the New Orleans media, and bought him a drink.

The final week of August was busy for me and Lee. He was already aware that his documented pro-Castro views and activities could be used to frame him in the murder of President Kennedy, which the right-wing cabal was planning. Bioweapons, spies, lies, betrayals and talk of assassinations started to have an effect on both of us. We found ourselves surrounded by evil. One evening, we discussed it.

"I AM A MARXIST"

—Lee Harvey Oswald, August 21, 196

With these words, a few weeks before President Kennedy' assassination, Lee Harvey Oswald sketched the indelible ou line of this Self-Portrait in Red.

HEAR OSWALD'S OWN VOICE AND LEARN:

What did Oswald really think of President Kennedy?
Hear the only recorded statement in existence, as Oswald gives his own opinion of President Kennedy.

Was Oswald alone?
Listen to this record, as Oswald defends the Fair Play for Cuba committee. Then decide for yourself.

Was Oswald insane?
Listen to this record . . . then judge for yourself.

What did Oswald call his enemies?
Hear Oswald pin a label on people he dislikes, and smear the State Department and the CIA.

Whom did Oswald admire?
Hear Oswald's own suggestion, that the United States should have dropped weapons "into the Sierra Maestra where Fidel Castro could have used them."

How did Oswald explain his three years in Russia?
Listen to this record, and hear his revealing reply.

This Album cointains the authentic, unedited recording of the now famous " versation Carte Blanche" interview, origi broadcast live on Radio Station WDSl New Orleans, just a few weeks before P dent Kennedy's assassination.

This is a 33.1/3 r.p.m. high fidelity recording playbac R.I.A.A. characteristic.

Introduction by . . .

Hon. T. Hale Boggs, Congressman from Louisiana and House Majority Whip, in whose District the debate was held, and who supported the INCA TRUTH TAPES program from the outset.

Impression by . . .

Dr. Alton Ochsner, world famed surgeon and President of both the Alton Ochsner Medical Foundation and the Information Council of the Americas (INCA), who was perhaps the only listener who knew of Oswald's defection before the debate.

Analysis by . . .

Edward Scannell Butler, Executive President of INCA and panelist on the f evening, who has interviewed scores of re from communist colonies, and who was the propaganda specialist ever to confront Osw person.

This is the original Oswald Self-Portrait in Red. Accept no substitutes

Narration by Marshall Pearce   Mastering by Cosimo Recording Studios   © Copyright The Information Council of the Americas (INCA)

This is when I learned more about Lee's passive resistance techniques. He said that he had learned this skill from the Quakers, and from reading Ghandi.

The marks on his chin and ears were still present, but he dismissed all that: "They were just defending their beliefs," he said. "I don't hold it against them."

That's how our discussion began.

"When I was eleven," Lee said, "I venerated comic book heroes. I vowed to stand against evil. I slipped along the way a lot, but I still have that dream."

"When I was fifteen," I responded, "I felt the same. I wanted to be a saint."

"Well," Lee told me, stroking my hair, "good for you. As for me, I haven't had much success 'fighting evil' so far. Instead, I've had to fight the evil I've found in myself, as you well know."

"But you're winning the battle," I said earnestly.

"Yes!" he answered, proudly. "I am. I'll be 'demmed' if I'll help give the world another Hitler. I prefer to offer myself as the Scarlet Pimpernel, or maybe Zorro. Wearing my mask."

"But Zorro was a Don. And Lord Blakeney was a baronet — "

"Oh, I have a little money," Lee said modestly. "My friend George is in charge of it."

"I hate money," I told him.

"I, as well," Lee agreed. "I despise those who live off the labor of the poor. It's one reason I chose to do menial work. I was gravitating too quickly to a life of ease."

"But you hated working at Reily's."

"God, yes! The heat, the noise, the lack of respect."

"By the end of the century, they say the average American worker will only have to be on the job thirty hours a week."

"I hope so," Lee said. "If we keep men like Kennedy in office, who don't owe their souls to cartels and corporations, and will keep us from blowing ourselves to hell."

Lee had been trying to make me care about President Kennedy as much as he did. He now brought up Kennedy's July 26 speech on a treaty with Moscow to ban nuclear tests in the air, water, and in space. The speech had infuriated ultra-conservatives who thought Kennedy was displaying weakness in the face of Communism. But Lee praised the President for his foresight. We have forgotten how brave Kennedy was.

JFK announcing the nuclear test ban, July 26, 1963

As for Lee and me, we wanted to abandon the rat race to others. "We'll leave their money and corruption behind," Lee said. "We'll be like Lord and Lady Blakeney. We'll play the old part."

"And what if they kill you?" I asked.

"We're forewarned," he said. "That's a mighty good advantage."

He had adopted the light, devil-may-care voice and manner of the Scarlet Pimpernel, but both of us knew we were in deep trouble.

We now walked along slowly, wrapped in silence, heading toward Audubon Park, holding hands, aware of the rings that touched and made the tiny clinking sound that meant we were still linked to others. But soon, we would leave our rings behind! After awhile, we began talking again, mostly about Dave's recent parties, when he'd promised not to have any until September. True, he put away the breakables — and of course the mice vanished. I wondered where they went. It had to be close by.

"The two Cuban kids know," Lee replied.

"But why couldn't we just work over there, instead of having to go through all of this hassle at Dave's?"

"He doesn't want you to see the others," Lee said, with a sharp look.

Sometimes you can be so close to something that you lose perspective. Lee had pinpointed the problem. The entire reason for working in Dave's apartment had to be because I was not supposed to meet whoever else was involved. I had seen initials, and even a few names as sign-offs on some reports, but who was in charge of what? Dr. Mary had mentioned that some cultures might be stored in liquid nitrogen as back-ups. In that state, they could be kept dormant, but alive, at minus 200 degrees C. The process, in essence, immortalized those deadly cancer cells. They could be used any time in the future.

The thought gave me chills. Our goal had been to turn the attention of those who wanted to assassinate Kennedy back to taking over Cuba after Castro's demise. We were trying to help save a president on the cusp of extinction. But how naïve was that? Who would willingly give up such a weapon, once available? It would be there waiting to be activated, when needed. I confided these fears to Lee.

"There's nothing you can do about it, Juduffki," Lee said, trying to comfort me. "It's not your fault, either. Who would you complain to?"

Lee was right. I couldn't even prove there had been a lab at Dave's, even though I now went to his apartment almost daily. We'd been so careful. I had no contacts with anyone, and little proof of

PLAZA 7-2700

HAROLD S. DIEHL, M.D.

Senior Vice President for
Research and Medical Affairs   AMERICAN CANCER SOCIETY, INC.
and Deputy Executive Vice President   521 W. 57 ST., N.Y. 19, N.Y.

having done anything. Dr.
Mary couldn't defend me
without losing her posi-
tion. I knew her standards
were high, and I was determined to talk to her about
my suspicions. But I al-
ready knew the answer: the
project had taken too long
and had cost too much to
simply throw away after-
wards. Not when the cells
could live forever.

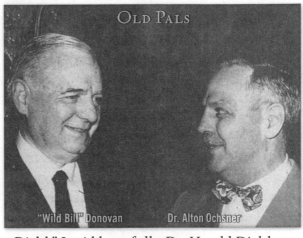

OLD PALS

"Wild Bill" Donovan   Dr. Alton Ochsner

"Maybe I could talk to Dr. Diehl," I said hopefully. Dr. Harold Diehl
had been fond of me, and I knew I could to talk to him in private. He
had concerns for safety in cancer research. I found his card in the re-
cesses of my black purse.

But Lee pointed out that Diehl, the Senior Vice President for Research for the American Cancer Society and Ochsner the former ACS
President, had been pals for many years. Their friend, "Wild Bill" Donovan (who died of cancer despite Ochsner's efforts) had been a leading
ACS official, too, and was the founding father of the CIA. Diehl would
probably do nothing.

Lee said we should wait until Dave came back from Miami again
before trying to tackle yet another problem. Before his trip, Dave had
helped draw anti-Castroites away from Lee on August 9th, by holding
an anti-Castro demonstration a few blocks further up Canal street,
and before that, he'd spent time in bars and nightclubs with Lee, helping to spread rumors of Fernandez infiltrating the anti-Castro camp.

"As I said, I had to hang around those bars, myself," Lee said. "Think
of my sufferings!" he went on. "Instead of playing chess, reading a good
book, or making love to you, I had to encourage grown men to drink
until they vomited. Come on, let's have some fun before going home."

"I don't have much time left."

"It won't take that long. It's one of my favorite places," he added,
putting his arm around me, "and it's close, a place that made me happy
when times were tough."

By now, we had arrived at a tall grassy embankment in Audubon
Park which I'd seen before.

"I've been exercising," he said, as we gazed at the hill. "Bet I can keep
up with you all the way up this thing!" After hiding my purse in some
bushes, up the hill we went, Lee ahead all the way. As we stood panting
at the top, I remarked that it wasn't fair: his legs were longer, and he did

not have a pair of breasts weighing him down. Lee said, on the contrary, he was weighed-down by all that equipment between his legs! Exploding with laughter, we kissed.

Monkey Hill was built for all the kids of New Orleans, Lee said, especially poor kids who had never left the state and had no idea what a free-standing hill might look like. I remember I was wearing my tight olive green skirt, and actually believed Lee when he said any grass stains, if I rolled down the hill with him, would not show. Wrong! But Robert didn't notice my stained skirt when I got home. Still fascinated with Hitler, he was busy reading *The Rise and Fall of the Third Reich*.

"Mr. Rat has been home again all day," Susie said, anxious for me. "When is he going to get a real job?"

"He's trying to sell encyclopedias at night now," I told her. Late that night, when he got home, I finally told Robert that my job at Reily's was over.

"I couldn't promise them that I would stay after the summer was over, so they made me resign," I told him. Lies again, but they worked.

After learning that I had immediately landed a "job" at Rev. Jim's, Robert calmed down. I handed over the "earnings," most of which was actually money given to me by Lee from Clay Shaw. Once he had the cash in his hand, Robert told me how his job was going.

"I came home early today," he answered, lighting up a cigarette. "I had no luck. If I can't sell something, we'll go to Florida, and move in with my folks until school starts."

"We don't have to leave early," I objected. ""We're getting along OK on my art earnings." Angry at myself for getting into this situation, I stared helplessly at Robert's cancer stick. He knew I hated it when he smoked in front of me, and he had promised not to do so. I had given mice lung cancers with the same stuff Robert was sucking into his lungs, and blowing all over me.[16]

Wednesday, August 28, 1963

This was the day that Rev. Dr. Martin Luther King, Jr. delivered his "I Have a Dream" speech in front of the Lincoln Memorial in Washington, DC to a live audience of 200,000, and a television audience of millions.

Hope swept across the land. It was a monumental date in American history, and a true watershed on the social landscape. Lee and I watched the news together at Susie's, as Dr. King quoted from the Declaration of Independence: "That all men are created equal." To the black population, it was an inspirational moment that gave them strength and

confidence to challenge the racist structure that had denied them their rights. To the white supremacists, it was a call-to-arms. Few places in the country felt the weight of this dramatic collision of perspectives more than rural Louisiana, where organizations like the Ku Klux Klan secretly controlled the voting apparatus, and illiterate blacks still toiled in the fields. This is exactly where our story goes next.

1. Prisoners were known to volunteer for transfers to Jackson for medical experiments. William Livesay, a former prisoner at Angola, has brought forth verified information for researchers. He was a New Orleans area resident incarcerated in Angola in 1963 after assaulting a patron at the Gas Light Lounge. Livesay kindly provided this statement:

    "...I was in New Orleans Parish Prison for nearly a year awaiting trial in 1962, then sent to Angola from 1963-5... *While at Angola several others & I volunteered for medical experiments to be held at Jackson.* There were 8 or 10 in my group to board the bus to the hospital. The only 2 names I remember are Dan Robertson & a guy with the last name of Mayes. After we were there for 4-5 days, Mayes walked out of the ward one night after seeing one of the hospital orderlies come in from outside & forgetting to lock the door. The next morning the bus came & took us all back to Angola. I remember we were given some pills every morning but I have no idea what the experiment was about. I learned later that half of us were given medicine & the other half were given placebos. Several years later I went to New Orleans at the request of Dan Robertson to testify on his behalf in a lawsuit he had brought against the State (or possibly the hospital) to show that the pills he took during that brief stay had caused him mental problems. *I remember the doctor from Jackson testifying also about the experiment.* If I can help further please let me know. Sincerely, Bill Livesay" (emphasis JVB)

2. Lee and I went to several hotels for our romantic activities a total of thirteen times. The number was easy for me to remember because thirteen is referred to as "a baker's dozen," and Baker was my married name! The hotels that I remember were the Roosevelt (just off Canal Street), the Monteleone (in the French Quarter near Canal Street), and the Royal Orleans (in the French Quarter near Jackson Square). When Lee and I went to the Royal Orleans, we often walked over to see St. Louis Cathedral and the artists in Jackson Square.

3. Both WWL-TV and WDSU-TV were located in the French Quarter, and the International Trade Mart where Lee would be leafleting was just across Canal Street, making it only one-half block outside of the French Quarter. *(See view from French Quarter on next page.)*

4. Marcello had recognized me from his 500 Club, on the night that Lee, Sparky Rubenstein and Clay Shaw arranged to smuggle in the shipment of rifles from South America. He had told Sparky to make sure I was only drawing pictures of animals, not the attendees at his secret meeting.

5. A couple of years ago, I failed to pick out my own daughter's face in a group photo she sent me. I was unable to pick out my own face in my graduating class mass photo. It's been a lifelong malady. However, I have an excellent memory for conversations and quotes. Getting lost all the time has kept me humble when I've been praised for my poetry, paintings, for my nearly eidetic memory of the past, or for my encyclopedic compendium of knowledge. Just don't ask me to go to the store for you. I might not make it back. I've always believed that my inability to recognize faces, and the big laugh Marcello had that day, had some weight later in saving my life.

6. Forensic evidence exists indicating that one of the people accidentally photographed with Lee in front of the Trade Mart on Aug. 16, 1963, was Chauncey Holt, who admitted on camera to making Lee's fake ID's and being present at the Trade Mart that day. Holt was a Mafia asset and disguise artist of many talents working with the CIA on projects such as Operation Mongoose. Many researchers now believe that at least six "tramps" were arrested in Dallas on Nov. 22. Three arrested together were widely photographed and known to have been questioned, but witnesses testified that they were then released (including Holt) without charges. Then, records found years later revealed that three tramps went to jail that day. The media next told the public that the three jailed tramps were the three famous tramps "erroneously reported" to have been released. But forensic data tell us the three "new" tramps do not match well the photos of the "famous" tramps. Holt, not the jailed tramp named Abrams, is the better forensic fit for the 'old tramp' seen in the famed photos. Skilled in disguise, Holt was capable of making himself look older than he was.

7. These were the same contact lenses given to me in a special set of different colors in late 1960 by Bausch & Lomb, an optics manufacturer whose test laboratories were then located in Sarasota, Florida.

8. Lewis and Quiroga hated each other, but after Lewis (who spoke out as a witness after his friend David Ferrie was found dead) reported to Garrison that he had been shot at, he later added that it was Quiroga, which was a fabrication, though he stated he saw his assailant (his original written statement never mentioned Quiroga). Lewis then failed a polygraph on the matter. This cast everything else Lewis told Garrison into doubt. Critics who state that David Lewis lied about Quiroga then try to say that therefore his wife, Anna Lewis, is (guilt by association) also a liar, since she stated on film that Lee and I double-dated with her and her husband. At the time of Garrison's investigation, Anna Lewis (pregnant) was threatened and finally left the city. Her whereabouts, according to her husband, were unknown. He was obviously trying to protect her, and of course would not reveal the relationship between Lee, me, and his family. As it was, Lewis was soon charged, after speaking out, with theft at Trailways, and was fired. His life and reputation destroyed, Lewis left New Orleans, divorced his wife, who was left to care for six children alone, and never spoke out again.

9. Dutz and his family testified to the Warren Commission that they made a point of hearing Lee's radio broadcasts and seeing his televised appearances. While I do not know how many family members learned Lee's secret (Dutz told the WC that he disapproved of his nephew's political views) one of his sons dared express admiration for Lee's intelligence to the WC.

10. It was 6:00 P.M. Maybe the store was closing.

11. These were the days before cable and satellite. There were only three networks, NBC, CBS, and ABC. WDSU was the NBC affiliate and about one-third of the television audience in New Orleans watched it. Bottom line: between 50,000 and 100,000 people saw the segment.

12. It turned out that Lee repeated the city's name some half dozen times in the Listening

Post recording, as he knew the broadcast would be truncated. Lee had corrected my mispronunciation several times. Persons who have claimed Lee was not a New Orleans native due to "mispronouncing" New Orleans should have listened more closely, because Lee also has said "AX" for "asked" in other recordings — a peculiar pronunciation typical of a New Orleans native-born speaker.

13. Edward Scannel Butler

14. A "transcript' of the `debate" is posted on the Internet — as relayed to America's trusting people by The Warren Commission. Read the official version below, and then read what Lee actually said, as preserved intact on the 1963 INCA record:

STUCKEY: Mr. Oswald... I'm curious to know just how you supported yourself during the three years that you lived in the Soviet Union. Did you have a government subsidy?

INTERNET VERSION OF LEE'S REPLY: OSWALD: ...I will answer that question directly then as you will not rest until you get your answer. I worked in Russia. *I was not* under the protection of the — that is to say I was not under protection of the American government, but as I was at all times considered an American citizen. I did not lose my American citizenship.

INCA RECORDING OF LEE'S REPLY: OSWALD: ...I will answer that question directly then, as you will not rest until you get your answer. I worked in Russia. *I was* under the protection of the — that is to say, I was not under protection of the American government, but as I was at all times considered an American citizen. I did not lose my American citizenship.

15. Ed Butler and Dr. Ochsner released a phonograph album early in 1964 about this debate called *Oswald: A Self-Portrait in Red*. Ochsner's photo and the INCA logo are on the back of the album, along with this quote: "Impression by Dr. Alton Ochsner, world famed surgeon and President of both the Alton Ochsner Medical Foundation and the Information Council of the Americas (INCA), who perhaps was the only listener who knew of Oswald's defection before the debate." Since Ochsner is identified as the "only listener who knew of Oswald's defection before the debate," researchers should ask how Ochsner came by that knowledge. Ochsner's voice is also heard in the background of the recording and could not be removed. He was present, despite his notoriously busy schedule, when the recording was made of this young, supposedly unknown person. Did Ochsner want to make sure that Oswald did not dare mention anything to do with him, or the project? It must be acknowledged by all that Lee Oswald was important enough to Ochsner that he took time from his horrendously busy schedule to attend the 'debate.' Is it then such a stretch to believe my assertion that Ochsner had previously interviewed Oswald at Charity Hospital?

16. In 1969, after the birth of our first child, Robert quit smoking – cold turkey – and never touched a cigarette again.

International Trade Mart viewed from Canal St.

East Louisiana Mental Hospital,
main building

CHAPTER 23

JACKSON

A s the final days of August arrived, most of the Project's goals had been reached. The deadly galloping cancer had been dramatically enhanced and successfully transferred from mice to marmoset monkeys and then to rhesus and African green monkeys, progressively working its way up the evolutionary scale toward humans. The next and final step was to test the bioweapon on a human.

I was told that the human was to be "a volunteer" from Angola Penitentiary, an infamous prison located near the banks of the Mississippi River, north of Baton Rouge. The test itself would be conducted about 30 miles from Angola at the East Louisiana State Mental Hospital in Jackson, Louisiana.[1] This was about 120 miles northwest of New Orleans, just below the Mississippi state line. Everything was carefully planned for this to happen on Thursday, August 29, 1963, which was expected to be a typical summer day in a small Southern town.

Lee and Dave had been properly trained to conduct the test. The components of the bioweapon were ready for travel. Alibis were in place to provide plausible deniability for key people. A reliable, air-conditioned vehicle was provided for the safe transportation of the team and the bioweapon. The car was a big black Cadillac — an automobile that oozed importance. They would wait for a signal at a staging area near the hospital. When the vehicles escorting the prisoner left Angola a phone call would be made to alert the team, which would intercept and slide into position behind the two State vehicles, creating the impression of an official convoy. In this way, the arrival of the test team would not be noticed. For this last step, timing and coordination were critical.

I personally trained Lee and Dave to handle the materials and prepared the bioweapon for safe transport to the mental hospital, but I did not accompany them on this first trip, so, what I report here is what Lee and Dave told me.

Thursday, August 29, 1963

Early that morning Lee, Dave Ferrie, and Clay Shaw entered the black Cadillac — which was registered to the International Trade Mart — to begin their journey to Jackson, Louisiana. The bioweapon had been placed inside two special Dewar jars. To an outsider, they looked like common lunch thermoses. A couple of sandwiches had been tucked in with them, inside an ordinary-looking lunch sack which Lee would carry. Shaw was at the wheel because only he could legally drive the Cadillac.[2] After crossing Lake Pontchartrain, they stopped briefly in Hammond, Louisiana, (Shaw's home town) where he checked on his ailing father and called his secretary, providing an alibi for himself should it be needed, to account for his rare absence from New Orleans.

From Hammond, Shaw drove north to Clinton, Louisiana, where they picked up a fourth passenger, an orderly who worked in the mental hospital in nearby Jackson.[3]

Discussions about Kennedy, Johnson and Castro stopped when the orderly entered the car, and an uneasy silence prevailed. Clay Shaw then drove the foursome to the courthouse in Clinton. There they were to wait for word of the convoy's departure from Angola penitentiary. Once there, Shaw again called his secretary, telling her that he was at someone's office, and gave her a phone number where he could be reached. He promised to call her back when he was leaving. But this "office" was actually a pay phone near the courthouse in Clinton, Louisiana where he had parked the black Cadillac. They waited for the phone call from Angola.

Secrecy was an important issue in this operation, and Clinton had been selected as the staging area because it was better than the small-

er town of Jackson, where it would have been difficult for a black Cadillac to park and wait without being noticed. The Clinton courthouse was accustomed to more traffic. Official-looking vehicles (like the black Cadillac) came and went all day.

When the trip was planned, it seemed like an excellent place. Jackson is approximately halfway between Angola and Clinton, so the distance was perfect for Shaw to rendezvous with the convoy. The presence of a known hospital employee in the black Cadillac, as well as Shaw's impressive business-like appearance, would add to the patina of legitimacy.

Once inside the hospital's gates, the orderly would direct the team to one of the many outbuildings on the hospital's campus, where the test would take place. Their plan looked good on paper, but there was a problem: Thursday, August 29th was no "ordinary day" in Clinton, Louisiana.

Just the day before, Dr. Martin Luther King, Jr. had delivered his historic "I Have a Dream" speech in Washington, D.C. His words ricocheted through the national media, and Dr. King was the talk of the town that day, either a hero or a villain depending which side you were on.

Hoping to leverage the momentum created by Dr. King's impassioned speech, the Congress of Racial Equality (CORE) held a voter registration drive in Clinton, a KKK-controlled bastion of White Supremacy which routinely denied blacks their right to vote. Emboldened by the massive outpouring of support in Washington and the presence of CORE observers in Clinton, the local blacks gathered peacefully, but defiantly, to stand in line and exercise their lawful right to register to vote.[4] The sun was hot and the delays were long, but it was no worse than a day spent picking cotton or digging potatoes.[5]

The whole of idea of "allowing" blacks to vote challenged the sensibilities of the conservative whites who ruled this Southern town. People were wary, and tensions were high on both sides. Local white folks watched with scorn as blacks eager to register stood in a line that barely moved. The local Registrar of Voters was stalling, trying to wait them out.

Clinton, Louisiana, 1964

Meanwhile, police officials worried about the possibility of violence erupting in the tense atmosphere.[6] Into this scene drove a black Cadillac full of strangers. After a while, Lee and the orderly got out of the car, and Ferrie moved into the front seat.

Lee said he got out of the Caddie because it was becoming an "object of interest" but he had to stay close to the car, in case the pay phone rang. Then he said he encountered an angry young black woman on the street who had just been denied her right to register. She was very upset, and told Lee she had been in line even before the office opened. When she got her chance at last, she produced her proof of residency and was then asked to read a section of the U.S. Constitution. When she did, she was told she had "failed" her literacy test. She had earned her degree in Business from Tuskegee Institute.[7]

Hearing this tale of injustice angered Lee and he returned to the car and made a bet with Shaw, Dave and the orderly that, because he was white, he could register to vote, even though he did not live in the parish.[8] They accepted the bet and Lee got in line to register, the orderly keeping him company. These two were the only white people in line. At one point, somebody who knew the orderly saw him and stopped by to talk.[9] That's when Lee heard about a job opening at the Jackson Hospital.

The hours wore on, but the pay phone still did not ring. There was obviously a delay at the prison in Angola. The Cadillac was essentially trapped in this amazing scenario.

After about two hours of standing in line, Lee finally reached the Registrar of Voters. He was polite and friendly. Lee took out his wallet and flashed his ID, asking if he could register to vote. The Registrar invited Lee to sign the roll book. Lee signed the roll book and then said he was glad he was now a bona-fide resident of East Feliciana Parish.[10] Realizing that Lee was flaunting the fact that he was not really a resident, the Registrar demanded to see Lee's ID again. As Lee showed him his ID (which indicated that he lived in Orleans Parish), Lee said he had heard there was a job opening at the mental hospital, and he was sure that having a local voter's registration card would improve his chances.

Angry that he had been taken in and suspicious of Lee's true intentions, the Registrar quickly erased Lee's ink signature as best he could and told Lee to leave the area, saying "Forget about a job there, you *belong* in a mental hospital!"[11]

Lee told me, later, "I did get registered, but it was only for two minutes. Then he erased me," Lee said, smiling.

"Well, you were registered longer than the colored girl," I replied.[12]

The town's curious sheriff eventually approached the Cadillac to investigate and asked the driver to identify himself. Shaw displayed his driver's license and said, "I am Clay Shaw from the International Trade Mart."[13]

Finally, the pay phone rang, and Shaw answered. The prison convoy was on its way: They had to leave at once in order to join it before the convoy came into view of the hospital's manned security gate. All went as planned, and they entered without a problem. Once inside the gates, Shaw parked the Cadillac in an appropriate place, and entered the main building to take care of some money transactions. The orderly then guided Lee and Dave to the clinic, which was located in a smaller structure well behind the massive administration building with its impressive white-columned facade. There they met the medical and technical personnel who would oversee the experiment.

Lee carried the bioweapon in his "lunch sack," with the sandwiches. The ordinary-looking thermos bottles had clear glass liners on which the cancer cells had been grown. The liners were, in essence, giant test tubes, easily pulled from the thermos bottles.[14] The cancer soup was decanted from one of these liners (to which it adhered, like slime) with trypsin, an enzyme, and was then prepared for injections into the volunteer. More injections from the same batch would follow, if the first injections "took." The second liner was for backup, in case the first batch got contaminated. We hoped this same setup would successfully transfer the bioweapon to Mexico City, and then to Cuba. No border inspector would guess that virulent cancer cells were being smuggled in, since the cells were invisible, and the medium itself looked (and even tasted like) weak chicken broth.[15]

Lee and Dave were both qualified to instruct other technicians as to how to handle and work with the bioweapon. At Jackson, Dave gave the injections and explained to those involved how further injections should be given, and when. Lee watched and listened, so he would be able to deliver similar instructions when he handed off the Product in Mexico City or Cuba.[16] Lee left after viewing the first round of injections, and only saw one prisoner, because he needed to go to the Personnel office. There, Lee filled out an employment application to establish a motive for his planned return to the hospital in about 72 hours, when he would have to drive me there to check on the progress of the experiment. Afterwards, Shaw drove Lee and Dave home.[17]

But here was the problem: I was originally told that the prisoner was terminally ill and had "volunteered" to be injected with cancerous cells, knowing his days were numbered.[18] But, a simple fact remained: in order to do my blood test, I had to know what kind of cancer the volunteer had so I could distinguish between "his cancer" and "our cancer."[18] Right before the Team left for Jackson, I asked Dave to find out what kind of cancer the prisoner had.

"Oh, don't worry about that," Dave said matter-of-factly. "He doesn't have cancer. He's a Cuban who is about the same age and weight as Castro, and he's healthy."

I felt a chill sweep through my body. My heart turned over. This revelation was sickening to me. We would be giving cancer to a healthy human with the intention of killing him. This was not medicine, it was murder. It was wrong, morally, ethically, and legally. They had gone too far.

Friday, August 30, 1963

We all have heard the spiels about "What do you stand for?" Would you have pulled the lever in the German gas chambers if the *Führer* told you to, like Adolf Eichmann did? Would you have killed Hitler, if you had the chance? These are defining moments. Who are we? What should we do?

I was the girl who hated cancer, because it killed her grandmother. I was the girl who dreamed of finding a cure to free humanity from this curse. I was the one who sang in church and prayed on both knees to ask God for his help in this noble task. I had thrown myself into the heart of this beast with all my conviction. I had suffered the solemn pain and exquisite sadness of watching those poor people (and animals) die at Roswell Park.

I knew what this weapon would do in terms that I cannot describe here. But now, I was participating in what could only be called premeditated murder. The question was remarkably clear to me: Was I a murderer? No, I was not. And I was not ready to become one. Not for Dr. Ochsner. Not for Old Glory. Not even to get my medical school education paid for. What they were doing was wrong. It was evil. They had lost their moral compass.

So I wrote a letter of protest to my former hero. Yes, he had told me not to write down anything about the Project. There was to be no paper trail: I realized that if the paper got into the wrong hands, the entire temple would collapse on us. But my righteous indignation was fired up and in high gear. Under Ochsner's direction, we were violating the Hippocratic Oath. We were going to kill this man with cancer as a practice exercise, just to see if the Product would work on Castro. I protested this corruption of the spirit. And it was the beginning of the end for my medical career.

My note to Dr. Ochsner simply stated: *Injecting disease-causing materials into an unwitting subject who does not have a disease is unethical.* I signed it with my initials, J.A., and hand-delivered it to Dr. Ochsner's office at his Clinic. But Dr. Ochsner's regular secretary was on vacation, so an older executive secretary was covering for her. She said that Dr. Ochsner was in surgery, and she asked if the matter was "urgent." I said it was. Then she said she would read it to Dr. Ochsner over the phone when he called in for his urgent messages.

As I turned to leave, I heard her open the envelope. My heart sank. I belatedly realized that I should have said it was "personal" or "private" rather than "urgent."[20] I left quickly, and because I was frightened, I headed for Dr. Mary's apartment. As soon as I arrived, Dave Ferrie called me. Dr. Ochsner had contacted him and was frantically trying to locate me. Dave said Ochsner was furious.

"He's your enemy now," Dave warned me. "He told me that you and Lee are expendable. He even exceeded my own prowess in profanity. He's looking for you even as we speak. Good luck, J."

Dave then hung up. I was thunder-struck. Before I could recover from Dave's call, the phone rang again. It was Dr. Ochsner. He began by telling me that I could forget about Tulane Medical School. I protested that he had promised, and his word was supposed to be his bond.

"I'll set something up for you in Florida with Smathers again," Ochsner said with an air of accommodation. "He still likes you. As for me, I've lost interest in you. And if you think I'm upset about your piece of paper," he added, "if you talk about this to anybody, you will regret every damned word you ever said. Have I made myself perfectly clear?"

Then he coldly reminded me that I had to go to Jackson tomorrow to perform my unique cancer diagnosis blood tests. This was not a request; it was an order. No one else could do the work, and it had to be done tomorrow. Intimidated, I promised to go. Then he became abusive again. "There was to be no paper trail!" he roared. "What in the name of God made you decide to write a letter?"

"Sir, it wasn't a letter. It was j…"[21]

"There was to be NO paper trail!" he bellowed again.

Dr. Ochsner told me that Lee and I would have to be separated. He also said that if something bad happened to me it would not be his fault, absolving himself from any guilt in advance. It would, somehow, result from my own actions. I remembered the word that Dave had used: "expendable." Now, I understood that my life was being seriously threatened. Only after Ochsner hung up did I realize that his three-minute phone call had just wrecked my entire life, as if I'd been nothing but an egg he'd decided to boil.

I sat down on the sofa with my head in my hands and cried. The phone rang again. It was Dr. Mary. She said that she had heard about Ochsner's wrath over my letter and had called him, saying that I should have been informed that the prisoner was a convicted murderer, as well as a certifiable mental case.

"I'm so sorry," she told me. "He's made a mountain out of a mole-hill." This was a hint that Dr. Mary was still on my side, which was a huge relief to me. I hoped she would give me good references to a medical school in Latin America, which was one of the plans Lee and I considered. The only positive note she had to offer was that Dr. Ochsner had agreed to a civil exit interview.

Soon after our conversation, Lee called, telling me to take a cab ASAP and meet him at the Fontainebleau Hotel. Dr. Mary would pay for it. Lee and I reached the Fontainebleau at about the same time. As soon as we met, Lee broke the bad news that, in a few hours, Dave was to drive me to Charity Hospital to face Dr. Ochsner and his "civil" exit interview. It would be a late meeting, because Dave was still in court with Carlos Marcello, and Ochsner had to talk to some other people first. While we waited for Dave, Lee and I ate dinner in the lounge of the Fontainebleau. Young William 'Mac' McCullough, whose mother worked at Lee's Coffee Shop, and who himself was as-sociated with Marcello's people, recognized us and crooned some songs our way with his velvety voice, as he played the piano. The lounge's early patrons had filled the room by the time Dave showed

up and joined us at our table. Lee then said he had to go home, but would walk over to Susie's later that evening. Then came the dreaded ride to Charity Hospital. As I got out of the car, Dave said, "Don't worry. I'll wait for you."

I entered Charity Hospital feeling very small and very alone. Soon I was escorted to a large, silent conference room, where for several min-utes I was left alone to ponder Ochsner's notorious reputation for...

He was coming — in all his fury. What did my pitiful stab at "mo-rality" mean to the great Ochsner? Nevertheless, he could hang me, if he liked. I'd never back down on this. Nor would I cower before him.

When Dr. Ochsner entered the room, the look on his face was un-forgiving. Without a word, he handed me some important blood work code sheets, with which to make my reports. Then, rising to his feet, he exploded into a flurry of unrestrained verbal abuses. It was unlike anything I had ever encountered. I felt that he was throwing me, my heart, and my soul into the gutter. Then, he suddenly stopped and sat down and regained his composure.

"When you finish your assignment at Jackson," he said, "Give us the results and consider your work for us over." After his fuse burned a little further, he said "Consider yourself lucky you're walking out of here with your teeth still in your head. Now get out."

I left in silence, grimly proud of not breaking down in front of him. As Lee had marched stoically out of Reily, so I marched out of Charity Hospital. Outside, Dave was waiting anxiously. At the sight of him, I burst into tears. Dave put an arm around me and said: "I'm sorry, J. He's done with you, isn't he?"

It was the first and only time Dave ever touched me kindly, in all those months. It must have been the priest in him. Dave walked me to his car and I got inside, slumping down in the seat as he tried to start the engine. It did not cooperate.

"Damn it!" he said. "The starter in this thing is driving me nuts." Suddenly, his mood shifted, and he said a prayer aloud about the engine. Then on his next try, the engine started. Dave shot me a sharp glance. "See?" he said. "God exists."

"Oh, shut up!" I told him.

"You're full of fear and trembling," he said. "Quo vadis?"

"I'm about to get my head cut off, just like St. Paul," I answered. "My future in medicine is finished, at least in the United States." I had reached my moral limit. I refused to duplicate the sins of the Nazis.

My world was collapsing. And what would happen to Lee?

"You did the right thing to let him know your opinion," Dave said. "A shame you wrote it on paper, though. They hate records that remind them of their mischief. That's why they invented all those terms like Need to Know, Eyes Only, and Plausible Denial."

When we got to my apartment, Dave got out to walk me to the door. I went inside to wash the tears from my face and Dave took that moment to talk to Susie. Then Lee arrived, and we sat with Susie on lawn chairs in the back of the house. Dave told Lee about his car problems, and then about my fate. Lee looked at Dave and said, "Now you can have parties on weekends again."

"It won't be the same without you guys," Dave said as he returned to his car. He drove off with flare, screeching his tires and honking his horn. I waved goodbye, not realizing I'd never see my eccentric friend again.

Lee handed me my purse and said, "You left it in the car. You must be very upset."

I took my purse and clutched it, letting the tears fall again. Susie brought us lemonade, then left us to ourselves in the humid night.

Lee took out his *Pocket Aristotle* to show me that he had been un-
derlining various passages, even numbering them. We'd been discussing ethics and, today of all days, we both need-
ed a good look at what was right and what was
wrong. We were vexed by life's evils.

Lee tried to hold me together in my crisis.
He spoke about ethics, kindness, and morality.
I began to see what riches Lee exhibited, in his
fierce struggle to rise above the turmoil, wick-
edness, and pettiness all around him. He had
matured since I met him, right before my eyes.
There was a youthful majesty about him, a spirit
fit for a young philosopher king who cherishes
his freedom and wants happiness for humanity.

All nations bring forth a few who are consumed by a lust for power and fortune, and
who force their rule on others, he stated. Such
men may be remembered in their infamy, but
the great ones are known by the good they do

Concerned about ethical issues, Dave Ferrie
had ordered this book for Lee and me, at Lee's
request. It had been flown in from New York
along with some unpublished medical journal
manuscripts — our last shipment of cutting-edge
information.

for their people. At the height of these musings, Lee put the Aristotle
book in my lap, took my hand, and looked into my eyes.

"My wife!" he said to me. "Tell me I'm your husband."

"You're my beloved husband," I replied.

Lee leaned over and rested his head against my breast, and I stroked
his hair.

After a few minutes, he said "I'm tempted to tell you the end of that
science fiction story, where Adam and Eve are fleeing for their lives."

"Tell me!" I urged him.

"Not yet," he said, smiling and sitting up. He brought out a large
envelope, which he had been carrying inside his shirt. "When we meet
in Mexico," he said, "then I'll tell you how the story ends." Shyly, he
handed the envelope to me. "Open it," he said. "I want to see your face.
Then I have to go."

I opened the unmarked envelope, which was unsealed. Inside were
twenty brand new $20 bills - $400 in all. "It's for you," Lee said. "Money so you can reach me, wherever I am. Money to go to school with in
Florida next semester, if we have to wait that long."

I tried to resist the gift, but he told me I had to take it, so I would
have the means to come to him when it was safe. He also added, bitterly, that Dr. Ochsner should have given me money to help keep my
cover safe. "And besides," he said, "you might need new shoes!"

"How am I going to account for this?" I asked. "It's too much to risk
hiding it."

"You'll have to find a way," he said. "I need my wife by my side down there."

The envelope fell into my lap, as we held each other in the deepening night. Then Lee got up and walked away, not looking back. I followed him wistfully as he headed out to the sidewalk. As I stood there, I noticed a garage and yard sale next door. I needed an ironing board, and spotted one on the porch, where a lady sat. I got my purse, paid fifty cents for the ironing board, and carried it home, still wondering how I would explain the $400 windfall to Robert.

Then I had an idea. I crumpled and ironed the bills so they wouldn't look so new, then put them back in the envelope and shoved it under the ironing board cover. I made sure I was ironing when Robert returned home at about 11:30 P.M. As I ironed, the envelope fell to the floor, and I showed it to Robert.[22] I told him that I had just bought the ironing board from the yard sale next door.

"Then it doesn't belong to you," Robert declared with finality. "We'll have to give it back." Morality from the Miser! I was proud of him. As much as he craved money, he wouldn't take it if it didn't belong to him. We could have used some of that morality on the Project.

Still, I dreaded the coming of morning. I knew Lee had sacrificed to pull together that much money ($4,000 in today's currency). Early next morning, as soon as the sale opened, we went over to check it out. We learned that half the items, including the ironing board, had belonged to a retired teacher who had died. She had never married and had no known relatives. The landlord was selling her things to collect overdue rent. I asked if the sale had made enough to cover everything. Yes, it had. They'd even made extra, by selling her car.

Robert and I looked at each other, shrugged, and left with the $400 still in my purse. He went back to bed, and I finished ironing clothes. I was feeling pretty low after my lashing by Dr. Ochsner, knowing that my medical career was on the rocks, but at least I had not lost the money, so I would have the funds to meet Lee in Mexico. Once Robert had fallen back to sleep, I quietly went back to the yard sale and bought a black and gold hunting knife and a collection of silk scarves, all of which I stuffed into my purse, so Robert would not see them and ask questions.

Saturday, August 31, 1963

Lee and I had a final important trip to make for the Project. We had to go back to the mental hospital in Jackson, Louisiana to do blood tests on the "volunteer" to see if the cancer had established itself in his system.[23] Lee came to Susie's apartment and waited inside for Robert to leave, and when he did, I went into her apartment. I told them that Robert would be out trying to sell encyclopedias until about 10:30 P.M.

Lee and I said goodbye to Susie and walked to an old car that Lee had parked about a block away. This was the same old Kaiser-Frazer that Lee had used to drive me to Churchill Farms for Marcello's gath-

ering. I still thought of it as the Eli Lilly car, because I had seen it parked near their building several times. Lee said it was more reliable than Dave's car, and it had no known mechanical problems. As I climbed in, I noticed a big basket in the back seat.[24] Lee said that Anna Lewis was pregnant and the basket was a bassinet that David Lewis had bought for their next baby. David put it in this car to protect it from his toddler, who wanted to play with it. However it got there, the bassinet had plenty of room to hold my papers and the materials we had to bring back to New Orleans after the blood tests. Lee then said that he had five gallons of extra gas, extra oil and transmission fluid in the trunk and five gallons of water, so we were ready for anything.

As we drove off, Lee said he had to mail some red-herring letters to obscure his intent to live in Mexico with me. He said that one was for the benefit of the Communist Party and stated his intentions to move to New York.[25] Another was sent to the Socialist-Workers Party, stating his intention to move to the Washington-Baltimore area.[26] Lee also told me that he had already written other letters which said he planned to move to Philadelphia and elsewhere, just to keep them guessing. He also said we would be stopping to pick up a back-up set of cancer cells on our way to Jackson.

Once we were on the highway, Lee told me about what happened in Clinton and at the Jackson mental hospital two days before. Once inside the hospital, he and Dave were escorted into the clinic by the orderly, deep within the compound.

The plan to kill Castro depended on two or three people: First, a doctor to influence diagnostics for the required x-rays, then an x-ray technician to rig the machine to temporarily deliver a dangerous dose, (creating symptoms of an infection and pulling down the immune system) and someone to contaminate the penicillin shots given to overcome the presumed 'pneumonia' or 'infection', with the deadly cancer cocktail. Reactions to the foreign material would bring on fever, with more x-rays to check for 'pneumonia' — and more penicillin or similar shots. Only one shot had to reach a vein, and it was over, if the X-rays had been used. For this was a galloping cancer: Castro's chances, if it worked in humans as it did in monkeys, were zero. It had killed the African green monkeys in only two weeks. Castro's death by cancer would be ascribed to "natural causes."

Lee told me that after the cancer cells were removed from their glass container, he then observed the volunteer being x-rayed and injected. After that, Dave asked him to leave. Why? This made Lee suspicious. What did they not want him to see? Were there more "volunteers" besides the one he had seen? Perhaps this was why the convoy was so late. Maybe it took them longer to get organized because there was more than one prisoner involved. Based on the size of the vehicles in the convoy, they could have easily transported more than one prisoner. We believed Dave went on to perform additional injections on more subjects, and that Dave didn't want this information passed back to me through Lee. Lee had expected Dave, who knew the layout of the main building, to take him to the Personnel office where he planned to fill out a job application. That would fit well with his statements to Clinton's Registrar of Voters: he wanted people to remember his interest in a job, not his presence at the clinic. Without Dave, Lee had to ask the clinic receptionist for directions.[27] The application also provided an excuse for Lee's return, when he had to drive me there. That's how I came to learn of the ploy.

Lee took a more direct route to Jackson this time, avoiding going through Clinton again where he might be recognized as the man from the black Cadillac. As he drove, I told him what had happened concerning the $400. He replied, "You're worth more than $400 to me. I once left somebody behind that I loved. They beat her, because she pined for me. Never again."

I said nothing and waited for Lee to open up a little more. But he didn't. Finally he added, "When it is time for you to come to me, just don't let me down." He gave me a quick glance, smiled, and added, "I hope you won't get lost."

"I won't get lost," I assured him.

"It was my whole month's pay, you know. So hold onto it," he said.[28]

I was stunned. We went on in silence for some time. I let him muse. Then he said softly, "Never again," as if speaking to himself.

I felt enough time passed that I could speak, so I said, "But without the money how will you — ?"

"I've been careful," he broke in, knowing I'd bring this up. "There will be just enough for everything. Besides, after I reach Mexico City, I'll have all the money I'll need. If I need it." He stated this firmly. "My friend Alex has agreed to fly you out of Florida and across to Mexico, but if that doesn't work, you can still take a commercial flight to Mexico from Tampa. I'll be there to meet you, if there's a breath of life left in me."

As we reached the outskirts of town, we stopped at a gas station. The attendant filled the tank to the brim, washed all the windows squeaky-clean, checked the oil, and made sure the tires had the proper pressure.[29]

While all that was going on, Lee went inside the gas station and came out with a paper bag and two Dr. Peppers. In the bag was a thermos containing the cancerous bioweapon. The thermos had been delivered to the gas station, along with a small cooler full of ice for preserving the blood samples I'd bring back from Jackson, since our car had no air conditioning. The timing was perfect: I was impressed.

On we went, crossing beautiful blue Lake Pontchartrain, and then heading west to Baton Rouge. From there, we headed north, driving through open country, with lots of clouds overhead to keep us cool.

Lee had also developed some ideas to hide the true reason for his second trip to the hospital at Jackson in less than 72 hours. In small towns, strangers and their cars get noticed. Lee would make a point of asking two well-known, popular people in Jackson how to get a job at the hospital, even though he'd already filled out an employment application two days earlier. Witnesses from Jackson and Clinton would recall the same question as a common denominator, deflecting speculations about any other reason for Lee to be in the area. It was quite clever.

I took out the *Pocket Aristotle* and began reading to him about ethics, righteousness, the characteristics of both great and petty men, and finally something about women. Lee stopped the car, took the book from me, grabbed a pencil and made a note in the margin, writing *"Feelings about women."*

"I don't want to forget where it's at," he said. "Dave told me Aristotle believed women were inferior, and that he agreed with him. But that's not what it says here."

"All I want is to accomplish something good and beautiful, instead of this thing!" I said to Lee as I pointed back to the baby basket that held my files and the backup thermos filled with deadly cancer cells.

"You were boxed in," Lee said. "I've been there, too. This is the last of it."

"It's got to be," I agreed.

As we approached Jackson, the car's engine started getting over-heated, so Lee said we would stop soon to let the engine cool down.

As we entered Jackson, we looked for a sign that would tell us where the hospital was, but did not find one. Lee decided to stop at the local barber shop.[30]

"Town barbers know everything," Lee explained. "I'll ask for a hair-cut, and let the engine cool down. And I can tell my little story here, about looking for a job."

Though it was late August, the weather was cooler than normal and the sky was overcast with clouds, making it possible for me to stay in the car.[31]

Lee came out about 20 minutes later. I looked at his hair and won-dered if the barber had even cut it. Lee said he'd gotten directions, and started up the car again, noting that we were right on time.

When we reached the mental hospital's main gate, the orderly who had been with Lee at Clinton was waiting for us. The timing of our arrival had been planned to coincide with the hospital's shift change, when lots of cars were com-ing and going through the gates.

E. Louisiana Mental Hospital main building

We were taken to a back entrance to the main building, where we took a service ele-vator upstairs. Only important persons were kept in this building. Obviously, our prisoner was special. Once he knew where I was going to be, Lee went to the personnel office to pro-vide an excuse for his presence at the hospital. I asked to interview the "client," but was told that no one was allowed to see him. This an-gered me, but like it or not, I had work to do.

I checked the blood work data while a cen-trifuge spun down the freshly-drawn blood

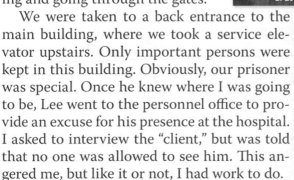

Back door, main building

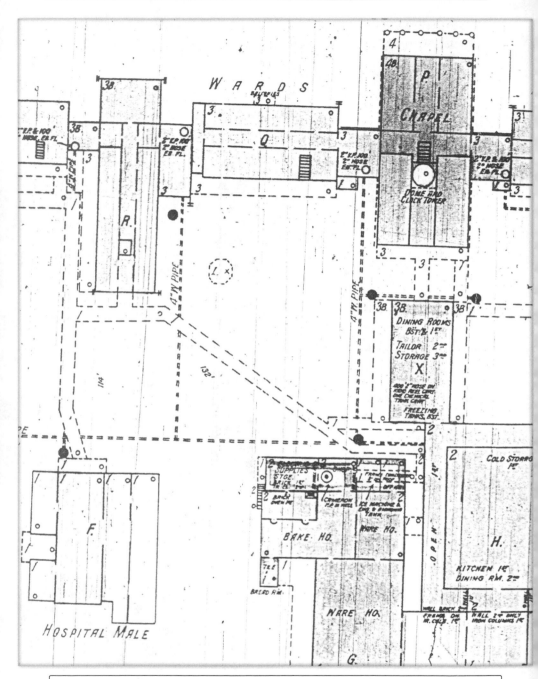

Map of East Louisiana State Mental Hospital, Jackson, as it was when Oswald delivered the bioweapon to the Men's Hospital ("The Clinic" in 1967). He observed injections, then asked a secretary directions to Personnel (Main Bldg), where he filled out an employment application, giving him an alibi for his reappearance when required to drive Judyth there. Witnesses testified in the Clay Shaw trial as to Oswald's visit to the clinic and his job application. Oswald should not have been allowed to enter the clinic. The fact that he asked for directions shows he had not yet been to the main building, where the "personnel" sign was prominent.

samples to pellets, inspecting slides and the blood counts already prepared for me. My task was to match the recorded data with the slides, and to look for any cancer cells there. A few were present — an excellent sign that the bioweapon worked. The original cancer cells had been tagged with a radioactive tracer. If any of those were also found in the pellets, the volunteer was surely doomed. But there were too many blood samples for just one client. I became more suspicious that there were others. The microscope work and centrifuging complete, I packed it all into the cooler for transport.

Having done that, I insisted I needed to observe the prisoner's current condition to see how he was physically reacting. The orderly reluctantly took me to the door of the prisoner's room, but said that I was not allowed past the door. The room was barred, but basically clean. Several storage boxes sat on the floor and some flowers sat on a stand next to the bed. The patient was tied to the bed and was thrashing around in an obvious fever. It was very sad and I felt sorry for what I had done, but I played my part and pretended to be pleased with his status.

We had spent no more than forty-five minutes at the hospital, and once back in the car Lee and I discussed what I had seen. I told him that I was almost sure there was more than one "volunteer." Lee asked me to describe the patient to him, which I did. Lee then pointed out that the hairline and nose were different from the patient that he had seen injected. Between Lee's comments and the number and variety of blood samples, I became convinced. More than one "volunteer" had been injected to test the effectiveness of the bioweapon.

Now we were ready to head to New Orleans. As we left the hospital campus, we could hear a hissing sound from under the hood. Lee pulled over to inspect the engine. There he found a pinhole leak at the connector end of one of the radiator hoses. Lee said we needed to improvise some type of "field dressing" to fix it.

I retrieved a rubber tourniquet from the cooler. Lee said that would help, but we still needed something to hold it in place, so I stripped off my nylon stockings and handed them to him. He smiled and took out his handkerchief, placing it over the rubber tourniquet and tying both into place with my nylons. It worked, at least well enough for us to continue our trip.

It was now twilight, and weather was kicking in. A strong breeze came up and some raindrops started falling. We hoped it would cool things down, but the engine was still overly hot.

Lee turned into a long driveway, and said, "We have to stop and let the car cool down." He parked under a big tree, near a nice house with a front porch. Lee said this was the home of Reeves Morgan, a state representative who worked at the hospital.

"I'll be right back," he told me, adding that we would have to let the radiator cool down enough to add water safely, and that it was best, as always, for me to remain unseen.

Lee went up to the house and was promptly invited inside. It seemed Mr. Morgan knew Lee, from his friendly greeting, but this may have just been the hospitality that rural Louisiana prides itself on.

As I sat in the car, I worked on my charts and checked the temperature of the cooler. At one point I looked up and saw a girl about my age standing on the porch looking in my direction. This was Reeve Morgan's daughter, Mary.[32] Since it was almost dark, I didn't think she could see me. But she did, and later testified that she saw a woman sitting in Lee Oswald's car.

After about 25 minutes, Lee came out of the house, got a gallon of water out of the trunk of the car, and poured it into the radiator. Conscious of Robert's pending return, and this being our third delay, we were behind schedule and tried to hurry home. Lee drove us back to New Orleans on the dark and wet narrow roads as fast as was safe, keeping a careful eye on the temperature gauge all the way.

We both knew that my work on the Project was now finished, and I would not be going to Tulane Medical School as planned. I would have to return to Florida with Robert, at least for a while, and Lee would need to finish his work for the Project. We talked about our future, and the obstacles we would need to overcome in order to start our life together as husband and wife.

Lee then told me that he had been ordered to break off contact with me after this trip. These were orders from Dr. Ochsner and passed to him by Dr. Mary. But Lee wasn't going to give me up any more than I would give him up. He and Dave had already figured out how to circumvent Ochsner's instructions without his knowing it. Lee said that Dave would set us up with a safe phone line, (one of the lines the Mafia used for sports betting) but until then, we should not communicate, so everyone would think Lee had made a clean break. We had acquired powerful and dangerous enemies, and we had to be very careful.

Lee said that he made it plain to Marina that he would leave, never to return.[33]

"I told her she had a hundred people in Dallas who would take care of her. She'd be happy there; or she could live with me, and never be happy." Lee felt divorce from Marina was inevitable, and they should go ahead and get it over with while the kids were young, so they wouldn't have a lot of bad memories of fights and arguments. He cried as he told me these things. He understood the weight of his actions, and they grieved him. His grief was real, and it helped me understand that his love for me was as real as mine for him.

Even though Lee had been ordered to break off contact with me, we had the right to say good-bye to each other one last time. So we planned to spend as much time as possible together tomorrow at our favorite hotel, the Roosevelt.

It was about 11:00 at night when we returned to Marengo Street, and we were happy to see that Robert's car was not there. But we expected him home at any minute, so Lee stopped his car down the block. Collie saw me get out of the car, and came running down the street to greet me, wagging her tail. As she did, another car rushed by and struck her. Collie yelped in pain!

I rushed to Collie, and Lee got out of the car and came over to the panting dog. We anxiously searched for broken bones and signs of internal bleeding, like pale gums, under the streetlight. Except for a bruised shoulder, she appeared to be all right.

Lee gave me a quick kiss goodbye and then left. He still had to drop off the reports and blood samples, buy a bus ticket to Texas (to use as soon as he was ordered to go to Mexico City), and return the car. I had been carrying Lee's *Pocket Aristotle* when we had seen Collie hit by the car, and now, finding it fallen on the ground, I put it in my purse and slowly walked Collie home.

When I told Susie what had happened, tears flowed. Collie was all she had left in her life. "Oh my, I could have lost you!" she told her dog, between her kisses. It reminded me how precious all life really was. I thought about the "volunteer" I had seen in the hospital. It was an emotional conclusion to a nerve-wracking day. And Lee and I had just one day left before our separation.

Worn out, I took a birdie-bath and went to bed. I'm not sure when Robert got home, but when he did, he woke me up, as always eager for *l'amour.*

Sunday, September 1, 1963

Around noon the next day, Lee and I met in the lobby of the glorious Roosevelt Hotel in downtown New Orleans. We spent almost the whole day together in our suite. We were almost giddy over being able to have so much private time together. I delighted Lee by dancing for him wrapped in my new collection of silk scarves, to the music from *Lawrence of Arabia*, teasing him to the brink. Though we loved to talk, we spent several hours doing everything we could think of to express our pleasure and delight in each other without words. I wore the black necklace he gave me, and little else. There was joy, laughter, love and happiness. I gave Lee the black and gold hunting knife, in anticipation of our meeting in Mexico[34]. Lee gave back the love letter that I had written him, and asked me to keep it for him. He said he could not keep it with his things and felt it was too precious to destroy. *(See letter in Appendix.)* He also asked me to keep the nice brown tie his uncle had given him, so he could wear it at our marriage ceremony.

To grow so close to another person, young, strong and clean as we were, with the uncanny electric sparks that flew between us, the way we kept catching each other's glance at the same moment, the way we relaxed with total trust: I now know this is rare and precious.

At one point, we were standing on the balcony overlooking New Orleans, which had been transformed for me from a dark violent nest of vipers into an incredibly romantic city filled with life, energy, and music: All because I got to see it through the eyes of someone who wanted me to see it the way he saw it. As our day slowly drew to an end we became solemn, knowing that a long period of separation was about to begin. It was painful to think about. Lee gave me some post-cards that he'd kept since his teenage years. They were places he wanted me to see someday. We were together from 2:30 until nearly 10:30 that night. As our last hour together approached, Lee and I held each other as if our hearts would break. Finally, and sadly, our day of delight was over, and I arrived back at Marengo Street.

Robert was not home yet, so I called Dave on Susie's phone and asked him to tell Dr. Mary we expected to leave in the morning. My heart was heavy. When I hung up the phone, I realized that my dream of finding a cure for cancer was dead.

1. The Warren Commission did not look into these events. In fact, they claimed that they did not know where Lee was during this time. The Clinton Incident, as it is called, was discovered and documented in the late 1960s by the Garrison Investigation and again in the 1970s during the HSCA Investigation. Some of the related documents were kept secret until the 1990s. Lee's account was unknown and unsupported for years, but is clearly supported today. A few details were also gleaned from witnesses who testified either in the Clay Shaw trial or the House Select Committee on Assassinations to present a more complete picture of the events.

2. Whether the vehicle was owned or leased is a point that requires more discussion. However it worked, it was the ITM's vehicle and only ITM personnel could drive it.

3. This man has been identified by other researchers as Estus Morgan, because he later stood in the voter registration line with Lee Oswald in Clinton. Since Morgan was a local, he was easily recognized by the witnesses.

4. The Congress of Racial Equality (CORE) workers were mostly student volunteers who were still on summer break.

5. They would be returning to their classrooms in just a few days. After they left, these newly registered African-American citizens, and even members of their families, of all ages, would be thrown in jail.

6. Ten days earlier, in nearby Plaquemines Parish, a number of CORE members staged a protest march in support of those who had been denied the right to register to vote. Over two hundred protesters were arrested and jailed, with help from Van Buskirk, a White Supremacist who frequently disrupted voter registration processes. Rumors abounded that Richard Van Buskirk was in town. So when an unfamiliar black Cadillac parked near the Voter Registration Office, it attracted attention. Was that the FBI? Or the press? Or Van Buskirk?

7. Now called Tuskegee University, the Tuskegee Institute was founded on July 4, 1881, in a one room shanty, near Butler Chapel AME Zion Church. Thirty adults were in the first class, and Dr. Booker T. Washington was the first teacher.

8. George de Mohrenschildt wrote in his manuscript, *I Am a Patsy! I Am a Patsy!*, that Lee "was sincerely and profoundly committed to a complete integration of blacks, and saw it in the future of the United States... Of course, he greatly admired Dr. Martin Luther King and agreed with his program... he frequently talked of Dr. King with real reverence." (p 198).

9. As it happened, the orderly's friend also worked at the hospital. He was using his lunch hour to pick up a friend who wanted to interview for a new job opening at the mental hospital.

10 The Registrar of Voters was later identified as Henry Earl Palmer, and is said to have been a high ranking member of the Ku Klux Klan.

11. One of Garrison's several investigators of the Clinton scene, Anne Dischler, clearly indicated that she saw a signature that was almost completely erased on a page in the Parish registration book. But when she returned a second time, the page, and then the book itself, disappeared. Dischler testified that "It looked like where Oswald had signed his name. You could make out part of the 'O' and while I was looking at the signature, Henry Earl Palmer (the Registrar of Voters) told me that 'this is where Oswald signed.'"

12. Despite the strong turn-out and the hours of waiting, only a few names actually made it on to the official register that day.

13 Professor Joseph Riehl, a New Orleans native with a high interest in the case, who initially helped give me courage to speak out, internet-posted an article by the *Morning Advocate Sunday Magazine* called "East Feliciana's Oswald Connection" ... CORE workers as well as the parish registrar of voters and the Clinton Town Marshall noticed some strange outsiders near the registrar's office ... in 1969 ... Clinton Town Marshall John Manchester testified that during the registration drive a black Cadillac parked outside the registrar's office was called to his attention ... he checked out the situation. In court, Manchester identified the defendant, Shaw, as the man in the driver's seat. Manchester testified Shaw said he was representing the International Trade Mart...At the trial, Palmer, the registrar, identified Oswald as one of only two whites in the long line of prospective voters. He said he passed Oswald in line at least six times. Palmer also identified Shaw and Ferrie as the occupants of the black Cadillac. Palmer testified that when Oswald reached the front of the line he made no attempt to register to vote. Instead, Palmer said, Oswald spoke to him about getting a job in East Louisiana State Hospital ..."

14. A special lid allowed filtered air to reach the living cells inside the bottles.

15. I created a unique pH indicator (yellow, going to lighter yellow) instead of the usual 'pink' phenol red, so the medium would look like chicken broth.

16. A similar transport and storage method would be used to get the materials to Mexico City,

from there the cancer cocktail would be out of Lee's hands, on its way to Cuba.

17. I do not know if Shaw drove them all the way back to New Orleans on the night of August 29, 1963, or if they stayed with a friend of Shaw's that night and came home in the morning. It is reasonable to point out that Clay Shaw's boss at the International Trade Mart was Lloyd Cobb, and he owned a farm near Jackson that occupied several thousand acres.

18. The volunteer perhaps congratulated himself that a few x-rays and shots would keep him from hard labor on a chain gang.

19. These were based on blood titer research I'd conducted at UF.

20. This was a serious error on my part, as it compounded my "sins." I had not only written a protest, but now a secretary knew the contents.

21. I had hoped to say that it was "just a note," but I did not get the opportunity.

22. My entire family would eventually learn of this $400 "windfall" that supposedly literally dropped into my hands from an old ironing board.

23. The "volunteer" was given a devastating x-ray treatment to destroy his immune system soon after the injected cancer cells were 'discovered' in his bloodstream (which would go on the prisoner's record). The slides and blood samples taken at that time proved he had cancer. Then came the x-rays, to see if tumors could be seen. Of course, there would be none, but this gave the x-ray technician the opportunity to rig the x-ray machine to assure an overexposure so strong that the volunteer's immune system would be severely compromised. Then he would be given shots to "strengthen him" — which would be labeled penicillin, for example, but which would actually contain more of the invisible galloping cancer cells. Only now, we believed his body would be unable to resist them. My tests would help determine if the cells were surviving. Ordinarily, a human would have little trouble destroying injected cancer cells. But this cancer was different: it was custom-designed to kill.

24. Jackson witness Lea McGehee would later recall seeing a "bassinet," but whatever one might call it, the basket was there, and proved useful.

25. WC Vol. XXII p. 169)

26. (WC Vol. XIX: p. 577)

27. Excerpt from Clay Shaw trial:...SCIAMBRA: Q: Please state your name for the record. A: Mrs. Bobbie Dedon. <snip> Q: Where were you employed in the summer of 1963? A: East Louisiana State Hospital...At the clinic as a receptionist. Q: ...I call your attention to late August or early September, 1963, and I ask you if anyone asked you for instructions — A: Yes. Q: — how to get to the personnel office. A: Yes. Q: (Exhibiting photograph to witness)...I ask you if you have ever seen the person in this picture. A: Yes...At my desk at the clinic...Q: Do you know who this person is? A: It is Lee Harvey Oswald...<snip>I just told him directions to go to the center building which is the administration building.<snip> Q: Where would a person go to apply for a job? A: At the administration building. Q: Can you remember about what time of day this was? A: It was around lunch, because I was getting ready to go to lunch. Note: Lee carried a lunch sack, but it was probably after 3:00. The witness could not recall if Lee wore a beard or not. This fact has been used to discredit her statements, ignoring supporting statements from witnesses in the personnel office that back her up, stating they saw a job application from Lee Oswald in their files — before it disappeared.

28. Lee received $200 a month from the FBI and $200 a month from the CIA. Besides these cash payments, he also received additional funds through American Express for special expenses he couldn't cover. Lee had told me he was "on loan" to the CIA

29. This type of full-service gas station was fairly common in the 1950s and 1960s.

30. Originally, Shaw, Dave, Lee and the orderly drove from Clinton to a rendezvous point that never included the town of Jackson, where they met the convoy and proceeded to the hospital.

31. Decades later, I interviewed Jackson's town barber, Lea McGehee. He'd never forgotten his encounter with Lee. Nor did he forget that there was an unusual car parked outside- a Kaiser-Frazer- with a young woman sitting in it, at the same time Lee so cordially met him. McGehee

was still running the same barbershop. He said the young woman he saw in the car (from the back) had shoulder-length dark hair, a fact he told Garrison's jury. In early 2001, Kelly Thomas — granddaughter of Charles Thomas (who had helped expedite Lee's passport)-helped me interview McGeHee on audiotape. First, McGehee gave me a little quiz, asking what kind of haircut Lee got. I told him that I didn't notice any difference when he returned to the car, so I didn't think Lee really got a haircut. "That's right!" McGehee said, pleased. He then agreed to be tape recorded. Rejecting photos of me with short hair, he said that as a barber, he remembered the length and color of the hair of the young woman: she had shoulder-length hair. I then showed him a photo of me with shoulder-length hair, and he agreed it was the correct length. The photo was taken July 20, 1963 — in Fort Walton — a month earlier. The other photos with short hair were taken in 1961. One researcher has since tried to insert a matron named Gladys (who didn't even like Lee) in the car with him there. But she also stated that Lee got into the black Cadillac after seeing McGeHee (what? leaving 'Gladys' all alone? Why would 'Gladys' drive Lee Oswald to the barber shop, to be picked up there in the Cadillac? It's all because the researcher insists Lee Oswald couldn't drive, though many witnesses have stated otherwise on the records). McGeHee said he was pressured to add the 'Cadillac' detail — never mentioned in his lengthy Garrison testimony years earlier — to his story, by the same researcher, telling him that the woman sat in the old car merely waiting for her laundry to get done (though this mystery woman was never interviewed). Since 'Gladys' lived in New Orleans, and the barber had never seen a Kaiser-Frazer in town, do the researcher's efforts to omit me from the scene make sense? Even so, she could not eliminate me from the same old car where I was spotted by Reeve Morgan's daughter, Mary, later the same day. Dr. Howard Platzman has written an essay exposing the gymnastics involved in trying to dismiss my testimony, available to any who inquire.

32. Both Morgan and his daughter, Mary, would always remember Lee's visit. Importantly, Mary was still on her summer break from college — more proof that the date Lee was seen in Jackson was before Sept. 2nd, after which most colleges began their Fall semester. Mary recalled spotting a woman sitting in Oswald's car — the second witness to report my presence "at the end of August or the first of September." Below are excerpts from the Clay Shaw trial testimony of Reeves Morgan, and an interview with Morgan's daughter: "(p. 45) Q ... how long did you talk to Oswald that day? A: Well, it wasn't too long, I would say maybe 20 minutes or 25 ... (p. 46) Q. Was anybody at home when Oswald was at your house, besides yourself? A. Yes, sir, my daughter was there…(p. 47) Q. Mr. Morgan, you say that this conversation took place either in late August or early September? A. To the best of my recollection. <snip> ... I was burning trash out of my fireplace, and it didn't feel too bad, it wasn't cold, it wasn't hot. (p. 49) Q. Was he clean and neat looking? A. Clean and neat, very well appearing fellow, nice appearance."

Andrew Sciambra interviewed Morgan's daughter for Garrison privately on June 3, 1967. This excerpt is from his January 29, 1968 report of that interview:

"I ...talk(ed) with his daughter, Mary Morgan, who had been at home at the time of the Oswald visit. Mary Morgan ... told me that when Oswald was in the house talking with her dad, she happened to walk towards the screen door and went onto the porch and just casually noticed that there was a dark-colored car parked under the tree in front of the house. It was rather dark and she didn't really pay much attention to the car ... it was an old car and the model was somewhere in the Fifties. She says that she remembers seeing a woman in the car."

33. Marina knew Lee was leaving for good: there is a piteous scene in McMillan's book when she and Lee said goodbye, in tears, when Ruth finally came to take her and Junie back to Texas. Even McMillan says that Marina never expected to see Lee again. This decision wasn't easy for him.

34. Lee kept only a few items in his small room at 1026 North Beckley, where he lived after being ordered to return to Dallas, but the Dallas police found the black and gold Imperial hunting knife I had given him. This deeply touched me when I learned of it in 2010. (Ref: Nov. 22, 1963 Report of Dallas Police Turner, Potts, Moore and Senkel.)

Chicago
Washington D.C.
St. Louis
Atlanta
Dallas
Gainesville
New Orleans
Houston
Tampa
Havana
Yucatán
Mexico City

— CHAPTER 24 —

SEPARATION

Monday, September 2, 1963

At dawn Robert got up and started to pack the car. He was anxious to leave, but we had to wait for the bank to open so he could withdraw all of our money. During his pre-trip safety check, Robert discovered a problem with the car and took it to a garage, hoping we still might be able to leave that day. But the repair took too long, and we had to spend an extra night in New Orleans.

Robert's parents called nervously when we didn't show up in Ft. Walton as planned. Obviously worried about whether I actually planned on accompanying Robert home, they tried to motivate me by saying I could earn $150 if I finished an architectural rendering of their new apartment buildings before we had to be in Gainesville on the 6th.

September 3, 1963

Once again, we prepared to leave. I hugged Susie goodbye for the last time.[1]

The bank would open at 9:00 A.M., so at 8:45, we left 1032 Marengo Street forever. As Robert braked to turn onto Magazine Street, I saw a tanned young man, dressed in a white T-shirt, and flip-flops, reading a newspaper. As the car turned, he looked up from the newspaper, and looked directly into my eyes — *Lee!* It was the last time we saw each other.

By 9:15, we were on our way to Ft. Walton Beach. On the 6th, we left for Gainesville, headed to a cottage Robert's mother found for us.[2]

September 6, 1963

Robert and I arrived in Gainesville after sunset and checked into our "furnished cottage." I was way too tired to care that the only furniture was a double bed, a little Formica-topped table, and a wooden chair. At least the mattress was clean.

The tiny cottage was on 62nd St., just west of campus, but it was too far from UF to walk. Robert's parents had told us it was "cute" — and it did have a little porch, draped with kudzu and passion flower vines.

The kitchen was the size of a closet and had a tiny oven where the roaches lived. Besides the creaky bed, the table and the chair, our little palace was well stocked with wooden crates, some planks of wood, and a bunch of bricks, out of which we fashioned a desk and bookshelf. The bathroom is best left undescribed.

Near our mildewed haven, on the right, were some new brick apartments where we met new friends. Ron Ziegler and his pretty wife, Karen, lived in one of them, and were newlyweds too. They bought a 'forest painting' from me, and sometimes I would visit them and watch TV.

Prior to our goodbyes in New Orleans, Lee had taught me a phone call scheme called a "call wheel," so he, Dave and I would know how and when to call each other using rotating call-times and pay phone numbers.[3] For security reasons, we would call Lee by the name of 'Hector' on the phone.

Lee set up the way for Dave to communicate with me in Gainesville. Dave had some contacts in Gainesville and one of them left a phone number for "J" at the Craft Shop in UF's Student Union, where I used to work. Dave told me Lee was confident that even I could find the Craft Shop again, since I had worked there for an entire year. We all knew Robert would be happy to drive me to the campus if it meant I would make some money, so I told Robert that my friend Don Federman was now an editor of *The New Orange Peel* (UF's witty student magazine) and that he'd pay me to do some illustration work for the magazine. After Robert dropped me off on campus on his way to class, I stopped by the Craft Shop and picked up the phone number I could use to call Dave for free and with privacy. This got the call wheel started.

When Dave called the next time, he updated me on the civil rights unrest in New Orleans, which was making Guy Banister foam at the mouth. Finally, Dave told me, "Hector was in Dallas." Lee had gone to Dallas briefly to prepare for his trip to Mexico City. He arrived in Dallas around lunchtime and proceeded to a large prestigious building downtown, where he met two men. One was his handler, "Mr. B" who had accidentally told him his name was 'Benton' when previously he'd said his name was "Benson." Disturbingly, now Lee heard this man addressed as "Bishop" by the anti-Castro Cuban who joined them. He now realized that only the letter "B" had been consistent in "Mr. B's" name. Lee had previously been informed that he'd meet not only his handler, but also the contact who would make sure the bioweapon got into Cuba, so he assumed the Latino was that man. No names were exchanged: it was an eyes-only encounter, and the meeting then abruptly ended. To Lee, this was a bad sign, showing inadequate respect for him. Not even invited to eat lunch with them,

Lee was immediately sent back to New Orleans with an empty stomach and was home before nightfall. It was obvious he was to be given as little information as possible, which made him feel extremely uncomfortable.[4]

Mr. B's treatment of Lee remained a nagging concern for him. He was also concerned because shortly after returning to New Orleans he was driven to Baton Rouge, where he found himself "inspected" by a military officer prior to entering a meeting. After that meeting some kind of cash account was set up for Marina and the children, so Lee could leave her behind without worry.

Next, Lee was ordered to keep nice and quiet in New Orleans, in contrast to his recent activities publicly touting Cuba and Uncle Fidel — a great relief.[5] Basically, he was to lay low until the prisoner(s) died, at which time he had to be ready to travel at once without being noticed. However, Lee still attended meetings, requiring quick trips to both Baton Rouge and Sulphur, Louisiana (a very small town with its own airport outside of Lake Charles), as well as a flight to Florida. The rest of the time, he sat quietly reading on the porch, on watch for any hostile anti-Castro visitors. Unemployment checks met his family's basic needs: he didn't dare take a job. During this time of peace, Lee still made it clear to Marina that she must go to Texas without him when Ruth Paine, who was visiting her CIA-employed relatives out east, came for her. Our split-up was a sham. Dave kept us informed.

As September progressed, Lee transformed himself into a quiet homebody. Neighbors noticed that he spent many hours reading on his porch. At night, he was often still reading by lamplight. Mrs. Garner, the apartment manager, testified that Lee couldn't possibly be working, as he was spending all his time reading books on the hot porch, clad only in yellow beach shorts and wearing flip-flops.[6] Best of all, Lee reported that he had reached a truce with Marina: "We don't even argue anymore." Back in Gainesville, Robert attended day and night classes at UF, and I worked at the Craft Shop in UF's student union all day, attending classes at night, so we saw little of each other. I wanted Robert to think I intended to stay, but under our bed a packed suitcase was ready.

As we entered the latter part of September, Lee awaited Ruth Paine's arrival in New Orleans, so she could transport his family back to Dallas. Lee wanted them out of New Orleans before he had to leave to courier the bioweapon to Mexico City, as soon as the prisoner died. There was no longer any doubt about the cancer cocktail's efficacy: it was only a matter of days. Ruth Paine's job was to take care of Marina and Junie in Texas, and she assured Marina that she would pick her up in New Orleans on September 20th.[7]

Friday, September 20, 1963

Once Lee dropped off the bioweapon to the contact in Mexico, he would have money to disappear and would send word for me to join him. He no longer fully trusted anyone he was working with, so he was anxious and suspicious most of the time.

When Ruth Paine did not arrive on the morning of the 20th, as planned, Lee's anxiety soared. What if the prisoner died today? Would he have to leave Marina and Junie alone in New Orleans the next morning? What if she went into labor while he was gone? Worried about these issues, Lee contacted Dr. Warner Kloepfer to help, should he need to leave before Ruth Paine arrived. Dr. Kloepfer was on the faculty of Tulane Medical School, so he had access to doctors in town. Both he and his wife spoke Russian, and they had already visited Marina and Junie twice, ostensibly because of their Quaker connections with Ruth Paine.

Later that evening, Ruth arrived with her small children and parked her station wagon in front of Lee's apartment on Magazine Street for the next few days.[8] After three days of packing, they were ready to leave.[9]

Monday, September 23, 1963

Lee got a phone call telling him to get ready to travel. The call meant that the prisoner had died, and that Lee must soon leave for Mexico City with the bioweapon. Marina and Junie would now have to depart, freeing Lee to go his separate way. Despite Lee and Marina's copious problems, they both saw this as a watershed moment in their lives. Neither thought they would ever see the other again. Their goodbyes were sorrowful.[10]

As for me and Lee, our planned escape and reunion seemed imminent. From this moment on, I could be required to disappear at anytime, and fly to join him in Mexico. Alex Rorke, a trusted friend, would bring a plane to Eglin Air Force Base.[11] Even I knew how to get to the nation's largest air force base! I would board, then he and his pilot would fly me to the Yucatan, where our new lives, undercover, would begin. I bought a .22 revolver for the trip.

Tuesday, September 24, 1963

Lee walked out of his apartment at 4905 Magazine Street for the last time and began a historic journey. Within 72 hours, he was in Mexico. Much of what we know about these 72 hours comes from the U.S. Government files which are fairly good at tracking people across borders and through the public transportation system.[12] They are accurate, by-and-large, because no one preparing them understood their significance. But there are some glaring gaps in the Warren Commission's account of Lee's movements during this time that have puzzled both investigators and researchers for decades. In brief, the Warren Commission says Lee took a bus from New Orleans to Houston, then from Houston to Laredo, where he crossed the Mexican border about 2:00 P.M. on September 26th.

There are two major problems with their account. I will explain these problems first, and then tell you what Lee told me to fill in the gaps. First of all, numerous witnesses saw Lee on the second leg of the bus trip (from Houston to Laredo), but no one saw him on the first leg (between New Orleans and Houston). Warren Commission investigators openly admitted they had no witnesses, nor direct evidence, to support the idea that Lee Oswald was on the bus during the first leg of the trip. They also admitted they only inferred that Lee was on that particular bus, because it was the only one that went from New Orleans to Houston during the time period in question.

As you will see shortly, Lee was not on the bus from New Orleans to Houston, but he did have a ticket for it and his suitcases were checked as luggage. The second problem for investigators was that two witnesses report seeing Lee in Austin, Texas and one reported speaking with him in Dallas that same day, at the same time Lee was supposed to be on the bus between New Orleans and Houston.

So how could someone do that? Austin is about 500 miles west of New Orleans. It takes over 8 hours by car. Then Dallas is several hours to the north. But everyone agrees that Lee got on the bus in Houston later that same day, because there are plenty of witnesses who saw him and talked to him. So if he was in Austin and Dallas, then he had to travel back to Houston. There is only one logical answer to this puzzle, and it involves an airplane. And not some puny single-engine job with a small gas tank. This one would take a larger, faster plane with a long range to complete the triangle of New Orleans-to-Austin-to-Dallas-to-Houston all in one day.

The task itself is not really the problem, because there were plenty of airplanes in south Louisiana providing logistical support to the oil exploration industry that could make this trip easily. In fact, they moved people and equipment across the oil belt of Texas and Louisiana constantly. Any company, like Schlumberger or Halliburton, that provides logistical support for oil exploration could easily accomplish this task if directed to do so. So the question is not how could it be done, but rather how would a lowly unemployed coffee-machine greaser like Lee Oswald have access to airplanes used by the oil industry? Here is the crux of the matter.

I will tell you what Lee told me about his trip, and I will combine it with what has been established by other sources to complete the picture. We begin with Eric Rogers, who lived in the 4907 apartment to keep an eye on Lee's family. He saw Lee leave 4905 Magazine Street and board the Magazine Street bus carrying two suitcases.[13] Lee visited his downtown post office box, picked up an unemployment check and cashed it, then headed to the International House were he spent the day in tactical meetings and slept there that evening. Lee called his uncle Dutz at that point to say goodbye. He was ready to travel.

Wednesday, September 25, 1963

Early in the morning, Lee, Guy Banister, Hugh Ward (Banister's partner and pilot), and an envoy from Texas met for breakfast at the International House. Banister explained that the envoy represented a "Mr. Le Corque" who was "in tight" with Lyndon Johnson.[14] Banister explained Le Corque's impressive background to the group. The story went back to an American fighter pilot named Claire Chennault,

 who went to China in the late-1930's to help Madame Chiang Kai-shek reorganize the Chinese air force in preparation for war with Japan. The result of Chennault's efforts was a legendary band of American guerilla pilots called the "Flying Tigers," which fought the Japanese military in air-to-air combat on a daily basis, but claimed not to be associated with the U.S. Government.[15] Somewhere along the way, Chennault acquired the title of General, though he had only been a Captain in the U.S.

Army Air Corps. The secret was that Le Corque was actually Thomas G. Corcoran, a member of FDR's inner circle who helped organize the Flying Tigers as a clandestine operation for the U.S. government. Le Corque was Chennault's main benefactor inside the U.S. Government and managed their covert relationship for years. Le Corque became very close to General Chennault.

After World War II, Chennault relocated his airplane fleet to Lake Charles to work with the oil industry in south Louisiana and southeastern Texas. A few years later, Chennault developed terminal cancer. As he lay dying in Ochsner Clinic, with his wife (Anna Chan Chennault) and Dr. Ochsner at his side, Madame Chiang Kai-shek and Le Corque came to visit General Chennault to thank him for all of his heroic efforts. After Chennault's death, Le Corque became involved with

Chennault's wife romantically and financially, winding up half owner of his substantial airplane fleet, before it was taken over by the CIA.[16]

Hugh Ward, the pilot who would be flying Lee around that day, complained about having to drop the plane off at the Chennault Air Field in Lake Charles instead of flying back to New Orleans. This meant that Ward would have a long bus ride from Lake Charles to New Orleans after spending the entire day flying. But the others at the table were not sympathetic to Hugh Ward's plea. There was pressure on the mission to leave as soon as Clay Shaw came to finalize details, so it was too late to change anything. In a few minutes, Clay Shaw arrived with a zippered bag like the blue one Lee owned. It held two thermoses: one contained the deadly cancer cells. The other contained a sterile medium for replenishing the liquid in the other thermos to keep the cells alive. There were also packets resembling packets of sugar to make more sterile medium, if necessary. There were also crackers and bananas in the bag, to make it look like a lunch pack that could pass a simple border inspection. If inspected visually, the cancer cells would look like chicken broth.[17]

After opening the blue bag and showing its contents to Lee, Shaw handed "Le Corque's" representative an envelope, saying, "This goes to Austin, too." Then Shaw gave Le Corque's envoy a stack of files to take to LBJ's lawyers in Austin, and shook hands with everyone, commenting that he had a personal interest in making sure Lee's trip was successful. Hugh Ward told Lee to grab something to eat off the table, because it was time to "hit the road." Lee said he loaded up a bag with warm cinnamon rolls, enough for both breakfast and lunch, reminding me that nobody loved cinnamon rolls more than Lee Oswald.

Everyone left International House at the same time. Banister drove Le Corque's envoy out to the Lakefront Airport where a plane waited to fly him alone to the Texas capital. Shaw headed to Hammond to spend the day with his ailing father, neatly obscuring his early morning absence from the Trade Mart. A car and driver was waiting outside of International House to take Lee and Hugh Ward to an airport in Houma, Louisiana (about an hour southwest of New Orleans). But first, they had to pick up a package from the nearby offices of Eli Lilly that needed to be delivered to someone in Austin. After getting the package from Eli Lilly, the trio headed to the Houma-Terrebonne Airport, known to locals as "the blimp station." Lee said they reached the blimp station without undue delay.

When Lee and Hugh Ward arrived at the Houma-Terrebonne airport, a twin-engine plane sat on the tarmac with a Hispanic man seated in the co-pilot's seat. The plane was a De Havilland "Dove," a work plane used by the oil field logistics teams in south Louisiana and Texas.[18] This one was owned by Schlumberger, the largest oil field services company in the world, and had just flown in from Hull Field in Sugarland, Texas on the west side of Houston. Normally equipped to carry two crew members and 8 passengers, half of the passenger seats had been removed to make room for cargo. This plane had a range of 1,000 miles and a top speed of over 200 MPH, so it could make the 450 mile trip from Houma, Louisiana to Austin, Texas comfortably in two-and-a-half hours on half a tank of gas. Its engines were warm,

Alex Rorke

its fuel tanks topped off, and it was ready for take-off. Lee and Hugh Ward climbed aboard. Hugh climbed in the pilot's seat, and Lee got busy securing his cargo. Just then a message came over the plane's radio. It was sent by a ham radio operator who worked with the Cuban underground. It said that Alex Rorke had "run into some trouble," and he and his pilot might be "missing."[19]

This was instantly a great concern to Lee because, not only was Alex Rorke one of his trusted friends from his nefarious anti-Castro world, he was also the man who was going to fly me from Florida to Mexico when it was time for Lee and me to disappear, which might be this week. After an anxious discussion, Hugh

said they had to get in the air to stay on schedule and encouraged Lee to lie down and get some sleep. Lee was tired from days of inadequate rest and curled up in Ward's bedroll, with the blue zippered bag and its insulated contents taped to the empty seat next to him.

The Dove flew at top speed all the way to Austin, arriving at lunchtime. A rental car awaited the team on the tarmac. Lee and the Latino entered in the car, and the Latino drove Lee to downtown Austin near the state Capitol, where Lee went to a lunchroom near the Texas governor's office.

What he did next is most perplexing. Despite all the precautions taken to secretly fly him to Austin while he was supposed to be on a bus headed to Houston, Lee walked into the U.S. Government's Selective Service office and started complaining about the status of his

Marine discharge.[20] He had already addressed this issue with attorney Dean Andrews in New Orleans and written letters to the Secretary of the Navy about it. And he would be leaving Austin in a few hours to move to Dallas, so why complain now? What could this accomplish? And wouldn't it blow the cover off the secret trip? As with many of Lee's actions, this one probably had another motive entirely. Perhaps he was doing the fake-alibi routine as he did in Jackson to scramble the time line, but there may have been a darker reason.

Another report had come in that Rorke's plane was missing, Lee was now certain he was being set up by people planning to kill the President, and he was concerned that another reason for his trip to Mexico City was to make him look like a Castro agent. If Lee believed that the trail to the plotters led to Austin, perhaps he wanted to leave a clue: a scrap of evidence to prove he was actually there that day. He told me it was to create an alibi to confuse the timeline, but I think there is room for questions here. He said he went to the Selective Service office first, but told the woman there that he had already been to the governor's offices. Then he gave his name as Harvey Oswald, and when she could not find his Selective Service card, he left.[21]

With at least one witness to his presence in Austin, and with his alibi in place, Lee waited for the courier; who soon arrived with an envelope full of cash. The courier told Lee that "nobody knew" where the money had come from, but they wanted to make sure they knew where it was going, so Lee had to sign a receipt for the cash. Lee said he counted the bills twice. The Latinos, meanwhile, were eating lunch with some anti-Castro friends and had promised to seek news about Alex Rorke. When they returned, they dropped Lee at the Trek Café on South Congress Avenue, where he waited for about forty-five minutes while they dropped off the package from Eli Lilly in the biology building at St. Edward's University.[22]

As Lee waited, his tension grew as he worried about Alex Rorke. If Alex Rorke had been killed, how would I be able to join him in Mexico? Lee worried about finding another pilot he could trust. Perhaps he could get Hugh Ward to help him. Lee ordered three or four cups of coffee as he drew on several napkins. He was the only person in the café, and there was only one waitress, so she couldn't help but notice how nervous he was, and tried to strike up a conversation, but Lee did not respond. He finally saw the Latinos waiting in the car outside. After briefly wondering if he was being set up to get robbed of the cash he had just received, he left the café, taking the napkins that he had been drawing on with him.

The point about the napkins is that in order to call me about the Rorke problem, Lee had to write out our call wheel from memory, then calculate the roll-out of dates and times, so he would know which phone to call and when. He wrote out another wheel to reach Dave.

The Latinos took Lee back to the airplane in Austin. Hugh Ward then flew them to Dallas where Lee said he had to meet with Jack Ruby. I had heard Jack Ruby's name from the strippers at the YWCA in New Orleans, but had no idea that Lee knew him.[23] However, due to Lee's connections with Marcello, this did not surprise me very much. Ruby apparently wanted Lee to get him some laetrile, a cancer drug that was legal in Mexico, but illegal in the U.S. Lee also said he had to make a reservation on an apartment in Dallas. Then, if things didn't work out for Marina at Ruth Paine's place, due to the pressures of the new baby, she would have a place to go. He planned to use the apartment himself for a quick return trip to Dallas after his baby was born, for Lee had a deep desire to see his baby before we vanished for an unknown length of time.

The plane arrived in Dallas near sunset, and Lee was met by two Latinos who drove him around on his errands. The airport in Dallas was so close to Ruth Paine's residence that Lee insisted on being driven past her house to see if Marina and Junie had safely arrived.[24] Lee was concerned that Paine's heavily-packed, travel-worn station wagon might not make it all the way from New Orleans to Dallas without breaking down. Lee was relieved to see the station wagon sitting in the driveway. It was twilight by then and the car had already been unpacked. Lee could now go to Mexico without fretting about his family's safety.

Then, Lee said, he went to meet a woman who was active in the anti-Castro community to see if she had contacts in Mexico City, and if he could get information about Alex Rorke's situation. I believe the woman that Lee went to see was Sylvia Odio, since she reported being introduced to Lee (as "Leon Oswald") by two Latinos at this time.[25] Lee said they spoke in Spanish, too rapidly for him to follow.[26]

Odio told several persons before the assassination that she met Lee Oswald, and that she later received a call saying Lee was 'loco' and would as soon kill Kennedy as Castro. Many researchers consider Lee's meeting with Sylvia Odio as the first overt attempt to frame Lee for Kennedy's murder. If Lee was already being set up as a patsy while on his way to Mexico City it raises serious questions about the real purpose of that trip.

Today, we know that Alex Rorke's plane crashed on the day Lee left for Mexico City after leaving Cozumel, where I believe Alex and his co-pilot, Geoffrey Sullivan, flew to check out where I could safely be dropped off. Then the plane took off on another mission, apparently near or over Cuba, where it was shot down. On Oct. 6, eleven days later, Gerry Hemming took Interpen members and hunted for the downed plane and bodies.[27] I find the timing of both the Alex Rorke rumor and his subsequent disappearance troubling.

Once his business in Dallas was finished, Lee boarded the Dove again and flew to Houston, landing at Hull Field in Sugarland, on the west side of Houston. There, he was handed a second blue zippered "lunch bag" and told that it contained fresh cancer cells which would give the Product two extra days of shelf life.[28] Then Lee swapped the lunch bags and took a long bus ride to Laredo. To the outside world, he seemed to have traveled by bus all the way from New Orleans.[29]

Dave called to tell me "Hector is in Houston." I knew that meant Lee was on his way to Mexico City, and I would hear from him soon, so I went to my designated pay phone at the designated time, and waited for Lee's call, hoping to get information about catching a plane and joining him in Mexico. Fortunately, Robert was busy day and night attending classes and studying in his carrel at the university library, so he did not interfere.

Finally, the phone rang. It was Lee calling from Houston. He began by telling me that Alex Rorke was missing. I could hear the stress in his voice. Lee said he was planning to meet Alex Rorke in Mexico City to discuss the best places to drop me off in the Yucatan. He would try to find out more about Alex's situation.

In the meantime, I should be ready to go to Eglin AFB. He would try to find another pilot. If not, I could take a commercial flight out of Tampa or Miami. Our hopes were still high, but the call was short. Lee said he did not have time to talk. He said he loved me and hung up. Later, Lee told me he had to hang up so fast because he had to call a "Mr. Twiford" to alert his network that he was headed to Mexico City.[30] Then Lee got on a bus headed for the Mexican border.[31]

That weekend, I took many short walks to the local grocery store, so I could pace back and forth near their pay phones at certain times. I couldn't help it. In between, I pored over the newspapers for clues about Kennedy's enemies.

AUTOBUSES
Transportes del Norte

OFICINAS GENERALES:
HEROES 271 PTE.   MONTERREY, N. L.

MEXICO, D. F.

DE

LAREDO, TEX.

A

CONEXIONES
GREYHOUND
Lines

CONTRASEÑA SIN VALOR

BOLETO DIRECTO

PRECIO: $ 93.75

Friday, September 27, 1963

Lee arrived in Mexico City in mid-morning, where the Warren Commission claims Lee checked into a well-known hotel, but Lee told me he rented quarters at a Quaker establishment, where he pretended he was a drug dealer working for the mafia. This seems to have terrified everyone, so they completely avoided him, which is what Lee intended. That evening, the big moment finally came — the handover of the bio-weapon. Lee went to the designated drop-off point — a souvenir shop, where he was supposed to meet a medical technician that would continue to keep the cells alive. But the technician failed to show. When Lee tried to contact Mr. Bishop, he was told that Bishop had flown to Washington, DC. Lee had been abandoned in Mexico City. His fears now escalated: he had justifiable visions of being arrested, interrogated, and tortured by the Mexican police, if anybody at the Quaker house reported him.

The years have faded some details, but I recall that Lee reached an emergency contact, a 'cutout' who said he'd try to help out. This was a blonde-haired young man with a Moped. He had friends at a local university medical school. Meanwhile, Lee tried to avoid looking like a drug dealer. He went to a jai alai match and a bullfight, where he finally met his blonde-haired emergency contact. Together, they decided to go to the Cuban Consulate, for Lee now wanted to try to enter Cuba, if he could, before the bioweapon expired.

Lee had a list of trusted contacts memorized, which he had been told to give to the medical technician, along with instructions on how to keep the bioweapon alive and how (and where) to make injections.

He was willing to risk his life to do so. To that end, Lee visited the Cuban consulate, along with his friend. I personally believe that no U.S. spy photos showing Lee at the Cuban Consulate were saved because he was not alone in these photographs. I believe he was accompanied by the blond contact. Hence, photos of a heavyset male CIA agent were deliberately labeled with Lee's name.

Either Lee's friend, or Lee, handed over his application for a transit visa to enter Cuba. At this time, an attractive young woman, Sylvia Duran, handled Lee's application. She later reported that "Lee" was a blonde-haired young man, most likely to protect herself, for Duran ended up being tortured by the Mexican police at the behest of the U.S. after the assassination, to force her to confess that she'd slept with Lee. I am sure she regretted ever meeting him. As new evidence has shown, after Kennedy's assassination it became too dangerous to implicate Lee as a pro-Castro, pro-Soviet agent, and it was decided that Lee would simply be known as "a lone nut." Duran was then released from prison.

Lee was impersonated by phone at this time as well, linking him to a Soviet spy known to be a professional assassin. As for Lee, because of his loyalty to Kennedy, and despite his belief that he was surely being set up to take a fall, he made a final attempt to get the bioweapon into Cuba. He must have played his part well, because Señora Duran invited Lee to a party — which is why the police were told to arrest her later. After the party, they went to Sylvia's place, where he spent the night[32] Lee told me that he slept with Duran to get her cooperation, hoping for vital information and help from her. He didn't have to tell me about her, but by now, we never hid things of that nature from each other.

But nothing "under the table" worked, and of course the Cuban consulate refused to approve Lee's transit visa request on such short notice. The hurry-up request had marked Lee as a suspicious character, so Lee put on a dramatic Scarlet Pimpernel act. He made a foolish spectacle of himself. Such a fool could not possibly be important, or dangerous! Even so, Lee might have been awarded the transit visa "under the table" — it was not unheard-of — by showing a dog-like loyalty to Castro. But the ploy, which never had much of a chance of success, failed. Lee was treated rudely by the consulate staff, who again denied his request.[33] With no transit visa and a biological weapon that was about to expire, Lee contacted the Mexico City CIA station, seeking further instructions. The CIA had previously promised Lee that he would stay in Mexico City and start a new career there as an asset. But now, Lee was ordered to return to Dallas for "debriefing." Life in Mexico would come later: he was not to be upset about the failure of the mission, he was told, because a deadly hurricane was approaching Cuba, disrupting everything. But because the timing was off — the hurricane had been no such threat on the 26th — Lee didn't believe a word of it. With a sense of impending doom, Lee prepared to return to Dallas. Everything had gone wrong in Mexico City, except Señora Duran.

Failure on an important mission like this was not in Lee's play book. In a last ditch effort to do something to advance the cause, he left the thermoses in the souvenir shop in a safe place, keeping the zippered bag because it matched the one left behind in Texas — just in case he would be asked to try again. He deposited one of his two suitcases in a locker in the bus station, so he would have some clothes to wear when he returned to Mexico. It was now obvious to Lee that he had been betrayed, and his actions at the consulate would further stain him as a pro-Castro fanatic, making him an even more convincing patsy in Kennedy's murder.

"They think I'm a blind fool!" Lee told me soon after. "If they don't want me for Cuba anymore, I'm better off dead than alive to them."

Lee saw that while his usefulness was over, his knowledge of names, faces and events was dangerous. It was a bad combination. Lee concluded that Mexico had become too obvious for us to hide in. We immediately changed our escape plans. We would flee to the Cayman Islands, wait a year or so, then move on to fulfill our dream of exploring lost Mayan cities. On his way back to Texas, Lee stopped in the U. S. Public Health Service office at the border and told a contact where he had left the deadly materials.[34] He also looked into quickie Mexican divorces in a nearby border town.[35] Once in Dallas, Lee was ordered to check in at the YMCA and not to tell his wife he was in town until after he'd been debriefed. It should be noted that Lee never mentioned going to Cuba again, despite his supposed obsession with the subject. His Cuban transit visa was actually approved less than a month later, which was almost record time, but he ignored it. The mission to kill Castro had failed, and his attention was now focused on what would happen to John F. Kennedy.

After his debriefing, Lee was able to call me at last. He told me "They said it was the hurricane," in the clipped way that he had when he was irritated.[36] "They said every demmed safe house was wrecked, and most of our contacts were scattered."

Lee was shown photos of the devastation Hurricane Flora had caused in the Caribbean. Several days before hitting Cuba, Flora hit Haiti, where it killed 5,000 people. The approach of that Category IV storm with winds gusts over 200 mph prompted Castro to send his medical staff, which was concentrated in Havana, all over Cuba to deal with the coming disaster.[37] A week later, Lee was shown more photos of the massive devastation caused in Cuba by the killer hurricane, making it obvious to him that his handlers were trying to allay his suspicions.

Lee didn't buy the Hurricane Flora excuse as the reason that his contact was not in Mexico City. "How dumb do they think I am?" he said. My intuition told me that he was right at the time, and today we know that Lee entered Mexico City on the morning of September 26th, and Hurricane Flora did not hit Cuba until October 4th. So it is not a plausible excuse for Lee's contact not being in Mexico City when he arrived.

The other point was that Alex Rorke had indeed disappeared on September 25th, as Lee had been told, but he was not informed until much later that Rorke and his pilot had been shot down over Cuba and might still be alive, held as prisoners. Lee's Latino contacts should have given him this information, but did not. This made Lee rightfully suspicious. We believed a deliberate effort had been made to keep me in Florida.

Lee's involvement in the bioweapon project was now over, as was mine. Though the transit visa to Cuba arrived on his birthday, Cuba was no longer on his assignment list, so the visa was ignored. Instead, he'd been assigned to spy on a band of right-wing nuts interested in killing Kennedy. In the meantime, Lee was told he could be "sent to Mexico at any time." We just had to be patient.

Thursday, October 3, 1963

Dave called and told me that "Hector" was back in Dallas. Then he told me that I needed to order a new birth certificate at once. If anyone looked at my birth records, he explained, the last known address would show "New Orleans," for I had ordered the certificate when living there. That had to be covered up. I obeyed, and ordered a new birth certificate for the second time in two months. The new certificate was sent to Gainesville, Florida.[38]

Sunday, October 6, 1963

Lee called to say that it had been confirmed that Alex Rorke and his pilot were probably dead. Rorke's plane was believed to have been shot down over Cuba sometime after taking off from Cozumel. Dave had promised to find another pilot to get me to Mexico when the time was right.

Monday, October 13, 1963

I asked Robert to drive me to a pay phone located on a high curb near a row of older homes so I could make a call about getting a job. The phone rang as I approached it, but Robert didn't notice. It was Dave Ferrie. He said I had been hired at Peninsular ChemResearch, a sophisticated laboratory located on an isolated campus just outside Gainesville, Florida. There scientists and their assistants created and tested "designer chemicals" for private and public concerns. The slogan was that there was not a molecule they could not make. Robert never even inquired how I could get a paying job at a highly-regarded chemical laboratory with only one college chemistry course on my official record, when dozens of top graduate students from UF's prestigious chemistry department would gladly have worked there for nothing, just to get that lab's name on their resumés.

"You'll be working a lot of hours," Dave warned me.

"So what?" I mused, thinking I'd be happy creating exotic chemicals for esoteric scientific projects. Dave had told me that some of these would be sent to New Orleans via such routes as the Mound Park Hospital in St. Petersburg, Eastman Kodak, and our familiar chemical supplier, Eli Lilly, including materials similar to antifreeze, which could be used to safely deep-freeze the deadly cancer cell lines, keeping them alive virtually forever. Oh, great! Eternal death. My greatest achievement.

Dave explained that he had persuaded Dr. Ochsner that my "appointment" at PenChem was necessary to help deflect the inevitable questions that would arise over my failure to do any more lab research. Ochsner conceded that I needed something interesting in Gainesville, or questions might arise about what had happened in New Orleans that made me abort my "holy mission" to defeat cancer. I would start on Wednesday.

My ultimate goal for that autumn was to escape with Lee, so I did not register for any important classes, since I'd have to leave with incompletes. Instead I would work at the well-regarded PenChem lab to provide an excuse for my absence from UF's labs.

Wednesday, October 16, 1963

Once again, Lee and I would start our new pre-arranged jobs on the same day, just as we had in New Orleans. Lee's new job was at the Texas School Book Depository, across the street from the federal court house in downtown Dallas.[39]

Lee probably called me at our University contact number (I think I was taking night classes on Tuesdays and Thursdays there). He had now moved into his "safe house" and had no plans to live with Marina again, though he would visit her and Junie on the weekends. He gave me his phone number at the Depository, where he would start work Wednesday morning as an inventory clerk.[40] The big building had been purchased recently by a Mr. Byrd, a close friend of LBJ and his Texas oil baron cronies, and a new company handling school books had moved in.

They were refurbishing the place, Lee said, and with so many people coming and going, it was easy for him to "come and go" as well. "It's just another temporary cover job," Lee told me. Mr. Truly, his boss, had been told Lee was working undercover for the FBI.

"I have the same kind of job freedom that I had at Reily's," Lee said. "But even better, because there's no time clock." Lee filled out his hours by hand, or would have a secretary do it. He came and went as necessary, just as he'd done in New Orleans.[41]

"Don't give up on me," he said. "I've been promised that I'll be sent back to Mexico City before long. Things are working out, Juduffki!" I remember that he also cautioned me about his appearance. "I've lost some weight," he warned me. "So don't be worried when you see me. I haven't been sick — I've just tried some self-discipline, like T. E. Lawrence."

Lee and I had been fascinated with Lawrence for not only his abilities as a spy and great leader, but also for his model of self-control and calm, no matter what he faced. Lawrence had trained himself to go without food or water for long periods of time, and now Lee told me that he had just broken a series of fasts, and long periods of meditation. So not to worry — he was now drinking lots of milk, and devouring hamburgers and cinnamon rolls!

Saturday, October 19, 1963

Friday had been Lee's 24th birthday. When I heard his strained voice, I realized that something sinister was blowing in the wind. It began when he told me that he cried when Marina and Ruth gave him a little birthday cake.

"I won't live to see another birthday cake," he said quietly, "unless I can get out of here. And if I don't do it right, we'll all get killed."

To my gasp of horror, he added, "I'm sorry. You have to hear it." I now learned that upon his return to Dallas, Lee had been invited to be an actual participant in the assassination plans against JFK.

"You know what that means," he warned me. I did.

"So, you're going to go through with it?"

"I'm going to have to go through with it. Who else is in position to penetrate this, and stop it?"

I started to cry, feeling both hopeless and helpless.

"Don't cry," he said. "It's killing me! I can't stand your crying like that."

I suddenly felt faint, and accidentally dropped the phone. When I picked up the phone again, we tried to comfort each other. But then Lee revealed that he had decided to send on any information he could about the assassination ring. He was convinced that his information could make a huge difference.[42]

Lee was spending evenings with men who were plotting the death of the President of the United States — men who would stop at nothing to gain more power. They might even be able to blame it on Castro, impelling Americans to war against Cuba, and thus killing two big birds with one big stone. Lee and I both believed that an invasion of Cuba could trigger World War III, if Russia moved in to defend her Communist ally in the Caribbean.

"I know you think I'm a good shot," he told me. "Truth is, I'm not that good. So why did they recruit me?"

Lee made a bitter laugh. "They'll set me up. You see how they hung me out to dry in Mexico City," he went on. "Now they've put off my return to Mexico until after Christmas. I'm going to be snuffed, just as I told you, way back."

But he felt he had to stay on, with so much at stake. There was now no way to persuade Lee to save himself. In fact, he would have thought it immoral of me to suggest it at the expense of President Kennedy.

Touching, to me, was another statement he made: "Marina hasn't had the baby yet. At least I'll be allowed to see my new son. That's something, you know."

"How do you know it's going to be a boy?" I asked him.

"Marina says it feels different," he replied. "So I think it's a boy."

So we talked, trying to lighten the fear and paranoia that from this time onward filled our days with darkness and dread.

Monday, October 21, 1963

Little Audrey Rachel was born on the 20th, weighing almost seven pounds, and the birth was quick and easy for Marina. Lee called me soon after, to tell me that he had another little girl, and that he was delighted. But I knew Lee well enough to sense that he was upset. He finally told me. After Marina went into labor on Saturday afternoon, Ruth Paine said she would drive Marina to Parkland Hospital, but she would "appreciate it" if Lee would stay home with her children and Junie, so they wouldn't be stuck in the hospital waiting room for who knew how long. Her argument was convincing: Ruth had arranged the payment plan, she spoke Russian, she was a woman Marina trusted, and besides, Lee's ride to work was the neighbor. If he stayed with Marina at the hospital, how would he get to work the next morning? And how would Junie feel, having to come back with Ruth, leaving both her mother and daddy at the hospital?

Lee reluctantly agreed, and forlornly watched his wife driven away to Parkland Hospital by "The Pain" a few hours later. To his shock, Ruth soon returned.

"She took Marina to Parkland — and just left her there!" he told me, bitterly. Marina had nobody who could speak Russian to her in her time of need. Nobody to be with her after the baby was born. Lee said he was so angry that he gave Paine some verbal insults, then went into the bedroom and refused to speak to her again, though he overheard enough from a telephone call she made to know that Marina had given birth and was okay. He had to go into Dallas to work the next morning, but got a ride back to the Paine house because Junie was alone, without her mother, for the very first time in her life.

"The Pain then offered to drive me to the hospital to see my new baby," Lee said. "I didn't want to be in the same car with her," he added, "but I wanted to see Marina, and apologize to her. And I wanted to see Rachel. She's very pretty." It was obvious to Lee that Ruth Paine's so-called "affection" for Marina was only skin deep.[43]

Lee had even less good to say about Michael Paine, Ruth's estranged husband, describing him as "nosy, and in the way." Convinced that Marina should have a car and learn how to drive, Lee said he had arranged for the Paines to find a used car, which they could offer as a present, celebrating Rachel's birth. News of the used car thrilled Marina. She didn't know that Lee was going to pay for the car 'under the table' — a fact he didn't reveal to her because it would indicate that he had other funds.[44]

Thursday, October 24, 1963

Lee made a short call to me on Thursday night after an anti-UN demonstration in Dallas, where he joined over a hundred protesters.[45] Adlai Stevenson was making a speech at the Dallas Memorial Auditorium when the protesters surged forward, waving signs, and spitting on him. One woman hit him on the head with her picket sign.[46] Lee was pleased to have helped. "Surely they will have to increase protection for the President in this city, now," Lee declared, proud of his part. "When the President comes next month," he predicted, "I hope this means he'll be safer."

---

1. I named our first child after Susie in 1968, puzzling both sides of the family, for there weren't any relatives with that name. Our last contact with Susie would be a cancelled check in late September for our share of the August electric bill, which I hid in an album, precious to me because it had her signature on the back. There was no reply to Christmas cards or calls: Susie vanished not only from our lives, but also from the 1964 telephone directory (compiled in October, 1963) after decades with the same address and phone number. It frightened me, and I could speak to nobody about it.

2. We waited for the bank to open, but Reily's check still wasn't there. Robert made out a check Aug. 29 for "balance of account," but until the Reily check came, we didn't know the final amount Reily decided to give me. Angry, Robert called Reily again and was promised the check really would be deposited later in the day. The amount was still unknown. After ordering the money to be sent to the Florida National Bank (my account, but Robert's name was soon on it), we left New Orleans broke. We didn't get the money until Sept. 6th, closing the New Orleans account the same day we arrived in Gainesville. *(See check in Appendix.)*

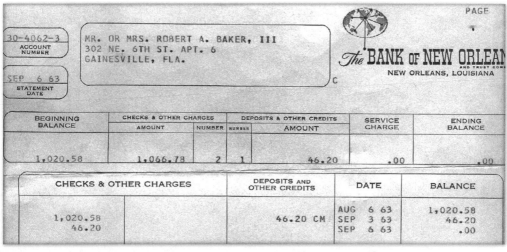

		PAGE
30-4062-3 ACCOUNT NUMBER	MR. OR MRS. ROBERT A. BAKER, III 302 NE. 6TH ST. APT. 6 GAINESVILLE, FLA.	*The* BANK OF NEW ORLEAN AND TRUST COMP NEW ORLEANS, LOUISIANA
SEP 6 63 STATEMENT DATE	C	

BEGINNING BALANCE	CHECKS & OTHER CHARGES AMOUNT	NUMBER	NUMBER	DEPOSITS & OTHER CREDITS AMOUNT	SERVICE CHARGE	ENDING BALANCE
1,020.58	1,066.78	2	1	46.20	.00	.00

CHECKS & OTHER CHARGES		DEPOSITS AND OTHER CREDITS	DATE	BALANCE
1,020.58 46.20		46.20 CM	AUG 6 63 SEP 3 63 SEP 6 63	1,020.58 46.20 .00

3. I've shown this clever, foolproof, yet simple rotating number and date system to researchers and *60 Minutes* investigators.

4. Years later, the veteran anti-Castro/CIA operative Antonio Veciana would tell the brilliant HSCA investigator Gaeton Fonzi that he met Lee, in the presence of "Maurice Bishop," Lee's erstwhile handler in Dallas. Lee told me the same name. "Mr. B" was now calling himself "Mr. Bishop."

5. Until now, nobody has offered a truly logical explanation as to why Lee suddenly stopped all his dedicated public activity promoting the FPCC and pro-Cuban interests. He'd obtained the newspaper articles and 'notoriety' needed to alleviate any suspicions, it was hoped, that he was anti-Castro — an image that had to be wiped out due to the training film. Since infiltrators were common, Lee had now "proven" via the staged events that he was 'actually' pro-Castro — necessary to help ensure his safety in Mexico City, where pro-Castro spies abounded.

6. Mrs. Garner never mentioned seeing a rifle. Neither did any of the neighbors.

7. Ruth Paine would say Marina had been living with her all along, so she could have her baby as a Texas resident, getting bargain basement prices at Parkland Hospital in Dallas. Though there were many hospitals in the Dallas-Fort Worth area, and despite the fact that the Paine home was in Irving, Parkland was the hospital where Lee's baby would be born.

8. Source is Mr. Garner.

Marina, with Junie in a stroller, and Ruth with her own two small children, went to Bourbon Street and through the French Quarter on one of these evenings, but Lee stayed behind, "doing errands." He failed to accompany the women to the French Quarter because Lee and I had been there so often it was possible that somebody might call out, "Oswald! Where's Marina?" The excursion without Lee is mentioned in Ruth Paine's WC testimony and in McMillan's 'official version' biography, *Marina and Lee.*

9. Please keep in mind that the rifle was supposedly placed in this crowded station wagon, then removed after the long trip and placed in the Paine garage, never being noticed. Michael Paine, an intelligent helicopter research engineer, said he thought the rifle, wrapped in a blanket, was heavy iron "camping equipment." He testified on March 17, 1964, that he lifted and held the bundle several times and even pushed it aside as it lay on the sawdust-strewn garage floor in full view (p. 437 WC). The rifle supposedly was kicked around, as Paine claims, for two months, until a few hours before Kennedy was shot. Michael Paine mentions sawdust on the floor, but the blanket had no sawdust on it, and the rifle had neither hairs from the blanket on it, nor any sawdust. Ruth Paine also stated she saw the blanket. Marina, after much questioning, said she once peeked inside and saw the rifle stock. She could not identify the rifle shown to her as belonging to Lee, though other times in her testimony, she said he sat on the porch in New Orleans "dry firing" his rifle for hours at a time — an activity nobody else ever mentioned. They only saw Lee reading.

10. McMillan writes how Lee and Marina wept, and how Lee held June and got her something from a vending machine, bursting into tears, convinced he might never see her again, just prior to Ruth Paine's removing Marina and June to Irving, Texas. Lee would go on to Mexico City, where we planned to marry after he completed his mission there. But the mission was called off. The promise that he would be able to stay in Mexico was broken. He was ordered to Dallas. Since Marina was expecting birth very soon, and he was given a new promise that he'd be assigned in Mexico after Christmas (though he no longer trusted such promises, and we made alternate, new plans), he reluctantly returned to Dallas.

11. Lee told me he had met Rorke, a CIA asset, in Florida. Rorke had also lectured students at Tulane in 1963, and Lee may have met him again at that time. But Rorke's association with Lee would soon spell doom for himself and his pilot: just after they had flown to the Yucatan (which was probably a dry run to check logistics for my trip), and at the same time Lee was in Mexico City, their plane vanished forever. I had been given a book by Dave Ferrie, one that belonged to the Eglin Air Force Base's library. The book had a contact name written on the

inside cover that I was supposed to use to get inside the base, and which would allow me to board the plane.

12. Warren Commissions's investigation.

13. Eric Rogers, in his July 21, 1964 testimony, also mentioned that Lee was wearing goggles as he raced to catch the bus, a comment never explained. These may have been his lab goggles, to be used while handling the cancerous cells. He probably grabbed them at the last minute as he rushed outside to catch the bus.

14. Today, thanks to researchers' help, I know that "Le Corque" had to be Tommy "The Cork" Corcoran. Noted historian Robert A. Caro, the fearless biographer of Lyndon Johnson, tells us that President Johnson had cash sent to Austin whenever it was needed, using people such as John Connally, Cliff Carter, or Tommy "The Cork" Corcoran as couriers. Tommy "The Cork" is mentioned in *Time* magazine's Dec. 6, 1963 edition, soon after Kennedy's death. In an article called "The Men Lyndon Likes" Corcoran was one of "four men "..."the new President ... counts among his most valued advisers..."

15. Today, we know that the U.S. Government financed these Flying Tiger operations, but for decades it denied all association because it was officially neutral and "not at war" at the time.

16. "Anna Chan Chennault, a vice chairman of the Republican National Finance committee and co-chairman of Women for Nixon-Agnew, had been born in Bejing and educated in Hong Kong. At the age of 23 she married Gen. Claire Chennault the founder of the Flying Tigers. She bore the general two children and became a U.S. citizen in 1950. After the war he founded China Air Transport and privatized the Flying Tigers. Gen. Chennault died in 1958 in his native New Orleans. She then sold the Flying Tigers and China Air Transport to the CIA, using the influence of Thomas ("Tommy the Cork") Corcoran...who was smitten with Anna...Tommy the Cork was so intoxicated by love for Anna that he didn't care if his favorite Democratic party was being maimed or not. Lyndon Johnson got wind of Anna's dealing and had the National Security Council bug her and determined that she indeed was fooling around in U.S. foreign policy...Tommy the Cork ended up doing service for both sides: ostensibly advising Anna, then ducking back to tell the Humphrey-Johnson people what the Republicans were doing..." Source: Tom Roeser, http://www.tomroeser.com/sectionlist. asp?Month=2&Day=12&Year=2008

17. Lee's original blue zippered bag held identical items which had been sent ahead to Houston, presumably by plane, along with batches of the cancer cocktail. Lee would replace the bag he had been given in New Orleans with his original blue bag, if time permitted. It would have a culture fresher by almost two days inside the "thermos." When Lee told me this, I wondered if M. D. Anderson Hospital's cancer research center in Houston had kept a copy of our bioweapon for itself. Had it literally flown from Ochsner's control, just as we had feared? The fact that later, in Dallas, Jack Ruby would claim that he had been injected with cancer cells — knowing that Jack had seen our lab and knew that the injections were painful. And that a larger bore needle was needed (so the cancer cells wouldn't clog the needle) makes me believe now that my suspicions were well-founded.

18. I remembered what kind of plane was used because I found it ironic that a "Dove" was used to carry the bioweapon.

19. Rorke was heavily involved in anti-Castro activities and worked for the CIA. For more information see http://www.spartacus.schoolnet.co.uk/JFKrorkeA.htm

20. Mrs. Lee Dannelly was interviewed by the FBI after Kennedy died. She said she arrived "a few minutes late..." from lunch on Wednesday, Sept. 25, to find Lee waiting for her.

21. After meeting with Mrs. Dannelly, Lee went to the Governor's offices, after having firmly planted the idea in the lady's head that he had already been there. He gave the name Harvey Oswald to Mrs. Dannelly that day. The name "Harvey" prevented Dannelly from finding Lee's card, for Lee had no intention of staying there long. FBI records tell us Mrs. Dannelly assiduously sought a card for "Harvey Oswald." Witness statements were thereby "timed wrong," reducing their credibility and helping to muddy the waters. Nor could Lee explain why he had come all

the way from New Orleans to straighten this out. No doubt the lady thought Lee rather dense, but lurking behind his façade of stupidity was "the Scarlet Pimpernel." This tactic was similar to what Lee had done in Jackson, when he asked both the barber (Edwin Lea McGehee) and State Rep. Reeves Morgan about how to get a job at Jackson's mental hospital after he had already filled out a job application at the hospital two days earlier.

22. The waitress Stella Norman recalled this to the FBI after the JFK assassination. [FBI 105-82555-NR 1950, 3.6.64]. Florence Estella Norman, widow, 4301 Bannister St., Austin.

23. Neither Lee nor Dave ever disclosed to me that "Sparky Rubenstein" and "Jack Ruby" were the same person. They probably forgot that they had never told me! So I had no idea when Lee talked freely of Jack Ruby that he was speaking about Sparky Rubenstein. It would be a great shock when I finally learned — only in 1999! — that these were not two separate men, and that the man that I knew cared about Lee had somehow been forced to shoot him. That Jack Ruby *did* care is evident from the fact that he actually risked a great deal by calling the Dallas police at least twice, warning them that Lee was going to be shot. His voice was recognized. The warning calls were ignored.

24. The airport is actually called the Dallas-Fort Worth airport because it is located between the two cities. Ruth Paine lived in Irving, Texas which is one of many small towns between Dallas and Fort Worth. For simplicity, we call this "Dallas."

25. What is certain today is that Sylvia Odio's testimony is taken seriously, since Odio told both her psychiatrist and her priest about the incident before the assassination.

26. One Latino witness personally wrote to me that he saw Lee that night in Dallas and knows Lee visited Odio.

27. Source: Interview with Gerry Hemming, by A. J. Weberman, Nodule 15.

    Their plane "officially" disappeared somewhere over the Yucatan on September 24, 1963, after taking off from Cozumel; but by October, Rorke and his pilot, Geoffrey Sullivan, were believed to be prisoners in Cuba after being shot down over Cuban territory. "Sullivan believes (her father) was "held in a Cuban jail for at least a decade and later executed as a spy. She was 5 years old when her father disappeared and has been investigating his fate for decades. The Department of Veterans Affairs has listed Sullivan as "missing in action."" Sherry Sullivan was awarded 21 million dollars in damages on Dec. 16, 2009 because the CIA had neglected to attempt to ransom her father, though others had been ransomed. Source: *Bangor Daily News*, Wednesday, December 16, 2009.

    A. J. Weberman reported (Nodule 15) that Marita Lorenz stated: "Alex wouldn't go along with the Kennedy assassination, he was a former Jesuit priest. Alex disappeared about two months before the assassination."

28. This is a troubling incident, since it raises serious questions. First, who prepared this second batch of cancer cells? And what happened to the first batch that Lee was given by Shaw? Did Lee, thinking he was following orders and instructions, actually leave the bioweapon in the hands of right-wing fanatics in Houston, while he carried a thermos of something else to Mexico City? Lee had been taught to check the condition of the cells — the medium that I'd designed would begin to turn clear as waste products built up. Lee could see the color changes that would inform him when to discard the old medium and add fresh. But what if the Houston thermos never contained the bioweapon? Whatever the answer, one thing was clear: Houston had its hands on it, and I doubted that they would easily give it up.

29. The Warren Commission: "there was no firm evidence of the means by which Oswald traveled from New Orleans to Houston ... he left New Orleans, probably on Continental Trailways Bus No. 5121, departing New Orleans at 12:20 P.M., on Wednesday, September 25, 1963, and scheduled to arrive in Houston at 10:50 P.M. That bus is the only one on which Oswald could have left New Orleans after noon on Wednesday, September 25, 1963, and arrived in Houston before midnight."

30. Memory can be peculiar: I remembered Twiford's name so many years because it was so similar to the TW-1 exchange of all our important phone numbers in New Orleans. Time

has dimmed my memory about much more: I had to ask researchers about "Twiford." It was probably 10:00 in Houston when Lee called the Twiford residence — late enough to assure he wouldn't be invited over. I think Horace Twiford, who was a Socialist Party official and a merchant marine, suspected Lee was an anti-Castro spy. I know Lee called to throw Twiford off track over something related to the leafleting of the Wasp. Twiford's wife answered the phone, saying her husband was out of town, which Lee already knew. Mrs. Twiford said Lee stressed his pro-Castro FPCC credentials, then said he was "flying to Mexico City." This would be reported to Twiford, who would pass the information to Communists there. Perhaps Lee was saying he was "one of them," with nothing to hide.

31. I remember one statement from Lee about that border crossing: "I didn't travel alone," he said.

32. Regarding Duran, Gerry Patrick Hemming confirmed Lee's actions to me, as well, when I met him face to face and asked him. How could I be too upset, when Lee knew that every night I was probably having sex with Robert? It was just a temporary matter we had to live with, to reach our final goals.

33. They later reported that Lee had threatened to kill himself. Who knows what actually happened in there. He was desperate.

34. Lee's visit to the USPHS office was reported to the press after the JFK assassination, but the poor soul who gave out the information was quickly encouraged to say otherwise. Ref: affidavits of Orin Pugh and William Kline were given to Warren Commission, 26 Aug and 31 Jul 1964.

35. After the assassination, The Warren Commission could not ignore reports (called "rumors" by the FBI) that Lee had asked about divorce laws at some border towns.

36. Hurricane Flora one of the worst Atlantic storms in history, killed 7,000 people,

37. Many Americans don't know about Hurricane Flora. It did not hit the U.S. mainland. After hitting Cuba, it spun around and headed off to the North Atlantic. To put the massive destruction of this killer storm in perspective, let's compare it to the worst natural disaster in American history, the Galveston Hurricane in 1900 which flooded the island and killed about 5,000 people. Hurricane Flora was a Category 4 storm (like Hurricane Katrina), and it killed 1,750 people in Cuba. Americans' near-complete lack of knowledge of this devastating storm is largely due to the dearth of press coverage of Cuban events in the American media in the early 1960s. They came from a secret photo processing spy unit in the Dallas area.

38. Those who try to dismiss my account should ask why I ordered another birth certificate only six months later, and kept both of them though they said "female infant Vary." In 1986, I finally got a third one when we had to move overseas — this time with my name on the dotted line.

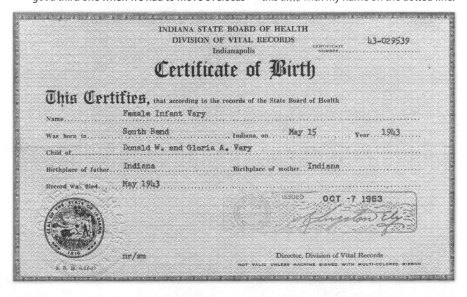

39. The TSBD job was his second job in a row located across the street from a federal courthouse — this one in Dallas. Reily's was also located across the street from the federal courthouse.

40. RL7-3521

41. In fact, Lee's record of his final day of work would declare he'd been there eight hours, even though he'd been arrested by police early that afternoon. It seemed business as usual, except Lee was getting involved with people concerned about the President's upcoming trip to Dallas.

42. I believe he was lured into position by the very people he thought he could trust.

43. The documentation for this unexpectedly coarse treatment of Marina by Ruth Paine has been found in Mary Ferrell's chronology:

    "Mrs. Paine takes Marina to Parkland where she is admitted at 8:56 p.m. and delivered by Dr. James F. Herd, 1114 N. Winnetka, of   Audrey Rachel Oswald, 6 lbs, 15 oz., at 10:41 p.m. The baby is #22347. (22:230,746; CD 210, p. 5) (Note that the birth occurred only an hour and 44 minutes later, but Ruth Paine did not stay with Marina, instead, returning to Irving almost immediately. Lee Oswald had remained at the Paine residence hoping Ruth Paine, who spoke Russian, would be there to support Marina, and Marina had agreed. Instead, Marina was left on her own. JVB)

    Oswald stays at the Paine house with June Lee Oswald and Mrs. Paine's two children. Mrs. Paine says Oswald goes to bed; she calls hospital after waiting "a proper time" and learns of the birth. *She tells Oswald the next morning.* (2:404,514; 3:39; 9:361,436; 22:746; 24:694; *Dallas Times Herald*, 11/28/63, p. A-38; *Detroit Free Press*, 12/7/63, p. A-3; *Redbook*, July 1964, pp. 85, 87) (This incident has been used to demonstrate that Lee Oswald had no feelings for his wife, which was untrue. The next entry depicts Mary Ferrell offering a possible reason why Lee Oswald 'did not want to go' to Parkland when she offered to drive him there the next evening. JVB)

    Oct. 21, 1963 (Monday) — Oswald returns to Irving with Buell Wesley Frazier after work. Mrs. Michael Paine takes him to Parkland Hospital, between 7:30 p.m. and 8:00 p.m., to see the baby. (3:40; 11:291; 22:746; 24:694) Mrs. Paine says Oswald did not want to go. (3:40) (Perhaps he feared he might be asked to pay something. Thus the subtle demonization of Lee Oswald, even in this chronology.)

44. The Paines knew Lee "had other funds." That means that they knew more about who Lee really was than they have ever admitted. As stated earlier, Lee avoided driving because he better played the "poor man" role that way, and also because his original Texas driver's license had been 'flagged' to say he was a Communist or subversive. Having returned to Texas, he 'put off' getting a new Texas driver's license, but that doesn't mean he was "unable" to drive, though Ruth Paine stated he received driving lessons from her. If he actually did, it was a la Scarlet Pimpernel.

45. Lee was openly attending all kinds of political meetings at this time. I've always wondered how the official version — that Lee was an antisocial lone nut, who stayed away from people — came to be believed by so many people for so long.

    Meetings Lee attended in late October, mentioned in chronologies, include:

    Oct. 23: "USA Day Rally," Gen. Walker, speaker, Dallas Mem. Aud. (Ruth Paine, witness) Oct. 24: "UN Day" Adlai Stevenson, speaker, Dallas. Mem. Aud. (Michael Paine and others, witnesses) Oct. 25: John Birch Society meeting with Michael Paine (Oswald self-reported being at the meeting when he spoke up at an ACLU meeting) Oct. 26: ACLU meeting with Michael Paine.

46. Wikipedia statement: "Stevenson was assaulted by an anti-United Nations protester in Dallas, Texas, on October 24, 1963…" This is an example of how history gets rewritten in the case. Stevenson was actually spat upon by several protesters, as well as assaulted, and over 100 protesters were involved. By minimizing the event to a single sentence, Wikipedia assists history re-writers in making the impression that Dallas wasn't 'that' dangerous for John Kennedy. But it was. Source: http://en.wikipedia.org/wiki/Adlai_Stevenson. The John F. Kennedy memorial Library recorded: "One hundred Dallas civic leaders sent a telegram of apology to Adlai E. Stevenson and President Kennedy, expressing shame that "extremists" struck and spat on the country's chief representative to the United Nations." Source: http://www.jfklibrary.org

Jim Garrison

Earling Carothers "Jim" Garrison was District Attorney of Orleans Parish for twelve years (1962 to 1973), and is best known for his investigation into the Assassination of President John F. Kennedy. He adopted the name "Jim" in the early 1960s.

In 1966, Garrison began his investigation into the activities of Lee Harvey Oswald in New Orleans at the request of Louisiana's U.S. Senator Russell Long. This investigation led him to 544 Camp Street, the nerve center of anti-Castro activities in New Orleans located in the heart of the U.S. intelligence community and eventually involved a colorful cast of new characters including Guy Banister, Jack Martin, David Lewis, David Ferrie, Dr. Mary Sherman, Dr. Alton Ochsner and Clay Shaw, a prominent businessman involved in international trade. The investigation also discovered that Oswald, Ferrie and Shaw had been seen together in Clinton, Lousiana that summer, and that Oswald and a young woman had been seen by several witnesses in nearby Jackson, Louisiana around the same time.

In early 1967, a leak to the press suddenly exposed Garrison's secret investigation and within days, his primary suspect David Ferrie was found dead in his apartment. A month later, Garrison arrested Clay Shaw and charged him with conspiring to murder President Kennedy. What followed was two years of criticism of Garrison and his investigation from certain quarters, particularly the local media as well as by *Time* magazine and NBC News.

But Garrison fought back by getting on national television and telling the American people that there had been a "coup d'etat" in America and that the Central Intelligence Agency had murdered President Kennedy. Garrison's attempt to present his case against Shaw in court was frustrated when over 50 of his extradition requests to retrieve witnesses from other states were denied. On March 1,

Garrison announcing Clay Shaw's arrest

1969, a New Orleans jury acquitted Clay Shaw of all charges after less than an hour of deliberation. A post-trial poll of the jury showed that, while Garrison had convinced them of a conspiracy to assassinate President Kennedy, they were uncertain of Shaw's role. Testimony had revealed that a man known only as "Clay Bertrand" had been overheard plotting against Kennedy but the judged refused to allow a jail card into evidence showing that Shaw had admitted to using the alias of "Clay Bertrand."

In the closing arguments of that trial, Assistant DA James Alcock said that two witnesses in Jackson, Louisiana had seen Lee Harvey Oswald with a young woman in a car and that their investigation had determined she was certainly not Marina Oswald. Alcock concluded his presentation with "I wish we could have identified her. I wish we could have brought her into the courtroom and presented her to you."

Garrison's prosecution of Clay L. Shaw remains the only trial brought in the murder of John F. Kennedy. Garrinson's investigation was documented in his book *On the Trail of the Assassins* and popularized by Oliver Stone's movie entitled *JFK*. He died in 1992 without every learning the identity of the young woman or why she and Oswald had been together that day in Jackson.

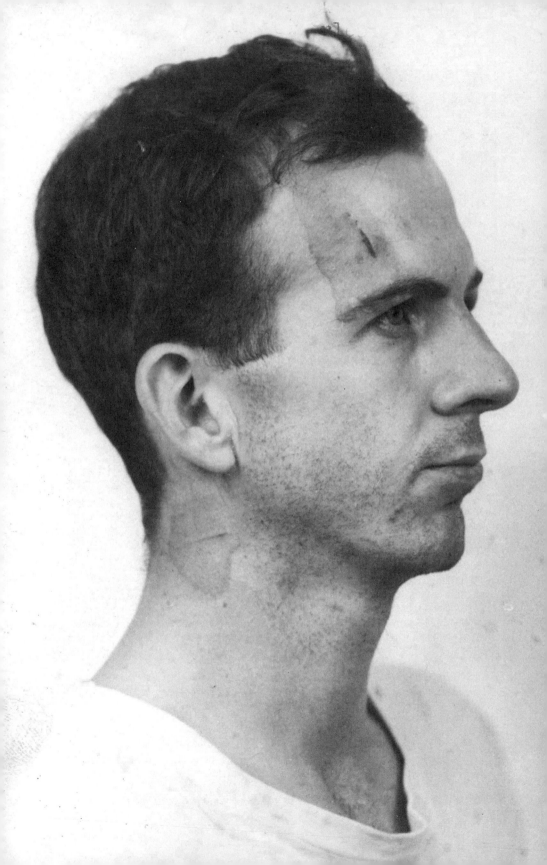

— Chapter 25 —

COUNTDOWN

The plot against President Kennedy thickened in November. By now, Lee had convinced me that Kennedy was a great President who sought peace, and I shared Lee's fear that his life would soon end. Lee had been recruited in the Baton Rouge meetings into the Dallas plot. He had penetrated the ring. Now, he was meeting with one or more of the plotters on a regular basis. "But I'm meeting too many new people," he told me. He said he felt he was being "treated like a dangle." He was given tasks to do, as if they trusted him, but he was never certain who was who.

A Secret Service agent sought his help in assessing the possible ambush sites that might be used when the President came to Dallas. Presumably, this was to afford protection for Kennedy, but of course, such work would also reveal which sites were best for murder.

One meeting in particular disturbed Lee: he called it the "trophy" meeting. It was held at the posh 3525 Turtle Creek address. Lee had not attended that meeting, but he'd been told about it. "Kennedy won't be killed on Turtle Creek Boulevard," Lee revealed, "because Mayor Cabell, Senator Tower, and Clint Murchison

DALLAS MAYOR EARLE CABELL
WITH MAJOR GENERAL EDWIN WALKER
NATIONAL INDIGNATION CONVENTION
DECEMBER 13, 1961

all have apartments right there, at 3525 Turtle Creek."¹ General Walker happened to live on Turtle Creek, too, Lee said, but farther away.

Lee said the motorcade would turn at the 3600 block "because the plotters want to show their power ... that they are in charge of their trophy."² They would also be taking trophy photos of the assassination.

At this time, Lee believed the kill site would probably be the Dallas Trade Mart — if Kennedy wasn't terminated earlier in Chicago or Miami. Sickening to me and Lee was their plan to circulate a photo of JFK's head, "dead, with his eyes left open."

Today, I wonder if Lee's contacts were fake agents, going through the motions to properly position him for his role as patsy — a possibility never far from Lee's mind since our showdown at Katzenjammer's. Was Lee thus kept from interacting meaningfully in Dallas with persons who might have been able to save the president? Or worse, did Lee give a fake Secret Service agent good advice on possible ambush sites, hoping to save Kennedy from execution, only to have them turn it around, and use it to kill the president more easily? These are questions that still haunt me.[3]

Saturday, November 16, 1963

Lee met with an FBI contact at a location unknown to me, revealing that a right-wing group was planning to assassinate President Kennedy during his visit to Dallas on November 22nd. Someone in the FBI took the information seriously and sent out a teletype message to field offices that night. William Walter, a clerk in the FBI office in New Orleans, saw this telex the following morning and later affirmed he had seen this document to Jim Garrison when he investigated the JFK assassination in the late 1960s. The FBI claimed it could find no copies of such a document, but that hardly surprises me.

There are many things that Marina and I might disagree on, simply because our situations and perspectives were different at a difficult time for both of us, but I am pleased to report that we agree on this important issue. Marina wrote a bold letter to the Chairman of the U.S. Government's JFK Assassination Records Review Board in which she said: "I now believe that my former husband met with the Dallas FBI on November 16, 1963, and provided informant information on which this teletype was based."[4] I don't know what led her to that conclusion, but I came to the same conclusion based on my own experience, since I was in near-daily contact with Lee at the time. Given that Lee knew J. Edgar Hoover was compromised by his relationship with the Mafia, he literally risked his life to try to use the FBI as a means of sending his warnings through the Telex.

James Hosty, early 1960s

True enough, Lee had several trusted contacts, but Dallas FBI agent James Hosty, who knew Lee was not to be bothered, was not on the list. He had begun hanging around Ruth Paine and Marina. "Hosty worries me," Lee told me. "He's been pretending he's trying to find me, but he knows where I work. He's actually picking up information from 'The Pain.'" Lee saw Ruth Paine as a real danger: he had caught her snooping through his things in New Orleans and knew about her CIA connections. He'd told me never to trust her, and Marina would be advised by the Secret Service to stay away from her because she was CIA.

Lee's most important achievement — temporarily saving Kennedy's life — was an accomplishment he only hinted at, typically understating what he had done.[5] I knew that Dr. Mary Sherman had given him the names of some trusted contacts, and that one of his warnings to save Kennedy had been successful. But I had no more information. I knew that Dr. Sherman's contacts were in Chicago, but I didn't know how that linked to Lee's successful warning until James Douglass kindly sent me his book, *JFK and the Unspeakable — Why He Died and Why It Matters.* Only then did I realize how important Dr. Sherman's role had been in the attempt to save Kennedy. I knew she must have been frustrated by our failed get-Castro project, which she had hoped would save the President's life. I now understood that Dr. Sherman had continued to work with Lee. Nor had she cut me completely off: she had promised to give me a recommendation to a medical school in the Americas. But I did not realize that Dr. Sherman's role — assisting Lee — had extended beyond New Orleans, back to her familiar territory in Chicago.

I now understood what courage Dr. Mary had. On July 21, 1964, only a few hours before the Warren Commission met in New Orleans to hear witness testimonies, she was brutally murdered.

Wall Street Journal

BEFORE BREAKFAST: Democratic legislators at the White House for meeting with President are, from left: Senator Carl Hayden of Arizona, Representatives Hale | Boggs of Hubert] press se

Woman Expert in Cancer Slain In Burned Louisiana Apartment

NEW ORLEANS, July 21 (UPI) — The police answered a fire call today and found the badly burned and repeatedly stabbed body of a woman expert in bone cancer.

The body of Dr. Mary S. Sherman, 51 years old, was on the floor of her apartment on St. Charles Avenue, a prosperous area. Neighbors had smelled smoke and called the police to investigate a fire.

A coroner's investigator, Sam Moran, said Dr. Sherman's body had apparently been set on fire in the bed and rolled off on the floor. She had been stabbed eight times in the left arm, chest and stomach.

The front door of the apartment had been forced and Dr. Sherman's purse looted. Her car was missing but was later found about eight blocks away.

Dr. Sherman did cancer research work at the Ochsner Foundation Hospital in New Orleans.

She was a widow and lived alone. Her apartment was the target of burglars several times in the last few years, and she had a burglar alarm installed. It was apparently not working last night.

Her maid said she last saw the doctor yesterday afternoon. She said she had been in good spirits and talked of a woman friend who might arrive for a visit.

Dr. Sherman was born in Evanston, Ill., and held two degrees from Northwestern University and a medical degree from the University of Chicago. She taught there before joining the Ochsner group in New Orleans 12 year ago.

She was a partner in the Ochsner Clinic and was director of the bone pathology laboratory of the Ochsner Medical Foundation.

A spokesman for the clinic described her as "an internationally recognized authority in bone and joint pathology." Much of her work dealt with cancer of the bone.

Turkey
Special
ISTANE
—The ma
Ankara a
21, 1960,
attempt 1
and cadet
mier Isme
was lifted
the martie
ating som
ernment

Sunday, November 17, 1963

Just before Lee hung up, he uttered one of the normal-sounding sentences we used to indicate when he would call again, on our call wheel. "I'll call back in a few days," actually meant the same night and the same phone, but three hours later in our code system. To miss a call "broke" the wheel, meaning I'd have to wait for my time to call him. Because we took risks to be at the phone when it was the proper time

ME & LEE

and day, and because Lee had never before failed to follow through, I became frightened.

As I waited, risking Robert's imminent return home from the university library, I reviewed how Lee had told me, in the flat tone of an undertaker, that Kennedy would be killed in one of three possible plac-

Governor Connally salutes the President and First Lady at Love Field

Front area of the Dallas Trade Mart where 2,600 people wait at a sold-out luncheon for the President

es: Love Field, the Trade Mart, or Dealey Plaza. Each site had its problems: Love Field was without good natural cover, making escape difficult for the perpetrators, but the large crowd expected there would provide some cover.

The Trade Mart had good sniper positions available inside and out, but it would be so heavily guarded that, again, escape would be difficult. That left Dealey Plaza, where several tall buildings surrounded what was essentially a fishbowl. However, the Dallas Police headquarters were located there. Unless the police were also involved, the mob of police certain to be present there to help guard the President should be able

to home in on the snipers and catch them quickly, unless the snipers shot from the overpass, or from the low hill near the end of the Plaza. Because I knew Lee would move heaven and earth to call me if he could, I was now terrified. What if somebody had overheard? *What if they'd killed him?*

The call wheel was now disrupted, and Dave, who called me about once a week, wasn't slated to contact me again until Friday evening. I would have to use the emergency numbers Lee had given me to reach him at the Texas School Book Depository (TSBD). It would be a per-

Texas School Book Depository

Elm St

Houston St

Main St

Dealey Plaza

son-to-person call, using the code word "janitor" — and Lee would refuse the call. This got the call wheel on track again, for the time that I called automatically told Lee where and when I would be available for his call back, that same day.

Wednesday, November 20, 1963,

The call wheel was like a clock that controlled our secure communications, but waiting for my turn seemed to make time stand still. Finally, during my afternoon break at PenChem, on Wednesday afternoon, I was able to call the TSBD, person-to-person, asking if Lee Oswald, the 'new janitor' was available to take the call. I hoped he would come to the phone, but I knew he got my message when the call was refused by Mr. Oswald.[6]

That night, Robert picked me up late from PenChem, where I worked overtime on Wednesdays and Fridays. He dropped me off at our cottage, and then, as he'd been doing all week, went back to the University library to study (or whatever!). I knew he wouldn't return until at least 3:00 A.M.[7]

I waited a dark and anxious hour near the pay phone by the 7-11 store, and at 11:00 p.m., Dallas time, Lee called, apologizing for not calling me back on Sunday. He'd never had enough privacy to do so. For the next hour and a half, we talked our hearts out. It was the most ominous and sorrowful call I've ever experienced. "How much can you say?" I asked, worried that he might have to suddenly hang up again. "We're safe," he said, "but I have meetings tonight, in two different places."[8]

Lee said that he was no longer alone, and an abort team had been called in to help him. "Even though they're going to try to kill him," he said, "I've sent out information that might be able to save him."

In his Scarlet Pimpernel voice, he added, as if it was all just another adventure, "That's worth dying for, you know!" I could close my eyes and imagine him smiling at me as he said that, full of bravado. But he meant it. This was the moment he had lived for. The chance to make a real difference with his life. But it was not a death wish. Informed that he was now 'part of the group' that would assemble in Dallas to shoot the President, and secretly the member of an abort team that would try to intervene, Lee said he would be required to obey orders from both sides.[9]

There was no way he could provide an excuse, he said, for not showing up where he was supposed to be. He was in too deep.

"Why don't you make yourself sick, by taking a laxative or something?" I suggested, as if escaping the plot to murder the President would be like playing hooky from school! We had a grim laugh over the absurdity of that one. "Juduffki!" he said, then "Minnie-Mouse!"

Hearing those pet names he loved to call me, I wanted to die with him.

"I want to come!" I begged. "I want to be there — with you!"

"No!" he replied. "You'll have to wait for a call from Dave."

"I want you to call me!" I told him. "I don't trust anybody anymore. And from all you're saying, it's too late to help Kennedy any more than you have. So just go!" I urged him.

"Even if I wanted to, which I do not," Lee said, his voice trembling, "I couldn't. We've talked about this before, Juduff. They'd not only do me in, they'd come after my family. They'd find you. You'd all die..."

What could I say? Lee was up against ruthless professional killers who followed the code of vendetta. If they were prepared to kill the President of the United States, anyone who got in their way would die, and if they couldn't kill Lee, they'd kill everyone he cared about.

Because time was so short now, Lee said there wouldn't be another call from him unless he reached Laredo.

"Lee," I said slowly, "you didn't say 'until.' You said 'unless.'" "I apologize," he answered. I heard him suck up his breath. We were both very close to tears. Then he asked if my packed suitcase was still ready, under the bed. He reminded me of all the wonderful places and things we wanted to see, and had dreamed about.

"You'll get on the plane," Lee said. "I'll make sure you'll be okay... I'll be there, if ..." We both feared the end of his sentence and froze in silence. "... if I don't make it out," he finished, solemnly, "Then you'll have to go on ... without me."

"How?" I asked. "Who could ever replace you, in my heart?"

"You love babies," he said. "Promise me that you'll have babies."

"I don't want to have babies with anyone but you," I protested.

"Oh yes, you will," he answered. "You take home baby birds and feed them. So I know you'll want to have your own babies. Promise me."

I knew in my heart that he was right, so I promised.

"I'll never forget you, as long as you live!" I blurted out. "That might only be until tomorrow," he said, with a tense laugh, as I realized that I had meant to say "as long as I live," but my emotions were overwhelming me and my speech was getting sloppy. "How much more can you tell me?" I asked. "Who are you up against?"

"I'll be talking to them tonight," he repeated. "Then I'll go to bed and miss you."

"And tomorrow?"

"Tomorrow, I'll go say goodbye to Junie, and Rachel, and Marina..." Lee took a gasp of air, as if he struggled to breathe. Warm tears started streaming down my cheeks again. Soon we were both crying. I wanted to hold him, but the only thing I could do was squeeze the phone tighter.

"Oh, my God! Lee!" I blurted out. I felt weak, helpless. I leaned against the pay phone with the midnight of the world spinning around me. I suddenly felt like Lee and I were standing at the flaming gates of Hell itself.

"Know how we wondered who my handler was?" Lee whispered. "Mr. B? Benson, Benton, or Bishop? Well, he's from Fort Worth, so it has to be Phillips. He is the traitor. Phillips is behind this. I need you to remember that name," Lee said, repeating it with cold anger. "David Atlee Phillips."

David Atlee Phillips

David Atlee Phillips was a CIA officer working in Mexico City in 1963, at the time of Lee Oswald's visit. On Nov. 20, 1963, Lee Oswald also told Judyth Vary Baker that he believed that David Atlee Phillips was coordinating the JFK assassination plot.

Born in 1922 in Fort Worth, Texas, Phillips fought in World War II as a nose gunner on a bomber and was captured, and became a prisoner of war in Germany. After the war, he moved to Chile and started an English language newspaper for South America. In 1950 he started working for the CIA and rose through the ranks, eventually becoming Chief of Operations for the Western Hemisphere.

In 1954 Phillips was instrumental in over-throwing the freely-elected president of Guatemala, Jacobo Arbenz, after he nationalized land owned by the United Fruit company. Phillips orchestrated a combination of propaganda and bribery, as well as financing of a rebel army which invaded Guatemalan from Honduras. In 1959 Phillips went to Cuba to work undercover after Castro took over. In 1960, he returned to the United States, helped to organize the Bay of Pigs invasion, and worked on a means of having Fidel Castro murdered. CIA's Richard Helms appointed Phillips as Chief of Cuban Operations, enabling him to roam the entire Western Hemisphere freely to coordinate secret operations to get rid of Fidel Castro. To this end, Phillips is said to have used the name "Maurice Bishop" while working with an organization of anti-Castro Cubans called Alpha 66.

In 1963 the CIA station head in Mexico called Phillips "the most outstanding Covert Action officer that this rating officer has ever worked with."

Phillips later served as CIA Station Chief in the Dominican Republic and in Rio de Janeiro. In 1970, he was called to Washington to lead a task force to prevent the election of a leftist President in Chile. The effort failed and Salvador Allende was elected President of Chile, only to be killed in a military coup in 1973. In 1975, Phillips retired with honors from the CIA.

Over the years a number of researchers have suggested that Phillips was involved in planning the JFK assassination. In 2007 a deathbed statement from former CIA officer E. Howard Hunt, who had worked with Phillips in Guatemala and in anti-Castro operations, named Phillips as a participant in the JFK assassination.

Maurice Bishop as described by Cuban informant

Lee then said there were two other names I needed to remember: Bobby Baker and Billy Sol Estes. He said the assassination itself was not their doing, but it was because of them, and I was never to forget their names.

My thoughts were racing every direction at once, as I frantically sought a solution. "Is there any way you could get out of this? Something you haven't thought of?"

"They'd just get another gun to take my place," Lee said. "If I stay, that will be one less bullet aimed at Kennedy."

Bobby Baker

Bobby Baker & LBJ

Robert Gene Baker was a powerful Washington insider and advisor to Lyndon B. Johnson, as his 1978 book, *Wheeling and Dealing: Confessions of a Capitol Hill Operator,* details. At the height of his political power as a Senate deal-broker he was often referred to as the "101st Senator".

Starting as a page in the U.S. Senate at the age of 14, he was befriended by Senator Lyndon B. Johnson and participated in LBJ's deal-making so much that he was known as "Little Lyndon." Baker obtained political information for LBJ who said: "He seemed to sense each man's individual price and the commodity he preferred as coin." Baker eventually became secretary to the Senate Majority Leader.

In the early 1950s Baker began a series of shady business deals, such as arranging for a Mafia associate of Meyer Lansky and Sam Giancana to become involved in a deal to establish casinos in the Dominican Republic. In 1960 Johnson was elected Vice President under JFK, and Baker remained as Johnson's secretary and political adviser.

In 1962 Baker had established the Serve-U-Corporation to provide vending machines for companies working on federally granted programs. The machines were manufactured by a company secretly owned by Chicago Mafia boss Sam Giancana and others. A lawsuit associated with this venture eventually generated so much press that an investigation was launched into Baker's business and political activities. Rumors that Baker was involved in corrupt activities prompted Attorney General Robert Kennedy to investigate further, and he discovered Baker's links to Clint Murchison and several Mafia bosses. In the process, evidence emerged that LBJ was tainted with political corruption involving a $7 billion contract for a Texas company to build fighter jets. Lawyer Abe Fortas represented both Lyndon B. Johnson and Bobby Baker and worked behind the scenes in an effort to keep this information from the public. (LBJ later appointed Abe Fortas to the U.S. Supreme Court.) On October, 7th 1963, Baker was forced to resign his post on the Senate staff.

News that the FBI had discovered that the Quorum Club, which Baker also ran, was providing women for liaisons to leading politicians expanded Baker's legal problems. As a result, JFK decided to drop Lyndon B. Johnson as his running mate in the 1964 election.

Joachim Joesten, an investigative journalist, wrote: "The Baker scandal then is truly the hidden key to the assassination, or more exact, the timing of the Baker affair crystallized the more or less vague plans to eliminate Kennedy which had already been in existence. The threat of complete exposure which faced Johnson in the Baker scandal provided that final impulse he was forced to give the go-ahead signal to the plotters who had long been waiting for the right opportunity."

In 1967 Baker was found guilty of seven counts of theft, fraud and income tax evasions, including keeping "campaign donations" intended to buy influence with various senators for himself. He was sentenced to three years in federal prison, but served only sixteen months.

His words seared into my soul: *"If I stay, that will be one less bullet aimed at Kennedy."* These were his exact words. They would stay with me forever.

"Maybe I can still do something," he added, grasping at a straw, "but what bothers me the most is that they're going to say I did it. They're going to pin it on me. And what will my babies think of me, when they grow up?"

"I hate the human race!" I wailed. This corruption was evil itself. The unmasked face of human hatred.

"Stop it!" he commanded. "I can still do something. Maybe I can fire a warning shot."

I was speechless. Did he really think that would work? Or was he just trying to make me feel better?

Billie Sol Estes

Billie Sol Estes was a Texas businessman best known for his involvement with a variety of scandals involving then Vice-President Lyndon B. Johnson. After amassing a fortune in various agricultural businesses in the 1950s, Sol Estes was arrested by the FBI in 1962 and charged with 57 counts of fraud which alleged he had swindled $24,000,000 from various sources using schemes that involved federal government programs for grain and cotton. The investigation lead to his relationship with LBJ, and other members of the Texas Democratic Party, and the charges had the potential of convicting LBJ of crimes that would not only destroy his political career, but put him in prison. President Kennedy was aware of these developments and is said to have privately decided to drop LBJ from his 1964 presidential ticket as a result.

As the investigation into Sol Estes activities continued, a total of seven witnesses suddenly died from carbon monoxide poisoning, though one was also shot five times. All were ruled as suicide. Sol Estes was defended by one of LBJ's attorneys, and though he was found guilty and sentenced to fifteen years in prison, he spent little time there, since his conviction was overturned in 1965 by the U.S. Supreme Court, which said excessive media coverage had deprived him of a fair trial.

Later in life, after LBJ's death, Estes admitted to secretly funneling millions of dollars to LBJ and that it was LBJ who had ordered the murder of President John F. Kennedy, Henry Marshall, George Krutilek, Harold Orr, Ike Rogers and his secretary, Coleman Wade, John Kinser, and even Josefa Johnson, the president's own sister. Sol Estes had his attorney write a letter to the U.S. Department of Justice stating, "Mr. Estes is willing to testify that LBJ ordered these killings, and that he transmitted his orders through Cliff Carter to Malcolm Wallace, who executed the murders."

It should be noted that it was Cliff Carter who called the Dallas Police Department from the White House and instructed them to bring Oswald outside for the television cameras on Sunday, Nov. 24, 1963, where Jack Ruby shot him. Further, Mac Wallace's finger print was found on a box of books stacked in the so-called "sniper's nest" on the 6th floor of the building where Lee Oswald worked on Nov. 22, 1963.

A Certified Latent Print Examiner with many years experience affirmed in a notarized affidavit that he found 14 matches between a National Archives "unknown" print, taken from what the Warren Commission designated Box A in the Texas School Book Depository, and a fingerprint card submitted "blindly" for comparison, which bore the fingerprints of Malcolm Wallace.

"The Secret Service will react," Lee said. "The Chief might react. Even the driver."

The thought of Lee firing a warning shot only to have the many guns of the President's Secret Service team turned on him terrified me into silence.

After the pause, Lee said: "I'll love you as long as my heart is still beating." He told me that when he came to me, he would be wearing the brown shirt I had bought for him, and that he would not be wearing "that demmed wedding ring."[10]

"Humans should live as long as oak trees!" I mourned, recalling a poem Lee had read to me about an oak and a lily.

"But lilies are beautiful, too," he countered. "Besides, I'm no dummy. As you said, yourself, I still have some tricks up my sleeve."

Then Lee asked me to pray for him. I said an "Our Father."

When I was finished, he said "I'm satisfied. It's a very old cry to God. Maybe He will hear it."

"I love you, Lee," I whispered, as I pressed myself against the pay phone, hoping to get inches closer to the man I loved, as he spoke the last words I would ever hear him say to me.

"Goodbye, Juduffki. I love you," he said. Then he hung up the phone, and the silence began.

It was around 2:30 A.M. as I walked back home alone, oblivious to the darkness around me, worrying only about the dangers that Lee faced. The next day was full of worry, but void of any incident worth mentioning here. I went to work as usual and played wife for Robert at home.

Friday, November 22, 1963

I went to work at PenChem, as I'd done every day for the previous six weeks. I tried to act normal, though I knew this was no ordinary day. At lunch time, I sat down in the laboratory to eat. Cabinets and shelves lined the walls. Sleek stainless steel counters were stacked with sophisticated equipment and orderly rows of test tubes.

I had brought a diet shake to eat for lunch. I dipped my milky diet drink into one of the large Dewar jars that held gallons of sub-zero liquid gas and it froze in seconds, yielding a taste like ice cream. I ate it with a spoon.

For some reason, our hour-long lunch break started later than usual that day. Mr. Mays, my boss, and Nancy, his assistant, greeted several chemists who came into our lab area for lunch. They seated themselves on tall stools at counters to watch the news on a television set which hung from the wall near the door. It was rarely turned on at lunch time, but today it was. The noon news was on. Other employees came in, too. It was unusual to see so many people crowded into our small lab. I wondered why so many people came in to watch the television when there was a volleyball game in progress outside.

As for me, I held dreadful secrets in my heart, and every minute crept by with increasing anxiety. Would President Kennedy die today? Would Lee? I felt so helpless. I was nobody. There was no one I could call. The only real information I had was the name of a CIA officer that Lee said was involved. The CIA killed heads of state, so what would they do to Lee and me if we got in their way? There was an 'abort team' out there. Perhaps Kennedy was already safe — perhaps the assassins had been located and arrested! After all, Lee had sent information and warnings. As the news program concluded, I could hear several men in the lab whispering tensely about Kennedy. One expressed his hope that somebody in Dallas would shoot him. I kept my mouth shut, feeling so paranoid and suspicious that I wondered if some of the people in the lab could be in on the plot.

When I finished eating, I started to work on logbooks, occasionally glancing over at the TV which had played clips of JFK and Jackie and Air Force One on the mid-day news. The leading chemists and technicians were still unaccountably sitting in our lab, discussing Kennedy. I heard somebody tell my boss that the president had arrived in Dallas and that his motorcade was currently parading through the city."

I reminded myself how important it was to show no interest or emotions, and to maintain my veneer of calm, but inside I was on fire. President Kennedy may have been the most charismatic leader in America, but in the Deep South, he was hated by the segregationists and anti-Catholics. Stories circulated about the president being soft on Communism and "a puppet of the Pope." Almost everyone I worked with at PenChem showed open disdain and even hatred for the "Yankee President."

As the minutes ticked by I gazed out the window, where the volleyball game was still in progress under some pine trees. I reviewed the lab schedule for the afternoon: optical analysis of a few test compounds with a ruby laser and an alkaline-halide crystal. By now, I could do that work with my eyes shut. A half-dozen scientists and technicians still congregated in the lab, chatting and listening. What kept them here, near the TV set? Did they know something about the plans in Dallas? After all, my job at this facility had been arranged by people like Dave Ferrie and Dr. Ochsner. Was there a connection?

Shortly after 1:30 P.M. Florida time (12:30 P.M. Dallas time), the television erupted with an announcement that the President had been seriously wounded by gunfire in Dallas. Soon, the network cut away from its regular programming. I can't remember the words; I only remember my horror. About a half-hour later, we heard news that a

Walter Cronkite announcing JFK's death

priest had given last rites. This news was greeted with cheers and whistles of approval in the lab. Tears started running down my cheeks, despite my efforts to hide them

"Good!" Mr. Mays said, slapping his big hand against his thigh.

"For God's sake!" I exploded, "This man is fighting for his life! What's the matter with you?!"

Seeing the expressions on the faces around me, I realized the terrible political error I had just made. I'd forgotten where I was, and who I was supposed to be. This was Florida! And I was a lab assistant.

I shrank under the malevolent glares, wiped my tears, and lowered my head. I had not only exposed myself as a Kennedy sympathizer; I could have jeopardized those who had sent me here. The poisonous whispers and sidelong glances at me continued, so I went to the sink and washed my face, put my lab coat up on a hook, and fell into a seat at the records desk so I could face away from the others.

After awhile, it was announced that President Kennedy was dead. I started crying quietly again as I opened the logbook, and tried to look busy. Maybe Lee had not been caught in the middle of this mess. As I wiped my eyes, I noticed my hands were shaking. OK, Kennedy was dead, but could Lee make it out of Dallas alive? Would he be found dead in the Depository with a rifle lying near his body? I preferred to hope that Lee was heading toward a small plane waiting for him at some small airport. At least, no arrests had been announced. No news was good news for the moment.

It was now about 1:50 PM in Dallas. My imagination ran wild.[12] In another half-hour, Lee could be in the air, headed for Houston. Dave had even promised to fly Lee to Laredo. Soon after, I could meet him in Mexico. We'd have our marriages annulled, change our names, and hide until it was safe to emerge again.

The television interrupted my daydream. A man hiding in the Texas Movie Theater had been arrested for killing a Dallas police officer.[13] The officer, J.D. Tippit, had been shot in Oak Cliff. Hearing this chilled me to the bone, since I knew Lee's apartment was in Oak Cliff.

Soon, the media's speculation began. Could this man also be the President's assassin? My hopes began to dim, remembering how Lee had said he went to tell his family goodbye on Thursday evening.

Then I heard the words I feared: "Lee Harvey Oswald." I flashed on Lee's comments from only 38 hours ago, telling me they were going to blame it on him.

By 4:00 P.M., the TV and radio had begun repeating the name "Lee Harvey Oswald" over and over. I shuddered, realizing he was being set up as the scapegoat, just as Lee had predicted. Everyone in the lab was glued to the tube.

I also noticed that the news announcers constantly used Lee's middle name, like it was a mantra. What was Walter Cronkite's middle name? Why did they have to say "Lee *Harvey* Oswald" with the same solemnity as when they identified President Lincoln's assassin as "John *Wilkes* Booth." It had the sound of finality about it. As if they were pronouncing a death sentence, writing an obituary, or engraving a tombstone.

Suddenly I began to worry about my own safety. What if the local police or federal agents burst into the lab and hauled me away? What could I say? Who would believe our government was being taken over from the inside? While Dave, Lee and others had done everything they could to eradicate all traces of my involvement, we knew we were fighting forces much bigger than ourselves. I whispered to myself: *Remember where you are. Stay calm. You have to survive.*

Finally, I saw Lee's picture flash on the screen. I could see he had been beaten. I gasped.

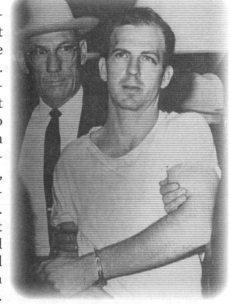

Mr. Mays noticed. "Are you a God-damned Communist?" he shouted at me. His assistant, Nancy, looked at me like I was mad. It was puzzling to them. First I cried because President Kennedy was killed, and now I was upset because they had "caught the man who shot him." But I had lost more than they could understand. Yes, in that moment, I had lost their esteem, my job, and my future with them, but more importantly to me, I had lost hope for Lee. As long as he lived, he could talk. But those who knew what Lee knew would not want him to talk. Lee was a dead man walking. At least he had not been shot on the street or during his arrest. Perhaps police custody would provide him some shield against those who wanted to silence him. The lab looked like a dreamscape to me. I pretended to work and hoped the day would end soon.

About 5:00 P.M., my colleagues began getting into their cars to go home. I had no car, so I had to call Robert for a ride. There was a pay phone outside by the compressed gas tanks. I reached it and called Robert, who was at home studying. I told him President Kennedy had been killed. As usual, he had few words to say: "That's bad news. What a shame. It's because he was for integration, you know." I told Robert the lab was closing down, and everybody was going home.[14] I asked him to come pick me up. But Robert, always practical, reminded me that if I worked an extra hour or two, as I usually did, then we wouldn't lose money today.

"I just want to go home," I told him sadly. I had no strength to work and no desire to fight. Robert, however, did. He argued with me, telling me that I wouldn't feel any better at the house than I did there. I began to feel resentful again towards Robert. Why wasn't he bothered by the shocking news that the president had been murdered?

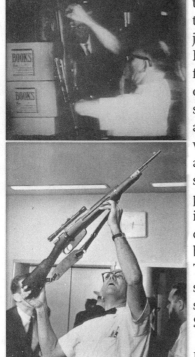

With no way to get home by myself, I sat in the lab and watched the relentless news as it unrolled across the screen. By now, it seemed everyone had jumped to the conclusion that Lee killed Kennedy. The images of the next two days flash in my memory, as they do in millions of others. The police paraded a rifle for all to see, announced that Lee had lived in Russia, and reported on his pro-Castro activities. I was appalled when I heard them refer to him as "the assassin," instead of "the accused assassin." What happened to "innocent until proven guilty?" Why was the media presuming Lee was guilty from the start? I knew Lee didn't kill JFK. Lee thought Kennedy was our best hope for peace. But what about Officer Tippit? While I couldn't imagine Lee actually shooting anybody, maybe Tippit had tried to shoot him, and Lee had to defend himself. Such is the weight of an accusation.

Suddenly, I remembered the call wheel. I always worked overtime on Fridays. If I'd gone home, I would have missed Dave's call! I checked the call-wheel schedule. It was time for Dave to call! I headed to the pay phone under the pine trees near the gas tanks. Surely he would have some inside news. The phone rang right on time, but as soon as I answered, Dave exploded: "Do you have my library card?" he demanded. "Jackass Martin called the police and told them Hector had my library card!"

Then it struck me. Dave wasn't talking about his card for the New Orleans Public Library; he was talking about his card from the Tulane Medical School library. That card would lead the police not only to Dave Ferrie, but straight to Dr. Ochsner. The Project would be exposed, and that would be disastrous for everybody involved!

Dave had lent me his TMS library card so I could check out medical journals, and I had given the card to Lee in David Lewis's presence when I needed Lee to return some medical journals for me. David Lewis must have told Jack Martin, as he always seemed to do, especially with information concerning Dave Ferrie. Lee, of course, had given the card back to me later, but David Lewis (and therefore Jack Martin) didn't know that. I had planned to give the card back to Dave Ferrie the last time I saw him, but that was the same night that I had the disastrous exit interview with Ochsner. I was too upset to remember Dave's TMS library card. It had remained lost and forgotten somewhere in the cellars of my cavernous purse.

"Do you have it?" Dave demanded frantically. "I've even been to Hector's apartment, and it wasn't there!"

"I have it," I replied.

"I want you to burn it! Right now! While I'm on the phone!" Dave ordered.

Here I was, standing in between a liquid nitrogen tank and a liquid oxygen tank, with "No Smoking" signs posted all around. I described the scene to Dave over the phone.

"Then dissolve it in sulfuric acid!" he commanded. I agreed to do just that, though I actually ripped it into tiny pieces and buried it in the sand under a pine tree.

"Thanks, J," Dave said, sounding a bit more relieved. "I'm okay now. I'll deny knowing anything about the card. I'm going over there (to Texas). The boys will be driving all the way. The good news is, we talked to Marcello's people at supper, and Lee's going to get some highpowered legal help."

Dave had spent the afternoon in court with Carlos Marcello. It was the conclusion of a long trial. Bobby Kennedy's people had tried to deport him, but they failed. At almost the same moment, they heard that JFK had died. Marcello was having a party for his victory over Bobby Kennedy, and as part of Marcello's inner team, Dave was required to attend.[15]

"We'll get Lee sprung," Dave exclaimed.

"Sprung?" I could hardly believe my ears.

Carlos Marcello and lawyer in front of New Orleans Federal Court House, 1966

"He's not the only one who got arrested," Dave said. "He's just getting all the publicity right now. You have no concept of how powerful the mob is in Dallas. Marcello's lawyers are on top of it right now. I give you my oath on a stack of Bibles. We'll get him out, or somebody will pay, big time."

I was used to Dave's hyperbole, but I did allow my hopes to rise a bit.[16]

Dave said he'd call back tomorrow when he knew more. It would be to a different phone and very late. Meanwhile, he suggested that I pray to St. Jude.

Saturday, November 23, 1963

The wait for Dave's phone call seemed like forever. Fortunately, Robert had fallen asleep watching the news with our friends the Zieglers, but we were young and kept late hours, so they were still up. We occasionally spent a long night with the Zieglers, and they were used to my going outside at night to take a look at the positions of the planets or to get soft drinks, so when I said I wanted to get some fresh air, they gave me some money to retrieve cokes from a vending machine down the street. As I walked to the pay phone, I was on edge and my hair raised at every sound in the dark night. I hoped my watch was in synch with Dave's, so I wouldn't have to wait around for his call.

The phone rang as soon as I reached it. Dave was as nervous as I was and apologized for calling a few minutes early. I told him I was glad he did. Then I heard Dave make a sound as if he were choking. I realized he was swallowing back his tears. "Oh, my God, J," he said to me. "I won't hide it from you."

Dave was crying. I started to cry, too. I didn't think I had any tears left, but there they were, stinging my eyes. I was so anxious to hear what he had to say.

"It's hopeless. If you want to stay alive," Dave warned me, with a strained voice, "it's time to go into the catacombs.[17] Promise me you will keep your mouth shut!" he added. "I don't want to lose you, too," he

Carlos Marcello & Santos Trafficante

said, his voice choking on his words. I felt weak all over. "If there is any chance to save him, we'll get him out of there, I swear to you. So play the dumb broad, and save yourself. Remember, Mr. T will watch every step you make."

Dave meant I was being watched by "Santos" Trafficante, the Godfather of Tampa and Miami. He was also the good friend and ally of Carlos Marcello.

Fortunately, Marcello liked me, which is why I believed I had a chance to survive any threats from that direction.

"I'll call you one more time. After that, I can't call anymore," Dave said. "And now I have other calls to make. So, *Vale, Soror*."[18] ("Be strong, sister.")

I returned to the Zieglers' house with four soft drinks from the coke machine. Nobody had moved from the TV set.

Sunday, November 24, 1963

I was still freaked out. The stress was unbelievable, and I couldn't sleep. Robert was surprised that I couldn't even cook. "I had no idea you liked Kennedy so much," he said. Luckily, all of America was transfixed by the tragedy, and everyone was watching their televisions, so the Zieglers were no exception, and I was welcome as always.

As lunchtime approached, we were watching the non-stop television coverage of the JFK assassination. Robert had left for the university library to finish an English paper. We all knew Lee was to be transferred from the city jail to another location, since it was announced the night

before. I was, of course, anxious for more information about Lee, and watched attentively. But there was delay after delay, and we were subjected to continuous replays of the interviews and endless discussions of the President's upcoming funeral. In this mix, there were also brief clips of Lee saying "I didn't kill anybody … I haven't shot anybody" and "I do request someone to come forward to give me legal representation."

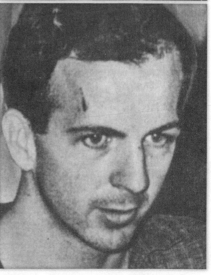

The transfer was dangerous. I was afraid, because I had heard how corrupt the Dallas police were. I also knew that there was real anger out there over the murder of the president, and much of it was being directed at Lee. So I was afraid of those who might want to take revenge on Lee. I didn't dare leave the set, or rest my eyes, though I hadn't had a bit of sleep. My heart ached as I realized that millions of people were seeing a face they recognized only as the killer of a beloved president.

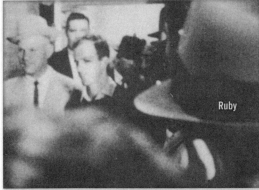

Now the time had come for Lee's transfer to a place out of the public eye, where I feared that he would be tortured to force a confession. But I knew Lee would never confess to such a thing. I watched with immense concern and tried to stay awake. Then I saw Lee come out!

At first I was relieved that they had given him a sweater to wear. Then I realized Lee was now dressed all in black, like a villain or a hit man. How crowded the place was![19] It was practically a mob scene. My eyes searched to see Lee. You could hear the excitement rippling through the crowd in the basement. There was a throng of reporters. Now I could see Lee, handcuffed and flanked by two giant Texas marshals hanging onto his arms. His face showed the strain of hours of interrogation.

A horn honked, as a vehicle suddenly moved into place, distracting everyone's attention for a split second. I held my breath as Lee was brought forward through a throng of shouting reporters, as cameras flashed. Lee glanced briefly to his left as if he saw someone he recognized. Suddenly, a dark, hulking figure lunged from the direction Lee was looking and threw himself against Lee. A gunshot was heard.[20] I saw a bit of Lee's face, twisting with pain as he gasped, and then collapsed, buried under a pile of thrashing people. The basement exploded into

chaos. There were shouts, and pandemonium broke out as police and reporters rushed forward. I screamed. It was the most terrible moment of my life. I can't remember a thing after that, except vomiting in the bathroom. Then everything blanked out. I can't recall how I conducted myself. I remained that way for hours, if not days. I recall only a deep and relentless presence of anger and outrage that kept me on my feet when I went to work the next day, despite my overwhelming grief.

No, Lee did not confess during his long hours of interrogations, nor as he drew his last pain-wracked breaths.[21] To his last gasp, Lee insisted that he shot nobody. He was taken to Parkland Hospital where President Kennedy had died.[22] He was even wheeled into the same

emergency treatment room, but objections arose, and a precious minute was lost, moving him to a different room.

Lee was cut wide open without any anesthesia. His lung, liver, aorta, kidney, spleen, and a blood vessel to the lung had been cut by the single bullet, which didn't quite exit his back. After 45 minutes of traumatic physiological stress, his blood-deprived and overburdened heart finally faltered, and stopped beating. The man I loved more than anyone in this world was dead, and I would never see him again. Never hear him again. Never touch him again. Never have his babies. Never look into his blue-gray eyes again. They had taken my true love away from me, in front of the whole world. And they did it in a police station, where law and order should prevail. The perverse irony of it all was only overshadowed by my anguish. It was the worst day of my life.

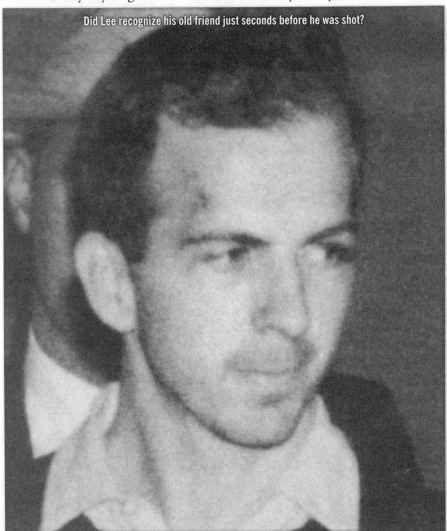

Did Lee recognize his old friend just seconds before he was shot?

The shooting of President John F. Kennedy

On November 22, 1963, at 12:30 PM local time, President Kennedy was fatally wounded while traversing Dealey Plaza in Dallas Texas in an official motorcade. Kennedy had come to Texas in hopes of increasing his popularity in anticipation of the 1964 presidential election.

The President spoke early that Friday morning in Fort Worth, then flew to Love Field near Dallas by mid-morning. His motorcade then drove through downtown Dallas on his way to the International Trade Mart where he was scheduled to speak at a business luncheon. The protective bubble-top had been removed from the limousine for the day, and the weather was clear.

As the motorcade moved down Main Street, the crowd gave JFK an enthusiastic welcome. Texas Governor John Connally and his wife rode in the limousine with President and Mrs. Kennedy. The parade was to end at Dealey Plaza, a historic park edged on one side with courthouses and police stations.

After passing the Dallas Sheriff's Office, the motorcade then turned right on Houston Street, went one block, passing the county jail, and then turned left on Elm Street, making a 130 degree turn which slowed the Presidential limousine down to 11 mph as it passed in front of the Texas School Book Depository (TSBD). Proceeding past the TSBD down Elm Street, several gunshots were heard. Both President Kennedy and Governor Connally were hit by bullets, but Mrs. Kennedy, Mrs. Connally and the two Secret Service agents in the front seat were not. How many shots were fired, by whom, and from which direction, and from what type of weapons, has long been the center of much of the JFK assassination debate.

Kennedy and Connally were rushed to nearby Parkland Hospital where Kennedy was pronounced dead at 1:00 pm of a gunshot wound to the head. Governor Connally, who had serious wounds to his chest, survived.

Within the next hour, a Dallas police officer was gunned down in Oak Cliff, a residential neighborhood a few miles from downtown Dallas. Police arrested

a 24-year old Lee Harvey Oswald in a nearby movie theater for the policeman's murder (although evidence has since surfaced indicating that Oswald was in the theater during the Tippit shooting). Later that afternoon, it was announced that Oswald worked in the Texas School Book Depository Building and had been in the building when Kennedy was shot, and that he was being charged with murdering both the President and the police officer.

Two days later, Lee Oswald was murdered in the basement of the Dallas Police Station by a local nightclub owner and Mafia bagman named Jack Ruby. The President's murder was recorded by numerous spectators' movie and still cameras, and Oswald's murder was broadcast live on national television.

1. Lee did not give me a numerical address where these dignitaries lived: I looked it up years later.

2. The route scheduled to be driven was as follows: left turn from the south end of Love Field to West Mockingbird Lane, right on Lemmon Ave, and just after passing Lee Parkway (ironic name), make a right turn at the Robert E. Lee Park, onto Turtle Creek Blvd. From 3525 Turtle Creek Blvd., you could view the motorcade as it turned onto Turtle Creek Blvd. The motorcade then proceeded down Turtle Creek, which turned into Cedar Springs Road, then turned left on North Harwood Street, turned right on Main Street, turned right on Houston Street, then made the deadly, sharp left on Elm Street, and through the Triple Underpass. The rest of the route would have included a right turn up the ramp to North Stemmons Freeway, to the Dallas Trade Mart at 2100 North Stemmons.

3. Douglas Horne's five books, *Inside the ARRB,* James Douglass' book, *JFK and the Unspeakable: Why He Died and Why It Matters,* and Vince Palamara's fine research all point to Secret Service involvement in the plot to kill JFK.

4. Marina Oswald Porter, April 19, 1996, letter to Mr. John Tunheim, Chairman, JFK Assassination Records Review Board, 600 E Street NW, Second Floor, Washington, D.C. 20530, (Certified Mail No. P 271 942 632)

5. Ref: Douglass, James: *JFK and the Unspeakable: Why He Died and Why It Matters*, p. 200-201, 213-217, as reported by Abraham Bolden and his wife, and corroborated by official records.

6. I estimate I made the call to the TSBD at about 1:00 PM Lee's time, knowing he always showed up after lunchtime to check his schedule. Our calls on the Mafia racing line went through the Covington exchange, near New Orleans, as arranged by Dave Ferrie for us, and previously, the operator sending on the call was never a problem. But this time, the operator gave me some trouble. She would later tell investigators that a woman with 'no accent' asked for "Lee Oswald" the 'new janitor' (the middle name 'Harvey' was added to the document after it was typed) at the TSBD and that Oswald did not accept the call.

7. I found records that I attended night classes on Tuesdays and Thursdays at this time, but because of the trauma of what happened, I withdrew before the end of the trimester. I own a document showing that I withdrew for 'health reasons,' which was certainly the case: for almost two weeks, after the horrible events of November 22-24, for the first and last time in my life, I considered suicide.

8. Any mention of "meetings" made by Hector (Lee) while on the phone meant telephone calls, not physical meetings. I therefore assume Lee would still have to make two more phone calls before he could get to bed, or we would probably have talked for at least another hour. Anyone who is close enough to me to have endured my phone calls knows they can last for hours. But in our final call, we could no longer follow the rules or easily control our emotions. I called Lee by his real name, and he tenderly called me all sorts of silly pet names.

9. I was not in Dallas on the 22nd, so I can only speculate how Lee ended up in the TSBD — his own workplace — that fateful day at lunchtime. Employees had a 45-minute lunch break, and Lee usually ate alone, then went for a walk outside the building. He did not go for a walk on November 22. I wonder if Lee was ordered to stay inside his own workplace, which I think would have proven to him that he was going be set up to take the blame, just as he suspected. He was supposed to have a 'spotter' with him, who instead of helping him would likely kill him if he didn't cooperate. It seems that Lee was left to himself in the TSBD. His handlers may have hoped he would panic, or otherwise seem to be involved, and then could be shot on the spot. By being ordered to stay inside the TSBD, he would also have no way to contact the abort team. A close examination of the events that day reveal that Lee Oswald was not expected to survive arrest. But they were dealing with an intelligent man who knew how to stay calm in the throes of a hurricane.

10. What he did wear was his U.S. Marine Corps ring, with its motto "semper fi" — always faithful. Imagine how I felt, seeing that reddish-brown shirt on him, in pictures I saw many years later. All photos I'd seen were black and white on the 22nd, showing a ripped-open shirt. For 36

years, I wouldn't look at even the smallest newspaper article about any of it. Then, in late 1999, I finally gritted my teeth and looked at the pictures. Oh, so many lies about Lee! So many words, and so little understanding.

11. I knew that Jackie was wearing a pink suit and had been given red roses. For years, I thought I had seen the Kennedys arrive at Love Field on TV, remembering her pink suit and the fact that the red roses would look nice with it, but the Love Field arrival clip was played over and over that weekend. I recall that transistor radios were all over PenChem, and some radio stations made news broadcasts every half hour. That's probably when we heard the comments on Jackie in her pink suit in Kennedy's motorcade that was 'now' going through Dallas.

12. Lee would leave that plane at the airfield at Alief, Texas, and travel to nearby Hull Field, where Dave Ferrie, or a trusted associate, would arrive six to twelve hours later from New Orleans, by car or plane depending on the weather. A storm was plowing across southern Louisiana and the Gulf Coast, but Dave would fly if able; he was willing to take some risks.

13. The Texas Theater was owned by Howard Hughes, who had strong ties with the CIA. The fact that Lee moved around, seating himself next to several people, including a pregnant woman, within a few minutes suggests he was trying to find a contact. Whoever sent him to the theater betrayed him. A witness reported seeing an "Oswald double" leave the back door of the theater, and enter a police car. For years he thought Oswald was arrested and taken out through the back door of the theater until he was told that Oswald was escorted out the front door.

14. PenChem only 'closed down' totally for Christmas and the 4th of July. But very little was getting done today, and by volunteering to finish experiments for others so they could go home at 5:00, I could add an extra hour or two to my work load. I worked overtime three times a week, and had earned keys to both open up and close down my lab, including keys to the compound's gate itself, for everything was fenced in for security reasons. I was also allowed to create some special chemicals which eventually, by roundabout means, reached New Orleans.

15. Dave also told me that Marcello had rigged not only the jury, but also fixed the date of the last court session so he could celebrate JFK's, death as well as his victory, "to rub it all in Bobby's face." Marcello was certain Kennedy would die that day. With the use of the mafia by the CIA, and with Lee's seemingly strong links to Castro, the government's role in the coup was well hidden, except for the actions of the Secret Service and the Dallas police. Only later would the FBI's complicity become obvious.

16. Dean Andrews would later admit he'd received a call to help Lee, then retracted his statement after Garrison went for the jugular.

17. This was one of Dave's religious references to the early days of Christianity when the Christians hid and buried their dead in vaults underground.

18. The Latin word "vale" is a farewell, like "take care" or "be strong." "Soror" means sister and is the root word in "sorority."

19. I learned that seventy of Dallas' finest — plus uncounted reporters — were present, yet not one man was placed in front of Lee to protect him from a frontal attack, and neither man "guarding" Lee had a firearm ready.

20. The blast sounded muffled like a silencer. The shot was fired so close to Lee that his body muffled the sound of the gunfire.

21. President Johnson called the Parkland emergency room and requested that they get a death bed confession out of Lee.

22. While waiting for an ambulance, Lee was carried, still handcuffed, into a small room where we only have the police version of what happened. They said they urged him to make a deathbed confession, but he shook his head and remained silent. The receipt below shows that Lee Oswald, though mortally wounded, received no oxygen in the ambulance — an unconscionable omission.

Judyth, 1964

CHAPTER 26

SILENCE

If I was going to live, I had to leave the past behind. But the emotional trauma I experienced watching the murder of the man I loved was devastating. It torpedoed my soul. Awash with feelings of hopelessness, I felt like the walking wounded staggering off a battlefield. The images of Lee getting shot played in my head over and over again. Each time, I could hear myself scream in the soundtrack, and thoughts of suicide flooded my head. I barely had the energy to fight them off. The joy had been sucked out of my life, and a cold shroud that I had never known before settled over me. What life? What was left of it? My promising medical career and my hope to cure cancer was reduced to ashes. The only man I ever truly loved was murdered before my eyes, and I could say nothing of what I knew.

I measured my loss repeatedly: there would be no more moonlit carriage rides, no glances between us as we walked together, I would never again gaze into Lee's blue-grey eyes or hear him affectionately call me "Juduffki." I gradually unpacked the suitcase under my bed; there would be no sudden departure to a new life of adventure. My life was now with Robert, a man who for weeks failed to notice my condition. Robert would never buy me begonias, nor yearn to read my poetry, nor would he want to climb Chichen-Itza with me. As I combed my hair, I remembered how Lee had caressed it, and could not bring myself to cut it. He had loved it long and free. In place of thoughts of suicide, I sank into an abyss of depression.

I could not share my situation with Robert. To his usual concerns about sex and saving money, a third was added: making good grades so he could quickly get into a Master's program in geology. I easily convinced him to get this degree right where we were at the University of Florida, citing how expensive it would be to move to New Orleans. Of course I had no choice but to continue working as a lab assistant at PenChem, but I found myself without the will to continue my night classes at UF. I went to a doctor and he agreed that my health was precarious: the university gave me "H" grades, allowing me to drop out of school for health reasons.

For the next five weeks, I struggled to hide my emotions from those around me. I did my best to follow familiar procedures in the lab, but was unable to concentrate on new material, and the quality of my work suffered. It mattered little: my boss had told me that my days at PenChem were numbered. I would be terminated as of December 31st.

Any mention of Lee's name or the JFK assassination, even accidental encounters like news on the radio made my heart race. I made a conscious decision to guard what was left of my ability to conceal my heartache by refusing to watch, read or listen to any news on the subject. But it was impossible not to hear that they had blamed it all on Lee, and that they had identified his killer as Jack Ruby.

I knew there would not be an honest investigation. Powerful elements of the government were involved on too many fronts to allow that, and the American Media was steeped in a tradition of blind obedience to the government line. The American citizenry was likewise a naïve and unwitting accomplice. They would easily swallow the lie that Lee killed Kennedy in a solitary act of insanity.

I knew differently, but what could a college student do about it? Besides, I believed I would be murdered if I spoke out and, if I died, how would Lee's children ever learn the truth about him? They had the right to know that their father had not killed Kennedy, that Lee had lost his own life trying to save the President. They needed to know that when Lee had a chance to flee and save himself, he stood his ground to protect them from retaliation by the monstrous forces he faced. These were my thoughts at the time and though I wasn't there in Dallas that day, I will always believe in Lee's innocence.

I realized that my work here on Earth was not yet finished, and resolved to go on with my life in hopes that one day I might be able to set the record straight, at least for Lee's children. Lee would have wanted

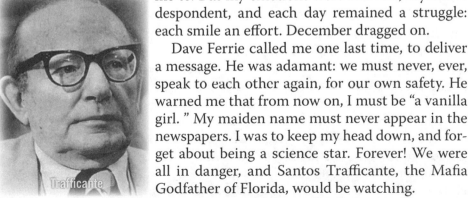

me to. But my emotions were still raw, my mood despondent, and each day remained a struggle: each smile an effort. December dragged on.

Dave Ferrie called me one last time, to deliver a message. He was adamant: we must never, ever, speak to each other again, for our own safety. He warned me that from now on, I must be "a vanilla girl. " My maiden name must never appear in the newspapers. I was to keep my head down, and forget about being a science star. Forever! We were all in danger, and Santos Trafficante, the Mafia Godfather of Florida, would be watching.

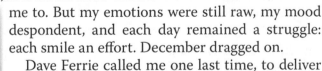

Trafficante

"I've stuck my neck out by calling you, " Dave said, at the end. "But Lee would have wanted me to. " Then he said "Goodbye, J."

He hung up. I listened to the silence and realized that my privileged contact with Lee's underground maze was over. I was no longer part of their world and, if I kept my mouth shut, maybe they would stay out of mine.

On the final day of the year, I went to work at PenChem as usual. Mr. Mays, my supervisor, showed me the incomplete entries in my tear-stained lab book, and reminded me not to return after the holiday.[1]

I entered 1964 depressed and unemployed, but at least I no longer wanted to kill myself. I retreated into painting, sitting in our decrepit little cottage, placing my dark thoughts on bleak canvases. Even Robert finally noticed. He told me to enroll in classes again, so I could see the university psychiatrist for free. When I did, I was diagnosed as suffering from depression. The doctor noted that it was a common symptom for girls on birth control pills. As a result, I was prescribed a lower dose. It was suggested that I take niacin, and I was told to stay in school, that the combination would eventually work. It did. Over the next several months, I slowly pulled out of my depression.

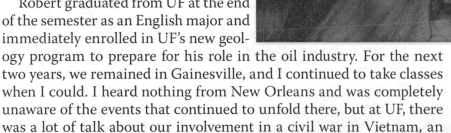

Robert graduated from UF at the end of the semester as an English major and immediately enrolled in UF's new geology program to prepare for his role in the oil industry. For the next two years, we remained in Gainesville, and I continued to take classes when I could. I heard nothing from New Orleans and was completely unaware of the events that continued to unfold there, but at UF, there was a lot of talk about our involvement in a civil war in Vietnam, an obscure little country in Southeast Asia. In the election of 1964, with 80 percent public approval of his Vietnam policy, Johnson buried Goldwater in a landslide.

By 1965, my own work at UF was starting to shine again and my spirits were raised by an award for outstanding creative achievement from the Phi Beta Kappa Society. I also earned an Associate of Arts degree.

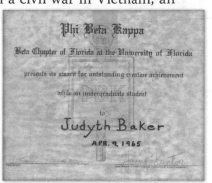

Phi Beta Kappa

Beta Chapter of Florida at the University of Florida

presents its award for outstanding creative achievement

while an undergraduate student

to

Judyth Baker

APR. 9, 1965

Late in 1965, Robert finished his M. S. in geology, and we moved to Austin, Texas where he continued in graduate school, working toward his PhD in geology and statistics. While Robert had little interest in foreign countries, Dr. A. F. Wedie, his director, wanted him to work on

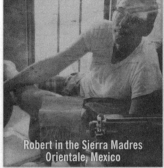
Robert in the Sierra Madres Orientale, Mexico

stratigraphy in Mexico for his dissertation. I encouraged the project and made sure I was able to accompany Robert there. We'd be living in the same country Lee and I had planned to explore together. In 1967 we moved to the Sierra Madres Orientale mountains in north-eastern Mexico where we had neither television nor English language newspapers. There I became pregnant and had my second miscarriage. Upon returning to the states, I became pregnant again. Since I had

not yet had a successful pregnancy, the doctors feared I would have another miscarriage, so I was confined to bed a great deal. Even back in Austin we took no newspapers, nor did we have a TV set. I missed the news coverage of Jim Garrison's investigation into Kennedy's assassination. I was not even aware at the time that Garrison had arrested Clay Shaw and charged him with conspiring to murder the president. I certainly had no idea that his investigators were trying to identify me (the young woman seen with Lee Oswald in Jackson, Louisiana by two separate witnesses), or that my friend Anna Lewis had protected me by lying to Jim Garrison about knowing Lee.

Some have said that Anna's bold lie saved my life, and I agree with that assessment. I should also mention that Mr. Monaghan (my boss at Reily's) and Dean Andrews (Lee's attorney), both of whom knew me, neglected to mention me in their Warren Commission testimonies. Whether they did this to protect me, others, or just to protect them-

Judyth, 1968

selves, I cannot say, but I am glad they did.

In mid-1968 we had our first child, a girl I named Susan (we always called her Susie). Susie was named after my dear friend Susie Hanover from 1032 Marengo Street. Ten days after Susie's birth, Robert had to return to Mexico for another 10 weeks to finish his field work, so I went to his parents' house on Santa Rosa Island in Florida. Though very elegant, the house was still under construction and it was a stressful time, especially having to deal with Robert's stern mother, who believed that babies should "cry it out, " and when she was home at night ordered me not to feed Susie until she stopped crying. I now under-

1969

Dr. Mary

Guy Banister

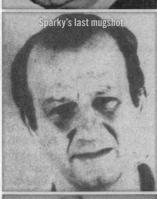

Sparky's last mugshot

David Ferrie just days before his death

stood why Robert was so unemotional, and this healed some of the distance between us. When Robert came back, I returned to Austin very grateful for his non-interference in child-raising.

Meanwhile, those who knew about the Project started dying off. On December 9, 1963 (only 17 days after JFK's assassination) Mary Richardson died suddenly of a massive cardiac arrest, though she was still in her 40s. She was the preacher's wife who had helped me that terrible night of the police raid in May of 1963. She had provided lunch for Lee and me and, while waiting for Lee to arrive, I had told her about Drs. Sherman and Ochsner. She had even driven Lee and me over to Susie Hanover's house at 1032 Marengo Street. Mary Richardson was the only person outside the Project who knew the connection between the players. What did she do when she saw Lee arrested in Dallas? Did she contact the authorities to share what she knew? If so, was her death the price she paid for her honest intentions?

In July of 1964, Dr. Mary Sherman was brutally murdered. The true circumstances of her death were not released to the public. Guy Banister also died a few months later, and there is still some question about the cause. Banister's pilot and partner, Hugh Ward, died in a mysterious plane crash. Sweet Susie Hanover disappeared, and we do not know what happened to her. Even Lee's Uncle Dutz died that same year.

By the end of 1966, Jack Ruby was in Parkland Hospital dying of galloping lung cancer while awaiting re-trial outside of Dallas, but not before he told his jailer that he had been injected with cancer. Ruby's sudden death on January 3, 1967 has always been considered suspicious by critics.[2]

David Ferrie also died under suspicious circumstances a month later, in February 1967, soon after it was announced that New Orleans District Attorney Jim Garrison was investigating him. Meanwhile, dozens of other witnesses, that I did not personally know, also died mysteriously, including Dallas County Deputy Sheriff Roger Craig who saw a rifle found in the Texas School Book Depository building that he insisted was different from the one reported to the Warren Commission. Then there was Lee Bowers, whose observations from the railroad control tower overlooking the parking lot atop the Grassy Knoll at Dealey Plaza contradicted the Warren Commission report.

In 1969, Robert's hard work and advanced education finally paid off. He got a job working as a petroleum geologist for Esso, now Exxon. We moved to Houston, Texas. Robert was making good money now, and our standard of living improved. He entered an exciting new world and traveled a lot, often speaking at professional conferences about his advanced work in computerized geology.[3] In July, we finally bought a television set so we could watch the Moon landing.

Later that year, I had a remarkable personal experience that changed my life dramatically. One night, I had a dream in which Jesus appeared before me and, being disappointed with my sadness, let His pure love flood over me, forgiving me for everything in my past. It was amazing. Just like that, my faith was restored, and I was no longer an atheist. What a change! I was filled with a new sense of joy and a new purpose for my life. I had hope for our family, and began to look forward again. As it happened, Mormon missionaries knocked on our door. "Here's a coincidence, " I thought. I invited them in, and they soon persuaded me to join the Church of Jesus Christ of Latter-Day Saints. Suddenly, a very large circle of new friends entered our life.

Robert was fascinated by my new friends and impressed by the dramatic change in my self-esteem. Soon he, too, joined the Latter-Day Saints in December 1969, which surprised even me, since he had been disinterested in religion since I'd known him. Robert proved to be flexible enough to join the LDS church, but there his flexibility ended. Once convinced, that was it: he would never leave the church.

As the 1960s ended, anti-war protests, psychedelic drugs, promiscuity, and bra-burnings still raged on in America's youth culture. With my hatred for LBJ, I had written for underground newspapers under pseudonyms, and had even marched for peace, but there was so much work to do as Mormons that Robert and I were nearly overwhelmed.

We were welcomed, however, into a clean, ethical, conservative community that was family oriented, encouraged childbearing, and had plenty of love to share. No more birth control pills for me! Time to make babies. I felt my new Mormon community was the family I had lost, and I was back in the grace of God.

Our membership in this new religious community freed Robert to roam the planet helping Exxon obtain and develop oil wells, while I lived safely and securely in a bedroom community in Stafford, near

1970

Houston. Robert traveled to Australia, South America, Malaysia and Norway, while my life was filled with hard work and fresh food. I was surrounded by dear friends, all of them pious Mormon women with burgeoning families. Yes, my new Mormon life isolated me from the outside world, but I was happy.

Strengthened by Robert's professional success and our proud roles as new parents, Robert and I summoned the courage to visit our families at Christmas of 1972. Before going to Fort Walton Beach, we went to Bradenton. It had been ten years since my father tried to have me arrested when I left for college in 1962. The event had ruptured our relationship so badly that I had I boycotted family events. Besides, I was afraid to have my maiden name mentioned in any newspaper articles.

In 1964, Grandpa Whiting was in the VA hospital in Tampa again, and I was determined to visit him. When I entered his room, Grandpa lay there wheezing, staring at the ceiling. He was on so many painkillers that he scarcely recognized me. After we hugged, he asked me to check out the lumps under his arms. They were giving him radiation, and he was feeling horrible. "They still won't tell me it's cancer," he said. "But you'll tell me. " It was so obvious. With tears in my eyes, I told him. "Hand me that damned rosary! " he commanded. "I've got some work to do." When I called my mother to tell her Grandpa was dying, she begged me to spend the night "at home."

My sister was still not in college, and my parents had no intention of helping her to get there. When our parents started drinking, a fight ensued, and I took Lynda back with me to Gainesville. There, on November 24, 1964 — the anniversary of Lee's death — overwhelmed with sorrow, I told my dear sister that I'd had an affair with a man I dearly loved, even though we were both married. I prayed she would not judge me.[#] She didn't. Lynda married a wonderful guy who graduated from UF. Though I was thrilled for her, I didn't dare attend her wedding in Orlando. By then, Grandpa Whiting was dead — I didn't attend his funeral, either. And when my aged Grandparents Vary passed away, again, I was too afraid to go to their burials.

However, after nine years of being a "vanilla girl" and "keeping my head down" to avoid having either my maiden name or my connection to cancer research being reported in the press, I now believed it was safe enough to return to Bradenton. We arrived with little Susie and our baby son to see my parents, my sister and her husband, and my cousin Ronnie and his new wife. At last, a family Christmas!

But the legend of the girl from Manatee High School who wanted to cure cancer was still alive and well. On Dec. 28, 1972 an article appeared in the local newspaper, which began with "From the time she was a child, Judy Vary hated cancer." Then it proceeded to summarize my scientific activities from "Magnesium from the Sea" to the American Cancer Society, to Roswell Park Cancer Institute, to the University of Florida. It went on to say that I was married to Robert A. Baker III from Fort Walton Beach, who was currently employed by Exxon Corporation in Houston, Texas, and that we were members of the Church of Latter Day Saints. It even listed the names and ages of our two children. Talk about blowing my cover! At least it did not mention New Orleans, or how my research career abruptly ended there. But ignorance was indeed bliss. I left town shortly before the article was published, unaware of its existence until researchers found it years later.

Fortunately, time does change some things: after J. Edgar Hoover died and his blackmail files had been destroyed, Congress finally investigated the intelligence operations of the CIA and the FBI. Senator Frank Church chaired the committee, and in 1975 he likened the CIA's murder machine to a "rogue elephant stampeding out of control." He described the FBI's COINTELPRO program as "illegal and contrary to the Constitution." The next year, as the United States celebrated its 200th birthday, the U. S. Congress decided it was time to take a second look at the JFK Assassination, so they established the House Select Committee on Assassination (HSCA). The HSCA sought testimonies from anyone who might have information concerning the President's assassination, but at that time I was deeply involved in the Stafford Bicentennial Commission's activities. I was also busy having more babies and raising children, and not the least bit interested in exposing

---

'JUST A Wife And Mother...?' — 12/28/7? Brad. Herald

She Is A Woman Fulfilled

Dec. 28 1972

By MAGGIE CHANCE

From the time she was a child, Judy Vary hated cancer. Her grandmother, two aunts and an uncle had died of the dread disease, and young Judy burned with the desire to discover a cure.

The budding scientist started winning honors in her junior year at Manatee High School. She took first place in the school science fair for her exhibit, "Magnesium from the Sea." then went on to win the county - wide competition. She took her exhibit to the State Science Fair, and took two firsts, one in the chemistry division and one in the physical science division. But she didn't stop there: a trip to the National School Fair in Indianapolis garnered her a fourth-place win.

In her senior year at MHS, Judy concentrated on cancer research. An unexpected gift from Fred Langford supplied her with 100 white mice (there were 99 females and 1 male, and soon, she says, they had over 400!).

She induced cancer in the control animals, using substances from tobacco and filters of cancer. Then she treated them, using the method she developed. Irradiation had long been used in the treatment of cancer, but had been accompanied by undesirable side effects: in some cases, the radiation treatment had actually caused the adjoining cells to become cancerous. Her theory was that by the use of anti - radioactive agents and non-toxic stearates injected beneath the cancers, spread of the disease to other parts of the body would be retarded.

Her work in this field brought her more national honors; was the first girl named as a member of the honors group in the Westinghouse Science Talent Search, she was a guest writer at the National Science Writers Seminar at the invitation of the Florida Division of the American Cancer Society, she received an American Cancer Society scholarships and one from the Florida Medical Society, and was awarded a summer job in research at the Roswell Park Memorial Cancer Research Center in Buffalo, N.Y. She also received scholarships to several colleges, but ended up at the University of Florida. It was there the direction of her life changed radically. She met and fell in love with Robert A. Baker III, fellow - student from Fort Walton Beach. He was majoring in English, but her interest in science fired his interest in geology. Simultaneously, his interest in writing reactivated her creative talents. (During her senior year at MHS, she had taken top art award in a student show.)

Bob went on to become a geologist and statistician for the Exxon Corporation in Houston, Tex.; Judy now devotes her not inconsiderable talents to homemaking (the Bakers have two children) and her true vocation, art. Yearly, she designs Christmas cards, printing about 1,000. She also designs advertising logos for Atlantic Richfield and for Arco Corporation.

But her pride in her husband and his accomplishments overshadows her own. Visiting her Bradenton parents, Mr. and Mrs. D. W. Vary, over the Christmas holiday, Judy said "I'm just a wife and mother. It's Bob who is the genius in the family." She laughed "I married a walking computer." She is particularly proud of his most recent computation; he has determined how many grains of sand there are in the world! Asked for the figure, Bob just smiled and said "There-are as many as stars in the sky." Queried further, he said that, when he'd finished his calculations, another statistician in his office had also just finished computing the number of stars, and startlingly enough, the figures were the same.

Judy credits her abiding religious faith for much of her happiness and serenity, for her acceptance of her change of life direction. A member of the Church of Latter Day Saints, she laughed, "We've only just started our family. We have two children, Susan, 4, and Josiah, 10 months. Eventually we want at least 7."

The Bakers were planning to visit with his parents in Fort Walton Beach before returning to their home in Texas.

them to the darkness of an assassination, an extra-marital affair, and the horrors of a cancerous biological weapon.

Fearing the stress and attention which my testimony could generate, I decided to maintain my silence. Lee was still being blamed for Kennedy's murder, and I understood that those who killed JFK could still easily eliminate me. I did not want my innocent children to become motherless.

Someday, I told myself, I will become brave enough to tell the world the truth about Lee, so that the children he adored will know what their father really stood for — but not yet. I was still too young and too frightened. So I did not step forward. (And, of course, nobody asked me to.)

Twelve years had passed since the JFK assassination, and some things were changing. The Warren Report had been dissected by experts, and its flaws were beginning to be chronicled and exposed. Jim Garrison's trial of Clay Shaw had come and gone, and though it was soft pedaled and marginalized by the press, it inspired another generation of independent JFK assassination researchers to challenge the official version. But I knew nothing of any of that. All I saw was the mainstream media spin, which I still tried to avoid as much as possible. They had burrowed into their lies deeper than ever. I noticed that their language morphed in an Orwellian fashion: the words 'accused assassin' became 'the assassin.' The question "Did Oswald shoot Kennedy?" became "Did Oswald act alone? " Outrage burned inside me, stoked by every accidental encounter with their deception. How could the truth be turned so upside-down? How perverse was it that a man who gave his life trying to prevent President Kennedy's assassination would end up in history books as his lone killer?

No one knew what I knew. And only a few knew that I knew it. The only person capable of pulling down the Temple might be me. But if I did, that massive construct of lies could easily fall on me and my family. So I vowed never to buy a single book, nor bring home a thing that might crack my veneer of apathy concerning the subject. As far as my family was concerned, I would pretend that the nation's sorrows did not touch me personally.

I ended up with five children, living in the safe Mormon world where I had respect and standing. I continued to avoid my past with the same tenacity I had used to block out pain in the hospital as child. I was afraid that if I looked into the face of that Medusa, I would lose control and reveal my dark secrets prematurely. I continued in this mode for years. As time went by, my fear of losing control of my emotions gradually abated, and the temptation to speak out grew less compelling. I had blocked it out of my life once again.

By 1977, I had made a kind of peace with my father. Then he suddenly died — on my birthday of all days — and I returned to Bradenton briefly for his funeral. I buried a lot of things that day: a new era of communication commenced with my mother and her family. She went on to re-marry a fine man and lived several more decades in comfort.

In 1980, we had a party at our house. It was a family-type affair with children and adults, and we were watching the Winter Olympics. We watched the hockey game between the US and USSR. There were about 35 people in the house, and the party was in full swing. The men were crowded around the TV set in our cavernous living room, and the game was getting quite intense. Amazingly, we were winning! Everyone was excited: I was busy serving snacks, when our thirsty 8-year son noticed that there were no more glasses in the cupboard. But he knew where there was one more glass. He headed to our tall bureau, climbed on a chair, opened one of the three vertical glass doors. When I saw him remove a large green tea glass, I called out, "Stop! Not that glass! That's the one Lee Oswald gave me!" OOPS.

A handful of my Mormon female friends stopped their conversation and looked at me to ponder the curious comment. I gently removed the glass from my son's hands and improvised, "Oh, didn't I tell you? I used to work with Lee Harvey Oswald ... a long time ago, in New Orleans. We used to ride the buses and streetcars to work. He gave me this glass. It's a keepsake. "

I quickly shifted their attention to cookies and the game, but the cat was out of the bag: from then on, I decided to occasionally tell a close friend that I owned such a glass so that no 'mystery' would seem to be attached to it. It became common knowledge in our family that I had known Lee Oswald in New Orleans, and he had given me the green tea glass that sat on the top shelf of the bureau.

By the early 1980's, my faith in the Mormon Church started to fade, but not my faith in God. I had welcomed their control of my life, but I was concerned about their inordinate control over my children's lives and their futures. I wanted them to have more freedom, and frankly, I was ready for some myself, so I began the long, difficult process of extraction.

Robert had recently been spending a lot of time in Norway and, in 1985, our entire family moved there. I met born-again Christians there (also in the oil industry) who helped me break my ties from the Mormon community, which was not nearly as strong in Norway as it had been in Texas. In 1986, about the time Susie left for college at BYU, I returned to Houston to finish my B. S. in anthropology. While there, I was baptized at Lakewood Church in Houston and officially left Mormonism after seventeen years. Robert, however, did not share my conversion, nor did four of my five children. He refused to read the letters I wrote explaining why I believed the LDS church was not for us. It triggered a show-down in our family. As a result, I took two of the kids and headed back to Houston. The other two stayed with their father in Norway.

Leaving the Mormon Church meant that I lost contact with hundreds of friends and the support structure I had grown to love. It was not only a personal loss, like losing a second family, but also a logistical loss, since I still had children to raise. I decided to move back to Bradenton to be near my mother and a beloved stepfather. I bought a house there and enrolled my children in schools near Manatee High School. Robert divorced me in November 1987, and only two months later married a woman recommended by the Mormon Church. Six months later, the two boys who had been living with their father and his new wife came to live with me. Lawsuits ensued and various legal battles dragged on for years, but I was determined that my children would have freedom to choose for themselves what religion they wished to embrace. I even drove them to Mormon services, if they wanted to go. With their father, there had been no freedom of choice.

As a well-compensated oil geologist, Robert had plenty of money for the custody battle. But I spent every cent I had fighting to keep the four children: I eventually lost our house in the process. In the end, my lawyers were so disgusted with Robert's tactics that they worked for free.

During the years with Robert, I had avoided anything to do with the JFK assassination, but once he was gone, I gave myself permission to quietly remember what had happened back in 1963. So in November 1987, on the anniversary of the assassination, I got out the green glass and the black necklace that Lee had given me years before, and let myself start remembering again. I got out the newspaper clippings, photographs, and documents from my youth, leafing through them for the first time since 1963. My children had never seen any of these items. To this day, most of them still haven't.

I re-read the articles about the girl who dreamed of finding a cure for cancer. And, yes, I cried. The old wound was open once again, and I felt it was finally time to face it. From that day forward, at the end of each November, I would write memory-jogging items on small sheets of paper: our conversations, the sights and the sounds, the little things that Lee had said to me. I recalled the day I was banished from cancer research by Dr. Ochsner, and Lee encouraged me to "uplift hearts instead of bodies" and to "create beauty" with my paintings. Confronting the shortness of his own life, Lee said "Now, I'll never have the time to read and learn everything I want to." I asked him not to talk like that, adding: "You're not dead until you're dead." "Ah, Juduffki," Lee answered, "there are walking dead all around us."

Eventually, I organized my collection of documents into 3-ring binders. But I still did not talk to my children about any of this. These were my personal secrets. I kept them to myself. I wanted to protect my children from them, at least while they were young.

As the 1980s ended and the 90s began, my children worked hard to get to college without any help from their father: every one of them would win full scholarships and many awards. I was very proud of them and, though I was stretched thin with full-time jobs and single parenthood, I made special efforts to help them have some fun on weekends.

On Saturday nights, my living room was full of teenagers piled on pillows and sofas watching videos. The kids would rent a popular video of their choice from the local store and bring it home. They would watch the movie, while I served snacks and kept a cheery eye on the proceedings. I was teaching and counseling at that time, and all the kids felt at ease with me. Besides, this was the only chance I had to see movies!

One Saturday night in 1992, it was time for our movie party. My oldest son was home from college between semesters, and was responsible for selecting the movies that night. Our only rule was that it not be something grossly inappropriate. The kids arrived, and once everyone settled into their spots, the movie began. Busy at the back of the room preparing treats, I kept one eye on the screen to see what they were watching. I heard a familiar but dated voice announcing something like a news broadcast, and I looked at the screen to see the initials "JFK" appear in white letters on a black background. It was Oliver Stone's film! With a sinking heart, I realized I couldn't handle it. Not in a room full of teenagers! Without saying a word, I got up and called a neighbor, asking her to keep an eye on our house and kids. Something had come up — I needed to leave. I got in my car and drove to my church, where I prayed for strength.

A few hours later, I returned to a room full of curious teens who wondered where I had gone. I dodged their questions: I was not ready to talk about it.

As a result of Oliver Stone's film, the U. S. Congress passed the Assassination Records Act and set up the Assassination Records Review Board (ARRB) to de-classify many of the surviving documents surrounding the JFK assassination, as well as to collect additional testimony from anyone who had relevant information. But I was still in the middle of a bitter legal battle with my ex-husband. Can you imagine the impact on a custody fight that stepping forward and telling the

ARRB my story would have had? I didn't dare speak up. I still had precious children to raise, and until they were out of the house and on their own, I had to maintain my silence.

By 1994 I lost my house, and my youngest child and I moved to Orlando where two of my sons attended college. I returned to college myself, and in 1996 earned an M.A. in English. Later that year, I was offered a fellowship at the University of Southwestern Louisiana and moved to Lafayette, Louisiana with my youngest daughter to work on my Doctorate. In a wave of nostalgia, I had applied there with the idea of living in the same state where Lee had been born. For the next several years, I taught college classes. By 1998, I had completed all my advanced courses in writing, 18th Century Literature, and linguistics and would soon pass all my comps. I became what academics call ABD: All But Dissertation.

In December 1998, my youngest daughter married and went on her honeymoon. Finally, I was alone. The next day I rented *JFK* and sat down to watch it in earnest. Needless to say, watching Joe Pesci's dramatic portrayal of Dave Ferrie and Gary Oldman's amazing depic-  tion of Lee was a surreal experience for me. It was like watching a dream, but knowing you were not asleep. I noticed funny things, like Joe Pesci's voice had a higher pitch than Dave's, and Lee didn't stutter as much as Gary Oldman showed him doing, but beyond such trivia, it was a fairly good re-creation of the world Lee and I had known. I was amazed that it was acted mostly by people who had never met Lee, Guy Banister, or Dave Ferrie.

But what struck me most deeply that day was the inscription at the beginning of the film. The words were seared into my brain:

"To lie by silence when we should protest makes cowards of men."

I knew that I had been "lying by silence." If I did not speak up, then I was a coward. Could I tell my children that we were all cowards — that there are no heroes left? It was a watershed moment. I soon began writing a detailed chronology of everything I could remember in a series of letters to my oldest son. Letters that I had no intention of giving him: he might find them after my death. I still planned to go to my grave without saying a word out loud. Still, it was a small step forward.

It had been 35 years since 1963. Hundreds of books had been published, with a wide range of theories. I didn't know the names of any of them, but it was time to start learning what people had been told about both Lee and the JFK assassination. So I read two books that I found in the city library: *Oswald's Tale* and *Marina and Lee*. I was shocked at the lies and distortions about Lee, but there was an even bigger shock when I learned who Jack Ruby really was.

He was not just the man who had murdered Lee. His real name was Jacob Rubenstein, and in his youth, his old mob buddies from Chicago called him "Sparky" because of his short temper. Jack Ruby was "Sparky" Rubenstein! Lee's friend! The man whom I had met at Dave Ferrie's apartment in New Orleans! Could life really be this perverse? It was Sparky who told me that he had known Lee since he was a child. It was Sparky who had given me a $50 bill as an apology for losing my rent due to the police raid at Mrs. Webber's boarding house. It was Sparky who had taken us to dinner at Antoine's (and to Clay Shaw's house) the night that Lee saved us from the menacing sailor. And it was Sparky who had hosted our evening at the 500 Club with Carlos Marcello. Sparky was Carlos Marcello's friend Jack Ruby — the one the strippers at the YWCA told me about! And it was Sparky who had marched into the basement of the Dallas Police Station, pulled out his 38 caliber pistol and killed Lee.

When I realized Lee had been murdered by a friend he had known since he was a child, my eyes were opened to the corruption that rules our nation. I recalled that in his last phone call to me, Dave had tried to explain why Jack Ruby had to kill Lee — that Lee would have been tortured to extract a confession, or they would kill him in the attempt, once they got him out of the public eye. Dave had forgotten that neither he nor Lee had ever told me Sparky's current name. Dave had tried to convince me that Lee's murder was a mercy killing. He wanted me to accept that, so I wouldn't tell anybody what I knew about Lee's killer, and his knowledge of the project. Of course, I never did. Learning that Jack Ruby had died of cancer while awaiting re-trial, perhaps even due to the same cancerous bio-weapon that Lee and I helped develop, gave me no satisfaction. No one deserves to die like that. But having heard Dave Ferrie tell Jack Ruby about our cancer project, I knew that Ruby was fully aware of its potential, and in fact, he was probably supplying money for it. With that in mind, I found it very interesting that Ruby died 28 days after being diagnosed with cancer, just as the prisoner in Jackson had done, and that shortly before he died, Ruby told family and friends, "I have been injected with cancer cells."

The hour had come. I wanted to remember it all. Record it all. Leave my memoirs for my children, and for Lee's. I called my sister and asked her to go with me to New Orleans. After more than 35 years I was ready to go back and confront what had happened. With our friend Debbee in tow, we headed to New Orleans to visit the places burned into my brain by the events I lived through. When we did, I had vivid and painful flashbacks. Some were overwhelming. At one point, when

Debbee & Judyth

we were riding on a streetcar down St. Charles Ave., I was suddenly overcome and burst into tears. I began sobbing hysterically and got off the streetcar, followed by a puzzled and worried sister and friend. It terrified me to realize how much pain was still locked inside. Now I knew that the very act of speaking up would be difficult for me emotionally. Would I break down and start crying in the middle of interviews? Could I maintain my composure enough to get my story out?

Nevertheless, I was determined to break my silence. But, how? Where do you go to tell a story like mine? And to whom?

In 1999, I contacted a TV documentary program and they asked producers at *60 Minutes* to interview me. While these telephone interviews were being conducted, I obtained a literary agent and gave him a teaser book, for I was afraid of who might sue me or try to hurt me. I told him that later I'd give more information. With my daughter gone, I was able to get more access to the Internet and I decided to find people within the JFK research community who might help me present my story to researchers, publishers and the press. I observed that Dr. Howard Platzman and Martin Shackelford were not "anti-Oswald" as were most on the newsgroup I was reading about. I contacted Dr. Platzman, who worked for an insurance company in New York City. By this time I had found several witnesses, a few of whom consented to be taped or filmed. Among them was Anna Lewis: her husband, David, had died of cancer. I was pleased to learn that she had told her family about having known Lee and "his friends" for years.[4] When I told Platzman and Shackelford about how Lee and I had double-dated with Anna and David Lewis, we decided to meet in January, 2000, so they could meet Anna Lewis face to face, along with Dr. Joseph Riehl. I regret that I did not share as much information with Dr. Riehl as I should have – he was my dissertation director at the time, and I was too fearful of conflicts of interest. He did offer a shoulder to cry on!

By then, I had confirmed much of what Edward Haslam had written about the secret labs and the Project – I had learned of Haslam's little-known book, *Mary, Ferrie, & the Monkey Virus,* late in 1999 and obtained a copy in November. I was amazed how Haslam had ferreted out so much that I thought had been buried forever, out of reach.

Dr. Platzman invited Debra Conway, who was an executive with JFK Lancer (they run conferences and sell books about the JFK as-

sassination) to attend our January meeting in New Orleans. She and Shackelford brought their video cameras. I hadn't been aware that any filming would be conducted, and thought we were simply going to have interviews and then do a tour of the various sites.

By then *60 Minutes* had hired Dr. Platzman and others to investigate my story, which they did for 14 months. Everyone's expectations were high. *60 Minutes* had the ability to get the story into millions of households in a single day. They interviewed me repeatedly in New York and elsewhere, as their investigators scoured the National Archives to find evidence that might support my story. They paid expenses for me and two investigators to visit New Orleans, but unfortunately one of them was Brian Duffy: he had written glowing reports about Gerald Posner's *Case Closed.* He said it was too hot to tour the city as I wished, stayed in the shade and went nowhere, as did the trip to New Orleans. In 2001, after three promises that the story would be aired, *60 Minutes* backed out. What a disappointment! A few weeks later, I saw an email from Phil Scheffler, one of the producers, who said that their investigation into my story was the "longest and most expensive investigation" ever conducted in the history of *60 Minutes.* Respected producer Don Hewitt, who created *60 Minutes*, sent me an apology.

Not airing the story must have been a grave decision after making such an investment. When C-Span asked Don Hewitt about their decision a year later, he said, "[We] were convinced that we were about to break the biggest story of our times… but the door was slammed in our face. "

For the next few years, I struggled to tell my story and earn a living. I was having difficulty holding a job because my name was now out there on the Internet, with websites telling lies about me. Several times I was fired from a teaching position due to being 'notorious.'

One incident that was both a success and a set-back occurred in 2003. As the 40th anniversary of the Kennedy assassination approached, I was contacted by Nigel Turner, a British film and television

producer who had developed a well-respected series called *The Men Who Killed Kennedy*. The six episodes had become a fixture on the A&E's History Channel and were shown several times a year, but with special emphasis each November. Turner was planning to add two new episodes when Gerry Hemming, whom I had visited, told Turner about me. Turner looked into my past and then interviewed me for days. In the end, he asked the History Channel to allow him to make a third new episode about my relationship with Lee.

After interviewing me on tape, comparing that with his notes, and doing more research, Nigel came to my house in Orlando again and interviewed me on camera for 38 hours over the next several days. The result was reduced to a 46-minute-long segment called "The Love Affair" that aired five times, along with his two other segments ("The Smoking Guns" and "The Guilty Men") on the History Channel in November, 2003.

The show was extremely successful and over 50,000 copies of its DVD were sold by the History Channel the following week. However, one of the two episodes that had accompanied "The Love Affair" had made the unambiguous claim that then Vice-President Lyndon B. Johnson had cooperated in the assassination of President Kennedy. Though Johnson was dead, his wife was alive, wealthy, and angry. She and other LBJ supporters, including two former Presidents, Jack Valenti (President of the Motion Picture Association of America) and Disney's distributors, attacked the History Channel with threats of law suits. All three new episodes were hastily withdrawn and the masters were supposedly destroyed, though there was no specific allegation about the content of "The Love Affair" itself. Yes, this was a major disappointment but, fortunately, irrepressible renegades have repeatedly posted videos of the episode on the internet to get the story out. The History Channel has never aired it again.

Frustrated, I tried to communicate my story on the Internet. What a disappointing experience that was! I figured that anti-conspiracy opponents who believed that Lee had killed Kennedy would argue with me, but I did not anticipate that they would resort to rude, personal attacks in an effort to discredit me... or drive me away. Yes, it hurt. But they only drove me away from their websites, not from my goal of getting the truth out about Lee. But what really surprised me was the volatile reaction of many pro-conspiracy JFK researchers, some of who were heavily invested in their own theories (and in their book sales). New eyewitness testimony of Lee Oswald's involvement in a bio-weapon project forced them to rethink everything and challenged their views. I learned, rather late in the game, that such people can say almost anything on the Internet without having to back up their accusations with hard facts. One researcher claimed I changed my family name from 'Avary' to 'Vary' because I did not like my family name. Another one solemnly declared that I had been diagnosed with a mental illness by a psychologist friend (who had never met me). I learned that the groups and forums on the internet, whether pro-conspiracy or anti-conspiracy, were basically fan clubs led by a handful of leaders who wished to promote their books, theories and personal beliefs. They like to argue and want to win. It's a sport for them. If they 'like' a new witness, who fits their theories, all is well. If they don't like you, watch out.

Along the way, however, I made some good contacts with JFK researchers like Pamela Brown, who has simply kept reminding people to consider my story without preconceptions. Jim Marrs interviewed me in person and on camera on several occasions, as have more iconoclastic researchers with open minds such as Dr. Jim Fetzer, Wim Dankbaar, and Harrison Livingstone. Peter Devries, the Dutch investigator who uncovers frauds and criminals, has also filmed me as a witness after investigating me. These people took the time to study the evidence and then embraced my story. I also met other witnesses (e. g., Gerry Patrick Hemming and Dan Marvin) who had worked in Lee's covert world themselves and understood its rules and rhythms. But it was *60 Minutes* that introduced me to author Edward Haslam, who had been doing his ground-breaking research into the death of Dr. Mary Sherman and her connections to David Ferrie and his cancer research project for over a decade before I met him.

Haslam studied my documents in detail and interviewed me extensively and repeatedly (in person, on the phone, and by email) before deciding to include my story in his 2007 book *Dr. Mary's Monkey*, which helped people to understand the players (like Dr. Ochsner) and issues (like anti-Communism) behind our bio-weapon project in New Orleans.[5]

Today, convincing evidence continues to emerge that is exonerating Lee from the lies of 1963 and beyond. First, we know that Lee could not have killed Dallas Police officer Tippit, which is what he was originally arrested for. At the time Tippit was shot, Lee was already sitting in the Texas Theatre, which is where the police arrested him minutes later. Further, the shells found at the scene of the Tippit murder had been fired from a semi-automatic pistol, not a revolver like the one the police said they wrestled away from Lee in the theatre that day.

Second, Lee could not have shot President Kennedy, because witnesses saw Lee on the second floor of the Texas School Book Depository moments before and after President Kennedy was shot. Lee was seen in the second floor lunch-room, where he bought a coke from a vending machine, not on the six floor as has been claimed. If there were multiple snipers on the sixth floor, as some have claimed, Lee was not one of them.

Third, Doug Horne, a former military intelligence analyst who worked on the staff of the Assassination Record's Review Board (ARRB), published a comprehensive five-volume series entitled *Inside the ARRB,* which presents evidence to support his conclusion that the U. S. Government's evidence (including the x-rays and medical evidence) was tampered with and falsified. In the process, Horne revealed that critical frames from the Zapruder film, which showed the exact moment Kennedy had been shot, had also been altered to hide visible damage to the back of Kennedy's head – damage caused by a bullet from the front. Extremely high resolution blow-ups of these frames, presented to Horne by Sydney Wilkinson, whose team of professional film restoration experts ("The Hollywood Seven") found evidence of gross tampering in the Zapruder film, including the fact that the back of Kennedy's head had been crudely painted black to hide a shot from the front. As Sydney told me herself on the phone, "He didn't do it, Judy! This proves it!"

And finally, in his well-researched and powerfully written book, *JFK and the Unspeakable,* author James Douglass explains why powerful forces inside the U. S. Government decided to kill JFK. Before looking at the event itself, he establishes the context of the assassination. In the process of tracing the story step-by-step, he reveals that a plot to assassinate Kennedy in Chicago on November 2, 1963, had been foiled thanks to a tip from an informant named "Lee." Douglass poses the question: Was this "Lee" really Lee Harvey Oswald? Suddenly, I understood the cryptic comments that Lee had made to me in October about getting a "trusted FBI contact" in Chicago from Dr. Mary Sherman. If Lee had not warned them about Chicago — and if Kennedy had been killed in Chicago on November 2 — then he would never have come to Dallas. Lee would never have been accused of assassinating him, nor been murdered himself. Due to Lee's heroic actions, Kennedy lived three extra weeks, and Lee died as a result. Such was the cost of his courage.

I have paid my own price for speaking up. Not only have I been subjected to rude insults and conspicuous harassment on the internet, I have experienced mysterious car crashes that appear to have been efforts to discourage me from telling the world what I know. I have experienced death threats so terrifying that I applied for political asylum in a Scandinavian county; while under their protection, I had to miss my own mother's funeral. For my own safety, I now live outside the United States year-round, and members of my own family have disowned me. I'm only in touch with two of my children now, and I haven't seen any of my seven grandchildren for years. One son, who now refuses to speak to me, asked me to publish my story as "historical fiction." I refused. This story is true, and I have told it as accurately as I can.

Now I leave my testimony in your hands.

Judyth Vary Baker

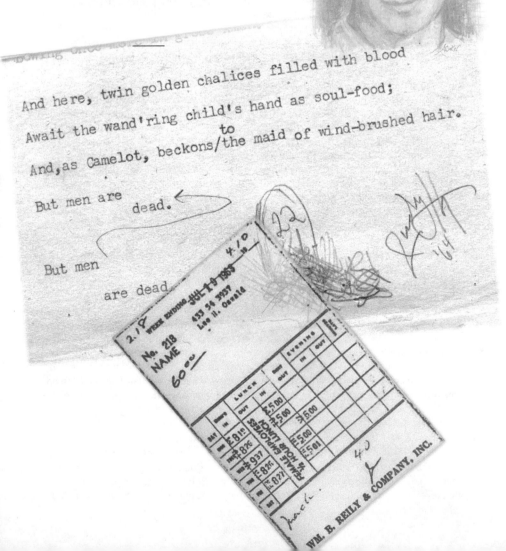

And here, twin golden chalices filled with blood

Await the wand'ring child's hand as soul-food;

And, as Camelot, beckons/the maid of wind-brushed hair.
to

But men are dead.

But men

are dead.

I placed a little note inside the green glass, where it sat for many years next to Lee's handwritten "receipt." The note explained where my evidence files were hidden, with instructions to take the files to our family attorney in case I was found dead. My sister wrote a long letter describing what I told her:

Subj: memories Date: 05/16/2000 1:29:29 AM Central Daylight Time From: bxxxxxxx) To: electlady63@aol.com (Judyth V. Baker) Dear Judy, I am sorry for not writing you sooner, but with my new job and school, it has been quite hectic. I don't need to tell you about hectic because I think you wrote the book on that already. Speaking of books, I told you I would write to you about what we shared in conversations many years ago... I believe in the fall of 1964 when I lived with you and Bob in Flavette at U of F. I remember on one particular evening, we were reminiscing about our past and what we hoped would be in our future lives, and that was the night when our conversation turned to even more serious talk about you. I remember we stayed up very late, and you were quite concerned about whether or not you should tell me something so serious in nature that you weren't sure if we should continue our discussion. But, you know me, I egged you on to tell me what was so important that you couldn't share it with me. I remember you told me that if I wanted to know what you were keeping to yourself, I had to swear to secrecy and never tell anyone about this. You said if anything ever happened to you.... such as an early or premature death, then I should tell anyone that would listen about what you were about to tell me. I swore to you I would keep your secret, and up until this day I have done that. Now, because of the writing of your book, and with your permission, I will repeat what you told me so many years ago. You told me you were afraid for my well-being, but felt I needed to know what had transpired in your life at that time. Here goes..... You told me that you had a love affair with a man who was trying to help our country and he was involved in very secret and covert activities for our country. You said you met him when Bobby left you all alone after you were married and you fell in love with each other. You told me if anything ever happened to you, I was to look for a green glass that he had given you as proof of what you were telling me. You said that my life might be in danger if I ever mentioned this to anyone and made me promise that I would never speak of this conversation again unless something happened to you. I was full of questions, and you were very hesitant to give me many details, other than you and he had shared a common interest in saving our country and the President, and that you were both very much in love. You said you wanted to be buried next to him some day, and someday you would tell me the whole story about the two of you. You said you worked closely together and had some close friends who were also working with you. You said the friends were also in danger and you wouldn't tell me much more. You said someday I would know everything, but it would mean you probably would not be alive if that knowledge came to me. I remember I was frightened for you and didn't understand what it was all about, but I also knew you were in pain and hurting over this man you loved so much. You reminded me about the green glass several more times during our conversation that night, and wanted me not to think badly of you for being in love with another man when you were already married to Bobby. I told you I would never judge you, Judy, and I never have. I have kept this secret all these years, including how you and he had loved each other so much and how you wanted to be buried next to him when you die. I now know why you wanted to protect me and not tell me the details of you and Lee... and I also know why you feared for your life for all of these years and wanted to protect me and your children from any danger. I know what you told me was the truth back then, and I still remember the fear and at the same time the love in your voice when you told me this information. I hope people will believe you and me as well, because I swear what I have just written is true. I love you honey, with all of my heart. Your sister, Lynda

1. Mr. Mays said I had erased some data and changed it. But only ink-written data was permanent. Data written in pencil was double-checked, then re-written in ink.

2. Jack Ruby's death on January 3, 1967 has been considered suspicious since the day it happened. The main suspicion has always been that Ruby had been injected with cancer to prevent him from speaking more freely about what he knew during his upcoming re-trail

outside of Dallas. Many discounted this claim since giving somebody cancer by an injection was not considered to be medically possible at the time. In his book, CROSSFIRE, Jim Marrs addresses "The Mysterious Death of Jack Ruby" (p. 429) and notes that on October 5, 1966 the Texas Court of Appeals overturned Jack Ruby's conviction and on December 7, 1966 ordered a new trial to be held outside of Dallas. Two days later, Ruby became ill and entered Parkland Hospital where doctors initially thought he had pneumonia, but quickly changed their diagnosis to lung cancer. Before the week was over, the Parkland doctors announced that Ruby's lung cancer had advanced so far that it could not be treated (meaning it had spread to other parts of the body — Stage IV). The median survival time of a patient with Stage IV lung cancer is eight months, but twenty-seven days after the onset of his initial symptoms of cough and nausea, Jack Ruby was dead. Deputy Sheriff Al Maddox was Ruby's jailer at the time. He later told researchers that Jack Ruby told him of being injected with cancer and handed him a note making that claim. Maddox also remembered what he described as a "phony doctor" had visited Ruby shortly before he became sick. A second law enforcement officer said Ruby had been placed in an x-ray room for about 15 minutes with the x-ray machine running constantly, an action that would have certainly compromised his immune system. The autopsy found the main concentration of cancer cells to be in Ruby's right lung, but noted that cancer cells had spread throughout his body. These cells were sent to nearby Southwest Medical School for closer scrutiny using an electron microscope. Bruce McCarty, the electron microscope operator that examined Ruby's cells there, told Jim Marrs that he was surprised to find Ruby's cells had microvilli (tentacle-like extensions that grow out of the main cell), since microvilli were not normally seen in lung cancers. A decade later, however, cancer researchers at the Albert Einstein College of Medicine in New York noted that when cancer cells of various types and origins were suspended in specialized liquids they would form microvilli extensions "when settling on glass." This is consistent with my description of the need to separate their suspended cancer cells from the sides of the glass thermos every couple of days.

3.   Robert A. Baker III of Stafford, Texas was awarded at least five patents by the U.S. Patent Office for his innovations in seismic science during his career. They were: US Pat. 6014344 - Method For Enhancing Seismic Data, US Pat. 7013218 - System And Method For Interpreting Repeated Surfaces, US Pat. 12041767 - Method For Editing Gridded Surfaces, US Pat. 6775620 - Method Of Locating A Surface In A Three Dimensional Volume Of Seismic Data, and US Pat. 6675102 - Method Of Processing Seismic Geophysical Data To Produce Time, Structure, Volumes. He also invented numerous patented processes that are held solely by Exxon Corp.

4.   David Lewis said he had seen Banister, Ferrie and Lee together in 1962. People assume Lee never left the Dallas-Fort Worth area in 1962 after returning from the USSR, but he was estranged from Marina for weeks at a time, and his whereabouts are mostly unknown. Anna Lewis stated she remembered seeing Lee in the fall of 1962. These people were not lying: Lee told me in April '63 that he had recently been in Florida. From New Orleans, Lee flew to Texas and reputable witness Antonio Veciana told HSCA investigator Gaeton Fonzi that he met Oswald there at a time when Marina insisted her husband never left town.

In a debate between Jim DiEugenio and John McAdams on Black Op Radio it was stated, "You get people like David Lewis, who absolutely insisted he saw Oswald with Ferrie and Banister, but he insisted it was in 1962 — well, that was shot out of the water." No, it was "shot out of the water" only for those who refuse to consider the eye-witness testimony of David Lewis, Anna Lewis, Judyth Baker and Antonio Veciana.

5.   When I first talked to Edward T. Haslam he told me he had met a woman in New Orleans in 1972 who said her name was Judyth Vary Baker, and that she had been a close friend of Lee Oswald. Whoever this woman was, it was not me. Once we met, and he saw I was not the same woman, Haslam accepted that someone had gone to the trouble of presenting him with a double in an attempt to mislead him and discredit me.

Afterword

By Jim Marrs

On November 22, 1963, I was working toward a degree in journalism at the University of North Texas near Dallas. I started my investigation into the JFK assassination that same day by obtaining every edition of the local newspapers to capture the story as it unfolded.

I obtained my Bachelor's Degree in journalism in 1966 and, following some graduate studies, was working as a professional newsman in the Dallas-Fort Worth area two years later. For the next 40 years, I continued my investigation, interviewing witnesses, collecting books and documents, poring over the 26 volumes of the Warren Commission, and trying to find sensible answers. In 1976, I was asked to teach a course on the JFK assassination at the University of Texas at Arlington, which I did every fall and spring semester until my retirement in 2007.

I have interviewed hundreds of witnesses, like Dallas Police officers who told me of a mysterious letter they had received about two weeks before the assassination from an A. J. Hidell (Lee Oswald's alias) warning of an attempt on President Kennedy's life when he came to Dallas. This letter disappeared when FBI agents descended on the Dallas police station following the assassination and scoured every conceivable file, locker and even motorcycle saddlebags. Since this letter is now missing and there is no proof it existed, I have not previously mentioned this story publicly.

I studied the testimony of a Dallas Deputy Sheriff, Roger Craig, who was on the sixth floor of the Texas School Book Depository building immediately after the shooting and watched fellow lawmen as they discovered a 7.65 mm Mauser rifle. I found it curious that it was not until the next day that the rifle was suddenly identified as a 6.5 mm Italian Carcano, which could be traced to the sole suspect, Lee Harvey Oswald.

I also spent many hours with Lee Oswald's mother, Marguerite, who told me her son was an agent working for the U.S. Government. She also told me about the time a military officer accompanied Lee home from junior high school and told her he was just the sort of lad the U.S. military needed.

In the fall of 1964, just a month after the release of the Warren Commission Report, I interviewed retired Army General Edwin Walker in his Dallas home where he told me that Oswald knew Jack Ruby and that the Warren Commission would have to start over on that one fact alone. Walker also said that the bullet fired through his window on April 10, 1963 was a 30.06 caliber and could not have come from Oswald's 6.5 mm rifle.

My interviews came to include Sen. John Tower, former House Speaker Jim Wright (who told me he heard shots from the area of the Grassy Knoll), Nellie Connally, Sen. Ralph Yarborough (who rode in the same car as Lyndon Johnson, saw smoke drifting from the Grassy Knoll and denied the story of Secret Service Agent Rufus Youngblood vaulting over the front seat to protect LBJ), and witnesses such as Jean Hill, Charles Brehm, Bill and Gayle Newman, James Teague, Phil Willis and Dallas surveyors Robert West and Chester Breneman, along with many Dallas policemen and city and county officials.

I bought the entire 26 volumes of the Warren Commission Report, which I found filled with much extraneous matter; yet it omitted some of the pertinent testimony that I had heard in Dallas.

From Chester Breneman, I obtained a copy of the original survey map he and Dallas County Surveyor Robert West made of Dealey Plaza for the Warren Commission on May 31, 1964, to make sure I knew every conceivable distance, angle and height that might affect an analysis of the shots fired. The information on his copy of the original plat map was at odds with the Warren Commission's published document. Today, I distrust any computer simulation of the assassination based on the commission's figures, which I know to be altered and inaccurate.

In 1989, I finally condensed my two decades of investigation into a book entitled *CROSSFIRE: The Plot that Killed Kennedy.* It was successful and made it to the *New York Times* Best-Seller list for nonfiction. In my book, I published a list of more than 100 names of persons who were in some way connected to Oswald or the assassination. Many died premature and sometimes mysterious deaths, which I merely termed "convenient for anyone not wishing the truth of the JFK assassination to become public."

The 1991 Oliver Stone film, *JFK,* viciously attacked by the major corporate media even prior to its theatrical release, was based on *Crossfire* as well as Jim Garrison's autobiographical book *On the Trail of the Assassins.*

In 2001, when I heard that a woman had emerged from the shadows, 38 years after the assassination, claiming to have been in close personal contact with Lee Harvey Oswald on a day-to-day basis during the summer of 1963 and that her name had never once appeared in any document or any report, I was skeptical, to say the least. My first question was: If what she says is true, how is she still alive?

When I finally sat down with Judyth Vary Baker, I heard a familiar collection of names such as David Ferrie, Guy Banister, Jack Martin, David Lewis, Clay Shaw, and Carlos Marcello, all common figures in many JFK assassination books about Lee Oswald's time in New Orleans. She could have easily read them and sewn them together into a story. Her tales of Oswald were rambling and exhaustively detailed, and during the telling, she waxed and waned through a broad spectrum of emotions. At times, her story was confusing, hard to follow and peppered with technical medical jargon and references to people who were highly placed in the world of science. I also heard less familiar names, like Dr. Alton Ochsner, who had published a record album about Lee Harvey Oswald, and Dr. Mary Sherman, who had been on my list of mysterious deaths in *Crossfire*. Then Judyth told me about a secret cancer project in which she had been involved with Mary Sherman, David Ferrie and Dr. Ochsner, which was intended to create a biological weapon to kill Fidel Castro. Before I could recover from this revelation, she informed me that she and Lee had eventually become lovers. I can certainly understand the disbelief of those who hear her story for the first time, or only catch bits and pieces of it.

Could it be true? I pondered. How could a 19-year-old college student have been dragged into a covert operation to develop a cancerous biological weapon? And if she had, how did this involve Lee Oswald, who officially was supposed to be a lone nut and a Communist who dreamed of living in Cuba?

As I considered her story, I knew that either this woman was telling the truth or she needed to be in Hollywood writing screenplays, because her ability to concoct an absorbing story out of thin air was truly amazing.

But her story of a personal relationship with Lee Oswald helps us to understand her motivation for risking her life to tell us this story and helps us explain how she was in a position to learn the things that she knows. But primarily, Judyth's story paints a clear picture of the events that transpired in New Orleans in the summer of 1963.

This was a perplexing period, confused by the conflicting evidence presented to the public by the Warren Commission and its defenders. Oswald handed out pro-Castro literature one day; the next he was offering his services to anti-Castro Cubans. Described as an anti-American defector to Russia who detested the U.S. Government, when arrested in New Orleans he nevertheless requested to speak to an FBI agent and gave agent John Quigley virtually a full report on his activities in that city. Oswald finally got steady work at the William B. Reily

Company, but then slipped out almost daily until it cost him the job. What was this all about?

Judyth's well-supported account places all these events into a comprehensible context as well as helping to explain why Jim Garrison's investigation was so threatening to people in high positions of power.

There is no evidence that Ferrie, Banister, Clay Shaw, Dr. Ochsner, Dr. Sherman, Jack Martin, David Lewis or any of the New Orleans characters ended up in Dealey Plaza. The only person who can conclusively be connected to the scene of the shooting is Oswald. In other words, if Oswald was not the shooter, then it is questionable if the plotting in New Orleans actually resulted in the assassination. The New Orleans plot was real enough but the true assassins remain masked behind the smoke from the Grassy Knoll, the objects of never-ending research and theory. Oswald was a patsy and New Orleans is a red herring. But the events in New Orleans in the summer of 1963 reveal the murderous interconnection of the major players in the assassination. It is this backdrop of anti-integrationist businessmen, oilmen and corporate leaders, obliging and corrupt politicians, anti-Communist Cubans, vengeful Organized Crime bosses and loose cannons within the U.S. military, CIA and FBI that everyone involved felt had to be kept from the public.

Judyth Baker has never claimed to know who killed Kennedy, only who did not. While her story does not reveal the identity of Kennedy's assassins, it nevertheless presents a broad outline of the participants in the background.

Me & Lee is not a dry academic treatise nor is it an obtuse government report. It is a vibrant and emotional personal narrative from the standpoint of one who obviously cares greatly for the story she is telling.

The basic question, of course, is whether or not her story is true or untrue. It is either one or the other. Even if it is only partially true, it speaks volumes about the activities of Lee Oswald and many others in New Orleans during the summer of 1963.

Let's assume for the moment her story is untrue: why would Judyth Baker concoct such a tale? Was it for fame, fortune, and a chance to insert herself into history? If so, she failed miserably. She has made no money, been involved in freak accidents, viciously attacked on the Internet and finally forced to flee the United States to live abroad in poverty – hardly incentives to insist on her involvement with a man who arguably is more universally despised than Osama bin Laden.

Her promising scientific research career was prematurely terminated in New Orleans. Why? In the summer of 1963, she was under the wing of the great Dr. Alton Ochsner, and due to attend Tulane Medical School on a full scholarship. Then she returned to Florida, worked at Pen Chem Laboratories in Gainesville for about four months, was fired on December 31st, and completely abandoned her dream of curing cancer. What happened in New Orleans that summer?

Having interviewed Judyth on several occasions and carefully studied her documentation and other materials, I can say that I have found her to be both internally consistent and forthright in her statements regarding her knowledge of events in New Orleans. Furthermore, her account has been largely confirmed from several separate sources.

Contrary to some claims on the Internet, when I visited Mary Ferrell, that Grande Dame of assassination researchers, at a Dallas convalescent home shortly before her death, she exhibited a continuing confidence in the basic truth of Judyth's story.

I further challenge anyone to recall details of their lives almost 50 years ago with the clarity and attention to detail of Judyth Baker. Her recollections which can be verified -- and there are many -- substantiate her claim of a photographic memory.

Baker's collection of news clippings, documents, employment time cards and even bus tickets is impressive and fully support her account. In fact, the only real obstacle to my accepting her tale was her claim of a passionate love affair with the man vilified by history as a traitorous defector, lone "nut," and the assassin of President Kennedy. Where are the love letters and snapshots of the loving couple?

The answer lies in the prudish early '60s. No married person seeing another would have left behind incriminating photos or love letters. And, considering this case apparently involved undercover agents working on a dangerous and clandestine project, the need for secrecy was intensified tenfold. In this light, it is truly amazing that Judyth has retained the documentation that she now holds.

Still, what was really needed was a living witness who could place Judyth and Lee together and provide some insight into their relationship. I finally got to see an interview recorded by Debra Conway, who has been actively involved in the JFK assassination community for many years. She interviewed Anna Lewis, who worked as a waitress at Thompson's restaurant in 1963, and was married to David Lewis, who worked for Guy Banister and knew Lee Oswald through that office.[1] Anna Lewis and her husband socialized with Lee Oswald and Judyth Vary Baker on several occasions, and often saw them together at Thompson's restaurant. In her taped interview, Anna Lewis made it abundantly clear that she did not particularly care for Judyth, yet, when asked about Judyth's relationship with Lee, she plainly stated, "I would say they were lovers." For me, this answered the question about the true nature of Judyth and Lee's personal relationship.

For those who continue to question her legitimacy, one can only ask: who was the Judyth Vary Baker claiming knowledge of Oswald who met author Ed Haslam in 1972 in New Orleans? (See *Dr. Mary's Monkey* for details) It was clearly not the same Judyth Baker of today.[2] Someone was impersonating Judyth, who had left New Orleans nine years previously, which lends great support to the idea that a very dangerous secret was being preserved through cover-up and misdirection at a high level.

Anyone who has studied the JFK assassination in any depth has come to the realization that a massive cover-up has taken place at the level of the Federal Government of the United States. This was accomplished for many different reasons, some benign and others not so benign. The covert cancer work, which may well have perfected a cancer-causing virus, may well be an even more sensitive government secret than the assassination.

Adulterated polio vaccines, a cancer-causing medium, virulent anti-integrationists and anti-Communists, Mafia crime bosses and thugs, corrupt politicians and a runaway military-industrial-intelligence complex all combined in a dangerous mixture that led to the murder of the chief executive. And it reached all the way to the top of the American power structure. It was a very deep and ugly can of worms, which no one in authority wished to open. This aversion has continued up to the present day.

Will anyone in government finally tell the public the truth about the Kennedy assassination? It is highly unlikely.

Jim Marrs

But can we ever really know the truth? I say yes, by studying the wide array of information now available, thinking for ourselves, and listening to the impassioned, unflinching voice of Judy Vary Baker.

For once, I agree with one of her constant critics, who wrote, "If Judyth Vary Baker is telling the truth, it will change the way we think about the Kennedy assassination." For those who know the facts behind her story, I think it already has.

1. Thompson's Restaurant was located at 133 St. Charles Ave. in the Central Business District of New Orleans. It is mentioned many times by Judyth in *Me & Lee,* and by Garrison witness Carlos Quiroga as a meeting place for anti-Castro Cubans.

2. In 1995, I read an obscure and self-published book by an unknown author named Edward T. Haslam, the son of a New Orleans doctor, who decided to investigate the murder of Dr. Mary Sherman, a physician who had worked with his father at Tulane Medical School. Haslam had also mentioned Ochsner, Sherman, Ferrie, Oswald and a plot to kill Castro. I called Haslam, and asked him if he had ever heard of Judyth Vary Baker. He had. At the time I also questioned his claims regarding the polio vaccine contaminated by a monkey virus. Today that scandal has been confirmed and reported by mainstream news outlets.

   I met with Haslam in Dallas on two separate occasions (2002 and 2003) to interview him on camera about Judyth. Haslam said that in 1972, as a college student at Tulane in New Orleans, he had met a woman who said her name was Judyth Vary Baker, and she had been a close, personal friend of Lee Harvey Oswald. She also had questioned Haslam closely about any information he might have concerning the JFK assassination. The problem was that, years later, when Haslam was introduced to the real Judyth Vary Baker by 60 Minutes, he realized the first had to have been an impostor, since Judyth did not live in (or visit) New Orleans at the time. So who knew about JVB's connection to Oswald in 1972, and why would they go to such lengths to impersonate her? Haslam did not have an answer, but he was determined to find out more about the curious woman.

Bradenton Girl Wins Top Award

MELBOURNE (AP) — A boy who lives near Cape Canaveral and a girl from Bradenton won the top awards at the State Science Fair which ended Saturday.

Robert Baum, Melbourne High School senior, took first place in the senior biological science division with his study of chemical control of human heredity.

Judyth Vary, Manatee High School junior, came in first in the senior physical science division. She worked out a method for extracting magnesium from sea water.

Both youngsters will enter the National Science Fair to be held next month at Indianapolis. Each received a $100 defense bond. Baum also will be given a two week cruise on a Navy ship. Miss Vary was presented with an encyclopedia.

The state fair will be held at Lakeland next year and at Pensacola the following year.

First and second place winners by divisions and categories:

Senior — zoology, William Adkins II, Melbourne; Chris Cherniak. Botany, Baum; David Muchow, Winter Haven. Physiology, Kirk Middleton, Fort Pierce; Marshall Crosby, Gainesville.

Physics — engineering, George Adcock, West Palm Beach; Russell Norell, Miami. Mathematics, Miklos Wass de Czege, Gainesville, James Benson, Vero Beach. Geology - astronomy, Gordon Midgett, Tallahassee; William T. Starks, Tampa. Chemistry, Miss Vary; Ronald Isaacson, Miami Beach.

Junior — biology, Kenneth Webb, Titusville; Bruce Chappell, Gainesville. Zoology, Chappell; Donald Shreve, Tampa. Botany, Sara Bush, Ocala; Barbara Louise Corbett, Haines City. Physiology, Kenneth Webb. Titusville; Michael Zinner, Coral Gables. Physical science, Archie Carr, Gainesville; Michael Diogo, Orlando. Physics and engineering, Diogo; David Kerns Jr., Tallahassee. Mathematics, Billy Nixon, Gainesville; Susan Johnson, Winter Haven.

Geology - astronomy, Carr; Cecil James McCullers, Live Oak. Chemistry, Nancy J. Worth, Miami; Bruce Landsperger, Tallahassee.

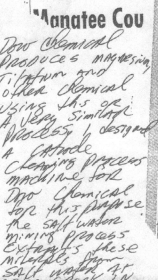

FIRST PLACE PRIZE in the Manatee County Science Fair chemistry category was awarded to 16-year-old Judith Vary for exhibit, above, illustrating the process of obtaining magnesium from seawater. The process was developed by the Manatee High School Junior after experimenting in class and is patterned after the same procedure us... laboratories, but with som... cess utilizes a gallon of s... except magnesium and, t... ing and electrolic action, r... nesium oxide or 1.2 gra... Photo by King.)

JUDY VARY IS TOP STATE YOUNGSTER IN SCIENCE FAIR

MELBOURNE — Judy Vary, a junior at Manatee High School, yesterday captured a first place honor in the State School Science Fair for her exhibit 'Magnesium From The Sea.'

She won first place in the Chemistry Division and first place in the Physical Science Division to cop an all-expense paid trip to Indianapolis, Ind., site of the National School Science Fair. Her awards today included a $100 U.S. Savings Bond.

The exhibit won first place in the Manatee High School Science Fair, then took first honors in the County School Science Fair at the Agricultural Center in Palmetto.

Reports from the fair were incomplete, with a chance that other Manatee County entrants might capture honors in the state competition.

Texas Rattler Steak

(handwritten notes): Dow Chemical produces magnesium, Titanium and other chemical using this or a very similar process. I designed a cathode cleaning process machine for Dow Chemical for this phase of the salt water mining process. Extracts these minerals from salt water at Oyster Creek in Freeport Texas.

BL Austin Design Engineer ✳ 1-13-2002

1960 Newspaper Clippings from Melbourne, Florida covering the 1960 Science Competition. Of the dozens of students listed, only two experiments were described: Judyth Vary's magnesium extraction method and Robert Baum's chemical control of human heredity. Note that the boy was given a cruise on a Navy ship, and the girl was given an encyclopedia.

APPENDIX

ADDITIONAL DOCUMENTS CONCERNING JUDYTH VARY BAKER'S STORY,
ARRANGED APPROXIMATELY IN CHRONOLOGICAL ORDER.

1959 Report Cover for Judyth's report on Education in the USSR that she did in Feb. of 1959, when she was in 10th grade at Manatee High School.

1960 Envelope from a bank account set up for donations to Judyth's cancer research project. It is covered with her chemistry notes (which is why the envelope was saved).

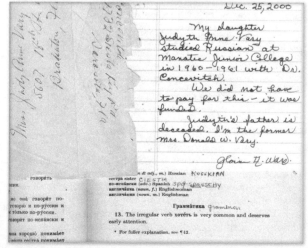

1960-61 Russian Studies are discussed in this Christmas, 2000 note from Judyth's mother. She wrote this note to verify that Judyth took the course, and that her family did not need to pay (it was funded by military officers in Col. Doyle's circle).

WALTER REED ARMY INSTITUTE OF RESEARCH
WALTER REED ARMY MEDICAL CENTER
WASHINGTON 12, D. C.

IN REPLY REFER TO: MEDEC-ZOA   2 September 1960

Miss Judyth A. Vary
5607 18 Street, West
Bradenton, Florida

Dear Miss Vary:

We are very pleased to learn of your interest in protecting
against radiation injury.

I am arranging for two chemicals to be sent to you under separate
cover. These chemicals are mercaptoethylamine as the hydrochloride.
This material should be administered to mice intraperitoneally in a concentration of 13 milligrams of free base per milliliter about fifteen
minutes before irradiation. A solution of greater concentration may be
used. The solution is prepared by dissolving the chemical in distilled
water and adjusting the pH to 7.4. This should be done relatively soon
before you use it, since air will tend to oxidize the compound to the di-
sulfide, in which case it will have somewhat less protective activity.
This chemical as well as the other one I am sending to you is hydroscopic;
that is to say, it will take water from the air and turn into a liquid.
You should therefore, keep it inside a desiccator so that the material
will remain dry. The chemicals that I am sending to you are packed in a
jar with desiccator around them. If the desiccator turns pink you can
put the desiccator only in the oven to regenerate its original blue color.
The second compound is aminoethylisothiourea bromide hydrobromide. This
should be given intraperitoneally in a dose of 350 milligrams per kilogram
as a double salt, i.e. as it comes from the bottle. The solute injected
should not exceed more than half a milliliter in volume and it also must
be adjusted to a pH of 7.4. If it is injected at a pH of around 1 or 2
it will have an irritant effect in the mouse. If it is injected around
pH 4 to 5 then the compound will rearrange to a structure which is not
quite as useful as that which is injected around pH 7.4.

The protective activity of these two compounds is somewhat different.
The aminoethylisothiourea is somewhat more effective in protecting mice against
radiation then is mercaptoethylamine. However, we think the mechanism of
the isothiourea derivative is appreciably different from the mercaptoethylamine

I am enclosing both in case you wish to use two sets of mice for protection studies. My thought is you should use the isothiourea initially;
if you have good luck then use the mercaptoethylamine.

I am interested in your studies on hypothermia and in the work that
you are doing with the stearates. We have some similar work going on in
tissue culture with hypothermia which I would be very pleased to talk over
with you sometime. Furthermore, if you have difficulty in obtaining some
of the stearates let us know what you're interested in. We will be pleased
to send them to you if we have them available.

We look forward to hearing from you again as to the results of
your studies. And look forward to facilitating your work on this interesting
experiment.

Very sincerely yours,

DAVID P. JACOBUS, M.D.
Chief, Department of

September, 9, 1960, Letter from Walter Reed Army Institute of Research.
The question is often raised: Did the U.S. Army really collaborate with Judy Vary's high
school cancer experiments? This two-page letter from David P. Jacobus, M.D., Chief of the
Department of Radiobiology at Walter Reed Army Institute of Research shows that they
did in 1960. Dr. Jacobus not only sent Judyth exotic chemicals to protect her laboratory
animals from radiation, but he expressed interest in her research on hypothermia and stearates, offered to facilitate her work, and requested to hear the results of her experiments.

PRESIDENT JOHN F. KENNEDY,
1600 PENNSYLVANIA AVENUE,
WASHINGTON, D.C.

FEB. 14, 1961

JUDYTH VARY,
4402 POMPANO XXX
LANE,
PALMETTO, FLA.

ans ack mr 5-20-61

DEAR PRESIDENT KENNEDY;

I KNOW THAT YOU HAVE RECIEVED PROBABLY THOUSANDS
UPON THOUSANDS, OR MILLIONS, OF CONGRATULATIONS FOR BECOM-
ING OUR NEW PRESIDENT. BUT I WANT TO CONGRATULATE YOU AGAIN.
YOU HAVE HELPED TO PARTIALLY WAKE AMERICA FROM HER HORRIBLE
AND DANGEROUS APATHY. YOU HAVE LIT THE LAMP THAT REVEALS
THE RATS AND THE BROKEN WINDOWS IN OUR SUPPOSEDLY SECURE
HAVEN FROM WORLD STRIFE. I HOPE YOU CAN PATCH UP THE HOLES;
YOU SAID IN YOUR MOMENTOUS INAUGURAL SPEECH THAT 'ASK NOT
WHAT YOUR COUNTRY CAN DO FOR YOU, BUT WHAT YOU CAN DO FOR
YOUR COUNTRY'...WELL, I WOULD LIKE TO KNOW WHAT WE, THE VOTE-
LESS, TEENAGE MINORS, WHO CARE ABOUT THEIR COUNRRY, CAN DO?
     I KNOW THAT MOST OF US WOULD GLADLY LAY DOWN OUR LIVES FOR
OUR COUNTRY. THE VOTELESS, TEENAGED MINORS IN BOTH WORLD WARS
HAVE. SIR, FRANKLY, WHAT CAN WE, AS CITIZENS AND AMERICANS,
DO? IN THE LAST ELECTION, WE YOUNG PEOPLE CUT OUT PAPER DON-
KEYS WITH 'GET OUT AND VOTE' SIGNS ON THEM; ELEPHANTS, TOO,
FOR THAT MATTER. IT WAS VERY DISAPPOINTING TO SEE HOW FEW
RELATIVE TO THE POPULATION ACTUALLY VOTED. IT WAS EVEN MORE
DISHEARTENING TO REALIZE THAT, WHEN CONFRONTED WITH VARIOUS
QUESTIONNAIRES ON WORLD AFFAIRS, ETC., WE TEENAGERS FOUND THAT
THE PEOPLE AT LEAST IN THIS AREA DON'T EVEN CARE ABOUT WHAT
IS HAPPENING ABOUT THEM. ALL THEY SEEM TO CARE ABOUT IS SEG-
REGATION, RELIGION, AND TAXES. I THINK THAT THIS IS NOT UNI-
VERSALLY SO (I HOPE TO GOD IT IS NOT!), BUT SURELY SUCH APATHY
AND SUCH PREJUDICES SHOULD NOT EXIST IN THIS SUPPOSEDLY PRO-
GRESSIVE NATION. PRESIDENT KENNEDY, WHAT COULD I, AS A TYPICAL
TEENAGE CITIZEN, DO? WHAT CAN MY FRIENDS DO? WE ARE VERY INTER-
ESTED IN OUR COUNTRY'S WELFARE,--WE'RE NOT ALL JUVENILE DELIN-
QUENTS! WE REALIZE THAT TODAY OUR COUNTRY IS BEING CHALLENGED
BY SEVERAL NEW POWERS,--BEING HUMILIATED, TOO, IN SOME CASES,
BEING CONFOUNDED, EVEN SCORNED. I PROMISE YOU THAT A LOT OF
US DO CARE, AND WE'RE BEHIND YOU ALL THE WAY! IT TAKES COURAGE
TO FACE SUCH PROBLEMS AS YOU MUST FACE NOW. IT TAKES COURAGE
THESE DAYS TO EVEN ACKNOWLEDGE THE FACT THAT THEY EXIST, I
GUESS. MAY GOD BLESS YOU! MAY YOU 'STICK TO YOUR GUNS'. I HOPE
THAT YOU WILL LET US ENTER THE RANKS OF THOSE WHO WANT TO FOL-
LOW YOU INTO THE FEARFUL BUT PROMISING 'NEW FRONTIERS'! WE
PROMISE TO DO WHAT WE CAN. I DON'T THINK THAT THIS NEW GENERA-
TION 'TEMPERED' BY WAR AND DEPRESSIONS AND EDUCATED TO REALIZE
AND DECIPHER THE HANDWRITING ON THE WALL, WILL LET YOU DOWN.
WE'RE BEHIND YOU, MR. PRESIDENT! LET US BE YOUR VAN GUARD!
                              SINCERELY YOURS,
                              JUDYTH VARY.

February 14, 1961, Letter to JFK: Judyth's thoughtful 1961 letter to President Kennedy
shows her political views clearly. Describing herself as one of the "voteless teenage minors"
who would "gladly lay down our lives for our country," she concluded by saying, "We're behind you, Mr. President! Let us be your vanguard!"

The train (leaving Penn. station now) is pleasant. But I fret. I se
a Sister of St. Joseph sitting across from me. She is fortunate in the
she has so conquered her desires for approval, and instincts for rat-
living in such a wonderful and exemplary manner. I don't have such
power of character. If only I did. But, one must do what he can.
I'm doing mighty little, but, God, o Patient One, maybe someday I'll
lose this horrible selfishness, conceit, and pride in my heart. A small
child sits in front of me eagerly, for he hears the chattering of my
two little companions--the parakeets, Billie and Dolly--who HAD to
come along! I wish we all could have the rank curiosity, the frankness
and honesty, of a young child who has not yet learned, nor been taught
the guiles, deceits, and daily disillusioning actions that tell others
you are a wholly Super-Duper, Orthodox and Remotely Remote Typical
Rude, Vesty, V.I.P. (Nobody else turns to watch them; they pretend that
parakeets are always to be found on overnight trains; they ignore.).

a great part. Orlanda is coming right along, I would like to see her
eventually use all her talents not only for self-expression, but for
self-illumination and help for others. She is a fine, little one;
along with a few other little ones, am attempting 2 help man.

July 12, 1961

A general seminar conducted at Roswell Park M.I. in Buffalo is a
model of democracy in action. Tis quite a shame governmental systems
couldn't thus be made in such an orderly, sensible, polite and good
manner.

                                                          total
Note: 80% of irradiated mice after 5-6 exposures(@ 400 Rs)will develop
leukemia cancer incidence is higher where cosmic ray incidence is
higher; also where radioactivity in minerals R consumed by population.
Exposed thus 2 high overall radiation effects, C3H mice demonsrate
relatively high incidence of spontaneous cancer.
Hyaluronidase--concentration
                      depolymerization of polymerized ground substance in cel
use 5% hyaluric acid (high viscosity), 4/kg atropine, 350-550 cc. for
1-2% area of spread.

Summer 1961: Two clippings from Judyth's Typewritten Diary.
The first section was written in mid-June about her trip to the Roswell Park Cancer Institute.
This passage speaks of a train ride from New York City to Buffalo, NY, just after Mrs. Watkins
had left. It shows some of her inner-thoughts about her own character and compares these
to the nun on the train. She also ponders some children seated nearby and the parakeets
which accompanied her on the trip. The second section was written a month later and discussed her work at the cancer lab in Buffalo. Of interest is her statement about using radiation to cause cancer and about cosmic rays causing cancer.

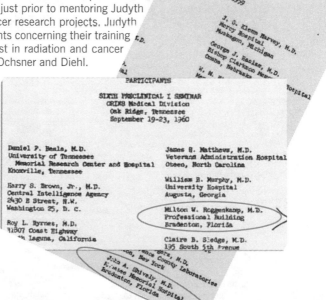

Summary 1961: Judyth's Lab Notes from her time at Roswell Park Memorial Institute in 1961 show various doses of a variety of ingredients used in cancer experiments which involved the cell growth medium (RPMI 1640) which she used in her cancer experiments at St. Francis University, at the University of Florida, and in New Orleans. Especially interesting is the reference to FCS (Fetal Calf Serum) at the bottom of the sheet. Now called FBS (Fetal Bovine Serum), it helps to grow human cancer cells in the lab. Bovine means "cow" or "cattle," and recent studies by virologists have shown structural similarities between BIV (Bovine Immunodeficiency Virus) and both HIV-1 (Human Immunodeficiency Virus, aka AIDS) and SIV (Simian Immunodeficiency Virus). In Jan. 2002, *AIDS* magazine (pp. 123-125) described a "Chimeric Virus" which they labeled BIV/HIV-1. Today, the FBA requires cattle in the U.S. to be inoculated, and 40-60% have BIV.

1959 & 1960: Two document portions show that two of Judyth's doctor-mentors in Bradenton were trained to handle radiation and tissue cultures ("pre-clinical") with CIA participation, just prior to mentoring Judyth in her high school cancer research projects. Judyth has additional documents concerning their training and Oak Ridge's interest in radiation and cancer research through Drs. Ochsner and Diehl.

Miss Judyth Vary
4402 Pompano Lane
Palmetto, Florida

Saint Francis College
Fort Wayne, Indiana
June 23, 1961

* Return address
lowered & inset to
allow enlargement
of letter.

Dear Miss Vary:

Thank you for your letter of June 10. We regret the delay in answering, but my absence from campus for some time has resulted in belated correspondence.

We are happy to know that you have selected Saint Francis as the college of your choice, and we are pleased to renew our original full-tuition scholarship offer of #350.00. This scholarship is renewable each year (provided that you maintain the required scholastic index), amounting to a total of $1400.00.

Since our college is comparatively small, we do not have facilities for extensive laboratory research at present. Some experimentation with white mice or other small animals will be possible. We have plans for a new science building in the near future and will begin construction of a new residence hall and a new classroom building this summer.

You may be interested in knowing that four of our science and math instructors have received National Science Foundation Grants or Fellowships within the past two years and are currently pursuing research or doctorates at Indiana University, University of Notre Dame, University of California, and the University of Louisiana at Baton Rouge. Three of the four will return to the campus as instructors in September.

You may like to know that resident students who must earn a part of their expenses may engage in part-time employment on campus. A student who works ten hours a week can defray approximately $225.00 of her expenses per year.

The college also maintains a student loan fund. Worthy students may arrange for a partial or full-expense loan. Our interest rate is four percent, and the student need not begin refunding the loan until one year after graduation.

Saint Francis College has now added "The Tuition Plan" to its student aid program. Literature explaining this convenient way of meeting college expenses will be sent to you within the next month by our Tuition Plan representative. We feel that some or all of these student aids will be of interest to you.

We are sending application forms and our catalog by ordinary mail. These items should reach you by Monday or Tuesday.

In reference to several of your questions, we do have advanced placement in languages. There are opportunities for "overloads" for students who maintain a 3.5 cumulative average. We are cognizant of originality of thought, and we feel that we are reasonably (sometimes extremely) strict.

Distance may prohibit your visiting Saint Francis College, but we do want you to know that you are most welcome any time. We wish you and your family could meet some of the faculty and students and also see the residence hall with its attractive accommodations for the girls. You will like the truly Franciscan spirit of joy and friendliness that prevails on the campus in both classroom and extra-curricular activities, uniting the students into just one big family.

We would appreciate hearing from you soon to learn about your plans. May the Holy Spirit guide you in the choice of a college suited to your needs and interests. God bless and love you always.

Sincerely in St. Francis,

Sister M. Veronica

Sister M. Veronica, OSF
Director of Admissions

Letter from Sister M. Veronica: Letter showing that Judyth could do research at St. Francis College with small animals such as white mice, etc., which the college later denied was ever possible, or that Sister Veronica ever existed! Researcher Rom Rozoff, not satisfied with that, interviewd others at St. Francis who did remember Sister Veronica. He was surprised that he was lied to.

HALE BOGGS, M. C.
2D DISTRICT, LOUISIANA

COMMITTEES:
WAYS AND MEANS
CHAIRMAN, SUBCOMMITTEE ON
ADMINISTRATION OF FOREIGN
TRADE LAWS AND POLICY
JOINT ECONOMIC COMMITTEE

Congress of the United States
House of Representatives
Washington, D. C.

FOR IMMEDIATE RELEASE
Thursday, March 15, 1962

WASHINGTON, D.C.---- President Kennedy will fly to New Orleans, La., on Friday, May 4, to deliver a major address on foreign economic policy, Rep. Hale Boggs(D.-LA.), the House Majority Whip, announced today.

The International House of New Orleans will sponsor the President's visit to the Crescent City, Congressman Boggs said.

Dr. Alton Ochsner, president of International House and an internationally famous surgeon, will be in charge of arrangements in New Orleans for the President's visit, Boggs noted.

President Kennedy probably will deliver his address in the city's Municipal Auditorium about 11:00 A.M. on May 4. Howeve further details of the visit will be determined by the President at a White House conference with Boggs and New Orleans Mayor Victor H. Schiro next Tuesday morning (March 20).

More details of the President's trip to the Crescent City probably will be announced after the White House meeting, which has been scheduled for 10:00 A.M., Boggs stated.

Shortly after his speech on foreign economic policy, President Kennedy is scheduled to depart for Eglin Air Force Base, Florida.

XCongressman Boggs said that all members of the Louisiana Congressional delegation will be invited to accompany the President on his flight to New Orleans.

(MORE)

March 15, 1962, Press Release from Hale Boggs says Dr. Alton Ochsner is to be in charge of arrangements for visit to New Orleans. At the time, Ochsner was president of the International House, one of the city's most important trade associations. Boggs was the Congressman from uptown New Orleans where Ochsner lived and was appointed to LBJ's Warren Commission to oversee the government's investigation of the JFK assassination. Members of Dr. Ochsner's political organization, INCA, provided the media coverage for Lee Harvey Oswald in 1963.

note: I know someone that knows somebody that knows you and thats' perhaps nosey. C - U - ?
soon.. get your sore foot well so we can dance! How do you spell your last name?

1962 Letter: Written to Judyth by her father in April 1962 when she was a student at the University of Florida. This was several months after he tried to have her arrested in Gainesville. First, he scolds her for "not thinking soundly" and for "believing in fairy tales," but then he implores her to come home for Easter so they can celebrate the holiday "as a family together."

UNIVERSITY OF FLORIDA
GAINESVILLE

UNIVERSITY COLLEGE
OFFICE OF THE DEAN   August 6, 1962

Miss Judith Anne Vary
4402 Pompano Lane
Palmetto, Florida

Dear Miss Vary:

Congratulations on your successful participation in the
University College Honors Program last semester. Your
achievement results from the kind of intellectual curiosity,
enthusiasm for learning, and willingness to work hard that
we are always pleased to see in students at the University
of Florida. I hope that you will continue your excellent
efforts, so that you may receive the Associate of Arts
Certificate with Honors or High Honors.

                                    Sincerely,

                                    Byron S. Hollingshead
                                    Dean

August 6, 1962, Letter: From the Dean of the University of Florida congratulating Judyth on her high academic performance during her first semester at University of Florida. At the same time, Judyth's official transcript reported that she had a "D" in chemistry. Such discrepancies were typical of the administrative games being played with Judyth's paper trail at the time.

COFFEE PLANT WILL BE BUILT

Luzianne Production to Be Consolidated

A new $1¼ million roasting and ground coffee plant will be erected in New Orleans by William B. Reily and Co. Inc.

Construction will begin this fall on the new plant adjacent to the firm's present instant coffee facility on the Chef Menteur hwy. at Jourdan Rd.

Occupying part of an 11-acre site, the masonry building will contain 75,000 square feet of space. It will be ready for use in 1964.

The plant will replace the firm's present ground coffee facility at 640 Magazine St. Managerial offices will remain on Magazine St.

John C. Clark will serve as vice-president in charge of operations at the new plant, which will consolidate all of Reily's Luzianne brand ground and instant coffee processing in one location in New Orleans.

Other plants in Baltimore, Charleston and Los Angeles will continue to serve those areas.

Architects for the new plant are Curtis and Davis of New Orleans.

In announcing the new facility, William B. Reily Jr., president of the New Orleans-based firm, said, "This ultra-modern building will double the present ground coffee output of Luzianne and will enable our company to maintain its expanding position in the

Coffee Plant to Be

THIS IS DRAWING of the new Luziar ground coffee plant after expansion of present instant coffee section at Chef M teur hwy. and Jourdan rd. The broken I indicates the separation between the old a

Shot Is Fired

PECOS, Tex. (AP) — Pranksters or terrorists fired a bullet into the rambling residence of convicted swindler Billie Sol Estes on Friday night and the family prepared to flee Saturday.

The shooting was the third incident in a week around the residence.

Pam Estes, 15, oldest of the five

planted a l Klux Klan s) on Estes' pulled loose tric sign on ing, "Home Newsmen culated in P firmation th sell his hom

---

1963 Newspaper Article, "Coffee Plant will be built": This article shows the new Luzianne Coffee production plant that Reily Coffee was building in 1963. Mr. Monaghan used the prospect of new employees to bait Mr. Desmare at the Retail Credit Company to facilitate the approval of background checks for Judyth Baker and Lee Oswald.

Guy Banister Associates, Inc. GBA   531 LAFAYETTE ST. •   523-4532

NEW ORLEANS 12, LOUISIANA

March 27, 1963

Honorable Edwin E. Willis
U. S. House of Representatives
House Office Building
Washington, D.C.

Re: Leon Norbert Weiner.

Dear Sir:

You will recall that Dr. William R. Sorum positively
identified the above named individual as a top Communist
Official in New Orleans, in his testimony on February 15,
1957, before the House Committee on Un-American Activities.

Weiner now heads a construction company in
Wilmington, Deleware. A member of the City Council has been
accused of soliciting a bribe. The person from whom the bribe
is alleged to have been solicited is Weiner.

Is there available to me any documentary proof of
membership in the Communist Party, on the part of Weiner, in
the files of the HCUA?

The same is true of membership in the Progressive
Party or of any cited Communist front.

Does the HCUA plan to release the testimony of
Dr. Sorum, given in executive session?

With kindest personal regards, I am

Sincerely yours,

Guy Banister

Guy Banister

GB/dpr

March 27 1963: One of the few extant letters by Guy Banister available to the public.

Judyth obtained this letter from a desk in the office of Congressman Willis during one of her visits there for Bill Monaghan. Willis' New Orleans office was across the street from Reily and Judyth carried messages from Monaghan to Willis' office, which was in disarray because it was being moved to a new location. She saw the letter among a stack of correspondence and took it to show to Lee Oswald because it mentioned Dr. Sorum and showed Banister's activities connected to Willis.

In the letter Banister describes Leon Weiner, a home-builder from Maryland, as a "top communist." When Weiner died, the *New York Times* described this chairman emeritus of the National Housing Conference as a national advocate of affordable housing for those of modest means and the elderly. The newsletter of the National Association of Home Builders called him "the conscience of the housing industry." President Johnson appointed him to the commission helping write the Fair Housing Act of 1968, and he later served as a delegate to the White House Conference on Aging. This is an excellent example of the kind of political activist that Guy Banister believed threatened America. Dr. Sorum, who "positively identified" Weiner as a communist for HUAC, was a psychiatrist.

Banister's letterhead had never been published until Judyth posted this letter online. She donated the original and now only owns the original carbon copy. She still owns the reply where Willis replied to Banister's request after conferring with the CIA. She also has copies of documents showing HUAC's Willis was working with the CIA regarding how to handle defectors.

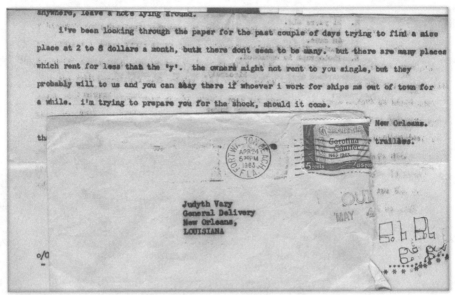

anywhere, leave a note lying around.

    i've been looking through the paper for the past couple of days trying to find a nice place at 2 to 8 dollars a month, but there dont seem to be many. but there are many places which rent for less than the 'y'. the owners might not rent to you single, but they probably will to us and you can say there if whoever i work for ships me out of town for a while. i'm trying to prepare you for the shock, should it come.

New Orleans.

th   trailers.

Judyth Vary
General Delivery
New Orleans,
LOUISIANA

o/c

Letter & envelope postmarked April 24, 1963, from Robert Baker. Referred to on page 125-26.

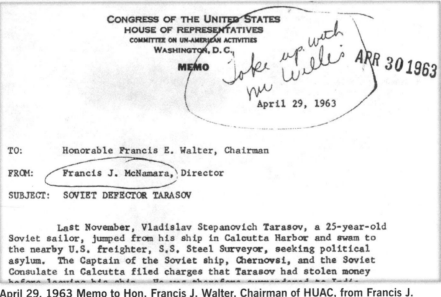

CONGRESS OF THE UNITED STATES
HOUSE OF REPRESENTATIVES
COMMITTEE ON UN-AMERICAN ACTIVITIES
WASHINGTON, D. C.

MEMO

Take up with Mr. Willis

ARR 30 1963

April 29, 1963

TO: Honorable Francis E. Walter, Chairman

FROM: Francis J. McNamara, Director

SUBJECT: SOVIET DEFECTOR TARASOV

    Last November, Vladislav Stepanovich Tarasov, a 25-year-old Soviet sailor, jumped from his ship in Calcutta Harbor and swam to the nearby U.S. freighter, S.S. Steel Surveyor, seeking political asylum. The Captain of the Soviet ship, Chernovsi, and the Soviet Consulate in Calcutta filed charges that Tarasov had stolen money

April 29, 1963 Memo to Hon. Francis J. Walter, Chairman of HUAC, from Francis J. McNamara, Director, regarding Soviet defector.
Excerpt from correspondence directed to Francis Walter, the HUAC Chairman stepping down, on how to use a defector. It was handed to Willis before he became Chairman. Rep. Willis also worked with the CIA regarding defectors and knew Lee Oswald's true history.
In the upper right-hand corner "Take up with Mr. Willis" is written in Walter's handwriting, circled to get attention. Walter would soon step down because of illness and Willis, the Acting Chair soon after, would take his place in mid-May, 1963.
  The "Tasarov letter" shows that HUAC's Willis was thoroughly "in the CIA loop" regarding defectors. He was made Acting Chair, then Chairman, of HUAC at the time former Soviet defector Lee Oswald was employed across the street from his office, at Reily's. Here Willis is asked to decide what he wishes to do with the Russian defector, Tasarov.

P.C. IV-4-61

THE STATE OF ALABAMA,
MOBILE COUNTY.

PROBATE COURT

I, V. R. JANSEN, Judge of the Probate Court in and for said State and County, hereby certify

that the within and foregoing _____ One (1) _____ page/

contains a full, true and complete copy of the Marriage License as issued to Robert Allison Baker,III to inter-marry with one Judyth Anne Vary together with certific of solemnization of Matrimony,

as the same appears on record in my office in White Marriage License

Book No. 1963 Page No. 5469

Given under my hand and seal of office this 2nd day of May , 1963.

V. R. JANSEN
Judge of Probate.

BY
Recording Clerk

May 2, 1963, Marriage License: Robert Baker attempted to marry Judy Vary in New Orleans on May 1, 1963, but discovered that Louisiana had a waiting period to discourage sudden marriages. Robert decided to drive Judy to Mobile, Alabama to get married because Alabama did not require a waiting period. Robert had to leave for long-term offshore work in the Gulf of Mexico within 24 hours of their marriage in Mobile – the reason for the quick trip to Alabama

Monday

My Darling Judy,

Today I was thinking forward to the time when I'll be working in town and happened across a scheme that might save us bread money. Dont stop reading just because I'm writing about money. If you get a Transfer going and coming on the bus, you can use the Transfers the next day on the ST Charles line. Perhaps you should ride one line in the morning and the other in the afternoon. It may not work for one reason or another, like the color of the Transfer, but it might. If we both do it, it'll save a whole dollar per week.

May 24, 1963, Letter: From Robert "Bob" Baker mailed to his new wife "Mrs. Robert A. Baker III" at Judyth's 1032 Marengo Street address. The letter begins "My Darling Judy" and goes on to explain his scheme to save her money on the transit system in New Orleans. The letter itself is written on a document from Dixie Dynamite, a company that supplied explosives to Evangeline Seismic Company for whom Robert worked. The return address shows "Hopedale, Louisiana" which is little more than a operational harbor for the oil industry along the Intercostals Waterway which was cut through the remote marshes of St. Bernard Parish about 50 miles southeast of New Orleans. The letter, however, is postmarked from Schriever, Louisiana, which is about 100 miles southwest of New Orleans. At the time, this disparity between Hopedale and Schriever caused Judyth to suspect that Robert was traveling around south Louisiana on his time off, instead of coming home to New Orleans to see her.

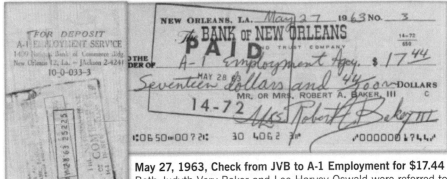

May 27, 1963, Check from JVB to A-1 Employment for $17.44
Both Judyth Vary Baker and Lee Harvey Oswald were referred to Reily Coffee by the A-1 Employment Agency in May 1963. This check is a payment by Judyth to them for their services.

Lee Oswald is on record as having registered at A-1 employment prior to being hired at Reily's. Judyth reported that she accompanied Oswald to A-1 on several occasions. Judyth was charged for a 'referral' that was extracted wrongly from her by A-1.

To remedy the situation and reduce the fee, Oswald visited A-1 employment on May 15th, Judyth's birthday, pretending he was not yet employed. A-1 gave Oswald a referral to a photography company but, already employed at Reily's, he never showed up for the appointment. But he got Judyth's fee reduced. The contract (as can be seen in the WC record) shows Judyth's A-1 payment was reduced by more than half. This check shows Judyth's signature as "Mrs. Robert a. Baker, III" which she used to obscure a paper trail. However, her husband had opened the bank account as "Robert A. Baker, III or Judyth A. Baker." Judyth had this changed to "Mr. or Mrs. Robert A. Baker, III." The notation on the check "Judyth A. Baker" was made by the bank to note Judyth's name change.

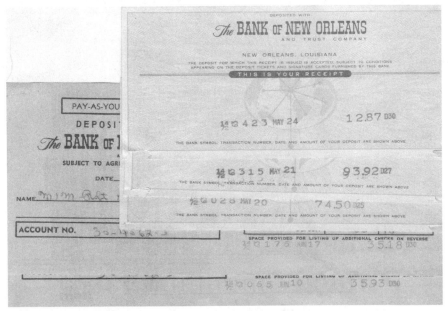

1963 summer: Judyth's deposit slips from Bank of New Orleans.

Robert A. Baker's W-2 form and a paycheck stub showing his employment (with free room and board) with Evangeline Seismic, as well as some checks to himself cashed for unexplained reasons while gone.

My dearest love, ♡   thou...
                                      bestowed.

you have brought such sweet joy to a life that was empty: may your lifelong wishes come true! it's not that I weep with all my love shaking inside like flowers blown by the wind, it's that your life should touch my own so gently, so lovingly, so surely, like the gentlest raindrops on parched seeds, which then burst asunder, put up green, green arms, and grow to that flower. You are sun, moon, stars. You are forever immortal because of what we have between us. And as the miracle of it continues to astound me, so I weep with all this happiness. A lifetime of sorrow could lie ahead for us, but what difference? Together, today, we live forever. I won't forget! And I love you forever, dearest beloved, no matter what! ♡ kisses and love Judy

July 29, 1963 letter written by Judyth to Lee. Lee had recently returned from the meeting at the Jesuit Seminary and met Judyth for lunch at Katzenjammer's Restaurant, next door to Guy Banister's office. It was there that Lee first informed Judyth that he believed that he was being set up to be the patsy in a plan to assassinate President Kennedy. Judyth was so distraught over the news that she bit her lip so hard that it bled; the bite was so deep into the flesh that it required stitches to stop the bleeding. Later that day, she returned to her desk at Reily's and wrote this highly emotional letter to Lee. Both her sense of impending doom ("A lifetime of sorrow could lie ahead for us") and her love for Lee ("I love you forever") are obvious. Darker still are her implied references to his death, calling Lee "forever immortal" and saying "Together, today, we live forever. I won't forget." See p. 416. She gave the letter to Lee in person. He read it, thanked her for it, and returned it, saying that he could not have a letter like that lying around.

The torn section at top right where the words "thou…" and "bestowed" remain, had a quotation that was, approximately, "My love's thoughts, only to thee bestowed." There was no name or address in that torn fragment.

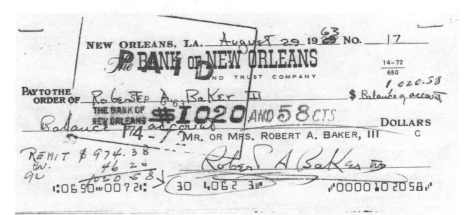

```
Miguel M. Cruz, M., age 18                Patn. F. Wilson
2526 Mazant St., Apt. C., NO, La.         Patn. F. Hayward
                                               1st Dist.

who having been duly sworn, doth depose and say:
       That on  Friday    the    9th    day of  August    19 63 , at about
    o'clock  P  M., on  700 Blk. Canal St.  Street, between
                                        Streets, within the jurisdiction of this Court, one
    Lee H. Oswald, Carlos J. Bringuier, Celso M. Hernandez and Miguel M.
                        Cruz...
       and there wilfully violate Ordinance No. 828 MCS  Section 42-22 relative to
    disturbing the peace by Creating a Scene...

        the peace and dignity of the City of New Orleans.
```

August 9, 1963: Portion of Oswald's arrest record for disturbing the peace.

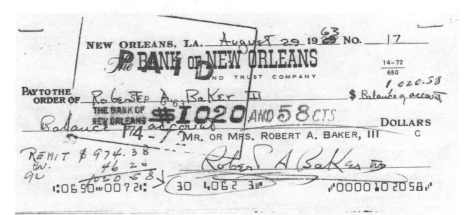

September 2, 1963: A check "for balance" was written by Robert A. Baker (who was preparing to leave New Orleans) to close out the New Orleans bank account, but he asked the bank to not process It until the final Reily settlement check was deposited ($46.20). The bank statement (and other records) show that as soon as the Reily check was deposited, the account was closed with a conversion of funds to the Florida National Bank on the same day the Bakers arrived in Gainesville. *See bank statement on page 507.*

September 17, 1963, Portion of application for Tourist Visa to Visit Mexico.
Lee's application shows that he stated his religion was Catholic, the same as Judyth's.

Lee Oswald's Time Cards

The President's Commission on the Assassination of President Kennedy, known unofficially as the Warren Commission, was established on November 29, 1963. The commission published a ponderous 26-volume collection of findings which, on the surface, appears to include every conceivable piece of information imaginable about Lee Harvey Oswald's life (including his pubic hairs) and every person who came in contact with him. The information net was so broad that a study of the teeth of Jack Ruby's mother was included. A more critical look at these same volumes exposes that, despite the large volume of documents presented, there were conspicuous omissions. One such omission was Lee Harvey Oswald's time cards from Reily Coffee Company, where he was employed several months before the assassination. So where were Oswald's time cards? And why were they not presented in the WC volumes?

Immediately after Kennedy's assassination, FBI agents scooped up all of the documents and evidence that they could about Lee Harvey Oswald. In New Orleans, FBI agents walked down the block to the offices of Reily Coffee Company and picked up Oswald's employment records, including his time cards. So the FBI had Oswald's time cards from day one, but the time cards were not displayed anywhere in the Warren Commission's 26 volumes. Why didn't the FBI give Oswald's time cards to the commission?

What the FBI did give to the commission was a typed list of Oswald clock-in and clock-out times. The list, Commission Exhibit 1896, was prepared by William Monaghan, VP of Finance and Operations at the Reily Coffee Company. Monaghan was also former FBI Special Agent #005074 (1942-1945), a member of INCA (with Eustis Reily and Dr. Ochsner), and Judyth's boss. This omission of the time cards is odd when considering the testimony of Oswald's supervisor at Reily in which he complained that he could never find Oswald when he needed him and that he learned Oswald had been leaving the building without permission while clocked-in.

> the signature of employee.
>
>   Mr. MONAGHAN also furnished data taken from time punch cards of employee, LEE H. OSWALD. The following is a compulation reflecting the time OSWALD arrived at his place of employment and the time he left each day while employed by the William B. Reily and Company, Inc., as reflected on these time cards:
>
> | DAY | TIME IN | TIME OUT |
> |---|---|---|
> | Friday, 5/10/63 | 7:59 AM | 4:30 PM |
> | Monday, 5/13/63 | 8:24 AM | 5:00 PM |
> | Tuesday, 5/14/63 | 8:18 AM | 5:00 PM |
> | Wednesday, 5/15/63 | 8:23 AM | 5:00 PM |
> | Thursday, 5/16/63 | 8:29 AM | 5:00 PM |
> | Friday, 5/17/63 | 8:25 & 9:57 AM (stamped twice) | 5:00 PM |

So why would Oswald's supervisor continue to approve his time cards if he thought Oswald was skipping out of work? Did Oswald's supervisor even approve his time cards? And if he didn't, who did? Where were their initials? And who were they? Seeing the actual time cards would have raised these questions and could have helped answer them, but the cards were missing.

In the 1990s, after the JFK Assassination Records Act opened the government's files concerning the JFK assassination, Oswald's time cards were found in the FBI's files. A quick look at Oswald's time cards reveals a prominent "J" that appears on many of his cards. So, who is "J"? Evidently, "J" is the first initial of Bill Monaghan's secretary at the time that Oswald worked at Reily: Judyth Vary Baker. She admits that she approved Oswald's time cards despite his absences, and her narrative account of her handling of Oswald's time cards, explain the disparity between the inconsistent clock-in times and the consistent clock-out times stamped on his time cards.

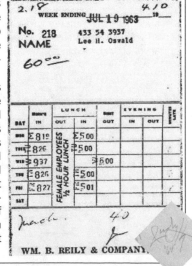

Lee Oswald's clock-in/out times

After May, my clock-outs for Lee were almost all at exactly 5:00, 5:30, 6:00, or 6:30, for nobody noticed or cared. I'm glad now I was so precise because it helps prove I clocked Lee out. The general precision of clock-out times before May 31 was because I could get immediately in line as Monaghan's secretary, so there was no waiting for clock-outs at 5:30 or later. Note Lee's time card was stamped at exactly 5:00 PM eight days in a row (May 13-22). For June 7-July 11, there are 17 clock-outs in a row at exactly 5:30. **Only two clock-outs in all eleven weeks of Lee's employment at Reily's varied more than a single minute from the hour or half-hour.** This, despite the fact that other employees' clock-outs varied as much as 15 minutes, depending on the length of the line. Note that Lee's clock-in times varied greatly. This is strong statistical proof that Lee's clock-outs were rigged, evidently by someone with the signature "J."

Note that, when Lee had to work with Guy Banister in May and early June on college campuses, he was consistently very late those mornings. After classes let out for the summer, he generally clocked in an hour earlier.

Lee's official clock-in time was 8:30, though he was originally supposed to come to work at 8:00, as he did exactly once during the entire time he worked at Reily's: his first day.

DATE	IN	OUT	HOURS	IN LATE	OUT LATE
May 24	9:58 AM	6:30 PM	8.5	88 Min.	118 Min.
May 27	9:53 AM	6:35 PM	8.6	83 Min.	113 Min.
May 28	8:50 AM	5:31 PM	8.6	20 Min.	50 Min.
May 29	9:45 AM	6:30 PM	8.75	75 Min.	105 Min.
May 30	9:00 AM	5:30 PM	8.5	30 Min.	60 Min.
May 31	9:53 AM	7:32 PM	9.6	83 Min.	113 Min.
June 3	9:47 AM	6:30 PM	8.75	77 Min.	107 Min.
June 4	9:50 AM	6:30 PM	8.8	80 Min.	110 Min.
June 5	9:58 AM	6:30 PM	~9	88 Min.	118 Min.
June 6	10:05 AM	6:30 PM	9.1	94 Min.	125 Min.
June 7	8:57 AM	5:30 PM	8.5	27 Min.	57 Min.

(semester over)

DAY	TIME IN	TIME OUT	DAY	TIME IN	TIME OUT
Monday, 6/3/63	9:47 AM	6:30 PM	Monday, 7/1/63	8:59 AM	5:30 PM
Tuesday, 6/4/63	9:50 AM	6:30 PM	Tuesday, 7/2/63	8:49 AM	5:30 PM
Wednesday, 6/5/63	9:58 AM	6:30 PM	Wednesday, 7/3/63	8:53 AM	5:30 PM
Thursday, 6/6/63	10:05 AM	6:30 PM	Thursday, 7/4/63	--------	--------
Friday, 6/7/63	8:57 AM	5:30 PM	Friday, 7/5/63	8:53 AM	5:30 PM
Monday, 6/10/63	8:52 AM	5:30 PM	Monday, 7/8/63	8:47 AM	5:30 PM
Tuesday, 6/11/63	8:44 AM	5:30 PM	Tuesday, 7/9/63	8:49 AM	5:30 PM
Wednesday, 6/12/63	8:56 AM	5:31 PM	Wednesday, 7/10/63	8:54 AM	5:30 PM
Thursday, 6/13/63	8:50 AM	5:30 PM	Thursday, 7/11/63	8:58 AM	5:30 PM
Friday, 6/14/63	8:29 AM	5:30 PM	Friday, 7/12/63	8:27 AM	5:01 PM
Monday, 6/17/63	8:53 AM	5:31 PM	Monday, 7/15/63	8:19 AM	5:00 PM
Tuesday, 6/18/63	8:53 AM	5:30 PM	Tuesday, 7/16/63	8:26 AM	5:00 PM
Wednesday, 6/19/63	8:53 AM	5:30 PM	Wednesday, 7/17/63	9:37 AM	6:00 PM
Thursday, 6/20/63	8:52 AM	5:30 PM	Thursday, 7/18/63	8:26 AM	5:00 PM
Friday, 6/21/63	8:53 AM	5:30 PM	Friday, 7/19/63	8:22 AM	4:30 PM
					(terminated)
Monday, 6/24/63	8:57 AM	5:30 PM			
Tuesday, 6/25/63	8:58 AM	5:30 PM			
Wednesday, 6/26/63	8:54 AM	5:30 PM			
Thursday, 6/27/63	8:53 AM	5:30 PM			
Friday, 6/28/63	9:01 AM	5:30 PM			

Clips from page two of
Commission Exhibit 1896

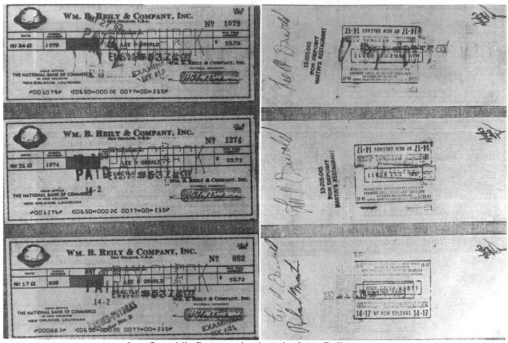

Lee Oswald's first paycheck stubs from Reily.

Judyth's first paycheck stub from Standard Coffee (division of Reily), followed by paycheck stubs directly from Reily for her position as Bill Monaghan's secretary.

DATE	HOURS WORKED	SALARY	COMM. OVERTIME	TOTAL EARNINGS THIS PERIOD	EXPENSES	FEDERAL O.A.B.	INCOME TAX	MISCELLANEOUS AMOUNT	ITEM	BOND
JUL 12 63		46.00		46.00		1.67	8.40	1.05	INS&LATE	

WM. B. REILY & COMPANY, INC.
NEW ORLEANS, U.S.A.

EMPLOYEE'S STATEMENT OF EARNINGS AND DEDUCTIONS

DATE	HOURS WORKED	SALARY	COMM. OVERTIME	TOTAL EARNINGS THIS PERIOD	EXPENSES	FEDERAL O.A.B.	INCOME TAX	MISCELLANEOUS AMOUNT	ITEM	BOND
JUL 19 63		46.00	.4	46.43		1.68	8.40	.20	LATE	

WM. B. REILY & COMPANY, INC.
NEW ORLEANS, U.S.A.

EMPLOYEE'S STATEMENT OF EARNINGS AND DEDUCTIONS

DATE	HOURS WORKED	SALARY	COMM. OVERTIME	TOTAL EARNINGS THIS PERIOD	EXPENSES	FEDERAL O.A.B.	INCOME TAX	MISCELLANEOUS AMOUNT	ITEM	BOND
		46.00		46.00		1.67	8.40	.20	LATE	

WM. B. REILY & CO. INC.
640 MAGAZINE ST.
NEW ORLEANS LA. 70160

72-0297940

WITHHOLDING TAX STATEMENT
1963 Federal Taxes Withheld From Wages
Copy B-To Be Filed With Employee's Tax Return

Type or print EMPLOYER'S identification number, name, and address above.

Type or print EMPLOYEE'S social security account no., name, and address below.

Judyth Anne Baker
511 East Brooks St.
Ft. Walton Beach, Fla.

	No. of Dependents	Single	Married	Excludable Sick Pay	City Tax Withheld
				(If None, Enter "0" or "None")	

SOCIAL SECURITY INFORMATION		INCOME TAX INFORMATION		State Tax Withheld
$ 18.82	519.07	$ 92.60	519.07	
F.I.C.A. EMPLOYEE TAX WITHHELD, IF ANY	TOTAL F.I.C.A. WAGES PAID IN 1963	FEDERAL INCOME TAX WITHHELD, IF ANY	TOTAL WAGES* PAID IN 1963	

FORM W-2—U. S. Treasury Department, Internal Revenue Service *Before payroll deductions or 'sick pay" exclusion.
EMPLOYEE: This is not a tax return but you must file it with Form 1040A, or Form 1040. See instructions on other side and on back of Copy C. If you expect to owe more income tax for next year than will be withheld if you claim every exemption to which you are entitled, you may increase the withholding by claiming a smaller number of exemptions or you may enter into an agreement with your employer to have additional amounts withheld. See Form W-4.
APP. I.R.S. 11-29-62

FOR USE OF INTERNAL REVENUE SERVICE
Employee's Copy and Employer's Copy compared ....

Judyth's 1963 IRS W-2 form from Wm. B. Reily & Co. Inc., above, reflecting her total earnings also seen on her final paycheck stub, shown below.

WM. B. REILY & COMPANY, INC.
NEW ORLEANS, U.S.A.

EMPLOYEE'S STATEMENT OF EARNINGS AND DEDUCTIONS

DATE	HOURS WORKED	SALARY	COMM. OVERTIME	TOTAL EARNINGS THIS PERIOD	EXPENSES	FEDERAL O.A.B.	INCOME TAX	MISCELLANEOUS AMOUNT	ITEM
AUG 9 63		9.20	1.29 519.07	10.49		.38			

Final paycheck stub issued to Judyth by Reily. The afternoon of August 9 Judyth was fired by Bill Monaghan after she was seen associated with the activities leading up to Lee Oswald's arrest for disturbing the peace earlier that day on Canal Street in New Orleans. *Ref: Chapter 21.*

Fall 1963, Pay-stubs and W-2 form: Judyth worked at Peninsular ChemResearch, Inc. in Gainesville for the last several months of 1963, the same year she worked at Reily Coffee Company in New Orleans. **In both cases, she omitted her maiden name "Vary" from her W2 form as she had been instructed by David Ferrie.** She listed a Fort Walton address on the Reily form, so that her tax statement would be mailed to Robert's family at the end of the year, but she listed her Gainesville address on the PenChem document, since she lived there at the time. The Social Security Numbers match, though they have been blocked out here for privacy issues.

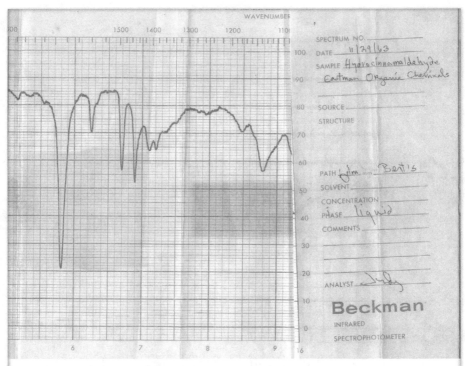

WAVENUMBER

SPECTRUM NO. _____
DATE 11/29/63
SAMPLE Hydrocinnamaldehyde
Eastman Organic Chemicals

SOURCE _____
STRUCTURE

PATH film mm Bert's
SOLVENT _____
CONCENTRATION _____
PHASE liquid
COMMENTS _____

ANALYST _____

Beckman
INFRARED
SPECTROPHOTOMETER

November 29, 1963, Graph: Judyth worked as an assistant in a high-tech lab with gas chromatography, a hydrogen halide laser and mass spectrometry equipment at Peninsular ChemResearch, Inc. in Gainesville, Florida, after she left New Orleans.

Judyth printed this chromatograph upside down in order to save a personal printout of Hydrocinnameldehyde, an aromatic compound yet to be fully investigated. Judyth thought this aldehyde should be tested to see its effect on lung cancer cell growth rates in vitro.

Note "Judy" signature above the word "Beckman" and the 11/29/63 date, which is one week after the JFK assassination.

Some of the equipment Judyth worked with at Penn Chem, 1963

NEW ORLEANS STATES-ITEM

LARGEST AFTERNOON CIRCULATION IN LOUISIANA

RED FLASH

Listen to The States-Item Chimes at 9, Noon and 5

VOL. 88—NO. 35　Associated Press, Advance News service, North American Newspaper Alliance and AP Wirephoto　TUESDAY, JULY 21, 1964　Entered N. O. Post Office as Second Class Matter Under Act of March 3, 1879　PRICE 5c

Orleans Woman Surgeon Slain By Intruder; Body Set Afire

Guerrillas Ambush 2 Viet Units

SAIGON, Viet Nam (AP)—Communist Viet Cong guerrillas, using standard ambush tactics, crippled two and possibly three government units near the tip of South Viet Nam today in a series of battles that continued into the night.

Reliable American sources said as many as 60 government troops had been killed and possibly 100 wounded in paddy fields and mangrove swamps of Chuong Thien province about 130 miles south of Saigon three hours before here in Saigon.

The battles were fought near the mud-walled fort of Vinh Chan, the center of a major engagement last week in which more than 200 government paramilitary personnel were either killed or wounded.

The Communists control two ambushes on the 10th anniversary of the Geneva agreements that split Viet Nam and set the Northern section up for Communist rule

AT LEAST 18 troops were rescued in the ambush of a battalion-sized force, military wending its way south from

See VIET—Page 6

French Vessel Carrying 28 Burning at Sea

NEW YORK (AP) — The French freighter Margaret was burning today off the coast, some 295 miles east southeast of Cape Race off Newfoundland, the Coast Guard reported.

The ship was en route from Montreal to Lisbon with about 28 men aboard, the Coast Guard added.

The "Mary Day" call said "Fire aboard, need assistance," a spokesman said.

The Coast Guard said Campbell, about 305 miles from the freighter, was heading for the area.

The Coast Guard said five merchant vessels were within 100-mile radius of the stricken freighter.

A Coast Guard plane on base patrol also was headed for the scene.

CHECKING THE SPOT WHERE THE BODY of Dr. Mary Stults Sherman was found... Detectives FRANK HAYWARD, left, and ROBERT TOWNSEND JR.

NEIGHBORS—REPORT—PREVIOUS—INTRUDERS

Scene of Slaying Reveals Interrupted Busy Routine

By ROSEMARY POWELL

In Dr. Mary Stults Sherman's kitchen a single place setting of china and silver with a tea bag in the cup, were laid out on the serving bar this morning, in evidence of a busy orthopedic surgeon's breakfast.

Just across the hall was the evidence of a well-organized bedside...

Fired Warning Rockets Across U.S. Ship—Reds

MOSCOW (AP)—The Soviet Union denied today that Soviet vessels fired warning rockets across the bow of a U.S. American grain ship in the Black Sea.

Clues Lacking In Killing of Dr. Sherman

By KERMIT TARLETON

An intruder entered his way into a fashionable St. Charles ave. apartment early today, stabbed a prominent woman orthopedic surgeon to death and set fire to her body.

Police apparently had virtually no clues to the identity of the slayer of Dr. Mary Stults Sherman, whose body was found about 4:10 a.m. on the floor of her smoke-filled bedroom in the Patio Apartments, 3101 St. Charles.

The 51-year-old police research specialist had been stabbed eight times in the left arm, left chest and stomach, police said, and her body was badly burned.

HOMICIDE DETECTIVES SAID the front door to her apartment had been forced open, her wallet was empty and her 1961 automobile was missing.

Dr. Sherman was an orthopedic surgeon at the Ochsner Clinic and was director of the bone pathology laboratory of the Ochsner Foundation Hospital.

Police said apparently the body was set on fire in the bed, but rolled over onto the floor where it was found lying on the floor face.

Juan Valdez, who occupies another apartment on the second floor of the apartment complex, reported that he smelled smoke and turned on the alarm.

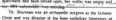

SAM MORAN, SPECIAL INVESTIGATOR for the Orleans Parish Coroner's office, said the front door had been forced open and an unsuccessful attempt made to open a jewelry box. Some rings and a watch were found inside the box, he said.

Mrs. Elinore Peterson Segen, a maid who had been employed by Dr. Sherman for the past 15 years, said the doctor's apartment had been burglarized several times in recent years and a burglar alarm had been installed.

MRS. PATERSON SAID BURGLARS stripped Dr. Sherman's apartment 18 months ago while she was on a visit to England.

The maid said that when she left Dr. Sherman about 4:30 p.m. yesterday she was in good spirits and talked of a woman friend who was expected here for a visit.

Hospital attaches said Dr. Sherman worked in her laboratory yesterday morning, but was off duty yesterday afternoon. She kept a dental appointment in the afternoon and was soon returning home at 5 p.m.

DR. MARY STULTS SHERMAN

Police Slaying Bulletin

Here is the text of the police bulletin on the slaying of Dr. Mary Sherman:

"Victim: White female, identified as Dr. Mary S. Sherman, 3101 St. Charles ave., Apt. J. Time of Occurrence: Between the hours of 1:30 p.m., 7:19-64, and 4:12 a.m., 7-21-64; Weapon used, undetermined at present time; wanted subject or subjects, unknown."

Here is a message on Dr. Sherman's missing automobile:

"Attempt to locate the following described vehicle, believed involved in a homicide committed at 3101 St. Charles ave. this date..."

Cancer Work Slain Doctor's Main Interest

The most avid field of interest for Dr. Mary Stults Sherman, who was stabbed to death early today in her St. Charles ave. apartment, was bone cancer treatment and research.

Dr. Sherman, who had a large following of physicians who respected her work in the field of bone pathology — primarily the study of tumors, benign and malignant, of the bones and joints, was director of Ochsner Medical Foundation's bone pathology laboratory.

IN HER PRIVATE life, the attractive 51-year-old widow seems to have had a passion...

Disarm Conference Holds 200th Meet

GENEVA (AP) — The seventeen-nation disarmament conference met for the 200th time today...

Where to Find It

UPTOWN APARTMENTS WHERE WOMAN DOCTOR WAS SLAIN

July 21, 1964: Mary Sherman's murder was an above-the-fold story on the front page of both New Orleans newspapers, first in the *New Orleans States-Item* in the afternoon of July 21, 1964, and then in the *Times Picayune* on the morning of July 22, 1964. Both newspapers continued daily coverage of the story for two weeks, and both said she had been stabbed multiple times and that her body had been set on fire, but neither mentioned the main forensic fact of the case – that Dr. Sherman's right arm and thorax were entirely missing. The photo of her on the front page of the *States-Item* was actually not Mary Sherman, but a photo of one of her sisters that the press found in Sherman's apartment. And contrary to the headline, there was no evidence that "the intruder" murdered her. See *Dr. Mary's Monkey* for more information. Judyth was in Gainesville and had stopped communicating with anyone in New Orleans, so she did not hear about Dr. Sherman's death until much later.

Oswald Tipsters Silent; Autopsy Excludes Murder

New Orleans (AP)—David W. Ferrie's death created fear yesterday among some people who claimed to have information relating to Ferrie or Lee Harvey Oswald in connection with the assassination of President John F. Kennedy.

Storm Rages In Europe; Toll Mounts

Hamburg, Germany (Friday) (AP) — Disaster emergency crews, called into action by siren and cannon fire signals, fought early today against flood tides from violent storms sweeping northern Europe.

The violence of weather was described in some places as the worst within living memory.

Hours before dawn 11 persons had been reported killed by the storm.

HAMBURG WAS threatened with what might be the worst flood disaster since 1962 when 312 persons died.

But the dikes have been built higher since then and there were hopes they would

Ferrie, labeled by District Attorney Jim Garrison as a prime informant in his investigation of the assassination, was found dead in bed Wednesday. A preliminary autopsy report attributed death to a brain hemorrhage. A coroner's report yesterday ruled out murder, leaving suicide, natural causes or accidental death as possibilities.

A woman who was about to give the Associated Press details she said related to Oswald's activities in New Orleans was frightened into silence. She warily greeted a reporter at her home.

"You see that," she said, directing attention to a snubnosed .38-caliber revolver placed on a nearby chair. "I don't say anything might happen to me. But I just won't talk to you. I have nothing more to say."

Another person on the periphery of the case, David Lewis, a bus station baggage clerk, dropped out of sight Wednesday night. Neighbors said the Lewis family had suddenly left town. Lewis had

told newsmen he feared for the safety of his wife and four children because of his knowledge of a possible conspiracy to kill President Kennedy.

HOWEVER, Lewis appeared at the district attorney's office yesterday. Before going into Garrison's office he said:

"I'm not worried about myself, but I am about my family. Maybe there has been too much said about me already, but they know my name and know what I look like and they know where I work, so that's it."

A onetime private investigator, Lewis claims to have known Oswald, the man named by the Warren Commission as President Kennedy's assassin.

Another figure in the case, Miguel Torres, was removed at his own request from a jail cell to the hospital at Orleans Parish Prison.

WDSU-TV SAID it had been informed by "a source" that a relative of Torres claimed to have received a telephone call threatening the man's life.

Criminal Sheriff Louis Heyd Jr., had no comment other than to say Torres wasn't sick.

Torres, a Cuban exile, was returned to New Orleans from the Louisiana State Prison at Angola in January and has been questioned by Garrison's investigators. Torres lived a block away from Oswald's residence here.

Coroner Nicholas Chetta ruled out murder as a possible

February 1967 Newspaper Article about David Ferrie's Death: Appearing in the local newspapers of New Orleans, this article discusses reaction to the death of David Ferrie in light of that fact that he was a suspect in Jim Garrison's investigation into the JFK assassination. The article mentions that David Lewis knew Lee Oswald and that, upon the announcement of the Garrison investigation of David and Anna Lewis, he suddenly left town because he feared for the safety of his wife and children. Later in the article, it says that Dr. Chetta, the Coroner, ruled out murder as a possible motive in Ferrie's sudden death.

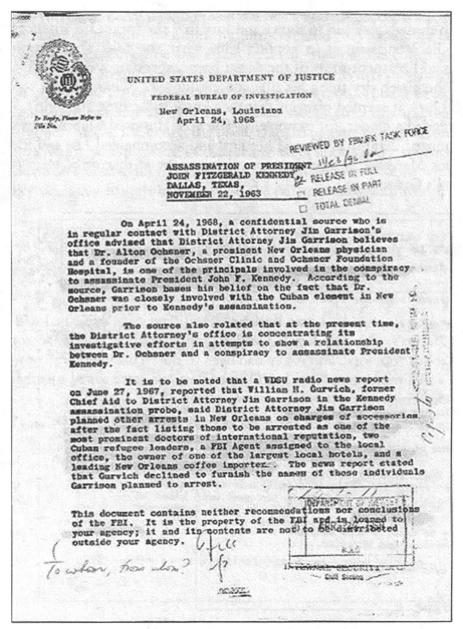

UNITED STATES DEPARTMENT OF JUSTICE

FEDERAL BUREAU OF INVESTIGATION

New Orleans, Louisiana
April 24, 1968

REVIEWED BY FBI/JFK TASK FORCE

ASSASSINATION OF PRESIDENT
JOHN FITZGERALD KENNEDY,
DALLAS, TEXAS,
NOVEMBER 22, 1963

☐ RELEASE IN FULL
☐ RELEASE IN PART
☐ TOTAL DENIAL

On April 24, 1968, a confidential source who is in regular contact with District Attorney Jim Garrison's office advised that District Attorney Jim Garrison believes that Dr. Alton Ochsner, a prominent New Orleans physician and a founder of the Ochsner Clinic and Ochsner Foundation Hospital, is one of the principals involved in the conspiracy to assassinate President John F. Kennedy. According to the source, Garrison bases his belief on the fact that Dr. Ochsner was closely involved with the Cuban element in New Orleans prior to Kennedy's assassination.

The source also related that at the present time, the District Attorney's office is concentrating its investigative efforts in attempts to show a relationship between Dr. Ochsner and a conspiracy to assassinate President Kennedy.

It is to be noted that a WDSU radio news report on June 27, 1967, reported that William H. Gurvich, former Chief Aid to District Attorney Jim Garrison in the Kennedy assassination probe, said District Attorney Jim Garrison planned other arrests in New Orleans on charges of accessories after the fact listing those to be arrested as one of the most prominent doctors of international reputation, two Cuban refugee leaders, a FBI Agent assigned to the local office, the owner of one of the largest local hotels, and a leading New Orleans coffee importer. The news report stated that Gurvich declined to furnish the names of those individuals Garrison planned to arrest.

This document contains neither recommendations nor conclusions of the FBI. It is the property of the FBI and is loaned to your agency; it and its contents are not to be distributed outside your agency.

April 24, 1968, Gurvich Letter: Found in the FBI files by CBS's 60 Minutes researchers in 2000. It is on letterhead from the New Orleans office of the FBI, but it is addressed to no one, is unsigned, and refers to comments of an unidentified source. But it does mention Dr. Alton Ochsner. The problem with the document is that it is known that the federal government was tampering with Garrison's investigation into the JFK assassination. It is difficult to say if this document really represented Garrison's intentions or whether it was just another strut in the array of disinformation that was constructed to frustrate Garrison's efforts to investigate the JFK assassination.

Anna Lewis: Witness to Judyth's relationship with Lee Harvey Oswald

Judyth (left) and Anna Lewis in 2000.

Anna Lewis and her husband David Lewis socialized with Judyth Vary Baker and Lee Harvey Oswald on numerous occasions during the summer of 1963. Many of these activities were basically double-dates strolling the streets of the French Quarter, but others were more sinister, such as a visit to The 500 Club, where Lee Oswald introduced Anna and David Lewis to Carlos Marcello and Jack Ruby. Therefore, David Lewis' association with Lee Oswald was well known to the New Orleans underworld, which included both the local Mafia and the intelligence agents that lurked around Lafayette Square near where both David Lewis and Lee Oswald worked.

After the JFK assassination, those who knew about David Lewis' association with Lee Oswald were very concerned about what he might say. As a result, Anna and David Lewis were repeatedly harassed and threatened by various sources, most of whom wanted them to remain silent and by a few who wanted them to speak out. In the midst of this dark circus, Anna Lewis continued to raise her batch of young children.

In 2000 Judyth Vary Baker told several JFK researchers about a woman that she had known in New Orleans in 1963 who could confirm that she knew Lee well, if the woman could be located and if she was willing to talk. The researchers tracked down Anna Lewis and in Jan. 2000, researchers Joe Riehl, Howard Platzman, Martin Shackelford, Debra Conway and Judyth were present when Anna Lewis was interviewed on camera.

The results of that interview were 34 minutes of video, which has been widely distributed and which was subsequently posted on the internet for public viewing. The essence of that video is presented here: In 1961, Anna moved to New Orleans. Still a teenager, she got a job as a waitress at Thompson's Restaurant on Saint Charles Avenue, near Lafayette Square where Guy Banister's office and many federal offices were located.

In Dec. 1961 she met David Lewis and Jack Martin who came into that restaurant as customers. Both men were working as private detectives for Guy Banister at the time. Anna soon began dating David Lewis who urged her to be careful about what she said around Lafayette Square because the place was crawling with undercover cops, FBI informants, and other secret operators. It was there in Lafayette Square that David Lewis introduced Anna to Lee Harvey Oswald in the winter of 1962.

In April of 1962 Anna and David Lewis moved to Houston where they were married. Later that same year, Anna and David moved back to New Orleans, where Anna resumed her waitress job at Thompson's Restaurant and where David began working as a luggage handler at the Trailways bus station. David told Anna that he was no longer working for Guy Banister, though she did notice that he still hung around with Jack Martin and others associated with Guy Banister. One day, Lee Oswald walked into Thompson's Restaurant alone and took a seat at a table near the window. Anna recognized Lee and remembered meeting him in the park the year before, so she greeted him in a friendly manner when she went to his table to take his order. But Oswald would not talk to her and simply ordered a cup of coffee.

For the next half hour, Oswald stared out the window. Then two men arrived and sat down with Oswald. Anna saw that "papers were exchanged" between the men, then Oswald got up and walked out of the restaurant. The next time she saw Lee Oswald was when he came in Thompson's Restaurant accompanied by continued next page

Anna Lewis (continued from previous page)

a young woman. When her husband David joined them he introduced Anna to the couple. The young woman was Judy Baker. Anna heard much of the subsequent conversation, about the political situation in Cuba and about plans to go to Cuba to kill Castro. Anna did not take the talk seriously, considering it to be little more than the bravado of boys. To her: "It was a joke."

Lee Oswald and Judy Baker became frequent customers at Thompson's, and Anna greeted them when they came in the restaurant. Before long, the Lewises started socializing with Lee and Judy. In Anna's words: "Judy Baker and I, and David and Lee, would walk the streets of New Orleans together. It was walkin'-and-talkin'. We used to go to the old Preservation Hall to listen to the jazz music together. We used to hang around Thompson's together."

During the interview, Anna was asked what she thought was going on between Judy Baker and Lee Harvey Oswald, and she replied, "Well, when two people, which is male and female, are together the way that they were together, and acted together they way that they did, there is only one conclusion you can put to this: She was his mistress. And when you is his mistress, you got be in the bed with him." One night... Lee Harvey Oswald's wife called the restaurant and asked Anna if her husband was there."I told her, Honey, my job is to serve your husband, not to tell you who he is with. And I hung up."

Anna clearly did not like Judy at the time. In her words: "Judy was a stuck-up little girl. She thought she was better than anybody else, and she hung onto Lee Harvey Oswald's arm like she thought I wanted to steal him from her." Anna went on to describe Lee Oswald as "a very quiet man who would listen to what other people had to say, but never commented on anything. But when he spoke, you had better listen to what he had to say because he did not like to have somebody talking when he is talking." She concluded her comments about Lee with "To tell you the truth, he was not my type."

David Lewis later told Anna that Lee Oswald had some guns and rifles in a closet in Guy Banister's office, but Banister became unhappy with that arrangement and ordered Lee to move the guns upstairs. One evening Lee Oswald took Judy Baker, David Lewis and Anna to the 500 Club and introduced them to both Carlos Marcello and Jack Ruby. Anna described The 500 Club as a place for high-class people and noted details of the interior of the 500 Club, such as a two-way mirror above the bar positioned so that Carlos Marcello could sit in his office and "watch the people there to make sure they ain't stealing from him."

Anna was obviously charmed by Marcello and described him as "a very nice, distinguished-looking gentleman. If you did not know what he was – that he was involved with the Mafia – then you could have really fell in love with him." Anna also met David Ferrie at The 500 Club but was not impressed with him: "He didn't like me. I didn't like him either. I didn't like his toupee. It looked like a rug." Anna considered Ferrie a con-man who manipulated others, but she did acknowledge that she was once in his apartment where she saw microscopes and other odd paraphernalia, saying: "I thought he was a druggy. He had things that he would burn his stuff in, like that, and I thought he was a druggy." Anna confirmed that "Lee Harvey Oswald did not consume alcoholic beverages, neither did David Lewis."

Thompson's location was at the heart of the anti-Castro community in New Orleans, and Anna had overheard so much "kill Castro" talk at Thompson's that when Anna first heard there had been an assassination on Nov. 22, she assumed that it was Castro who had been assassinated. Upon hearing that it was Kennedy who had been killed, Anna called her husband David Lewis at work. Upon hearing the news, David simply said "Oh, shit." And when Anna heard that they had arrested Lee Harvey Oswald as JFK's assassin,"that's when reality hit."

Anna Lewis (continued from previous page)

Later that same day, David Lewis's friend Jack Martin was pistol-whipped by Guy Banister. Anna said that a strange man marched into Thompson's and told her: "Tell David to keep his mouth shut, if he knows what is good for him."

"After the Kennedy assassination happened, the trouble started in New Orleans... They hounded us."

Six weeks later, on Dec. 31, 1963, Jack Martin told David Lewis to get out of town because things were "getting hot in New Orleans." David Lewis said he knew things were getting hot, but he could not afford to leave. Then someone fired a gun at David Lewis while he was walking down the street in New Orleans. Frightened, David went to the bus station and caught the next bus to Baton Rouge, only to get on another bus and return to New Orleans that same day where his wife and children were. Then someone kidnapped David Lewis off the streets of New Orleans and took him to a hotel in Houston, only to let him return to New Orleans by bus a few days later.

Next, Anna said men from the FBI entered her house, rummaged through her mail and searched her personal possessions, all without a warrant. When Anna encountered them and complained to them about their entering her house, they said that her small children had let them in so they did not need a warrant. Jack Martin then came to her house and told Anna and David that their phones were bugged.

When Jim Garrison began investigating the JFK assassination, television cameras filmed Anna and David Lewis leaving their house and broadcasted the footage announcing that the Lewises were leaving town. Anna only learned about the story when her sister called her house to check on her.

The next day undercover agents from the DA's office followed her to work. Annoyed by this unwelcome attention, Anna flagged a police car on the street and told the police officer that the men in the car following her were soliciting her for prostitution. As the police detained the car, she escaped on the bus. Then District Attorney Jim Garrison himself called her on the phone at home and told her she had to give a statement on what she knew. Anna told Jim Garrison that she did not know Lee Harvey Oswald. Upon hearing this, Garrison told her that would have her picked up and brought to his office, but Anna threatened Garrison right back, saying that she was five months pregnant and if she lost her baby, she would be suing him personally and his office over the loss of her baby. So Garrison left her alone.

David Lewis decided to cooperate with the DA's office, at least to a point: "When he started talking to the DA and it all came out that he (David Lewis) knew him (Lee Oswald), I guess that is when he put his life on the line." But David Lewis survived the threats of the 1960s and died on May 5, 1998 of cancer. Anna emphasized several times during the interview that she never heard any talk about plans to kill President Kennedy from David or Lee, and that Lee Oswald did not look like a man who was going to assassinate anyone.

Note: Critics of David Lewis contend he sought money by speaking out, as Jack Martin made a tape of Lewis' statements and tried to sell it. Lewis feared Carlos Quiroga, falsely blaming him for the shooting incident. After Lewis failed a lie detector test on the matter, Garrison dropped him as a witness. David and Anna fled New Orleans due to threats and their marriage ended. Quiroga also failed a lie detector test, testing false about not having seen the weapons used to kill JFK, denying personally knowing Oswald, and denying he knew Oswald's FPCC organization was bogus.

To Whom It May Concern: Dec. 26, 2000

Regarding "Oswald":

My mother, Judyth Anne Vary Baker, expressed very little interest in the Kennedy assassination or in Lee Harvey Oswald. We had no books on the subject at the house (out of 1000's). When the movie, JFK, was released I offered to take her to see it — but she refused. When she finally spoke of this in late 1998 — it came as a complete surprise. In my opinion, to the best of my knowledge, my mother never followed the Kennedy assassination nor showed any interest. In fact, in retrospect this seems odd because we spoke of so many political topics.

Sincerely,

Josiah R. Baker

Christ Baker
witness 12/26/00

Note from Josiah Baker, Judyth's oldest son, about his mother, Lee Harvey Oswald, and the JFK assassination. He and his sister, Sarah, also wrote statements concerning knowing about the "green glass" for years.

... use ... me. She took the glass and said it was her "Oswald glass"! At that point, several women in the room were interested and they talked about it. Mom admitted that she and Oswald worked together, they were friends, and went home from work everyday on the street cars in New Orleans.

JOSIAH R. BAKER   Christ Baker 12/26/00
                            witness

Index